North American Distribution

Publishers Group West
Berkeley, California
(800) 788-3123
PGW Rocks!

Translations & Foreign Editions

Brazilian Edition by
Leganto-Comercio Direto de Livros
Rio de Janeiro, Brazil

Croatian Edition by
Mozaik Knjiga
Zagreb, Croatia

Czech Edition by
Alpress
Prague, Czech Republic

German Edition by
Goldmann (Bertelsmann)
Munich, Germany

Hebrew Edition by
Babel Publishing House
Tel Aviv, Israel

Hungarian Edition by
Athenaeum 2000
Budapest, Hungary

Italian Edition by
Nuova Pratiche Editrice
Milan, Italy

Korean Edition by
Darimedia Publishing House
Seoul, South Korea

Norwegian Edition by
Pax Forlag
Oslo, Norway

Polish Edition by
Swiat Ksiazki
Warszawa, Poland

Russian Edition by
Eksmo
Moscow, Russia

Serbian Edition by
Alfa-Narodna Knjiga
Belgrade, Serbia

Slovenian Edition by
Presernova Druzba
Ljubljana, Slovenia

United Kingdom & South Africa
Vermilion (Random House U.K.)
London, England

Elsewhere in the Federation by Goofy Foot Press
www.goofyfootpress.com

Guide To Getting It On!

The Universe's Coolest and Most Informative
Book about Sex

for adults of all ages

author
Paul Joannides

illustrator
Dærick Gröss Sr.

Goofy Foot Press

Oregon, U.S.A

Guide To Getting It On!
Fourth Edition
V. 4.2 October, 2004

Publisher's Cataloging-In-Publication
Joannides, Paul N.
Guide to getting it on! / Paul Joannides, author;
Daerick Gross, illustrator.-- 4th ed.
p. cm.
Includes bibliographical references and index.
ISBN: 1-885535-67-8
1. Sex instruction. 2. Sex. 3. Man-woman
relationships. 1. Gross,Daerick. 11. Title.

HQ31.J63 2000   613.9'6

Goofy Foot Press
P.O. Box 1719
Waldport, OR 97394-1719
www.goofyfootpress.com

printed in
Saline, Michigan
McNaughton & Gunn
Made in the U.S.A.

Bed of
CONTENTS

Warning & Disclaimer

Read it and weep!

Hard as we tried, this guide isn't perfect, nor was it intended as a final authority on sex. There will be times when it is better to consult your beautician, bartender, or best friend. You might also speak to a physician or licensed sex therapist. Ultimately, it is your body and your sexuality — venture beyond the bounds of common sense at your own peril. Also, this book talks about sex acts which are illegal in some parts of the planet. Know your nation's laws about sex; break them at your own risk.

No one involved with the writing or publishing of this book is a physician or licensed sex therapist, although members of these professions have been consulted on thorny issues. The people who have contributed ideas to this book are mostly psychologists, psychoanalysts, social workers, lawyers, teachers, writers, a couple of surfers, and even a prostitute and a priest. The actual writing was done by a mental health professional. Just because some of these people have college degrees doesn't mean they know any more about sex or sexual relationships than you do. They all struggle at times. Still, their perspective might be helpful and even refreshing.

While the techniques mentioned in this book work well for some people, they might not be good for you. Check with a physician or licensed sex therapist before attempting any sexual act that you are unfamiliar with, or do so at your own risk and with the understanding that bad things might happen. Consult with a physician if you have any condition which precludes strenuous exercise or sexually exciting activity.

All readers, except those who are trying to get pregnant, are encouraged to use birth control and to adopt a medically sound strategy for avoiding sexually transmitted infections. However, no form of birth control is foolproof, and diseases have been known to outsmart even the finest of barriers. These are normal consequences of having sex and are not the fault of this book.

This book was written to help expand the consciousness of its readers. Neither Goofy Foot Press nor any of its minions shall be liable

Operating System: Mac OSX
Software: Adobe InDesign CS/3.0
Headers: Cooper Black/Adobe Systems
Text: Fairplex Wide Book/Emigre Graphics
Icons: Many by P22 Type Foundry & Galapagos
Drop caps & Headers: Cooper Black/Adobe Systems
Book Interior Design & Type Consultant: Dmitri Siegel
Cover Consultant: Denise Westmoreland
Copy Editing Consultant: David Hoffert
Cover Font: Grouser/PizzaDude
Captions: Advert/Font Font

Goofy Foot: When a surfer leads with the right foot instead of the left. Results in a different orientation toward the wave.

This book is dedicated to Sisyphus.

The Alpha Chapter

Chapter 1

Sometimes I think life is just a rodeo,
The trick is to ride, and make it to the bell
But there is a place,
Sweet as you will ever know
In music and love
And things you never tell

Rock and Roll Girls by J.C. Fogerty, Wenaha Music Co.

O kay, so this guide isn't like other books on sex. It doesn't have pictures of male or female private parts that look like they were taken from a cadaver, and it doesn't hide behind a wall of fancy sex terms or read as though it were from *Mr. Rogers.*

This guide encourages you to explore dimensions of sexuality that people in our country usually aren't told about—from the emotional part of getting naked together to why a guy who takes his penis too seriously might have trouble pleasing his sweetheart. It covers subjects like hand jobs and heart throbs, kisses above and below the waist, vibrators, friendship, and even sex on the Internet.

But most important of all is the Goofy Foot Philosophy, which says that it doesn't matter what you've got in your pants if there's nothing in your brain to connect it to.

Do with It What You Want

Since this is a book about sex, it might be a good idea to include a definition of what sex is. But trying to define sex is a lot like trying to insert a diaphragm: just when you think you've got it in, the thing turns ninja on you. For instance, here are only a few of the issues that need to be addressed if you are trying to define the term "sex:"

 People think of intercourse as the ultimate sex act, the real thing—*ipsum fuctum.* But if intercourse is the ultimate act, then how come making out or holding hands is sometimes sweeter and more meaningful?

 Almost all sex acts can be painful, obnoxious, or boring unless you do them with someone who turns you on. Does this mean that the mental part of sex is more important than the physical part?

 Why does one couple find a particular sex act to be highly erotic while another couple finds the same act to be downright disgusting?

 A person has sex and an orgasm, but doesn't feel sexually excited. The next afternoon he or she catches the brief but intense gaze of a total stranger and nearly bursts with sexual feeling. How can a brief glance make someone feel more sexual than an orgasm?

 You are getting a physical exam. You are naked and your genitals are being touched. Neither you nor the examiner is aware of any sexual excitement. However, if you were naked and being touched in this way after a romantic date, it might be incredibly sexual. How much do we rely on the context or situation to tell us what's sexual and what isn't?

 Two sexually-experienced people are having cybersex. They have never met in real life and have only masturbated with each other on webcams. Yet they say this is the most intense and satisfying sex they have ever had. How can this be?

 How can a song, car, or piece of clothing be sexy?

Needless to say, we have given up on trying to pin a tail of definition on the big donkey of sex. It seems that any definition of sex needs to fit who you are as an individual as well as your particular situation. Instead of pretending to know what that might be, consider this:

> *Learning about sex and intimacy is a lifelong task. Even with years of experience, we still blow it on occasion. The best we can do in the pages that follow is to tell you what we wish we had known about sex twenty years ago. Do with it what you want.*

Morality & What's in Your Pants

In much of America we still try to equate morality with whether you keep your pants on. We also associate morality with religion. But the truth is, there are Christians, atheists and Jews who are moral people, and Christians, atheists and Jews who are immoral people. The same is true for people who are sexually active and for those who aren't. Morality, from this guide's perspective, is your ability to respect and care for your fellow human beings. It has little to do with the way you enjoy your sexuality, unless what you do breaks a special trust or violates the rights of others.

Hmmm. A Book on Sex

In doing research for this guide, we reviewed a number of sex books that were written between 1800 and 1960. How to describe these books? Imagine if the abstinence-only people perfected mind-control and took over the world. We're talking line after line of really strange advice. Sex books of the past gave a girl a psychiatric diagnosis if she masturbated or wanted to be on top, and some even said that married couples shouldn't have sex more than once a month. Yet the writers of these books considered themselves to be paragons of reason. They were sure they had the right answers. So please be aware that books on sex don't often pass the test of time, and this is a book on sex.

Whether it is this book or anyone else's, there are no *Ten Commandments of Sex.* Books on sex are merely a reflection of the time and culture that spawn them. Who knows what the sexual fashion will be by the time today's toddlers have reached middle age?

Birth Control & Gnarly Sex Germs

This book's chapters on birth control and sex germs talk about everything from scruffy sex rodents to things you can do to make a rubber feel right. Hopefully, their perspective on sex will help you avoid things like unwanted pregnancies and an early funeral. In the meantime, it might be helpful to remember that just about anything in this world that's worth doing will kill you if you're stupid about it. Having sex can be far less risky than driving on the freeway or even driving across town. It just depends on how smart you are about sex and how badly you drive.

How It Fits In

There are many different reasons why people have sex, some having to do with love, others not. For instance, many of us have sex because it can be a great deal of fun, especially with someone whom we care deeply about. It's also an activity that couples do when they have a primal urge to get physical or need to relieve erotic tension (a.k.a. horniness). Some individuals offer sex to please or placate a partner, and some use it as a way of gaining security or status. In addition, people have sex when they want to have a baby. Baby-making sex has an added dimension which can bring partners incredibly close, as long as you're not going to a fertility clinic.

Sex can mean different things at different times. For instance, you might find yourself in a situation where the sex helps to expand and deepen your love for each other. In another relationship, the sex can leave you feeling anxious and empty. Early in a relationship, the lovemaking might excite you and rev you up; at another point it might be a source of comfort and calmness. In most long-term relationships, there will be stretches where the sex is boring. Sometimes it gets better on its own; other times, it requires a massive effort.

For those of you who are younger, people sometimes refer to matters of the younger heart as puppy love and treat it with disrespect. That's silly. The most powerful feelings in life are often puppy love. Cherish them. As for having sex with your puppy love, far be it from this guide to say yes or no. It might be wonderful, but then again, maybe not. Just be aware that there's usually more to a good carnal experience than the hydraulics of sticking hard into wet. For some people, what separates the good sexual memories from the bad are intangibles like fun, friendship, love, and caring.

It might also be helpful to remember that as you get older, your expectations about sex may change. For instance, if you just turned seventeen, getting laid in and of itself can be a huge thing. But by the time you turn thirty-four, you'll have more experience under your belt. By then, you might want your sex life to take you some place different than when you were younger. Perhaps you will be searching for different qualities in a partner as well. Hopefully, you will want sex to be special no matter what your age.

A Red Flag—Matters of the Heart

On an emotional level, sex can be as powerful as you want to make it. But good luck if you are trying to have sex *without* it becoming emotional.

The emotions that accompany sexual relationships can be magical, enchanting and wonderful. Then again, they can be really awful. For instance, a cherished relationship can fizzle and go flat, leaving you empty and hollow. Or it can suddenly crash and burn, causing you so much heartache that you might wish you were dead. The tears can pour from a place so deep that you'll wonder if they will ever stop.

Lovemaking can also be a way of working through fears and crises, as well as a place for growth, forgiveness, fun, and friendship.

No Assumptions Here

Most of us make assumptions about the sex lives of other people. For example, consider Tim, a quiet, college-aged computer geek, and Jake, a well-liked twenty-seven-year-old shortstop on his company's baseball team. Tim is biceps-challenged while Jake looks like he just leapt from the pages of *Men's Health*. Yet Tim-the-geek has a wonderfully creative and fulfilling sex life with his girlfriend, while Jake-the-god is a virgin. Jake lives in fear that someone will discover his entire sex life consists of masturbating to porn in cyberspace.

This book is just as much for Tim and his girlfriend as it is for Jake and Rosie. It makes no assumptions except that you are curious about sex and might want to enjoy it even more.

The other thing to keep in mind is that no matter how old you are, there is still time left for you to have a rewarding sex life.

Charts, Graphs & Sex Surveys

This book has no charts or graphs. If you are the type who's bamboozled by such things, consider the following: how do you graph the value of a loving glance or heartfelt hug? Yet try to enjoy sex in a long-term relationship without them. Rather than assuming which graph is best for you, this guide tries to accommodate a full range of sexual tastes and beliefs, be they conservative, eclectic, or kinky. Are any of us just one or the other?

In addition to charts and graphs there are sex surveys. These are published every couple of years, each claiming to be the ultimate sex census. But think about it: big as it is, the federal government has trouble doing an accurate census of its own citizens, and the only two questions it needs to ask is if a person's heart is still beating and what his or her address is. Imagine a team of five or ten researchers trying to document the sexuality of 250 million people! Even if all you do is masturbate, your sexuality is probably too complex to be summarized by charts, graphs, or surveys.

Readers' Comments

To solicit readers' comments for this book, we sent out more than seven-hundred questionnaires to men and women who ordered prior editions of the *Guide*. We have also received 4000 surveys from people who have visited our website at www.BoinkCentral.com.

We received far more responses from women than men and the women's responses were a hoot to read. The men's responses were, for the most part, a bit uncreative. Are these the same guys who brag about their sexual prowess? Even the women in the office who helped read and tabulate the responses snored through most of the men's answers, while thoroughly enjoying the sexual creativity of their own gender.

Since there was nothing scientific about the design or distribution of our questionnaires, it is impossible to jump or even crawl to conclusions. But in case you wonder why this book has more comments from women than men, it's because their responses were more interesting, instructive and sexy.

Final Alpha Note

Most people would probably agree that sex is best when it's honest, caring and fun. The same should be true for books on sex. Hopefully, you will never find a more honest assessment of love and sex than in the pages that follow, or a publication that has more respect for its readers than this one does for you.

A Brief History of Sex

Chapter 2

This chapter provides a brief history of sex in America: from the 1950s to the turn of the millennium. Don't worry, it's not like having to read about George Washington crossing the icy Delaware, although people have been known to do things just as drastic when they haven't had sex in a really long time.

Some writers give the impression that there was no sex in the 1950s and that sex wasn't even invented until the 1960s, when humanity supposedly started making love instead of war. This is not true. There was plenty of sex in the 1950s. It's just that couples often waited until they were married before having intercourse. Also, couples usually dated for a longer time before getting sexual. Since a woman's virginity was more of a commodity then, it's possible that unmarried couples shared more hand jobs and oral sex than intercourse.

Sexual expression was sometimes a challenge for single women in the 1950s, since they were often expected to put out enough to keep a man interested, but not so much as to gain a bad reputation. Have things changed all that much? Some women used this double standard to their advantage, while others found it oppressive.

Virgins with Breasts like Missile Silos

While virginity was an important commodity for a young woman during the 1950s and early 1960s, she was also expected to wear bras with names like "The Torpedo" or "The Bullet Bra." These bras had one purpose and one purpose only—to make her breasts stick out like sexual weapons. Talk about mixed messages.

The Rolling Stone Orgasm, Circa 1966-1977

For young people in the late 1960s and 1970s, there were at least three different types of sexual experience.

The first type of sexual experience was getting yourself off by hand. This provided a really intense jolt of sensation that left you feeling relaxed and settled. It required little social skill or effort. (Some of us who went to religious school would try giving up masturbation for Lent, which is how Palm Sunday got its name.)

The second kind of experience was better. Much better. The second kind of sexual experience was what happened when you were lucky enough to have a sweetheart. It happened when your eyes met, when you held hands, when your lips touched, and when you talked on the phone. The second kind of sexual experience sent a herd of butterflies somersaulting through your stomach and made you feel happy just to be alive. It tugged at the edges of your heart and nearly tossed you off your still-clumsy feet.

The third type of sexual experience is what happened when the second type of experience started to include intercourse. It's what happened when you went "all the way."

Did the third type of sexual experience rate as being the best of times? Sometimes, but not always. Sometimes it was over before it started. Sometimes it wasn't as much fun as playing football in the mud or breaking local laws and ordinances. Too many times it didn't give you the simple calming comfort of a summer night with your head in a lover's lap, gazing at her moonlit face outlined by a billion stars from the sky above. But sex was progress, and it helped us put tracks on our innocence—as if that wasn't going to happen soon enough on its own.

In the '60s and '70s, sex before marriage became acceptable. For many people, it was great. With the introduction of the birth control pill, they had more freedom to do what came naturally. Other factors that helped change the sexual climate included the invasion of rock'n'roll bands from Britain, the use of LSD and other psychedelic drugs, the media, marijuana, the mini-skirt, the women's movement, and the anti-war movement.

A Few Yams & 25,000 Gallons of Policemen's Urine

Just shoot us now for trying to discuss the history of the birth control pill in three paragraphs. But you can't even begin to think about sex during the past forty years without putting it in the context of the birth control pill.

With the release of Viagra, you would think the big drug manufacturers are the best friend of the hard penis and wet vagina. But fifty years ago when researchers desperately needed funding to continue their work on the birth control pill, America's drug companies refused. They worried that their reputations would suffer irreparable harm if they provided funds for something as disgusting as birth control. Being associated with birth control of any kind was so looked down upon that Goodyear Rubber, which produced $150 million worth of condoms in 1958, refused to acknowledge it. (We might still call them "rubbers," but the people at Goodyear made sure we would never call them "Goodyears.")

Birth control pill researchers in this country needed to be careful. As late as 1953, it was still against the law for scientists in Massachusetts to do studies or research on contraceptives. And even if there hadn't been political roadblocks at nearly every turn, there were significant scientific limitations. For instance, in 1930 it took the ovaries of 80,000 pigs to extract even the tiniest bit of estrogen. In order to harvest enough hormones to fit on the head of a pin or two, German biochemists had to collect and distill 25,000 liters of urine from the police barracks in Berlin. A huge leap occurred when researchers learned how to synthesize the hormones needed for birth control pills from yams grown in Mexico.

You might think that when the birth control pill made it to market in the 1960s, it was college-aged women who flocked to buy it. Actually, the strongest impact of the pill was probably on mothers in their thirties and forties with three to six children. These women lined up at doctor's offices the moment the pill became available.

Highly Recommended: For an excellent history of the pill, see *Sexual Chemistry, A History of the Contraceptive Pill* by Lara V. Marks, Yale University Press, 2001. Also: Andrea Tone's *Devices and Desires, A History of Contraceptives in America,* Hill & Wang, 2001.

The Clitoris, 1966 A.D.

Aside from landing an astronaut on the moon, science in the 1960s also introduced men and women to the word "clitoris." While the clitoris was by no means an invention of the 1960s, few people knew what to call it, and many men as well as some women were ignorant of its function.

An unfortunate aspect of this "new" discovery was that people started to describe the clitoris as a mini-penis. As a result, men who were earnestly trying to please their partners began rubbing the clitoris with the kind of intensity that they wished women would use when rubbing their not-so-mini male penises. Of course, rubbing a clitoris in this way can result in extreme discomfort for a woman. Who knew?

If men had learned only one lesson during the 1960s, it should have been to ask a lover what feels best. Instead, we often thought to ourselves "I gotta find her clitoris" and went for it like bears to honey. Still, with the discovery of the clitoris there was simply no turning back. Or so we thought.

A Note on Clitoral History: They knew what to call it in 1918! A British Court in 1918 ruled that a tabloid newspaper had not libeled an actress when it ran headlines claiming that she was part of a secret "Cult of the Clitoris." The writer of the tabloid article claimed that German spies were using sodomy, sadism and lesbianism to undermine British wartime resolve and to sap the strength of the British people. The article said that women with enlarged clitorises might be doing the Kaiser's bidding.

Sex from the 1980s to Now— Love Takes a Backseat to Cash Flow

Much can be learned about sex from the 1980s through now by considering the plight of a conservative and popular United States president who held office during that time. During the 1980s, this president spent millions of taxpayers' dollars to establish an executive office of celibacy, a governmental agency whose job it was to sell the American people on virginity. However, during the 1990s, this same president's flesh-and-blood daughter could be found posing buck naked, legs spread, in a popular men's jerk-off magazine. Go figure.

Not to be outdone, a more recent U.S. president who was trying to boost his own moral image fired the surgeon general for expressing an opinion about masturbation. This same president signed into law bills that allocated millions of dollars for abstinence-only sex education—but who would know better than he, since one of the bigger legacies of his second term was to introduce the words "oral sex" into the vocabulary of nearly every first-grade child throughout the land.

And that's how sex has been here in America during the past decade or three: a kind of Siamese twin with one head being puritanical and the other hedonistic. Or maybe that's how sex has always been, but TV and the media are now highlighting it in a way that is harder to ignore. Whatever the case, it is now a sad truth that people who hear the word "sex" are just as likely to think of disease as fun or healing, and the 1960s notion of sexual freedom has given way to warnings about sexual abuse and harassment. And while young teenagers who haven't even started to grow pubic hair are now having intercourse, college students on some campuses in the midwest are proving to be more conservative than their grandparents were in the 1950s. Who knows how to summarize what's going on in this country sexually, except to say that there are many different people with many different points of view.

If ever there was a time when we needed to be tolerant of each other's sexual tendencies, whether they involve total celibacy or the occasional weekend threesome, now seems to be it.

Sex in the Media

The message we often get from the media today is that we're supposed to be sexual athletes. And if for some reason you don't have an Olympic symbol tattooed to your labia or scrotum, there are commercials about pills or a hormone-filled patch that you can slap on your rear. That way you can always be hard, always wet, and always happy.

Don't be fooled by the content of today's sex-filled media. It might cause your great-grandmother to sigh and declare that we're all going to hell, but it doesn't encourage us to be any more intimate about sexuality today than in the 1950s. Then, the problem was embarrassment. Today, people are trying to replace the need for love and understanding with something you can get at your local pharmacy or adult toy store. ("I've got my blue thrill-pills to keep my dick going and a gel-filled vibrating butt plug to stick up her booty—she's gonna want me tonight!")

While we don't have any problem with pills if you really need them or plugs if you both enjoy them, keep in mind that nature gave you all you need to have an incredible sex life with. It's sitting above your shoulders.

Learning about Sex from the Past

Learning from history is often important, but it seldom happens when the subject is sex. For instance, can you imagine a grandmother telling her sixteen-year-old granddaughter or grandson: "I didn't start having multiple orgasms until I was forty-five, after your grandfather started reading books on how to help it happen..." or "If you masturbate right before a date, it might help take the edge off the evening," or "It wasn't particularly easy being pregnant at seventeen; I wouldn't recommend it."

If we had to tell you what we've learned about sex from history, you wouldn't find any concern about how much, what way, or even when. Yet those are the things that people seem to worry about the most. Instead, here's what we'd say:

There isn't a feeling in the entire universe that you and your sweetheart don't have stored somewhere in your bodies, feelings that are waiting to be touched, shared, and released. Yet the extent of your current lovemaking is to stick your tongues down each other's throats, tweak each other's nipples a perfunctory number of times, lick each other's genitals because that's what the sex books say you should do, and then thrust away until one of you goes 'Ooo-ahh, ooo-ahh,' and the other goes squirt, squirt, squirt. For a lot of people, sex is still an extension of grabbing for the cookie jar, which is fine as long as your expectations aren't very high.

Fortunately, there are a lot of wonderful dimensions to sex besides just huffing and puffing while the bedsprings squeak. Sharing sex with a partner allows you to discover where the different emotions are stored in each of your bodies, where your hopes and dreams are hidden, where the laughter and pain reside, and what it takes to free the fun, passion, and hidden kink. To achieve that level of sharing you have to take the time to know someone, to feel what they are feeling, to see the world through their eyes, and to let a partner discover who you are in ways that might leave you feeling vulnerable. This can be scary.

Granted, there will be plenty of times when all you want from sex is a quick jolt of sensation, but if that's all you ever expect from sex, then you might be coming up a bit short.

The Next Chapters

One of the problems with adult sexuality is that few of us started with a philosophy or overview. The next couple of chapters attempt to remedy that. Please be aware that the Goofy Foot Press has about as much passion for philosophy as for rattlesnakes and flat cola. Hopefully, you will find the philosophy chapters to be fun, interesting and relevant.

End of Chapter Notes: Is it a contradiction to be criticizing the drug companies for trying to sell you pills for sex, and then saying how amazing the birth control pill was? If one could see signs of consciousness or social responsibility at the big drug companies, that would be one thing. But the birth control pill was forced on them, and they only went along once they could see the huge profit margins. As for today's sex-enhancement drugs, it's one thing to make a pill available to help some men who are having real problems with erections or premature ejaculation; it's quite another to have an understanding or appreciation for how complex our emotions and sexuality can be. Special thanks to Beatrice Fontanel and her *Support and Seduction—A History of Corsets and Bras,* Harry Abrams, New York, 1997 for the term "Breasts like missile silos."

For updates and more information,
Please visit us at
www.BoinkCentral.com

The Dirty Word Chapter

Chapter 3

You might be wondering why a chapter on dirty words would be stuck so close to the front of an otherwise fine and upstanding book. Perhaps there is more to this chapter than just dirty words.

Whether you agree with this guide's observations about dirty words is not the point. This chapter, like all of the others in this book, was written to encourage you to think.

Hans, Sven & Yellow Snow

We at Goofy Foot Press probably use the word "fuck" more times each day than the pope says Amen. The sad thing is, we mainly use our fucks to express anger or frustration. Seldom do we use them in the fun way. This is often the case with sexual slang here in America, where swear words and sex words are often one and the same.

In Sweden, a culture that is more sex-friendly than our own, sexual slang is not usually used to express anger or frustration. If Sven or Hans are really annoyed, they are more likely to yell something about yellow snow than sex. Even our own Pueblo Indians had no history of using sexual slang for hurling insults. If a Pueblo Indian was really bent out of shape, he or she might have implied that the offending party was a lousy farmer or kept a sloppy wigwam. But then again, the Pueblos had a less repressive attitude about sex than some of our forefathers.

Calling People by the Female Genitals

Back when he was a kid, the worst thing your author knew to call another person was a "cunt." He never could bring himself to use the word, but then again, he had yet to work with anyone in the entertainment industry.

Another slang word that kids often use is "pussy." While pussy is a term that refers to the female genitals, it is also an expression that boys use to taunt other boys who are being wimps or cowards.

Why does our culture associate cowardice with being a woman or having a woman's genitals? And why would we want to discredit the very female genitals that so many of us craved (and still crave) to touch and know more about? What kind of number is our culture doing on us, anyway?

Mother-Fucking, Titty-Sucking, Blue-Balled What?

A researcher by the name of Warren Johnson studied how normal eight-year-old boys and girls use slang. According to Johnson, the children's favorite expression when out of parental earshot was "mother-fucking, titty-sucking, blue-balled bitch." Johnson hadn't expected to find America's eight-year-old children capable of outswearing his former marine troop.

Of particular interest is Johnson's observation of an eight-year-old girl yelling "Suck my dick!" to another child who was annoying her. As long as she was going to use sexual slang for swearing, why didn't the little girl yell the more anatomically correct "Eat my pussy!"? Perhaps even an eight-year-old child knows that the way to insult someone in our society is to tell them to take the woman's place in a sexual act, with terms such as "You cocksucker!" "Screw you!" and "Get fucked!" being crude ways of saying, "You're the woman in sex, you piece of garbage!"[1]

It is difficult to understand how something as sweet and delicious as sex could be linked to anger or frustration. It is equally difficult to understand why being the woman in sex is a put-down. Yet these are the premises about sex that we Norte del Americanos grow up with.

When Eight Turns Eighteen

What's going to happen when the little girl who yelled "suck my dick" gets older and wants to share sex with a boy? How is she supposed to enjoy performing the very insults that our society has taught her to hurl at others? Is she going to require the young man to swear

---

[1] It could be argued that the implied insult behind terms like "fuck you" or "suck my dick" is that the receiver of the insult is homosexual. But wouldn't that be just as true for the hurler of the insult, who seems to be inviting the act? If someone wants to imply that the offending party is gay, there are plenty of expressions that do just that and few people hesitate to use them.

undying love and adoration before she blows him? Will she extract a measure of revenge by making him deliver on goods or promises? Will she use sex as a commodity, weapon, or way of achieving security? Will she learn to hide her sexuality, or perhaps become numb to it? Will she turn men into sex objects? Worst of all, will she pretend that giving a blow job isn't really sex?

Equally disconcerting is what this attitude does to boys. The message is that you either screw or get screwed, the former being associated with winning, the latter with losing. This turns sex into a performance or competition.

Sluts, Whores, Virginity & Sewers

Western religions have never done too well with the notion of women and sexuality. For instance, early Christians taught that a virgin daughter occupied a higher place in heaven than her mother, since the mother must have had sex for the daughter to have been born. And around 400 A.D., Christianity's St. Jerome wrote, "Though God can do all things, He cannot raise a virgin after she has fallen" (Epistles 22). Not even God can help you when you lose your virginity, if you are a woman anyway. It's never been a problem for men, but then again, we're the ones who wrote the scriptures. (You don't have to be religious to know that when a boy has intercourse for the first time, he becomes a man. Yet a girl who has intercourse loses her virginity and is no longer pure as the driven snow, assuming she was in the first place.)

Rigid as St. Jerome may have been about women's virginity, he was quite the feminist compared to some of his Christian and Jewish predecessors. For instance, one early church father described women as "a temple built over a sewer," with *sewer* referring to their genitals. Men who made statements like these were later declared saints.

Perhaps it's no coincidence that many adult women who are unable to have orgasms were raised in households where the temple/sewer notion still holds sway.

To this day people still equate a woman's personal reputation with her appetite for sex: if her sex drive is too low, she is cold or frigid; too high and the sewer floods the temple, in which case she is called easy or a slut, whore, ho, or nympho. In Britain, the term is "slag." While young men are free to strut their sexuality, young women learn to carefully regulate theirs. Otherwise, they risk being called dirty words.

NOTE: Contrary to what makes sense, women are often the first to accuse other women of being sluts or whores. Men may have been the bozos who wrote the anti-woman theology, but women can be its cruelest enforcers. Also, scripture tells us that Jesus of Nazareth was loving and respectful toward women. Why did the church fathers who followed him have so many problems with this? And if the human body was made in the image and likeness of God, as scripture says, why were church leaders so rejecting of women's genitals and sexuality? Had God been drinking the day He crafted the clitoris and vagina?

Dicks, Pricks & Morons

Why do we refer to a person who is being a total jerk as a "dick" or "prick"? A dick should be someone who brings pleasure, but that's not what our culture teaches us.

For instance, adults will praise a young boy for his latest drawing or for making it to the toilet on time, but if he proudly displays his pint-sized boner, throats get cleared. Boys in our society are encouraged to spend eons learning how to make a baseline jump shot or to hit an A-minor flat nine on a guitar, yet they are taught to ignore their own sexuality in hopes that it will simply go away until they get older. Maybe that's why many of us grow up having more sensitivity for what happens in music, art, or sports than for what happens in bed.

Power-Booting & Name-Calling at Dartmouth

While our culture encourages its straight men to strut their sexuality, this doesn't mean we always do. For instance, the following story tells of how the term "faggot" is used by straight guys to deride other straight guys for preferring women to beer. It is from Regina Barreca's fine book, *They Used To Call Me Snow White But Then I Drifted*, Viking/Penguin, New York, New York, 1991:

> When I started my first year as a student at Dartmouth College, there were four men for every woman. I thought I had it made. Dartmouth had only recently admitted women, and the administration thought it best to get the alumni accustomed to the idea by sneaking us in a few at a time. With such

terrific odds in my favor socially, how could I lose? I'd dated in high school and although I wasn't exactly Miss Budweiser, I figured I'd have no problem getting a date every Saturday night. But I noticed an unnerving pattern. I'd meet a cute guy at a party and talk for a while. We would then be interrupted by some buddy of his who would drag him off to another room to watch a friend of theirs "power-boot" (the local vernacular for "projectile vomiting"), and I realized that the social situation was not what I had expected.

Then somebody explained to me that on the Dartmouth campus they think you're a faggot if you like women more than beer. This statement indicated by its very vocabulary the advanced nature of the sentiment behind it. If a guy said he wanted to spend the weekend with his girlfriend, for example, he'd be taunted by his pals, who would yell in beery bass voices "Whatsa matter with you, Skip? We're gonna get plowed, absolutely blind this weekend, then we're all gonna power-boot. And you wanna see that broad again? Whaddayou, a faggot or something?"

While many boys who end up at colleges like Dartmouth have intercourse by the age of sixteen, a fair number remain crude in their ability to value friendship with sexual partners. While they may be coordinated enough to guide a penis into a vagina, on an emotional level some still belong in the arms of their drinking buddies. Equally puzzling are the young women who agree to have sex with these emotional giants.

Sexuality here in America remains a confusing entity. A "just say no" mentality thrives in a culture that uses sex to advertise and sell everything from soap to beer. As a result, there are times when we flaunt our sexuality, and other times when we deny it completely.

Bitch Versus Faggot

While the dirty words aimed at women often speak to how they regulate the space between their legs, it's almost always assumed that women are heterosexual. Even if a woman is being aggressive, a male who feels threatened is more likely to call her a "bitch" than a "dyke."

On the other hand, insults at men are aimed at a different level. Guys are always needing to demonstrate a pick-up truck kind of quality that we call manliness. If we slip up, we're called a faggot or queer, even if the only dick we've ever held is our own. There's a knee-jerk response that teenage boys have whenever another boy steps outside of the fragile notion of what's considered masculine; they call him a "fag."

On the surface, the insults for men and women have the same premise: each likes dick too much. But a woman who is being insulted is usually allowed to remain heterosexual. The guy, however, has his sexual identity called into question.

A woman is usually considered to be heterosexual to the core, while a man's heterosexual status is something that knows no rest. It has to be earned and constantly demonstrated or he risks falling off the stilts that define him as straight.

Origin of the Bimbo & the Stud

"Bimbo" and "stud" aren't dirty words per se. But they achieve dirty-word status when you consider the following observation made by a female friend of the author who was sitting on the beach:

> A father was standing a few feet into the surf with a young boy on his right side and a young girl on his left. The children were the same size. Whenever a wave came in the father would keep his right arm rigid. This helped the boy brave the oncoming splash. At the same time, the father would lift his left arm, pulling the girl into the air so she could avoid the splash. The little boy was being taught how to face the wave; the little girl was being taught to expect a man to rescue her.

Bimbo training starts early in our country. All too often, the first step is getting little girls to believe that they are more fragile than boys. Then, ads in women's magazines spawn the belief that there is something unsexy about the female body unless it's plugged with a scented tampon and accessorized with perfume and high heels.

Seldom does our society encourage boys and girls to value and respect each other. More often, boys are taught to protect girls because the latter are supposed to be weak, while many girls are still taught that their worth is determined by the desirability of the boys they date.

Blow Jobs & Bounced Checks

Consider the following statement by a modern American wife of five years:

> My husband's going to be furious when he finds out about the check I bounced, so I better give him a really good blow job tonight.

As you will discover in the chapters that follow, this book has no problem with really good blow jobs, but not when they are motivated by fear, lack of power, or crass manipulation. Yuck. This sort of thing gives blow jobs a bad name.

Naturally, after this was first published, protests from female readers flooded in. Trading blow jobs for money is one of the few ways that women have had throughout the ages to even the score economically. Trading sex for money brings far more joy into the world and is less destructive than the ways that many men earn their paychecks. And what about the possibility that the above-mentioned housewife finds the situation to be a sexual turn-on and might totally enjoy giving the payback blow job?

Rearranging the Bed Sheets on the Titanic
With the New Word "Foreplay"

The term "foreplay" was invented by people who write books on sex. Foreplay is what you are supposed to do to get a woman wet enough so the two of you can have intercourse. It may seem strange that this book considers foreplay to be a dirty word, since caring guys are usually encouraged to embrace the concept. Yet there is nothing caring about the underlying premise of foreplay: that women are somehow a little retarded and need to be warmed up before they want to become sexual. Shoot, you have to warm up the old Ford on cold days, so why not the woman you love?

Most sex books forget to mention that a woman who is masturbating can get herself off just as fast or slow as a man. Perhaps the problem isn't that women have a slower warm-up time, as the notion of foreplay seems to imply. Perhaps the real problem is our culture's concept of sexuality, where being a woman (e.g. getting fucked) is a common insult, where "scoring" makes a boy feel like a man, and where respect, friendship and caring are not necessary conditions for sex.

Unfortunately, the concept of foreplay implies that tenderness is little more than a tollbooth on the highway to intercourse. Nonsense. Tender kisses and caresses do not need to be trailed by intercourse to justify their importance or necessity. They are just as important as intercourse, if not more so.

If you can't get past the notion of foreplay, try to think of it as everything that's happened between you and your partner since the last time you had sex. How you treat each other with your pants on has far more impact on what happens in bed than carefully planted kisses minutes before intercourse. This is just as true for the way that women treat men as for how men treat women.

Why Even Care?

Studs, bimbos, bounced checks—why even care? How can you not care? These are the myths about each other that we take to bed with us. They're what gets in the way.

END OF CHAPTER NOTES: Regarding the wigwam comment at the start of the chapter, were you on your feet? Pueblo Indians don't live in wigwams. Their homes are either adobe/stone pueblos or caves. Unfortunately, life on the reservation has not been good to the sexual habits of the Pueblo, and incidents of rape are now being reported. 🐌 In unnatural settings like prisons and expensive private boys schools, heterosexual males sometimes coerce other males into having sex as a sign of power or superiority. Or sometimes they simply do it because it's intimate and it feels good. Once men are returned to the mainstream of society, the object of their desire becomes women and the sex is referred to as "making love." 🐌 Did the little girl mentioned earlier in this chapter actually understand the premise of the slang phrase "suck my dick" or was she simply mimicking the correct social usage? Does it matter? Is there any difference in the long run? 🐌 Expressions like "Fuckin' great" are examples of how sexual slang is used in a positive sense. They tend to be role neutral and refer to the act of intercourse itself. 🐌

Special thanks to the writings of Ira Reiss, Paul Evdokimov, David Schnarch, Regina Barreca, Carol Tavris, the late Bob Stoller, and many others for inspiring concepts used in this chapter. Thanks also to Paul Kroskrity, anthropology professor at UCLA, for the information about the Pueblos. And finally, thanks to the famous sex researchers who originally suggested that people should think of foreplay as everything that happened since the last time you had sex. Perhaps giving foreplay a name was an improvement over what had come before, or so it is said.

Swearing in Other Cultures

It is beyond the scope of this book to compare and contrast swearing and slang in different languages and in different cultures. Here are a very few examples from languages that you might find interesting:

Armenian:

I fuck your soul; I masturbate on your chin; Let the rats cum on you; I fuck your Turk mother; Your father smokes my penis; My dick in your sister; You are eating sperm ice cream; May your grandfather fuck your mother; I'll hand you your mother's vagina.

Albanian:

(Insults from this region seem to be less sexual and based more in economics or religion): May darkness consume you; May God take your seed away; May you not produce children or ever have wealth; May you die as a dog shot in a vineyard; May the thunder fall in your toilet; May you go insane; May your child drown in his/her own blood; May you get fucked by a blind dog.

Bengali:

Your mom has sex with goats; Your mom has ten tits; The brother of your pussy is my dick; A woman whose pubic hair has dandruff;

Your grandson is a fuckhead, your dad is a rickshaw-puller, and your mother is a whore; An elephant's dick up your mom's vagina.

Flemish:

If my dog had a head like yours, I would shave his ass and teach him to walk backwards; If my ass looked like your face, I'd be afraid of taking a shit; I believe you were born while your mother was standing; Your mother is the mattress of the town; (there are also many non-sexual references to being dumb or stupid).

Greek:

A strand of her pubic hair can pull ships; I'll shit in your sister's mouth; What happened? Can't find your cock?

Hindi:

Your mom got fucked by 100 dogs, the 100th one being your dad!; The fly that sits on the ass of a whore; I will fuck your mom in your sister's vagina and your dad will bring a lantern; Your sister has a dick made of rubber!; Pig (very offensive to Muslims); Your mother sucks donkey dick; A bamboo up your ass; An elephant's trunk in your mother's vagina; I will put a bed in your mother's vagina and fuck your sister on it; Born into this world from a dick; Result of a torn condom.

It is worth noting that in many cultures, the premise of the worst insults has to do with the sexual indiscretions of one's mother or sister. Why should having sex with someone's sister or mother be used as an insult?

The insults listed above are a few of the thousands you can find at www.insultmonger.com. This fascinating website has collected insults from 133 countries. If you spend some time at insultmonger.com you will see that there are interesting nuances to be learned about a culture from the way it hurls its insults and slang.

Hi! I'm Labby...

...and I'm Pud!

We were just wondering,
Whadda ya doing with your
pants still on?

Bras, Briefs, Barbie & Vibrators

The Next Four Chapters

The chances are good that at one time or another you've seen or touched a bra, a vibrator, a Barbie doll, and a man's underwear. They all have something to do with sex, but in ways you may have never thought about.

For instance, you may feel sexy in your new bra and silky panties, but there was nothing sexy about the bra when it was first introduced in the 1860s. Women didn't like it, and a hundred years later, feminists wanted to burn it. The mere fact that a bra and panties might be sexy makes an interesting statement about how we view femininity. After all, not many of us would look at a pair of men's briefs that were lying on a bed and use the word "sexy."

Many of the things that help to define our sexual likes and dislikes have interesting and unusual histories. Some of the things that we hold dear in a sexual way resulted from decisions that were made in business offices rather than in anyone's bedroom. They were decisions made by people wearing suits and ties rather than people who were naked and breathing hard.

After reading these chapters, you might have a little more appreciation for what's behind the "sexy" in sexy lingerie, and maybe you won't walk down the doll aisle at Toys'R'Us in quite the same way. Keep in mind that these are only four of thousands of objects that are part of our sexual consciousness—objects with their own unique history; objects that fit together to give our sexual landscape its color and texture.

Barbie the Icon
No Parents & No Panties

Chapter 4

This chapter is about Barbie. You might be wondering what a cultural icon like Barbie is doing in a book on sex. Perhaps the following statements by our female readers will be helpful:

When you were a little girl, did your Barbie doll ever have sex?

"I had lots of Barbies. She and my giant panda bear got naked and 'did it,' and my sister and I dressed her up in Ken's clothes. Unfortunately, you can't dress up Ken in Barbie's clothes. We tried." *female age 18*

"My basement was a temple to Barbie and all her relatives. Barbie lived in a soap opera complete with abortions, sex changes, and adultery. She and Ken frequently got naked in their Laura Ashley canopy bed." *female age 24*

"Barbie and Ken had a very active relationship and 'sex' life. It's hard to say it was a sex life without any genitalia. I guess I used them to emulate the adults around me. Barbie and Ken often went skinny dipping at the ocean, and slept nude most times." *female age 35*

"My Barbie had Ken on her ALL the time. If I knew then what I know now, Barbie would have been on top more often."
female age 44

"My friend had a Ken and we used to make them have sex by making their little plastic bodies rub against each other when they were lying in Barbie's little nylon bed. We were about ten and were disappointed that Ken's underwear was glued on."
female age 22

"You know those parts in movies that parents were always trying to hide from younger children? I got a slight peek one day, but all I saw were sheets moving. After I saw that, Barbie and Ken made those sounds and simulated those actions. But I wasn't sure what they were really doing." *female age 22*

"She had kinky fantasies and a lot of BDSM. Barbie was a fun girl." *female age 18*

"Not Barbies but definitely with my Lego men. Don't ask me why, but those spacemen certainly had interesting encounters when I sent them on missions. I was pretty inventive for a seven-year-old." *female age 19*

While these women's experiences by no means represent that of most girls, it is likely they represent a significant number. (See more reader comments on their Barbie's sex life at the end of the chapter.)

Eleven Inches of Attitude

The year was 1959. The place was the Toy Fair in New York that's held every February. Mattel's new toy named Barbie was falling flat on her face, or would have if such a thing had been anatomically possible.

Since the beginning of time, toy buyers in America have placed orders for their Christmas inventory at the annual Toy Fair. It was the moment that would determine which toys would make it to toy store shelves the following Christmas, and Barbie was getting the cold shoulder.

This was nearly fifty years ago, and the radical new doll named Barbie shattered everyone's idea of what a child's toy should be. The price she paid for her uniqueness was to be ignored by toy buyers. Buyers for toy stores in 1959 were placing orders for dolls that were soft and huggable, dolls whose souls were made from rags.

Believe it or not, Barbie had a plastic mother named Lilli who was made in Germany. In the late 1950s, Lilli caught the eye of Ruth Handler, co-founder of the Mattel toy company. Lilli was a sexpot of a doll who was marketed to horny German males. She looked like a German streetwalker. Lilli was originally part of an adult comic strip where she appeared as a comical gold-digger and barfly.

Both Barbie and Lilli were 11½ inches tall. The apples did not fall far from the tree when it came to looks, but Ms. Handler made sure that Barbie was born into an entirely different social class. Lilli was more like Anna Nicole Smith, while Barbie was Jackie Kennedy. Interestingly, Barbie's place of birth (at least the address of Mattel) was

Hawthorne, California, the same city where America's other sex idol, Marilyn Monroe, was born.

Large Breasts and No Panties

In 1959, toy store buyers wanted what they knew—dolls that reflected our society's idea of what a good girl should be and what she would hopefully become: a selfless mother, teacher, housewife, and nurse. They didn't get it when they saw Barbie, a doll who has been described by author Christopher Varaste as:

> "An 11½ inch glamour queen with exotic features in a striking black and white swimsuit. She was everyone and defiantly no one. She seemed ageless, though she was supposed to be a teenager. She was beguiling, mysterious, and yet innocent. She was a symbol of a culture struggling to find a suitable identity. As a toy for young girls, her rather severe look took some getting used to. Her Asian eyes, curly bangs, and big red lips could have belonged to a wide range of ethnic backgrounds. She was, in a word, peculiar." (From Christopher Varaste's incredible book of Barbie photographs *Face of the American Dream—Barbie Doll, 1959 - 1971*)

If it hadn't been for a stroke of marketing genius, Barbie could easily have gone down in flames. But Mattel's strategy for selling Barbie to the American public was as unique as their product. They were one of the first companies in history to make television commercials that were aimed at children viewers.

From the very first commercial, Barbie was portrayed as a human being with a glamorous and adventurous life. She was never described as a doll and she was never burdened with trivial limitations such as parents or a husband.

Mattel aired their first Barbie commercial during the wildly popular Mickey Mouse Club TV show. If parents didn't know what to make of Barbie, their American daughters certainly did. Once the summer of 1959 started, every Barbie in every toy store was bought as quickly as it arrived.

Barbie's official name was Barbie Millicent Roberts. When Ken was released a few years later, his name was Ken Carson. It is fitting

and telling that Barbie and Ken's namesake was Carson/Roberts. Carson/Roberts was Mattel's advertising company that played such a dramatic role in Barbie's success.

Not Your Normal Housewife

Barbie's persona was created by two women who had both violated the housewife norm of the 1950s. One had co-founded a large corporation, the other was a tall, striking, unmarried veteran of the fashion industry. Unlike any doll before her, Barbie was created as a young woman whose life didn't revolve around a husband and a family. Her limitations were as thin as her waist and her possibilities as large as her breasts.

Early in Barbie's evolution, someone wanted to make a miniature vacuum cleaner that Barbie could use to vacuum the house. But Ruth Handler, Mattel's co-founder, refused to allow this. During the era when Barbie was born, it was automatically assumed that a woman's role was to be a housewife and raise babies. Keeping Barbie vacuum-clearner-free was an important statement to little girls. It was a signal that they could exceed the boundaries that our culture had traditionally placed on them.

Barbie Is Nobody's Wife

Islamic leaders in Iran have described Barbie as being satanic. They have expressed concerns that "the unwholesome flexibility of these dolls, their destructive beauty, and their semi-nudity have an effect on the minds and morality of young children." Plenty of American parents have felt the same.

However, if you read Mattel's press releases for Barbie, you'll see that when she dresses to the nines, it's not to capture the gaze of some guy or even girl. Mattel's Barbie dresses for Barbie. She has no need to please anyone but herself. This is one of the many Barbie qualities that throws feminists for a loop: they detest the emphasis on glamour, yet no one can ever accuse Barbie of coddling to the whims of a man. The Barbie that Ruth Handler created doesn't care if she goes home alone and she doesn't need the approval of a male to make her feel good about herself. That's been as much a part of her message to little girls as the big boobs and tiny waist.

Here's another part of the Barbie mystique that upsets feminists: Barbie succeeds and succeeds well in traditional male professions. But whether she's being a firefighter or a physician, an astronaut or a police detective, Barbie always pulls it off with her femininity fully intact. Some women have said this sets an impossible standard for little girls, but it also tells little girls that you don't have to grow balls to have balls. Barbie has shown little girls that they don't have to surrender the things that they like about their femininity to compete in a man's world. Barbie has provided a way for little girls to experiment with the positive messages their parents and teachers are hopefully giving them. She also provides a way for little girls to be selfish and mean, as all children can be.

Mattel's Barbie has come with so few of the traditional limitations that any little girl can make her do and be anything she wants.

Less Fighting, Better Play?

Researchers have studied what types of play lead to more bickering and what kinds lead to less. One thing they didn't expect to find was that girls who are playing with Barbie dolls tend to fight less and display more advanced levels of play than girls who are playing with traditional dolls. The range of activities that Barbie play provides is much greater than a doll that you simply hold, feed, and change. Barbie has friends, activities, and a whole life that's as expansive as her different outfits and hairstyles. In addition, Barbie's presence invites the involvement of mothers, aunts, gay uncles, and even grandmothers who had their own Barbies when they were growing up.

Barbie was never intended to be the *Leap Frog* or *Hooked On Phonics* of children's play. The fact that Barbie inspires a high quality of play and better language development was not Mattel's goal. Mattel's emphasis has been for people to buy more Barbies and especially more Barbie accessories, perhaps in the same way that companies who make computer printers hope to nail you for the cost of the pricey replacement ink cartridges. It is fascinating how Mattel has managed to achieve this goal without limiting the persona of Barbie.

For instance, Mattel has never married off Barbie. Yet Mattel has sold millions of Barbie wedding dresses and thousands of Dream-Bride

Barbies or Wedding-Fantasy Barbies. The hitch has been that the wedding idea is all just a big Barbie dream or fantasy. Keeping Barbie from really being married allows little girls to marry and unmarry her as often as they desire. Being perpetually single keeps Barbie footloose and fancy free.

Mattel never wanted Barbie to be pregnant, but plenty of children wanted her to have a baby. So they devised a "Barbie Baby Sits" kit which contained an infant and other childcare objects.

As much as Barbie has been associated with fashion and glamour, Barbie has never defined fashion nor been at the cutting edge. She has always been a year or two behind, like most women who can't afford this year's Paris originals.

Femininity and Masculinity Constructed

In children's play, symbols can be far more important than words. As Barbie expert M. G. Lord tells us, Barbie's outfits have usually included purses or other container-like objects that are symbolic of female genitals. And Ken's outfits have had obvious phallic objects. For instance, in Barbie's cookout set, she has a spoon and a spatula, while in Ken's cookout set he has a long fork that is skewering a big pink weenie. Ken's hunting outfit has a massive rifle, his baseball outfit a really long bat, and his doctor's outfit a stethoscope with big long tubes.

Keeping Barbie a Moving Target

Few people will dispute that Barbie has become an American icon. Given her icon status, you would think she would appear the same today as she was in 1959. Not true. Since the very beginning, Mattel has made Barbie change and evolve. Some of these changes have been technological, like using different vinyls, skin tones, and hair. Other changes have been purely stylistic.

Barbie's face has changed as well. The first Barbie's face was a combination of her harsh-looking German mother and the Geishas of Japan, the country that first manufactured and helped to refine her. You can also see how the vinyl used in the #5 Ponytail Barbie of 1961 contained an oily compound that makes her look like she has a greasy face or is perspiring. Unfortunately, the more recent Barbies have been given a bubbly, wide-eyed generic smile rather than the more intriguing streetwalker-Geisha expression of the early years. The faces on the early Barbies were all hand-painted in Japan, while the latter ones are machine stenciled.

A Cock-Ring Ken?

Ken was an afterthought to Barbie. He was released in answer to the demand for a Barbie boyfriend, but he was always expendable.

When Ken was being conceived, the two women who had created the persona of Barbie wanted him to have a bulge between his legs. The male executives at Mattel were horrified and embarrassed at the suggestion. They wanted Ken to have the same crotch as Barbie. The women held out and Ken got a compromise bulge, although no one would ever accuse him of holding a candle to a doll with the masculine persona of GI Joe.

In the mid-1960s, Mattel released a "Ken a Go Go" doll, where Ken played the ukulele. Not long after that, Ken was euthanized. He reappeared in 1969 with an extreme makeover that Mattel hoped would revive his dismal sales. Then, in 1993, Mattel released the truly amazing "Earring Magic Ken." This Ken was literally swept off the shelves by a stampede of adult gay males. "Earring Magic Ken," also known as "Cock Ring Ken," was dressed in a lavender vest and had a necklace around his neck with a cock ring on it. The cock ring was not only the spitting image of the cock rings that men at gay male rages were wearing around their necks, but it was scaled to the exact dimensions as well. (It seems that someone in the design department at Mattel got one by the corporate brass.)

The more recent Kens have actually appeared as if they might be straight and even have a bit of a hunk factor. If Ken really is up for servicing Barbie, Mattel should consider making a Viagra Ken. That's because the average Ken has at least eight Barbies that he needs to put out for.

Late Breaking News—Does Ken Have Alzheimer's? Is Barbie Doing a Hunk Half Her Age?

At the 2004 Toy Fair, Mattel executives announced that after forty-three years together, Barbie was dumping Ken. It seems that Mattel might be pushing one of their newer boytoys named Blaine in Barbie's direction.

The Kens of late had been looking considerably more manly, while some of the Blaines look like Southern California mall-rat druggies. Poor Ken: he finally turns straight and now Mattel is putting him into assisted living.

As for how well Blaine might be equipped, in one of his earlier packagings he was holding an electric guitar with a neck that was so long it was at least the equivalent of a 9" penis.

Barbie and Your Sexual Needs...

According to our adult readers, plenty of their Barbies liked to have sex. So imagine if Barbie were an ambassador for your sexual needs now that you are grown up? For instance, if you were in a new relationship and were thinking of having sex, you and your partner could get a couple of Barbies and maybe a Ken or even a G.I. Joe. They could do a show and tell, where they would answer questions such as the following:

What sorts of things turn Barbie on?

How does Barbie like to be kissed?

Does Barbie masturbate? If so, does she use her fingers or a vibrator?

Does Barbie go down on Ken or G.I. Joe? If so, how can the guys help it to be a good experience for everyone?

Does Barbie swallow?

What kinds of sex does Barbie like the best?

Does Barbie like to initiate sex?

Does Barbie like to sleep with men, women, or both?

What kinds of signs does Barbie use to let her partner know what she likes and what she doesn't like?

Does Barbie like to have her breasts played with? If so, can she show what feels best?

Can Barbie show Ken exactly how she likes to have her clitoris touched?

If Barbie likes intercourse, does she have favorite positions?

If one of the dolls is a male, he can answer similar questions about his own sexuality.

Barbie and friends could say things to each other that the two of you might feel too embarrassed to say in real life. Perhaps they could show each other things that you can't quite put into words.

You and your partner could also have fun creating sex scenarios for Barbie and her lovers. Maybe she could pick up another Ken or Barbie and have a threesome. Or maybe she and her partner could play strip poker, or one of them could be dominant and boss the other around. Like Barbie herself, the possibilities abound.

Parents & Barbie

What follows is the ultimate discussion of Barbie by the parents of a young girl. It is from Margaret Atwood's piece *The Female Body*:

> He said, I won't have one of those things around the house. It gives a young girl a false notion of beauty, not to mention anatomy. If a real woman was built like that, she'd fall flat on her face.

> She said, If we don't let her have one like all the other girls she'll feel singled out. It'll become an issue. She'll long for one and she'll long to turn into one. Repression breeds sublimation. You know that.

> He said, It's not just the pointy plastic tits, it's the wardrobes. The wardrobes and that stupid male doll, what's his name, the one with the underwear glued on.

> She said, Better to get it over with when she's young.

> He said, All right, but don't let me see it.

> She came whizzing down the stairs, thrown like a dart. She was stark naked. Her hair had been chopped off, her head was turned back to front, she was missing some toes, and she'd been tattooed all over her body with purple ink, in a scrollwork design. She hit the potted azalea, trembled there for a moment like a botched angel, and fell.

> He said, I guess we're safe.

The Female Body by Margaret Atwood, originally printed in Vol. XXIX, No. 4, Fall 1990 issue of Michigan Quarterly Review, edited by Laurence Goldstein.

Excellent Resources: This discussion of Barbie has provided only a small sketch of the truly rich and fascinating history of this cultural icon. If it has peaked your interest, you are strongly encouraged to check out at least two excellent books on the subject. One is M.G. Lord's exceptional *Forever Barbie—The Unauthorized Biography of a Real Doll*, 1994/1995, Avon Books, New York, New York.

One of Lord's many fine observations can be found in her discussion of Barbie's friend, Midge: "If plastic dolls could kill themselves, I'm sure Midge would have tried."

Regarding the second highly recommended book, *Face of the American Dream, Barbie Doll (1959-1971)* by Christopher Varaste, Hobby House Press, 1999. Who knew that photos of the early Barbie could be so fascinating and compelling? Barbie's face and expression during this period was much more interesting than now, and Varaste does an exceptional job capturing it.

Reader's Comments

"Ways Barbie impacted my femininity? She made me hate clothes."   *female age 21*

"Ways Barbie impacted my femininity? I dress better now."
female age 20

"My sister and I were a little obsessed with Barbie. We turned old dressers and coffee tables into Barbie mansions. I played with Barbie from the time I was 4 until I was 11 or 12. I'm not sure when Barbie and Ken started having sex (they weren't just sleeping in the same bed), maybe when I was 7, that's when I learned what intercourse involved. Mostly, I got the dolls undressed, put them in bed and twisted their bodies back and forth. They couldn't really do anything since Barbie didn't have a vagina and Ken didn't have a penis. However, once Barbie and Ken started having sex, they never stopped. Every night. That's how I thought it was done, only at night, only in bed. Several Barbies went through a sex change. I got her ready for the operation (remember Dr. Barbie?), wheeled her into the operating room, and when she came out, she'd been replaced with a Ken doll. All of Barbie's friends talked about her behind her back when she got the change—her mother (grandma Barbie) had a hard time coping. I'm being glib, but I did act all of this out. My Barbies had detailed conversations, had intimate family lives, detailed jobs, etc. There was a lot of adultery in Barbie's world which resulted in divorces, private investigators, and alcoholism. All the adultery was acted out in full detail, from Ken coming on to his secretary at work to the act itself to Barbie throwing all of Ken's clothes out the window... Barbie helped me act out my own questions about being an adult. I'm a feminist now, I have a healthy relationship, earn more than my spouse, don't wear make-up or high-healed shoes, and my husband helps with all the housework. It's okay to let little girls play with Barbie." *female age 24*

"Ways Barbie impacted your femininity and/or sexuality: There was one summer when I was fairly obsessed with the fact that Ken had no dick. Beach Ken had a totally inaccurately placed suggestion of one, but no balls." *female age 21*

"My cousin and I were addicted to our Barbies, from as early as I can remember. I think I was seven or eight when our Barbies started having all sorts of high-drama romances, and there were ALL SORTS of different sexual experiences going on. My cousin and I were very creative with our Barbies' sexual escapades. I remember mine even having some homosexual experiences, which my cousin thought was weird. I actually think that my Barbies were a big outlet for my sexual curiosity growing up. When I was a teenager and no longer played with Barbies, I wondered if maybe it was odd that I made my Barbies have all sorts of sexual experiences when I was so young. But as I've gotten older, I've realized that sexually, I'm a very open and curious person, and I think it's just that I've always been that way. When I played with Barbies with my cousin though, I almost always had to play Ken. I find myself now very comfortable filling a lot of traditionally masculine roles in my relationships. The two may or may not be related."

female age 22

"Ugh, as much as I hate to admit it, yes my Barbies had sex. And since I also had a twelve-inch Luke Skywalker doll, they did it A LOT. I also played with a girlfriend at the time. We did sex play with our dolls." *female age 34*

The Historical Breast & Bra

Chapter 5

An early reader of this chapter said, "I'd rather be flogged with my Wonderbra than read a boring chapter on bras and breasts. I'm going straight to Chapter 22 where I can learn how to give a better blowjob."

Imagine that, a woman who takes her Wonderbra for granted! Before the 1920s, women were skeptical about bras. They preferred to wear corsets. As for bras being thought of as cute or sexy, that wouldn't happen until World War II.

There's hardly a woman in Western culture who doesn't have a bunch of bras, including a favorite one or two that she wears when she wants to feel extra sexy. She can also make a sexual statement by not wearing a bra. And what teenage boy doesn't equate success in dating with whether a girl let him put his hand under her bra?

This chapter looks at breasts and the bras that hold them up. It begins with a peek at breasts in different times and different places. It then focuses on the fascinating evolution of the bra: how it came to be in 1860, and how it eventually came to have a sexual edge. There's even a section on how to properly fit a bra, which is as much to help guys know more as girls. Later in this book, there's a separate chapter on touching and kissing breasts once the bra is off the chest and on the floor: Chapter 26: "Nipples, Nipples, Nipples."

The Ups and Downs of the French Breast

In the time of Renaissance France, it was believed that breast milk was made from blood that flowed from the vagina. This notion was handed down from the ancient Greeks, with Leonardo DiVinci eventually making a diagram of it (as redone here by our own Daerick DiVinci).

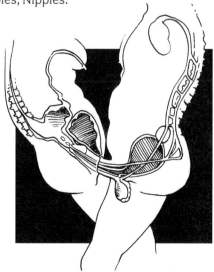

Since it was assumed that breast milk rose up from the vagina, intercourse was thought to curdle the breast milk supply. Perhaps the French believed that a penis going in and out of a vagina was like a paddle churning buttermilk. Whatever the case, women who were nursing babies weren't supposed to have intercourse. The gory details are shown in the illustration on page 39.

Given how the upper-class French women would rather have sex than nurse babies, the nursing job was pawned off on the women of the lower class. This caused there to be a distinction between the breasts of the lower class and those of the upper class. Breasts of the lower class were expected to be large and lactating, while upper-class breasts were expected to be small and perky. (They must have assumed that poor women didn't like sex, so their milk was safe.)

Before the revolution, women used the same kind of makeup on their breasts as they used on their faces. The goal was to make their breasts look exceptionally white. Older women would paint blue veins on their breasts to make them look like the more transparent skin of the younger girls. Unfortunately, the makeup they used on their faces and breasts was a compound that contained lead. Not only did it corrode the skin but it contributed to cases of lead poisoning. Not to be outdone by their sisters from the past, today's runway models sometimes paint nail polish on their erect nipples as a way of keeping them erect.

In time and with the coming of the French Revolution, the heads of many upper-class French women became separated from their perky breasts. Eventually it became not only fashionable but a sign of patriotism for all French women to nurse their babies.

Saggy and Happy in Papua

In Papua, New Guinea, grown women parade their saggy breasts with pride. It's considered a sign of childishness or immaturity for a woman in Papua to have the kind of breasts that Americans value. In fact, when ladies in Papua are getting catty, they might accuse someone of having the taut round breasts of a younger woman.

To the traditional Papuan male, the surgically-stuffed breasts of American actresses would be a big waste of time and money. And the traditional Papuan woman would think to herself, "Why would a woman want to do something crazy like that to her breasts just when they were starting to sag?"

In our culture, breasts have been often been regarded as the crown jewels of feminine appeal. For whatever reason, American breasts are covered in public. But in Africa and the South Pacific, women have walked around for centuries with their breasts bare. The men in those cultures don't get much of a rise from women's breasts. Instead, it's the parts that are covered up, namely the buttocks, that the men tend to find erotic.

Imagine what a dent it would have put in the lingerie, porn and plastic surgery businesses if women in America were always top-less and breasts weren't considered sexy? The entire Playboy empire would have never been, and Victoria's Secret would have started with thongs instead of bras.

War Bonds and Liberty's Breasts

To see how breasts were starting to be sexualized in America, consider World War I "Liberty Bonds" posters featuring Lady Liberty.

In the first poster, Liberty is a sturdy woman with the sexual appeal of a truck driver. The only way you can tell she is a woman is by the endless yards of drapes that are covering every inch of her body except for her manly, muscled arms and her stern, angular face. John Ashcroft could have relaxed around this Lady Liberty. After the release of this poster, bond sales continued to sag.

Months later, the next poster was released. Liberty had become less manly and she was even a bit sensual. A year later, by the time the fifth "Buy Bonds" poster was out, Liberty was quite feminine and scantily clad. She looked like she had been dressed by the people at Trashy Lingerie instead of being outfitted in a drapery shop. While her breasts were by no means large, they were taut and had an erotic edge. You actually had to look twice to see if any material from her nearly see-through gown was covering them. By the end of World War I, Uncle Sam was learning what it takes to sell bonds.

Twenty years later, during the second World War, American sol-diers consumed six million copies of *Esquire Magazine*. Perhaps this is because it showcased Vargas girls with their massive, gravity-defying bosoms. It was during World War II that pinup girls became famous.

The corset has a rich and interesting history. Contrary to what you often hear, very few women who wore corsets did a practice known as "tight-lacing." Tight-lacing is a fetish where the person wearing the corset laces it up so tight that his or her waist becomes unnaturally small. Many women in the early 1900s were hesitant to give up wearing corsets. Switching to a bra or "bosom supporter" might have been like a woman today going from panties to a thong.

The women who prepared the pinup models for the photography shoots would stuff the models' bras with layer after layer of felt pads. They felt this would help lift the soldiers' morale, among other things.

Birth of the Bra

For several centuries, the corset was the undergarment that supported the weight of women's breasts. The first brassiere wasn't patented until the time of the Civil War and it didn't appear in the marketplace until the late 1800s. It would be another twenty years after the end of the century before the brassiere would win widespread acceptance among American women. Several elements needed to converge for the bra to knock out the corset.

According to Jane Farrell-Beck and Colleen Gau in their excellent book *Uplift—The Bra in America*, here are some of the changes that needed to occur in women's lives for the bra to become popular:

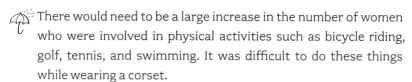 There would need to be a large increase in the number of women who were involved in physical activities such as bicycle riding, golf, tennis, and swimming. It was difficult to do these things while wearing a corset.

There needed to be a major change in the number of women in the workforce. For instance, there were virtually no female telephone operators in the 1880s. By the 1920s, with the explosion of telephones, there were huge numbers of female operators. These operators needed to reach across large switchboards to plug in cords to complete each call. This would have been difficult to do while wearing a corset with bones sewn into it.

The materials and design of the bra had to improve. Bras needed to fit better, have adjustable straps, be able to fasten easily, and they needed to have soft cups with underwiring to help lift and separate the breasts. The latter, when first introduced in 1910 by brassiere visionary Madeleine Gabeau, seriously clashed with the monobosom or monobreast look of the day. The monobosom look made women appear as though they had no defined breasts or cleavage. It was the bodice equivalent of wrap-around sunglasses. Needless to say, there needed to be significant changes in women's fashion for the bra to nose out the corset.

This is our illustrator's interpretation of a 1950s bra ad. The ad copy read "Perma•Lift, the lift that never lets you down! New, exciting, exquisite. Secretly processed Perma•Lift cushioned insets. Achieve the permanent uplift." Sounds like an ad for car tires!

———————————

 Women needed to start wearing ready-made clothing rather than having clothes custom made, and the price of the bra had to come down to fit the budget of the "new" working woman.

 A further stumbling block to acceptance of the bra was the lack of a universal sizing code. It wasn't until 1933 that a bra manufacturer proposed sizing bras according to cup sizes A, B, C and D.

World War II—Bad for Adolf, a Boon for the Bra

Before World War II, many American women had never worn pants. But once women began manning America's War Machine, pants are what they wore. This took many women by surprise, and some by shock. Articles began appearing in women's magazines giving tips and suggestions for how to wear pants. With the changes brought about by World War II, American women weren't just wearing pants and bras, they were punishing them.

This is the first time in history that welders, riveters, and ship builders wore bras, or admitted to it anyway. Bra design needed to seriously evolve to accommodate the range of motion of the new female workforce. Yet the supply of bra-making materials such as rubber, cotton, metal, and rayon was now rationed and in short supply.

For instance, it required 1,000 pounds of rubber to build an airplane, 1750 pounds of rubber to build a tank, and 150,000 pounds of rubber to build a battleship. Yet America's main supply for rubber had been through Asia—a trade route that evaporated with the beginning of hostilities. Without rubber there was little elastic with which to make bras. It was not easy for bra manufacturers to make it through the war!

Not only were bras keeping Rosie the Riveter's breasts from flopping, one bra manufacturer was given a secret contract by the government to produce special vests that carrier pigeons could wear. The vests, which employed much of Maiden Form's bra technology, allowed paratroopers to parachute while holding carrier pigeons. The pigeons were used for communications when radio silence was essential, such as right before D-Day.

Along with making pants a new part of women's wardrobes, World War II also gave the bra, with it's increasingly pointed cups, a new name: the Torpedo.

Foundations Start to Shake & Bras Become Sexy

By the end of World War II, actresses started sprouting seriously pointed breasts. It was as if the sultry Vargas Girl drawings were suddenly hopping off the pages of *Esquire* and coming to life. Books like Peyton Place were bringing small-town sleaze into the public eye, and the Kinsey reports on the sexuality of American men and women shocked and intrigued the masses. Sex was in the air!

Shortly after World War II, the Sweater Girl started to appear. When viewed from the side, Sweater Girl actress Lana Turner's breasts came out at a 90 degree angle. This was achieved by a bra which was the latex equivalent of the Golden Gate Bridge. A similar two-cupped engineering marvel called the "Bullet Bra" sold in the millions.

1947 was the year when Frederick Mellinger opened the first Frederick's of Hollywood. Millions of Americans were seeing his sexy magazine ads and receiving his Frederick's catalogue. Frederick's teased and titillated customers with items such as their Peek-A-Boo brassiere and half-moon stick on brassiere.

By 1949, Maidenform had begun its Dream campaign, which showed women wearing bras and flowing skirts saying things like, "I dreamed I danced all night in my Maidenform Bra" or "I dreamed I won the election in my Maidenform Bra." One of the Maidenform ads from 1962 showed a sexy young woman wearing only a bra with a bare midriff, a long tight skirt, and elbow-length gloves. She was standing next to a large bull with one hand sensuously stroking one of the bull's big horns. The caption read, "I dreamed I took the bull by the horns in my Maidenform Bra." Only a blind person would have missed the sexual innuendo of the ad. Many of today's feminists would have concerns about this notion, saying that women's power was dependent on their sexuality or sexual allure. Nonetheless, like their gutsy mothers who built our planes and tanks in World War II, women in the 1960s with their Maidenform bras were a force to be reckoned with.

The 1950s also gave birth to the inflatable bra, which gave a woman the option of pulling a tube out of each breast cup and filling it up to the desired level of allure. This was also helpful if the woman was flying in a plane and it went down over the ocean.

In 1970, Victoria's Secret emerged to grab the sexy-bra baton from Frederick's of Hollywood. Frederick's had acquired a sleazy edge, while Victoria's Secret screamed "classy and elegant." Victoria's Secret suddenly worked its way under women's blouses and into their pants. American women no longer needed to blush or make excuses to enter a Victoria's Secret as they had in the later Frederick's years. And if the thousand-or-so Victoria's Secret stores weren't enough, millions upon millions of Victoria's Secret catalogues have been read by American women and men from coast to coast. Unfortunately, there has been a price to be paid for the new elegance and sexual allure—a bra from Victoria's Secret often costs two or three times more than a similar design from Sears or Target.

Our drawing of a 1950s WonderBra ad. The copy reads: "She's Adorable..." "She's Bewitching..." "She's Delightfully Deceiving..." "She's Exclusively Elegant..." With the way the ad is written, it is hard to tell if it is referring to the women, their breasts or their bras. But that was the point. If you bought the bra, you got it all!

The bra is the final outpost that separates the outside world from the sensuous breast. Because of what it covers, the bra has achieved a kind of fetish quality for both men and women. That fetish quality has reached new heights in the last few decades when rock icons like Madonna started wearing designer underwear on the outside rather than on the inside. Foundations were shifting once more.

Crossing Your Heart from 1920 to Today

Bra and breast fashion has yo-yo'ed over the years, going from boy-like breasts to the Torpedo, and back again. In the 1920s, the flat-chested look was in fashion. By the 1930s, the full-busted look was back. By the 1940s, women started calling the brassiere a "bra." Bras and panties were now populating underwear drawers nationwide—a trend that continues to this day.

During the first wave of 1960s feminism, the popular saying *Burn Your Bra* came into being, as if bras were a ball and chain placed on women's chests by male jailers. Yet women hold almost half of the bra patents that have been awarded, and women have owned a number of bra-manufacturing plants. There's never been a glass ceiling holding women back from the higher ranks of corporate bradom.

Since the 1970s, some women have been trading in their natural breasts for surgically-enhanced models where the Torpedo Bra of the 1940s seems to be sewn into their chests.

Far from being something that holds women back, the bra was designed to hold parts of them up. It was made to help women deal with the discomforting pull of gravity. Of course, when you consider that breasts weigh from eight ounces to ten pounds, gravity has meant different things to different women.

The First Falsies

In case you think that insecurity about the size of body parts is a newly-acquired disease in America, some of the first falsies could be ordered through the Sears Catalogue in the late 1890s. They were called "bust pads" and were described as helping to "plump up the bosom." The same Sears, Roebuck & Co. catalogue with the bust pads also sold "The Princess Bust Developer, a New Scientific Help To Nature, If Nature Has Not Favored You." The Princess Bust Developer promised to enlarge and shape the bosom. It included a cream that was called "Bust Cream or Food, Unrivaled for Enlargement of the Bust," and a pump that looked like a toilet plunger. This sort of thing is still being advertised in magazines and on late-night TV!

For those of you who think that body-part insecurity only belonged to women, dozens of ads from the Police Gazette in the 1890s promised solutions for enlarging the penis (see pages 88-89).

No Room for Misfits

It is estimated that 80% of women aren't wearing the right bra. It's not like they accidently put on someone else's bra, but they might as well have. It takes a real effort to get the right bra size. Bra cup sizes can range from A to H, with stops in between at B, C, D, DD, E, F, FF, G and GG. There are also a large number of options for rib cage and back sizes.

If you compare the chests of two women who wear 36 C bras, their breasts can be shaped very differently. One woman's breasts might be shaped like eggplants, another's like cones.

Many women ignore that their breasts change size and shape over time. Just because you were a 36-B two years ago doesn't mean you are a 36-B today. Some breasts undergo significant changes in tenderness and size at different times during the menstrual cycle. A bra that might have been just fine on day one might be uncomfortable on day 27. Also keep in mind that your breast size can increase if you go on the birth control pill, and might decrease if you go off of it.

Bra shopping is not the sort of thing you should do by mail order, and you would be well-served to seek out a lingerie shop where the sales help has been fitting bras since the beginning of time. Avoid the sales clerk who is chewing gum and hasn't finished high school. Also avoid bras where there are bulges in the armpits or if the bra makes your breasts go out to the side. Your breasts shouldn't bulge along the top of the cups. And keep in mind that one company's 40 DD might be another company's 38 E.

Not only do you want a bra that fits and feels great through a full range of body motions, but you want one that holds up to repeated washings. It needs to support you in a way that keeps the ligaments in your breasts from stretching. Otherwise, there's not much point in wearing one.

Whether breasts are large or small, they are attached to the chest by suspensory ligaments. These ligaments are not elastic. Once they stretch they don't snap back. In her *Breast Book*, Dr. Miriam Stoppard recommends that young girls be given good supporting bras to wear, and that a woman should not go braless for long if she does not want her breasts to sag. (This would be a hard sell in places like Papua.)

Purchasing a bra isn't something a woman should do on the fly, and she shouldn't try to do it with two small children in tow. A caring partner will make sure that a woman has plenty of time to try on every bra in the store if she needs to.

Highest Recommendation: You will be hard-pressed to find a more interesting, better-written book on the bra than *Uplift-The Bra in America* by Jane Farrell-Beck and Colleen Gau, University of Pennsylvania Press, 2002. This book is the kind of marvel that should be—but seldom is— the staple of America's university presses. It is better researched than most of the other books on women's foundations, but it doesn't insult the reader with poor editing or incomprehensible sentences. In addition to exploring changes in fashion, *Uplift* shows the evolution of the bra within different social and economic contexts. If you want a good read about a fascinating subject, *Uplift* is a great choice.

If you are interested in more about corsets, consider the highly intelligent writings of Valerie Steele. She has managed to anger male corset enthusiasts because she calls their practice of wearing women's corsets a fetish. (Where would she ever get a silly idea like that?) Males who are strapping themselves into women's corsets are concerned that Ms. Steele is giving them an undeserved stigma. She's also managed to anger some of the academic feminists, because she has discussed how wearing corsets has had erotic associations and how the dangers have been blown out of proportion. They see her as being an apologist for the "corset torture" of women. It would be interesting to know how the corset-wearing women from the eighteenth and nineteenth centuries would weigh in on this matter.

Men's Underwear
The Fruit in Your Loom

Chapter 6

What would you think if a guy phoned his partner and said, "God, honey, I start to get hard when I think about the new briefs I'm wearing." Contrast this with a woman who calls her partner and says, "God, honey, my nipples start to get hard when I think about the new bra that I'm wearing."

In our culture, it's cool for a girl to get excited about her lingerie, but we'd consider a guy who talked this way about his own briefs to be a little strange. Of course, if he just spent $18 for a single pair of tightie-whities with a fancy name on the waistband, we'd hope the darned things would give him a rise.

Calvin Klein—The New Jockey in Your Underwear Drawer

In the early 1980s, manufacturers like Calvin Klein teamed up with famed homoerotic photographers like Bruce Weber to help make men look sexy in their traditional white briefs. Needless to say, the men they used in their photo shoots would have looked sexy wearing a loincloth made of cornhusks. Some people might say that the real emphasis of these ads boiled down to the bulge in the crotch—with all visual roads in those huge billboard ads drawing your eye to the sausage behind the fly.

The Calvin ads had two primary targets—gay men and straight women who buy underwear for their husbands and boyfriends. Nail these two groups, and straight guys are putty in the corporate hand.

In these underwear ads, the hazy image of a penis behind the fly was sexier than if the guy had been naked or if his penis had been hanging out. With his penis behind a white cotton veil, the model was able to give attitude in a way that a man who is buck naked can't. The combination of attitude and mystery about what's inside the briefs was fuel for many a fantasy. So while all roads led to the bulge in the briefs, it wouldn't have worked if the briefs had been pulled down to the hunk's knees. Women were being exposed to the same kind of "babe-in-a-lacy-bra" eye candy that's stimulated men over the ages, only with a fascinating urban contemporary edge.

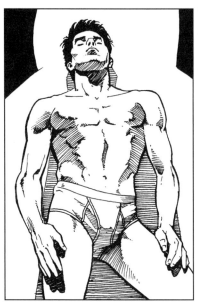

What Were Some of the Subliminal Messages in These Ads?

Wouldn't it be something if a woman could buy a pair of Calvin briefs for her man and have him suddenly look like the models in the Calvin ads? And wouldn't it be amazing if a man could slip on his Calvin briefs and suddenly feel like the Calvin Klein version of the Marlboro Man, minus the horse and the lung cancer?

Of course, if one of the models in the early Calvin ads walked into a room full of straight women, he would have no trouble finding a place to spend the night, even if his day job was collecting trash and he wore $2.00 briefs from WalMart.

The New Girl Underwear—Finally, a Fly for Your Clitoris!

There have been a few interesting changes in the underwear scene in the past two decades. For one, manufacturers have started making men's underwear for women. This has been perceived as massively cool. The boybrief as worn by women even has a fly or the suggestion of a fly in the front.

If you are in gender studies, you might assume that girls enjoy wearing boybriefs because it's a girl's way of taking the patriarchy's pecker and making it her own. Wearing boybriefs with a fly in the front makes the message even clearer.

But something more practical is involved. Women in our culture receive far more encouragement to explore and experiment with fashion than men do. For many women, fashion is a great adventure, and they have adopted zillions of styles throughout the ages—from some that were hideous to some that were elegant. Few of these had anything to do with trying to assume dimensions of masculinity. Quite to the contrary, much of women's fashion is designed to win the awe and delight of a girl's female friends.

As you will see in the next section, the road to making men's underwear cool for women to wear is much different from the road to making women's underwear safe for men to wear.

Men with Bikini Briefs, Trimmed Pubes, and Waxed Backs

Over the last decade, males in university settings have started teaching courses on men's studies. Of the many things they worry about, trying to define masculinity is near the top of their list. They often say that a defining hallmark of masculinity is that it tries to be the opposite of anything that's feminine.

Perhaps these scholars haven't noticed that straight guys have been doing a lot of girly things as of late, such as wearing earrings, and having the hair on their entire upper body waxed or zapped with lasers. Some even shave their legs, and plenty have taken to trimming their pubes and wearing underwear that's like a woman's bikini bottom.

Since this chapter is about underwear, we'll save the earrings and shaved scrotums for another day. What are some of the factors that have made it safe for men to wear women's bikini bottoms?

The Speedo Coefficient. We've had generations of incredible-looking Olympic male swimmers and water polo players who wear nothing but Speedos, which are basically g-strings on steroids.[1] Hard as you might try to keep looking straight ahead, Speedos have a built-in device that forces your eyes to stare at the guy's crotch and butt, even if this would be followed by a scream of horror if the man in the Speedo was sixty-years-old and ninety pounds overweight. Clearly, there is a precedent for a straight guy to wear girl's bikini bottoms for underwear. It's called the Speedo Coefficient.

Men-With-Pro-Balls Effect. It didn't hurt the cause of the male bikini when professional male athletes were hired to be in magazine ads and on posters in their bikini briefs. These half-naked athletes had women swooning, and they reassured men that they wouldn't risk being seen as gay if they wore women's bikini bottoms.

---

[1]Swimming at the Olympics recently took it in the shorts as a spectator sport when the men's traditional Speedos were replaced by a cross between bicycle shorts and a wetsuit.

The "Honey Do" Influence. A guy would have less resistance to wearing girls' bikini bottoms if his wife said, "Honey, I think you'll look sexy in these." This fact wasn't lost on the underwear manufacturers, as the ads with the male athletes in their bikini briefs were clearly aimed at women.

Penis-Over-The-Top Factor. The transition to bikini underwear for men had a good deal of practical significance. That's because when we pee, a lot of us don't pull the penis through the fly in men's briefs or boxers. Instead, we yank the elastic waistband down and pull the penis over the top. So the fly is totally useless for a lot of men and having the lower waistband makes the process of peeing easier.

Briefs and Bras in Perspective

Publications in gender studies tend to focus on subjects like violence, rape, and the truly awful things that some people do to others. They would consider our look at men's and women's underwear superficial. However, "superficial" means "on the outside." In the last two chapters, we took your shirts off and pulled your pants down.

If we had a Gender Studies course here at Goofy Foot University (a.k.a. Goofy F-U!), students would spend the first week playing with Barbie, GI Joe, Legos, and Matchbox Cars. They would then be asked to consider the relationships between play and gender identification. The next week, they would have to strip down to their undies and free-associate about what's masculine and what's feminine.

The most important lesson, however, is that a hundred years ago, no one would have been able to predict that the bra would ever be sexy. And as little as fifty years ago, no one would have been able to predict that men would feel manly wearing women's bikini bottoms. Look at all of the effort that went into turning these pieces of cloth into a part of our sexual fabric.

END OF CHAPTER NOTES: Most male surfers wouldn't be caught dead in Speedos. The only commonality between many male swimmers and surfers seems to be water, and the water of the former smells like chlorine while the water of the later tastes like salt.

"30,000 Thrilling, Invigorating, Penetrating, Revitalizing Vibrations per Minute"

Chapter 7

Throughout history, hysteria has been the most highly diagnosed disease in women. By the end of the 1800s, hysteria was such a major player in the medical mind that physicians assumed more than half of all women had it. Historian Rachel Maines says this is significant when you consider that physicians often treated women with hysteria by using genital massage—hands on, drop-your-knickers-in-the-doctor's-office genital massage.

Finding a definition of hysteria depended on who you asked. Symptoms ranged from anxiety, depression, or insomnia to feeling irritable, having sexual fantasies, or generous vaginal lubrication. One could argue that men had hysteria as often as women, but instead of going to a physician for genital massage, they walked one block south to receive this service from a prostitute.

The connection between hysteria and the female genitals was first made during the time of the ancient Greeks, when they proposed that hysteria was caused by a uterus that wandered inside the body. Intercourse, horseback riding, hydrotherapy, and genital massage have been but a few of the recommended treatments.

By the late 1800s, a big chunk of many physicians' and midwives' private practices involved treating hysteria with genital massage. There were several elements that made this treatment socially acceptable and medically sound. For instance, it wasn't considered sexual because the hands were placed on the vulva and nothing went inside the vagina. There was much greater controversy in the 1800s over the use of a speculum, which some physicians considered to be sexually scandalous because it went where the penis was supposed to go.

Proper medical practice was to massage the clitoral area with lubricated fingers. It was not unusual for the physician to keep massaging the woman's genitals until the table began to shake due to the patient's trembling response. The resulting orgasm was called a "paroxysm." This kind of massage was not regarded as a sexual act any more than having your back cracked by a chiropractor is today.

Why didn't they simply suggest to the woman that she mastur-bate? Masturbation by either men or women was considered a debili-tating disease, and physicians in the 1800s did not approve of it.

If you consider that the lion's share of the physician's or midwife's day could be spent in treating hysteria, imagine how receptive they were in the 1880s when the electric vibrator was invented. The neces-sary "hysterical paroxysm" (orgasm) could sometimes be achieved in less than ten minutes rather than in the hour that manual stimulation might require.

Two Birds with One Stone

During the 1800s, most physicians considered electric currents to be healing. Some also considered physical vibrations to be healing. Since the vibrations from the vibrator came from electric currents, using a vibrator on a hysterical vulva was the medical equivalent of winning the daily double.

Vibrators became available for home use at the end of the 1800s. According to Dr. Maines, they were advertised in publications from Home Needlework Magazine to the Sears, Roebuck Catalogue. They were said to stimulate the circulation and soothe the nerves. Vibra-tors were advertised under titles such as "Aids that Every Woman Appreciates".

The magazine ads for vibrators were often on the same page as ads for sex books or other personal matters. The vibrator ads included statements such as "It makes you fairly tingle with the joy of living," "The pleasures of youth will throb within you," and "30,000 thrilling, invigorating, penetrating, revitalizing vibrations per minute."

In addition to electronic vibrators, water-powered vibrators were also available. The advertisements for the water-powered vibrators boasted that they cost less than being treated at the doctor's office and they had the privacy of being used in your own home. However, once public utilities started putting water meters on private homes, the water-powered vibrator lost some of its appeal.

Hydrotherapy was a very popular treatment for hysteria in the mid-1800s. The effect was similar to masturbating with the jet of a hottub or by sitting under the spigot of the bathtub with your legs apart. Women in the 1800s seemed to enjoy hydrotherapy a great deal. However, the equipment was expensive and not readily available, and going to one of the spas that provided this treatment cost more than most women could afford. The electric vibrator brought many of the same benefits to women who couldn't afford the expensive spas.

For a well-documented, fascinating and unique study of this subject, check out *The Technology of Orgasm—Hysteria, the Vibrator and Women's Sexual Satisfaction* by Rachel P. Maines, Johns Hopkins University Press, 1999. Be forewarned that Dr. Maines writes to an academic audience and pretty much feels that men have been the scourge of all creation. She didn't spend much time exploring the possibility that some women may have felt better after their visits to the doctor's office. Dr. Maines might say that this would have been okay if the woman's desire for sexual contact hadn't been part of a medical diagnosis, or if medicine had been controlled by both sexes.

A Different Rub on Male Hysteria

The men who saw action in the trenches of World War I were exposed to some of the most brutal and frightening warfare known to humankind. As a result, there were thousands of mental health casualties who were said to suffer from shell shock. Symptoms included weeping, depression, nightmares, and anxiety attacks. Shell shock was considered by many to be a male form of hysteria.

While hysteria in women was often treated with genital massage, men who had this condition were treated with harsh electric shocks that were thinly disguised attempts at torture. The purpose was to shock the shell-shock victims into acting manly. It did not work.

If there had been any kind of equality or fairness in the way the sexes were treated, the male shell-shock victims would have had their genitals massaged in order to give them the healing "paroxysm" that the female hysterics received. Instead, modern medicine tried to shame and torture them into behaving like men once again.

Sigmund Freud was one of the people who spoke out against this kind of treatment. He did not feel that psychiatrists could or should torture a person into giving up a natural response to terror.

Time to Change Gears

We would have been happy to have done several more chapters like the four you have just read on Barbie, the Bra, Briefs and Vibrators. Then again, maybe you're thinking "I'll slit my wrists if I have to read another of those things. Let's get on to the SEX stuff."

And so it will be, starting with romance.

Romance

Chapter 8

Dear Paul,

This romance thing is making me crazy. I'm dating a wonderful girl named Valerie and last night I took her to a romantic night out at an expensive restaurant. I spent more than $100 for the two of us. She seemed to be having a good time. I figured that before the night was over my Little Willy would be seeing some serious action. But when I took her home all I got was a thirty-second good-night kiss. At this rate, I'll have to spend at least $2,000 on a weekend in Acapulco just to get a hand job. Do you have any suggestions?

Randy from Norfolk

Dear Randy,

You might be confusing romance with prostitution. This is a bad mistake, unless the woman you are romancing also enjoys turning tricks on the side. If what you are looking for is sex, you shouldn't have any trouble finding a woman who will give you more than a hand job for $100. If what you are looking for is romance, then sex should not be the goal. That's because romance has its own special universe that resides somewhere between Platonic love and carnal lust. Sure,

romance can evolve into sex, but it's just as possible to have a perfectly romantic evening and end up in bed alone. When that happens,
you do what the rest of us have done since the beginning of time: you
lather up Little Willy with his favorite brand of lotion and romance
him that way.

———————

Dear Paul,

*Romance is that mushy stuff that fills Harlequin novels. It is an
entirely feminine construct. Men only become romantic when sheer raw
sex is assured. Every time I see those pathetic diamond commercials,
I nearly throw up on my television. Has any guy ever been romantic
without the possibility of sex hanging in the balance?*

Lennie from Leadville

Dear Lennie,

Do you realize there is not a woman in the entire universe who
would date you if she knew you submitted this question? Were you
abused as a child? You won't believe this, but research done in Atlanta
shows that women who read romance novels have sex twice as
often as women who thumb their noses at the bodice-ripping genre
(*Archives of Sexual Behavior:* June 1984; 13(3):187-209).

In your defense, many of us associate romance with capital
outlay—the proffering of diamonds and stuff. Although we consider

ourselves to be free thinkers and quite the amazing philosophers, when it comes to romance we are witless puppets of the mass media.

TV and magazine ads constantly distort the notion of romance, given how we hardly see it portrayed without some credit card being hyped in the process. None of the huge corporations (or small ones) make a single dime when you do something simple but thoughtful for your partner. They don't want you to know that the possibility even exists.

Contrary to what your television is telling you, romance does not need to cost a thing. Romance has a lot more to do with thoughtfulness, kindness, and fun than spending tons of money. It has to do with special gestures, like taking the time to help your partner do taxes, or scouring the tile in her skanky-looking shower, or getting him a bottle of his favorite beer, or taking a whole day to help her organize a troublesome closet or garage. Maybe it's washing her car and getting the oil changed, or leaving a note on the refrigerator or car seat saying "I love you." Maybe it's telling him how much you appreciate how hard he works.

There's not a single thing about being romantic that should require the folks at MasterCard to increase your credit limit. Perhaps you are deluding yourself if you think that the only way you can be wildly romantic is by increasing the national debt.

Romance in Long-Term Relationships: Finding a Mix that Works for Both of You

When it comes to long-term relationships, all the romantic gestures in the world are meaningless if you aren't trustworthy and don't help maintain the mutual nest. Cooking a special dinner or sending an unexpected card won't get you far if you didn't do any of the chores that your partner was counting on you to do.

For romance to work in a long-term relationship, it certainly helps if both of you are reliable and trustworthy. Then, the kind and thoughtful gestures have a footing on which to stand. They help take your relationship beyond the functional and into the sublime.

On the other hand, when you hear people who have been together for a long time say that the sparkle is gone in their relationship, they have sometimes worked so hard on being reliable that they forgot about the little gestures that help make a relationship fun.

———————————————

Dear Paul,

My husband of fifteen years is the most trustworthy and hard-working man on the face of the earth. He's a great father to our kids and I love him dearly, but the romance in our relationship is gone. I can't remember the last time I received flowers from him that weren't for Mother's Day. The big trouble is, I've been noticing the pool man a lot

more than I should. He compliments me on what I am wearing, asks me about the projects I am working on, and makes me laugh. By the time he leaves every Wednesday, I find myself wetter than the pool deck! It's not that he's some sort of physical ten or that we've had sexual contact, it's just his wonderful attitude and the way he takes the time to notice me. How do I get my husband to do the same?

Waiting in the Sun

Dear Waiting,

I'll be hand-delivering this reply next Wednesday afternoon, right after Mr. Chlorine pulls out of your driveway. Here are some things to consider: It's quite possible that in your husband's mind, his way of being romantic is by working his tail off for you and the kids. Worse things have happened. Be sure that at least a couple of times a week you tell him how much you appreciate how hard he works. Do this from now until the end of time. Next, think back over the past fifteen years and come up with a couple of things that both you and he have enjoyed doing together—without the kids. Hopefully, it will have nothing to do with his work or yours. Maybe it's river rafting, maybe it's shopping for antiques or going to a carnival. Whatever it is, plan it for just you and him. Don't expect much from the first five or ten excursions; rusty wheels take a long time to loosen. At the end of each of your special outings, give him the best blow job he's ever had. It might help to pretend you are doing the pool guy. When you're done, tell him something like, "When you work so hard for us, it makes me love you. And when you spend time with me like you did today, it makes me want to have sex with you. I'd really like to do this again next week." Come up with your own variation of this theme, but do something that will help thaw the glacier that your relationship has become. Of course, if you and he are locked into some kind of unconscious struggle where you are acting out stuff from your respective childhoods, best to get marital or individual counseling.

Of course, my response has been a traditional one that doesn't reach beyond my own comfort zone. What if you were asking advice from someone who liked to swing? Swingers tend to see sex in threes and fours where the rest of us see it in ones and twos. A swinger might suggest that you broach the subject of trying a threesome with you, your husband, and the poolboy. However, stick-in-the-mud me would remind you that swinging is more apt to work if the primary couple has a solid and satisfying sexual relationship to begin with. I wouldn't recommend a threesome to jumpstart your sex life, unless your husband is secretly lusting after the poolboy as well.

What Readers Have to Say about Romance

"Romance is being kind, gentle, and thoughtful. Sometimes intense as when making love, sometimes only on pilot light, but never off." *male age 70*

"Romance is when we go roller-blading together at the beach." *male age 32*

"Romance is kissing at every red light while on a date, or feeling tingly when you see each other again after being apart for hours or days." *male age 38*

"Romance is when she and I can absolutely forget that the rest of the world exists. Just today we both had a million things to do to prepare for the coming workweek but I turned on the CD player and played a great Spanish song about a bull that falls in love with the moon. Soon we had dropped our work and were spinning each other around the living room like two people who had no idea how to dance flamenco." *male age 25*

"Romance is being naked in the sun."   *male age 42*

"What is romance? Stroking my hair, holding my hand, help-ing me with the housework, cooking, talking, sharing the day with me."   *female age 43*

"Romance is waking up in my partner's arms and being told that he loves me."   *female age 27*

"Romance is sitting on a hammock together reading our books."   *female age 26*

"Romance is talking to each other when we are frustrated or upset and then making love."   *female age 27*

"It's bringing home a single rose or a little something to say I was thinking of you today."   *female age 34*

"Doing things that show he values me as a life partner and not just a bed partner."   *female age 45*

"Being a friend AND a lover!"   *female age 37*

"For romance, I enjoy a great bubble bath together with candles and wine, lots of great smelling scents whether it's perfume, incense, or just the smell of my man."   *female age 36*

"If he brings you flowers or jewelry and he's not there in any other way, it's not romance."   *female age 45*

Hundreds of fun and romantic date ideas are waiting for you on our free website. Click on the "Dates" button.

www.BoinkCentral.com

Kissing–Lip-Smacking Good
Chapter 9

This chapter is about kissing on the upper body as opposed to kissing on the genitals, although one often leads to the other. A lot of couples mix the two together—a little peck, a little suck, a little peck, a little suck.

Sometimes kissing is used as a starter, to help stir up your body fluids. Sometimes kissing is all there is. Kissing can be awkward at times, especially at the start. But even if your lips are so experienced they could dock space shuttles for NASA, you might find some helpful reminders in the pages that follow.

The Power of Talking in Tongues

It's funny how kissing a partner on the lips usually makes more of an emotional statement than kissing him or her on the genitals, even if the latter sometimes feels better. For instance, one woman who makes her living by having sex with different men reports that she won't let anyone other than her husband kiss her on the lips. And when a relationship starts to go sour, couples usually stop kissing on the lips long before they stop having intercourse.

There are reasons why lip-locking is sometimes more intimate than getting into a partner's pants. From the moment we are born, most of us are kissed constantly by moms, dads, aunts, uncles, grand-parents, and anyone else whose approaching lips we can't success-fully dodge. At the same time, our genitals were virtually unkissed or unsucked, in most families anyway, until we could get old enough to talk a friend or partner into doing it.

Another reason for the added power of kissing is so many of the major senses have their outlets on the human face. There are vision, smell, hearing, and taste, and the lips and skin are exquisitely sensi-tive to touch. There are so many sensory apparata located on or near the human face that we have terms such as "You're in my face" or "Get out of my face" to express annoyance or social discomfort.

Interestingly, the ability to have an orgasm is not considered one of the basic senses, although it overwhelms the other senses when it actually happens.

When Kissing Is the Main Course

Kissing is often a prelude to other things, but there are plenty of times when kissing is all you get. Like when you are sixteen and necking all night long. Or when you are older but want to feel like you are sixteen. But don't for a moment think that extended kissing sessions are kids' stuff. Some people experience make-out sessions as hotter than a lot of the intercourse they've had.

If all you plan on doing is making out, be sure to put your gum in a safe place where you can find it afterward. It will help take the edge off until you can go home and masturbate.

Readers' Smooch Advice: The Basics

"Please don't eat my mouth. A good kiss can make me wet with desire, with only the softest touch." *female age 23*

"Kissing is not just a preliminary to fucking. Gently explore with your tongue, lightly suck on her lips and tongue. If she is into it as much as you, kiss with good suction, not lazily." *female age 45*

"When you're kissing, be gentle; don't swallow a woman's entire face into your mouth or dig your teeth into her cheeks." *female age 36*

"Start really light. Barely brush your lips against hers. Be very aware of her response. Increase the pressure ever so slightly when she begins to meet your lips. Eventually, touch the tip of your tongue to her lips. If she opens her mouth, you can let your tongue enter just the smallest bit, but try not to force her mouth open." *male age 25*

French Kissing

French kissing is the oral version of spelunking. The reason it is called "French kissing" is it was the only way the French could find to make each other stop talking.

French kissing is not a tongue-to-tonsils regatta. Try swallowing first and don't go shoving your tongue down your partner's throat. Pretend your tongue is Baryshnikov instead of Rambo and you will do just fine. There is always time for tonsil sucking later.

When you are French kissing, keep in mind that mouths enjoy variety. Don't cling to your partner's mouth like it's a New York City parking space. Bring your tongue out for air and change the pace with a little lip-to-lip or lip-to-neck action before re-probing the deep.

"Take it slow and easy, but not too easy." *female age 26*

"Don't jam your tongue down someone's throat until she invites you in." *female age 38*

"Getting deep throated for fifteen minutes at a whack is no fun." *female age 48*

Breathe or Die

When you are new to kissing, you might find yourself holding your breath. Sometimes there are good reasons for this, but usually it's a bad idea. When you are kissing, your mouth is often busy, while your nose is mostly in the way. Breathing through your nose gives it a purpose and keeps your partner from feeling like you are attempting mouth-to-mouth resuscitation.

El Niño You Are Not

People who are new at kissing sometimes ask what to do with their noses when they smooch, and whether they should kiss with their eyes open or closed. We don't know. As for the issue of serious salivary action, take these comments to heart:

"Turn off the water works! There is nothing worse than a big slobbery wet kiss." *female age 27*

"Try not to slobber!" *female age 25*

"An overly wet mouth is a turn-off." *female age 32*

"Girls love slobber. At least that's what they tell me. Maybe that's 'cause I slobber, though. Hey, wait a second!"

male age 22

Lip-Sucking Good

Keep in mind that eyelids, ears, noses, cheeks, and foreheads are sometimes excellent areas to kiss. And for heaven's sake, don't forget the neck. We're not talking vampire action, but something this side of raising a hickey might help create a welcome reception in body parts further south.

What about Hickeys?

Hickeys are what happen when a lover sucks on your neck or other body parts with enough force to cause internal bleeding. The hickey is the resulting bruise. Some people are proud of their hickeys and display them the way bikers do tattoos. Other people feel mortified when they discover a brownish or bluish blotch that wasn't there the day before. They even wear turtlenecks in the middle of summer to cover the things up.

Keep in mind that people with certain skin types hickey-up worse than others. As for hickeys between the legs, who much cares unless you are going to the beach or having an extramarital affair?

One woman who called a radio talk show said that her boyfriend had given her a hickey in the middle of her forehead. How do you explain that one, unless you lucked-out and got it the night before Ash Wednesday?

How to Hide a Hickey: Concealing a hickey with make-up is by no means a straight-forward procedure. The first thing to understand is that you need green to neutralize red. So if the hickey is redish in color, dab a green concealer directly over it first. Then use your regular skin-color foundation or concealer and powder on top. If you don't neutralize the redish blotch with green, the hickey will usually triumph.

Be sure to dab the concealer on rather than rubbing it in. If you don't have green, use an oil-based concealer that is lighter than your natural skin color, as the hickey color will cause it to look darker. But focus the application of the lighter concealer only on the hickey area. Otherwise, the area around the hickey will look like a big smudge and everyone will know. Scarves and high-necked collars can help.

Flossing, Brushing & Garlic

It is raunchy to kiss with pieces of food stuck in your teeth. Flossing and brushing can make you far more attractive than wearing expensive cologne or sucking on a fistful of breath mints. If you are concerned about bad breath, check with your dentist. Dentists know all about bad breath, as many of them seem to have it. Ask if you should scrape the surface of your tongue with the edge of a spoon.

If you are eating food with garlic or onions, make sure the person you plan to smooch shares some large bites. Flossing and brushing

won't put a dent in breath that's laced with garlic. Your only defense is to share the offense.

If You Are Wearing Braces

For people who have braces with rubber bands, consider taking the rubber bands out ahead of time. One reader barely escaped mid-smooch tragedy when a rubber band on his sweetheart's braces came unhooked and nearly shot him in the uvula. A direct hit would have triggered the same reflex that causes projectile vomiting.

Also, be aware that a tongue entering from the outside might get scratched or caught on metal edges that don't pose a problem for you. You might even tell your partner that you are concerned about this and would feel much better if he or she slowly and thoroughly explored the inside of your mouth with his or her tongue. WOW!

Great Kissing Advice

"The best thing you can do during a good kissing session is to ask your partner to kiss you the way he or she likes to be kissed. It really works. Just sit back and let him or her take over; you'll learn all kinds of things." *male age 26*

Kissing on the Edge of Town

In nearly every community where people have lips, there tend to be special places where the locals go to make out.

In the town where your author grew up there were two favorite places where people went to kiss and grope—well, three if you count the local drive-in, but that was more like an extra bedroom. One of those favorite places was at the river east of town. Another was in the orange groves. Each had its own hazard, which merely added to its allure. The road to the river twisted along a steep mountainside, which sometimes posed a problem if you were either low on gas or high on beer. As for the orange groves, a busted ditch or recent watering could result in hidden mud traps. Tires could spin aimlessly until your best friend's dad arrived to tow you out.

Eskimo Pies & Eskimo Kisses: Kissing in Other Cultures

You may have heard that Eskimos don't kiss like we do. Instead of kissing on the lips they allegedly rub noses. What's closer to the truth is that Eskimos put their noses in close proximity to inhale the breath

of a loved one. Perhaps they do this to keep their lips from freezing together. They may avoid oral-genital contact for the same reason.

Eskimos find that inhaling the breath of a lover is erotic; those of us from more temperate climates prefer exchanging wads of saliva. People raised in different cultures don't always agree on what's sexy.

The Real Estate between Your Neck & Knees

This guide places way too much emphasis on the standard Blue Chip kissing zones—lips, nipples and genitals. Lovers who enjoy each other will often go from head to toe, discovering and rediscovering where a partner loves to be kissed. Here are a few areas to consider:

Skin Folds The places on the body where the skin folds or creases tend to be very sensitive and love to be kissed. These include the backs of knees, the fronts of elbows, the nape of the neck, under breasts, on eyelids, armpits, crotches, between fingers and toes, and behind ears.

Bellies & Navels Think of the navel as a little vulva rather than a collecting point for lint. Some people love to have their navels licked and caressed. Others become seriously annoyed. Also, try kissing the landing strip between the navel and the genitals, and don't forget the hip bones.

Long Licks Don't hesitate to get your tongue really wet and take a long lick up your partner's body, from hip to armpit or tailbone to neck (known as "Australian" in some circles.)

Lower Back & Buns The lower back and rear end can be exquisite places to kiss and kiss again.

Human Serving Tray Fruits, dessert foods, and certain liquors can be served on various parts of the body with pleasing results.

Love Bites Teeth on skin can feel really nice or really ugly. If this is what you would like to try, lube your lover's skin with oil or saliva so your teeth glide along the surface. Then raise your lips up like Dracula and gently run your teeth back and forth. You might try a little biting action on large muscle groups such as the shoulders or buns. Be sure to get lots of feedback from the bitee, and for heaven's sake, stop short of violating cannibalism statutes.

Be Sure to Ask

Kissing is such a powerful thing, yet we seldom take the time to ask a partner how he or she likes to be kissed. Maybe he or she is turned on more by delicate little butterfly kisses than by some overly dramatic lip-lock that you saw at the movies. You'll never really know unless you ask, and it's a shame not to ask.

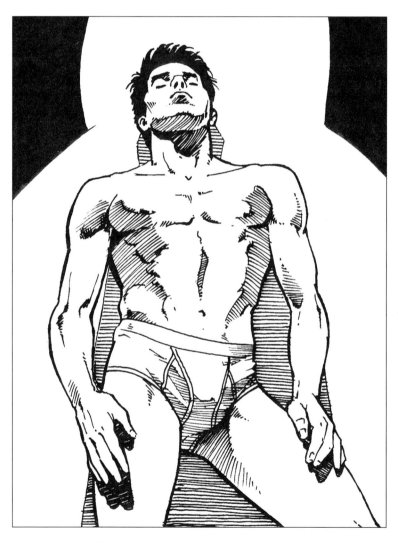

Readers asked if there was a bigger version of the brief boy from the Men's Underwear chapter. This seemed like a good place to put him, between Kissing and Getting Naked!

The Importance of Getting Naked
Chapter 10

In human relationships, there are different kinds of nakedness. For instance, in one-night stands, getting naked means exposing skin. Lots of skin. While this kind of sex can be exciting, a steady diet of it may leave some of us feeling a bit trashy and wanting a partnership with more depth. That's when you might start seeking a lover with whom you can get emotionally naked as well as physically naked, or maybe that has been your goal from the start. Whatever the case, this chapter talks about taking your clothes off, and suggests a kind of nakedness that has emotional as well as physical grit.

Getting Naked—An Overview

For some people, getting naked in front of a lover is as easy and natural as drinking a glass of water. For others, getting naked can cause distress or embarrassment. There are even people who engineer situations where they can get it on without taking their clothes off in front of the other person. Perhaps this gives you an idea of how powerful getting naked can be, and how vulnerable we can feel about our bodies.

As a culture, we are so uptight about nakedness that we don't have street-corner fountains with fat marble cherubs peeing into large pools of water or public paintings of naked Botticelli babes. The mere mention of a Thomas Kincaid frontal nude is enough to make most people squirm, and a bare crotch on network television is about as common as a snowstorm in Siam. At the same time, we are clearly interested in nakedness, given how so many ads and images in our society drip with prurient fury. Perhaps we have learned to cope with all of the mixed messages by becoming more aroused by near-naked images than by actual nakedness. Or near-nakedness might simply allow more space for our fantasies to imagine what might be under there. Whatever the case, with its suggestion of impending nakedness, the picture on the next page may have more intrigue than if the couple in it were buck naked.

The Naked-Nipple Rule

In North America, a woman isn't really naked unless her nipples are showing. In fact, we sometimes take the naked-nipple rule to extremes. For example, during the half-time show at a recent Super-bowl, one of the singers managed to let her nipple out. Even though her crotch was covered well enough to get her into Sunday School, the fact that her nipple saw the light of day caused a major furor. However, in Europe, they would have been wondering what the big fuss was all about?

Hopefully you will feel free to do your own half-time show at home, violating the naked-nipple rule as often as you please.

Getting Naked—Hidden Possibilities

If you and your sweetheart are in the process of becoming more physical, you might consider some of the hidden possibilities that getting naked has to offer. A lot of honesty and trust can be generated when you are naked together, something that rarely develops if the sole purpose of taking your clothes off is to have intercourse. It's how you can learn to relate physically with more than just your crotches. It's how a guy can learn to have his penis resting on a woman's soft, warm skin without feeling like he has to perform with it.

Naked Logistics

If it feels like your relationship is ready, you might consider planning a time and place where the two of you can work on getting naked. Some couples enjoy undressing each other, while others make a game out of taking their clothes off—from playing strip poker to light-hearted wrestling. There are occasions where one partner blindfolds the other before undressing him or her.

Sometimes getting naked just happens naturally if you go skinny-dipping or hot-tubbing, and some couples enjoy undressing each other while dancing, slow or fast. If you try this, be sure to have birth control handy in case you suddenly find yourselves doing the polka.

Occasionally, people find it helpful to tell each other some of the things that they do and don't like about their bodies. Some women worry their butts are too big or their breasts are too small or big. Some guys worry they aren't hung well enough, or they might be hung too well, or that their penis might bend the wrong way when it gets hard. Just getting your fears out in the open will usually help you feel more comfortable.

For couples who are particularly self-conscious, writer Jay Wiseman suggests getting naked in total darkness. Each partner then takes turns examining the body of the other with a small flashlight—one of those little penlight things that excites just enough photons to light up an area the size of your thumbnail. This can be a fun game that taps into all sorts of fantasies as well as help to decrease the anxiety of being seen naked all at once.

Another way for the shy at heart to share their nakedness is by getting a fun top or T-shirt to wear, with nothing on underneath. Or maybe you'd like to try a pair of silk boxers.

Guys Worry: Wood Good, Wood Bad?

When it comes to getting naked, men sometimes worry about whether they should or shouldn't have a hard-on. It doesn't matter. It's fine if you have one, it's fine if you don't. The whole point, if there needs to be one, is learning to associate nakedness with something other than just sex or taking a shower. With a little work, you might discover that being naked helps create the kind of space where you and your partner can talk about important things.

Some people don't have the slightest hesitation to get naked for sex, but if it's getting naked just to talk or hold each other, good luck. They sometimes become fidgety and fire off a rapidly dismissive "Sure, we'll have to try that sometime...." Perhaps that kind of nakedness feels too intimate.

Naked & Getting Off

While getting naked together doesn't need to include orgasms, some couples find it uplifting to have one or two somewhere along the way. So plan your naked time to include lots of holding and touching, an attempt at an orgasm or two, and then even more holding and touching afterward. (One reader comments, "Good luck on this one. I've spent a lot of lonely time while my partner sleeps immediately after orgasm.")

Coming is usually the last thing that couples do when they are having sex. Yet it might be nice to spend extra time holding and touching each other after you have orgasms, rather than simply rolling over and falling asleep or running off to work. That's because coming clears the senses in a way that allows many of us to share a special kind of warmth and tenderness.

Sex Tips with a Cranky Marxist Edge

Sometimes a half-peeled banana is more exciting than one with no peel at all, or so we've been led to believe. This type of philosophy has helped fuel the multimillion-dollar lingerie business, which for years has made a handsome profit selling flimsy wisps of underwear to women under the name of lingerie. Now manufacturers are gouging men with similar intent. They embroider the name of some fancy clothes designer or tennis-shoe manufacturer into the spandex band of men's briefs and suddenly charge $10.00 to $20.00 for a pair that you could otherwise buy at Sears for $2.50.

Anyway, if you find underwear to be erotic, here are a couple of possibilities:

 Women who wear nylons and garters might consider putting their panties on over the garter belt instead of under, so their panties can come off while leaving the stockings and garters intact. Fine tips such as these can be found in Cynthia

Heimel's classic, *Sex Tips for Girls*. Her lingerie chapter offers insight about women's underwear that no male writer short of a transvestite would ever get right.

A common garter faux pas, according to Los Angeles' Trashy Lingerie store, is wearing the rear garter all the way back instead of to the side. On the right leg, the front garter should be worn at dead center (12:00) and the rear garter should attach to the nylon at 3:30-4:00 as opposed to 6:00. On the left leg the front garter attaches at 12:00 and the rear garter at 7:30 or 8:00. This helps keep the seams straight. The "Western Woman" pictured on page 451 almost has it right, although her rear garter is closer to 5:00 than 3:30-4:00.

 Another Trashy Lingerie tip: if you are wearing a push-up bra, put it on and then reach across your chest with your right hand. Grab your left breast from under your armpit, lifting it up and dropping it into the bra cup. Do the same thing with your left hand and right breast. Another bra misdemeanor: incorrectly adjusting the straps so the bra rides up too high or droops down too low.

 Here's a piece of advice from the 1960s that will make some feminists cringe.... When going out, a woman might let a man know that she is not wearing any underwear, or reach into her purse and pull out a pair of panties while saying, "Oops, guess I forgot to put these on!"

 When sitting down to lunch or even for a long plane flight, some women briefly hike up their dress and intentionally adjust a garter in view of a man whose salivary glands they hope to make flow. The art of doing this, of course, is in the ability to disguise the purposefulness of the act. Reaching for something in the overhead compartment can achieve similar results if you are wearing a dress or skirt that's short enough.

 Here's a way to add a bit of variety and challenge when doing oral sex: Go down on your partner while she or he is still wearing underwear. You can reach under the material with your tongue, push it to one side for proper access, or pull it off with your teeth. You'll probably need a fingertip assist, but the gesture is what counts!

 If you're having a quickie, you might keep your underwear on and try working your way around it. Also, some couples enjoy having oral sex and intercourse while one or both partners is wearing crotchless underwear.

Dry humping with only your underwear on can be fun. So can taking a shower or bath while still wearing your underwear. Plenty of dry humping gets done at the beach when it's not very crowded and people are wearing swimsuits, assuming they aren't sporting a nasty sunburn.

 Women shouldn't hesitate to take their lovers with them when shopping for lingerie. Shopping for a new bra or skivvies might seem mundane to a woman, but it could be a fun treat for a man. It will also help give him ideas for when he wants to get you a special gift. If it's possible, ask him to accompany you into the dressing room.

 For guys, the next time you are in a big department store with your sweetheart, nudge her into the men's underwear department and ask her what style and colors she thinks might look best on you. This can make for added pleasure the next time she reaches down and pops the buttons on your blue jeans.

Dear Paul,

I get seriously turned on when my girlfriend is wearing pantyhose. There's something about the feel of them on her legs that makes Mr. Winky pop straight in the air. Any advice about this?

Seamless in Seattle

Dear Seamless,

Given how most of our mothers wore nylons or pantyhose, and considering how often our toddler selves stood next to them with arms wrapped around their legs, it's a wonder more guys aren't stirred into action by the feel of a woman in pantyhose.

Assuming your girlfriend is understanding and willing, ask her to cut out the cotton crotch on a pair of pantyhose. Thanks to the new ventilation system, you'll be able to go down on her as well as have intercourse while she is wearing her customized pantyhose. Make sure she cuts out the crotch on the inside of the seam so they don't unravel. Also, consider helping her to arrive orally first, because it isn't likely that you'll be lasting for long once the intercourse begins. If she isn't handy with scissors, she can purchase crotchless pantyhose in some stores, but probably not Target or Sears.

P.S. You're going to love the illustration in the "Kink" chapter!!! Also, it appears as though your girlfriend wrote in asking if you might have a fetish. I go to bat for you at the end of that chapter.

Men's Underwear

Men have a choice of wearing briefs, boxers, nothing, or even women's underwear if they're of that ilk. Most of us end up wearing whatever our mothers bought for us as kids, usually briefs or boxers. Each provides a different kind of feeling that a man gets used to, thus casting him for life as either a briefs guy or a boxer guy, although there are probably some men who are switch-hitters. While a briefs guy might experiment with boxers for a couple of months or even years, there's a tendency to go back to what he started with. Same with a boxer guy. A woman shouldn't push the issue one way or the other, unless the man doesn't care or is the type who tells her when to wear a bra.

Cramped Penis Alert

A guy's penis usually hangs downward when it's soft, but as it stiffens it needs extra head room to accommodate the expansion. Yet if a man is wearing jeans, the expanding penis often gets trapped in a downward position (ouch!) or is stuck in a horizontal pickle. So if you are fooling around with your clothes on, the penis will usually need a quick assist to rise above it all. While it might be a bit presumptuous for a woman to lend a helping hand if you are making out on a first date, this can be a really nice gesture once you are on groping terms. When the bulge starts to grow, just reach inside his pants and pull the penis up so its head is pointing toward the man's chest, unless it naturally bends down.

Jocks & Cups

Some men like to wear athletic supporters for erotic purposes. Perhaps one reason for this is the athletic supporter emphasizes a man's rear end by keeping it naked while highlighting his genitals by keeping them covered. While this might be more prominent in the gay community, some straight women get turned on by seeing a lover in an athletic supporter, as long as he isn't wringing wet from playing four hours of rugby.

Special Lingerie Supplement—Learning from Lady Lawyers

During the 1970s and 1980s, a large number of lady lawyers in this country suddenly began to penetrate the traditional male lair. Being confused about how to be taken seriously, most of these women started wearing boring wool suits with blouses that had floppy bows (the lady lawyer uniform). The intent was to look as nonsexual and unalluring as humanly possible, as femininity was considered to be some sort of liability when arguing matters of law. Short of wearing a body bag to court, most of the women succeeded handily. Interestingly, some of these lady lawyers made it a point to wear steamy lingerie under their boring suits. It was a way of saying to themselves, "At least some part of me is still feminine."

In our society, wearing lingerie has been an important way for women to feel feminine. In fact, some women feel sexier wearing lingerie than they do being naked. Some women feel better masturbating while wearing lingerie or underpants.

As for guys feeling more masculine while wearing boxers, briefs, or jockstraps, some do and some don't. What feels best of all is when a lover pulls off a man's briefs or boxers.

Note: Thanks to the writings of Barbara Keesling, Linda Levine, Lonnie Barbach, Cynthia Heimel, and Jay Wiseman for naked inspiration. Ditto to the folks at Los Angeles' Trashy Lingerie.

At Work

At Home

On the Penis & The Man Behind It

Chapter 11

This chapter was written for women readers, although the men who have seen it claim to be amused. The topic is boys and their toys. Hopefully the following pages provide some insight into the love, and sometimes hate, relationship between a man and his weenie.

Toys, Pain & Pleasure

As a woman, the first thing you will find out about penises and testicles is that most guys take them way too seriously. There are reasons for this:

The penis is the only childhood toy that a guy gets to keep and play with throughout his entire life. It is the only toy he will ever own that feels good when he tugs on it, that constantly changes size and shape, and is activated by the realm of the senses. Try to find that at Toys'R'Us.

One of the first things a man does when he wakes up in the morning and the last thing he does at night is to touch his penis and testicles. It's a male ritual of self-affirmation that has little to do with sexual stimulation. A daytime extension of this is known as pocket pool.

The average male pees between five and seven times a day. Each time he pees he has a specific ritual, from the way he pulls his penis out and holds it, to the way he wags it when he's done. When he is peeing alone a guy will often invent imaginary targets in the toilet to gun for. An especially fine time is had when a cigarette butt has been left in the commode. Floating cigarette butts are the male urinary equivalent of the clay pigeon. While this may be a difficult concept for a woman to fully grasp, it does make for a certain amount of familiarity, friendship, and even self-bonding between a man and his penis.

You wouldn't believe how often the human male experiences a jolt of pain in his testicles. It is a discomfort that gives a guy the kind of extra-personal relationship with his reproductive equipment that menstruating women have with theirs. The source of agony can be anything from an elbow during a game of basketball to simply bending over and having your pants crimp the very life force out of you. One of the great culprits in male testicular angst is the horizontal bar on the bicycle frame. Why is it that girls' bicycle frames are V-shaped when it is guys who need the V? Not only did this confusion among bicycle makers result in our younger selves not getting to look up girls' dresses when they were mounting their bikes, but many of us still have the word Schwinn engraved on the underside of our testicles from each time a foot slipped off the pedal.

This may be difficult to fully appreciate, but there is the matter of the unwanted hard-on. The unwanted hard-on usually strikes with predictable ferociousness first thing in the morning. Not only does it interfere with the ability to relieve a full bladder, but it provides logistical problems for a guy who has to traverse shared hallways to get to the bathroom. The unwanted hard-on can be particularly excruciating and even painful for its most frequent victim, the adolescent male. The unwanted hard-on is much less of a problem after a man turns thirty, and by the time he's forty it is an event accompanied by a sigh of relief and a moment of thanks.

When guys are naked together we sometimes glance down to check each other out. Do women make similar comparisons regarding their breasts? Since we males do it among ourselves, we figure that women check us out in the same way. This can make us extra conscious about what we've got between our legs.

When life is full of despair, the one thing that a guy can usually count on for a good feeling is his penis, unless matters are totally out of hand, in which case he needs to consider something stronger like tequila or prayer.

Our society teaches us that sexual pleasure between a man and a woman depends on the man's ability to get hard and stay hard. What a demented view of sex. This puts a lot of pressure on guys to be consummate cocksmen. It makes us more dick-oriented than necessary, at the expense of everyone.

These items aside, the most important thing for a woman to know about a penis is how it figures into a man's concept of his own manliness. Ridiculous, but important.

Weirdness in the Locker Room

You might think that a man's primary concern about penis size has to do with what a sexual partner might think. Yet when we asked men if they feel comfortable about being naked in the locker room, the majority answered the question as if it was specifically about penis size. The question had nothing to do with the penis or its size!

How do you feel about being naked in the locker room?

"I used to feel uncomfortable back in my freshman year of high school. Then I realized that I was really a little bigger than average. I always used to think I was inadequate. However, after having sex with a few girls and definitely not receiving complaints, I'm completely content with my size."
male age 21

"I used to think that my penis was really small and so I was shy about it. As it turns out, I'm on the high end of average when erect: I'm just not a hanger." *male age 32*

"I have an inferiority complex about the size of my penis. I don't care how many studies tell me that I am right in the middle of the curve, I will always feel small." *male age 25*

"I was raised in a fairly strict and religious environment, so nudity of any kind was a no-no. My equipment is pretty small and I was a late bloomer. All this adds up to being very shy about my own appearance. In junior high and high school, when 'naked locker time' was mandatory, I would arrive as early as possible and change quickly so that others wouldn't see me. If others were around me without clothes on, I gave myself tunnel vision or imaginary blinders so I wouldn't see other guys' equipment. I didn't want to be perceived as gay, and glancing around was a good way to get yourself taunted at least, beat up at worst. Yes, that sort of thing happened all the time at school, and the coaches let it ride. All a part of growing up and being a man, dontcha know." *male age 41* (And this guy was straight!)

The men who said they were comfortable in the locker room often made reference to their penis size as well, saying it was a good size. You could almost predict how a man feels about being naked in the locker room by asking how he feels about the size of his penis.

The National Police Gazette: New York

From the Police Gazette, A Popular Magazine in 1892

The ads above were in the Police Gazette of 1892. Not a word has been changed. In 1892, "excesses of youth" meant masturbation, and there was no cure for syphilis. The ads on the next page are from the back of a current magazine printed in 2004—more than a century later.

Today, the Ads Still Work, Even If the Pills Don't

The pills and promises are totally ineffective, yet men keep buying them. The print ads have now broadened their web to include late-night TV infomercials and Internet "enhancement" spam. The spam often has misspellings to keep it under the radar of filters.

Manliness — A Goofy Definition

Masculinity and femininity are inventions of culture that have little foundation in science or nature, yet they remain powerful forces in the way we view ourselves and each other. In our society, everyone has an idea of what a real man is, but few people know how to define it. This guide suggests that there are at least two influences which help a boy become a real man:

> A parent figure who provides physical and emotional tenderness without being too controlling, and someone with a solid sense of values and work ethics whom the boy can look up to and believe in.

These are the same ingredients that are essential to raising a real woman. They lead to the following definition:

> A real man in American culture is a fairly responsible person who can stand alone when the occasion demands, but who can also be warm, comforting, and kind; a person who doesn't need to prove his masculinity by trying to scare or intimidate others.

Of course, there are plenty of males who have none of these qualities, but appear to be total studs nonetheless. These are the guys who usually take their penises way too seriously. That's because the only way they can convince themselves that they are real men is by performing manly activities or drinking lots of beer or doing drugs, and then having a vagina nearby that they can stick themselves into.

While most of us resort to these behaviors on occasion, some guys make a lifestyle out of it.

Penis As Camouflage: Why It's Difficult to Be Satisfied By a Guy Who Takes His Penis Too Seriously

A hard penis is sometimes used to camouflage what's missing inside a man, as well as what's missing in a relationship between a man and a woman. If a guy is all hung up about his penis being a symbol of his manliness or demands that it have a disproportionate amount of attention, then it gets in the way of his being at one with a woman. The same is true for a guy who needs to always play a manly role. He sometimes feels more warmth for his car or computer than for his wife.

Unfortunately, a lot of women grew up thinking that a distant, self-involved, dick-centered type of guy is what manhood is all about. As a result, they end up being attracted to guys whom they can never really get close to, and spend the rest of their lives bellyaching about what duds we men are.

Narcisso 'Gasms

Biologically, most women can have a couple of orgasms to the average man's one. This is just fine with most men, since most of us would like to see our partners have as much pleasure as their hearts and loins desire. But for a man who takes his penis too seriously, orgasm giving sometimes becomes too important. A partner's orgasms become reassurance that he's a total guy. We all do this to some extent, but for some it's a matter of narcissistic life and death.

If your man is like this, you may discover that your main function in life is to look good and have lots of orgasms. Or maybe it's just to look good. Consider yourself an offering to the great Dick God.

The Penile-Pumping Regatta

Some men lose emotional connection once intercourse begins. The woman starts to feel like she's become a masturbation machine. Sex becomes a pumping regatta in order to prove dick-worthiness. This can be really boring for both partners.

To give you an idea of how much insecurity is involved in all this, consider the words of a twenty-nine-year-old man who is starting to question why he takes his penis so seriously:

> "It's like, I attack sex. I'm afraid of slowing it down. If I'm gonna be fucking, I'll fuck like crazy, gotta have a huge dick and fuck like crazy to avoid dealing with whatever's making me anxious. Women have always said to me, "God, you can't get enough." But I think the reason I can't get enough is that if I slow down, the fears start to crowd in on me. Does this woman really want to be with me? Is she going to leave? Is my cock good enough? It's hard for me not to use sex as a seal of approval. (In Harry Maurer's *Sex: An Oral History*, Viking Press, 1994)

Of course, there are plenty of women who have their own insecurities. Is getting breast implants or wearing a padded bra all that different from this guy's need to have a big penis?

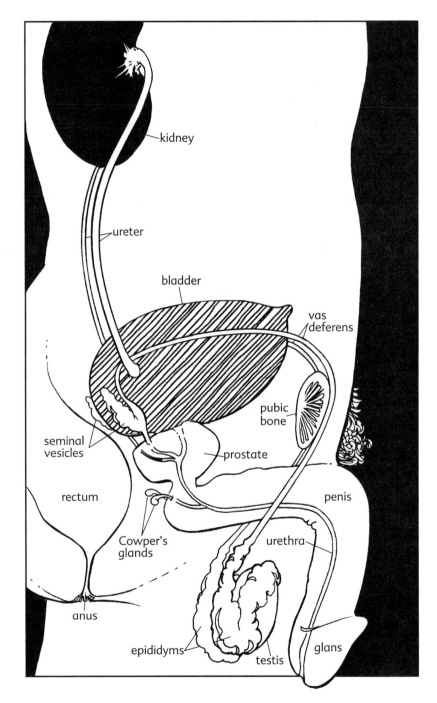

kidney

ureter

bladder

vas deferens

pubic bone

seminal vesicles

prostate

rectum

penis

Cowper's glands

urethra

anus

epididyms

testis

glans

What's inside a Guy, Plumbing-Wise

The Diagnosis & Cure

How do you distinguish a man who takes his penis too seriously from one who doesn't?

The man who doesn't take his penis too seriously is able to be kind and caring and doesn't beg out when it comes to doing the dishes. He may have various passions in life, often sports, music, business, or trying to fix things (sometimes successfully), but these usually help to center rather than isolate him. Sex with him is a natural extension of your friendship that makes all the sense in the world.

As for "curing" the kind of man who takes his penis too seriously, you can't. Hard as you might try, no human being has ever changed just because someone else wanted him or her to. It's something that has to come from within. Friends and lovers can sometimes help if they are willing to call the guy on his nonsense, but they can't make the changes for him.

Sexual Awareness: Hood Ornaments vs. Wet Triangles

When it comes to sexual awareness, the penis is positioned like the hood ornament on an antique car. It's difficult to ignore what your hood ornament is telling you when it's making a tent in the front of your pants. Sometimes we guys aren't even aware that we are sexually aroused until we feel ourselves starting to get hard.

Women are not conditioned from early childhood to associate sexual arousal with specific body cues in the way that men are. While their genitals often swell and lubricate, no flags get waved. Most of the changes happen on the inside and can be chalked-up to a nice tingly sensation between their legs. Besides, "good" girls are often taught to ignore their body's sexual cues.

While the penis can be a reliable indicator of sexual excitement, it does have its share of false positives and negatives.

Unwanted Wood

"For some reason, out of nowhere, your penis starts to get hard and it is extremely difficult to stop."   *male age 25*

"It's totally embarrassing. You just want to get up and go, but you can't. So you start pulling on your shirt or sweater to try to cover up the bulge. You become very self-conscious; you think everyone is looking at your crotch." *male age 43*

"It's like being in an elevator with an umbrella that will not go down." *male age 42*

"It can physically hurt when your penis is trapped in your jeans pointing downward and it suddenly gets hard for no reason whatsoever." *male age 26*

"Most of my memories of unwanted erections were at school, generally during class, and I was terrified that someone would notice." *male age 24*

"I travel a lot for business and sometimes wake up erect after a flight. It's terribly embarrassing. If I can't think the damn thing down, then I have to go through the tricky maneuver of flipping it up, trapping it under my waistband without being noticed, and then keeping my briefcase in front of me when I stand." *male age 25*

Women usually assume that the presence of a hard-on means that a man is sexually aroused, and that no rise in his pants means he isn't. If only it were that simple. Consider the occurrence of the unwanted hard-on. The average teenage male is capable of getting a totally unwanted hard-on in the middle of an algebra test for absolutely no reason, unless he is a member of that rare breed who finds polynomial equations sexually arousing.[1,2] When you are a young man,

---

[1]Fear of an unwanted hard-on might be one reason why teenage guys instinctively wear their shirts untucked. As for the issue of being aroused by polynomial equations, one woman recently recalled that her first orgasm as a teenager occurred spontaneously during a high school algebra test. She thinks it had more to do with the way she was sitting than the subject matter. She was so astonished and overwhelmed by the flood of sensations that she left the entire test blank, although she was an A student and well-prepared. She suspects her female teacher understood what was happening, since nothing was ever said and she wasn't marked down. With more experience and self-awareness, this woman's earlier sense of being overwhelmed by her orgasms evolved into feelings of delight and amazement.

[2]Unwanted erections aren't helped by sitting, since sitting can cause the veins that carry blood out of the penis to be pushed shut.

hard-ons just happen; nobody is more befuddled than the possessor of the penis. To say that all hard-ons are a sign of sexual arousal badly overstates the case. One reader took a bad grade in an early-morning high school class because he couldn't go to the board due to his unwanted erections. His only thoughts were of frustration, not sex.

In addition to getting unwanted hard-ons, there are times when a man can feel highly aroused, yet either fail to get hard or have it go limp when he needs it the most (floppus erectus).

False Negatives: When Gravity Dings the Dong

> Confucius says: If limp dick is worst thing that happens to your relationship, you live charmed life.

Hopefully your lovemaking isn't solely dependent on the man's ability to get hard. If it is, your sexual relationship might be somewhat limited. It's also disconcerting to think that your entire sex life might be centered on the whims of the average penis, hard or soft.

Regarding the biology of erections, it is perfectly normal for a hard penis to partly deflate every fifteen minutes or so. Regarding the psychology of erections, be aware that hard-ons have been known to fly south for varying periods of time, from a single day to who knows how long.

The most unhelpful thing a woman can do when a guy can't get it up is to become defensive. Women often assume that erection failures mean the man doesn't find them attractive or that he might be gay. These are possibilities. But there are about a billion and ten other reasons for not being able to get an erection, from fearing that you won't be good in bed to what just happened on Wall Street. Given the stress of living in the modern world, it's a wonder we men are able to get it up as often as we do. And given the lack of tenderness or excitement in some relationships, an unerect penis might be a signal that the man and woman need to get closer emotionally before anything more can happen.

While most of us have been raised to think of a limp penis as a sign of failure, perhaps it might be more productive to view it as an opportunity to bring a man and woman closer. For more information, please see Chapter 54 "When Your System Crashes," which discusses

THE GOOFY DICK GAME
Real Penises of Real Guys

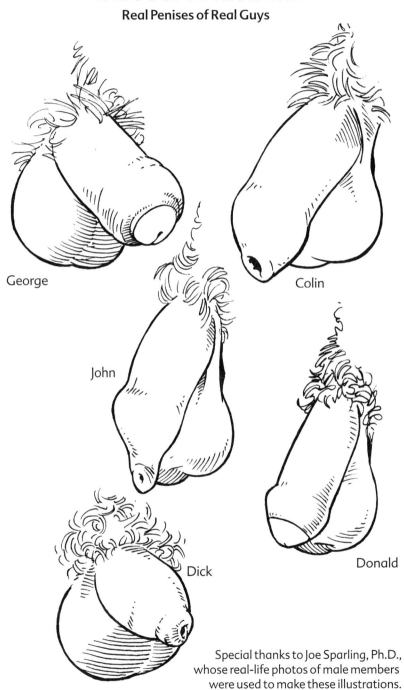

George

Colin

John

Dick

Donald

Special thanks to Joe Sparling, Ph.D., whose real-life photos of male members were used to make these illustrations.

Match Each Soft Penis On The Other Page With Its Erection On This Page

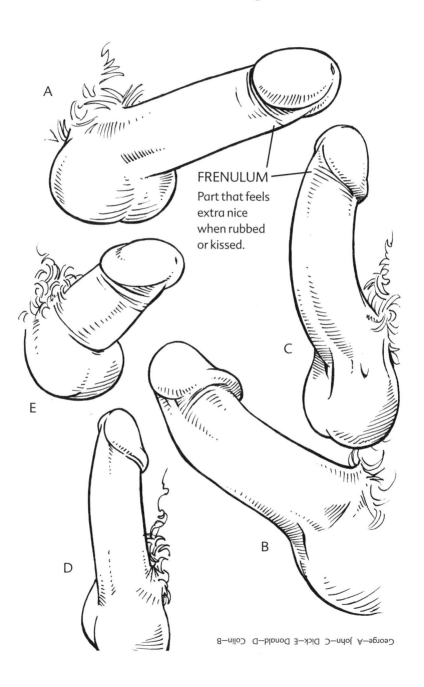

FRENULUM
Part that feels extra nice when rubbed or kissed.

George—A John—C Dick—E Donald—D Colin—B

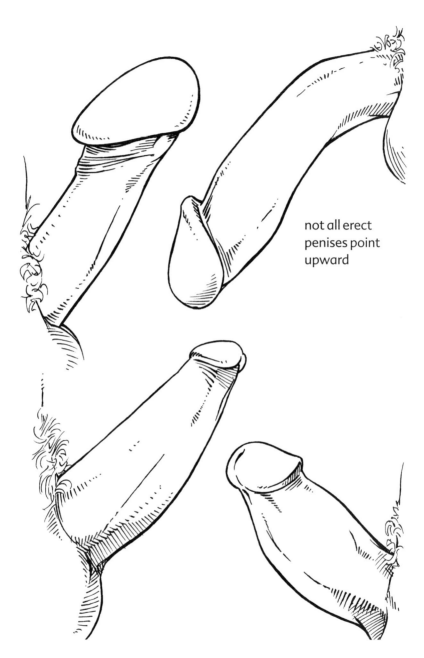

not all erect
penises point
upward

Shape: *From these drawings of real-life erections, you can see that terms like "6 inches" and "normal" are somewhat meaningless. All of these penises are "normal," yet very different from each other.*

Different Penises,
Different Erections

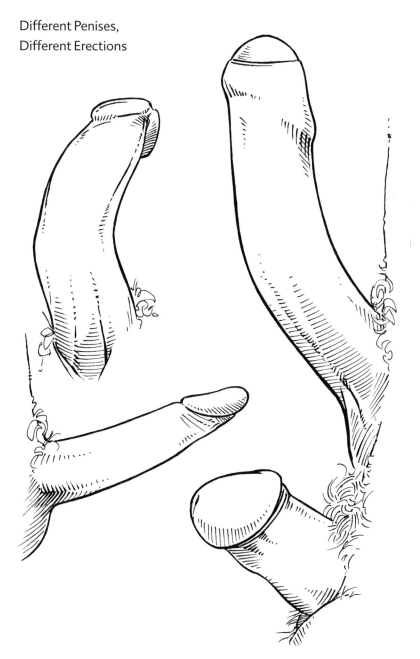

Size: *According to a study at the University of California at San Francisco, the average length of a flaccid penis is 3.4 inches, while the average length of an erect penis is 5 inches. Most guys are within 2 inches of these figures.*

the penile nose-dive and other forms of male hydraulic failure. In long-term erection failures, one should first rule out physical causes which can range from the side effects of prescription drugs to failing arteries in the penis because of cigarette smoking or diseases of the circulatory system. However, modern medicine wants us to believe that all erection failures have a physical cause. That's because it's much easier to prescribe a pill than to really listen.

Author's Note: Many years ago, when I was still in school, I was fortunate to have been under the guidance of one of the most highly regarded pediatric neurologists in the world. I still remember one of the rare days when I ever saw him express anger. There had been a leadership change (or "coup" as he called it) at the National Institute of Mental Health. He said that much of what we worked for would be over, and that research funding in all areas of mental health would soon be focused on finding a pill for everything. He feared this change would have a profound effect on the future. Time has proven him right.

Betty on Dick

The following passage is from Betty Dodson's neat book, *Sex for One*, Harmony Books, New York, 1996. In addressing the issue of misbehaving penises, Ms. Dodson speaks with welcome concern:

> Although I ran only a dozen men's groups, the experience helped me to let go of my old conviction that men got a better deal when it came to sex.... I thought they could always have easy orgasms even with casual sex, and I envied their never having to worry about the biological realities of periods or pregnancies. But the truth is that not all men are able to be assertive studs who make out all the time.... The most consistent sex problem for many men in the workshops was owning a penis that seemed to have a will of its own. An unpredictable sex organ that got hard when no one was around and then refused to become erect when a man was holding the woman of his dreams in his arms....

If this situation sounds familiar, tell your man that there probably isn't a woman alive who wouldn't be happy to receive a long, lingering back rub and oral sex in the place of intercourse. In other words, if his woody won't work, let him know in no uncertain terms that there are plenty of other ways to please you sexually. This guide's philosophy: *Never ever let a recalcitrant penis ruin your time or his!*

Dick at Dawn

Guys often wake in the morning with erections, which are usually left over from dream sleep. Contrary to what you might think, a man's first feelings upon waking with an erection aren't necessarily sexual. They are more along the lines of "I wish this stupid hard-on would go down so I can pee," or "Damn, I hate having to wake up this early." While some men enjoy having sex first thing in the morning, not all men associate early-morning erections with horniness. In fact, a man who wakes up in a grumpy mood might feel seriously annoyed if a woman assumes that his early-morning wood is for sex. She may need to coax him into having sex, although his penis is rock hard.

Dear Paul,

My boyfriend always wakes up in the morning with an erection. But when we start having intercourse, it goes down. He doesn't have this problem any other time. What's up?

Gretta in Marietta

Dear Gretta,

Sometimes a dog barks when he's happy, sometimes he barks when he's upset. It's a wise owner who knows the difference.

Contrary to how it seems, the kind of erection your boyfriend has when he first wakes up is little more than a limp penis trapped inside of a raging hard-on. It happens because he wakes up while in the middle of a dream.

Dream-sleep erections occur no matter what a man is dreaming about. He could be dreaming that he's being chased by a pack of hungry wolves and the thing would still be hard as a rock. Although it appears otherwise, it's not the kind of erection that your boyfriend gets when he's been thinking about you all day.

Although it may look and feel like it's ready for action, treat it like a floppy penis that needs to be aroused. Try kissing or playing with it before jumping your boyfriend's bone(s). This will help turn it into a waking-state erection and might help prevent it from going down.

Since his erection was not born from sexual desire, don't assume that your boyfriend feels like having sex. He might feel better if he could pee and brush his teeth. On the other hand, he may feel just fine having sex with a full bladder and dragon breath.

A Wet Warning—Ain't Love Grand!

Every once in a while a girlfriend will ask a guy if she can stand behind him and hold his penis while he pees. This is a completely normal request born of completely normal curiosity. But be fore-warned that you are sometimes giggling so hard that the entire bathroom becomes a target. On the other hand, women sometimes do a better job of aiming the thing than we men. As for penile calligraphy skills, one female friend of this Guide loves grabbing her husband's penis and writing their names in the snow with its amber stream.

Men Checking Out Other Men

Guys often have a powerful curiosity to check each other out. You might assume that this curiosity is greatest when they are kids and decreases as they get to be adults, but a recent study by a group of Ph.D. students disagrees. These students hung out in restrooms at a San Diego Padres game and secretly studied a hundred different men who were peeing. They claim that most guys made an attempt to check out the equipment of whomever was peeing next to him. Furthermore, men who were well-endowed went out of their way to show their meat to the other men who were peeing. Of course these tendencies might be more true of Padres fans than, say, Detroit Tigers fans, who are usually too busy weeping in the men's room to check out anyone else's wood.

As for generalizations, if you are a guy who has ever glanced down at another guy's penis when you are peeing, you can take comfort in knowing that you are probably normal.

First Ejaculation

Before starting puberty, a guy can stroke his little pecker until it nearly falls off and his orgasms will mostly be dry except for maybe a few drops of clear, slick, slightly viscous fluid. Sometime during puberty, this changes. He starts to produce an adult-sized wad when he has an orgasm. Instead of being clear and thin, it's white and thick, and instead of being a drop or two, it's a teaspoonful or two that oozes all over the place. (See Chapter 19, "The Glands Down Under" for an examination of what happens during ejaculation, and the changes that occur in the male pelvis during puberty.)

The process of going from a few drops to a full wad can be quite wonderful if you know what to expect and know that it's normal. It can be a little disturbing if a guy doesn't have a clue. It can be particularly disturbing if he hasn't been told about ejaculation and masturbates for the first time after entering puberty, since by then he's fully loaded and ready to shoot. Perhaps porn on the internet is so prevalent these days that some young guys might be better prepared for the big wad wammy than some of these readers were:

> "I didn't really know what I was doing. I was about eleven and discovered this new feeling when I rubbed this silky part of my blanket over my penis, so I kept doing it. Eventually, I got this intense feeling in my groin and then there was this goop everywhere. I was completely freaked and grossed out. I thought that I broke myself, but was too afraid to tell my parents."   *male age 24*

> "I was sure anything that felt THAT good had to be sinful, and that my ejaculate was evidence that I was damaging my insides. Each time I'd masturbate (almost daily) I would feel horrible guilt afterwards and swear to God that I would never do it again."   *male age 44*

> "I had heard about masturbation while sitting in the back of the school bus. When I tried it just the way the kids told me, it was almost like pain. For weeks I would stop short of actual orgasm for fear that I would do some sort of internal damage to myself. Finally, one day I kept rubbing through my fear and found that I enjoyed the hurting tremendously."
>
> *male age 25*

The Couch-Potato Penis

As they get older, many things start to petrify or harden. This is true for logs, fossils, and the human brain. Unfortunately, it is not true for the human penis. In fact, as a penis approaches its fifth decade, it tends to petrify less fully than it did earlier in life. It also squirts less fluid during ejaculation. Some women will cling to this information like a ray of distant hope, while others will be disappointed. Whatever your situation, it shouldn't make much difference. That's because as the bearer of the penis gets older, he becomes wiser in the ways of love. By then, he can hopefully compensate with wit and wisdom for whatever he loses in hardness or volume.

Also, older men seldom make an effort to stay in good shape. It's being out of shape, rather than increasing age, that often causes the couch-potato penis and decline in libido. However, age alone is responsible for changes in ejaculation, with the middle-aged man sometimes feeling nostalgic for his teenage genitals, which sometimes could propel ejaculate up to three feet.

Bebop & Squirt — Men & Multiples

Most males experience orgasm as an overlapping two-part process—sensation and ejaculation. Some guys have learned to separate the two events, experiencing a series of orgasmic sensations before they finally ejaculate. According to Dr. Marian Dunn, who interviewed a number of men with this ability, the one common thread was that their partner remained in a state of high sexual excitement after the man's first feeling of orgasm. This seemed to provide an essential path of feedback that he could feel in his penis as it remained inside her vagina. Beyond that, some guys had small ejaculations with each orgasm, some didn't ejaculate until the final curtain. Some of these men had been able to do this all of their lives, others had learned it recently. Those guys who had always been able to do it assumed that all men could and were surprised when a sexual partner pointed out the difference.

This should not be confused with *delayed ejaculation,* a situation where the man wants to have an orgasm but is unable to. If you want to pursue books on male orgasms from a Taoist sexuality perspective, check out the writings of Douglas Abrams and Mantak Chia.

Hormone Advisory

Plenty of people feel that testosterone influences sexual behavior as well as aggressive behavior. Since males have higher levels of testosterone than females, and since males commit the lion's share of aggressive criminal acts, this connection might make sense. However, researchers have found that low levels of testosterone are associated with higher levels of aggression in men, and higher levels of testosterone have been associated with calmness, happiness, and friendliness.

Women have less testosterone than men—as little as one-fifth as much. People who don't know much about women have said that this explains why the sex drive of women is lower than that of men. While women may have less testosterone, their testosterone receptors are more sensitive than men's. So less goes further in women than in men. As for the notion that women have a lower sex drive than men, good luck proving that generalization on women in this day and age.

In the lab, researchers are starting to explore the possibility that it's the male mouse's ability to respond to estrogen that causes his natural aggressiveness. While both men and women have estrogen, women have more of it. However, it's possible that men's estrogen receptors are more sensitive than women's. Does this mean that Mighty Mouse gets his "might" from the hormone that people associate with the female body?

Hopefully this will add a bit more complexity to your thinking about hormones and sexual behavior. Just because this hormone or that is circulating in the body doesn't mean a whole lot. There's the matter of hormone receptors, and of how the person has been socialized to behave when he or she gets a rush of this or that. It is also possible that hormone levels rise or fall in response to a social situation or context. So when it comes to sexual behavior, it might be our hormones that respond to the sexual feelings we are having rather than them being the things that cause a particular feeling.

On Men's Hormones

Research indicates that men have mood shifts every bit as strong as women. This makes nonsense of the myth that men are more emotionally stable than women. Researchers are also finding that sex hormones affect the moods of different men in different ways. Some men become irritable or depressed when their testosterone level is elevated. Others appear to become calmer. How men respond to the increase in hormone level is an individual matter which may have more to do with social conditioning than biology.

As for hormones and sexual desire, a certain level of male hormone is necessary for sexual arousal, but it isn't very high. Increasing the amount of male hormone above this level doesn't make men any hornier. The only time when added hormone increases a man's horniness is when his testosterone level is below the minimum to begin with. Do not take things like testosterone and DHEA without first having your blood levels tested, and then under the direction of a skilled physician if lab results show a deficiency.

Guys & Horniness

It is sometimes assumed that the average male wants to have sex each and every hour of the day as long as the opportunity presents itself. There are some guys for whom this axiom simply doesn't apply, at least around here. Maybe it's a problem with our masculinity, maybe we're latent homosexuals, or maybe we have nervous systems that are sensitive enough to be impacted by some of the really disturbing things that happen in the world. Or maybe we are really tired and need a good night's sleep. Whatever the case, it is sometimes difficult to drop everything and have sex. There are plenty of times when it's just as nice to cuddle up close to a sweetheart and enjoy falling asleep in each other's arms.

The Vicissitudes of Mercy Sex — Making a Man Come Sooner

Let's say you are getting your man off as an act of kindness and aren't particularly into it, or you really need a good night's sleep but won't be able to get one until his glands have sneezed. Here are a few suggestions that might be helpful in making a man come sooner. The latter suggestions which deal with increasing his level of mental excitement will probably be more effective, but they might be more taxing on you if you're not particularly into it.

Tighten the Foreskin Pulling the foreskin taut around the base of the penis can cause a man to feel more sensation when his penis is stimulated.

Focus on the Frenulum The frenulum is the most sensitive part of the penis. It's just below the head of the penis, on the side where the seam runs up the shaft. During oral sex, you might focus on this area. If doing him by hand, make sure that your fingers run over this part of the penis with a fair amount of pressure during each stroke. Pumping too quickly may numb out the penis and be counterproductive. Also, using a well-lubricated hand rather than masturbating him dry might help to speed up his ejaculation.

Adding a Squeeze or Twist Try giving a well-lubricated hand job where your entire hand wraps around the penis and twists up and down it as though it were following the red stripe on a barber's pole. Try a similar twisting motion with your head during oral sex. Just a slight turn of the neck is all that's needed, nothing to give you whiplash. At the same time, work the area between his testicles with one of your hands.

Visuals If the man is turned on by your naked body, for heaven's sake, crank up the lights and park the parts he enjoys most in full view. If there's a particular bra that gets him going, wear it during the sex.

Play with Yourself Never hesitate to play with your nipples or vulva. Some men will be so turned on by watching you play with yourself that they will begin to masturbate and finish themselves off with their own hand.

Pleasure Toggles Some men have a spot along the part of the penis that is buried beneath their testicles or all the way back to the rim of their anus which deepens the degree of sensation when pressed upon. Knowing your man's sexual anatomy and keeping a finger on this spot may help move up launch time. Women who give superb blow jobs often work these areas with one hand while tending to the end of the penis with their tongue and lips.

Nipples Some guys' nipples are quite sensitive; others aren't. If your man's are, tweaking them with your fingertips or caressing them with your lips and tongue can speed up arrival time.

On or Up His Rear A wet finger on or up a guy's anus can speed some men up considerably.

Extras If he gets turned on by you talking dirty to him, do it if you're in the mood. If he likes X-rated movies, load his favorite in the VCR or DVD. If you're having intercourse, try slowing down the thrusting rather than speeding up, or change his pace. If he's thrusting shallow, have him thrust deep. If you usually do it in the bedroom but are able to switch to the kitchen or living room, a change in routine can help increase the level of excitement and speed up launch time.

If His Weenie Goes Pop

So let's say you are riding your cowboy in a sexual way and you suddenly fall off, or you rise up a little too high and cream his penis on the way down (not the fun type of creaming) or you are trying one of those ridiculous intercourse positions that some artist put on some Pharaoh's tomb. Or perhaps you've had a wicked week at work and the kids have the flu and the last thing in the world you want sticking inside of you is your partner's penis, but he has the nerve to insist nonetheless. Whatever the cause of the calamity, should your man's erection suddenly bend in a direction that nature didn't intend and makes a cracking sound or goes POP, get it to a hospital right away. Although rare, the pop might be from the snapping of a ligament in the penis that acts like the suspension cables on the Golden Gate Bridge. If it breaks, internal bleeding that might permanently damage the penis can result. Urologists can usually save the wounded soldier within the first few hours post-pop, but wait more than a day and your guy could end up going to the grave with a penis that's shaped like a deflated circus balloon, or worse yet, an Allen wrench.

An erect penis can also be damaged if it is repeatedly bent midshaft. This sometimes happens during sloppy intercourse and might eventually lead to Peyronie's disease. Peyronie's disease can cause painful and/or bent erections. Some physicians believe that Peyronie's disease results from patches of calcium that collect on the penis at points where it has been torqued. The calcium or plaque decreases the elasticity of the expanding penis, which is like pinching together the side of a balloon when you are blowing it up. This condition can be improved with vitamin E in approximately 30% of cases. Some urologists say that vacuum pumping can also help to straighten out a penis that is bent out of shape.

Your Penis On Drugs!
(hopefully)

We promised no cadaver-like illustrations, but couldn't help it when Daerick-the-illustrator came up with this. After getting over the stark harshness of this drawing, perhaps you will be able to see how the different levels of anatomy fit together.

Warning: The intercourse position that can cause the most potential damage to the penis is when the woman is on top. Be sure to use lots of lube and understand that bad things can happen if she pulls it out too far and then sits back down on it when the head's not inside the vaginal opening. Any kind of genital pain that lasts more than ten minutes needs to be tended to by a physician. Serious long-term damage can often be averted if you get medical help right away.

Dear Paul,

Why are guys always touching and grabbing at their genitals?"

Eva from Evanston

Dear Eva,

When the skin on the balls sticks to the thighs, and the skin on the penis sticks to the balls, you get a claustrophobic feeling. It's like if you had to keep your arms pressed against your sides all the time. Try it for just five minutes without lifting them. When it happens with a guy's balls, he's gotta dig to lift and separate or it starts to feel like he's going to go nuts. Body powder can sometimes help. Underwear that doesn't fit right can make matters worse.

———————

Dear Paul,

When guys are peeing, why can't they aim it right? Would it kill them to get all of it in the bowl?

Nancy in Niagara Falls

Dear Nancy,

The problem is not with the aim, but with the unpredictable nature of the stream. It tends to break up about as often as the signal on a cellular phone. Sometimes a rebel tributary will appear and shoot off to the side, sometimes a healthy stream will suddenly turn into a spray, and sometimes it goes exactly where you aim it, but the toilet water splashes up and makes a mess on the rim.

Of course, this is no reason why a guy shouldn't grab a wad of toilet paper and clean up after himself (bowl, floor, walls, shoes, ceiling). This is something that parents should teach their sons. Also, I don't know if you are aware of the first law of fluid dynamics, but a man never pees on his pants leg unless it is one minute before an important meeting or job interview.

———————

Dear Paul,

The skin on the shaft of my husband's penis is a lot darker than the skin on the rest of his body. Is this normal?

Amber from Brownsville

Dear Amber,

It's perfectly normal. Penises vary as much in skin tone as they do in size and shape. One guy's penis might be darker than his normal skin color, another guy's might be lighter, and a third guy might even have freckles on his. You can't predict until his pants are down.

———————

Dear Paul,

When my husband's penis is erect, it almost points down instead of up. Is this normal?

Diane in Bend

Dear Diane,

A lot of guys point up, at approximately a 30-degree angle from their stomach, assuming they don't have a big hanging beer belly. But plenty of guys stick straight out, and others point down. You might try an intercourse position where you are on top but facing his feet. From this position, he may be able to tickle parts of you that a man with an "uppie" would miss. Most important is that you and he experiment with positions that feel good for both of you.

———————

Dear Paul,

When it comes to pleasing guys, why are they so focused on their penises? There's so much of the body that feels good when it's kissed and touched, yet they seem to want everything to focus on the penis.

Flabbergasted in Frankfurt

Dear Flabby,

Let me start by asking you a few questions. Let's say you've just cooked your lover a romantic, candlelit dinner. You've gone to the gym, feel really good about the way your body looks, and are wearing a killer dress with your sexiest whatever on underneath. You want him to want you more than he wants his car, a new computer, or Monday Night Football. But when the lights finally go down, much to your surprise, his willy is nilly. No matter what you try, he's not able to have an erection. So tell me, what's going through your mind? Are you thinking that he's not interested? That he doesn't find you attractive? Let's say you call it a wash and go for it another time. If he still has no erection, are you thinking maybe he's a wimp? Gay? If you are married, do you start to wonder if he's having an affair?

The sad truth is, if a man can't get it up, there's no end to the negativity that follows. And as much as you aren't aware of it, you are just as focused on the penis as he is—as the ultimate indicator that you are attractive and that he is excited about you. So once a penis gets hard, a guy figures he'd better start doing something with it ASAP. And if the thing suddenly goes down, especially if it deflates while your legs are wrapped tight around his waist and you've just cried out, "Fuck me harder," heaven help the poor boy. He'll be a big disappointment to you and an even bigger disappointment to himself. All of your hard work—the day, the beautiful dinner, the romantic evening—will be ruined because of the focus that you, he, and the rest of us place on his penis. So while you make a point that I clearly laud, there's more to it than meets the eye.

I'm still simplifying this way too much. There are plenty of other issues involved, like the way many of us have learned to focus on our penises since it wouldn't be manly to do otherwise. Honestly, if you heard about a woman taking a leisurely bath and playing with her nipples for half an hour, you'd probably say, "cool." So would most men. But what if you heard about a guy taking a leisurely bath and playing with his nipples for half an hour? I know what you'd be thinking. While male nipples might be wired the same as yours with the same potential for sensation, we certainly don't think of them in the same way. Besides, unless it's a hottub, men are supposed to take showers.

And finally, whether it's due to our biology or simply the things we teach ourselves about sex, a man sometimes feels a strong need to ejaculate once he becomes aroused. This need is much more pronounced if he is in his teens or twenties than later in life. It makes us focus on having to do something with that darned penis rather than being able to enjoy what's going on around us.

In Praise of Geeks!

"I don't know about other women, but I have discovered that the *geek* crowd which doesn't often get laid in high school has a great deal of time to contemplate what they'd do if they ever got their hands on a woman. They are far better lovers because they've taken the time to contemplate something other than *scoring.* Plus as a friend of mine used to say, 'Nine-tenths of sex happens in your mind, the rest is all in your head.' Geeks think, jocks avoid it at all costs because in high school thinking is not cool. Besides geeks know how to be passionate rather than just *stoked.* Give me a geek any time."

female age 35

Recommended Resources: If you want to learn more about the penis, here are two excellent books to consider: *A Mind Of Its Own—A Cultural History Of The Penis* by David M. Friedman, The Free Press, New York, 2001, and *Dick—A User's Guide* by Michele Moore and Caroline de Costa, Marlowe & Co., New York, 2003.

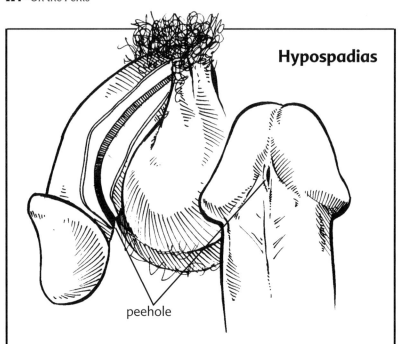

Hypospadias

peehole

Hypospadias is a birth defect where the young dude's peehole doesn't come out the end of his penis. Instead, it is located along the underside of the shaft anywhere from the bottom part of the glans (a minor case) to near the scrotum (a more pronounced case). In some situations, the urethra doesn't form in the penis at all and comes out behind the scrotum. Hypospadias is fairly common, impacting approximately 1-in-250 males. If one male in a family has it, there is a 20% chance that his father or brothers will have it.

In hypospadias, the canal that carries the urethra doesn't go all of the way through the penis to the end of the glans. The biggest problem tends to be when the man needs to urinate. He will often have to pee sitting instead of standing. Unless he has had surgery, his penis will often work as well as the next guy's, but his ejaculation doesn't go out the end. While physicians will often recommend surgery, this is usually a very bad idea except in the worst of cases. If your son wants to have surgery on his penis, let it be his own decision when he is an adult and can make an informed decision after reading the stories of other men who have had the surgeries.

What's Inside a Girl?
Chapter 12

Most books on sex present female genitals as though they were a static entity that is easy to comprehend. They give you a few carefully illustrated diagrams and proceed to speak of women's genitals as one would a carburetor. This is a big mistake.

Of course, some people might say this puts women down since it implies their genitals are more complex or more mysterious than men's. Nonsense. This is simply acknowledging that if a man approaches a woman's genitals in the same way that he does his own, he and his partner might be missing out on a lot of fun.

This chapter approaches women's genitals differently than most books on sex. It begins with a boy's quest to discover what's between a woman's legs. It then discusses some of the realities and myths about women's sexuality, although it is nearly impossible to separate the two in our society. Then it talks about various body parts and sexual sensations. It ends with women describing how it feels in their genitals when they are aroused or wet.

Instant Pussy

What follows is an experience that the author of this book had with women's genitals back when he was eleven years old and very, very curious.

He had been in the big city visiting relatives and it was time to return home. Since the northbound bus didn't leave 'til noon, he had extra time to spend in the Greyhound depot. Eventually, he found himself using the men's room, which was a far cry from the one-seater he had grown up with. For instance, right next to the towel dispensers sat three different vending machines.

One of the machines had men's colognes in it; you could spritz yourself with Old Spice or Brut for a dime. Next to that was a machine that contained a product which was totally baffling. And next to the mystery machine was a dispenser that said *Instant Pussy—2 Quarters*. To put this into proper perspective, back then candy bars weren't

much more than a nickel, and two quarters amounted to a near fortune. But then again, the front of the machine promised a facsimile so exact that you couldn't tell instant pussy from the real thing.

For the next hour or so, the young boy pondered the ultimate existential question: ten candy bars or instant pussy, ten candy bars or instant pussy, ten candy bars or instant pussy. A rush of guy hormones apparently kicked in and he returned to the smelly porcelain palace with two shiny quarters in hand.

The rest of the day was spent in quiet anticipation, with thoughts of instant pussy overwhelming whatever interesting sights and sounds the big city had to offer. Finally, after he had arrived home and done his chores, the anxious boy opened the small box and read the instructions. "Place capsule in a large glass of warm water." He spent the next half-hour trying to decide just how warm the water should be. He even took out the thermometer and tried to make it a perfect body-heated 98.6. Then came the big moment. He crossed himself and revved up his courage. With an Enola Gay-like swoop, his trembling fingers dropped the capsule into the glass. Then he waited. And waited. And waited.

Forty minutes went by before the gelatin capsule finally melted and revealed a thin piece of sponge in the shape of a cat.

A grown man would have known to go for the candy bars. But the young boy was still clinging to the hope that there were answers out there somewhere to questions that felt so much bigger than he.

What's Inside a Woman?

A fine way to learn about what's inside a woman is to hold her. For hours. Your skin against hers, the weight of her body and emotions pressing against yours. And if you really want to learn about a woman, consider having babies and raising them together. Hopefully you will like what you discover, although there are no guarantees for either of you. As for understanding a woman's sexuality, some women will let you deep inside of them; others will only have sex with you. It's no different than with men. Just because it's sex doesn't mean it has emotional depth, even if you are married and having intercourse the prescribed 2.3 times a week.

Myth #1 Men Are Hornier than Women & Men Peak Sexually In Their Late Teens Whereas Women Peak in Their Late Thirties

There is a silly notion in our society that young men are hornier than young women and that the cause is biological (hormones, chromosomes, or the will of God). It is also said that women don't reach their sexual peak until they are in their late thirties.

It is interesting how these myths don't exist in cultures that are more accepting of women's sexuality than our own. Perhaps it's not until American women get into their late thirties that they start to realize what a crock of sanctimonious nonsense they have been swallowing all their lives about themselves and their sexuality. That's when they start to let go of their silly illusions about men being hornier and begin seeking their fair share of pleasure. Unfortunately, by that time a lot of their male contemporaries have gotten fat or are simply out of shape, which makes them less receptive to anything that requires physical effort and stamina.

Myth #2 Tampon-Related Insanity: Rosie the Riveter Has PMS?

The next biological myth, one that is more prevalent now that doctors and pharmaceutical companies can make a lot of money off of it, is that women become incompetent or emotionally unstable during "that time of the month." To this day, PMS remains such a loosely defined concept that most men qualify as having it. Perhaps the concept of PMS has become so bloated that it no longer resembles reality.

During World War II, when the bulk of American males went to war, millions of American women manned the nation's industrial war machine. Our female-dominated workforce turned out an armada of planes, tanks, ships, and guns that was unprecedented in history. It wasn't until the men returned from war and needed their old jobs back that the myth of women's so-called hormonal instability began to rear its head once again. It's a myth that fit well with our society's need to get women out of the workplace and back into the home.

One reason PMS is such a negative concept is that it helps fuel the notion that women as a group are flakier than men. Just as flaky, yes; flakier, no. While menstruation may not feel wonderful, it doesn't make a woman emotionally unstable unless she's depressed or fragile to begin with. (Around 3% of women are emotionally unstable, the

same number as men.) While most men don't menstruate, we do have just as many mood swings each month as women.

The following quote from Harriet Goldhor Lerner helps put the hormone matter in proper perspective. This quote was found in Carol Tavris's excellent book *The Mismeasure of Woman: Why Women Are Not the Better Sex, the Inferior Sex, or the Opposite Sex*, Peter Smith Publisher, Magnolia, Massachusetts, 1999:

> Let's face it. Do you stay off the streets at night because you fear attack from uncontrolled, irrational women in the throes of their Premenstrual Syndrome? Probably not. We stay home at night because we fear the behavior of men.

Myth #3 Wrestling with the Concept of "Womanhood"

People make all kinds of assumptions about womanhood, yet not many of these assumptions hold up to scrutiny. For instance, a conservative female's definition of womanhood might not have much in common with that of a radical lesbian feminist, which might not have much in common with that of a heterosexual feminist. And that's just the opinions of women; most of us men gave up trying to define womanhood sometime around 1970. Still, it might be instructive to consider some of the contradictions about womanhood:

Intuition is said to be a defining element of womanhood. Yet there is not a single respectable study on intuition that has ever shown women, as a group, to be any more or less intuitive than men. Besides, you don't have to know too many women who date and marry total jerks to have serious doubts about the assumption that women are the more intuitive gender.

In the past, motherhood was thought to be an essential element of womanhood. Yet we all know plenty of women without children who are far from deficient in the area of womanhood, whatever womanhood might be.

It is often assumed that women are the less aggressive gender and that men's aggression makes them more bullying or controlling than women. Yet what about those women who rule the roost with an iron fist, or a matriarch who manipulates everyone around her by being the consummate martyr, or those women who nag, whine, or

criticize with an intensity that's the psychic equivalent of physical violence? While women don't always do it with bullets and knives, there are just as many aggressive, controlling, and unpleasant females as males. And when you adjust for the number of miles driven by each sex, there are just as many aggressive female drivers as male drivers. Aggression, or the lack of it, is not a defining element of womanhood.

One female professor-type penned a bestseller that claims there are significant style differences in the way men and women express themselves. Perhaps this is a defining element of womanhood. Yet when an interviewer noted that this woman's own style was more like the men she describes in her book, she fully agreed and added that her husband's style is more like a woman's. It's a good thing she didn't include herself and her husband in her studies.

There are women who equate womanhood with their ability to create desire in a man's eyes. In other words, if he wants her, she feels like a woman. If not, she starts to feel sexless. Being so dependent on the approval of men (or other women) makes it scary to have a strong opinion or to speak your mind.

So what do men wonder about womanhood? One totally normal heterosexual male said he wondered what it would be like to have women's breasts with sensitive nipples, apparently subscribing to the myth that all women's nipples are like detonators of nuclear bombs. Another straight man said he wondered what it would be like to have women's genitals, to have a penis inside of you during intercourse. A third man whose wife had recently given birth wondered what pregnancy would feel like and what it is like to nurse a baby who had grown inside you from the time it was a single cell.

Why do these men focus on the body as the thing they wonder about womanhood, leaving out the social and political features that a professor of women's studies might include? Perhaps they are being predictable clods, or maybe they have known and dated enough women to appreciate the huge range of personalities, capabilities, and perspectives that different women offer. Perhaps they think that women's minds are similar enough to their own that it wouldn't be such a big deal to wonder about that. Maybe the only unifying attribute they can ascribe to "womanhood" is having a female body.

It's possible that some of today's women feel equally challenged in trying to define womanhood for themselves. Hopefully you and your sexual partners will feel safe enough to be whatever you need to be, whether it is society's stereotypes of manly, womanly, boy-like, girl-like, passive, active, or bits and pieces of each.

Women's Sexual Anatomy — The Nerve of It All

In the late 1950s, a scientist named Kermit Krantz explored how women's genitals are wired. It is difficult to find a single research report on the topic of women's sexuality that is of more value than the one produced by Kermit Krantz, who painstakingly dissected the genital regions of eight dead women. He found a great deal of variation in the way the nerve endings were distributed throughout the different women's genitals. While there tended to be a higher concentration of nerve endings in the clitoris, the amount varied significantly among the women; that is, some had more nerve endings in the labia minora (inner lips) than in the clitoris, and some women's nerve endings were highly concentrated in one area while other women had nerve endings that were spread out over a larger area. To quote Dr. Krantz:

The extent of innervation in different females varies greatly.

What this suggests is that no two women get off sexually in the exact same way. Each woman needs to explore her own unique sexual universe, from where to touch to the kinds of fantasies that get her off. One might love oral sex and be so-so about intercourse, while the next craves a penis in her vagina. No matter how experienced her partner might be with other women, he won't know exactly what she likes until she tells him. It's not the sort of awareness he is going to assimilate during a one-night stand. A female reader comments, "Talking about this is as much her responsibility as his." A male reader says, "Sex is a hundred times better when a woman can actually show or tell you what she wants.

For a man, prior experience can be as much of a hindrance as a help. Stimulating his current partner's vulva in the same way that used to drive a former lover wild could be about as effective as calling her by the former lover's name.

Show & Tell

Most guys know what other guys' penises look like. That's because male genitals stick out. You can't help but notice them when you shower or pee together. But women have no subtle way of looking at each other's genitals, even if they are buck naked. One would have to sit with her legs apart for the others to see. One female reader comments: "While women speak to each other in graphic terms about things like menstruation, blow jobs, and the ratio of penis size to male ego, we usually don't talk to each other about what our crotches look like; not that we'd necessarily want to."

Still, some women have found it reassuring to see what other women's vulvas look like. They are often surprised to find that there is a lot of variation. If you are a woman who would like to know what other women's vulvas look like, there's plenty of free porn you can see on the Internet, or buy yourself a couple of men's jerk-off magazines.

There are also photo books on vulvas which have been published by feminists. Interestingly, the muff shots in some of the politically correct beaver books have a clinically sterile edge that's not particularly arousing. In fact, these mug shots of women's crotches are every bit as un-erotic as mug shots of men's crotches. Makes you wonder if it

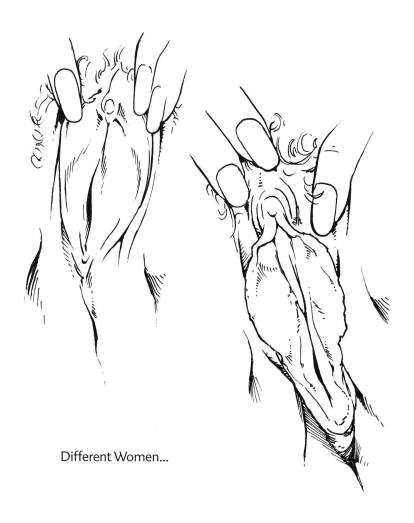

Different Women...

isn't the rest of the picture or the sexual situation, rather than just our genitals, that makes us sexy.

Perhaps the missing element in some of the feminist beaver books is an attitude that says, "What we have between our legs is a good thing. It's fun, it's sexy, we like it." Maybe that's the difference between a picture that's clinical and one that's erotic. Of course, some women will claim that men should value sour pusses every bit as much as happy ones. But some of us enjoy knowing that women find their

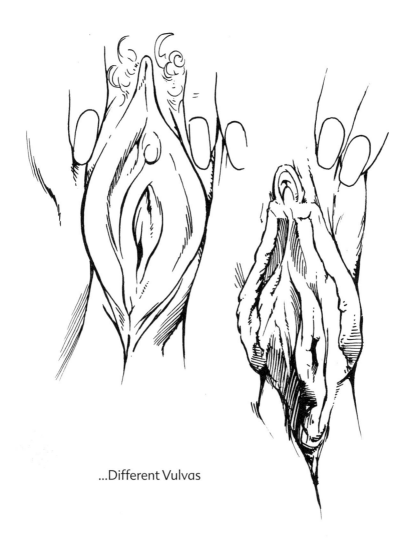

...Different Vulvas

own genitals to be sexy. Perhaps that's why a lot of us nearly ejaculate on the spot if a partner enjoys masturbating and lets us hold her or watch while she's doing it.

In our culture the vulva is usually wrapped with anything from silk to spandex and leather to lace. This wrapping is known as lingerie. Lingerie is thought to give a sense of allure, like the wrapping that covers a precious gift. Or perhaps the allure is in knowing that the woman finds her genitals sexy enough to cover them in an erotic way.

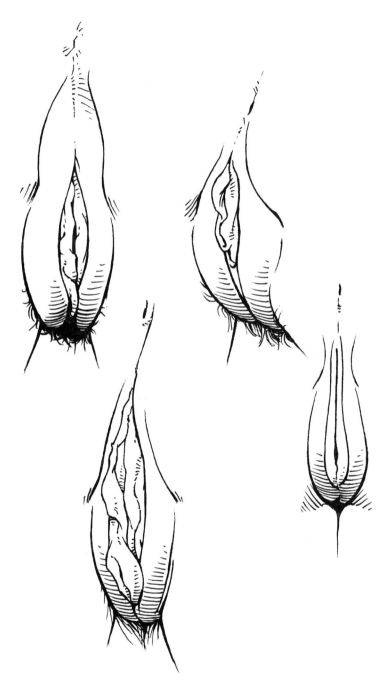

View from behind.
What? Aliens stole their anuses?

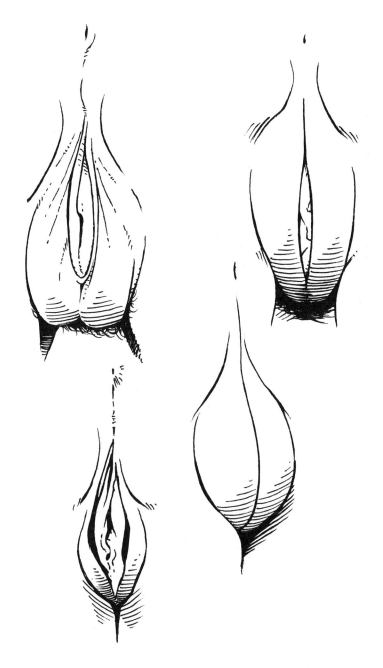

One way to find out how your vulva looks is to sit on a large Xerox
copy machine, lean forward, and press the copy button.
The cover is glass, so sit very gently, and be sure you have the
permission of the machine's owner!

Dear Paul,

My girlfriend thinks her genitals are ugly. Is there anything I can do to help her change her mind?

Bobby in Beaver Falls

Dear Bobby,

It's the strangest thing how even the most politically-liberated woman can harbor negative feelings about the way her crotch looks.

Even Betty Dodson, champion of female masturbation during the past three decades, used to feel that her genitals were deformed. She assumed they were deformed due to childhood masturbation. Finally, a male lover insisted that this wasn't true. He brought her porn magazines so she could see that her genitals were like other women's—and how much variation there could be in the way the lips are formed.

What's interesting is that men end up knowing more about what women's genitals look like than most women.

Strange as it might seem, a lot of girls don't look at their own genitals until they're old enough to start having sex. The only way a guy would wait that long to look at his genitals is if he were born blind or was paralyzed from the waist down and didn't know they were there.

Also keep in mind that our society doesn't want girls to be curious about their genitals. While it is natural for a child to fall asleep with a hand between his or her legs, parents often assume that this kind of self-comforting will turn an innocent girl into a slut-in-the-making. Heaven help a young girl who is caught bringing her fingers to her mouth or nose after touching herself "down there." Talk about being threatened to within an inch of her life—all for exploring how she tastes or smells.

In working on the latest edition of this book, I was seriously shocked by what college health care workers told me. After hearing about the new NuvaRing birth control device, I thought the benefits of only having to pop this thing inside a woman's vagina once a month would bring women flocking. While it appears to be the thing that will make the pill obsolete for many women, the student-health workers had concerns that college-aged women wouldn't use it because a lot of them find it disgusting to put their fingers inside their own vagina.

What in the blazes are we doing in this culture of ours when we raise intelligent young women to think it's "Icky" to stick their fingers inside their vaginas? They're fine to let some guy do whatever he wants in there with his fingers and penis, and half of them don't even consider giving a blow job to be sex, but birth control experts are worried because so many college women won't put their own fingers in their own vagina one or two times each month—I just don't get it.

I recently received a video showing one of Betty Dodson's workshops where women check out each other's equipment. One of the women here at the Goofy Foot Press, who prides herself on her independence and liberation, felt uncomfortable when she first saw the tape. Fortunately, she remembered that she's just fine with porn tapes where guys's dicks are wagging all over the place, so she made a serious effort to relax and watch the tape. By the time it was over, she said that watching it had been instructive in all sorts of ways. She had never realized her own discomfort with women's genitals.

How can you help your girlfriend have a positive experience with her own genitals? First, begin by realizing this is part of a larger cultural disease. Then, perhaps with patient and creative encouragement on your part, maybe she'll start to realize that what's between her legs isn't so bad after all.

Vulvas, Vaginas, Beavers & Bears

While many of us can correctly label the male genitals, we usually don't know stem from stern about the female organs of sex. For instance, people refer to everything between a woman's legs as her vagina. Yet this is far from true. What sits between a naked woman's legs is her vulva.

You might ask, "What difference does it make if you call it a vulva or vagina?" One female educator answered this question by asking another: "What if parents taught their children that they had no eyes, ears, nose or mouth, but instead gave them one word for their entire face and called it 'tongue'?" This would be confusing and limiting. It might even suggest that parents are afraid of faces and all the wonderful things they can do.

The following page has a list of the different vulva parts.

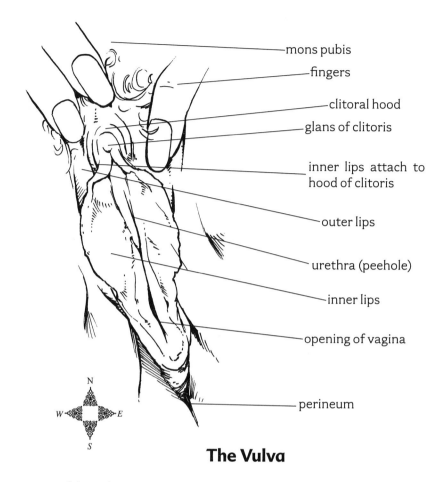

mons pubis
fingers
clitoral hood
glans of clitoris
inner lips attach to hood of clitoris
outer lips
urethra (peehole)
inner lips
opening of vagina
perineum

The Vulva

Parts of the vulva:

The outer lips (labia majora)

The inner lips and the clitoral hood (labia minora)

The clitoris, which is made up of four different parts.

The urethral opening (peehole). Good luck finding it!

The opening of the vagina. (Spread the lips to see it.)

The mons pubis is a fleshy little mound that sits on top of the pubic bone. It is usually covered by pubic hair, unless the woman has been trying to wear a string bikini with grace or simply likes to have her pubic area trimmed, close-cropped, or cleanly shaven. The mons pubis is a wonderful lovemaking ally that men sometimes ignore.

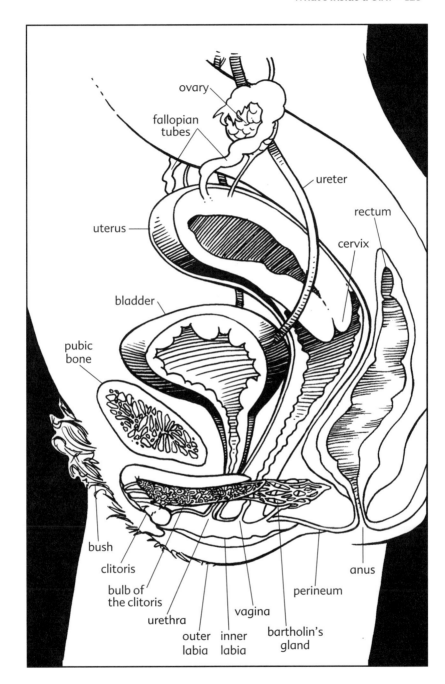

What's Inside a Girl?

An Important Note: Please be advised that even sex therapists don't know as much about women's genitals and sexual pleasure as you would think. For instance, Adele Clarke, associate professor of sociology at the University of California, San Francisco, recently searched the database Medline and found 1,611 articles on the penis but only 78 on the clitoris. Perhaps this says something about the state of concern in modern medicine about women's sexuality. Another part of the problem is when the government is putting millions of dollars into sexual abstinence education, you don't get a lot of quality research on what makes sex feel good. This has been going on since the time of Ronald Reagan. So while we've tried our best in this chapter to bring you the latest information, don't be surprised if by the next edition we take some of it back and sheepishly say "Ah, sorry, folks..."

Lips, Lips, Lips

Wouldn't you know it, but even the ancient Romans got it wrong. They named the outer lips "labia majora" (big lips) and the inner lips "labia minora" (small lips). But in a lot of vulvas, the outer lips aren't particularly prominent, while the inner lips fan out in all kinds of ways and shapes. In fact, if you look at enough vulvas, you'll find that it's the size and shape of the inner lips that give them their unique personalities. As a result, we've chosen not to call them *big* lips and *small* lips. Instead, we call them *inner* and *outer.*

The outer lips often have hair on them, while the inner lips are as bald as can be. For most women, the inner lips are more sensitive than the outer. A lot of women play with the inner lips or gently stroke them when they are masturbating. Perhaps one reason for this is the inner lips connect to the hood of the clitoris. Tugging on the inner lips may provide a more pleasurable way of stimulating a clitoris that's feeling extra sensitive. When you give the inner lips the right kind of attention, they often swell, open, and deepen in color.

During intercourse, the inner lips are pushed and pulled with each stroke of the penis. This makes them become one of the media that help transmit sensation to the glans of the clitoris.

Clitoris—Point Guard for Women's Genitals

If you don't know a clitoris from a bunion, ask your sweetheart to show you. If you don't have a sweetheart, maybe you have a female

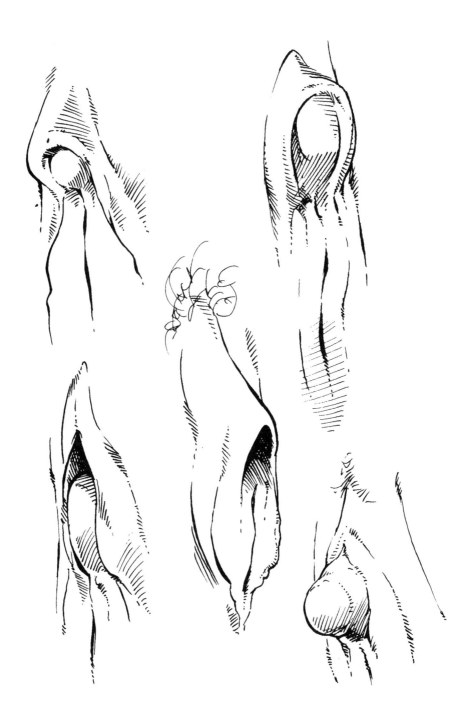

friend who's up for show'n'tell. Or maybe you'll learn in your own due time. Here's the definition of clitoris from the Goofy Glossary:

> **clitoris** — Latin for "darned thing was here just a second ago."
> The only organ in either the male or the female body whose
> sole purpose is pleasure, which, from a biological perspective,
> might indicate that the female genitals are more highly evolved
> than the male's. 2. Sometimes regarded as the Emerald City of
> women's orgasmic response. 3. Not to be approached in haste.
> 4. Sometimes wants to be caressed with vigor; other times
> can hardly tolerate being breathed upon.

The clitoris is made up of three or four parts, depending on which school of thought you subscribe to. These parts are the glans, the shaft, the crura, and the vestibular bulbs (the wild card in different people's definitions). There is only one glans and shaft, but the crura and vestibular bulbs branch off into two legs.

The Glans & Shaft Of The Clitoris

The part of the clitoris that you see in porn movies or when a woman is in front of you with her legs spread is only the glans. You might see some of the shaft if you pull back the hood. This is only a small part of the clitoris, yet it's what we assume is the whole thing.

Sometimes a glans will nearly pop out at you and shake your hand; others can hardly be seen. Some are extremely sensitive; others aren't. Some change sensitivity with the time of the month, others keep an even keel. The sensitivity of the glans has nothing to do with its size, which can range from 2 to 20 millimeters in diameter.

The glans of the clitoris is made of soft tissue that expands and becomes firm when it receives satisfying stimulation. It's the same kind of material that's in the glans of the penis. It has little glands beneath its surface that provide oil to keep it shiny and slick. It's this oil that allows the hood of the clitoris to glide back and forth over the glans without it feeling abrasive. If there isn't enough oil, the surface might eventually become rough like the glans of a circumcised penis. Pulling the clitoral hood over a dry glans can be extremely painful.

As a woman approaches orgasm, her clitoris often disappears or seems to retract. This can be confusing for the man who is trying to stimulate the clitoris by hand or mouth. The confusion is in knowing

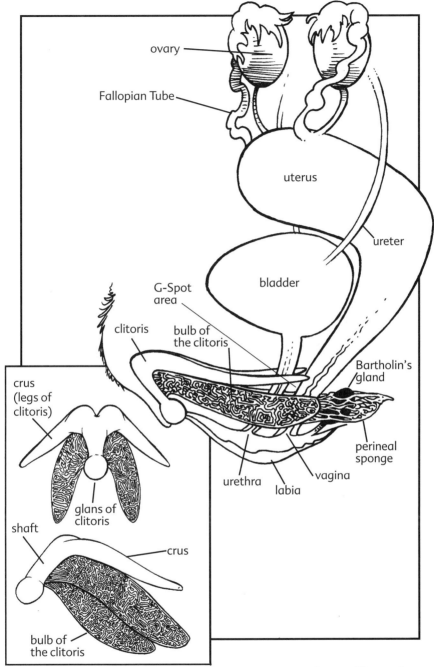

ovary

Fallopian Tube

uterus

ureter

bladder

G-Spot area

clitoris

bulb of the clitoris

Bartholin's gland

crus (legs of clitoris)

perineal sponge

glans of clitoris

urethra

labia

vagina

shaft

crus

bulb of the clitoris

The Clitoris

whether to play Hercule Poirot and give chase, or to simply wait until the clitoris returns.

The truth of the matter is that right before orgasm, extra blood collects in the back part of the clitoris. This causes the shaft and glans to straighten out and salute. If you are stimulating the clitoris with your finger or tongue, it might feel like the clitoris suddenly starts to hide or retract. It's a very bad strategy to push harder to try to find it. If whatever you were doing managed to get her to this point, for heaven's sake, don't change now. What seems like a game of cat and mouse is just the clitoris straightening out right before having an orgasm. The penis does this as well. Right before ejaculation it gives a brief cough or throb which lets you know the wad is on its way.

Of course, it's certainly possible that as a woman becomes more aroused, she may want you to stimulate her in a different way or on a different spot. You'll never know what feels best unless the two of your are able to discuss it together.

There is a foreskin or hood that covers the shaft and glans of the clitoris. Manipulating the hood of the clitoris is an art form that is discussed in the chapter "The Zen of Finger Fucking."

The Crura of the Clitoris

The crura look like the legs of a wishbone that run beneath each of the labia. The wish of a sex partner often seems to be "I hope I get some, I hope I get some." To keep us a little off balance, a "crus" is an individual leg or part of the wishbone, while "crura" is what you say when you are referring to both of them.

The crura are made up of erectile tissue that is called corpora cavernosa, just like the cylinders that are inside the penis. If you add in the length of the crura to the length of the glans and shaft, the entire clitoris is about four inches long.

The illustration on the previous page shows how the crura actually surround the urethra in the area that some women experience as the G-Spot. The bulb of the clitoris is also a major player in that particular area. Since the G-Spot seems to expand as it is stimulated, it might be possible that the erectile tissue in the crura and the bulb of the clitoris are contributing factors.

The Bulbs of the Clitoris, a.k.a. The Vestibular Bulbs

Bet you didn't know that Mother Nature planted a pair of bulbs inside her favorite garden. These are special bulbs that grow and blossom each time a woman is sexually aroused.

The bulbs of the clitoris are also called the vestibular bulbs. They fill up with blood when the woman is sexually aroused, and can make the opening around the vagina feel more tight or firm.

If an anatomy book even shows the bulbs of the clitoris, it will call them the vestibular bulbs. Urologist Helen O'Connell suggests that the vestibular bulbs be renamed the *bulbs of the clitoris.* Her research shows that the vestibular bulb is made of erectile tissue, is attached to the glans of the clitoris, and is very much a part of the clitoris. Also, in comparing the sexual anatomy of corpses of different ages, she found that the amount of erectile tissue in the younger women was greater than that in older women. Yet researchers who study anatomy usually are only able to work on the bodies of women who were much older at the time of their death. Perhaps they have been under-reporting just how large the entire clitoris is in most women.

A Moment of Reflection

Take a moment and look at the diagrams of the clitoris. See the placement of the crura and the bulbs? Do you think it's possible that you're wasting a big chunk of time and energy if all you do when you play with a woman's clitoris is focus strictly on the tip or glans? Some women actually find it a treat if you do a really deep massage of the tissue that's beneath the large lips. It may seem like it would be painful since you are reaching all the way down to the pelvic bone, but what you are really doing is stimulating the rich vascular beds in the hidden parts of the clitoris. Of course, you should never do this without direct feedback from the woman, and while some will find it takes them to a different place, others would rather stay just where they are.

Urinary Meatus, More Fun Than It Sounds

You might think of the circle of tissue around the end of the urethra as not too significant. But it is sensitive enough that some women rub it instead of the clitoris when they are masturbating. The official term for this tissue is "uretheral meatus," which is Greek for "pee and play".

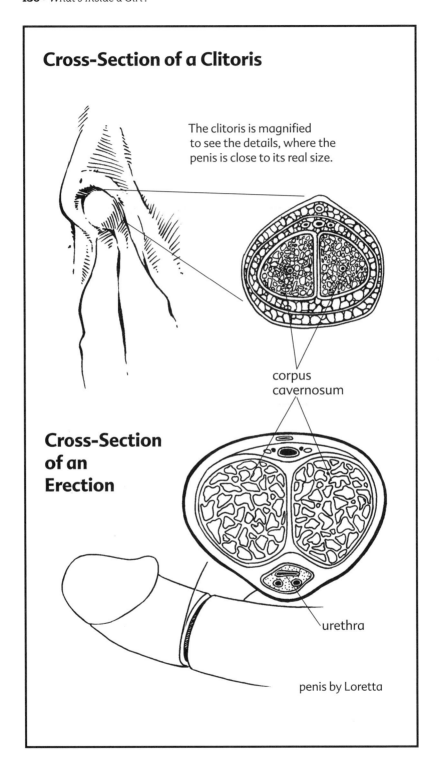

Cross-Section of a Clitoris

The clitoris is magnified to see the details, where the penis is close to its real size.

corpus cavernosum

Cross-Section of an Erection

urethra

penis by Loretta

Clitoris during Intercourse

The glans of the clitoris is seldom positioned to rub noses with an incoming penis. This is why a number of women enjoy the added stimulation of a finger or vibrator during intercourse, or sometimes push the clitoris against the shaft of a sweetheart's thrusting penis or grind it against his pubic bone while his penis is all the way inside. Other women do just fine with thrusting alone. It all depends on how the man's anatomy interfaces with the woman's, where the particular nerve endings are located, how long the man is able to last, and, perhaps most importantly, the woman's level of desire and arousal.

However, if you consider the total structure of the clitoris as having the same volume as the penis, and you look at how the bulbs and the crura wrap around the opening of the vagina, it's possible that the penis makes more contact with the clitoris than meets the eye.

A Final Note on the Clitoris — How Do You Pronounce It?

One day the author of this book found that he had to address a classroom of students and might need to say "clitoris." There he was, with almost twelve years of college under his belt, not knowing how to pronounce the word "clitoris." To prepare, he wrote "clitoris" on one card and "penis" on another. He then asked friends of both sexes to say the two words out loud.

No one had any hesitation in pronouncing penis, but almost everyone approached clitoris with a perplexed look and said, "Well, here's how I've always pronounced it…" Some said cli-TOR-is, others said CLIT-or-is. As he was exploring his own usage of the word, he realized that the only time he had referred to it was in bed with a woman, and then he called it "it." (One dictionary says that either pronunciation is correct, although it lists CLIT-or-is first.)

Papa Freud & The Viennese Vagina

Not too long ago, Freudian psychiatrists proclaimed that women had defective egos if their orgasms didn't originate from deep inside the vagina. Sex researchers in the 1960s did society a huge service in showing that the majority of women's orgasms involve the clitoris rather than the vagina. However, they may have gone too far in discounting the vagina as a source of pleasure. In fact, some women feel that having something in the vagina (penis, dildo, fingers) during orgasm changes the character of their orgasm and makes it more of a full-body experience. It's not necessarily better, just different from an orgasm that's all clitoris.

Busy Little Beavers

People often think of the vagina as being passive or inactive. Not so. Consider the following:

The human body is made up of many different tubes. The favorite tube of many straight males and lesbians is the vagina, a hollow canal with walls that contain nerves and blood vessels. When not aroused, the walls of the vagina lie flat against each other like a firehose without water. When aroused, a vagina often straightens out and puffs up even more than an erect penis, often doubling in length or depth.

When sexually aroused, the first third of the vagina becomes narrower while the back part expands and sometimes balloons open, a little like the bottom half of an hour glass.

The first third of the vagina is often sensitive to touch, while the back two-thirds are more sensitive to pressure. The walls of the first third tend to have more tiny folds, while the back two-thirds tend to be smoother.

For some women, the back part of the vagina expands before orgasm and then contracts. This might cause a longing to have something inside the vagina which the rear walls can grasp during orgasm. It has been suspected that this has certain religious or spiritual connotations, since during this process women have been known to call out the name of the Lord.

We could try to map out a vagina for you, but why not make your own vaginal love maps? What nicer way to spend an afternoon than exploring the tender shoals of a lover's warm, moist vagina.

Sponges in the Vagina?

Believe it or not, there are two sponges or spongy areas above and below the walls of the vagina. One is called the urethral sponge, the other the perineal sponge.

The urethral sponge is the bed of tissue that surrounds the entire length of the urethra, which is the tube that takes the urine from the

Balloonis Vaginis

Here's an example of how much the vagina can expand when the opening of the vulva is held closed around the nozzle of a douche. (This should not be done at home, as water or air can be forced into the abdomen.)

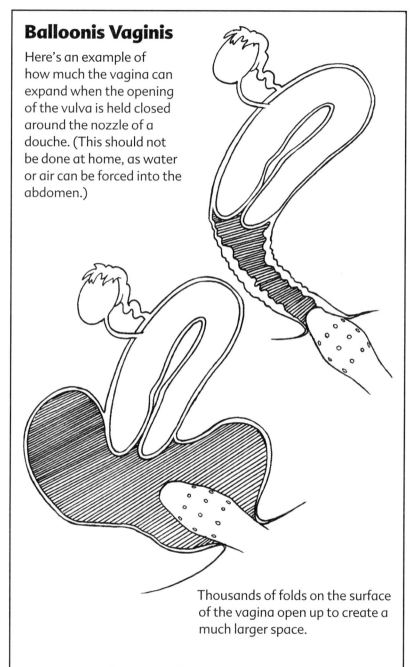

Thousands of folds on the surface of the vagina open up to create a much larger space.

This example shows how the vagina can expand to accomodate a penis or a baby. It was drawn from an illustration in the 1949 classic *Human Sex Anatomy* by Robert Latou Dickinson.

bladder to the outside. It runs along the roof of the vagina. You might think of it as looking like the foam insulation that protects certain pipes. The tissue that makes up the urethral sponge includes the peri-urethral glands, which make fluid. Some people compare them to the small glands that are embedded inside the tissue of the male prostate. It is thought that some of the female fluid or ejaculation comes from these glands.

You can feel the urethral sponge by sticking a finger or two inside a vagina and making a "come here" motion. This will cause your finger to wrap around the pubic bone. You will actually be pressing the urethral sponge against the pubic bone. This can make some women feel like they have to pee. It's the kind of motion that is involved in stimulating the G-Spot area, which is basically where this is.

A good way to feel the perineal sponge is to put a thumb inside the vagina and push down into the floor of the vagina. You will be pushing into a bed of highly vascularized tissue, which means a lot of blood can gather down there. Your thumb will be pushing into the area that's between the Bartholin's glands.

Variations in Preference

"I have orgasms fairly easily, but have never had one with a penis inside. I'm happy with that, but men seem disappointed that I don't need a penis."   *female age 57*

Some women like coffee first thing in the morning; others don't. Some like tomatoes; others find them slimy and odd. The same is true for intercourse: some women can't get enough of it; others prefer their crotches just as they are without a penis begging to enter. This has little to do with a woman's sexual orientation, but rather with her sexual perspective, which is determined by a combination of physiology, temperament, and prior life experiences; or experiences from prior lives, if you are into that sort of thing.

As for variations, one woman might prefer oral sex to intercourse. Another might prefer masturbating while her partner either holds her or masturbates along with her. A third woman might not feel satisfied unless sex includes intercourse. And a fourth woman might prefer oral sex with John, but intercourse with Bill.

Variations in Wetness

When sexually aroused, some vaginas get so wet that the woman needs to wring out her underwear. Other women can be every bit as aroused, but their vaginas remain dry. Also, some women become wetter during certain phases of their menstrual cycle.

Men shouldn't be so silly as to gauge a woman's level of sexual arousal on vaginal wetness alone. And a woman shouldn't feel there's anything wrong with her if she puddles her pants during the day from thinking about sex, or if she seriously drenches the bed when she lets go and has a really hard come. The range in wetness is enormous, has extremes from wet to dry, and should not be overinterpreted.

Women who remain dry even when highly aroused are smart to keep a tube or bottle of water-based sex lube handy. Some women insert a glycerin suppository or similar product into the vagina to make it wet and sensually sloppy. And no matter how wet the woman gets naturally, she should consider using lubrication when her partner is wearing a condom or is inserting a dildo or sex toy.

*What does it feel like in your genitals
when you are sexually aroused?*

"Tingling starts in my clitoris and spreads to my labia. My whole vulva starts to throb, literally. The throbbing is extremely pleasurable. Then my vulva gets swollen and almost hot. Once it is swollen, every slight touch sends lightning bolts of pleasure all around my whole body." *female age 23*

"Sometimes it's an ache not unlike having a full bladder. Other times, a sensation of heat and congestion in my labia, clitoris and vagina. If I'm highly aroused, or if my clothing is tight, I'll be able to feel my pulse between my legs. Sometimes I'll feel my tendons and muscles twitching as well." *female age 36*

"My labia feel swollen and tight; my clitoris becomes hard. Sometimes my clitoris feels like it's huge, and it sort of throbs. If I am extremely aroused, my whole vulva feels as though it's pounding, with my clitoris as the center." *female age 26*

"You know the feeling you get right before your leg or arm falls asleep? I mean, before it's annoying or hurts. It's a really intense tingling feeling. It makes my whole body feel warm and excited. There are moments, however, right before my partner enters me, when my vagina actually aches." *fem. 27*

When did you first make the connection between being sexually aroused and being wet?

"When I was around ten or eleven, while watching a sex scene in a film. My panties got wet, and I realized that was why. If I'm really turned on, I'll drip down to my ankles." *female 25*

"I first connected being wet with sexual arousal when I was thirteen. I was watching a silent, vintage erotic film with a friend. When I went to the bathroom, I was soaked!" *fem. 26*"

"The first time I connected wetness with sex was when I was nine or so and got all wet and throbby when I was watching a couple kissing at the beach. But I don't always get wet when I feel aroused; it isn't an indicator for me."   *female age 38*

"When I first masturbated, I only touched myself on my clitoris, so I was very surprised when I eventually felt my vagina and it was dripping fluid."   *female age 23*

Comments about being wet...

"Being wet is hard to explain. I don't know if I can offer insight because it just happens. The most annoying thing is that if you don't wear panties and get wet, it tends to be very messy, but arousing!" *female age 36*

"For me, the degree of my wetness varies greatly from time to time and seems to be largely affected by how mentally 'into' having sex I am at that given time." *female age 34*

"If my boyfriend just starts kissing me and wants to have sex, I am not automatically wet. I need to be turned on. This could be by way of slowing down and paying attention to my body, or it could be by talking sexy, reading, looking at, or listening to erotica." *female age 26*

"It does not work when my partner concentrates solely on doing mechanical things to get me wet. Yet a simple very tender kiss can do it...." *female age 48*

"I enjoy sex a great deal, but seldom get wet." *female age 32*

Four Scores & Seven Vaginas Ago

If you have had the good fortune to experience sex with a number of women and were of a clear mind when doing so, you may have noticed that not all vaginas are created equal. Not all penises are created equal either.

For instance, steam might be billowing out of your ears at the mere sight of a certain woman, but after having intercourse with her your penis complains that jerking off in the shower feels better. At the same time, a woman who seems quite plain on the surface may be the one whose vagina you remember most throughout life.

Vaginal Farts

"My boyfriend was performing oral sex on me and fingering my vagina. When I sat up, all of the air in my vagina came rushing out and made a huge fartlike noise. I was totally embarrassed; it was completely unexpected. I looked at my boyfriend with shock on my face, and then we both started laughing."

female age 25

Occasionally, air gets trapped inside a vagina and makes a fartlike noise when it comes out. This happens all the time. It's nothing to be embarrassed about. Both of you created the situation and hopefully you had a fine time doing so. Besides, it's just normal room air that's seeping out, nothing that's going to peel the paint off the ceiling.

Vaginal farts are more likely to happen after you have had an orgasm and the rear part of your vagina which had ballooned open during arousal begins to collapse into its normal resting state. The Irish apparently utilized this principle to create the first foghorn.

The Cervix

The cervix is a fleshy little dome in the top rear part of the vagina. Nature put it there as a valve or gatekeeper that joins the uterus and the vagina. The cervix can be as small as a cherry in a woman who has not delivered a baby through her vagina, or it can be much bigger. It has a little dimple in the center that female fluids flow down through and male fluids flow up. The cervix sometimes feels softer during ovulation, when mucus passes through it and bathes the vagina. This keeps it clean and more acidic, conditions which encourage conception. At the point when conception is most likely to occur, the mucus becomes clear and slippery. Danger! Danger!

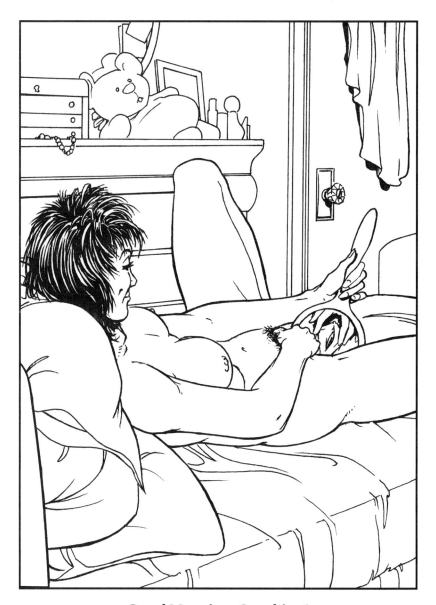

Good Morning, Sunshine!

The cervix has a space around it that is called the fornix. This is a delightful area to explore with a finger. It is also a good space to know about when the woman's vagina isn't particularly deep or her lover has a long penis. Couples in this situation might want to find intercourse positions that encourage the penis to slither under the cervix and into the rear fornix. This will add an extra inch or two of runway space. Rumor has it that some women find stimulation of the space around the fornix to be quite pleasing; others will surely hate it.

See Your Cervix, Learn the Hidden Wonders of Nature

There are at least two ways to see a cervix. The first is the traditional way, by using a speculum. This is a metal or plastic device that physicians insert into a woman's vagina to help push the walls apart. This allows the physician to see parts of a woman that most boyfriends and husbands never do. If you have a healthy sense of curiosity, get a speculum from your physician or medical supply store. Lubricate it with KY jelly, gently insert it into the vagina, and add the krypton beam of your favorite flashlight. You will then need to bounce all of this off the front of a hand-held mirror. This will give you a bird's eye view of the cervix.

A statement of disbelief that is often made upon seeing the small slit in the cervix is "A baby is supposed to fit through that?"

Another way of seeing inside a vagina is to get an acrylic dildo with a view port that is optically designed to give you 5X magnification. These aren't cheap. Once you insert it, the cervix should be in there somewhere. Or skip the speculum and just grab a hand mirror. You won't be able to see your cervix, but there's plenty you can see.

Ovaries

A man's testicles tend to announce themselves wherever he goes. Not so with a woman's ovaries. In fact, it's possible to have a long-term relationship with a woman and not even know her ovaries are there, except indirectly through events like pregnancy or menstruation.

Assuming you want to, the best time to feel a woman's ovaries is when she is lying on her back and is in an "It's okay if you feel my ovaries" kind of mood. Otherwise, don't even try. Rest one hand on her lower abdomen below her belly button. Place a lubricated finger or two from your other hand deep into her vagina. When you encounter the rear wall of her vagina, veer to the left or right and push up gently while pushing down with the hand that's on her abdomen. You will need to rely on her instructions from there. If a woman doesn't know where her ovaries are, she might ask her gynecologist to show her during her next exam.

While some women enjoy having their ovaries explored, others experience it in the same way that a man does a pop in the balls. It might also depend on where she is in her menstrual cycle.

While exploring your partner's ovaries during her menstrual cycle is a concept that some couples will relish, those of us with a less gothic bent might let the opportunity slip by. No matter what sorts of things you are into, keep in mind that some women prefer different types of sexual stimulation during different phases of the menstrual cycle. This can be particularly true for nipple and breast stimulation. Learning about these variations can take months or even years, but good luck if you don't.

Redbootie & Glamour Puss — Charms? Quarks? G-Spots?

Some people swear by the G-spot, others aren't so sure. Hopefully you will appreciate that everyone's body is different, and what pleases one person might not please another.

The biggest problem with exploring for a G-spot isn't whether you have one, but what your expectations are. If you are exploring just to explore, this is a fine thing. If you are exploring because you think you are deficient, then you are misleading yourself.

Just so you'll know, the writers at the women's magazines routinely call to ask about this spot or that spot—the G-spot, the C-spot or the X-Y-Z-spot. It's never enough for them if you say, "Sure, that might feel really good for some women, but not so good for others." These writers have been assigned to write a story that will validate the kind of cover copy that will sell the magazine—come hell or high water, they're going to deliver on that headline that reads "The One HOT Spot Every Woman Has!"

The covers of women's magazines are designed to make you feel bad if you don't buy them. They want you to feel that you will lose your spouse to some other woman who did buy this issue of *RedBootie* or *Glamour Puss*.

So please, if you do want to explore different parts of your vagina, approach it as you would a game of Scrabble or Monopoly, as a fun game, and not as if you'll be sexually inferior if the latest this-spot or that-spot turns out to be no spot at all.

G-Spot Orgasms

For the sake of exploration, let's say there are at least three kinds of orgasms that a woman can have. The first is clitoral, the second is vaginal, and the third is a combination of the two which is called a blended orgasm. It seems that feelings in the clitoris get to your brain by way of the pudendal nerve, while the vaginal orgasms are transmitted through the pelvic nerve. And then you've got your blended orgasms which is a bit of both. The G-spot orgasm is thought to be a blended orgasm. Perhaps this is why women who have G-spot orgasms describe them as being pretty intense.

Theoretically, the G-spot is made up of tissue that surrounds the urethra. This places it on the roof of the vagina about a third to three-quarters of a finger deep. Some people say the G-spot is close to a small patch of vaginal tissue which might feel rough. The roughness is from several small folds in the tissue. Others refuse to get specific and seldom mention landmarks. Some people say the G-spot is small when unaroused (about the size of a pea), but grows bigger when fully aroused (about the size of a quarter). That's inflation for you.

Some women feel a slight discomfort or bladder fullness with G-spot stimulation. G-spot aficionados suggest that women let go of their concern about bladder fullness and allow their muscles to relax in order to enjoy the benefits. Why not put a couple of towels down just in case? Then it won't matter if you have a gusher. Also, it's best to wait until the woman is fairly aroused before exploring for G.

One way of stimulating the G-spot is by inserting a finger or two into a wet and awake vagina and making a "come here" motion. A woman who is exploring on her own might find it easier while squatting. In addition, there are vibrator attachments and special sex toys that are designed for G-spot stimulation.

One intercourse position that you might try when exploring for G is as follows: the woman kneels on the floor next to the bed and leans on the mattress. She is leaning on her elbows and her upper body is diagonal to the mattress. Her partner enters her from behind. Experiment with various types of thrusting, shallow to deep. If it's more comfortable, she might try this standing, with her elbows resting on a

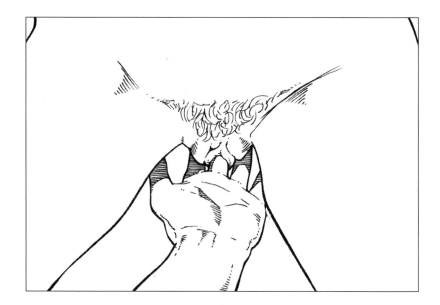

table or dresser. The point is to somehow get the ridge on the glans of the penis rubbing back and forth over the special G-button.

As for the feelings that accompany G-spot stimulation, some women enjoy them tremendously while they don't do much for others. Also keep in mind that sexual satisfaction is part of a much larger process. How you treat each other when you aren't having sex will probably impact your level of satisfaction far more than simply romancing a woman's G-spot will.

Female Ejaculation vs. Bum Bladders

Some women ejaculate right before or after orgasm. The amount of fluid can range from a few teaspoons to what appears to be a pint or more. There is lots of speculation, but virtually no science, about what the fluid is and where it comes from.

The biggest problem with female ejaculation is that women who do it sometimes feel embarrassed and try to prevent it. As a result, they keep themselves from fully relaxing and can't have orgasms. Most guys are happy to have a partner ejaculate, especially when they realize it means she may have had a really deep orgasm.

If you happen to be a gusher or a bed-drencher, please don't think that any guy in his right mind is going to have a problem with it. Why not have fun shopping together for extra sets of towels?

The New G-Spot Book—Goddess-Speak & PseudoScience

It's unfortunate there's so little genuine research on sexual pleasure. But this failure does not justify attempts to invent science in the name of women's sexuality. Such an attempt can be found in a new book on female ejaculation & the G-spot. We're talking Goddess-Speak and PseudoScience to the extreme.

We should have known something was up when the book's only review came from an Associate Professor of Political Science at some college that nobody's ever heard of, and when the book's foreword by a well-known author turned out to be a thinly-veiled apology and disclaimer for what was to follow.

Look, if you want to write a book on the G-Spot and female ejaculation and say "This is a really cool thing to explore, why not give it a try?" more power to you. But when you take a cup of your own "ejaculate" to your family doctor and he agrees it's got other stuff in it besides pee, this is not science. When you suggest that most women already ejaculate, but into their bladders, this is not science. When you say that with a little practice, any woman can launch her own load of ejaculate, this is not helpful.

Science knows next to nothing about the male prostate gland, yet the new G-spot book declares that all women have a prostate gland and it can supply up to a cup or more of ejaculate a day. One of the few things we do know about the male prostate gland is that it supplies about a third of the volume of each male ejaculation, or about a third of a teaspoon. So this female prostate must be a whopper!

If any women readers really do have a prostate gland, take some sound advice and keep quiet about it. Otherwise, surgeons will start cutting yours out as fast as they're trying to cut ours out. And if you don't have a prostate gland, be glad. You won't believe the problems a prostate gland can cause.

Women have been having some pretty outrageous sex for centuries now without knowing squat about the G-spot. So if you can't find yours, all is not lost. And if you don't ever ejaculate, what's the big deal? Think of the mattress covers you'll save.

If you are looking for a sane book on the subject, try Cathy Winks' *The Good Vibrations Guide to the G-Spot*, Down There Press, 1998.

Women & Multiple Orgasms

"Usually I am too sensitive following an orgasm for any stimulation. But occasionally, when I've had a real shake-the-walls, body-mind-soul climax, I'm still in a state of high arousal and if my husband stimulates me again a few seconds later I go off with a bang. Sometimes this can happen two or three times in a row. It feels like a fire-cracker exploding without any prior warning, and we often start laughing at the surprise and delight of it." *female age 47*

"It feels like having a baby, except all the pain is replaced with pleasure." *female age 34*

"It was very intense, almost too intense, like my body was out of my control." *female age 45*

Giving a concise definition of multiple orgasm is not easy. It's like trying to describe a sunset. One hitch is that people usually associate "orgasm" with the type of orgasm that men often have. Adjectives like "multiple" need to be added to make it fit the kind of experience that women sometimes have, although multiples don't necessarily feel like a bunch of singles. Another problem in defining multiple orgasm is that the experience varies from woman to woman. Whatever the definition, here are a couple of reasons why some women are capable of having multiple orgasms. Please keep in mind that plenty of women are perfectly happy with their single orgasms and don't want or need anything more.

Anatomy Despite the extreme sensitivity that may follow her first orgasm, a woman's genitals might stay primed and ready for more. This gives some women the potential to have an extended wavelike orgasm or separate orgasms with little time in between.

Physical Awareness Recent surveys of nurses and healthcare providers show that nearly forty percent of these women have or have had multiple orgasms. This is much higher than among women who aren't healthcare providers. Perhaps familiarity and awareness of the body may contribute to the kind of orgasms a person has.

Emotions Gynecologist David Cheeks did a series of hypnotic regressions on a number of his women patients. One group of these women routinely enjoyed multiple orgasms, while another group had difficulty reaching orgasm at all. ("Hypnotic regression" means to explore early childhood memories while under hypnosis. Whether such memories describe what really happened or are simply metaphors for early emotional experience is a subject of much debate .)

Upon recalling their childhood feelings, the women who were able to have multiple orgasms could remember wonderful sensations in their genitals that were present not only during events like baths or diaper changing, but also during moments of happiness and joy, especially when parents expressed love or acceptance for the child. These women had no memories of being scolded for playing with their genitals. This contrasted sharply with memories of the nonorgasmic women, who recalled few early associations between happiness or joy and sexual sensation. Under hypnosis these women could often recall being scolded for playing with their genitals.

It doesn't take a genius to figure out what this suggests. On the other hand, there are plenty of women with rather hideous childhood sexual experiences who love sex and get a tremendous amount of comfort and joy from it. Unfortunate or tragic early experience needn't shackle one for life.

Possible Parallels Between Girl 'Gasms & Giving Birth

Some people claim that a woman's sexual experience can transport her into another dimension, one that incorporates aspects of Disneyland, the Taj Majal, and maybe an orbit or two around the moons of Jupiter. Perhaps some of the parallels between a woman's ability to bear children and her sexual response might give the latter extra kick. For instance, consider the following associations which were culled from the writings of an early feminist by the name of Niles Newton:

During early sexual arousal and the first parts of labor, a woman's breathing often becomes deep and slow. Then, at the point of orgasm and the second stage of labor, her cervix opens up and her breathing pattern becomes interrupted. Her face often tenses and strains, and she experiences uterine contractions. (Uterine contractions, whether part of orgasm or childbirth, are thought to be triggered by the release of similar hormones.)

A woman's clitoris is usually engorged (swollen) during orgasm and immediately following birth, moments when women often experience a sense of joy and well-being. Some women have orgasm-like experiences after giving birth.

 During both sex and childbirth, a woman's behaviors and expressions become less inhibited. She is less aware of her immediate environment. If the sex is good, anyway.

Uterine contractions and nipple erection often occur during orgasm and while nursing a baby. There are accompanying changes in the skin temperature of the breast during both orgasm and nursing, and it's not unusual for a woman to experience sexual pleasure while nursing. Some of the same hormones mediate both milk release and uterine contraction. Also, some babies respond to sucking on the breast with rhythmic movements and penile erection. Many of us grown-up guys do the same.

Some women enjoy rubbing their clitoris while in various phases of labor. They say it helps to relax them. This makes sense when you consider that orgasms help release the body's natural painkillers.

Here is one that Ms. Newton may have missed: Some women who have really powerful orgasms push down as they are coming, perhaps a little like a woman who is pushing out a baby.

Perhaps these parallels allow a woman access to sexual feelings that are different from a man's. Then again, the sexual journey could be an individual matter that has little to do with whether your sex.

Dear Paul,
I am a 30-year-old sexually active woman. I was recently having intercourse with a gentleman of large stature (big penis). I felt no pain, but started bleeding. I have had intercourse with other men, and assumed my hymen had torn long ago. Is it possible it didn't tear until now? My female physician didn't seem to know much about hymens, and said it might bleed some more.

Mary Anne from Mt. Hood

Dear Mary Anne,
It doesn't surprise me that your physician is hymen-challenged. Some of the better studies on hymens have only been done in the last couple of years, and some of these seem to contradict each other.

The hymen is a thin membrane that is located at the front of the vagina. Hymens are like dresses: some are nearly nonexistent, others cover everything. Most are somewhere in between.

Folklore has it that a woman's hymen stays intact until she has her first intercourse, during which time it supposedly bleeds. It has been said that in some cultures, the marriage could be called off and the woman even stoned to death if there was no blood on the sheets of the wedding bed. To this day, there are physicians who perform minor surgeries where the edges of the hymen are stitched together, creating the appearance of "virginity." One medical journal describes a surgery where a small capsule of bloodlike substance is attached to the hymen, assuring that there will be blood on the sheets the morning after. Women in the olden days would insert a blood-soaked sponge or a small fish bladder full of blood—several times a day in brothels that promised virgins.

A recent study has shown that the hymen isn't necessarily torn after intercourse. Nineteen percent of the sexually active women in this study had no visible abnormalities of the hymen. Most physicians would have declared these women to be virgins—even if they had been boinking their brains out the night before. In its conclusion, this study states, "So-called rupture and bleeding of the hymen is not to be routinely expected after first sexual intercourse."

Some women are born without hymens. Hymens can also be torn or stretched during exercise or heavy petting, with nary a penis in sight. And contrary to what you might think, studies also show that tampon usage does little to stretch or tear a hymen.

For most women, the first intercourse causes very little hymen-related discomfort and or bleeding. What usually causes the pain is tension and lack of sexual arousal. Plus, there's a lot of rearranging that goes on in the pelvis during the first intercourse.

As for your question about your hymen bleeding after several years, this seems quite possible. If you experience any further discomfort or bleeding during intercourse, see a gynecologist. You want to be sure that something else isn't causing the problem.

Finally, in case you were wondering what a hymen is worth, courts in Korea ordered a hospital to pay a female patient $6,200 for tearing her hymen during a gynecological examination. And for those

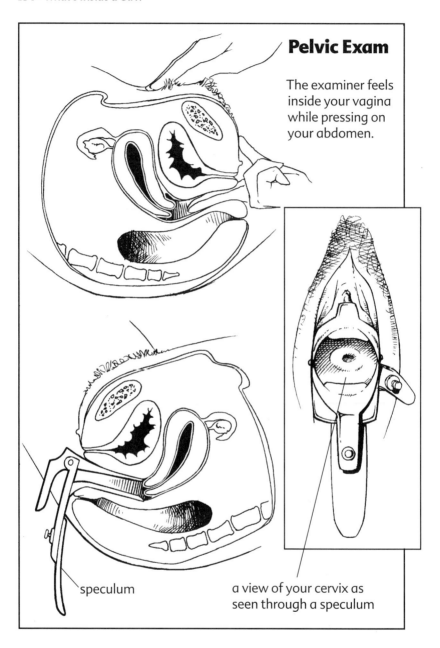

Pelvic Exam

The examiner feels inside your vagina while pressing on your abdomen.

speculum

a view of your cervix as seen through a speculum

of you with a bee in your bonnet, there is the *Journal of Hymenoptera Research*. Hymenoptera refers to a class of insects that we know as bees, wasps, and ants, and would only relate to your genitals if you had ants in your pants.

Dear Paul,

I lost my virginity at 16, a relatively painless experience. I didn't feel the tearing or separating that I have heard described. He just felt very large. Several years and several partners later, I noticed that something felt very different down there. Something inside was swollen. It turns out I had aggravated a "hymenal tag," or a remnant of my hymen.

This tag is just like any of the other folds of skin there, except it looks like a pointy little bit of skin where there probably should be smoothness. My GYN said it could be snipped off with no major complications, just a bit of bleeding, but didn't recommend it if this was just one isolated incident. (No snipping for me!!) Apparently, hymen tags are fairly common, but most women never detect them because they are rather far up in there, and they don't feel any different from any of the other delicate folds.

Tagged in Tucson

Dear Paul,

My friends have gone recently to their first gynecologist exam and the stories they told me really scared me. One girl said it was really uncomfortable and the other one said it was downright painful, she was actually crying. Both mentioned something about the doctor sticking their whole hand inside them, is this true? I am starting to worry because I can't even get a tampon in there, last time I tried it was too painful and I gave up. Do some girls have unusually narrow vaginas?

About to Have My First Pelvic Exam

Dear About to Have,

For the exam itself, you will go into a room and trade your shirt and blue jeans for a paper gown—sometimes purple, sometimes blue, whatever is the latest in disposable gyno fashion. Usually a nurse and doctor will come in for the exam. They will ask you to lay down on an examination table. You will put your heels in metal stirrups and scoot your bum all the way to the end of the table. They will then shine a light on your beautiful genitals. The doctor will put a speculum in your vagina to help expand it and insert a little stick-like device to scrape some cells from the walls of your vagina. This won't hurt at all, but you still might feel something. The cells will be put on a slide and sent to the lab for testing. Then they remove the speculum and the doctor will

insert one or two fingers inside your vagina to feel your cervix, ovaries, and whatever else mother nature put up there. She will also feel
the outside of your abdomen with her other hand. Most doctors will
examine the lips of your vulva and some doctors will do a brief rectal
exam. The doctor or nurse will also do a breast exam. Here's some
advice for you from women who visited our website:

> "I remember how scared I was my first exam. The best thing
> to do is to tell the doctor that you are anxious and ask him
> or her to explain what is going to happen before the exam
> begins. A good doctor will explain things in as much detail
> as it takes to help calm your nerves. The worst part for me
> was the feeling of embarrassment that someone was looking
> at me. A pelvic exam should not hurt and if it does for some
> reason you should tell the doctor immediately so that he or
> she can stop. As far as tampons are concerned, I have the
> same problem and you might want to check out the tampons
> that are marketed as slim fit or even the ones that don't use
> an applicator. I find that these work best for me. Also try to
> relax. The more nervous you are the tighter your pelvic mus-
> cles will be." *female age 22*

> "It's not that bad, and no MD has EVER put his or her whole
> hand in me for a regular exam. Your friends are probably
> being overly dramatic." *female age 18*

> "He doesn't put his whole hand in there darlin—it just seems
> like you are very full because of the speculum. It is pressing
> you open from top and bottom and it is what you mostly
> feel. Also not all girls are a straight shot in. I had some dis-
> comfort on a regular basis until a male doctor pointed out
> that my cervix was tilted to the right hand side of my body.
> I now know to tell the doctor about this before going in so I
> don't get banged in the wrong direction. Unless the doctor
> is using one of the new disposable speculums they do come
> in different sizes as well. I am very petite and know that a
> smaller size will be more comfortable. Some of this comes
> from experience, but it is your part to speak out on these
> issues with your doctor." *female age 33*

"I am a very small woman. My first pap was done with the instruments they use to test small children for molestation, if that tells you anything. I have since had many pelvic exams, all of which have been done with standard equipment. Breathe deeply and try to think of other things, and let the doctor do her job. And don't let them give you an exam while you're on your period. It's uncomfortable for you, take my word for it." *female age 22*

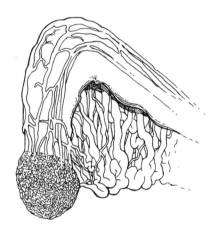

Glans and shaft of the clitoris, as inspired by Robert Dickinson's fine work from the 1930s and 1940s.

End of Chapter Notes: Some of the illustrations in this chapter were strongly influenced by:

Atlas of Human Sex Anatomy, Second Edition, Robert Latou Dickinson, The Williams & Wilkins Company, Baltimore, Maryland, 1949

A New View of a Woman's Body by the Federation of Feminist Women's Health Centers, Illustrations by Suzann Gage, West Hollywood, California, 1991. If you found the drawings in this chapter helpful, you are strongly encouraged to purchase the classic *New View* directly from the authors' website at www.progressivehealth.org

Carol Tavris and her classic book *The Mismeasure of Woman* should set the standard for any chapter on women or any of women's body parts. *The Mismeasure of Woman*, by Carol Tavris, Peter Smith Publisher, Magnolia, Massachusetts, 1999

Kermit Krantz' work arrived via a book titled *The Classic Clitoris*.

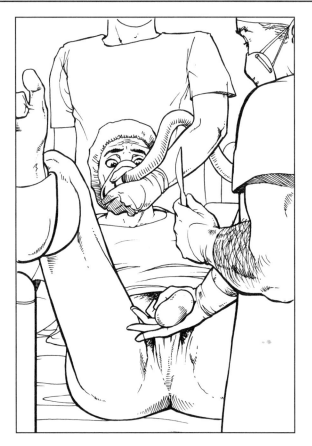

Does the Thought of This Make You Uncomfortable?

If a woman in our society has her reproductive organs removed, no one takes much notice. It's an everyday surgical event. But if a man has his testicles removed, we gasp in shared pain. Are a man's organs more important?

Until the 1990s, when managed health care started taking a closer look at surgeries, approximately 665,000 hysterectomies were performed each year on women at an average age of 42.5 years. A university professor who was a second-opinion expert for Blue Cross reported, "The patients who had the recommendations for the hysterectomies either had no pathology whatsoever or had pathology that was so minimal it was inexplicable to me how anybody could have recommended surgery."

Sunsets, Orgasms & Hand Grenades
Chapter 13

"Define orgasm? It's somewhere between a hand grenade and a sunset."

Mr. Billy Rumpanos, lifetime surfer
and early friend of Goofy Foot Press

One of the many neat things about sharing sex is having orgasms, also known as coming. This chapter describes what an orgasm might be and where it might come from. It talks about the sometimes fine line between pleasure and pain, styles of coming, faking orgasms, and how some people use orgasms for control rather than pleasure (orgasm dementia).

Perhaps it might be helpful to begin with a few comments from Dr. Frieda Tingle, the world's leading expert on sex:

Q. *Dr. Tingle, what do you think of sex in America?*

A. I think it would be a good idea.

Q. *Do you think Americans are too concerned about orgasms?*

A. Whose? Their own or their neighbor's?

Q. *In general.*

A. Orgasm is very important for many Americans because it tells them when the sexual encounter is over. Most of these people enjoy competitive sports, where some official is forever blowing a whistle or waving a little flag to let them know the event has ended. Without orgasm, they would be fumbling around, never knowing when it was time to suggest a game of Scrabble or a corned-beef sandwich.

Q. *What kinds of things affect a person's ability*
to have an orgasm?

A. One important factor is diet. Many times I have been told that it is impossible to have an orgasm after eating an entire pizza. I assume this has something to do with the Italian religious taboo against sexual abandon. Another factor is the weather. Many patients have told me that if the window is open and they are being rained on, it is particularly difficult to have the orgasmic experience...

(Dr. Frieda Tingle is the alter ego of Carol Tavris and Leonore Tiefer.)

Orgasm Defined

The best way to define orgasm is to put your hand in your pants and give yourself one. But this assumes that you are able to give yourself orgasms and that you don't have six different kinds. Perhaps you will find the following definition to be helpful:

Orgasms are extra-special sensations that people sometimes experience while being sexual, either alone or with a partner. They occur after a certain threshold of excitement has been crossed and can last from seconds to minutes or longer. A sense of well-being or relief often follows. This might be due to a release of pain inhibitors following orgasm. For instance, studies have shown that people with arthritis sometimes get pain relief for three to four hours after having an orgasm.

Orgasms often feel as if they are being broadcast from the genitals or pelvic floor, although there is no reason why they can't come from other parts of the body.

Some people experience orgasm as a single, tidal-wavelike surge of sensation with a couple of brief aftershocks; others experience orgasm as a series of waves, genital sneezes, or bursts of light, color, warmth, and energy. Some describe orgasm as creeping up on them, slowly flooding their senses, and some refer to it as a change in consciousness. Some of us experience it as an explosion while others call it a whisper. People occasionally use the term "congestion" to describe the feelings in their genitals just before orgasm; this should not be confused with nasal congestion, unless it's the kind that makes you sneeze.

Some orgasms make you feel great; others can be wimpy and disappointing. Some orgasms are strictly physical; others are physical and emotional. Some reach into the body; others reach into the soul. Some are intense and obvious; others are diffuse and subtle.

The way an orgasm feels can vary with different types of sexual activity; for instance, oral sex orgasms might feel different from intercourse orgasms. Masturbation orgasms are often the most intense, but not necessarily the most satisfying.

In our dreams!

Orgasms with the same partner are likely to run the gamut from totally spectacular to downright disappointing. It depends on the particular day, and whether your worlds are colliding or are in sync.

Some people have orgasms when a lover kisses them on the back of the neck; others need a stick or two of dynamite between the legs. The amount of stimulation needed to generate an orgasm has nothing to do with how much you enjoy sex. Orgasms which require more effort are sometimes more intense.

When shared with someone you love, the feelings that follow orgasm can make it possible to experience a special kind of intimacy.

Some people feel pleasantly amped or energized following orgasm, while others feel mellow and might want to sleep. For some people, one orgasm begs for another or at least calls for more hugging and tenderness.

Genitals can become extremely sensitive after having an orgasm. Stimulation that may have felt wonderful moments before orgasm often feels painful or abrasive immediately after. It never hurts to ask your partner about this, since it's true for some but not all.

Some people are easily derailed on the road to orgasm. For others, the phone can ring, the earth can shake, and a dam can break—they come no matter what.

A philosopher named Sartre noticed that as he was having orgasm he entered his own private orbit which caused him to lose awareness of his partner. Some philosophers make up for this temporary separation by feeling extra-close right after orgasm.

It is not necessary or even desirable for partners to come at the same time. For instance, it can be wonderful to feel or watch your partner have an orgasm, which is difficult to do if you are coming simultaneously. On the other hand, it might be nice to occasionally blast off together. Just be aware that not many couples are able to pull this off.

Some people have orgasms with their legs squeezed together, while others come with their legs wide apart (innies vs. outies). People who prefer coming one way sometimes find it difficult to come with their legs the other way. Do you have a preference?

Your Partner's Orgasms

We often assume that a partner who has an orgasm is fully satisfied, while one who doesn't is somehow disappointed. This assumes that you want nothing more from sex than orgasms. For instance, most of us can give ourselves really intense orgasms when we masturbate, but not many of us can get feelings of closeness, friendship, and love when we do ourselves solo. For some people, these latter feelings are the most important part of lovemaking. So try to be sensitive, but not too paranoid, about your partner's orgasms.

Women, Orgasms and Intercourse

If wanting orgasms were the sole reason for doing a particular sex act, not that many women would bother with intercourse. Only about thirty percent of women have orgasms from intercourse alone. Plenty of women who have orgasms during intercourse need extra clitoral stimulation in addition to thrusting, or they need the guy to ride high so his pubic bone rubs against the right places. Lots of women prefer having an orgasm before intercourse. They say that the intercourse feels better after they've come.

Things that increase the chance of orgasm: being seriously into your partner, exercise and a healthy diet, reading romance novels and seeing erotic images, and anything else that turns you on or increases your level of excitement.

Things that decrease the chance of orgasm: being annoyed or angry with your partner, smoking (chemicals in tobacco constrict blood flow to the genitals and may lower the level of testosterone in both men and women), stress (notice how you tend to have more sex while on vacation), not sleeping enough, taking certain drugs (antihistamines will dry up more than just your nose, and there's a huge list of drugs that will dent your libido or seriously delay your orgasm), and being Catholic (nearly sixty percent of Protestant women report they nearly always have an orgasm during sex, while twenty-six percent of Catholic women do). Perhaps one problem for Catholic women is the Catholic church's strident prohibition against touching yourself, which is how a lot of women learn to have orgasms.

Expressions, Decibels & The Way People Come in the Movies

Some people worry about how they behave when having orgasms. Some are self-conscious because they lose control. The answers? There are none. There is no correct way to come. Sexuality is an altered state of mind; what you do with it is strictly a matter of personal choice.

Some people fear that they will look weird if they allow themselves to be overwhelmed by an orgasm. They fear that their partner will laugh or find them ugly. Quite to the contrary, it is far more likely that a partner will think something like the following:

> "WOW! Her face got all twisted and contorted when she came. She looked like Whistler's mother on a really bad acid trip. She must have had a major orgasm. Maybe I'm not so bad in bed after all..."

Of course, there are plenty of people who have sensational orgasms but hardly show it at all. Their orgasms are an internal phenomenon that remains hidden from the outside world. Unfortunately, many of us assume that women are supposed to make a lot of noise when they are coming. Actually, there is little correlation between decibels and delight. Some women sound like freight trains when they come; others become rather quiet except for an occasional twitch and sigh. The same is true for men. If your partner comes in a quiet way and you would like to know more about it, why not ask?

Keep in mind that many of us learned to come quietly at a very young age. That's because there might not have been much privacy where we masturbated; letting out a large bellow would have informed the entire household. This was particularly true if you shared a room with siblings, and even worse if you had the top mattress in a bunk bed. The same difficulties are faced by people living in dorms, sororities, fraternities, and military barracks, where roommates often sleep only a few feet away. In these situations, we pretend to be asleep when masturbating—a funny notion when you consider that our roommates are probably doing the same thing.

The great sex-noise dilemma is also faced by moms and dads while making love (or trying to) when there's a household full of kids. Depending on the ages of the children, their response to hearing mom and dad can range from "Mommy sounds upset" to "That's so GROSS, turn up the stereo!"

Is It Possible to Have Too Many Orgasms?

Some of the various Tantric types nearly hemorrhage at the notion of a man ejaculating more than once or twice every ten years. They think that the male body is seriously depleted when it ejaculates. As a result, they hoard the white sticky stuff like generals do weapons-grade plutonium. Some even teach themselves to have dry orgasms.

Is there much reality to this seed-spilling fear? It has been written that the Nazis pondered this same question. To test it out they forced a prisoner of war to masturbate every three hours, day and night, for the duration of World War II. Thanks to the Allied invasion, the prisoner finally got to stop jerking off. He apparently went on to father several children and lived to a ripe old age, certainly as old as most seed-retaining monks if they didn't fib about being 128 when they are really only fifty-five. As for other living examples, one male friend of the Goofy Foot Press is now in his early seventies, but his mind is incredibly sharp and he doesn't look a day over fifty. He currently has at least five ejaculations per week, down from the ten or so he has been having since he was a teenager. According to semen-retention theories, he should either be dead or a zombie. On the other hand, Doug Abrams, one of the healthier-looking guys on the planet, has co-authored a book that presents the Tantric position of coming without squirting. Doug clearly practices what he preaches, and it is our hope that his prostate doesn't suddenly explode one day.

Regarding women and orgasm: nobody in his or her right mind has ever worried about a woman having too many orgasms, except for the people who live next door or in the apartment below.

Where Does Coming Come From?

The following quote is from a woman who had a spontaneous orgasm while riding public transit —a rather scary thought if you have ever taken the bus in places like Los Angeles or Detroit:

> I've perfected this wonderful ability to orgasm without touching myself. It started one day on the BART train when I was ovulating, and I felt myself throbbing. I started running a fantasy in my mind and discovered I could bring myself to orgasm. The only trouble with a public place is you have to control your breathing…. (Words of a former high school homecoming queen from the Midwest, as found in Julia Hutton's great little book, *Good Sex*, Cleis Press, San Francisco, CA, 1992.)

Sex therapist Herbert Otto writes about the time in college when he and his friends were talking about different ways of masturbating. One fellow said that he could ejaculate without touching his penis. Naturally, bets were made. The room became quiet and he pulled his penis out of his pants. After his eyes were closed for a while, his penis became erect. Eventually, he began breathing faster, and suddenly he had an ejaculation. This student became a well-known physicist.

Not only is it possible for some people to have an orgasm without genital stimulation, but it can even happen without sexual thoughts. For instance, some women have spontaneous orgasms during highly charged debates or intellectual discussions that have nothing to do with sex. One female reader had her first orgasm as a teenager while her hair was being brushed, and as a forty-year-old she still has orgasms when her hair is brushed.

While not many of us are able to have orgasms without genital stimulation, the existence of hands-free orgasms does suggest that there is more to orgasm than genital contact. For instance, there are plenty of people who have suffered nerve injuries and can no longer feel sensation in their genitals, yet they learn to have orgasm feelings in other parts of their bodies, such as their faces, arms, necks, lips, chests, and backs. They often find that these feelings are as satisfying as their former genital orgasms. This indicates that the power to experience an orgasm resides somewhere in the senses and not simply in the groin. (One woman whose clitoris and vagina were removed due to cancer surgery was able to experience the same kind of intense multiple orgasms after the surgery as before.)

People who have lost one of their senses do not suddenly grow new ones to compensate. Rather, they are forced to better use the senses that remain. This suggests that many of us could achieve greater sexual pleasure from other parts of our bodies if we learned to allow it. One way of doing this is mentioned later in this guide, where the woman stimulates her partner's penis with one hand while using her other hand or lips to caress another part of his body not normally associated with sexual feelings.

Orgasm Chapter Letdown

One of the failings of this book is that it doesn't define "orgasm" more broadly. For instance, in talking about a guy's orgasm, we assume that it's the kind that happens when his penis gets squeezed, stroked, or sucked. But what if he's capable of having an intense full-body orgasm when his partner kisses his neck or sucks on his earlobes for hours? In assuming that an orgasm needs to squirt out of our genitals, we keep ourselves from exploring other possibilities.

Unfortunately, to include the full range of possibilities would add another hundred pages to this book, and if that doesn't make you cry out in horror, nothing will.

Pain Next to Pleasure

Receptors for pain and pleasure are located next to each other throughout our bodies. These receptors often fire at the same time. It is our brain's job to decide whether the overall experience feels good or bad. To make a decision, it will sort through its data base of everything from whether we are ticklish to how we feel about people with brown hair and green eyes. As a result, each of our brains makes its own unique decision about what is pleasurable and what is painful.

For instance, while one person might enjoy masturbating to the fantasy of seeing Johnny or Amber naked, the mere hint of Johnny or Amber's presence might make another person feel sick to their stomach. Or one person might find spanking to be painful and a turn-off, while another might find spanking to be painful and erotic. The stimulus is the same, but how we feel about it depends on how our brain interprets it.

The way we interpret pain is also impacted by our level of sexual arousal. For instance, people who enjoy an occasional slap on the rear during sex usually don't like the pain unless it's done when they are sexually aroused. Being aroused causes the brain to throw routine caution to the wind, converting feelings that are otherwise painful into feelings of pleasure.

One by Land, Two by Sea

There seem to be at least two different neural pathways that transmit signals from the groin to the brain. So let's say your penis or clitoris is tied into one set of pathways, and your vagina or rectum are tied into another. And let's say that orgasms that are triggered by stimulation along one pathway feel different from orgasms that are triggered along the other pathway. And then to really throw a monkey in your wrench, what about Heather who brings home Josh and Zack for a glass of wine after work and ends up getting her different pathways lit up at the same time? The new term for this, besides "lucky," is a blended orgasm.

Possible Assist for Women's & Men's Orgasms

When women are about to come they often pull in or tighten their pelvic muscles. Yet doing just the opposite, pushing out, might make their orgasms more intense. Some women will hesitate to do this from fear that it might cause them to pass gas, but what the heck, you'll both live if she does. And if you consider the gas-passing habits of most couples, chances are she owes him a few.

Whether you are male or female, you might occasionally experiment with relaxing the muscle tone in your pelvis when you come. For instance, some men find that they can prolong the feelings of orgasm if they relax their crotch and anus as orgasm is about to come. Other men find this to be uncomfortable.

What Was It Like?

Lovers sometimes ask each other if they came, but not what coming feels like. Granted, sexual experiences are hard to put into words, since they often exist on the cusp between physical and emotional sensation. But asking a partner to describe what an orgasm feels like might lead to some interesting insights and discussions.

Guys Faking Orgasm?

Back in the winter of '96, when the first edition of the *Guide* was published, the section on faking orgasms assumed that it was women who did the faking. Not anymore. It seems that up to 30 percent of young adult males are faking orgasms at one time or another. These are males in the middle of their so-called sexual prime.

Researcher Karen Yescavage found that guys fake orgasm for reasons like: "I was tired," "I faked it so she wouldn't see me go limp," "So she would think she was doing a good job," or "I wanted to get it over with." The reasons women gave for faking tended to fall into the "I was tired, bored, or it was hurting" category.

The good news is that even the people who admitted to faking orgasms didn't fake them very often. Also, a number of people who faked felt it helped increase the intimacy in sex. For them, the intimacy was more important than whether they really came or not. Other people feel that deceiving a partner is wrong no matter what the justification. They can't see how you can lie and feel more intimate at the same time.

Interestingly, lesbians faked orgasms as often as straight white women, while straight white women faked orgasms twice as often as Hispanic women. One possible conclusion is that lesbians and white males may expect their partners to have more orgasms than Hispanic males do, and so the white females and lesbians felt more compelled to fake orgasms.

If Your Partner Fakes Orgasms

One of the worst things you can do when a partner fakes an orgasm is to try to help him or her to have one. This usually makes matters worse.

There is sometimes a fine line between helpful concern and obnoxious fretting, especially if the reason why you need your partner to have an orgasm is for your own reassurance that you are a good lover.

Rather than trying to help your partner have an orgasm, why not try to discover the things that give him or her physical comfort? Contrary to what you think, this might simply be holding each other for an extended time or not grabbing for your lover's crotch the minute you feel horny. If your partner has suggestions about technique, all the better, but this might not be where the problem lies.

While it is almost always a good thing to want to give a lover sexual pleasure, it can be counterproductive to assume that pleasure and orgasm are the same.

Far more relationships crumble from a lack of emotional pleasure than from a lack of orgasms. As long as you are able to give each other the former, there are plenty of ways to achieve the latter. This book lists several hundred.

Orgasm Dementia

Sometimes it's fun to count orgasms and go for it like pigs to mud. But for some people, orgasm production and/or procurement has a suspicious edge. Here are a few reasons why:

Some people get a sense of smug superiority by claiming how many orgasms they either had or "gave" a partner. They confuse sex with pinball.

Some people use pleasure-giving as a way of controlling a partner. They might hardly come at all while making sure that a partner comes several times. While this might not sound like such a bad problem to have, keep in mind that partners who won't surrender the reins sexually are sometimes very controlling in other aspects of life as well.

There are people who expect their partners to supply them with numerous orgasms. This can breed resentment over time.

Some people need to have sex or masturbate several times a day to help numb a chronic sense of anxiety or ease feelings of deadness. Having a constant stream of orgasms can be their way of keeping an emotional funk at arm's length. Do not confuse this with sexual pleasure, even if they do.

Reinventing the Sexual Wheel—Marketing & Orgasm

In order to sell books and tapes on sex, publishers want us to feel sexually inept if we don't buy whatever sexual experience they are hocking. For instance, during the last couple of years we were supposed to buy books and tapes on G-spot orgasms, female ejaculation, extended orgasms, one-hour orgasms, Tantric sex orgasms, extraordinary orgasms for boring people, and now, orgasms through herbal enhancement. It's only a matter of time before publishers start to sell *Better Orgasms for Your Dog and Cat,* and try to make you feel like a pet sadist if you don't plunk down $29.95 for the videotape.

Many of us would enjoy having bigger and better orgasms if we could. But sometimes the consumer simply has to say "enough is enough." On the other hand, sex can be a fun topic to learn more about. Since you are the physicians of our own sexuality, it wouldn't hurt to at least stay current.

Readers' Comments

For Men: What does an orgasm feel like?

"My knees get weak and I tingle everywhere. It feels like I am numb all over."   *male age 21*

"Like an energy emanating in the soles of my feet, up the back of my legs, in and through my rear end, to my belly button, and out through my balls and penis. Awesome, warm, exhausting."
male age 26

"When I'm getting close, it feels like every ounce of fluid in my body has been forced into my penis. My whole body is in anticipation of the moment when my penis can no longer take the incredible pressure and bursts. Flames envelope the entire

thing and the shock reverberates throughout my entire body."
male age 25

"Orgasm makes me feel very connected to my lover, like I'm
becoming a part of her." *male age 39*

"It feels like all your vital matter collects in your penis and then
shoots out of you!" *male age 22*

For women: What does an orgasm feel like?

"Every orgasm I have is different! Sometimes I feel like I'm just
melting, floating away. Sometimes I feel like I'm running or
pushing into the orgasm. Sometimes an orgasm will sneak up
on me; other times I will be able to control its arrival and duration." *female age 45*

"All my orgasms seem to be the same beast, but with varying levels of intensity from 'Gosh, was that it?' to an ache so
sharp it's almost hard to bear. My most intense orgasms tend
to come from using a vibrator but, oddly enough, they're not
always the most satisfying." *female age 36*

"Orgasms range for me from a simple response in my genitals,
without much sensation and even some numbness, to a mind-
blowing, explosive force of nature that permeates my whole
body, mind, and emotions, encircles my partner and fills the
room around us. Sometimes it's the physical sensations that
are the most intense part of orgasm; other times it's the emotional quality and being with my partner that take top billing.
Even when the physical sensation isn't very intense, I generally feel much more whole and integrated after an orgasm."
female age 47

Your first orgasm...

"With a vibrator at age thirty-eight. Finally!!!" *female age 49*

"It didn't happen until seven months after my first sexual experience. I had no idea what was happening. We were through
having sex. When I began to put my clothes back on, I started
to tingle and fluids started flowing out. It felt great, but I was
actually kind of scared and embarrassed." *female age 21*

"I had an electric shaver that had an attachment which was a massager. After about an hour of moving it around on my clit (and praying that the pillow between my legs was muffling the sounds so my parents didn't hear) I had an orgasm. I'd already had sex many times with my boyfriend, but I felt like I was really sinning now!" *female age 25*

"I didn't really know what I was doing. I was about ten or eleven and discovered this new feeling when I rubbed this silky part of my blanket over my penis, so I kept doing it. Eventually I got this intense feeling in my groin and then there was this goop everywhere. I was completely freaked and grossed out. I thought that I broke myself, but was too afraid to tell my parents." *male age 24*

"My first orgasm took place at age eighteen, when my fiancé introduced me, despite my initial revulsion and disbelief, to the delights of cunnilingus. I thought he was depraved. I was sure I was going straight to hell. I couldn't wait for it to happen again!" *female age 55*

"I had my first orgasm during one of my first menstrual periods. The feeling of a clean pad against my genitals made me feel a warmth I had never experienced before. I rubbed against it to see if I could prolong the sensation, although I had no idea what the sensation was. I just knew it felt good!"

female age 45

"I didn't know what was going on. My body felt like it was convulsing. I tried not to let the guy know this was happening. I didn't know at the time I was supposed to let myself go and enjoy it." *female age 26*

"The first one I had was clitoral—it tickled (I was probably ten). The second type of orgasm I had was when I was twenty. I felt it more in my vagina. It was overwhelmingly emotional and I came in a flood, and I do mean flood. I thought I had peed all over my partner. Now I have both kinds of orgasms. I get to pick, let's see, lobster or steak?" *female age 26*

"My first orgasm was when I was making out in the back seat of a car. I was on top of my boyfriend and there was a lot of bumping and grinding going on and I just climaxed, with my clothes on." *female age 49*

"I was surprised by how sensitive my clit was, but I wasn't sure the actual orgasm was an orgasm because it didn't seem nearly as explosive as what happened in the bodice-rippers I'd been reading. I couldn't believe I'd gone through all this work for that. Happily, many years of practice improved the results!" *female age 36*

"Age twenty. One morning before arising I was idly rubbing my clit and fantasizing, and from out of nowhere excitement began building more intensely than it ever had before. I rubbed myself quite vigorously and for a very long time, until suddenly there was a mind-blowing explosion. I was certain that everyone in the house figured out what I was doing. I was very embarrassed. However, I repeated the experience every night—it took over an hour of heavy-duty stimulation at first."
female age 51

"My first orgasm was by a male friend (not a lover). I told him that sex was not that great. He used his fingers to teach me what it could feel like. I remember thinking 'Oh God, this is an orgasm!'" *female age 48*

Dear Paul,

I would like to know some techniques on how to make a girl have an orgasm. My girlfriend is like a brick and doesn't tell me nothing. What should I do?

Evan in Illinois

Dear Evan the Bricklayer:

I'm sitting here scratching my head, thinking back over the women I've dated, and I can't remember a single one who I could "make" do anything, let alone have an orgasm.

One of the worst things that ever happened to sex was the idea that we needed to give a partner an orgasm. It would have been much better if we had simply set our sights on trying to please each other. Lord knows, that would have been challenging enough.

Wanting to give a partner an orgasm seems harmless enough on the surface. It's only when she doesn't cooperate that we start to get frustrated and our good intentions turn into something like "You'd better have this orgasm or it's going to make me feel like I didn't please you." Nasty, nasty, nasty. Likewise, guys who boast, "I never come before my partner does!" don't realize the subtle pressure they are putting on their partner to hurry up and come!

Another problem with the concept of giving a girl an orgasm has to do with ownership. If you are the one who is giving the orgasm, then it's not really her orgasm until after you have given it to her. So whose orgasm is it anyway? Hers or yours?

And finally, what if you feel the need to give her an orgasm, but she would rather you stroked her hair or gave her a long, loving foot rub? You know what happens. You'll do a half-assed job of stroking her hair or rubbing her feet because your dick won't stay hard forever or she might fall asleep from the sheer bliss of having her feet rubbed and you'll end up having to jerk off like some poor guy without a girl-friend. Get used to it, Evan.

You asked and here's what I suggest:

1. Stop trying to give her an orgasm.

2. Start trying to discover things that give her physical pleasure. For instance, does she enjoy it if you give her a foot or hand massage? Does she like it if you gently run your fingertips up and down her arms or legs? What about her hair? How about gently massaging her fore-head and face, or planting tender kisses on her shoulders and back? When you are in the shower together, do you lather each other up and hug and kiss while your bodies are soapy and slick?

3. Do you relate to her physically without trying to get each other off? For some strange reason, a woman likes to know that a man can have a hard-on without always needing to plug up one of her body cavities with it. Maybe she needs to know that the two of you can hug and share moments of tenderness without it automatically leading to

sex. Otherwise, she might start to tense up each time you are close or get wood.

4. If you are living together, it also helps to do your share of the vacuuming and dishes. There's no way she's going to let her body relax in a sexual way if she's holding onto anger at you for freeloading—although, as far as housework goes, the biggest slobs I've ever had for roommates were females, so I don't mean to perpetuate any myths in that area. Just keep in mind that guys who do their fair share of the housework get laid more often than those who don't.

Evan, you wrote to me about orgasms, and I'm responding with suggestions about foot rubs, romance, and housework. Actually, I'm trying to broaden your thinking about orgasms, which is much greater than simply knowing what part of a partner's anatomy to rub or suck.

Dear Paul,

My current girlfriend doesn't like me to play with her breasts, and the only way she can have an orgasm is when I give her oral sex. My former girlfriend didn't like me to give her oral sex, but sometimes had an orgasm from breast stimulation alone. Both women enjoy sex, but seem so different. How come?

Confused in Kalamazoo

Dear Confused,

For some people, you play with their breasts and BOOM! their genitals are on fire. For others, you are better off reading them their constitutional rights than tweaking their titties.

As for why the different responses, I'd like to share with you an idea that is being proposed by Herbert Otto, author of *Liberated Orgasm.* He feels that the kind of orgasms we experience are in part determined by what our culture teaches us to expect.

For instance, in the 1950s, a lot of teenagers enjoyed extended kissing and petting sessions, but intercourse before marriage was seriously frowned upon. So a woman who was a teenager in the 1950s might have learned to have orgasms from necking and nipple-play sessions in the front seat of a car—without a single touch or lick below the belt. This same woman's unmarried granddaughter pays no social price for messing around with her pants off. She has read *Cosmo* since she was twelve and feels that nothing short of a partner's mouth welded to her clitoris is going to give her an orgasm. And so her body responds differently than her grandmother's. Of course, this doesn't explain why your former girlfriend doesn't like oral sex, unless she's your current girlfriend's grandmother.

As for our current belief that the clitoris is the generator of all female orgasms, consider recent findings from Sudan, where female circumcision is done to young girls to prevent them from masturbating or getting horny. In Sudan, the clitoris, inner lips and part of the outer lips of the girl's genitals are removed. What's left is then sewn together. You would think that if any woman on the face of the earth would not have an orgasm, it would be a woman who had experienced this kind of clitoridectomy. Yet in a study of more than 300 Sudanese women who had been circumcised, at least half reported having orgasms and sexual pleasure. It's clear these orgasms aren't being generated by some guy kissing their clitoris. (Oh please, if any of you honestly think I'm condoning female circumcision, use the energy to write someone else a nasty letter.)

There are dozens of other reasons why one partner might prefer attention above the waist while another prefers it below. In responding to your question, I've focused on some of the less-obvious factors that sometimes play a role.

Now, did you ever wonder if your girlfriend has written in asking why YOU like something one way and her former lover liked something else?

Sex Fluids & Lube
Chapter 14

In order to enjoy sex, you need to feel okay about getting wet and slobbery. That's because no matter how you sort it out, sex is a wet adventure, an erotic monsoon of sorts. Various body fluids get sloshed around during sexual encounters. Some of these fluids, like ejaculate, arrive abruptly, while others, like saliva, sweat, and lubrication, are more constant in flow. Also, menstrual fluids can double as sex fluids, but there's an entire chapter on lovemaking during periods later in this book.

Fluid Understanding

Sex fluids mean different things to different people. For instance, one woman might find it wonderful when her lover ejaculates. It leaves her feeling valued and powerful being the one who makes his fluids flow. Another woman might find her boyfriend's ejaculate to be a sticky mess that she would rather not have to deal with.

Men usually welcome women's sexual wetness, although there are exceptions. For instance, the author of this book can remember a conversation from his freshman year of high school with a fellow member of the track team who had just felt up a woman for the first time. The young man described "it" as being wet, sticky, and yuckie. He indicated that "her thing" accommodated nearly half his arm. Considering this was a farm town, it seems likely that the woman in question may have been a cow.

Some young men who ejaculate for the first couple of times worry they might have broken something inside. Proper education about masturbation can help alleviate most of these fears. Single moms who want to explain ejaculation to their sons might find it helpful to know that prior to puberty, male ejaculate is clear and there is not much of it, perhaps a drop or two. After puberty it becomes white and there is more, about a teaspoonful. Whatever his age, it might be nice if a young man were taught to respect his own ejaculate as the catalyst for new life as well as a sign of his sexual maturity and pleasure—all three being good things that should bring pride as well as new levels of responsibility.

As for women's feelings about their own sexual wetness, most seem to enjoy it. However, young women who don't understand their body's sexual response may feel uncomfortable if they suddenly find themselves getting wet while in the middle of a meeting at work.

Other Sex Fluids

Two other body fluids that switch-hit as sex fluids are saliva and sweat. These flow in steady and sometimes subtle ways, unless propelled by a sneeze or when it's hot or humid and you are sweating like swine. Another body fluid that some people think of as a sex fluid is urine. (See "golden showers" or "water sports" in the glossary.)

Believe it or not, urine from most healthy humans is more sterile than saliva. In fact, urine is considered to be a mild antiseptic, although you might not want to replace the bottle of Bactine with it.

The Sex-Lube Lowdown

Hand Creams (avoid) Most hand creams and moisturizers are designed to be absorbed by the skin so people won't feel like greased pigs after they use them. This means that the macro-molecules that make up moisturizers are designed to go flat fast. As a result, most hand moisturizers are poor performers for sex or massage.

Jerking Off Whether it's for giving your partner a super-dooper hand job or for just jerking yourself off, you'll want a potion that leaves a woody wet and slippery for as long as possible. Try an oil-based lubricant, such as canola, corn oil, coconut oil, vegetable oil, mineral oil, almond oil, baby oil, various massage oils, and hair conditioner when you're wanking in the shower. A popular and nearly legendary jerk-off lubricant is a facial cleanser called *Albolene.* A newer substance that feels similar is called *Men's Cream. Elbow Grease* has been a guy's jerk-off standard since 1979. They also make a newer "light" version. For those of you who like roasting your nuts but have no open fire nearby, there's *Elbow Grease Hot* with menthol. A newer guy's masturbation lotion is called *Boy Butter.* **Note:** If you've invested a major part of your stock portfolio in companies whose main product is men's masturbation lube, keep in mind that a whole generation of uncut males is about to enter puberty in the US. Uncut guys don't need lube to jerk off with. They use what nature so wisely provided—the foreskin!

Women's Genitals Massaging the outside of a woman's genitals with oil-based lubricants is usually fine, but not so for the inside. Consider keeping a water-based lubricant handy for anything that goes inside a vagina—from fingers and dildos to penises and anything that's wearing a condom. Most water-based lubricants mix nicely with a woman's own natural lubrication, and a few drops of water or saliva can be added if they start to dry out. **Orifice Advisory:** Try not to use Vaseline (petroleum jelly) inside a vagina, as it blocks the ability of the vagina to cleanse itself and may result in infections. Scented lotions should be avoided because they can cause irritation, and women who get yeast infections should avoid lubes that contain glycerin. Lubes that contain nonoxynol-9 may cause irritation.

Water-Based Lubes These are the latex paint of the lube world. They wash up with water and don't have any pore-clogging oil in them. They don't harm latex condoms. *KY* is the mother of all water-based lubes, and they are now making special *KY Personal Lubes for Sex* in addition to the old fashioned *KY* for exams and surgical instruments. It seldom rates highly among the boutique sextoy shops, but maybe that's because it's the one lube you can buy at Target or WalMart. Also, unlike most other lubes, it is made by one of the biggest pharmaceutical houses and is FDA inspected and approved. **Orifice Advisory:** A few years ago, researcher Bruce Voeller analyzed a number of lubes and found chemicals that were not listed on their ingredient labels, e.g. mercury. Bruce recommended that people only buy lubes that were used for medical procedures because they had to be produced under the highest FDA standards. Otherwise, you don't know what you are getting. Also, some lubes and moisturizers say they are *water-soluble.* These usually have oil in them and should never be used with latex condoms or in the vagina.

Silicone Lubes The "newest" kind of sex lube has silicone in it. You might say, "I've heard that silicone is unsafe in breast implants. Why would I want to stick it in private places?" If you've ever been on the receiving end of a penis that's wearing a pre-lubricated condom, you've had silicone inside of you. That's because the lube on pre-lubricated condoms contains silicone. As for the safety of silicone, silicone molecules are supposedly too large to be absorbed into the body. The problem with leaky boob implants is that the silicone gets trapped inside your chest. That won't happen with any body cavity that you can safely stick a penis or tampon into.

Most silicone lubes are water-based, which means you can use them with latex condoms. The silicone keeps the lube from drying out, which is a problem with other water-based lubes. Another advantage of using silicone is if you are having sex in the bathtub or hot tub. The water in tubs washes away the body's natural lubrication, making intercourse difficult. The silicone-based lube is slow to wash off and will help keep your piston pumping longer. Slop some on your genitals while they are still dry. Intercourse in water may be more enjoyable.

A possible problem with silicone lubes is their effect on silicone sex toys. The silicone in the lube gradually dissolves the silicone in the toy. If you are using a silicone lube, put a condom on your silicone sex toys first. Also, if you are into electric sex, the serious kind with probes and electrodes, do not use silicone-based lubes. The silicone acts as an insulator.

Lubes & Licks Most commercial lubes taste awful. There are exceptions. For instance, the folks at Blowfish highly recommend the *For Play Succulents* flavored lubes. They are said to taste good when mixed with vaginal juices. They come in a number of flavors including champagne cocktail, chocolate truffle, cinnamon toddy, egg nog, juicy fruit, lemon drops, navel orange, passionate pumpkin, peachy peach, pink grapefruit, watermelon, and whipping cream.

Anal Intercourse You need a thick, goopy lube for anal play, and you'll probably need to reapply it a couple of times. Oil-based lubes have been the traditional standard for butt play, but you'll need to use them with polyurethane condoms instead of latex. Nobody's done any studies on the long-term effects of petrochemicals in your rectum. Fortunately, there are plenty of water-based lubes that will do the job without your butt oozing grease like the grill at McDonalds. Thin water-based lubes like *Liquid Silk* or *KY* may work for some highly experienced couples who have a doctorate in anal-spinchter relaxation. But the average butt that's about to get a good pounding will thank you for squirting something thick into it like *ID, Slippery Stuff Gel, Wet, Probe (Thick and Rich)* or *Maximus*. You might also experiment with silicone-based lubes like *Wet Platinum, Eros* and *ID Millennium*. Some couples like them, some don't. They share many of the qualities of oil-based lubes but don't have the nasty side effect of melting latex condoms. LUBES TO AVOID: Be careful with lubes that have pain killer in them, like *Anal Ease.* These are meant to numb your bum so anal sex doesn't hurt. But this is like disabling the smoke alarms in your home because they bothered you once when you burned the toast. Pain during anal sex is an important indicator that you aren't doing it right. Pain lets you know you are being too rough, aren't relaxed enough, turned-on enough, or whatever. Plus, if something numbs your anus it will numb his penis, setting the stage for a marathon run in your rectum.

Anal Fisting In a word: *Crisco.* Use nitrile gloves. *Elbow Grease* original is another standard. Some people recommend *Probe.*

Vaginal Fisting Keep it water-based, but as thick as possible.

For vaginal intercourse without a condom, plenty of couples don't need store-bought lube. If you are fine without it, don't buy it!

When a Woman Feels Too Wet

Some women on our sex survey say they get so lubricated naturally that they can't really feel the penis going in and out. If you are having this problem, the people at Touchofawoman.Com suggest taking an over-the-counter antihistamine to help dry up your natural lube just a bit. If you have the opposite problem and are taking an antihistamine, be sure to try using some store-bought lube.

Dear Paul,

While I don't usually have problems getting wet, my boyfriend and I can only see each other on weekends, and there are times when I could really use an assist by Sunday afternoon. Is there a lube that you can suggest?

Dusty in Slippery Rock

Dear Dusty,

There are times when nature's own sex fluids are spread too thin and people need a store-bought assist. This is especially true if you are using condoms, taking certain medications including anti-depressants and antihistamines, or are having weekend-warrior sex.

When considering what type of lube to use, it depends on the kind of sex you are having and the kind of feeling you and your partner enjoy. This is because different lubes leave different sensations.

For instance, since you and your partner are cramming seven day's worth of sex into two, you might consider a lube that lasts a long time and doesn't have any taste. A lube like *Eros* has a slight cushioning effect, is perfectly safe to use with condoms, and has a light oily feeling that some people enjoy. If you rub it between your fingers, you can still feel the ridges. If you put it in your vagina, you can still feel the skin on your boyfriend's penis going to and fro.

Let's say your boyfriend moves back home and you need an excellent all-around lube. *Liquid Silk* really does have a silky feeling. It is close to the way a woman's natural lubrication feels and it does not contain glycerin. (The people at Blowfish.com say it's the best lube they have ever encountered, and they sell several different brands.) *Liquid Silk* is not as slick and "fast" as some other lubes. You'll get plenty of lubrication but also plenty of sensation. *Liquid Silk* tends to soak into the skin so it won't feel like you need to wash it off. It also helps moisturize vaginal tissues. Some physicians recommend it for menopausal women. Tell your mom to massage it on her outer lips and one or two inches inside of her vagina twice a day.

Lubes that are glycerin-based tend to be slicker than most which means if you rub them between your fingers, you won't feel the ridges as much as you will with *Liquid Silk* or *Eros*. People who prefer these lubes say they feel "really fast." Interpret that any way you like.

And what if you and your boyfriend are fisting, doing anal play or swinging with other couples? Good lubes might be *Maximus* or *Sex Grease*. These are thicker than most lubes and won't dry out as fast. They provide a light cushion and stay exactly where you put them.

Johnson & Johnson who makes *KY* have come out with their new line of personal lubes made just for sex, *KY Personal Lubes for Sex*.

Places that sell sex lubes each have their favorites. Why not have fun trying samplers that have different brands? Find which lubes work best for you. (Thanks to Ellen at A Woman's Touch for one of the most intelligent conversations about sex lubes that I've ever had.)

Dear Paul,

When I have an erection, it starts dripping like I've come before I actually come. Is something wrong with my penis?

Marty from Manitoba

Dear Marty,

Sounds like precum. Unlike your regular ejaculate, it's clear and sort of drips out gradually instead of shooting across your chest. It makes the head of your penis slippery and more disposed to slide kindly into the vagina of the love of your life. It also helps make the urethra less acidic so your ejaculate is more likely to get her pregnant! You can tell precum from urine by touching it with your fingertip and then pulling your finger away. Precum will stay connected to your finger, making a cool-looking spindle, a little like bubble gum when you pull part of it out of your mouth. Precum can ooze out with a morning erection or when you've got unwanted wood in the middle of a class or at work. Any other fluids of an unknown origin that drip out of your penis, especially if they are a bit green or puslike, should be checked out by your healthcare provider.

Dear Paul,

Whenever I stand at a urinal, I can't pee if there's anyone else around. This puts me in a pickle, since I enlisted in the Marine Corps and ship out this summer, and there is absolutely no privacy in basic training. I currently live in a college dorm and using the shared bath-room has not been easy. Sometimes I have to walk up three flights of stairs to find a bathroom that's empty. Is there anything you can think of, or any direction you can point me in that might help?

Standing But Not Delivering

Dear Standing,

The problem you are describing is called paruresis or bashful bladder syndrome.

For those of you who don't have a bashful bladder, try imagin-ing what it's like never being able to pee while you are at a concert, baseball game, or when dining at a restaurant. Imagine what it's like when you seriously need to relieve yourself and your bladder freezes up whenever someone walks into the restroom.

For millions of Americans, this happens each and every time they try to urinate when they are not in their own home. The only safe place they can go for vacation is to the beach. Or maybe someone else's swimming pool.

Paruresis comes in different degrees: some people who have it can pee in a public restroom as long as they are in a closed stall. Others are unable to go in a restroom if anyone else is there, and some can't urinate at all if they are anywhere but home. They won't even try to enter a crowded restroom after a movie, between classes, or during an intermission at a large event.

You might have the idea that this sort of thing is a wimp's disorder, e.g. "a real man could just whip it out and pee." I once had a patient with this problem who was tough enough to take on the average marine. He had no shortcomings with women or sex, and was in high demand on both scores. Not only was it impossible for him to go in a public bathroom, he had to sit when he urinated at home for fear the stream would make noise and someone would know he was peeing.

The problem often starts before adolescence. A lot of people with shy-bladder problems can remember back to a specific event that triggered the anxiety. For instance, a kid having to use a group urinal in a football stadium with a bunch of grown men who are standing around him peeing out two quarters worth of beer. For others, the causes can be more unconscious.

Far more men have shy bladder syndrome than women, but few women are asked to urinate next to each other without being in an enclosed stall. Guys are expected to go where other guys can watch, casually discussing the weather with each other while whipping it out and doing their business.

The best way to deal with the problem is with desensitization techniques. For most people it can at least provide a decrease in the severity. These exercises are described in an excellent book on the subject *Shy Bladder Syndrome—Your Step-By-Step Guide To Overcoming Paruresis* by Soifer, Zgourides, Himle and Pickering, New Harbinger Publications, Oakland, CA: 2001. Also try www.paruresis.org.

The How-To Part

Chapter 15

There's one way that dogs do it, one way that sheep do it, and one way that each kind of bug does it. This is also true for elephants, lemurs and wildebeests. Unicorns need to be extra-careful when it comes to oral sex, and the female praying mantis eats her male sex partners—to death. So does the black widow.

The animal with the greatest potential for a varied sex life seems to be the human. Human brains are a bit beefier, which means that our minds have extra room for sexy thoughts. But they also have room for strange thoughts as well. For instance, there are people who actually believe that giving or receiving a blow-job isn't sex. Does this mean we should we rip out both chapters on oral sex? Should we take out all of the tips and suggestions on how to give exceptionally good oral sex? Who wants to go on living if oral sex isn't sex, anyway?

For whatever reason, we are the only animals who do our sex indoors and in private. Unfortunately, this makes getting it on a bit of a mystery.

The upcoming chapters attempt to shed light on the mystery of sex. They describe tips and techniques for giving your partner monster amounts of pleasure. Hopefully you will find these techniques useful. But first, it might be a good idea to mention a few things about give and take, shame, and the *Guide's* policy on when to call it quits.

Give and Take

Author Julia Hutton interviewed eighty people to find out how each person defined *Good Sex*. Needless to say, she got eighty different answers. According to Ms. Hutton, "The interviews suggest that sexual savvy depends less upon how-tos than on self-knowledge, which evolves slowly, awkwardly and through many different routes."

Please keep Julia Hutton's words in mind as you read the how-to part of this book. *How-to* will only get you so far when you should be asking *how-come.*

Also, people usually assume that if both partners are sexually amped, then all they need to do is get naked and good sex will follow.

Would it were that easy…. Even when the sex is great, it often takes time to feel comfortable with a partner. For example, consider the following quote from a 29-year-old kindergarten teacher whose comments appear in Julia Hutton's excellent book *Good Sex,* Cleis Press, San Francisco, California, 1992. Chris is her husband:

> With Chris, I like having him in me, that warm good feeling. I've discovered I can ask for what I like, that there's nothing wrong with wanting your nipples pulled taut. I've learned that keeping a vibrator by the bed is not a crime. I've learned that Chris can come, and then I can come, and we can both enjoy watching each other come—as opposed to having this simultaneous orgasm that's supposed to move the world. If we have intercourse that's fine, if we don't that's fine. Sometimes we come home weary from work and it's: what do you want? Do you want to masturbate? Do you think you can focus enough for intercourse? It's negotiation, which I never thought it would be. I always thought it would be this mystic experience, but it's become a verbal experience.

While some couples have good sex from the start, other couples take months and sometimes years to find a satisfying groove. In addition, most couples report that their sexual desire for each other waxes and wanes, although sometimes it just wanes.

Shame between the Sheets

> *Because Ford never learned to say his original name, his father eventually died of shame, which is still a terminal disease in some parts of the Galaxy.*
>
> From Douglas Adams's *A Hitchhiker's Guide to the Galaxy*

Guilt and shame are funny things. We tend to become sloppy and unmotivated without them. Yet with too much guilt and shame, we are at war with ourselves.

Plenty of us might do better in bed if we felt a little less guilt and shame about what turns us on sexually, assuming it does no harm to others. This is especially true for people who are too bashful to tell a partner what does and doesn't feel good.

Hopefully, you will feel comfortable sharing this book with a lover if your guilt and shame are getting in the way.

When It's Okay to Go for It

Here are a few words about relationship hygiene, or when it's okay to go for it and when it's not.

The Guide's Policy on When to Call It Quits

If a potential partner doesn't want sex every bit as much as you do, go home and masturbate. At least you will still have your self-respect. If the relationship is worth it, phone the next day and talk it over.

If you need to convince someone to have sex with you, then it's the wrong person, time or place. If someone needs to convince you to have sex with them, then it's the wrong person, time or place.

If you don't have that much self-control or the ability to know when another person doesn't want to have sex with you, nothing this book says is going to help. Still, here are a few answers to questions from inquiring minds.

To Mindy at the College of the Sequoias: You say that you want him in the worst way and you can feel him getting hard, but it's no enchilada when you reach down and rub his crotch. He pushes your hand away. Just because a guy is hard doesn't mean that he automatically wants to have sex with you. Believe it or not, there are rare but important times when a man actually pleads with his penis to stay soft, but the thing goes BOING just to spite him. Mindy, there are reasons why we refer to genitals as "private parts." Maybe he has his reasons for not wanting your hands all over his. Did you ask? I'll bet you a milkshake and chili fries at Mearle's that you're moving way too fast.

To Mark at the University of Georgia: Dude, when it comes to sex, we've all been misled (or led on) at one time or another. Some of us have even misled others. We live in a society that is so weird about sex that it's not unusual for a person to appear incredibly seductive, but become confused or angry if you actually go for it. You end up feeling like some sort of pervert, when from all appearances it seemed like she wanted sex as much as you. In the future, why not make sure that it's your date who makes the first move—she kisses you first, she takes off your shirt before you reach under hers, and she unbuttons or unzips your pants before you touch hers. And while we wouldn't want to cramp your style, have you talked with her about the subject of sex when you both have your clothes on?

To LouAnne at Texas Women's University: You say that you and he had been "slamming down Kamikazes in his bedroom and he was wearing blue jeans three sizes too small in all the right places and had on one of those little half-length T-shirts that was exposing each and every one of his washboard abs..." LouAnne, it wouldn't matter if he were buck naked and had a red tassel on the end of his penis, when a person says "No more" you need to respect his wishes. None of us has a right to ignore another person's protests, no matter how hot, horny, hard, wet, willing, stoned, drunk, or sexually amped we might be. And even if a person has their tongue halfway down your throat for the better part of an hour, if they suddenly pull it out and wag it in a way that says "Stop," then you'd better be ready to stop. The same is true even if the two of you have been married for ten or twenty years.

To Randy at Fairleigh Dickinson University: You had been flirting with each other for weeks before you met at the party. You had both been drinking before your blood-shot eyes met from across the blurry room. After speaking for less than ten minutes, she said "Let's go upstairs, find someplace private, and have the sex we've always dreamed about." The following Monday, you find yourself arrested for rape. How can this be? "Informed consent" implies that your partner was sober enough to make a rational decision. If you knew she had been drinking, it doesn't matter if the two of you had been flirting for weeks and if she was the one who initiated the sex. If she was not sober when she put the move on you, it is you who can be charged with a crime.

The Zen of Finger Fucking
Chapter 16

"Rubbing lightly is what I do when I masturbate, so I like it even more when my boyfriend does it. I love it when he runs his fingers along my inner lips, up and down. I also love my genitals to be rubbed and tickled when I wear jeans or corduroy. I can come from that kind of stimulation." *female age 23*

Some men, especially younger ones, take the term "finger fucking" quite literally. They think that a woman's idea of a good time is having a man cram his fingers up her vagina. Other men attack a woman's clitoris as if it were a hydraulic pump, believing that the more they rub it the closer she gets to the big "O." (The only "O" she will sometimes experience is "OUCH!" rather than orgasm.)

The truth is, finger fucking is not something a man does *to* a woman, but something he does *with* a woman. It's all of him—his smile, kiss, laughter, strength, and tenderness focused in the ends of his fingers.

What follows is a great deal of information about pleasing a woman with your fingertips. Hopefully you will find some of this to be helpful, especially if you are able to leave your bulldozer behind and are willing to feel things with your fingers that maybe you've never felt before.

A Note on Terms of Art

In order to help some sentences read better, this guide occasionally does minor violence to the English language by using words such as "masturbate" incorrectly. For instance, while masturbation is something you do with yourself, expressions such as "masturbating a partner" or "masturbating yourself" are sometimes used, although "masturbating a partner" is a contradiction in terms, and "masturbating yourself" is as redundant as saying white cow's milk. We also refer to the tip of the clitoris as "the clitoris" as if that's all there is of it. Yet one of the reasons why genital massage feels so good is it massages other parts of the clitoris that are beneath the surface.

Coaching, Patience & Practice

"I had to learn how to touch her clit... I can remember being clumsy about it early on. She'd have to stop me — I was going too fast, going too hard. I can remember her saying, 'You're in the wrong place.' Well, show me where. I mean physically, show me... Rub so I can see it. Okay, now I understand. Over time, I've learned where the places are. I can find them in the dark now. But early on I couldn't. I'd say, 'Okay, show me. Are you sure?' Other times she would take my hand, or my finger, and she would put it right exactly where it was supposed to be, and she'd move it the way she wanted me to move it, and she would apply pressure to the back of my fingers, the amount of pressure she wanted, until I got the hang of it, and then she would take her hand away. If I got out of sync or something, she'd put her hand back and show me until I got it right. A few weeks later I might need some re-education, so she'd show me again." From Harry Maurer's *Sex: An Oral History*, Viking, New York, New York, 1994.

A truly civilized way of learning how to get a woman off by hand is to make an agreement with her that she will provide lots of coaching and patience and you will provide an eager willingness to learn.

That's because hands that are used to throwing a baseball, digging with a shovel, or torquing down engine bolts tend to get a little frustrated when it comes to finessing a woman's genitals; and that's only part of it. There's the additional matter of knowing when to speed up, slow down, push harder, or stay your course. For instance, some women might prefer that guys stimulate them with a constant speed and rhythm as they are approaching orgasm. This might not make sense to a man, since when we masturbate we sometimes speed up as we get close to coming. Other women cherish variety. They will want your fingers to go slow, fast, soft, hard, and have more speeds than a Kenworth big rig, or a Ferrari if you grew up on the rich side of town.

Differences in Attitude

"I've seen a couple of guys masturbate. I can't believe how rough they are with themselves!"   *female age 26*

Take this woman's comment to heart. The reason she can't believe how "rough" we guys are with ourselves is because she would never dream of finessing her genitals that way.

The best thing you can do when it comes to giving a woman pleasure by hand is to forget everything you know about giving yourself pleasure by hand. Do not even think for a moment about stimulating her clitoris in the same way you do your penis.

With a penis, you can slap it, yank it, and nearly choke it to death, all it does is get harder. In fact, think of how you squeeze or wag it when you are finished peeing. Try approaching a clitoris with that kind of careless abandon, and you're likely to be a dead man.

When it comes to touching a woman's clit, assume that softer is better. Always err on the side of tenderness. Push just hard enough to move the skin back and forth over the shaft of the clitoris, assuming you can find the shaft of the clitoris. And don't even get near a clitoris until you've paid your respects to everything else down there.

In time, your lover may want you to be more vigorous. For instance, some women enjoy it if you put your fingers on the outside of the big lips and push all the way down so you can roll the entire vulva between your fingers. This is more like a deep-tissue massage of the entire crotch, but there can be a time and place for it if your lover's feedback is reliable and forthcoming.

Showing Instead of Telling

> "When women moan or gasp, it encourages me to press harder or faster on the clit. Always with poor results."
>
> *male age 41*

Be aware that a woman's understanding of her own sexuality is sometimes on a body level and may have few words. Our society wants it that way and often teaches women from day one that they aren't supposed to tell men about their sexual needs. Getting all frustrated and yelling "Just tell me" does absolutely no good. She probably would if she could, but it's a little like asking someone to tell you the meaning of life. She may simply have to show you by putting her own hands over yours and guiding your fingers as they go. Or maybe she might say, "Please keep trying different ways—I'll let you know when it feels right" or "Maybe it wouldn't be so shy if you didn't press quite so hard…" or "Try it here."

One reason why feedback is so helpful is a woman might say "harder" when she actually means faster, or vice versa. And most guys make the mistake of thinking that if a little pressure feels good, a lot of pressure will send her through the ceiling. This is true, minus the metaphor. Guys also reason that if slow feels good, fast will feel even better. This kind of thinking is seriously flawed. If faster is what she wants, work together on establishing signals that will let you know.

Mix-ups will happen. You can get really frustrated, or you can view this as a cool learning curve. Besides, it's not like anybody's going to die or lose their job because you confused harder with faster!

Suggestion: A woman might try using her partner's fingers or penis to masturbate with. That way he'll get a good feel for the different kinds of speed and intensity that she likes, and how she wants the process to unfold.

Intrigue along the Inseam

"I like to wait until I can't stand it and beg him to put his fingers inside of me." *female age 25*

Men make a big mistake when they forget to give their fingers a sense of humor. Fingertips that tease and dance will find an especially warm welcome between a woman's legs. For instance, gently running your fingertips up and down a woman's inner thigh is about a zillion times more enticing than shoving your middle finger up her crotch. When she's ready to have your fingers inside of her, she will let you know in no uncertain terms, and even then it's sometimes wise to hold back and tease and play some more.

Finger fucking is definitely more effective if your fingertips are playful and melodic rather than serious or hyper.

Zen Boot Camp — Learning Her Style

"It's not a dish of salted peanuts down there, don't just grab and hope for the best. It's very sensitive. Even the slightest movement can produce a reaction, good or bad."

female age 45

The latter part of this chapter is dedicated to special types of fingerplay that a woman probably doesn't use on herself when she masturbates. But first, it helps if you can learn how to stimulate her in

the same way that she stimulates herself. (What if she doesn't masturbate? Then both of you can learn together.) With time, you will add your own special twists, but it's a big mistake to get fancy before you learn the basics — her basics. Give yourself at least a month or three in finger-fucking boot camp with your sweetheart as master and you as grasshopper. If you have a partner, you might ask her to put a small red heart in parts of this chapter that speak to her nether regions. Here are a few suggestions that might be helpful:

Make sure there are no rough edges on your fingernails.

Sorry, but finger fucking does not necessarily mean pushing your finger in and out of your partner's vagina. For some it will, but others will want a more schooled approach.

When a woman masturbates, she often rests her wrist on her lower abdomen just above the pubic bone. If this is what your partner does, try to do the same, since it will definitely influence the way your fingers feel on her vulva.

Lie next to your partner and reach your arm over her body until your fingers are touching her crotch. This allows your fingers to approach her vulva in the same way that her own fingers do when she masturbates. Or try sitting like the couple on the previous page. The worst way to masturbate a woman is while sitting between her legs, facing her vulva. This can be a fine position to use for genital massage, which is discussed later, but it's ineffective if you are trying to imitate the way she touches herself.

Let the vulva come to you. Men who are more experienced at lovemaking often begin with light, gentle caresses that barely touch the inner thighs and pubic hair. They don't go much further until a woman's legs spread open and her pelvis begins to arch upward. They tease and caress until the lips of her vulva invite their fingers inside.

Too often, a man's focus is to get his fingers on a woman's clitoris or to go mining up her vagina. Never hesitate to interrupt a bout of clit-play by running your fingertips up and down her inner thigh, or by massaging her mons, gently pulling on her pubic hair or reaching down a little lower and giving her inner lips a gentle massage or tug. Predictability is the hobgoblin of finger fucking.

The tip of the clitoris is often more sensitive than any single part of the penis. You don't want the rough skin of your fingers rubbing across it. This is why some men gently push and pull on the clitoral hood and labia (lips). Using the inner lips as leverage can provide pleasing stimulation without painful friction. Also, the inner lips attach directly to the clitoral hood, so tugging on them can provide a level of stimulation that's just right for some women; not too rough and not too light.

When your partner masturbates does she like to dip her fingers inside her vagina? This is sometimes done to bring her natural lubrication up to the tip of the clitoris.

Does your partner use extra lubrication when she masturbates, such as saliva or KY? Never be shy about using extra lubrication, especially if you'll be at it for long periods of time.

When men try to masturbate women, they often use just one finger. However, when a woman does herself she might incorporate her wrist into the motion, even if only one finger is actually touching her vulva. This can be a subtle but important detail, and it may require practice.

Find out if your sweetheart has a favorite side of her clitoris or labia that she likes to stimulate. Be sure to follow her lead. This is a lousy time to be dyslexic!

You wouldn't be worth a darn as a basketball player if you didn't know how to use a backboard. The same can be said for a lover who doesn't know how to utilize his lady's pubic bone — inside as well as out. It's a fine perch for a tired hand and offers all sorts of leverage when caressing a woman's genitals.

The mons pubis is the fleshy mound at the top of the vulva just above where the lips begin to open. It usually has hair on it. It's easy to ignore the mons and head straight for the clitoris, yet some women masturbate by putting moderate fingertip pressure on the mons and making a circular or back-and-forth motion with it. Your partner might want you to try this while the fingers of your other hand are rubbing her clit or stimulating the roof of her vagina. Some women enjoy it when a partner kneads the mons or taps on it with his fingertips.

There are women who might want you to pull back the hood of the clitoris. This will allow for much higher levels of stimulation. But for a lot of women, especially those with hypersensitive clits, this is a finger-fucking felony. If you are looking for amplification, it's much wiser to pull up on the mons with the fingers of one hand while gently tugging on the inner lips with the fingers of the other.

An excellent way to learn more about pleasing your partner is to rest your fingers over hers while she is masturbating herself. Then do the reverse, with her fingers acting as guides for your own. A woman shouldn't hesitate to take a man's fingers and put them exactly on those parts of her body where she likes to be touched. Most men will appreciate the assist!

Another advantage of having your arm resting across your partner's body is that it allows you to feel when she is tensing up, when her hips start to arch, and if her body begins to writhe or twitch as it sometimes does when highly aroused. These are important signals, because as a woman becomes more aroused she may need you to stimulate her in a different way. This is the lovemaking equivalent of learning how to type without looking at the keyboard.

When they masturbate, some women direct the stimulation to just one spot. Others might stimulate themselves in a more global way, tugging and pulling on the surface of the entire vulva. Plenty of women use a circular motion when rubbing their genitals, while others move a finger side-to-side or up and down like plucking at a guitar string.

You might try to achieve a certain tempo and rhythm as your fingers transverse the vulva. That way if she says "faster" or "slower," you'll have a point of reference to work from. While one woman might want you to maintain the same rhythm and hand motion from start to stop, another might need an array of tempos because she quickly habituates to the same finger motion and it loses its effect. Finding the right rhythm and tempo may feel awkward and be a challenge, but you will learn when to mix it up and when to stay your course. Helpful indicators include the little sounds she makes, changes in her breathing, the way her body moves—especially her hips and legs—changes in her vulva, and changes in her clitoris.

Does your partner like to have something inside of her when she comes? Your fingers, a dildo, etc.? Ask. Also, some women have sensitive spots inside their vaginas which they love to have stimulated with one hand while you do their clitoral hood with the other. Try doing the hood with whichever hand you use for writing, since it requires more fine motor skill than massaging a vagina. Simple pressure often works well in the vagina once you learn where to touch.

You never want to surprise a woman's vagina by suddenly shoving an entire finger into it. A more satisfying approach is to ease your finger in one joint at a time. For instance, once you get the signal that she wants your finger inside of her, slide it in as far as the joint that's between your fingernail and middle knuckle. Use it to make sensuous circles inside her vagina, gently tugging the tissue this way and that. After a while, she'll give you a cue to up the ante. Then glide your finger in a little further until you reach the middle knuckle. Stop and play some more. At that point, she might want it to go all the way in, or maybe she'll prefer the added fullness of a second finger. She might want you to do an in-out motion with your fingers, or maybe she'll want you to stimulate the roof of her vagina. Perhaps she'll want you to jiggle your hand or pull upward with it as your finger makes an "L",

with the fingertip part inside her vagina and inner knuckle part pulling up against the shaft of her clitoris. There are many different options.

There are women who enjoy being touched from behind, when they are lying on their stomach or on all fours or while leaning over something. You simply reach between her legs from behind. This changes the angle that your hand makes with her genitals. It's also a neat way to massage the roof of the vagina with your thumb!

Some women love having their nipples caressed, sucked on, or pulled while being masturbated. The added nipple pleasure makes it easier for them to come. Others find this annoying. Be sure to inquire.

While lying next to your partner, rest your arm across her body with your fingers on her vulva. Separate her labia with your first and third fingers and stroke between her inner lips with your middle finger, bringing lubrication up from the bottom of her vaginal opening. If she isn't already wet, lubricate your finger with saliva or store-bought lube. Try to be gentle, since the belly of the clitoris is sometimes extremely sensitive. Some women like to have their vulvas tapped with fingers, and some even like to be lightly slapped on the genitals — but only a moron would try something like this if his partner hadn't requested it.

The outer lips often have hair on them; the inner lips don't. The outer lips are usually more prominent, although sometimes the inner lips are. Some women like to have the man clasp each lip between his thumb and forefinger and tug on it. Some like this to be done very gently, others with more force than you might think. Do this very gently at first, increasing the tension to the point where your lover finds it most pleasing.

There's no reason why a woman shouldn't lube up a favorite part of her lover's body and rub against it with her vulva. Some women like to do this on a man's back or thigh. (There are women who think the penis would be more useful if it had been mounted on the front of man's thigh instead of between his legs. There is even a special dildo harness that mounts a dildo on the thigh, achieving this very feat in an amusing way.)

Some women enjoy using the head of a sweetheart's penis for masturbating. This can be an invigorating experience for both partners. Keep in mind that even if the male doesn't ejaculate, unwanted sex germs can be passed on or the woman can get pregnant from such activity. You can greatly diminish these risks if the man is wearing a rubber that is well-lubricated with something like KY.

If getting pregnant or sex germs aren't a consideration, some women like to use a man's ejaculate as a lubricant to masturbate with. This might be fun to do when he comes first. She might add some saliva or her own lube; otherwise it's likely to dry up.

Some men follow the same protocol each and every time they have sex. It never hurts to experiment with new ways to touch your partner, both with your fingers and with your heart.

Agony vs. Ecstasy

We recently had to take a friend to the emergency room. From another part of the ER there was a young man who was moaning in pain. He would pepper his moans with an occasional "Oh God". If you had changed contexts and heard these exact same moans coming from a bedroom window, you would have smiled in envy, sure the man was at the height of sexual ecstasy.

How is it that extreme pain and extreme sexual pleasure can sound identical? They certainly don't feel the same, not for most of us anyway. Maybe the sounds we make when our bodies are spinning out of control tend to be similar, whether we are spinning toward ecstasy or agony.

Keep in mind that it may be difficult for a partner to know when you are feeling pleasure as opposed to pain. It's up to you to help your partner learn the difference.

The Extra-Sensitive Clit

Some women have a clitoris that is super sensitive to touch. This kind of clit is simply too sensitive to be even the slightest bit forgiving, and if you don't appreciate the sensitivity of it you will start to assume the woman is way too finicky and not worth the effort. This is unfortunate. Read this chapter with her, and have her mark some of the things she thinks might work. Make sure she is highly aroused before your fingers go anywhere near her clit, and be mindful of how quickly it can go from being too sensitive to totally numbing out. Also,

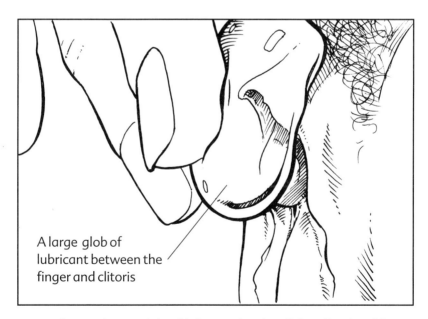

A large glob of lubricant between the finger and clitoris

Never fear trying a glob of lube on the tip of the clitoris. This can be a helpful way to approach a clitoris that is hypersensitive. (This illustration was inspired by the impressively diagramed "Illustrated Guide To Extended Massive Orgasm" by Steve and Vera Bodansky, Hunter House, Alameda, CA, 2002.

try to become a master of indirect stimulation, e.g. is it better if you caress her crotch when she's wearing blue jeans or underwear than when she's naked?

More Than a Peace Sign

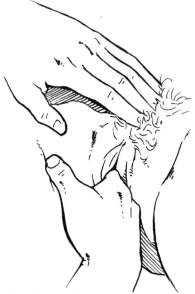

In reviewing porn movies done by lesbian producers, author Jay Wiseman noticed that when lesbian performers feel each other up they almost always use two fingers—not one or three. Wiseman asked a number of women about this, and most replied that two fingers simply feel better. Some of this guide's women readers said they enjoy one finger, three fingers, an entire fist or a big toe, but most agreed that two fingers is a fine number. The number of fingers a woman wants inside of her will also depend upon her level of arousal and sometimes upon her body's menstrual status.

You might consider wearing latex gloves when spending long periods of time with your fingers inside a woman's vagina. The smooth latex surface sometimes feels nice for the woman and helps to keep your fingers from stinging when they marinate in vaginal fluids, which are fairly acidic. Try putting a dab of water-based lube inside each fingertip of the glove and see if it makes any difference for you or her.

Female Readers' Advice on Fingers in Their Vagina

"I like it if he inserts one finger until the opening relaxes, then adds a second finger. When I begin to breathe faster, he should start flexing his fingers. The motion is similar to when you are signaling a person to 'come here.'" *female age 32*

"When I am sufficiently wet, I enjoy two fingers. I like it when he puts them in gradually and 'fucks' me with them gently. But no fingernails and no rushing!" *female age 35*

"Start with one finger, then go up from there. To find the G-Spot, put your thumb over my clitoris, then insert your first finger into my vagina and feel for the rough spot on the upper wall. Rub this spot!!!"   *female age 26*

"I like a finger in there, but please, don't dig for China." *fem. 48*

"I don't necessarily care for fingers in my vagina. I'd rather have a penis in there."   *female age 43*

"I like him to rub the entrance of my vagina in a circular fashion, but don't like a finger all of the way inside."   *female age 30*

Women's Genital Massage

Vulva Massage vs. Finger Fucking

Giving a woman a genital massage differs from giving her traditional hand play in a couple of ways:

You often use massage oil or lubricant.

You sit facing her, either between her legs or to one side.

You are not trying to imitate the way she masturbates.

What you learn about a woman's vagina from massaging her genitals can be used to increase her pleasure during intercourse. The sensitive spots or areas that you find in her vagina can sometimes be massaged with the head of your penis.

Think Clocks

Close your eyes and imagine a clock—the old-fashioned type that has a big hand, a little hand, and a cuckoo bird where the tip of the clitoris should be. There are six or seven clocks or pelvic time zones to consider when massaging a woman's genitals. An effective way to explore a woman's vulva and vagina is to imagine each part as having a clock face over it. The clock face will be your fingers' roadmap.

Working the Steps

What follows can take a day or it can take a year. Don't be a slave to protocol. If you have your finger at one o'clock and she suddenly starts moaning and her whole body contorts and writhes in pleasure, why not keep it there? If you don't get to two o'clock for another month, who cares?

If you are using massage oil, nuke the stuff for a few seconds if it is cold, or rub it between your hands to warm it. Then put your hand over your lover's genitals and slowly drip the oil on your fingers so it seeps through them and onto her vulva.

Sit facing your partner's crotch, either between her legs or on the side of her body that allows you to easily touch her genitals with the same hand that you use to jerk off with.

When massaging different parts of a woman's genitals, apply just enough pressure to move the skin back and forth over the tissue that's under it. Press harder if she asks.

Place an imaginary clock face around the hood of your partner's clitoris. Then put your fingertip at twelve o'clock, press lightly, and stimulate as long as she likes. Do this at each hour on the clock face. Hopefully your sweetheart will let you know when you hit a fun spot by saying something profound such as "There!" You can then say "two o'clock?" and she might reply "try one forty-five." Go back and forth until you have it just right. Instead of having to say something out loud, she might prefer to hold your penis, ankle or big toe in the same way that a kid uses a joy stick. She can then squeeze with her hand to indicate a direct hit.

When they masturbate, some women focus their finger on the inner labia or on the inner part of the larger labia rather than upon the clitoris proper. Be sure to explore the parts that are clitoris-adjacent.

Finding a man's peehole is not a particularly taxing exercise; finding a woman's can take a bit of work. Why would you want to? Because the little dome of tissue that surrounds a woman's urinary opening has sometimes been compared to the head of the penis. Some women might enjoy it if you stimulate this area; ask.

Lay your free hand over the lower part of your lover's abdomen. Experiment by applying different kinds of pressure with the top hand while fingers from your other hand are inside her vagina.

Think of the vagina as a tube that's about four inches long. Start at the rim (opening) of the vagina. Put pressure on each part of the tissue as your finger eventually makes a complete circle. Then move the imaginary clock face deeper inside and do the same thing all over again. Keep repeating this until you have done the whole thing. It helps to be extra thorough about clocking the first third of the vagina, because that's the part that is most sensitive to touch. Pay special attention to the roof of her vagina between 9:00 and 3:00. A number of women report pleasurable responses in this part of the vagina.

Some women feel a certain dull but enjoyable sensitivity around the base or deepest part of the vagina, a full finger deep. This part of the vagina is more sensitive to pressure than touch.

The urinary tube runs along the ceiling of the vagina from the outside of a woman's body into her bladder. It's a bit like an air-conditioning duct that is above a suspended ceiling. The urinary tube is surrounded by a special type of tissue that is called the urethral sponge. Some women refer to this area on the roof of the vagina as the G-Spot and find its stimulation to be quite pleasurable. One way of stimulating it is by making a "come here" motion with a finger that's put inside the vagina.

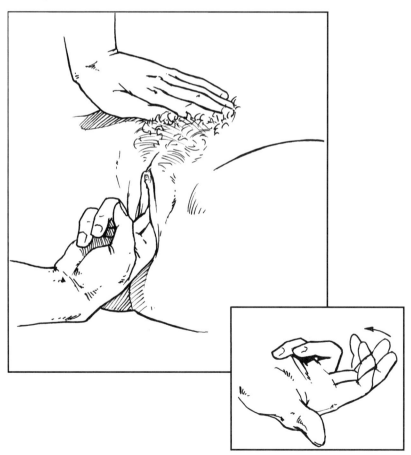

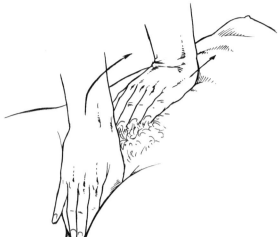

Place a well-lubricated hand between the woman's legs with your fingertips resting below her vulva but not touching her anus. Pull the hand all the way up to her belly, with your fingertips gently separating her labia with each stroke. Then do the same thing with your other hand, alternating strokes.

A woman's cervix can usually be found in the upper rear part of her vagina. It is easily felt if she is on all fours or brings her legs to her chest. The cervix feels like a little dome of tissue that's fun to run your fingers around. It may also have a small cleft in the middle, like your chin. Carefully stimulate the area surrounding the cervix. Some women may enjoy this and want you to do it more often; others won't. Cervical sensitivity can vary with a woman's menstrual cycle; massaging it may release some blood if she is close to her period.

The perineum is the groin's version of a demilitarized zone that separates the anus from the vagina. Push into the surface with your fingertips and explore.

The ring of the anus contains a multitude of nerve endings. Women and men who don't have aesthetic problems with anal stimulation might enjoy a clocking of their rectal areas. You may find that one part of the anus is more sensitive. Putting a finger on it generates pleasure. But be careful about going from a woman's rectum to her vulva without washing your hands.

The Lip Part of Erotic Massage

Women's genitals have two sets of lips—the inner lips and outer lips. The inner lips form the hood of the clitoris. In erotic massage, much time is spent with the inner and outer lips.

After lubing the area up, it might be nice to begin with one of the larger outer lips. Put your thumb and forefinger around the lucky lip, clasping it at the base where it attaches to your partner's crotch. Then run your fingers or fingertip from the lower to upper part of the lip, as though you were tracing one side of a parenthesis. Repeat this as long as your partner's feedback is positive.

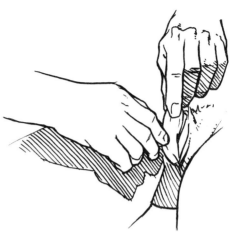

Another form of genital massage is done by holding a lubricated lip between your thumb and forefinger. While squeezing just a little, pull your fingers straight away from the woman's body. Your fingers will end up in the air an inch or two above her body, as though you had pulled them off the edge of a sheet of paper .

What Did You Discover?

It will take time to explore a woman's genitals. Maybe you will find one special place, or maybe ten. You might want to stimulate these spots while having intercourse or oral sex. Experiment with different positions that will allow you to reach them with the head of your penis. Or try stimulating an outer spot with your tongue while using your fingers to reach a spot that's deeper inside. The sensations won't necessarily pack the kick of a mule, but the overall effect can be quite pleasing.

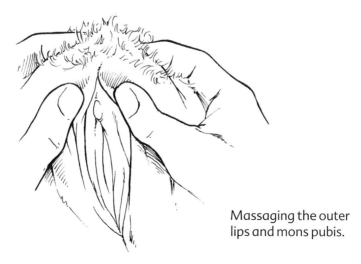

Massaging the outer lips and mons pubis.

Contradiction—Aquatic Sex Is Dry Sex

Many couples find it sensual to grope each other in the shower, hot tub, or bath. However, water tends to wash away natural lubrication. For a non-intercourse grope in a hottub, a good solution is to keep a plastic squeeze bottle with oil in it next to the tub. Stand and lube the outside of your dry genitals with vegetable oil, then ease your way into the water. This will help keep your genitals slick and slippery during aquatic hand play. For intercourse while submerged, try a silicone-based lube as mentioned.

Two advancements in hydrotechnology have been a boon to aquatic sex play:

Hand-Held Shower Head If you don't have one of these gadgets, consider getting one. It shouldn't take more than fifteen minutes to install, unless your plumbing is really rusty. Hop in the shower with your sweetheart and try out the various settings. Keep in mind that when you hold the shower head point blank against the skin it causes the water to bubble somewhat like the jet on a hot tub. This might feel good. Don't point a focused jet of water directly into a woman's vagina, as it might force air inside her body and could be dangerous.

Some men enjoy the feeling of the spray against the side of the scrotum. This might be one of those sexual experiences where the line between pleasure and pain is a fine but pleasant one.

Also, different brands of hand held shower heads create different kinds of spray. Some people might prefer one brand over another. You can often find them for under $30. Hardware chains generally put them on sale every month.

Powerjets in the Hot tub Check with your hot tub repair person about fitting an extension hose on one of the massage jets so you can direct the flow where you want. Tell him it's for your grandfather's hydrotherapy. Cut the air to the jets so it won't get into the vagina.

Also, there are now waterproof vibrators. These are tiny things which only have one conceivable purpose, yet the box shows a woman in a tub using the point of the vibrator against the side of her neck!

Winding Down

"The first time I felt a woman's vagina was with my first love. We were taking things very slowly, and when I would ask if I could go down her pants, the answer was no. I respected her wishes and we always did something else, usually making out. One day she finally told me I could proceed below the waistline. It was warm and wet and very soft. The wetness of her vagina was the most exciting feeling I'd ever had." *male age 25*

For some men, putting their fingers between a woman's legs is a moment that has its own wonder or magic. There's the woman's warmth, the start of her wetness, and how her body sometimes tenses and squirms.

Keep in mind that there are other parts of a woman's body where touch produces intense sensation. One reader reports that his lover has an area on the small of her back that is so erotically charged that her knees nearly buckle when he caresses it. He once nearly caused her to have an orgasm in the middle of a busy hardware store by caressing this part of her back. Another reader is so sensitive to having her fingers touched that getting a manicure feels like a sexual experience.

"It Just Snuck up on Me!"

Sometimes the nicest orgasms happen purely by accident. Let's say you've been stroking those special spots on her body, playfully caressing her thighs and tugging on her inner lips with the morning sun creeping through the blinds. Suddenly, one just sneaks up on her—and you. You weren't trying to give her an orgasm; you weren't stoking her clit; you were just kicking back, letting your fingers play and enjoy themselves. Maybe it's not the most intense orgasm she's ever had, but it's totally unannounced and it's nothing but pure lazy delight.

Final Words about Caressing a Woman's Genitals

As kids we used to hold sea shells up to our ears to hear the ocean. As adults, some men find themselves pressing an ear against a partner's chest while their fingers dance over the sweet spot between her legs. It might not tell you the meaning of life, but it's a start.

Whether you should roll the shaft of the clitoris depends on how long it is and how sensitive it might be.

Dear Paul,

How do you touch a woman between her legs? Based on my girlfriend's reactions, I'm clearly doing something wrong.

Klutz in Kalamazoo

Dear Klutz,

I still get confused about women's genitals. Sometimes they're too sensitive to even be breathed upon; other times, your most valiant attempt at mouth-to-crotch resuscitation won't wake the thing up.

To help me learn along with you, I pulled a video from the shelf titled *The Best of Vulva Massage.* While this was not done as a porn tape, it shows more up-close shots of women's genitals than any six editions of Hustler.

Klutz, if you learned how to do a fraction of the things they show in this tape, women would be lined up at your door. But herein lies the rub—with all the close ups of women's crotches, this isn't the sort of tape that most guys would grab if they wanted to be sexually aroused. And maybe that's part of the problem. If you touch a woman with the kind of pace that most of us want in a jerk-off tape, she probably won't like it. But if every once in a while you give her a full body massage and then gradually work your way up to a light and intimate genital caress, things might start to change.

If your partner can trust that she'll be getting something good from your new approach, she might be able to relax more during sex. This might help her be more receptive than she currently is, and perhaps it will allow the two of you to meet in the middle.

We all need gestures that encourage us to achieve a better space with our partner. Otherwise, we get entrenched and give up. We might not leave, but we give up.

HIGHEST RECOMMENDATION And Then Some: If watching this DVD or video were required of every high school boy in the nation, the state of American women would evolve. But retail stores wouldn't like this, because women would be too relaxed to do a single mall crawl. *The Best of Vulva Massage* by Joseph Kramer is a compilation of the best female genital massage tapes ever done. It would make a splendid graduation or wedding gift. You can get it at places like blowfish.com or goodvibes.com, or directly from eroticmassage.com where they occasionally put it on sale.

———————————

Dear Paul,

My girlfriend likes me to touch her genitals, but it takes a lot longer for her natural lube to flow than other women I've been with. Is there anything I can do to help the situation?

Sandy in Palm Desert

Dear Sandy,

I don't know if this has anything to do with your situation, but most of us guys start touching a woman's vulva near the tip of her clitoris. You are more likely to find lubrication near the bottom part of the vaginal opening, where the lips make a "U." Try dragging the fluid up from the bottom part of the vaginal opening with your fingertips. This assumes that you have spent plenty of time and effort to get the fluids flowing in the first place. Also, you might try using a water-based lube. Don't use the lube in place of extra kisses and caresses, but in addition.

Reader's Comments

"I would first tell him to approach slowly. Having someone just dive straight towards where they think my clitoris is becomes overwhelming. I like to be teased, I like a slow and sensual working up to where they think my clitoris is. If they are totally in the wrong area (just because it's hard doesn't mean it's my clit!) I have no qualms about giving directions."

female age 22

"Wait until I'm really turned on and I'm practically shoving your hand down my pants. Then, gently play around and see what I respond to. Once you've found my spot, start out slowly with only a little pressure. Don't focus exclusively on the spot, because that gets annoying and it makes me less sensitive. As I get more turned-on (which you can tell through body language like hip thrusting and my vocalizations), increase the speed but not the pressure."

female age 22

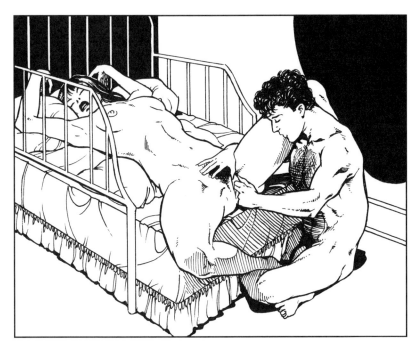

Snow White and the Prince trying tips from this chapter while the Dwarfs are away in the forest.

"There's no point in approaching my vulva and clit unless I'm aroused. Touching me there is not the way to arouse me."

female age 23

"Always get your fingers wet before touching where there isn't thick hair. Never, ever touch my clit dry. It hurts! Go ahead and play with my pubic hair. I keep it trimmed, but it means that every time you brush it, it sends a ripple of sensation through me. When I start arching up towards you, slip your finger just inside my outer lips and press gently, with a little circling motion. If I spread my legs more, please touch me! You should probably re-wet your fingers, either at my vagina (if I'm wet enough), or with some lube, or with your own saliva. I love being teased. Run your fingers along the edge of the inner lips, with just a little pressure. When I start moving against your fingers, caress my clit. Just barely touch me, that feels best. Again, that finger has to be very, very wet. In a very short while I'll be calling your name and God's!

female age 20

"The key word is GENTLE. At least in the beginning. Caress the pubic hair, then you could slightly penetrate with a finger near the vaginal opening. Gently move your hand forward till you find the clitoris. Never directly stimulate the clitoris, it's way too sensitive. Instead position your finger(s) on top of the hood and gently manipulate it side to side. Be sure no matter what you are doing that there is plenty of lubrication, either from my natural supply or from a bottle."

female age 35

"Before you even think about coming near me with your fingers, please make sure that they are smooth. Long nails aren't fun, neither are sandpaper hands. I know that many men are very rough with their own members, but I do not need that. You'd be surprised what the lightest touch can accomplish. There is no need to "grind" your fingers into me. And please, when you find a pace that has me moaning, don't decide to switch to a different pace. That gets annoying."

female age 20

Hand Jobs
Different Strokes for Different Blokes

Chapter 17

The hand job is like the Swiss Army knife—a fine, multi-purpose tool that is useful in many different situations. For instance, there's the classic hand job. Its goal is to bring the man to orgasm—rub rub, squirt squirt. This is usually most effective when you are able to do him in the same way that he does himself. He will think you are brilliant.

At the other extreme is the type of hand job where you use techniques that most men don't even know about. The goal of this type of hand job is to make every stroke an experience in and of itself, turning a man's entire body into one giant sex receptor. Rather than racing toward orgasm, the intent is to delay ejaculation while building erotic tension. In this type of hand job, there is no need for the man to have a full erection. It might be better if he doesn't.

Why Give Him a Hand Job? You'll Never Be Able To Do Him as Well as He Does Himself

It's always amazing to hear women discount the value of a hand job. They figure a guy has done it a million times so why bother. Or they'll never be as good at it as he is. But this is the very reason why it feels so good when someone else does it.

Imagine what it feels like when you rub your own shoulder as opposed to when someone else does it. You probably don't say to them "I know exactly what I like and my body gives me instant feedback, so thanks, but I'd rather rub my shoulders myself."

Did you ever think that it might feel really good to him because he doesn't get an instant feedback loop? He may actually be more aware of your hand on his penis than his own because it's not predictable. Plus there's the different skin texture of your hand, and the chances are good he'll be much more aware of the warmth of your hand versus his own. The same is true when you caress his testicles.

Yes, there is a learning curve just like there's a learning curve when he tries to caress your genitals. Limiting yourself to oral sex and intercourse is like limiting your wardrobe to only black. It looks great, but.... So what if you go so far as to tie him up and give him a slow, lingering hand job? Talk about walking a man on the line between agony and ecstasy.

Learning from Him

> "I could never move my fist that fast for so long. He really man-handles that sucker and it doesn't seem to hurt!"   *female 55*

Let's begin by explaining how men masturbate. This can be summarized with the following statement: *Grab it hard and whack it good.* Of course, there are variations, but this might help you appreciate the extent to which we men sometimes limit our range of sensual pleasure. This is something that sex therapist Herbert Otto drones on and on about:

> "It has been my experience that men, in general, are more rigid and less inclined to experiment sexually with their bodies than are women. Men appear to feel more insecure and easily threatened in relation to sexual matters, perhaps because of a perceived fragility of their manhood." *Liberated Orgasm* by Herbert Otto, Liberating Creations, Silverado, CA, 1999.

A lot of men view their body and penis as two different and sometimes unrelated entities, with the body merely being the chauffeur. Still, if you are going to find your way into a man's heart, the place to begin is by learning how to jerk him off. No matter how far you evolve past that point, being able to give a good old-fashioned hand job can be as comforting to a man as mom's home cooking.

How Men Masturbate

While each man might have his own unique spin on it, there are two basic ways that men masturbate. One is by doing it dry; the other is with lubrication.

Dry The man wraps one or two fingers around the penis at a strategically placed point, slightly below the head. He then moves the entire foreskin up and down with each stroke. Because the foreskin glides easily over the shaft that it covers, most guys clasp it more tightly than might seem comfortable. Much of the sensation occurs as the fingers move over the highly sensitive part of the shaft which is called the frenulum.

Lubricated Using lubrication results in a hand job that feels more like intercourse. When giving himself a lubricated hand job, the man often wraps his whole hand around the penis. The lubrication allows the hand to glide over the shaft and the head of the penis. A man who is circumcised is more likely to use lube. If you've still got your foreskin, there's no need to use lube when masturbating.

Dry vs. Lubricated With lube, a man who is circumcised tends to get more sensation from the head of his penis; when doing it dry, more of the focus is on the front of the penis below the head.

The lubricated hand job can be a more sensuous experience. However, plenty of guys prefer doing it dry and there are many times when masturbating dry is more practical. It's less of a production and it is easier to clean up with a tissue or sock.

What Does a Penis Feel Like?

When a penis is soft it feels a little like human lips. The skin has a silky smooth, almost translucent texture that slides over the tissue beneath it. A soft penis is extremely flexible. It can be warm or cold to the touch and feels more like a squid than a hotdog.

To know what a hard penis feels like, find a fairly buff guy who lifts weights and ask him to flex his arms. A hard bicep feels similar to a hard penis, although a hard penis won't be nearly as big around except in some guys' dreams. Poking a finger into a man's unflexed pecs will give you an approximate idea of what a semi-erect penis feels like.

Here are some women's recollections about the first time they touched a penis:

"It was sort of like 'Oh my God, what do you do with it?' I knew if you did something to it in the right way, that was good. I felt very, very careful, not sure what I was dealing with at all. It was like an alien creature that you were supposed to automatically know how to please. As I listen to myself describing it, I must have considered it as separate from the individual who it belonged to!" *female age 34*

"It was not a pleasant experience then, but it sure is now." *f. 42*

"I had intercourse a number of times but never touched it. I didn't get into that until much later." *female age 26*

"I didn't like the way it felt when flaccid. A couple of years later I finally got around to making friends with it, and it became exciting. When you make friends with a person, you make friends with his penis." *female age 21*

"It took me a while to figure out that you could really handle it, that it wasn't fragile." *female age 27*

Intent & Intensity

Some people say that the difference between giving a great hand job and a mediocre one is a matter of intent; if a woman isn't turned on by the situation, she can pump a penis till Tinkerbell commits a felony, nothing special is likely to happen. Other people say that giving great hand jobs is a matter of skill and endurance. Whatever the case, few women realize that they have the potential to control nearly every cell in a man's body with each stroke of their hand. Instead, they often just jerk away until things get sticky. One female reader comments, "Not true. Plenty of women are aware of the potential control they have, but choose not to pursue it."

Traditional Hand Jobs

Taking the Jerk Out of Jerking Off

This section is about giving a guy a hand job without lubrication. Ways of doing it wet are described later in this chapter.

Some women give hand jobs that are jerky. This is understandable, since it might appear that when guys masturbate we use a single upstroke followed by a single downstroke, all in rapid succession. But that's not how we do it. We usually have a more fluid motion. The hand doesn't stop or even slow down as it changes direction from up to down. The motion is smooth rather than jerky—which means the term "jerking off" is a misnomer.

Another potential problem occurs when a woman slows down or stops pumping as the man begins to ejaculate. While some guys may want you to stop right away, others will greatly appreciate it if you keep stroking for a few minutes after they ejaculate ("stroking through"). Some might even want you to proceed as though the penis were an udder, with you milking out each drop.

As the hand motion becomes more familiar, you might want to caress your man's testicles with one hand as you are jerking him off with the other. Your lover might also enjoy being kissed while you are giving him a hand job, perhaps on the lips, neck, or nipples. And touchy-feely types claim that orgasmic rapture is enhanced if you stare into each other's eyes as he is coming.

To find the optimal hand position, lie parallel to your man and reach across his body as he does when he is masturbating. Ask him to

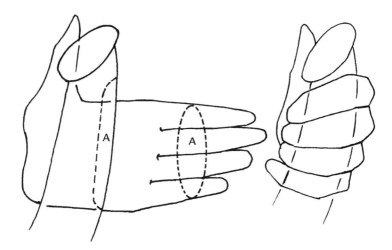

This is a rough approximation of where your hand should go when giving a hand job. Actual placement will depend on the size of your hand, the size of the object being grabbed, the amount of foreskin (tight circumcision, loose circumcision or no circumcision) and the preferences of the owner.

form your fingers around his penis in the same way he does when he's alone and thinking about you. The way he holds the penis and where he puts his hand on the shaft are more significant factors than you might think. Try to imitate the exact place where he grips himself. There are reasons for this. One of the most sensitive areas of the penis is called the frenulum. It's just below the head on the side that's away from the man's belly when he has an erection. It shows good form to rub a finger—not fingertip—over this spot with each stroke, especially if you plan on getting this over with sometime before next Christmas.

Wrap your entire hand around the penis so your thumb and index finger would touch if there weren't a big sausage in the way. Your hand should be in the same position as if it were holding a cup of tea. That's how we guys learn to masturbate, by drinking tea.

If your fingers were a belt, try to buckle them on the side of the penis and not in the front. Otherwise, your fingertips would go over the frenulum, which can be uncomfortable. It would not be hand-job cricket to have fingertips pressing into the frenulum.

Another reason to position your hand exactly where he does is because the foreskin is only so elastic—if he is circumcised, anyway.

If your grip is too high or low on the shaft, the foreskin will be pulled beyond its stretching point. Much confusion can be avoided if you ask him to place your fingers where he likes them. Then have him guide your hand up and down so you can see how high and low to stroke.

Variation Consider doing your man when he is standing or kneeling as opposed to lying on his back. This could be nice for both of you.

Pressure Chances are, your partner might want you to clasp or squeeze his penis more tightly than you were planning. Don't worry. It's unlikely you will choke it. It never hurts to ask if he wants you to squeeze tighter.

Ball Trick When masturbating, some guys push the little finger of the stroking hand against the lower part of the shaft near where the scrotum attaches. This causes the testicles to jiggle or vibrate with each stroke, which can feel really nice. But it's always best to seek your man's input when first trying to do this, since your finger might inadvertently poke him in the nuts.

Ultimately, it's unlikely you will get your sweetheart's hand motion exactly right unless you have him show you. That's because each guy varies in terms of grip, stroke, and rhythm—not to mention anatomy. Don't be surprised if it takes a number of tutorials before you get it right, especially if your hand is considerably smaller than his. If your own man is too uptight to teach you, it's likely that any number of his friends will be more than willing to let you learn the basics on them, or maybe one of your girlfriends can demonstrate on her boyfriend... Then again, she might use a banana. It can be both fun and helpful talking to your friends about their own special techniques for getting guys off, although you shouldn't assume they know better than you when it comes to the guy you are with.

In his wonderful books *Tricks: 125 Sex Tips to Make Good Sex Better, Vols. 1 & 2* (San Francisco: Greenery Press) author Jay Wiseman lists several tips to make a traditional hand job more fun. For instance, he suggests caressing the penis and balls for ten seconds with your fingertips, followed by one quick up-and-down hand stroke. Then caress for ten more seconds, followed by two quick up-and-down hand strokes. After every ten-second period of caressing, increase the stroke total by one.

Extreme Hand-job Techniques
For an Extremely Good Time

It's time to up the ante and consider techniques for doing it with lube. The next couple of pages explain the various strokes you can use for both the penis and the testicles. Then we talk about ways to help your man enjoy higher levels of pleasure.

Lubricating your hands and his genitals is essential when giving an extreme hand job. Any number of oils will work rather nicely, as long as you're thinking peanut oil instead of Penzoil or coconut instead of Castrol. It's a penis you are massaging, not a piston. Hand moisturizers absorb into the skin too quickly to be of any use.

Lube Him Up

The first thing to do is to get your man completely naked. This is usually not a difficult task.

The most civilized way of greasing a man's groin is to cup one hand over his genitals and drip massage oil over it. Gravity will pull the oil through your fingers and onto his genitals unless you are in outer space. Make sure that your man's testicles and penis are thoroughly basted with oil. To catch the excess oil, put a thick towel under him with a sheet of plastic under that. Plastic garbage can bags work really well. If cleanup is going to pose problems, use less oil.

From Where You Sit

When doing him dry, it's best to sit by your bronco's side so you can imitate his strokes. When giving an extreme hand job, you will be using lubrication, so you can do a fine job from wherever you sit unless it's across the room.

Different Massage Strokes

The strokes described below are simply possibilities. Perhaps one or two will seem fun to try. It can be nice to vary the pace by mixing and matching different strokes. You can certainly practice on a banana, but most guys would happily volunteer for beta testing. Also, it is not necessary for a man to have an erection for this to feel great. Many guys remain semi-erect when receiving penis massage. Some people think it feels best when the penis is sixty to seventy-five percent erect.

Fists Going Up   Be sure all skin surfaces are well lubricated. Wrap one hand around the base of the penis, squeeze lightly and pull

This position is great for hand jobs with lube, but not so good for doing it dry. Worse yet, her form is poor (fingertips on the frenulum) and his penis appears to be detachable!

it up along the shaft, over the head and into the air. As this hand is making its upward stroke, grab the base of the penis with your free hand, squeeze and do the same thing. Create a fluid motion with one hand constantly following the other. Be sure to slow the pace if the man shows signs of impending orgasm, lest he create fluid of his own. This technique is shown above. Some folks suggest giving a little extra squeeze or snap on the upward stroke just as your hand reaches the head of the penis. (See the illustration on the page after next.)

Fists Going Down Same technique as above, only in the reverse direction with your hands going from the tip of the penis to the base. Downward strokes such as these usually require an erection. Otherwise, the thing just flops there in your hand. Also, use a more open grip so you don't shove the penis into the body.

Thumbs Up While facing your man's crotch, clasp your fingers together as you might do when praying that the check you just wrote doesn't bounce. The only difference here is that your hands are clasped around your man's penis. Use the pads of your thumbs to massage the front part of the penis where nature left the seam showing. Spend extra time rubbing the area where the head attaches to the shaft, or just below it, as this is usually the most sensitive part of the penis. (Some people compare the sensitivity of this area to that of the clitoris, although they are probably overstating the case.)

Open Palm Rubbing Head of Penis Some guys might like this; others won't. Hold the shaft of the penis in one hand so it is sticking straight out from the man's body (perpendickular). Open your other hand flat and rub it in a circular pattern over the head of the penis, as though you were buffing it. Make sure that the palm of your hand is well-lubed.

Twisting the Cap Off a Bottle of Beer Hold the shaft of the penis near the base. With your other hand, grasp the head of the penis as though it were the cap on a bottle of beer. Twist it as if you were opening a beer bottle, with your thumb and forefinger running along the groove under the ridge where the head attaches to the shaft.

Wringing a Towel Dry Grasp the lower part of the penis with one hand and the upper part of the shaft with the other. There should be no gap between your hands unless mother nature mistakenly endowed your man with an elephant trunk instead of a penis. Twist your hands back and forth in opposite directions.

How to Pull the Foreskin Taut

The penis can usually be made more sensitive by stretching the foreskin. In fact, guys who masturbate with lubrication often use one hand to pull the foreskin taut while stroking the shaft with the other. This also helps keep the baggy skin on the scrotum from rising up onto the shaft of the penis. There are a couple of ways to achieve this:

Palm on the Side Clamp your thumb and forefinger around the shaft of the penis nearly an inch above where it joins the testicles (scrotum). Pull the skin down so your other fingers and palm rest on

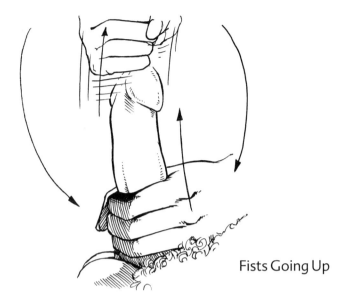

Fists Going Up

the testicles. This will make the foreskin taut. If the man is uncircumcised, reach higher up on the shaft to pull the extra skin down.

Taut Variation When he's doing himself and trying to keep his foreskin taut, it is possible that your partner hooks his thumb around the shaft of his penis and uses the other four fingers to cup, squeeze or caress his testicles. Then again, if he's the outdoor type with a history of running power equipment, he may need to improvise, depending upon how many fingers he still has left. There are many variations on this. Sometimes just the ring and pinky fingers lie over the top of the testicles; other times it's the index and bird fingers.

Strokes to Try When the Skin on the Penis Is Pulled Taut

Owie Ouch Alert! Remember, you only pull the foreskin taut when giving him genital massage if you are using lubrication.

Penis-Belly Rub The penis should be lubricated and resting flat against the man's belly. Pull the skin taut at the base of the penis as mentioned above. Open your other hand and lay it flat on top of the penis. Then drag the hand up toward the man's chest, as if you were trying to push the good feelings out of his penis and onto the skin of his belly. Repeat. As with any of these strokes, feel free to vary the angles, pressures and grips to form your own unique style. And don't hesitate to do a series of one stroke followed by an entirely different type of stroke.

The Corkscrew or Following the Stripe on the Barber's Pole Pull the skin taut at the base of your partner's penis. Wrap your other hand around the base of his lubricated penis. Squeeze lightly, and twist it upward as though you were following a corkscrew or the stripe on a barber's pole. If his penis is hard enough, do a reverse downstroke which should return your hand to the same position where it started. If there isn't enough erection to make the downward stroke work, just do a series of upward strokes.

When it comes to giving oral sex or lubricated hand jobs, don't hesitate to use a twisting motion up and down the shaft of the penis, especially on the ridge that's beneath the head.

Thumbs Up — Thumbs Down This may sound complicated, but it isn't. There are two ways to grasp a penis that is lubricated. One is with your hand facing up, so the little finger is toward the base of the penis and the thumb is toward the head. The other is with your hand facing down, so the thumb is around the base and your little finger is around the head end of the penis. It can be quite impressive when a woman alternates hand orientation with her stroking hand, so he never knows if the next stroke will be thumbs up or thumbs down.

Octopussy Fingers Pull the foreskin taut with one hand. Lay the palm of your other hand over the head of the penis and drop your fingers down along the sides of the shaft. (Your hand will look like an open parachute or an octopus when it swims.) Your fingers will stimulate the sides of the penis as you move your hand up and down. You can also twist your hand sideways, or do a corkscrew stroke that combines both motions.

Massaging under the Testicles

If the skin over the testicles is tight, heat the room and put a warm washcloth over them. Let the scrotum warm up for a couple

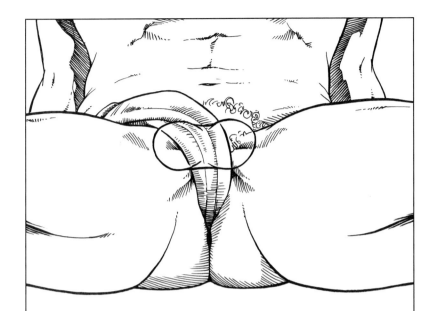

The Man with Invisible Balls

Women often assume that the penis is somehow glued or stapled to the front of a man's pelvic bone. In reality, it runs beneath his testicles and anchors inside his pelvis. Some men enjoy having the "invisible" part of the penis massaged. Push into the space between the testicles with your fingertips and gently rub, or massage the flat space behind his testicles.

of minutes until the testicles hang freely. Press into the middle of the scrotum with your fingertips. They should be touching the part of the penis that is covered by the testicles. Massage this area all the way back to where the man's anus begins. There is often a single spot on this part of the penis where a number of ligaments, muscle fibers, and nerve endings seem to converge. Putting fingertip pressure on this spot while massaging the "regular" part of the penis with your other hand can make the entire shaft—from the base of the pelvis to the head of the penis—experience a subtle, warm feeling that some men will find enjoyable. This might be on one side of the shaft rather than in the middle. You might also try massaging this area when giving a blow job.

A man's testicles will nearly cripple him with pain if they get hit, knocked, or flicked, but not when a partner caresses and massages them. Being massaged in this area can feel like getting a really nice back rub, only it's between the legs. Still, be gentle at the start, and keep in mind that while some men find the sensation to be delightful, others don't like to be touched there.

Massage that Includes the Testicles

Here are a few techniques to try on the testicles, as well as some strokes that include the testicles and penis. None of these strokes should cause any pain or discomfort. If they do, stop.

Simple Testicle Massage Explore with your fingertips the space between and around the testicles. Be gentle at first, and seek plenty of feedback. Once you find a form of massage that pleases the man, do it often. For some men, the sensation feels like it's part back rub and part orgasm. They might even prefer this to stroking their penis.

Ball Rub With the thumb and forefinger of one hand, make a ring around the part of your man's scrotum where it attaches to his groin. Squeeze gently until his testicles are popping out a bit, but not enough to cause pain. Run the fingertips of your other hand up and down the sides of his scrotum with a light tickling touch.

Penis Up, Balls Down Be sure that your hands are well-lubricated. Grasp the lower part of the penis with one hand. Clamp the fingers of your other hand around the base of the scrotum where it attaches to the groin. This should cause the testicles to pop out a bit and the skin covering them should become taut. Squeeze both hands lightly, and

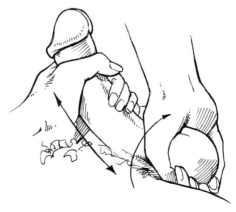

Penis Up, Balls Down

then do an upward stroke with the penis hand while the testicle hand pulls gently in the opposite direction. Find a tempo that works for both of you and keep repeating these strokes.

Flat-Handed Doggy Dig Straddle your partner's chest while facing his feet. Lay his penis flat against his belly with the head pointing up toward his navel. Place one of your well-lubricated hands between his legs with your fingertips resting below his testicles. Pull the hand all the way up to his belly, dragging your fingers over his testicles and penis. Repeat with your other hand, rhythmically alternating strokes as a dog might when digging in the dirt. This same stroke is illustrated in the chapter "The Zen of Finger Fucking," but as done on a woman.

The Point of No Return

When doing an extreme hand job, you might want to keep your man highly aroused for long periods of time without letting him ejaculate. No, we haven't lost our minds, it is possible.

Think about a scale of 0 to 10 where 0 means no sexual arousal and 10 is an orgasm. Let's say your partner starts to ejaculate when he reaches a 9 on this imaginary scale. Past that, there's no turning back. Try to keep him between 7 and 8 for as long as possible before finally letting him squirt, an event that might be rather powerful when it finally occurs.

One way to keep your man at such a high level of excitement is to learn his body language for when he is about to ejaculate. There are physical signs for when the well is about to blow: the veins in his penis may start to bulge or his penis might give a sudden throb, the color of the head might darken, his testicles may suck up into his groin, his muscles may suddenly tighten, his hips may thrust, and he might start to groan like a dying bull or invoke the names of the saints. Change the stroke or decrease the intensity when this starts to happen.

Some women find it very helpful if the man is able to report his levels of excitement by saying something like "6," "7," "8," or "9." Even the cues "more" or "less" are often enough. This will help you learn when to up the pace and when to back off. After a while you will become so familiar with his body language that you won't need him to actually tell you.

Ready, Set, Relax

It never hurts to begin genital massage by finding those parts of your partner's body where tension gathers. Who knows why, but the shoulders and back often become the body's collecting points for tension. There is no point in doing good work on a man's genitals when the weight of the world is parked between his shoulder blades. This is also true for women's bodies.

Some men believe that the only important part of sex is when a penis is being rubbed, sucked, or fucked. They might not care about the tension in their shoulders or even notice. They will sometimes direct your hands straight to their crotch with the idea that an orgasm will help relax them. While this is true, think of how much more pleasure they could receive if they were relaxed to begin with.

If your partner is getting too penis-oriented for his own good, go ahead and fondle his testicles with one hand. At the same time, repeat your request that he close his eyes and relax. Inform him straightaway that you will do to his body what you like, when you like, and how you like. If he still objects, slap him upside the head and remind him what you are holding in your other hand!

Spreading the Excitement — Pavlov Between the Legs

Extreme hand jobs can be used to help a man link the sensations in his crotch with other parts of his body. For instance, Hindu/Yoga types might have you stimulate the man's genitals with one hand while caressing various chakras (e.g. upper abdomen, heart, third eye) with your other hand. It might help if he inhaled deeply while you were doing this, as though he were sucking the warm glow from his genitals into the upper part of his body.

Western-psychology types might suggest kissing or caressing your partner's neck, shoulders, nipples, or chest while massaging his genitals. At various intervals, stop stroking the man's genitals but continue to kiss or caress the other designated body parts. If he were a dog and his name was Pavlov, he might eventually learn to have genital sensations when you caress these other body parts. Likewise, he might learn to have pleasant sensations in other parts of his body when his penis is stimulated. The ultimate goal is to help a man experience greater sensation over his entire body.

Helping a Partner Learn How to Please You

A man can help both himself and his partner if he will turn the lights up, get naked, and let her do an introductory physics lab on his genitals. The purpose is for her to tickle, squeeze, tug, and prod each part of the man's sexual anatomy so she can become more confident in handling his genitals. She can begin gently, increasing the pressure until the man says something earthshaking such as "Ouch!" At that point, the woman eases up until he says "Ah, that's perfect!" Here are a few specifics:

Penis Have her tug it, yank it, and squeeze it until she's able to distinguish your Ouch! zone from your Perfect! zone. Then help her learn how to grasp your penis to give you a hand job. Indicate how far up and down you like the strokes to go, as well as how fast to do them and how long you wish she would keep stroking after you come.

Testicles If the room is cold and your cojones are in frostbite mode, turn up the heat and put something warm over them until you have managed to coax them back down. Once they are hanging freely, let her tickle, caress, and play with them, letting her know what feels good and what doesn't. Then have her slowly squeeze each testicle until you say "Ouch!" Also, have her put a finger or two in the space between your testicles and push in until she is massaging the shaft.

Readers' Comments

What did you think the first time you saw a guy ejaculate?

"I did it right! Good job! I was proud of me. Then I thought, 'Geez, I hope my mom doesn't come home early.' " *female 22*

"I remember being disgusted and oddly fascinated at the same time, and I couldn't believe how far that stuff could shoot out!" *female age 32*

"It just kind of oozed out. For some reason I thought there was supposed to be more of a stream." *female age 37*

"I was jealous he could actually project it from his body and I couldn't." *female age 23*

"I was kinda grossed out by the whole thing." *female age 45*

"I was proud that I made him ejaculate, but I couldn't believe that people actually would let that go in their mouths. I was a senior in high school." *female age 25*

"I was a little shocked. I was young, 15, and I don't think I under-stood exactly what was going on. It's also when I realized that tissues weren't just for noses anymore." *female age 27*

"I wondered what it felt like. I wondered what it tasted like. Also, I wondered what it would feel like to have that happen inside of me." *female age 25*

"I vaguely remember thinking, it's amazing how their bodily pro-cess is. Also, there is what is needed to help form a human being." *female age 36*

Dear Paul,

My former boyfriend liked it when I gave him hand jobs without lubrica-tion; my current one wants it with lubrication. What gives?

Tina in Twin Cities

Dear Tina,

Some of us like to sleep naked, others wear pajamas. Some like the mountains, others like the ocean. The same is true for hand jobs, although I don't know why we have different preferences. I do know that most of us are extremely grateful when someone else's hand is doing the stroking besides our own.

Be aware that oil-based lubes are far superior to water-based lubes for hand jobs. That's because water-based lubes dry out and you have to keep squirting his penis with water or spit on it to keep the surface hydrated. Also, there's no need to buy an expensive lube. You can use anything from corn oil to coconut oil, as long as you remember to strain out the little brown pieces in case you've already used it to fry the chicken.

Try exploring different strokes that will keep your guy's gizzard going for a long time without letting it ejaculate. There's a fine video on this subject by a gay organization that will help any woman give amazing hand jobs, and who cares if it's a straight penis or a gay penis that's flopping all over the TV screen? Turn us guys over and we all look the same anyway, more or less. I do recommend this tape with the following caveats: 1. It takes itself way too seriously; 2. Watch it with the sound off; and 3. Fast forward through the first third or so, until you see the two guys demonstrating the actual strokes. This video is called *Fire On The Mountain.* They show a few previews of the different strokes on their internet site. Go to www.erospirit.org or call (800) 432-3767.

———————————————

Dear Paul,

What if a guy is uncircumcised? Do you give him the same kind of hand job as a guy who is cut?

Tina from Troy

Dear Tina,

There shouldn't be much difference when giving a dry hand job, except there's more foreskin so it will slide a lot better. In fact, a lot of guys who are uncut never need to use lube when they masturbate, since the extra foreskin does the job. With erotic massage, you'll be using lots of oil whether he's circumcised or intact. On the strokes where you pull the foreskin taut, you'll just have more yardage to pull.

Balls, Balls, Balls

Chapter 18

Balls usually take a back seat to the penis. One reason for this is the pleasure you get from your testicles is more subtle than the pleasure you get from your wang. But just because the pleasure is subtle doesn't mean it should be ignored. As one reader comments, "When my wife caresses my testicles and runs her hands up and down my thighs, it's one part excitement, two parts relaxation, and six parts bliss. I didn't appreciate this when I was in my twenties, but now I enjoy it as much oral sex. The sensation is different, but just as satisfying."

Ball Rules

Testicles are far more rugged than you might think and can usually be handled with impunity. You can squeeze or pull them with no problem, but pop them with a simple flick of a finger and you might have to peel their owner off the ceiling. Heaven only knows why. They should feel a bit like hard-boiled eggs without the shell, but they won't be that big unless your lover is related to the racehorse Secretariat.

As a man becomes aroused, his testicles tend to swell or become bigger. When he is highly aroused or just about to come, his scrotum and testicles will hug the shaft of the penis, like bungee jumpers on the upswing. Another thing to know about testicles is that they can easily go from feeling soft to feeling hard. It depends on the temperature and on the man's level of sexual excitement.

Testicle Embryology

In the womb, males and females start off with similar-looking genitals. These appear to be female. However, the genitals of male and female fetuses may have different concentrations of hormonal receptors, so the idea that all fetuses start off with the same "female" genitals may be out the window. Still, there are a number of ways in which our genitals sprout from similar fetal tissues.

For instance, the skin that makes up the male's scrotum starts from the same tissue as the lips of a woman's vulva. Have you ever noticed the seam along the center of the scrotum? If the guy with the scrotum had been born a female, that same tissue would have been used to make up the labia. So if a fetus is going to be a boy, nature glues the labia together to form the scrotum. This is a long-winded way of saying that a man's scrotum has about the same sensitivity as the lips of a woman's vulva.

What's Inside a Ball?

Technically, the testicles are glands that produce hormones and sperm. One is usually bigger than the other, and one hangs lower. Each testicle is a little factory. Sperm are produced in the tubules, stored and aged in the epididymis, and sent up into the abdomen through the vas deferens. Interestingly, sperm don't go straight from the testicles into the penis. Instead, they travel north, up into the pelvis to a place behind the bladder. That's where they make the connection with a tube that draws them in through the prostate gland. From there, they

Ball Plumbing

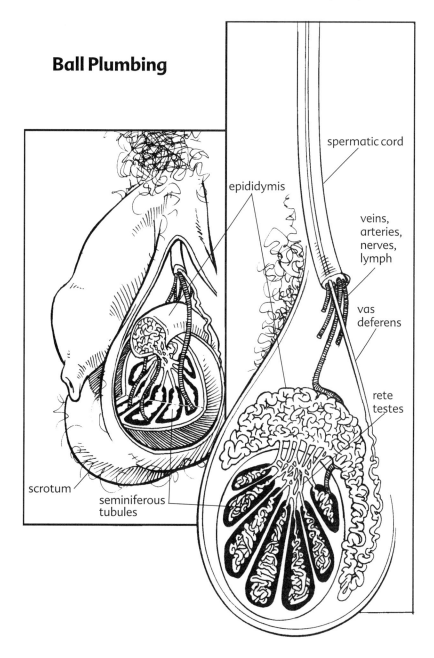

spermatic cord

epididymis

veins,
arteries,
nerves,
lymph

vas
deferens

rete
testes

scrotum

seminiferous
tubules

eventually shoot out through the penis. In the next chapter you can
read what happens when you have an ejaculation and where the sperm
go—before they leave your penis, anyway. The testicles are housed in
a pouch called the scrotum. The reason the testicles hang away from
the body is they need to run cooler than body temperature.

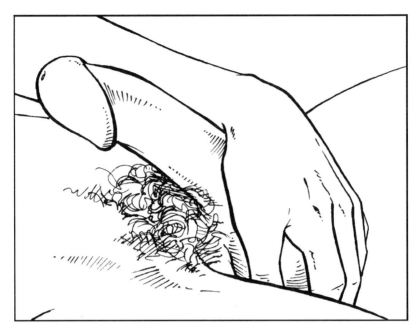

Try laying your wrist over the penis, as well.

Ball Tending

If you are out to give a guy's balls a good time, you might start by placing your fingertips on the sides of his scrotum and caressing lightly. Let his verbal feedback guide you from there.

You might also try resting the palm of your hand over his penis with your fingertips pointing down. Experiment with lightly massaging the back part of the scrotum, where it attaches to his body. As your fingers move, the part of your wrist that's resting on his penis will move as well. This should give his penis pleasure, which might mix nicely with the more subtle sensations that your fingertips are providing his balls. Some guys will find it pleasurable if you caress their testicles while they are face down or standing with their legs apart with you are reaching in from behind.

Intercourse Extra

You can handle a man's testicles during intercourse from some positions, like if you are on top facing his feet. Different rear-entry positions may also allow you to reach between your legs and caress his testicles. Experiment and see what you and he like best.

The Exquisite Brush-Off

Get yourself a makeup brush or a Japanese bamboo artist's brush, have your cowboy spread his legs and gently brush his inner thighs, testicles, penis, and abdomen. Doing repeated circles around the outside of his balls can feel especially nice. The sensation is subtle, somewhere between a feather and a fingertip. It can feel relaxing and titillating at the same time. If you enjoy taking control, you can always tie him up first. When brushing a guy, don't limit your strokes to just his genitals. Try his face, back, feet, and hands. If you're lucky, he'll grab the brush and return the favor.

Perineum

There is a patch of anatomical real estate between the testicles and rectum which is often ignored but has the potential for sensation. It is called the perineum. (Women have one, too.) Tantric and Hindu types get all excited about this particular area and regard it with the same kind of awe that we Westerners sometimes do the reset button on the computer. Place your fingertips on this area with just enough pressure so the skin moves over the tissue beneath it. Experiment and see what feels best.

Another Kind of Tenderness

If you are so inclined, don't hesitate to reach between your man's legs and cup or cradle his genitals at nonsexual times, like when watching TV or while falling asleep. Some men will find this to be extremely thoughtful and caring. Others will find it too arousing, and some may dislike this kind of tenderness.

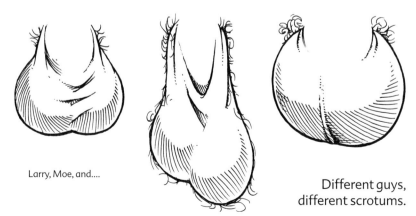

Larry, Moe, and....

Different guys, different scrotums.

Late-Breaking Ball News

Physicians are beginning to find that some guys who are sterile as adults got that way because they were playing sports without a cup and took a significant knock in the nuts. Any guy who is involved in a contact sport should wear a cup, whether he's an adult or a kid. Ditto if he's playing catcher in baseball. Fortunately, they have soft cups these days which are a lot better than nothing for the weekend warrior, and they'll make you look like you are really well hung. See "cup" in the Goofy Glossary at the end of this book for tips on wearing a cup.

Dear Paul,

When I was a kid I had the mumps and my testicles swelled up. I have heard this can cause sterility. Does this mean I am sterile?

Bill from Ball State University

Dear Bill,

Mumps is a virus that often causes swelling of the salivary glands (below your jaw) and sometimes swelling of the testicles (below your penis). About fifteen to twenty-five percent of guys who get mumps get swelling in one of their balls and sometimes in both. Even if your testicles were swollen due to the mumps, it is very unlikely that this would cause you to become sterile. Physicians use the words "rare" and "very rare" to describe the frequency of infertility from mumps.

While you probably aren't sterile due to the mumps, the only way to know for sure is to have your sperm analyzed or to get a woman pregnant. I encourage you to try the former.

Dear Paul,

My newborn son has an undescended testicle. What do you know about this?

Pam from Little Rock

Dear Pam,

The medical term for undescended testicles is "cryptorchidism," which is Greek for "hidden gonad." One way to get a case of hidden gonads is to go surfing during the winter; another way is to be born with them.

Contrary to what seems logical, the testicles in the male fetus don't form between his legs. Instead, they develop inside his abdomen and do not descend into his scrotum until a month or two before he is born. They make the journey from the abdomen into the scrotum through the inguinal canal.

Approximately 3.5% of males are born with an undescended testicle. This testicle often descends on its own without medical intervention, so that by one year of age, only one percent of males (1 out of 100 or 150) still have an undescended testicle. In ninety percent of these cases, it's just one of the testicles that is undescended.

If the testicle remains undescended after the boy reaches a year of age, the current practice is to treat it surgically. This is often done as an outpatient operation. Attempts to coax the testicle down with hormone therapy have unacceptable side effects and any gains are usually short-lived.

In any case, I would encourage you to get a second or even a third opinion from a pediatric urologist. As Dr. Joseph Dwoskin, a urologist from Texas Tech says, "There are as many opinions about testes as there are physicians who examine them."

———————————

Dear Paul,

My boyfriend was recently diagnosed with cancer of the testicles. Since it's hit so close to home, I try to tell guys to examine their testicles. Most just laugh. Maybe they'll listen to you.

Barb from Rock Island

Dear Barb,

The term "cancer of the testicles" is a misnomer. It should be cancer of the testicle (singular), given how it's usually only one testicle that gets the cancer. The good news is, we only need one ball to be fertile and to have a perfectly normal sex drive. The only reason for having the other ball is for playing pocket pool.

Cancer of the testicles is 97% curable if detected early enough. Unfortunately, the last thing a guy between the ages of fifteen and thirty-five thinks about is the possibility of getting cancer. After all, cancer is something that happens to people your parents' age, so it is beyond the average male's consciousness to check his nuts every month for lumps or changes in texture.

Another problem is that a lot of guys would rather sit naked on a fencepost than call the doctor's office and say, "I'm concerned about my testicle and I'd like you to check it out." So they wait until the cancer has spread all over the place before getting care. This isn't good, since some forms of testicular cancer can double in size in less than thirty days and you won't feel a bit of pain as it's happening.

A third roadblock in detecting cancer of the testicles is the extra meaning that we attach to testicles, as in the term "He's got balls!" Ever hear anyone say, "She's got ovaries!"? On a symbolic level, it's a big thing when a guy loses a ball, and I'm not talking over the fence. Most of us would rather deny the possibility.

Interestingly, it is often a partner who discovers the cancer. This can be a lifesaver, so I hope women readers will learn how to examine their man's balls in the name of health as well as pleasure.

The most common symptom to look for is a small lump or nodule on the side or sometimes the front of the testicle. It's usually not painful when you press on it. Another symptom is hardening of the testicle. Mind you, testicles swell and shrink, but it's time to get it checked when the entire testicle starts to lose its spongy texture.

Less common symptoms include pain or discomfort in the testicles, back pain, swollen breasts (guy breasts), or a kind of heaviness or unusual discomfort deep in your pelvis.

There are a number of things that can look like cancer. Most of these aren't and can often be treated with antibiotics. So don't assume that your doctor is going to present you with bad news.

It's very wise to do a routine ball exam once a month. The best time is when the scrotum is warm and saggy, like after a hot shower. Follow the instructions in the Ball Check chart that follows after the next page.

For a more complete discussion about cancer of the testicles, please see our website, www.goofyfootpress.com. Enter "cancer" in the Goofy search engine. We include links to the websites of men who've had cancer of the testicles. Interestingly, a lot of guys who have lost a ball to cancer don't have it replaced with a fake one, and are quite happy with their decision.

Dear Paul,

> *What is testicular torsion?*
>> *Twisted in Tennessee*

Dear Twisted,

Testicular torsion occurs when the testicle twists in the scrotum, causing the blood vessels in the spermatic cord to twist shut. It is very serious, and if emergency surgery is not performed within four to six hours, it is quite possible that the testicle will be lost. This is why any sudden or acute pain in the testicles that lasts for more than ten minutes should result in an immediate trip to the emergency room.

Torsion happens more often in teenagers, but adult males can get it as well. The potential for torsion is created when the testicle is not properly anchored in the scrotum. Below is an illustration of the three most common types of testicular torsion.

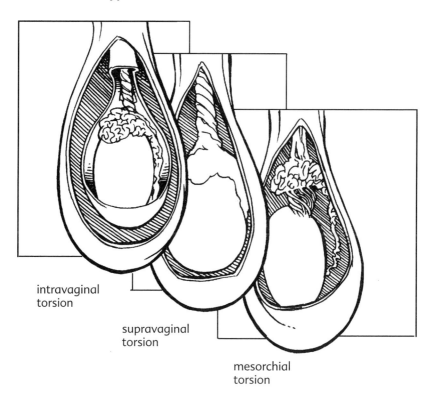

intravaginal
torsion

supravaginal
torsion

mesorchial
torsion

(Twisted balls are modeled after the illustrations in the excellent book *Imaging Of The Scrotum*, by Hricak, Hamm & Kim, Raven Press, New York, 1995.)

BALL CHECK!

① You need to do a ball check every 30 days or 3,000 strokes, whichever comes first.

The best time to do a ball check is after a warm shower.

②

Use both hands. Grab a ball. Roll it between your fingers. You are looking for any bumps or lumps. They can be smaller than a pea. Check the sides really well, and the top and bottom.

BALL NOTES *If you ever get popped in the balls and the pain lasts for more than ten minutes, have them checked by a physician. If not treated quickly, ball trauma can cause your huevos to become sterile. Also, one ball is usually bigger than the other. Nature made them that way.*

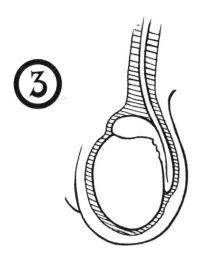

What You Are Feeling

When you feel your scrotum you may notice more in there than just two balls. There are a couple of spaghettilike cords that attach to each testicle at the back, toward the top. They are called the epididymis. They form a structure that is shaped like a comma. These might be fuller if you haven't ejaculated in a while. It may feel a little weird, but check out your comma for any little nodes, lumps or changes since the last check.

Squeeze that puppy. It should feel a bit spongy, although this varies depending on the weather and how horny you are. Be aware if the ball becomes extra firm or tender or starts to lose its spongy texture.

Grab your other nut, and have at it.

If either ball has any nodes, bumps or lumps, take it to a physician for a checkup. Chances are, it's only a cyst or infection, but that needs attention, too.

CONGRATULATIONS! You are done. Now go grab your favorite lube and reading material, and liberate a few million sperm.

The Glands Down Under
Chapter 19

One of the truly cool things about the prostate is that it's completely hidden. It's the one sex organ a guy doesn't have to worry about the size of when he's naked at the gym or when he's with a new lover. Prostates are measured in grams instead of inches, and a man has to be pretty neurotic before he'd worry about how his prostate stacks up against another guy's. In fact, you'd have to be chewing on some seriously strong mushrooms before you'd ever hear one woman say to another, "You won't believe the size of Bobby's prostate!"

Like the prostate, the seminal vesicles are important sex glands that are tucked inside a man's pelvis, but you don't hear as much about them because they rarely give a guy a hard time. The seminal vesicles sit on top of the prostate like a pair of rabbit ears. Without seminal vesicles and a prostate, there would be no wad when a man comes.

In this chapter, we'll discuss a range of prostate and seminal vesicle matters, like why a girl drips after intercourse and what happens when a guy gets his prostate groped. You'll even hear from a man who massages the prostates of 2400 pound bulls for a living. We'll also talk about prostate problems, including infections and cancer. But first, here's the skinny on the two sex glands that allow a guy to launch his load—and we're not talking the testicles.

How the Prostate Came to Be

You've probably heard how Zeus was the head of the Gods on Mount Olympus, and how he was a jealous sort with paranoid tendencies. What you probably don't know is how the prostate gland came to be. To make a long story short, there was a rather peculiar god by the name of Prostateus whose spit smelled like chlorine bleach. Zeus feared that Prostateus was scheming to overthrow him, so he asked his wife Hera to land Prostateus in the underworld near the River Styx. Hera didn't get the message quite right. She thought Zeus said to make Prostateus a gland by the river of shit.

To this day, you can still find Prostateus, who the Romans called Prostate, by sticking a finger about two inches up the male rectum. He'll be sitting just below the bladder, right where Hera put him. If you

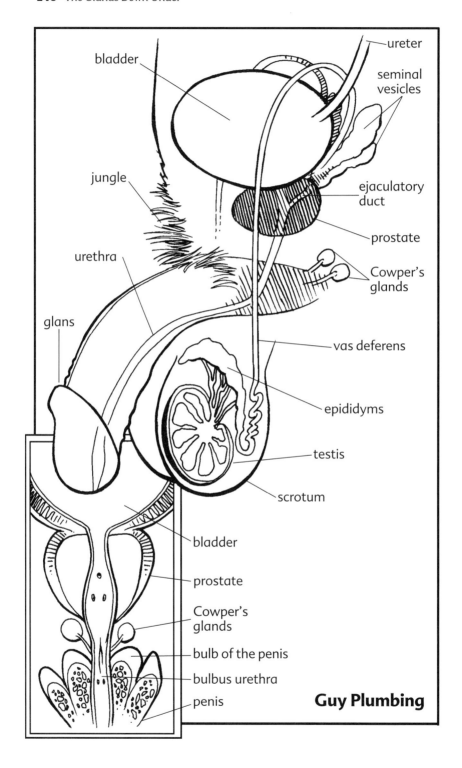

bladder

ureter

seminal vesicles

jungle

ejaculatory duct

prostate

urethra

Cowper's glands

glans

vas deferens

epididyms

testis

scrotum

bladder

prostate

Cowper's glands

bulb of the penis

bulbus urethra

penis

Guy Plumbing

reach in a little more, you'll find the two bota bags that Prostateus used to carry his wine in. They are now called the seminal vesicles.

From Marbles to Golf

If you take any fourth-grade boy, you can be pretty sure that his prostate is the size of a marble. If you take his dad, you're dealing with a prostate the size of a golf ball.

If the fourth-grade boy jerks off, he'll only produce a drop of two of clear sticky fluid. While he can still enjoy the nice feeling of an orgasm, he won't start to ejaculate until puberty begins. Until then, his small prostate and sleepy seminal vesicles are just a twinkle in the eye of his older, semen-producing self. It will take a jolt of juice from the teenage testicles to make the marble morph into a man-sized gland.

Geography of the Glands

The prostate is a walnut-shaped gland that's normally between the size of a walnut and a golf ball. It's located between the bottom of the bladder and the start of the penis. The urethra (tube you pee through) runs through the prostate like the Mississippi runs through the heartland. If you are thinking in three dimensions, the prostate wraps around the urethra like a donut around a straw, or your hand around your penis when your partner says, "Not tonight, dear."

The prostate is made up of smooth muscle fibers, connective tissue, small tubes, and clusters of glands that produce a clear fluid. If you find fruit metaphors helpful, the prostate is like an orange, with a tough skin and pulpy insides. The fluid from the prostate makes up around 30% of each ejaculation. As a guy is starting to ejaculate, the muscle fibers in the prostate squeeze the fluid from the tiny glands into the urethra.

The seminal vesicles are about two inches long. They sit above the prostate on the side of the bladder where the foul winds blow. They are long and narrow like a pair of puffy rabbit ears. The seminal vesicles have special cells that make a gelatin-type of juice that puts the "thick" in semen. The seminal vesicles manufacture about 70% of the volume that's in each and every wad.

NOTE: While the testicles are the master glands of the male pelvis, they contribute less than 1% of each ejaculation. The testicles are hugely important when it comes to keeping a male looking like a man, but they don't produce much of his wad.

Why Girls Drip after Intercourse without a Condom

Did you ever wonder why ejaculate shoots out of the spigot thick, but ends up dripping out of a woman's vagina as she tears out of bed and tries to get to work or class on time? The easiest way to find out why is to have a guy come in a glass. Then sit around and watch. In a few minutes, the thick whitish cum in the glass will start to morph into a thin watery fluid. If a woman who's had intercourse stands up when the ejaculate is in its thin-as-water state, it will drip. And drip.

So what's the trick? To find the answer, we'll need to explore what happens when a guy has an ejaculation.

When a guy is about to come and he reaches the point of no return, a couple of different things happen in his pelvis. It's like when you pour lime juice, tequila, triple sec, ice, and sweet'n'sour into a blender.

There's a blender part of the urethra that's located at the very base of the penis. It is called the bulbus urethra. When a man is about to have an orgasm, the ingredients that make up semen collect in the bulbus urethra. These ingredients include a tiny squirt of sperm, a big squirt of gelatin juice from the seminal vesicles, and a medium-sized squirt of prostate potion that contains an enzyme called PSA.

When the bulbus urethra fills with the different ingredients that make up semen, the pressure seems to trigger the muscles around it to convulse. This sends the wad flying through the penis and out the end; "Houston, we have an ejaculation."

As for explaining the trick in the glass, the key is the PSA from the prostate: when it mixes with the thick gelatin juice from the seminal vesicles it causes the gelatin juice to change its state from thick to thin. This makes the semen get watery. Scientists think this happens so the semen can more easily be sucked up by the woman's cervix. Evolutionists will say it's so other males will smell her dripping and will realize that their sperm has been out-competed. Marxists will complain that it's a capitalist plot to sell more tissue.

Prostate Has the Right Name, But Not the Seminal Vesicles

The prostate was given its name around 300 B.C. by Herophilus, the father of anatomy. The word prostate supposedly means "guard of the bladder." The prostate glands that Herophilus studied were apparently fresh and genuine, as he was allowed to do his dissections on criminals who were being put to death.

Herophilus also deserves credit for not spreading misleading information about the prostate. This was not the case for those who eventually found and named the seminal vesicles.

The name seminal vesicles implies that they are containers that hold the semen. But the seminal vesicles aren't containers. Even though they manufacture several ingredients that go into semen, seminal vesicles never see fully-mixed semen any more than an ice cream machine sees a hot fudge sundae.

If this seems confusing, take heart in knowing that it's taken four editions of this book before the author would even try to write about the glands down under, and even then it requires the aid of a Margarita and hot fudge sundae for him to get into the proper frame of mind.

Curiosity Will Not Kill the Prostate

Some people can read about the prostate and be perfectly content leaving well enough alone. Others will want to reach out and touch one. It probably depends on whether you view the prostate as a lump in a landfill or a jewel in a cave.

If you are interested in finding out more about the prostate and there's a guy around who is willing, get yourself some fingernail clippers, latex exam gloves (without powder), and KY Jelly or something just like it. Have the guy bend over, like in the illustration of the DRE (digital rectal exam) that you'll see after you turn the page.

Use the clippers to eliminate any claw on your fickle finger of fate. Stick your hand in a latex glove, and lube up your index finger and the guy's anus really, really well. In fact, there's no reason why you shouldn't get the ball rolling by treating the anus to a lubricated finger massage. This will help relax it and it might make him feel grateful.

Some books on the prostate say to have him push out like he's trying to pass gas, since this will help him to relax his anal sphincter. But his methane nozzle is a lot closer to your face than it is to his, so think long and hard before offering advice like this. Instead, you might use your free hand to pull one of his butt cheeks out a little.

A good way to approach is to pretend your finger is a hotdog that you are placing between the boy's buns. Your finger should be pointing toward his tailbone with the pad pushing against his anus and your wrist behind his balls. Of course, if common sense were leading the way, you would aim your finger straight in as if the prostate was a door bell button. But if common sense were ruling the day, you wouldn't be sticking your finger up some guy's asshole, would you?

Eventually, as you are pushing the pad of your finger against his anus, one of you is going to blink. This is your opportunity to push the pad of your finger farther into the opening. Simply flick the tip around and in. In the flicking process, your finger will suddenly go from pointing up toward his tailbone to pushing straight into his rectum. The quick flick can't really be seen because it happens as your finger is pushing into the anal opening. As long as you are gentle but firm there shouldn't be any need to peel him off the ceiling or call an ambulance.

Slowly push your finger in a couple of inches and start to explore the new neighborhood. The illustration on the facing page should be an adequate guide. While the prostate will be a lot bigger than the tip of your nose, the surface will probably feel a bit like it or like the padded part of your thumb as it meets your wrist.

If you explore the entire surface of the prostate from side to side, you might discover that it has a kind of indentation running down the center. Also, experiment with different levels of pressure. Be sure to get lots of feedback from the guy who is attached to the prostate.

For men who want to stimulate their own prostates, consider an S-shaped lucite sex toy (Crystal Wand) or a special butt plug.

Prostate Play vs. Prostate Massage

It's one thing when you are exploring a friend or lover's prostate. It's quite another when a guy is having prostate problems and a health care professional tries to do a prostate massage or milks fluid from it to study under a microscope.

One theory says that some types of prostate problems are caused by small pockets of infection that get trapped inside the gland. These pockets become surrounded with a hard material that encapsulates the infection. The purpose of a prostate massage is to push hard enough to burst these pockets of infection open. This requires a good deal of pressure and it's not any more sexually arousing than getting your breasts squeezed during a mammogram.

However, when you are stimulating a guy's prostate in a sexually exciting way, you are only pushing as firmly as he tells you to. There is no agenda and the motions are based on your mutual pleasure.

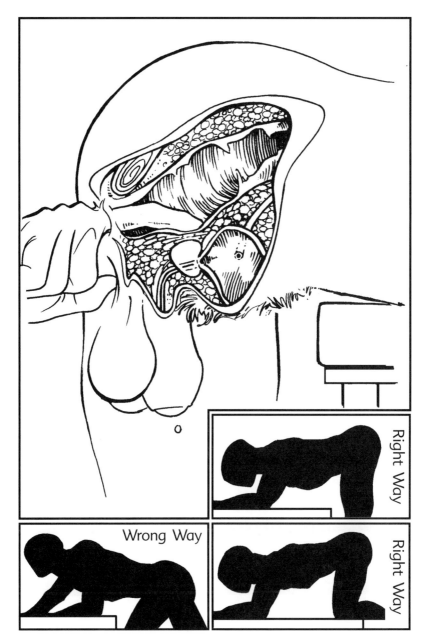

Right Way

Wrong Way

Right Way

DRE—Digital Rectal Exam

The examiner can only feel one surface of the entire prostate or about a third of the gland. The rest remains a mystery. One of the things a physician checks for is symmetry in the lobes of the gland. The only way to determine this accurately is if you are standing or squatting square, with your butt sticking up and out.

Stimulating a prostate isn't going to get most guys off, so if that's your goal, one of you will need to be playing with his penis. When he does start to come, his prostate might feel like it's starting to dome or swell. At this point, you might try rubbing your finger around his prostate or push down on it. Some guys like this, others don't. In the gay community, putting finger pressure on a man's prostate when he's coming results in an ejaculation that they call a "gusher."

Getting a Good Prostate Exam

Feeling a guy's prostate will help you appreciate what an art it is to do a good prostate exam. A lot of physicians who are too embarrassed to do a good exam tend to stick a finger up a guy's rear with lightning speed, touch it long enough to say, "Tag, you're it," and yank the finger out. It's a wonder why they even bother; they aren't doing the patient any good. This is the same thing as waving a wand over a woman's crotch and telling her she's had a pap smear.

One of the reasons why a "Tag, you're it" type of exam is useless is because on a really good day, the examiner is only able to feel along the surface of one-third of the entire prostate gland. He or she is trying to get a lot of information without being able to put a finger on most of it. Some of the things they are trying to determine are the size and symmetry of the gland, if there are lumps in it that might raise suspicions about cancer, and if it is spongy or hard.

Our medical consultant on this chapter estimates he has done more than 35,000 prostate exams during his career in urology. He says a thorough prostate exam takes time and concentration. For him to feel like he's done a good job, he has the man stand or kneel square with his butt pointing up in the air. He also tends to close his eyes once his finger reaches gland zero so he can focus better on the limited amount of information he is receiving.

So here you've got two grown men, one with his finger up the other's butt, both have their eyes closed, and each is hoping that when it's over, the man with the finger can give the man with the prostate a big thumb's up.

Note: It is certainly possible for a guy to feel his own prostate. With enough gymnastics, he can get a finger around it, but the notion of being able to do your own accurate self-exam is kind of silly.

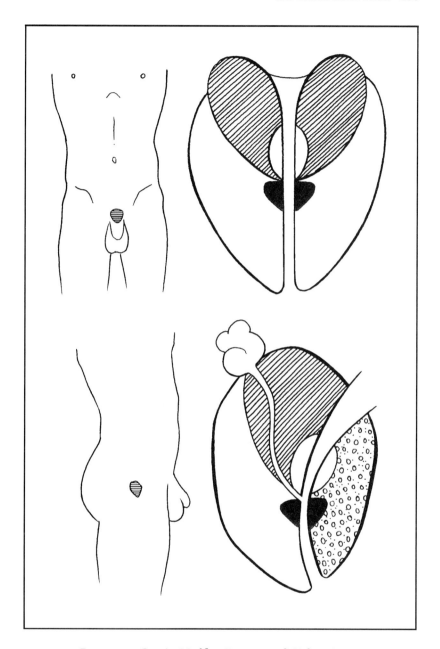

Prostate Cut in Half—Front and Side Views

Some people think of the prostate as a lump. However, as you can see from this diagram, the prostate is a complex organ that has a number of different parts to it.

Why Health Care Professionals Will Grope Your Gland

When a health care professional examines your prostate, it's called a DRE or digital rectal exam. There can be a number of reasons for this to happen. One is if you are a younger guy who is having pain or discomfort in his pelvis, or you are having trouble peeing and the doc is trying to rule out an infected gland as the possible cause. Another reason for having this done is called middle age. A white guy who is forty-five or older will usually receive a prostate exam during every routine physical. Black men get prostate cancer at a significantly higher rate, so they often receive prostate exams at a younger age. They will also do prostate exams on any man whose father or brother has had prostate cancer.

While a DRE isn't going to provide any answers by itself, it is one piece of information that might be helpful in ruling out conditions like BPH, prostatitis, and cancer. Yikes, did we say BPH, prostatitis and cancer?

Trouble in the Pelvis

Did you really think that a gland that's got to spend its entire life inside a guy's rectum isn't going to get uppity now and then? We're talking the equivalent of life without parole in a porta-potty. If the gland is going to start acting up, what are its options? First and foremost are the bladder and the urethra. With a little enlargement here and there, the prostate can nearly cripple a man's ability to do everything from peeing in a straight stream to making him drip for a long time after he pees. It can cause such an urgency to pee that he can't hold it for more than a couple of minutes and it can make him wake up three times every night. It can also mess with his ability to ejaculate without pain or to even walk or sit without discomfort.

Most prostates get bigger as a guy gets older, yet there's simply no room for expansion. As you can see from the illustration at the end of the chapter, if the gland grows one way it's into your bladder, the other way it's up your butt. Or, the growth might only be on the inside of the gland in the central zone, where it implodes upon the urethra and clamps it shut.

If this weren't bad enough, the prostate is one of the most under-studied parts of the human body. Scientifically valid studies on the prostate are few and far between. Although prostate cancer is the third most common kind of cancer that men get, there is little good science to guide physicians. Half of all men will at sometime have BPH or prostatitis, yet treatment remains more of an art than a science. While studies are now being done, it will be years before there is a decent body of findings to help health care practitioners make quick and accurate decisions.

Prostatitis

Prostatitis is a syndrome that can include pain in the pelvis, painful ejaculation, pain with erections, all sorts of peeing problems, and pain with life in general. Some men say it feels like they've got a golf ball up their butt, and it's not because they were bending over and someone forgot to yell "fore!"

Prostatitis is often described as a young man's disease, yet it can pummel the pelvis of any guy at any age. It can be caused by anything from an infection to chronic tension in the pelvis, although infection is found in less than 10% of all cases of prostatitis. To quote a recent article in the *Journal of Urology*, prostatitis is a syndrome that is "poorly defined, poorly understood, poorly treated, and bothersome." Or to quote our own prostate expert, "Prostatitis is a young guy's disease that is not diagnosed properly and is not treated properly."

If you've got a sudden, acute attack of pain in your pelvis, get yourself to a physician as soon as possible. This kind of prostatitis can usually be treated successfully.

If you have chronic prostate problems, educate yourself about prostatitis. A good source of information is www.prostatitis.org. Then, after you have an idea of just how many theories there are and how complex the problem can be, find yourself a good urologist. The prostatitis.org website usually keeps a list of urologists with whom people have had positive experiences.

Since chronic prostatitis tends to wax and wane, a lot of guys keep chowing down on tons of antibiotics, thinking that the antibiot-

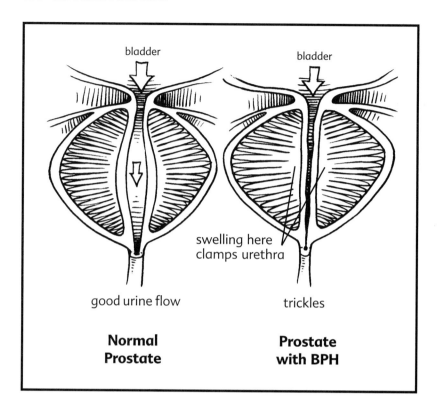

bladder

bladder

swelling here
clamps urethra

good urine flow

trickles

**Normal
Prostate**

**Prostate
with BPH**

ics helped it improve the last time around. This is not a good idea. You need to approach chronic prostatitis with patience and intelligence.

BPH—Benign Prostatic Hyperplasia

Let's say you are getting close to fifty and you notice that the wall doesn't shake anymore when you are peeing at a urinal. Or maybe you don't make it through the night like you used to. This could be due to a prostate that is getting larger as you are getting older.

It's called BPH when your prostate gland is enlarged and they don't think you've got cancer. The symptoms can range from mild to severe. One of the fascinating things about BPH is that the prostate can be greatly enlarged without you having any troubling symptoms, or it can be completely normal in size with you going through hell.

Although BPH and prostatitis are supposed to be two different things, a man who is under forty is likely to be given the diagnosis of prostatitis while a man who is over fifty is likely to be given the diagnosis of BPH, even if they have the exact same symptoms.

Prostate Cancer

It has been estimated that half of all grown men have an early form of prostate cancer called microcarcinoma. It usually stays where it is and you never know it's there. When this kind of cancer does go visiting, it often remains inside the prostate and is not aggressive. However, some forms of prostate cancer can be very aggressive. The challenge is in knowing which is which.

Prostate cancer is sometimes diagnosed on a wing and a prayer. One of the big challenges with prostate cancer is deciding when to treat it aggressively and when to take a "wait and watch" attitude.

One test that can possibly indicate the presence of prostate cancer is called the PSA test—with PSA being the enzyme that makes a guy's cum go from thick to watery. When the level of PSA in the bloodstream starts to rise, it might be due to cancer of the prostate. On the other hand, BPH can also cause the PSA level to rise, and some men who have prostate cancer show no rise in their PSA level at all.

At this point, scientists wonder if doing routine PSA tests are helpful, as they sometimes result in a wild goose chase. Please check with your doctor on a regular basis, since long-term studies are now being done that will offer more guidance.

If you are concerned about prostate cancer, educate yourself and check out numerous resources like some of the following:

1. *The Prostate Health Workbook* by Newton Malerman, Hunter House Press, Alameda, California, 2002. The title is misleading. This is a book for men who have prostate cancer and it's a good one. The author had prostate cancer and he's tried to provide answers to questions that others have been too embarrassed to ask or answer, such as "What Do I Tell My Grandkids?" "Do I Have to Shave?" and "What Is That Strange Thing Between My Legs?" The author has excellent suggestions such as the following:

"If you are diagnosed with prostate cancer or any other serious illness, take someone with you to your doctor's appointments. My wife was able to ask much clearer and tougher questions than I was. If you are single, or your spouse or partner is too emotional about what's happening, take a trusted friend or family member."

"If you are treated to a rough digital exam, find another urologist. The procedure is not too unpleasant if the doctor has a gentle touch."

2. Explore several websites, including www.phoenix5.org and www.ustoo.com. Some of your best help will come from other men who have been through it before you. However, be very aware of which companies contribute funding to the websites you are searching. It is unlikely that companies will be supporting websites that question the wisdom of taking their products.

NOTE: If you have cancer or BPH and if surgery or radiation is being suggested, ask if it will cause incontinence, impotence, a shorter penis, dry ejaculations and if you will squirt urine when you ejaculate.

A Healthy Prostate Diet?

Long term studies on diet and prostate cancer are just starting to come in. As of press time, it appears that a diet high in saturated fat is not good for the prostate. Men on high protein, high fat diets should take note. Two large studies at Harvard have shown that the prostate does better if you eat whole grains, fish, fruits, and vegetables. Omega-3 fatty acids from flaxseed oil do not appear to be good for the prostate, while omega-3 fatty acids from fish oil are good. Extra calcium might be bad for your prostate. Also, some men find that caffeine (coffee, tea, etc.), alcohol, and spicy foods can cause a flare up of prostate symptoms, as well as taking certain cold and sinus pills.

Smoking definitely causes bladder cancer, and it causes men with prostatitis to have worse symptoms.

Regarding sexual practices and prostate health, there aren't any studies to offer guidance. Having anal sex without a condom (barebacking) makes the guy who inserts vulnerable to prostatitis because E. Coli can cause prostatitis, and there's a lot of E. Coli in our rectums. There are also concerns that couples who are having vaginal intercourse can be passing some prostate infections back and forth, so if you have prostate problems, discuss this with your urologist.

The Bravest Men in America

We used to think that Joe Marzucco, our prostate consultant who has had his finger in the rectums of 35,000 men, was the bravest man in America. This was until we heard about Russ Page. Russ is involved in the artificial insemination business. He routinely sticks his hand up the rear ends of 2400-pound bulls. Not only does his hand go up there,

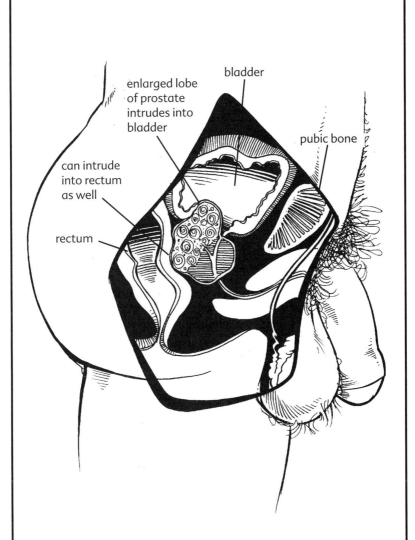

bladder

enlarged lobe of prostate intrudes into bladder

pubic bone

can intrude into rectum as well

rectum

When The Posterior Lobe of The Prostate Pushes Into The Bladder

This is what it looks like when a lobe of the prostate swells and pushes into the floor of the bladder. When a man tries to urinate, this enlarged lobe can push against the opening of the urethra and block the flow.

but he pokes, prods, and milks the various glands until he can get a squirt of semen to drip out of the bull's penis in order to examine the quality of it. This is the kind of job professors usually have their graduate students do while they take all the credit, but Russ doesn't seem to be university-affiliated. To quote a recent email from Russ answering our questions:

"The prostate of the bull is not a distinctly separate gland, but is incorporated into the shaft of the root of the penis. I start by gently massaging the seminal vesicles, which in the bull are three-to five inches and curved to each side. Next I start a rhythmic back and forth massage of the ampulla region (near the prostate) which I can then feel building tension. After about thirty seconds of this, the bull is usually ready to give me several drops of semen. I have been collecting semen this way for over ten years."

Russ prefers collecting semen like this, as opposed to with an artificial vagina that he would have to stick between a bull and a cow who is in heat. He says that bulls are instantaneous ejaculators (like many college males), and he would rather take his chances with his arm up the bull's behind when the bull is in a steel chute. Otherwise, when trying to collect sperm in an artificial vagina, Russ cautions:

"You must be quick and have thought out every move you will make in every circumstance, including where the closest, most sure escape route is, in case the bull's desire to hurt you is stronger than his desire to breed the cow."

And if you can find a more fitting ending to a chapter on the glands down under, more power to you!

THANKS! A very special thanks to Dr. Joe Marzucco, formerly of the Portland Kaiser Urology Department and now a sex therapist in private practice in Portland, Oregon. Thanks also to Russ Page, and to John Schulman, a sex educator in Corvallis, Oregon, who helps students learn how to do prostate exams.

Doing Yourself in Your Partner's Presence
Chapter 20

Alot of women have never seen a man masturbate, nor have many men seen a woman masturbate. Yet plenty of us, male or female, would find it interesting if not highly erotic to watch a partner masturbate. That's what this chapter is about: masturbating together or in your partner's presence.

In Front of a Partner

For straight people, masturbating in front of a partner can sometimes take a lot of trust. That's because masturbation tends to be more self-disclosing than other types of sex. It can also leave you feeling vulnerable if your partner finds you doing it. ("Oh, hi, honey, I was just sitting here in front of the computer jerking off.") Still, most of us continue to masturbate even when we are in a relationship, and being open about it usually helps to expand sexual enjoyment for both partners. Here are nine reasons why:

There is often something erotic and even forbidden about seeing your partner masturbate. This is just as true for women watching men as for men watching women.

If your partner can see how you please yourself, it might help him or her understand more about pleasing you.

Orgasms from masturbation are sometimes more intense than other kinds of orgasm. It might increase the level of intimacy in your relationship if you can ask your partner to hold you while you bring yourself to orgasm.

Masturbating together is an excellent way to share intense sexual feelings without the risk of unwanted pregnancy or STIs.

People often have unreal expectations that a partner can satisfy all of their sexual urges. There will be plenty of times when one of you is in the mood and the other isn't. There may also be times when your partner is so pleasantly drained by what you have just done (oral sex, genital massage, etc.) that he or she curls up and falls asleep on the

spot. If the two of you are comfortable about masturbation, then the spent one can simply offer to hold the horny one while he or she masturbates, or you can masturbate while your partner conks out.

There are times when people feel like doing it solo. If this is an accepted part of your relationship, you won't have to hide or feel like a weirdo when you want to control your own orgasmic destiny.

Sometimes your partner may want to lie down beside you and masturbate too!

Summers in the East, South, and Midwest are sometimes so miserably hot and muggy that the last thing you'll want to do is hug an equally hot and sweaty partner. Masturbating together is one way you can share sexual pleasure without full body contact.

When you do masturbate in each other's presence, don't forget that a partner's pleasure might be greatly enhanced with a special assist on your part. For instance, a man might enjoy it tremendously if his partner caresses or massages his testicles while he masturbates, and a woman might find it delightful if her partner licks her nipples or whispers sweet but nasty things into her ears while she masturbates. The possibilities abound.

Virgin Birth Alert! If you have male ejaculate on your fingers, be sure to wash your hands before touching a vulva. One woman actually became pregnant from masturbating right after giving her high school sweetheart a hand job.

Readers' Comments

"I wish he would do it in front of me more often. I've even named his penis Squeegy Loueegy." *female age 37*

"I never realized it was possible for a guy to be turned on by seeing a woman touching herself. Needless to say, once I figured this out about him, I put on a good show." *female age 45*

"It took a while for us to get comfortable with it, but I like to watch my husband stroke his penis. He enjoys watching me, too. I often masturbate as part of our loveplay because I like stimulation in more places at once than two hands are capable of doing." *female age 47*

"During intercourse one of us always has to touch me so I can have an orgasm, so in that respect, he's seen me do it. And we both chat about how we masturbate when we are alone sometimes." *female age 30*

"I masturbate in front of my husband, mostly with a vibrator. I still find it a bit embarrassing." *female age 35*

"I masturbate at least once a day. My lover loves it when I masturbate with him or beside him. He thinks it's one of life's great mysteries. I like to watch him masturbate, though sometimes it makes me jealous. I'd like him to take the time and attention he spends on himself and use it on me." *female age 24*

"I have watched her masturbate and even helped her, and she has done the same with me. It is fun and important for both of us." *male age 70*

Dear Paul,

I sometimes wake up in the middle of the night to find my boyfriend masturbating. He thinks I'm sleeping and don't know about it. Why would he be doing this after we just made love a few hours earlier?

Ann in Cheyenne

Dear Ann,

You won't believe this, but I recently received an email from a woman who said the sex with her boyfriend is extremely satisfying, but after they make love she still waits until he goes to sleep so she can masturbate. She loves their shared orgasms, but also enjoys her own.

There could be lots of reasons why your man masturbates after you make love, and maybe I'll be able to nail one or two. But first, let's talk about masturbation within a relationship.

Many of us have the fantasy that once we get into a relationship, we won't be playing with ourselves anymore. In some cases, that's how it is for the first couple of months or years. You either don't have the urge to masturbate, or can't remember why you used to do it so often. In other relationships, which can be just as satisfying, you don't really stop masturbating. And some women report that they actually start masturbating more once they are in a satisfying sexual relationship.

More often than not, it's impossible for us to fully satisfy each other's sexual needs. You might be worried about a project that's hanging over your head and the last thing you feel like doing is having sex. Or maybe there is nothing you are worried about—you just don't feel like getting physical. That's when it is really helpful if your partner feels free to masturbate.

As for your current situation with your boyfriend, here are some things to keep in mind:

- It is possible that he loves having sex with you, but wakes up horny and feels bad about waking you up, so he takes care of it himself.

- Maybe he wakes up in the middle of the night and can't get back to sleep. Plenty of us use masturbation as a natural sleep aid.

- It's possible that he enjoys giving himself orgasms in addition to the ones he has with you.

- Perhaps he masturbates several times a day to help with anxiety or depression. If that's true, it's best for him to get some therapy.

- Also, some guys aren't able to come with a partner, but are able to do so by masturbating. They might learn to fake orgasms so their partner won't think there is something wrong.

Whatever the reason for your boyfriend's midnight masturbation, it might help if you could talk to him about it. Otherwise, you will think there's something weird about the situation when there probably isn't.

The last thing I would do is confront the issue directly. Instead, try to create an atmosphere where it's safe for the two of you to disclose really private things about yourselves. For instance, you might raise the issue of masturbation in general, asking him if he would hold or maybe watch you while you gave yourself an orgasm. Most guys would think they had died and gone to heaven. Perhaps this would help make the subject of masturbation safe for conversation. Eventually, you can ask him how he does it and if he enjoys doing it in addition to the sex that the two of you have.

It sounds like you might be a little surprised at the statements of our readers that are listed below. We recently asked the following questions on our sex survey at www.goofyfootpress.com:

Is masturbation an important part of your life?
If you have a partner, does she or he know?

The vast majority of the men and women in sexually satisfying relationships answered "Yes" and "Yes." Here are some responses:

"How often? About three times a week, give or take. My partner does know, and we openly masturbate in front of each other." *female age 20*

"I masturbate regularly because in the fourteen years that I have been sexually active I have never received an orgasm from intercourse. The only way I can come is from a vibrator or by my husband performing oral sex on me. Sometimes I masturbate privately, other times in front of my husband right after intercourse." *female age 35*

"Masturbation is the act in my life that keeps me sane. My wife even helps me sometimes." *male age 38*

"My partner probably knows, but I do it more than he thinks."
female age 21

"I masturbate several times a week, and if she doesn't know after twenty-five years, well I'd be surprised." *male age 48*

"Sometimes, you just want to come and not have intercourse with your partner. It makes sense because you know how to make yourself get off better and faster than anybody else. You might also get to know yourself and discover new techniques."
female age 26

Nipples, Nipples, Nipples

Chapter 21

This chapter talks about ways of using your fingers and mouth to tweak your partner's titties. Plenty of women and men have mega nerve endings in their nipples. The sensations they transmit can be both pleasant and annoying.

For instance, one woman might find it heavenly when a lover barely breathes on her nipples, but convulses in pain if he is the slightest bit rough. So her partner learns to traverse her tender nipples like a butterfly and becomes a master at the art of subtle stimulation. Another woman wants her lover to handle her nipples with authority and doesn't find it erotic until his lips latch on like an industrial vacuum cleaner. Also, some women's breasts become more sensitive during certain stages of their menstrual cycle, especially if they are taking birth control pills. Know your lover's body and be sensitive to it.

In our society, it is assumed that men are the ones who stimulate women's nipples instead of it being a mutual experience. Too bad. Guys have the same variation in nipple sensitivity as women. Some men get an erection and nearly come when their nipples are caressed.

No matter what the sex of your lover, here are a few things to consider when kissing and caressing nipples and chests. Before getting into the parts about tips and techniques, let's look at what different women have to say about their breasts.

A Fascinating Take on Breasts

Here are some women's perspectives on their breasts as reported to Meema Spadola in her wonderful book, *Breasts—Our Most Public Private Parts,* Wildcat Canyon Press, Berkeley, CA, 1998:

"My preferences vary constantly. What feels pleasurable one moment can feel annoying the next. Sometimes I hit sensory overload and can barely stand to have my breasts touched."

Cecilia says, "My nipples are very sensitive and I could be aroused almost to the point of orgasm just by touching them, but only very gently, almost not at all." At the other end of the spectrum is Heather, who prefers a firm touch that includes clothespins and biting.

Then there is Carrie, who was known as the girl with the big boobs. "Guys were sometimes more attracted to my boobs than to me." One day when Carrie was wearing a large rain slicker which hid her breasts behind a wall of thick yellow plastic, she met a man from out of town and they seemed to hit it off. They talked on the phone and wrote letters for the first year of their relationship, with him never knowing that her bras were the size of saddlebags. Assured that he liked all of her and not just her mammaries, Carrie eventually married the man.

When breast-play isn't working, one woman reports, "When a man touches my breasts, I feel a little removed from the whole experience—as if he's on a date with my breasts." Another woman says, "My boyfriend loves to suck on my nipples, but sometimes I get this sense that he is focusing on them and tuning me out, and I can feel a wave of resentment, almost jealousy, when he latches onto my breasts." A third woman says, "I would feel like I had this 180-pound baby in my arms, and occasionally he'd fall asleep there sucking my breasts. I'm sure he thought he was giving me great pleasure, but it just didn't do it for me."

When breast-play is working, there are women who describe their breasts as being "a place of warmth and love," and "without breast stimulation, sex is purely physical with no emotional component." Another perspective comes from Scarlet, with 38DD breasts, who says, "I can't wait to take my clothes off in bed because I know that men will get excited; they always want to suck on my breasts. They think that I get incredibly turned on by it, but my breasts aren't as sensitive as men expect. Honestly, I could be balancing my checkbook while they're doing it. It's really not a big deal. But I do get turned on seeing them getting very turned on."

Finally, Ms. Spadola quotes a woman who has had sex with both men and women: "The men didn't seem to grasp that twisting them like radio dials does not work. They treated my breasts as something separate from my body. Women seem to know instinctively what to do with breasts. Women sense that there are times when you want your breasts to be touched, and times you don't. It didn't seem to occur to the men I was with that there might be mental and cultural baggage wrapped up there."

A Suggestion for Female Readers

Even if your guy has a big hairy chest, tell him you're going to touch and kiss his "breasts" the same way you like to have yours kissed, and then do it. If there are times when you like it gentle, tell him, "This is what I like when I say gentle." If there are times when you like it extra-rough, grab a pair of vice grips and let him know what you mean when you say rough. If you like your nipples tugged, show him exactly how and for how long. And please, don't get all bent out of shape if he requires refresher lessons. The learning process is not nearly as straightforward as you might think.

Techniques for Happy Breasts

There is no "one-size-fits-all" bra, and there are no sets of tips and techniques that will work for everyone. Here are a few to pick and choose from:

Size vs. Performance As with a clitoris or penis, the sensitivity of a breast has nothing to do with its size. Small ones can be like lightning rods, while big ones might not be sensitive at all.

Making the Nipple Taut Place your fingers on each side of the nipple, not quite touching the nipple but around the perimeter of it. Push down lightly and slide your fingers apart. This will make the nipple taut. Some people find that taut nipples are more sensitive.

In and Out Pucker up your lips and use them to make a gasket around the nipple. Then suck in and out without breaking the seal—so the nipple feels alternating currents of vacuum and pressure. This method is described in more detail in Ray Stubbs's book *The Clitoral Kiss*. It also works well on earlobes and the clitoris. However, if you are sucking earlobes in this way, be sure that earrings are removed first. As for jewelry in the nipples or clitoris, what's a boy to do?

Five-Finger Nipple Grab This works best if the breast and your hand are lubricated with massage oil. Rest the palm of your hand over the breast with your fingertips around its circumference. As you lift your hand, let your fingertips caress their way up the sides of the breasts until they are clasping the tip of the nipple. Pull on the nipple just a little or a lot, depending on what your partner likes and her level of arousal.

Nipple Between Your Index & Middle Fingers The ability to do this will depend upon the size and shape of the nipple. Cup your hand over the breast in such a way that the tip of the nipple rests in the space between your middle finger and index (or other) finger. Squeeze

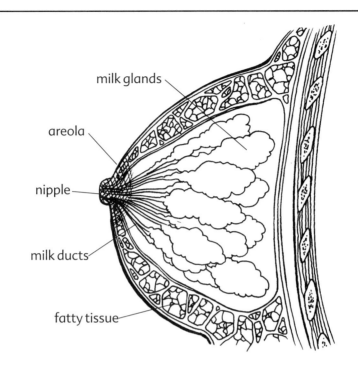

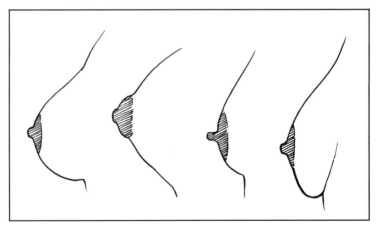

The breast is made up of glands, ducts, and surrounding fat. In younger women, the proportion of fat in the breast is usually lower, while with age, the proportion of fat tends to increase. It is the fat that gives the breast its unique size and shape. Because there is fat in the breast, it is completely normal for breasts to feel lumpy.

the fingers together so that when you lift your hand the nipple follows, pulling the rest of the breast up with it.

Nipple and Penis Some women find it highly arousing when a man caresses their nipples with the head of his penis. If he pulls apart the opening of his penis, he can sometimes stick the tip of an erect nipple into it. This is particularly true if he is uncircumcised.

The Whole Enchilada Women who like having their breasts and nipples caressed sometimes complain that men don't spend enough time doing this. Women who don't like having their breasts and nipples caressed sometimes complain that men spend too much time doing this. It's hard to lavish too much attention upon your partner's breasts if she enjoys it. Consider licking and sucking the entire breast and not just the nipple, and remember to alternate breasts every once in a while.

Hand and Mouth Chances are, your partner has two breasts and you have only one mouth. Perhaps she might like it if your fingers are caressing one breast while your lips are tending to the other or perhaps she would prefer your hand to be caressing some other part of her body. The best way to find out is to ask.

Variations in Sensitivity Sometimes one breast or nipple is more sensitive than the other. Find out if your partner would like you to spend more time on the sensitive side.

Different Temperatures An ice cube in the mouth can be a rousing way to greet a partner's nipples. Or for nipples that are already cold, drinking something warm just before licking or sucking them can feel quite exquisite.

Playful Plate Fruit salad, all kinds of fruits, dessert foods, and certain liquors can be served on nipples, chests, abdomens, backs, and other body parts with extremely pleasing results. Do what you can to keep sugars out of the vagina.

Getting to Watch Some people find it highly erotic to watch while a partner plays with her (or his) own nipples and breasts. So if you enjoy playing with your own nipples, there's no point in keeping it a secret.

Hard-Nipple Alert

Let's say you are playing with your partner's nipples and they get hard, is this a good sign? Sometimes yes, sometimes no. Until you learn more about your partner's body, don't assume that hard nipples mean happy nipples. Nipples can get hard from unpleasant stimuli such as roughness, abrasion, and cold—so be sure to ask your partner if he or she likes what you are doing. Also be aware that what a person wants in terms of nipple play can vary with their state of sexual arousal.

Readers' Comments

"Kissing my breast depends upon my mood. Sometimes I like being touched gently with fingertips and then gentle circles of a tongue followed by a very light sucking on the nipples."

female age 27

"Most of the sensitivity is in the nipple, but there are good feelings from having the whole breast caressed and sucked. Swirling your tongue around the nipple is good. Sucking the nipple is great! Biting the nipple is a MAJOR no-no." *female 34*

"Depending on how aroused I am, I like to be sucked hard and even gently bitten on the nipple." *female age 45*

"There doesn't seem to be any logical pattern or reason behind it, but sometimes even touching the breast area can hurt. Other times, pretty much anything is okay." *female age 32*

Dear Paul,

I am a twenty-year-old female and had to have a breast biopsy last year for a lump. I had not thought of my breasts as pretty before. They have always seemed too small compared to what all the boys were paying attention to. With a gain in self-esteem and self-respect and with the help of my current boyfriend, I've found that I really do think of my breasts in a whole new way, especially after going through the experience of surgery. My lump was benign, but it made me think about myself in a new way and what I really have to appreciate.

DD from Boulder

Dear Paul,

When I was a girl, my dad and I used to play and wrestle a lot. These are some of my fondest memories of childhood. Then, when I became a teenager, our physical closeness seemed to suddenly stop. Now that I'm older, I think it might have been because my chest started to develop and he began to feel uncomfortable. Is this possible?

Bella from Bellingham

Dear Bella,

I suspect you have hit the proverbial nail on the head. Growing breasts come between a lot of dads and their teenage daughters. Hopefully, dads will become aware of this and understand the huge loss to their daughters. Dads can gradually transform the physical closeness by being involved in other ways—with everything from playing catch to taking their daughter someplace special each week like a museum or out to lunch. The important thing is to maintain the intimacy which is so important to most daughters and dads while moving the physical relationship into something that's a bit more age appropriate.

Dear Paul,

My boyfriend wants me to lactate for him. I am not pregnant nor have I ever been and I don't know how to lactate. I don't know if it's safe or if it is going to turn me into a hormonal wreck. If you have any advice or know any books I would be really grateful.

Madonna in Montana

Dear Madonna,

For starters, what you are asking about is different from the breast play that couples often enjoy during lovemaking. You are talking about a situation where your breasts would be lactating and your boyfriend would be nursing on them at least two-to-four times a day, seven days a week. If he missed a nursing, you would need to pump or express the milk from your breasts.

Couples who do this sort of thing describe it as an "Adult Nursing Relationship." It usually begins after the woman has had a baby. The father may have started nursing alongside junior, or maybe mom encouraged him to take over once the baby was weaned. There are adult couples who keep nursing for years. Junior could be graduating from high school, and dad might still be sucking milk from mom's breasts.

The notion of having to nurse two-to-four times a day, seven days a week might be a jarring enough jolt of reality to cause even the most eager of couples to abandon the concept. However, couples who continue this kind of nursing seem to cherish the added closeness and mutual dependency. Not only is one partner dependent on the other for milk, but she is just as dependent on him to relieve her swollen mammaries. In fact, the woman's milk will often let down at the sight or sound of her partner's presence, just as a nursing mother's breasts will let down when she sees or hears her hungry infant cry.

There are two ways that someone who hasn't been pregnant can try to jump-start her non-nursing breasts. These methods have been pioneered by adoptive moms who are trying to breast feed their adopted infants. One method involves the use of drugs to trick your body into thinking you were pregnant and have given birth. The other involves a lot of seriously intense sucking on the part of your boyfriend, several times a day for several weeks in a row, and even then there is still no guarantee he'd be sporting a milk mustache when all is said and done.

If this did work, your breasts would probably get bigger so you would need to get new bras and blouses. As for the potential of getting stretch marks, I don't think it would be any different than with mothers who nurse infants.

Also, you would need to supplement your intake of calories and calcium just as a nursing mother does. Otherwise, your body might start robbing your bones of the extra calcium that your breasts need to produce milk. And if your boyfriend didn't cut calories in other ways, he'd probably start to get fat. As for the safety and impact of all this on your body—I'm not sure that anyone can say what it will be. Women have been nursing babies since the beginning of time, but does that have the same impact on your body as what you would be doing? I honestly don't know of any studies that have analyzed the outcome of women who lactate to fulfill adult fantasies.

Regarding the actual fantasy of nursing, I wonder if there are many couples who have had babies who didn't try it at least once? Beyond that, if couples are doing it, it's not the sort of thing they are likely to announce at Sunday's church social. So for more information, I would need to consult my second best source on such matters. Did it ever come up in one of the "Sex and the City" reruns?

For links on Adult Nursing visit the "Kinky Corner" on our free and mostly wonderful website
www.BoinkCentral.com

Oral Sex: Popsicles & Penises

Chapter 22

Some women enjoy giving oral sex to a man. It provides them with feelings of intimacy and closeness that can be both soothing and erotic. It also provides a feeling of power and control. Other women don't find anything special about doing oral sex, but will go down on a guy if he enjoys it. And some women would rather suck on a rusty old pipe than let their lips stray south of a man's beltline.

Whatever your preference, this chapter offers tips and techniques about giving oral sex to the male of the species. It starts with a candid discussion about male ejaculate and then offers techniques for giving splendid blow jobs. It also includes suggestions for the man who is receiving oral sex—things he can do to help make it a neat experience for both partners.

When Gay Guys Blow

Straight women often get the feeling that they need to swallow a guy's ejaculate in order to give a truly fine blow job. If this were true, you'd think it would apply just as much in the gay community, where the giver of the blow job knows exactly what it feels like to receive a blow job. But that's not true. Gay guys usually don't swallow when giving blow jobs. As one gay male reader says, "No way am I going to do all that work getting a partner to come and not watch him ejaculate. Besides, I don't exactly love the taste."

Of course, you might love swallowing whatever your man can pump. But do it only because you want to and not because there's some Emily Post of Blow Jobs who says it has to be.

To Swallow or Not to Swallow—That Is the Question

Considering what happens if you suck on a penis for long enough, a woman who gives oral sex eventually has to decide if she wants to swallow ejaculate. While some women don't mind swallowing, others find it weird. For many women the salient factors are how they feel about the guy and how they feel within the relationship. For others, it's a matter of taste and texture.

Different guys come in different flavors. They also have different textures and volumes. For instance, one man's ejaculate might be viscous while another's is thin. One man might taste good while another tastes bitter or salty, or as a female reader states: "My current lover tastes great, I like swallowing his ejaculate. But when my former boyfriend came, it felt like battery acid in the back of my mouth." Another reader comments that she has no problem with the taste or texture of male ejaculate, but that it sometimes upsets her stomach. A British sex expert with a Margaret Thatcher-like voice says that male ejaculate is an acquired taste, like swallowing raw oysters. She says it's nothing to get worked up over. We're not so sure, given how nobody around here likes swallowing raw oysters. As for the smell of male ejaculate, it's like a weak solution of Clorox—original scent rather than Lemon Fresh or Spring Rain.

Who knows what to advise about swallowing male ejaculate, except that a man shouldn't push the issue unless he is willing to swallow a mouthful of his own, although the actual amount is closer to a teaspoonful. Suggestions for how to give a really good blow job without swallowing are listed later in this chapter.

To Swallow or Not to Swallow: Hormonal Considerations

Women sometimes wonder if they are going to get a dose of male hormones when they swallow male ejaculate. Not to worry. While the testicles produce the lion's share of male hormone, these hormones are not released into a man's ejaculate. Instead, they are dumped directly into the bloodstream, where they can have an impact on the rest of his body. A woman is not going to sprout a beard or grow a big Adam's apple from swallowing her partner's cum. She will get more male hormone from giving him a hickey. As for the question of calories, the only way you will gain weight from male ejaculate is if it makes you pregnant.

Regarding the issue of health, ejaculate from a healthy guy has fewer germs than saliva. It seldom causes an allergic reaction. The main health concern about male sex fluids is whether the man has a sexually transmitted infection. For more on STIs, see the chapter, "Gnarly Sex Germs."

Quick & Easy

Going down on a man isn't as much a mystery as going down on a woman, given how the penis is pretty much in your face from start to finish. The childhood experience of sucking on popsicles will give you an idea of how to begin. However, popsicle sucking does not make for an excellent blow job unless your man keeps his penis in the freezer.

There are many different kinds of blow jobs. Some women like to give blow jobs that include lots of kissing and licking; others mainly suck on the thing and do fine at that. Using your hands while giving oral sex adds an extra dimension.

It never hurts to ask your partner what he likes, but these discussions are usually more productive after you've been down on him a time or two. The shared experience provides both of you with a point of reference. Then he can say, "I really liked it when you..."

Dozens of tips are listed in the pages that follow—just about anything you'd ever want to know about giving a really good blow job. But let's say you are late for a job interview and you need a quick primer in ten lines or less. You might start by tossing the lucky guy on his back. Lick his penis to get it wet with your saliva. This provides pleasure and lubrication. Then, make a ring around the penis with your lips. This will create a gasket. Slide your head up and down, but only as far as you feel comfortable. There is no need to suck. Each time you pull your head up, suction will build naturally in your mouth. But don't take our word for it. Try it first on one of your fingers.

Of course, there are about a hundred other factors to consider, from what to do with your saliva to keeping yourself from gagging.

Gag Prevention

Some women complain that they gag when giving blow jobs. When asked if they ever bothered to tell their partners about this, the gagging girls usually reply no. Perhaps their male partners were inconsiderate oafs, or maybe these men had trouble reading the women's minds. Whatever the case, many men would do back flips to please a partner if only they were told what she does or doesn't like. The last thing most men want is to hurt or displease a woman sexually.

What follows are four suggestions to help keep yourself from being gagged while giving a blow job, but the most important and intelligent suggestion is clearly the first:

Tell Him! If he thrusts and it gags you, let him know. Tell him that the two of you need to work on it, because you enjoy giving him blow jobs except for that part. Be specific! If a little thrusting is okay, help him recognize the difference between good and painful thrusting.

Fist on Shaft Make a fist around the shaft of your lover's penis, with your little finger resting on his pubic bone. This will give you four knuckles' worth of washer or buffer. If your man has an average-sized penis, there should be less than three remaining inches to go into your mouth. If your man is luckier than most, use two hands instead of one, as you would if swinging a baseball bat. As an added benefit, keeping your fingers around the shaft can be nice for him if you use them to pump the foreskin or pull it taut. More on the pleasure aspects later.

On His Back Some guys thrust involuntarily when they come. To deal with this, keep your bronco on his back and position your body between his legs. When he is close to coming, keep both of your hands around the base of his penis and your forearms flat against his pelvis. The weight of your body distributed against his pelvic region will help discourage any unwanted thrusting, and if he does thrust it will pull you up with him.

He behaves!

Gag. Yuck.

Don't Gag the Girl!

Get Him By The Balls Clamp your thumb and forefinger together around the upper part of the man's scrotum where it attaches to his groin. This will place the testicles in the palm of your hand. Some men find this pleasurable, especially if the woman gently pulls downward. If he thrusts more than you want, increase the downward pull, as though you were pulling back on a horse's reins.

Positions for Penis Sucking

A highly effective position for doing oral sex is to place yourself between your partner's legs, facing his body. This gives your tongue direct access to the most sensitive parts of his penis and scrotum, and the angle minimizes the tendency of the head of the penis to bang against your molars. It's a comfortable position for most women, and it lets a man watch you giving him head, which some men find to be reassuring, loving and a turn-on. Another variation is to sit, kneel or crouch in front of your partner while he is standing or sitting.

Some couples like the woman to straddle the guy's chest. In this position, she faces southward as she would if the couple were doing 69. This can be particularly nice for the guy if staring at his sweetheart's crotch and rear end provides an extra turn-on. But it places her mouth in a lousy position to give his penis maximum stimulation, as it puts her tongue in contact with the back side of the penis, which isn't as sensitive as the front.

In the positions mentioned so far, the guy lies still and the woman provides the up and down motion. Another way of doing a blow job is where the woman keeps her head still and the guy moves his penis in and out of her mouth. The fancy term for this that nobody but the pope ever uses is "irrumation," which is Latin for "altar boy, hold still!"

The position the woman usually takes in irrumation or "face-fucking" is on her back with her head propped up on a pillow. The man sits astride her upper body and gently thrusts his penis in her mouth. The woman lets the guy do some of the work and she has good access to his testicles and rear end, or she can easily masturbate while he's receiving the blow job. The couple can also alternate penis thrusting with French kissing. On the other hand, some women become bored or feel claustrophobic giving a blow job with the guy on top, or they fear that the man might be rough or thrust too deep. Putting your hand around the shaft of his penis while he thrusts will greatly decrease any chance that he might thrust too deep.

A final position that some couples enjoy is where they lie side by side, with the woman's mouth in front of the man's genitals. She can lay her head on a pillow.

Deep-Throat Myth

You wouldn't stick an entire popsicle down your throat, so why try it with a guy's dick? Truly great blow jobs have nothing to do with deep-throating a man. Deep-throating is more of a novelty than something that makes a penis feel great. If your man insists that you deep-throat him, go to the market and buy a vegetable that's the same size as his erect penis, hand it to him and say, "Okay, let's see you shove this thing down your throat!"

Also, don't confuse a penis with a clitoris and think that every square centimeter is packed with thousands of nerve endings. As was said in the porn film *How to Perform Fellatio:* "The most sensitive part of the penis is the top part, so stop wasting your time on the bottom," and the male actor who uttered this profound statement had a penis with a great deal of bottom part to suck if he had so wanted.

The average penis has certain parts that are sensitive and other parts that are mostly for show. For some guys, especially those who are uncircumcised, the head might be really sensitive. Find out how he likes you to suck or lick the head. Also, there is a sensitive nickel-sized area just below the head on the side of the penis that's away from his body when he has an erection. It's called the frenulum, and some guys can be brought to orgasm from stimulating this area alone. The seam of the penis that runs from the scrotum to the head usually responds to tender kisses, as does the entire scrotum.

If you still insist on deep-throating your partner, it might help if you position your body so you are either on top of the man in a 69-type position or are lying on your back with your head over the edge of the bed. These positions will help to straighten the pathway down your throat. They are better for deep-throating but not nearly as good for regular blow jobs.

Blow-Job Basics

Several tips and techniques are listed in this section for giving a really good blow job.

Slobber People who are neat freaks often try to swallow all of their own drool when giving blow jobs. Such people have been known to nearly drown. Smart women let gravity carry their saliva down a lover's penis. They can also use it as a lubricant for pumping the bottom part of the penis with one hand while doing the upper part by mouth. Don't hesitate to toss a towel under the man's rear or to wedge one beneath his testicles; that way there won't be a big wet spot or stain on the mattress, couch or seat of the Greyhound Scenicruisier.

If It's Still Soft Some women enjoy sucking on a soft penis and feeling it grow inside their mouth. Just because it's soft, don't think for a moment that each kiss, lick and suck doesn't feel exquisite. One of the few times when a man can be totally passive and feel no need to perform sexually is while he is receiving a blow job. Don't assume it's a negative sign if it takes a while to get hard or if it doesn't get hard at all. A man can still have a lovely time with a soft dick.

Lubrication for Licking When you first lick a man's genitals, coat your lips and tongue with extra saliva. This will make it feel better. Honest. If you suffer from the dreaded pre-blow-job dry mouth, try sucking on a mint beforehand to help kickstart your salivary glands. The mint might also help take the edge off the taste when the wad hits your buds.

Teeth Some women wrap their lips over their teeth when giving a blow job, given how the mere hint of teeth on the penis scares the tar out of some men. However, a set of sexy choppers can sometimes feel erotic, assuming the girl's not in a pit-bull kind of mood. Ask, experiment and see what you come up with.

Little Kisses & Flickering Tongues Never hesitate to lavish your man's genitals or any other part of his body with little flicks of the tongue or sweet little lip-locks. The kisses not only feel nice, but allow you to rest your jaw without having to yell "Intermission!" It usually works better if the area you are flicking your tongue over is already lubricated with saliva or massage oil, so get it good and wet first.

Twisting Your Head Twisting your head when going up and down the penis (in a corkscrew pattern) provides a higher level of stimulation, especially when focused on the upper half of the penis.

Twisting-Corkscrew Action (for the experienced) While on the upstroke, wait until you are halfway up the shaft and put the tip of your tongue under the ridge of the penis head. Not only does your tongue press against the sensitive frenulum while your head is twisting, but the tip of your tongue adds extra stimulation to the sensitive ridge below the glans.

A Shirley Temple You can lick the penis with the pointed end of your tongue, or you can soften your tongue and give it a long flat lick that covers more real estate. The latter is called a "Shirley Temple" because it's similar to the way a person licks a big lollipop.

Partners Who Aren't Circumcised #1 Without retracting his foreskin, stick the tip of your tongue inside his foreskin and run it in a circle around the head of his penis. You can hold the foreskin up with your fingertips as your tongue does circles between it and the glans.

Partners Who Aren't Circumcised #2 By varying the level of vacuum in your mouth, see if you can make the foreskin come up and down as you bob your head.

The Long Lick Mother nature left a seam on the penis that runs from just below the head to halfway down the scrotum. Never hesitate to take a long, wet lick from beneath your partner's testicles all the way to the tip of his penis, along the length of the seam.

Making the Foreskin Taut Using your hand to pull the skin taut over the shaft of the penis can sometimes enhance the pleasure of a blow job. It might also encourage the man to come sooner if that's what you want. Wrap your thumb and forefinger around the shaft of the penis an inch or so above the base. Then pull it down to the base. This makes the skin tighter on the penis and usually increases the sensitivity in the upper part of the penis. If he isn't circumcised, you may need to start higher up the shaft before pulling the foreskin down.

Pumping the Shaft While your lips are focusing on the upper part of the penis, there's no reason why you can't be pumping the bottom part of the shaft with your hand or fingers. Let your saliva flow down the shaft, lubricating both it and your hand, and start pumping. Some women synchronize the shaft pumping with their head bobbing, so their hand follows just beneath their lips at all times.

The Vacuum (Hoover Fellatis) Some men will like it if you draw a light vacuum with your mouth. One way to draw a vacuum is to take as much of the penis in your mouth as feels comfortable, make a seal around the shaft with your lips and suck some of the air out of your mouth. Then, as you pull your head back, a vacuum is created.

Na-Na-Na-Nipples Some guys have nipples that are highly sensitive. Caressing them with your finger while doing oral sex might add to the man's overall pleasure. The best way to find out is to experiment and seek feedback.

Inner Thighs and Other Places The inner thighs of both men and women can be extremely sensitive. There's no reason why you can't alternate a blow job with licking and sucking on your man's inner thighs, or caress them with a free hand.

Fingers in His Mouth When you are blowing him, you might try sticking your fingers in his mouth. Some guys will find this added touch to be very erotic.

Perineum (between the Testicles and Rear End) There is an area behind the testicles called the perineum that is often overlooked but has the potential for good feelings. Licking this area can light some men up. A gentle finger massage down here can also add an extra dimension to oral sex.

The Blow Hole You know the little slit in the head of the penis where the ejaculate comes out? It might be fun to explore it with the tip of your tongue.

Rear End Some men find that a finger on or up the anus when receiving a blow job can be enough to make the cannon fire. Some men claim that the most intense orgasms they have ever had occurred when a woman was giving them oral sex while putting a little pressure on their prostate. Other men hate this sort of thing. Also, a small vibrator up the rear might catch some men's attention, and some couples enjoy rimming (oral-anal contact).

Visual Assist There are plenty of men who enjoy watching a woman give them head. Some women might be offended by the notion, thinking that this has something to do with submission. The chances are that the man is way too appreciative to be thinking about gender issues when you are giving him a blow job. In her video on how to give blow jobs, porn star Nina Hartley comments, "It took me a long time to be able to do a blow job in the light and not get embarrassed." She apparently got over it.

Oral Intermission If your mouth gets tired, do him by hand for a while, or run your hair over his genitals. Or if you feel like playing with yourself, let him watch you do that. Some women say that they give their best blow jobs when they are just as turned on as their partners. Don't be afraid to let him know about it if you are. It may help speed things up.

Tap & Hum It might enhance the feeling of a blow job if you occasionally hum or tap the shaft of the penis when the head and frenulum are in your mouth.

Hot, Cold, Etc. Don't hesitate to suck on ice cubes to make your mouth cold, or drink hot liquids to make it extra-warm before and during oral sex. The same applies to licking nipples.

Going Down after Intercourse Some women enjoy giving blow jobs after intercourse. They find it highly erotic to suck on a penis after it has been inside of them.

A Little Help from Your Friends If you have a friend who is more experienced at giving blow jobs, consider asking her (or him) for pointers, but keep in mind that you will soon be evolving your own personal style. What you do will also vary depending on the guy you are doing it with and whether the friend you are asking used to sleep with him.

Oral Sex with Men of Size, And We're Not Talking a Big Belly

Oral sex may be problematic if your man's salami is on the enormous side. Never fear. The illustration on the following page shows how you can still lick and kiss it into submission. Use your hands to pump the shaft while focusing your efforts on the frenulum and head. Also, the chapter "Techno Breasts & Weenie Angst" lists a number of tips for having sex with the extra-well-endowed.

Cojones

What you do with your hands sometimes separates the good blow jobs from the great. Better blow jobs often include lots of finger and hand work. For instance, at the same time that your mouth is on his penis, consider caressing your partner's testicles. Also, there might be places along the lower shaft of the penis—the part that is covered by the testicles—that respond nicely to fingertip massage. Massaging this area with your free hand when giving a blow job can substantially increase the sensation. Make hand play an active part of the blow job, and he's not as likely to notice when your mouth needs a rest.

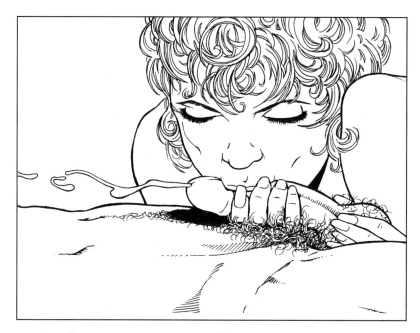

An Effective Way To Get Him Off Orally Without Swallowing

This feels so good that a lot of guys won't be able to tell that you aren't swallowing unless they are actually looking. The trick is to focus your lip action on the sensitive frenulum area while cradling the penis with your hand. This area is just beneath the head of the penis. Use lots of saliva and put plenty of tongue into it—almost like you are French kissing this part of his penis. Occasionally fill your hand with your hot steamy breath. This also works well if your lover's penis is a little on the huge side and you'd more easily fit a zeppelin in a one-car garage than get it in your mouth.

Two Balls, One Tongue

"I love my boyfriend's testicles. I like taking them into my mouth one at a time and sucking on them. The skin on the sack is really soft and feels great in my mouth."   *female age 23*

Some men will feel highly appreciative if you take one or both of their testicles in your mouth. Don't fear doing this. Just go slowly the first couple of times until you get the hang of it. The skin around the testicles (scrotum) also loves being licked and kissed. The sensitivity of the scrotum has been compared to the lips of a woman's genitals. If he doesn't have an erection, you might be able to fit his testicles in your mouth as well as his penis.

Right before He Comes

There might be certain things that you can do just before a man starts to come that will increase his pleasure. Some women wrap a hand around the bottom part of the penis so the entire shaft feels like it's inside a vagina. Others place their fingertips along the seam on the front side of the penis and apply a bit of pressure. They might be able to feel the ejaculate surge through the penis when they do this. Some men might appreciate it if you increased the vacuum in your mouth as they are about to come. Others enjoy it if you hold or caress their testicles or massage the part of the shaft that's beneath them. Since this is a highly individual matter, let him know that you would like to experiment with a couple of new things and seek his feedback.

An extremely intelligent and highly experienced prostitute who consulted on this chapter said she finds that many men like to have their nipples pinched as they are about to come.

Learn When He's Coming

If you know the right signs to look for, you can often learn when your man is about to come. This will give you options if you don't want to swallow.

Until you learn his body's signs, ask him to tell you when he's about to ejaculate. You might notice that his penis starts to swell and contort just before it spurts. You can feel this in your mouth. A hand over the testicles may be a good source of information, as they tend to draw closer to his body when he is about to squirt. Also, his body might tighten up or his hips might give a thrust when coming is inevitable.

If You Don't Like the Way He Tastes

If you know you're not going to swallow, keep a hand around the base of his penis while you are sucking on the upper half. As the signs of ejaculation present themselves, free your mouth from the line of fire, slide your hand up the shaft, to just below the head, and start pumping for Old Glory. Be sure your grip is firm and pump fast and furious. This is no time for a gentle touch.

Here are some other suggestions that you might find helpful:

Toothpaste or Mints Sticking a bit of toothpaste in your mouth before inserting a penis can improve the taste greatly. The same is true for sucking on a mint beforehand. The flavor of blow jobs can also be enhanced by sipping on your favorite sherry or liquor, or by glazing your man's yam with things like honey, jam or whipped cream. Champagne blow jobs can also be fun. While you might enjoy experimenting with minty liquors such as creme de menthe, do a small test patch on the side of the penis beforehand. While a little menthol on the skin can feel great, especially when you blow on it, too much can burn. It takes a few minutes for the full intensity of the burn to peak, so wait awhile before declaring your test a success.

Slobber and Punt When Old Faithful is about ready to blow, start to mobilize a pool of slobber in your mouth. When he comes, let the floodgates loose. The saliva will help thin the ejaculate, making it run out of your mouth faster. And for heaven's sake, don't worry about the mess. The more goo and slime running down the shaft, the better.

To the Rear If you are going to swallow but want to decrease the taste, place his penis as far back in your mouth as you can while still being comfortable. Then start swallowing fast. Unless he comes in buckets, it should decrease the amount of ejaculate that hits your taste buds.

Sublingual Ejaculation This tip is in the excellent book "Tricks— 125 Ways to Make Good Sex Better" by Jay Wiseman. When it feels like a man is close to coming, put your tongue over the head of his penis. He won't know the difference, but the first splash will hit the underside of your tongue where there aren't any taste buds.

Let Him Help Some guys won't mind finishing themselves off with their own hand if you have taken the time and energy to give them a really good blow job. It might be a special treat if you kiss or suck on their testicles while they pump themselves to orgasm.

Putting a Condom on with Your Lips

A competent prostitute can slip a condom over a man's penis with her mouth alone and he will never know it is there. This suggests that the problems some guys have with wearing condoms might be psychological. (So what else is new?)

In her book *The Ultimate Guide To Fellatio* (Cleis, 2002), Violet Blue suggests that you wet your lips and put the unrolled condom up to your mouth. Pull just enough vacuum to suck the reservoir tip into your mouth a bit. This should hold the rest of the condom, which is still rolled up, against your lips. Bend over the penis and pop the unrolled part over the head. Then walk the unrolled part down the shaft either with your lips or fingers. You might want to practice once or twice alone before embarrassing yourself in front of anyone else.

A key to all of this is getting non-lubricated condoms. Condom lube tastes absolutely awful, as do spermicides. Some condom brands to consider for oral sex include the *Durex Natural Feeling Non-Lubricated,* the *Trojan Regular Non Lube* (no reservoir tip, either!) and the *Trustex Flavored Condom.* As of press time, the word on flavored condoms is that they were pretty dreadful except for the *Trustex,* although some people will beg to differ. Either way, the flavor is just coated on and goes away fairly soon.

Other Approaches for Condom Balkers

Here are two approaches to consider if you want a man to use a condom while blowing him but he balks.

1. In a loud and clear voice, say, "Forget it, Charlie! If you think it tastes THAT great, suck on it yourself." Actually, he probably would if he could, and has maybe even tried a couple of times.

2. Try making the whole process of oral sex more fun and pleasurable for both of you. If he knows that the blow job is going to be lots of fun, putting a condom on won't be such a big deal. You might hock a small wad of spit on the head of a man's penis right before bagging it with a condom. Or if you are really prepared, use a drop or two of water-based lube. Once you have rolled the condom over his penis, squish the lube around the entire head.

During and after He Comes

This may sound like it's being too picky, but there are two things that happen in rapid sequence: while he is coming and after he comes. If you keep his penis in your mouth while he is coming, find out what he wants you to do while he's in the process of ejaculating. And then try to get a sense of how soon after that the head of his penis starts to get extra sensitive. After orgasm, the head of the penis can become painfully sensitive. What you were doing before he came might have felt great, but actually hurts after. Does he want you to keep his penis in your mouth, but to slow the action way down? Or maybe he's got calluses on the thing and wants you to keep going as if nothing happened. Another option is to keep the penis in your mouth, but to stop the sucking action and instead pump the shaft with your hand.

The only way to learn this is from experience and plenty of helpful feedback on his part.

What If He Doesn't Come?

This is a situation where one woman's blessing is another woman's curse. Some guys don't come from oral sex no matter how great your blow job. If that's the case, you and he will need to settle on how long the blow job should last.

Pre-Cum Jitters

Some people who are giving oral sex experience a brief paralysis or mini-dread right before the thing ejaculates. If this keeps happening, try to talk to your partner about it. Maybe he can give you plenty of warning before he's going to come so you can stop sucking and start pumping by hand. Or maybe it will help to put a condom on his penis while giving blow jobs, or perhaps you can switch into the position in the illustration a few pages ago, where you bring him off with your lips but the wad doesn't go in your mouth. With time and experience, it's likely any dread will go away.

Hands on Your Head

Men will often put their hands on a woman's head when she is giving oral sex. For most guys, this is a loving gesture which can also be used to let a partner know what feels good and what doesn't. However, some men will put their hands on a woman's head in an attempt to forcibly push it down onto the penis. This is rude and you need to tell him to stop.

Counterpoint: One woman says, "It can be particularly exciting, when a man pushes my head down on his penis. But I would never have sex with a man who I didn't love going down on. Also, you make a joke out of it when a woman grabs a man's head and pulls it into her crotch [next chapter under "Feeling Like a Crash-Test Dummie"] but call it assault when a man does this to a woman. You present a double standard that says we women are either more fragile than men or more easily offended when it comes to sex."

Research Findings

One of the more interesting research findings of all time is in an article about the hazards of oral sex. It was written by a group of dentists and published in a medical journal (Bellizi, Krakow and Plack, *Military Medicine* 145 (1980):787—honest, his name is Dr. Plack and he's a dentist). The article is titled "Soft Palate Trauma Associated with Fellatio."

The article tells about the daughter of an officer who was taken to the base hospital because she discovered a black-and-blue blotch in the back of her mouth. Several dentists eventually converged on the mystery blotch, trying to discover its origin. After eliminating all other possibilities, the dentists finally asked the officer dad to leave the room and then popped the big question: "Gotta boyfriend?"

In the back of the mouth near where the tonsils hang is a highly vascularized mass of tissue (highly vascularized means lots of small blood vessels). An erect penis hitting against this rather sensitive tissue can cause a bruise.

This isn't a common injury. It goes away like any other bruise, but it is a reminder that the woman, and not the man, should control the level of movement during a blow job. For instance, it's fine if she wants a lover to thrust in and out of her mouth, but the choice needs to be hers.

Ejaculate-Related Sinus Infections

When some women give blow jobs, they like to create a slight to moderate vacuum around their lover's penis. Men who enjoy this kind of sensation find it to be heavenly. However, a problem can occur when a man comes with the head of his penis in the back part of a woman's vacuum-pulling mouth. Apparently, the vacuum can sometimes draw ejaculate up into the woman's sinus cavities, creating what might be a cum-related sinus infection. If this is the case, the woman and her partner need to work on keeping the head of his penis in the middle part of her mouth when he is coming. Another solution, of course, is for him to wear a condom.

Lasting Shorter (as Opposed to Lasting Longer)

"Why is it when you are giving men head, they take forever to come, but are so much faster when having intercourse?"

female age 29

During vaginal intercourse, most guys make an effort to last as long as their partners want, sometimes successfully. While this might be a noble gesture during intercourse, it is not appreciated nearly as much during oral sex. That's because oral sex tends to tucker out the mouth of the giver. So if the purpose of the blow job is to get the man off, he shouldn't try to hold back his climax just to show what a stud he is. On the other hand, some guys love oral sex but can't come from it. The best course of action is to discuss this matter with each other. If the male is one of those lucky guys who can pretty much orgasm at will, he and his partner might devise a signal for when she'd like him to come. For the rest of us, the woman can ease up if we are approaching orgasm too fast, or she can try some of the measures listed on pages 106-108 to speed us up if her jaw is about to drop off.

Do Men Blow Men Better Than Women Blow Men?

In researching different sexual techniques, we have reviewed many videos on sex. Videotapes made by women, many of whom are bisexual or lesbian, are often (although not always) a good source of information. The absolute worst source of information is traditional straight pornography.

It wasn't until this book was nearly finished that we took stock of the fact that no gay male videos had been reviewed—except those on male genital massage. With this in mind, the following question about oral sex was posed:

Is it possible that gay men give better blow jobs than straight women?

Armed with several gay videos and lots of buttered popcorn, this question was examined by a small group of straight men and women, with the men being somewhat uncomfortable and the women being highly curious. The videos themselves caused a few unanticipated comments.

Most of the actors in the gay videos were exceptionally good-looking and appeared totally straight. At the very least, these men were far more buff, attractive, and likable than many of the actors in traditional straight porn movies. Upon making these discoveries, one female reviewer exclaimed, "It's a straight woman's nightmare: five naked men who are physical gods and I couldn't get one of them to look at me if his life depended on it!" Another woman viewer stated: "It's one of the few times in my life when I wish I had a penis. I'd let that cute blond guy with the dimples suck on it all night long."

As for conclusions, it seemed that these men handled each other's bodies with a kind of skill and effectiveness that some straight women might do well to imitate. The one technical difference was that the gay men used their hands more than most women do when giving blow jobs. However, the real difference in doing oral sex wasn't so much in technique but in intensity. It's difficult to put into words, but viewers had the feeling that the gay males (or gay male actors, anyway) seemed to form an intense relationship with the penis itself. No matter how much they might enjoy doing oral sex, few women make an emotional connection with a man's genitals in quite the same way as these gay men appeared to.

Granted, few people who have ever worked with actors consider them to be representative of average people. And this guide's methodology is lacking in scientific rigor, but the conclusion is, yes, it's quite possible that gay men blow men better than women blow men, at least in porn movies.

In turning the question around, it can be asked if women do a better job of giving oral sex to women. The answer? Who knows, although one female reader who is bisexual was kind enough to offer the following comment:

> "Having received oral sex from many men and women, I believe women's superiority at this activity is mostly myth."

An Oral-Sex Postscript over at the Beta House

Let's say a very straight, homophobic college fraternity man who prides himself on his conquests with women has just volunteered to take part in an experiment on sexual response. The researchers put EKG leads on his chest, blindfold him, restrain his hands and inform him that he is going to receive a blow job from "a very sexy blond." After receiving the blow job, he responds that she seemed to know more about how to please him orally than any sorority girl he's ever dated, and pleads for "her" phone number. The researchers then inform him that the sexy blond is a male who starred in one of the previously mentioned gay videos. As they show him a tape of this sexy blond doing him, the identity meltdown begins. Suddenly, our fraternity brother's enthusiasm isn't quite the same and he's not sure if the blow job was all that exceptional. More importantly, if this subject had been told the true identity of the sexy blond ringer before receiving the blow job, it is likely that he wouldn't have been able to get an erection or ejaculate.

In this hypothetical experiment, our subject's pleasure was determined as much by his fantasy of who was giving the blow job as the reality of it, assuming the blow job was competently done. MORAL: Never underestimate the role of the human mind in determining what does and doesn't work sexually.

Things a Guy Can Do to Help a Woman Who Is Trying to Give Him Oral Sex

Reread the sections about bruising, gagging and not lasting as long. Also try reading this chapter with your partner. The keys to a really good blow job are being willing to explore and give each other feedback.

Keep in mind that most women won't go down on guys who smell rank. Whether you are going out on a first date or have been married for twenty years, here are a few things to keep in mind: #1: Shower at least once a day, unless you are seriously into grunge or are a holdover from the court of Louis XIII, in which case bathing is irrelevant. #2: Don't wear the same socks or underwear for more than one day without washing them. If everyone including the dog and cat runs out of the room when you take your shoes off, use foot powder or spray. #3: While not particularly popular with the organic crowd, deodorant can be a wonderful thing. #4: Brush and floss your teeth often.

#5: Cut your fingernails and toenails often. #6: If you wear cologne, ask your partner or a woman friend how she likes the smell of it, as well as how much you should use. Maybe she will prefer you without cologne. Some guys smell great from just bathing alone. On the other hand, she might like you marinated with a bit of citrus or spice.

Pube Tug Tug on your pubic hair ahead of time so you'll pull out the strays that might end up in her mouth. It's now the height of straight male fashion to trim pubic hair as well. A few years ago this would have been considered weird.

Arrogance Don't assume that a woman automatically wants to suck on your penis just because it's there. (How would you like to suck some guy's dick?) Never take blow jobs for granted, and be thankful whenever you get one, even if your partner loves doing it. Tell her how good it feels. Also, it never hurts to ask yourself, "What have I done lately to deserve a blow job?" Did you give your partner a long lingering body massage? Did you help her with a project she's been struggling with? Did you do more than your share of the housework? Did you respond kindly in a situation where most men would have been jerks? Are you a loving partner and good friend?

Talk Oral sex requires a doer who is willing to accept helpful feedback and a receiver who is willing to give it. If words don't come easy, pick up a book like Violet Blue's *Ultimate Guide To Fellatio* and go through it together.

Mutuality Never, ever cop an attitude such as "My last girlfriend blew me really well. Why can't you?" There are reasons why you aren't with your last girlfriend. With enough mutual caring, love and experimentation, the chances are good that you will soon be receiving oral sex, but don't expect it to happen magically.

The Deep Throat Fantasy Ever since the *Deep Throat* movie, some men have been hyped up over the notion of having a woman do a sword-swallowing act with their penis. Get over it. A throat is not a vagina, and any extra thrills you might get from this are mostly psychological. Besides, why would you encourage your partner to do something that might trigger a natural gagging reflex? And if she gags on your penis, do you really think she's going to be excited about putting it in her mouth again?

He Who Gives, Gets A fine way to get great oral sex is to give great oral sex. This assumes that the rest of your relationship is in good shape. Do not expect that being a great lover will make up for being a selfish person. Some women will overlook bad manners and social lunacy for a good lay, but they have their own emotional problems and will make your life a living hell in other ways.

Asking vs. Not Asking

Every once in a while you might have a horrible day and are totally frazzled and in desperate need of a blow job lest you decompensate even further and have to be hauled off to the loony bin. If you don't abuse the privilege and have a loving partner who hasn't had an equally hideous day or week, she will usually do the mercy blow job even if she's not particularly into it. For this type of situation, it is fine to ask or beg for a blow job. However, in the course of normal lovemaking, it might not be such a good idea to routinely ask for oral sex. That's because some women don't take well to being pestered for blow jobs. Granted, they might love blowing you and will do so often, but only if it's on their own initiative. Of course, there are other women who are just fine with being asked.

Improving the Way Your Ejaculate Tastes

Some people claim that vegetarians, both male and female, taste better than their carnivore brethren, e. g., red meat makes men taste strongly and dairy products make ejaculate taste bad, but not nearly as bad as asparagus. However, it is likely that this is mere propaganda from the cows and chickens, or even the vegetarians. Also, smoking and/or drinking coffee might cause a guy's ejaculate to taste strong or bitter. Perhaps Starbucks can formulate a new blend of beans and call it "Ejaculate Lite" or "Sweet Wad." Regardless of their impact on the taste of semen, the combination of smoking and drinking coffee makes for bad-smelling breath.

One woman said that her partner's ejaculate tasted good unless he was under a lot of stress at work. Then it would start tasting bad.

One common suggestion for improving the taste of male ejaculate is to eat celery or fruit each day, especially pineapple and apples. The sugar in the fruit is supposed to give a guy's ejaculate a sweet edge. Perhaps this is useless folklore. However, if this is what a partner requested before doing more blow jobs, most guys would go to work each morning munching on stalks of celery and finishing their lunches with slices of fruit. Either way, if your partner is willing to be the taster, why not experiment with different combinations of food? Does ingesting a little cinnamon make a difference in the way you taste? What happens if you drink less coffee or eat less broccoli or garlic?

If your partner says that your ejaculate is really bitter, consider seeing a urologist to screen out the possibility of an infection in your prostate or glands down under. Although you might not be feeling any pain, it's still possible to have an infection. Unfortunately, in this day and age of HMOs, you will probably need to see a family physician or internist first, and it might be embarrassed saying, "Heather says my cum tastes bitter." Urologists, on the other hand, see genitals all day long, and it's usually easier to say something like that to them. In either case, rather than telling the receptionist or nurse the exact reason for the appointment, you might say that you'd like to rule out a prostate or urinary tract infection. Then tell the physician the real reason once you see him or her in private. And under no circumstances should you take antibiotics unless tests have been done and they show a problem. Antibiotics are not breath mints for the prostate gland.

Readers' Comments

"I am certain that women would give more blow jobs if they didn't feel like they had to swallow." *female age 43*

"Cum is not a gourmet treat, but not unpleasant either. I'd rather be eating mocha chip ice cream, but getting there isn't half as much fun. My partner's orgasm is often a total turn-on for me, and occasionally just a relief that the blow job is now over with." *female age 47*

"I don't find oral sex repulsive in the least if he is conscious of good hygiene. If he smells bad down there, it's a turn-off for me." *female age 34*

"I swear by pineapple; it helps take the bitter taste away." *f. 24*

"It feels funny when he squirts in my mouth. His cum often gives me an upset stomach so I usually spit it out." *female 23*

"If I'm in the mood it's really sensual. If I'm not it's like a job."
female age 43

"It is a major power trip for me if he comes in my mouth. I like knowing I have the ability to take this big strong man and turn him into a sack of Jello." *female age 37*

"It is great. I like running my tongue around the head and sliding it in and out of my mouth. I like to take his penis in my mouth as far as possible and rub my tongue on the underside of it, pushing the head into the roof of my mouth. It seems to drive him crazy." *female age 37*

"More than anything it feels so good because I am in control."
female age 23

"When it comes to blow jobs, let the lucky son of a bitch treat you like a queen, honey, because you are." *female age 48*

"I have to open my mouth wider than normal and it gets tired pretty fast. I don't really like it much, but he loves having it, so it makes me feel really good and loved to be giving him oral sex." *female age 32*

"I never was very good at blow jobs until I had a lover who had a small penis. Then I felt comfortable with him in my mouth."
female age 45

"I like to give head, so I don't need much persuasion. I get really wet from giving someone that kind of pleasure, and I always feel so powerful when I do it." *female age 23*

"It feels very sensual if he lets me take it at my own pace. I think the penis has the most wonderful velvety skin." *f. 38*

"I only like it if I can keep the hair out of my mouth. I enjoy it only because I know he enjoys it so much." *female age 35*

"I like it. I especially like the little leaks before he comes; it gets me excited to know he is so excited. I think cum has an interesting taste, sort of fizzy." *female age 38*

"I have discovered that we both find it erotic to have him come on my face or on my breasts when I give him head. I don't care for the taste of his semen." *female age 22*

"I find it helpful to open my mouth a bit when he's coming, then swallow quickly." *female age 26*

"I really don't like it when he comes in my mouth. I kind of gag on it." *female age 26*

"I used to tell my partner that I was semen-intolerant." *f. 26*

"It's okay as long as I can spit it out. I don't like to swallow." *f. 43*

"It's fun to take a limp penis, put it in your mouth and suck on it until it hardens." *female age 37*

"One thing that's really neat about sucking on a guy's cock is watching it change shape and color and get harder as it get's more aroused. You're right up there in the front row. You don't get that with intercourse." *female age 42*

"I've observed that not all guys come as much; some have very little, and others lots and lots." *female age 27*

"Never forget to caress and tickle the balls." *female age 44*

"Usually it's very erotic and sexy, especially if I'm particularly in the mood to suck him. Sometimes, rarely, it feels too much, invasive." *female age 48*

"My lover likes to hold my head and slowly slide in and out of my mouth. I trust him to do that without going too deep or choking me." *female age 37*

"My mouth and hand work as a team. As I pull away with my mouth, I twist my hand almost like a corkscrew." *female 26*

For Men from Female Readers

"Be very clean. Feel free to moan when you feel pleasure. Speak up if there is something I am missing." *female age 30*

"Keep your genital area clean and pleasant smelling." *fem. 34*

"Tell me what you like. If you want to grip the shaft or caress your testicles while I am sucking, go ahead and do so." *fem. 37*

"I love to give head, but I hate to feel pressured into doing it. Also, remember what goes around comes around. If I'm the only one going down, I'll be less likely to do so again." *fem. 26*

For Women from Male Readers

"Please don't do it like they do in the porno flicks, where the girl just about bobs her head off. Not a turn-on." *male 46*

"Don't be fooled by the name. Blowing has nothing to do with it." *male age 26*

Oral Sex: Vulvas & Honey Pots
Chapter 23

Having powerful feelings for a woman can leave some men with an insatiable need to kiss and lick her genitals. It's hard to explain why, but it's a primal need that can be triggered by a mere wink of her eye. Other men are happy to give a woman oral sex because it pleases her sexually, but aren't really into it. And some men would rather lick a cat.

Whatever your preference, this chapter is loaded with tips and techniques for giving a woman all of the oral pleasure her heart and thighs could possibly desire.

What's the Thing about Oral Sex These Days?

Whether it's giving a guy a blowjob or going down on a woman, it's hard to understand what *oral sex* means these days. For instance, some people give oral sex because they think they should and not because they'd die tomorrow from sadness if they missed the opportunity. Some people give it to avoid closeness, while others give it because they truly love the other person and it's a way of increasing their sense of intimacy. Two people might be intensely in love with each other but not enjoy oral sex, while another couple might barely be friends but are the oral-sex version of the Flying Walendas.

So while our oral sex chapters are pretty enthusiastic about the subject, so is our anal sex chapter but we'd be seriously twisted to say your relationship is in trouble if you don't enjoy taking it up the butt. The same is true about whether you like giving or receiving oral sex. Please don't view this Guide's enthusiasm as any kind of "should" or "shouldn't." You need to decide what works best for you in your private relationships without society telling you what to do.

The one thing we will say is that oral sex is just as much "sex" as intercourse, hand jobs or anal sex. Just because you decide to share it in a disembodied way (e.g. it's not really meaningful for you) doesn't mean it's any less sex than anything else you do when yours or someone else's pants are down.

Talking to Elvis from between Your Sweetheart's Thighs

It's a funny thing about oral sex, at least when you are a guy on the giving end. The woman whom you are giving oral sex to, a person whom you know and often love, sometimes just disappears. All that's left is a strange, twitching, moaning protoplasm which only partially resembles the person who was there just minutes ago. You are left virtually alone, with your tongue feeling like it's running the Boston Marathon. You might as well be talking to Elvis. After it's over, you might want to ask, "Hey, where did you go?" but you learn not to because she'll usually just give you a big smile and want to curl up in your arms.

A female reader offers a possible explanation. She says that when she is receiving oral sex, she isn't as aware of her partner's presence, so it's easier to let her fantasies run wild. She wouldn't necessarily want to tell him "where she went," since her fantasy might have been with someone else. Little does she know, guys who are sexually secure might get off on hearing about her fantasy escapades, even if they are with someone else.

The Way Women Taste

The previous chapter on blow jobs begins with a discussion of how guys taste. This chapter turns the tables and talks about the way women taste.

Most guys who enjoy going down on women know that some vulvas taste great, while others don't leave fond memories. Beyond that, men are fairly useless when it comes to discussing genital taste. Lesbian and bisexual women, however, will talk your ear off about the subject of how women taste. Their comments follow. But first, a brief discussion about female genital chemistry.

While most of the skin on the human body has a pH between 6.0 and 7.0, the optimal pH of the vulva and vagina is between 4.0 and 5.5. Vaginal secretions contain lactic acid, which helps maintain the lower pH.

A lower pH helps eliminate unfriendly bacteria which can cause anything from a rank odor to vaginal infections. Unfortunately, most body soap has a pH of between 6.0 and 14. This can raise the pH of the vulva and may challenge nature's system for eliminating unfriendly

bacteria. It might be why women who bathe more than once a day tend to get more vaginal infections.

Fortunately, there are now low-pH soaps with lactic acid that are made especially for women's genitals. They contain none of the artificial deodorants or scents that are in some products that go between a woman's legs. One woman who has been using the soap for almost a year says that it allows her genitals to stay fresh for a full twenty-four hours. Another says she no longer hesitates to let her husband go down on her twelve hours after her last shower. Physicians especially recommend this soap for women who have frequent infections.

These soaps are mainly being sold in France, Italy, Switzerland, and Ireland. Gynecologists in those countries can't agree on exactly which pH is optimal, so the soap is made with a slightly different pH in each country. (The fights in the gynecological journals must be interesting, with the Italians claiming to have invented love, the French claiming to have perfected it, the Irish raising a glass to it and the Swiss declaring neutrality on the matter.) One reader who started using a low-pH soap for her Canadian crotch now uses it from head to toe. She says it's helped to cure her dry skin!

There are low-pH soaps that North American women can find: Nature's Plus Natural Beauty Cleansing Bar (800) 937-0500, Sebamed Liquid Face and Body Wash (877) 732-2633 sebamed-in-canada.com, and www.herbalremedies.com. None are just for crotches, but some readers have tried them and would swear by them if they weren't so busy receiving oral sex.

Soaps aside, here are a few comments that bisexual women and lesbians had to say about the taste of their female lovers:

"One woman who I loved going down on suddenly began tasting different—not nearly as good. As it turned out, she had started taking vitamin pills. It was never a problem if she took herbs, but vitamin pills would ruin the way she tasted."

"A former girlfriend was a tennis pro. Sometimes she would play tennis for a few hours and I could go down on her without her taking a shower and she would still taste sweet. There are other women whom I have gone down on right after we showered, and they still didn't taste good. In making my own inquiries, I found that the sweeter tasting women didn't eat red meat."

"I watch my diet carefully, but I have to admit, the sweetest, best-tasting lover I ever had was a meat-eating, beer-drinking dietary disaster."

So much for consensus. Finally, a thought from the cleanest lesbian in all of Hackensack, New Jersey:

"Some women spend more time filing their toenails than they do taking care of their pussies. When I'm in the shower, I always separate the lips of my vulva and use a wash cloth to clean between them. I'm also careful about little bad-tasting pieces of gunk that might collect under my clitoral hood. These are what uncircumcised males get under their foreskin if they don't pull it back and clean it."

A Q-tip dipped in mineral oil works well to get rid of any "little pieces of gunk" that stick under the clitoral hood. As for how you taste and what to do about it, aside from perhaps trying a low pH soap, keep in mind the following tip from a bisexual woman from South Bend, Indiana: "A crotch in a spandex leotard is an unhappy crotch; nature meant for it to breathe." Nature also meant for it to get love, and that's what the rest of this chapter is about.

**Talking With Tongues—Suggestions for
Pleasing a Woman with Your Mouth**

According to some women, a smart and loving tongue between their legs can offer feelings of pleasure that fingers or a penis simply can't. Yet many a male merely pushes his face into a woman's crotch, sticks his tongue out like when the doctor asks you to say "ahhh" and wags away. What follows are suggestions to help cure a chronic case of tongue wagging.

On the Tip of Your Tongue

The human tongue, like the penis, can be made hard or soft. To understand the difference between a soft and a hard tongue, spend a few minutes licking the palm of your hand. This may not be as much fun as when Lulu Belle sits on your face, but a moment's practice on the palm of your hand can be a good way to learn about subtle variations in oral-sex technique.

First, if you've just been installing a new head gasket or fertilizing the lawn, it might be a good idea to wash your hands. Then, pretend your palm is a woman's vulva and give it a good licking.

Notice how quickly the end of your tongue goes dry. So much for the fantasy that the human tongue is automatically wet. A dry tongue creates drag or friction. Nature did not create the clitoris with a high tolerance for friction. In fact, nature did not create the clitoris with any tolerance for friction. None. Nada.

This is why you'll need to coat your tongue with saliva before licking a woman's private parts. Not so much that you drool, but enough to blow a good-sized bubble. After a few minutes, saliva from your mouth will automatically run down your tongue and keep everything well-lubricated, but not at the start.

Try licking your hand again. You may find that your tongue is somewhat taut with the tip hard and pointed. Try to let it go soft, in a way that would cause you to slur your words if you were attempting to speak. You may need to push your hand closer to your face, since a soft tongue is not as long as a hard tongue. Some women will prefer a softer, more rounded tongue when you are licking the underbelly of the clitoris, given how it isn't insulated by the clitoral hood. A harder, more pointed tongue can be a fine choice when licking the side of the clitoris or clitoral shaft, as these are protected by the clitoral hood and your tongue won't be making direct contact with the clitoris.

This may all sound like French if you have yet to go down on a woman. Not to worry; no matter how experienced you might be, she will still need to teach you where and how she wants you to lick. This can take weeks, months or years. Also, it's normal to feel clumsy when you are with a new lover or if you haven't done oral sex in a while.

The Initial Approach—Getting There

> "Gentle teasing brings me to an orgasm. I like him to start off gently, with light licks and kisses all over my vulva. I can't take too much pressure on my clitoris, though, and sometimes that ruins it for me."   *female age 23*

When you are shooting a free throw, you don't want to hit the rim. When you are landing a plane, you don't want to brush the treetops. When you are going down on a woman, it's an entirely different story. The best approach to a woman's genitals is anything but direct.

Once you've been with a woman for a while, you'll discover what body parts she likes to have licked. For instance, one woman might love it when you kiss her inner thighs or rear end, but hate it if you kiss her abdomen. Another woman might want just the opposite. Find the body parts that she likes having kissed, and spend plenty of time on them. Plant occasional kisses on her vulva, but only as a preview of what's to come.

An indirect approach helps assure a warm welcome when your tongue finally drops into your lover's saddle.

Your Goal: Orgasm or Pleasure?

Some men think they haven't pleased a woman unless they have given her an orgasm. That would be fine if sex were football and orgasms were touchdowns, but this kind of philosophy can spoil your love life. Instead of trying to delight your lover's senses, you'll always be playing to her clitoris. This can get tedious.

Of course, there are times when it's important to be single-minded about a woman's orgasm, but not as a rule. You'll do a lot better if you let yourself have fun, be close and want her dearly. If your lips convey this when they are between her thighs, you'll have a leg up on most other men.

Avoiding Beard Burn

When it comes to receiving oral sex, one thing that women often complain about is men's beards. Their advice: grow a full beard or keep your face clean-shaven. Grunge is not good on a woman's thighs.

If you're the kind of guy who grows a five o'clock shadow ten minutes after shaving, find a favorite set of towels and drape one over each of her legs, like mechanics do on the fenders of cars when they are working on the engine.

Three Oral Sex Caveats

Until shown otherwise, do not assume there are any similarities between the way you like your penis sucked and the way your partner likes having her genitals licked.

If your main exposure to oral sex has been through watching porn videos, forget all you have ever seen. Rather than showing the back of a man's head buried between a woman's thighs, the porn industry has invented its own version of oral sex. In porn oral sex, a woman sits with her legs six miles apart while some guy tries to lick her vulva without blocking the camera shot. While this is good for the cameraman, it's not necessarily going to please a lady.

A mediocre lover always knows what a partner wants without having to ask. An accomplished lover is a wise student who implores a partner to give him copious amounts of advice.

Body Positions

There are some oral sex positions that might look great, but don't work as well as others. What follows is a description of oral sex positions where your bodies are both pointing in the same direction. These provide the best face-to-vulva alignment, where your tongue has clear access to the tip and shaft of the clitoris. In this alignment, you will be licking in an upward direction. This gives you the most options, especially if she likes you to retract her clitoral hood once you get to the later innings.

To start with, imagine that you are standing in a swimming pool and the lucky lady is sitting on your shoulders. Only she is turned around so you are staring into her stomach and her feet are dangling over your shoulders, resting on your back. You are getting a mouthful of bathing-suit crotch material, but this beats the heck out of anything you ever learned in Red Cross swimming lessons. Envision yourself falling forward, so she lands on her back and you are on your stomach. You will be staring up at her navel, unless she hasn't been to the gym in about a hundred years, in which case her navel may be resting on the top of your head. One disadvantage of this position is that your head is looking up and this causes your neck to bend backward. This can be uncomfortable after awhile.

For the second oral sex position, which might be more comfortable than the first, go back to the swimming pool and imagine the two of you falling to one side or the other. You land on your sides, except for your head which is between her legs. Your mouth is on her crotch, and her inner thigh becomes a pillow for your head. Your neck doesn't have to bend backward as it does in the first position, since you can move your entire body to form more of a right angle to hers. One disadvantage of this "sides" position is that you don't have the full access and degree of control that you do when her legs are spread apart. So some guys will start off in the first position, when her clit is more sensitive and mouth and tongue control is more critical. Then they ask the woman to roll on her side so they can get into a more comfortable position and keep at it for as long as she likes.

In another oral sex position, she is "sitting on your face." Go back to the swimming pool and imagine you fell straight backward. You end up on your back and she's above you on all fours. The term "sitting on your face" is rife with deception. While it might look as if she is sitting on your face, she shouldn't be. It might feel good to have her in this position over your face, but the human face isn't the most comfortable object to sit on, unless the giver has been taking a lot of steroids and his face is starting to look like a park bench. As an alternative, she might want to stay on all fours, with you propping your head and upper body on a bunch of pillows to give your lips the necessary altitude.

Another good position for giving a girl oral sex is when she is sitting in a chair or on a stool, with you sitting or kneeling between her legs. She'll need to slouch so you don't get a mouthful of chair cushion, oak or leatherette.

There are other positions, like if you were doing 69. In these positions, your head is pointing in the opposite direction from hers and the alignment is not optimal. With time, you may evolve your own variations, but these are excellent no matter how experienced you are.

Pillows to the Rescue

As with any kind of sexual activity, a strategically placed pillow under your partner's bum can provide better access to her genitals. Also, don't hesitate to put a pillow under your head if it makes you more comfortable.

Some vendors such as Libida.com sell a special cushion wedge for help with oral sex called *The Liberator* (www.liberator.com). It is not cheap, but you might want to check it out. If you can't afford it, it is possible you've got something around that might work as well.

Ground Zero

Perhaps you are a total pro at giving oral sex, or maybe you know more about the dark side of the moon than licking a woman's genitals. Regardless of your experience, what follows is a blueprint for giving really good oral sex—as long as you get reliable feedback from the woman you are doing it with.

The tongue can be an abrasive little organ unless it is lubricated. Coat your lips and tongue with extra saliva as you approach your lover's vulva.

Doing oral sex tends to make your salivary glands sing. Instead of swallowing or letting it pool in your mouth, let your slobber flow wherever gravity wants to take it. That way, you're less likely to drown and you won't have to worry as much about pubic hairs wrapping themselves around your tonsils each time you try to swallow. Putting a towel under your sweetheart's rear will help to keep the mattress from turning into a giant sponge. Some women will appreciate it if you push an edge of the towel against the area that's just below their vulva so the saliva doesn't trickle down their butt crack.

When a woman flexes her legs, her pelvis arches forward. This will provide access to give good oral sex. A lot of women will do this themselves by putting their legs over your shoulders, or by planting one or both feet on your shoulders. Some pull their legs up to their chest. The guy can also wrap his arms around the back of the woman's thighs and push them forward.

As a woman becomes more aroused, she might want to change leg position or flex her thighs to help get her off. This could limit your access to her vulva, but if it's what does the trick, so be it.

Some women provide all the oral access a man needs by simply spreading their legs. On the other hand, you may want to separate the outer labia with your fingers. This gives your mouth better access to the inner lips, and can sometimes feel like the difference between kissing a woman whose mouth is open versus one whose lips are closed. Some women will offer a helping hand by separating the lips themselves. This can be highly erotic.

Lavish the outer lips with licks and kisses. Then try running the tip of your tongue up and down the furrows between the outer and inner lips of your lover's vulva.

The mons pubis is the little mound of flesh that sits directly above the labia. It is where the bulk of the pubic hair grows. Some women enjoy it if you rub the mons in a circular pattern. Also, pushing or pulling up the mons while doing oral sex can heighten the intensity for some women.

Some women will enjoy it if you run your fingertips through their pubic hair, and some will particularly enjoy it if you tug lightly on it or nibble gently on the mons.

The inner lips of women's genitals tend to be longer around the vaginal opening. Some are prominent enough to clasp between your fingers and tug upon gently. When a woman is highly aroused, she may enjoy this tremendously. Be sure to ask!

Her Clitoris

"Don't immediately dive into the clitoris and stay there. Warm up by licking all of the vaginal area. Suck on the labia. Then turn your attention to the clitoris. I like my clitoris to be licked, flicked and sucked. Sometimes I get off faster if my partner licks lower on the clitoris, rather than at the top of the hood. It makes for a different kind of orgasm." *female age 25*

No matter how small your penis is, nobody's going to have trouble finding it. No matter how large her clitoris is, nature designed it to play a mean game of hide 'n' seek.

After you kiss and caress the other parts of the vulva, some women will appreciate it if you focus your oral efforts in the vicinity of the clitoris. "Vicinity" might mean simply in the neighborhood, or it might mean knocking on the front door. Here are some landmarks describing different parts of the clitoris.

The shaft of the clitoris runs from the top of the labia to the tip of the clit. It might be anywhere from under a half-inch long to more than an inch. Pushing the labia apart and upwards with your fingertips will help to expose it.

The shaft of the clitoris wears a fleshy little wetsuit called the clitoral hood. This hood is similar to the foreskin on a guy who is not circumcised. It protects the shaft from the rigors of crotch life. Oral sex pros manipulate it to great advantage. With practice, the clitoral hood will be your friend.

The glans or tip of the clitoris is somewhere near the juncture where the clitoral hood splits into two. The tip of the clitoris can range from the size of a pen tip to a small finger, depending on the woman. Its sensitivity has nothing to do with its size. The tip is usually more sensitive to your tongue's caress than the shaft. This is why some women prefer it if you use a softer, more rounded tongue against the clitoral tip. Others will want you to lick with authority.

Sometimes all it takes to expose the tip is a single finger to pull the hood up. Sometimes it takes both hands and a litany of prayer.

To find the tip with your tongue, separate the outer lips with your fingers. Make sure your tongue has plenty of saliva on it for lubrication. Take a long slow lick from the bottom to the top of the vulva where the big lips meet. Somewhere along the way you will most likely feel a small knob or slight protuberance. Find out from your partner if this is the tip of her clitoris. Have her explain to you exactly how she likes it licked.

As your sweetheart becomes more aroused, it is likely that the tip of her clitoris will swell. Some swell predictably; others don't. This process can be challenging until you become more familiar with the way her clitoris changes. With some women, you learn to lick on a specific spot rather than relying on finding her clitoris with your tongue. You simply go on faith and past experience.

You might think that the surest way to arouse a woman would be to start at the tip of the clitoris, since that's where so much of the action seems to be. But this is not the way it usually works. For most women, you don't even approach the clitoris until you have planted plenty of kisses in the surrounding area. Then you might focus on the clitoral shaft, working the hood with your tongue and avoiding the tip. With some women, you never touch the tip at all. Of course, if your lover wants you to start by throwing a liplock on the tip of her clitoris, far be it from this guide to suggest anything different.

Some women enjoy it if you kiss their vulva in the same way that you do their mouth. Some crave a gentle nursing action on the clitoris. Some like it if you flick the tip of your tongue over the clitoris in a sideways direction; others prefer an up-and-down motion as though you were rapidly turning a light switch on and off, and some enjoy a circular motion. These different motions may seem awkward at first, but you will eventually learn to flick your tongue back and forth (or is it hither and yon) with enough grace to humiliate a hummingbird. Also, some women will want you to speed up or change locations as their arousal grows, while others prefer a constant motion.

Your partner might have a favorite side of her clitoris where she wants you to lick. To help improve access to the favored side, she might try flexing one leg while the other lies flat and a bit to the side.

The clitoris sometimes disappears right before orgasm. Who knows why, but it is almost always good news. With helpful input from your partner you will eventually learn how to respond; in the meantime, let The Force guide you. (When a clitoris disappears on you, you might try giving a little suck to pull it back out.)

After learning more about your partner's responses, you might experiment by puckering your lips around her clitoris and making a light vacuum. You can then push the clitoris in and out of your mouth either with your tongue or by reversing the suction every couple of seconds. Tricks like this can be found in Ray Stubbs's book *The Clitoral Kiss* Secret Garden Press, Tucson, Arizona.

Your partner's clitoris or the area around may begin to pulse once she is highly aroused. This is probably an indication to stay your course without any variation in speed, tempo or rhythm. Problems start when you assume that if she's pulsing at this speed, she'll love it even more if you double the tempo or do it harder. WRONG! These pulses happen every second or so and seem to be in direct response to the stimulus of your tongue. If you speed up, you will quickly lose them.

The contractions of orgasm are said to happen every seven-tenths of a second. Some men say that the best way to stimulate a woman's clitoris either by mouth or by hand is to use strokes that last seven-tenths of a second. Good luck making that one work.

Some women prefer to receive different kinds of stimulation depending on the time of the month. For instance, at one point in her menstrual cycle you avoid the tip or glans, but two weeks later you lick the tip silly. It's nothing you're going to learn in a one-night stand, and these changes don't apply for a lot of women.

Body Language Rather than Words

Some women reach a certain threshold of arousal where they can't tell which direction your tongue is moving. All they know is if it feels good or not. Be sure to pay close attention to your partner's body language as your tongue touches her exposed clitoris. If her body suddenly convulses or jolts, you have probably hit the right area but too early or with too much force. It never hurts to retreat and find a safe spot that's protected by plenty of hood. She will usually let you know when she wants more. The ways she might do this include telling you, pulling your head into her body with her hands, or grinding her crotch into your face. Hopefully she won't grab you by the ears, although men's ears make fine rudders for oral sex.

Her Vagina and Beyond

Using terms like "urinary meatus" or "the area around her pee-hole" can cause an aesthetic flat tire. However, the part of a woman's vulva between her clitoris and vagina which contains the urinary meatus is definitely worth exploring with the tip of your tongue. For some women its stimulation might be the difference between good oral sex and great oral sex. If you have aesthetic problems with this notion, think about what your lover dips the tip of her tongue into when she is sucking on the head of your penis. Also keep in mind that urine and the urinary passageway are more sanitary than the human mouth and that kissing her down here is more hygienic than kissing her on the mouth.

The opening of the vagina is in the lower half of a woman's vulva. A man might occasionally be swept away by an urge to stick his tongue far into his lover's vagina. This, of course, is ridiculous unless he has the same gene pool as Lassie. Still, it's a nice thing to do, or want to do. Realistically, your tongue will be able to stimulate the outer edges of your partner's vagina and maybe an inch or two inside of it. This is good, because it's the part of the vagina that responds best to touch. Reaching too far inside a woman's vagina can cause your tongue to get a nasty cramp and probably won't do much for her.

Some women may treasure a finger or two inside the vagina when you are doing oral sex, but usually not until they have reached higher levels of arousal. As for what to do with your fingers once they are inside, you will need to ask. Some women like them to stay perfectly still, while others will enjoy it if you twist, jiggle or thrust your fingers in and out. Also, there might be special spots in her vagina that your partner enjoys having stimulated.

The inner part of a woman's vagina often balloons open when sexually aroused. A number of women enjoy having this filled up. While a man's fingers will usually do the job, some women find that a silicone dildo works better. For some couples, inserting a dildo during oral sex can be a turn-on. Also, a woman might fantasize about having one man's penis inside her vagina at the same time that another man is licking her clitoris. Using a dildo while receiving oral sex can help satisfy this fantasy unless you are actually into threesomes. (There are actually oral sex dildos that strap on a guy's chin!)

One highly athletic advisor to this guide so loved doing oral sex on his women friends in high school and college that he was considered an important resource off the court as well as on. His secret? When a woman was about to have an orgasm, he would gently insert a finger-tip into her rectum. He says this would invariably launch a cascade of pleasure. There is no need to stick your finger in very far; just putting pressure on the rim around a lover's anus might light up thousands of nerve endings whose sole experience to that point has been to endure storms of methane and toilet paper abuse. A variation is to insert a small, well-lubricated plug or vibrator in the woman's rear while doing oral sex. Just don't put this or your finger in her vagina afterward.

You can always go for a triple play: lips on her clitoris, one finger in her vagina and one up her rear.

Some women push a man's head away from their vulva after they begin to come. Other women pull it in tighter. Don't fret if she pushes it away. This will give your tongue a well-earned rest. Also, some women are extremely sensitive after orgasm, when barely breathing on their genitals can feel overwhelming.

If She Starts Bucking

It's not unusual for some women who are receiving oral sex to start bucking their hips with pleasure. This kind of motion can knock a guy off the mound.

While it is important to discuss this with your partner, a response that some women seem to appreciate is as follows: Wrap your arms around her thighs from behind, as in the illustration earlier in this chapter. Put your hands firmly on her hip bones. The female hip bones provide a perfect handle and were clearly put there for this very pur-pose. Flex your arms so that she has to lift the weight of your upper body in order to buck. This shouldn't hurt her at all and will keep her pelvis still enough so you can give her more of what's causing her to buck in the first place.

Fun At The Y — Random Tips & Techniques

Find out if your sweetheart likes you to reach up and play with her breasts or other body parts while you are going down on her. One reader loves her partner to squeeze her toes when she's receiving oral sex—it can be the difference between coming or not for her.

One female reader suggests writing each letter of the alphabet with your tongue on your partner's vulva. Before long, she might start requesting specific letters or whole syllables!

Here's a game suggested in *Ultimate Kiss* by Jacqueline and Steven Franklin. Bring your lover to the edge of orgasm with oral sex and then pull your mouth away for a count of fifty. Then bring her to the edge again and pull your mouth away for twenty-five seconds. Then bring her to the edge and pull your mouth away for ten seconds. Do this once more, pausing for just a few seconds. Be sure to explain this game beforehand so she doesn't become seriously annoyed when you stop for the first fifty-second pause. One female reader suggests that this game can work equally well when masturbating a woman.

Sometimes it is fun to give a woman oral sex when she is still wearing her panties or bikini bottom. Start with your lips on her inner thighs, work them up to her crotch, and then sneak your tongue under the material. Eventually push the material to one side with your tongue, teeth or fingers. This will provide more working room.

Some women might like it if you blow warm moist air through the front panel of their underwear; others won't. But never blow air directly into a woman's vagina.

Consider pulling your lover's panties off with your teeth. But be careful not to leave any holes or rip the material, given how fancy little underthings often cost an arm and a leg; it's best that she not remember you as the one who destroyed her favorite undies.

It is difficult to do oral sex when a woman is standing. The access is too limited. Think nothing of crawling under her dress when she is standing to plant tender kisses in places where other guys only dream of touching, but she'll need to sit or lie down to receive your oral finest.

After she is highly aroused, place the tip of your tongue on the side or bottom of her clitoris. Then push the tip of a small vibrator on the other side of your tongue.

Separate the outer lips with your fingers and lay your tongue flat against her vaginal opening at the lowest part of her vulva. Take a slow, long, wet lick that lasts for about sixty seconds. This way, her clit gets a long, slow protracted licking as your tongue creeps its way up her vulva like a red-hot glacier.

Some women like so many pillows under their rear ends that their entire body is on an incline with their crotches angled up in the air. This provides wonderful access as well as an intriguing view. It may also cause lots of blood to rush into the woman's head.

A more subtle way of making your tongue vibrate is to hum while placing it on your partner's clitoris. A well-hummed aria can push some women into orbit. Others will start laughing hysterically.

On a hot muggy day, ice cubes can always spice up any kind of sex play. Some women enjoy an occasional ice cube in the vagina. If you try this, use small cubes that won't cause frost burn. During the cold of winter, sipping a warm drink before kissing a woman's vulva can leave her with warm and sensual feelings.

Some couples enjoy placing a slice of banana, mango or papaya inside a woman's vagina for the man to retrieve with his tongue. Honey and syrup should be used with caution. While they are fine on nipples and other parts of the body, residual sugar in the vagina might inspire its resident yeast cells to procreate with painful delight. This may not be a problem for most women, but is worth noting. Also, you may need to douche to get out any remaining fruit if your man is a sloppy eater.

There are special swings that are great for doing oral sex. They can be hung from a doorjamb or ceiling rafter. The swing spreads the woman's legs and places her at the perfect height for a man to give her oral sex while he is sitting upright. Beware that most swings are poorly made and uncomfortable. You'll need to shell out a lot for a good one.

Some couples occasionally pour champagne into a woman's vagina when her legs are elevated. (Vamosa?) Her partner then licks out the champagne, although this is not recommended for men in twelve-step programs or for women whose vaginal tissue might become irritated. (The sugar in the champagne can cause a yeast infection.) An extremely dry champagne with low residual sugar might be preferable. Avoid putting cold duck in a woman's crotch, although a loving goose on her rear is usually welcome.

Some women have a problem with being kissed on the face after being kissed on the crotch. If that's the case in your household, consider keeping a wet washcloth handy. Run it across your face before kissing above after kissing below.

Safety Note: It can be very sexy to blow warm moist air over your lover's vulva, but very dangerous to blow air into her vagina. Never lock your lips on your partner's vulva and blow air into it, unless your partner is made of plastic and is inflated that way.

Female Ejaculation

Some women who are highly aroused ejaculate fluid around the same time that they have an orgasm. One female reader who ejaculates says that her male partner finds it exciting. Guys who are ejaculate-shy should discuss it with their partners and explore ways of ducking when the tsunami begins.

If your partner ejaculates and you have a problem with it, take solace in knowing that you've done something incredibly right to get her to that point.

Feeling Like a Crash-Test Dummy

Some women are not particularly subtle when it comes to signaling their oral sex wants and desires. In fact, it is not unheard of for a woman in the heat of oral passion to grab a man's skull and yank it one way or another with enough force to cause whiplash.

If she grinds your face into her crotch with a nose-flattening swoosh, she probably wants you to up the tempo a bit. But don't be silly and let your tongue go full throttle, because this might cause her to whip your head in the opposite direction. Learning to shift tongue-gears gradually can add years to the life of your neck.

Neck Pain, Lock Jaw & Tongue Cramping

Tongue cramping and jaw paralysis are common side-effects of giving oral sex. These usually occur just moments before the woman blurts out, "There, that's perfect, don't stop!" Being able to continue when every ligament and muscle fiber from your neck up is screaming for mercy is what separates the oral sex men from the oral sex boys.

With experience, you will discover which positions land you in traction. Do not suffer in silence. Discuss this with your partner so you can find positions which are mutually pleasing. That way you'll be able to give her more of what she likes. And don't hesitate to give your mouth a breather by gently replacing the tip of your tongue with the tip of your wet finger.

Damn Those Dental Dams & Latex Beaver Tarps

Several years ago, some bozo decided that the way to safely go down on a woman was to spread a dental dam over her crotch. Why not just use neoprene or Naugahyde?

Lately, they've come up with an alternative that's supposedly thinner and more lick-friendly. Hmmm. It may be made for vulvas instead of molars, but good luck. First of all, you have no clue what you're licking. It might as well be the President's face under there. And then there's the texture problem. Try whipping your tongue back and forth over latex. No matter how much slobber you throw on it, your tongue drags and your RPM rating goes to hell. Giving a woman oral sex through even the thinnest of latex barriers makes you appreciate how much subtlety is involved when making her little lips sing.

A more satisfactory barrier is Saran Wrap. You can see through it, it doesn't slow your tongue action, and you can always use it afterward to cover the Peach Melba or Apple Brown Betty.

When a Woman Doesn't Like Her Own Body

"I have a lot of hang-ups about oral sex because I think the guy wants to get out of there as soon as possible. So I need to be reassured you really enjoy it. The orgasm I have with oral sex is the most wonderful, but it often takes a long time and would try the patience of anyone." *female age 38*

Some women don't like their bodies and are uncomfortable when a man has a close-up view. If this is the case in your relationship, it might help ease your partner's mind to do oral sex with the lights out. On the other hand, if your partner is looking for an excuse to feel bad about herself, she will assume that you turned the lights out because you find her body ugly. Either way, it never hurts to talk about this.

One possible solution is to start doing oral sex when the two of you are in the shower. She might feel more comfortable with this, reassured that she is clean enough for you to enjoy.

Maintaining a Hard-On While Giving Oral Sex

If a guy is giving his sweetheart oral sex, it might be nice if he kept doing it long enough to at least get her off. But once he feels his hard-on starting to go, a man will sometimes surface from between a woman's legs and try to have intercourse before it's "too late." Otherwise he feels unmanly about going soft.

So why does a man sometimes lose his erection while going down on a woman? First of all, doing oral sex requires the kind of concentration that isn't always conducive to maintaining an erection. It's a little like playing catch or strumming a guitar, things that can be immensely enjoyable but don't necessarily make a guy hard. Also, for some men, doing oral sex on a woman can bring up all sorts of primal feelings that aren't fully in sync with getting a hard-on. These can be pleasant and even deeply moving feelings, but they might not be the stuff that erections are made of. For other guys, it's instant wood when tongue touches thigh.

There is also the matter of mouth fatigue. It's not easy to keep a hard-on when your tongue and jaw start cramping. On the other hand, it's kind of fun to see how far you can lick a lover into an altered state of consciousness even if you can't talk too well afterward.

Whatever the cause, it's not unusual for a man to lose his erection when he is going down on a woman, but not because he is unhappy or a wimp. Women might consider what a drag it would be if they had to stay hard while doing oral sex. Nobody ever gets on their case for losing an erection.

Things a Woman Can Do to Help a Partner Who Is Going Down on Her

Here are suggestions for women who like to receive oral sex:

Tugging on Your Bush Take a moment to tug on your bush before your man goes down. You'll pull out the lose hairs that would otherwise end up sticking to the back of his throat.

Trimming Your Triangle While some women feel that trimming the triangle defiles the natural appearance of the female body, others take pride in showing off more of their genitals. A woman so inclined shouldn't hesitate to put her lover in charge of muff maintenance and coiffure. Many men find this a joyful duty.

Labia Laundering Separating the labia and washing between them once a day will help to keep your genitals clean and tasty. Douching usually isn't necessary nor advisable.

Not Helpful Women who think that their own genitals are dirty or not likable seldom do themselves any favors when it comes to oral sex. For instance, a guy might be having a wonderful time kissing and caressing his partner's genitals when she suddenly pulls him up because she's decided that he surely can't be enjoying something "as gross as that." If a woman fears that her genitals don't taste good, she should ask her partner. And if she feels there is something bad about her genitals, she should tell her partner lest he feel hurt by her rejecting behavior. Perhaps his reassurance will be helpful. On the other hand, if it's something that genuinely makes her feel uncomfortable, then he shouldn't keep trying to do it.

Information As long as it's done with sensitivity, most men will appreciate any input or suggestions that a woman has about giving her oral pleasure. If you feel shy, hand your lover a copy of this chapter or Violet Blue's *Ultimate Guide To Cunnilingus* and ask if he'll read it with you. And if your man's ego is so fragile that he can't handle your input, perhaps he would do better with a mindless partner who has no input to give. If you aren't equal partners in sex, you aren't equal partners period. Is that what you want?

Masturbating Don't hesitate to reach down and masturbate while your partner is doing oral sex. Of course, this may be more easily said than done, so be sure to let him know that you want him to keep licking while you masturbate. While this can be fun, it may require some interesting tongue-finger logistics.

Attitude Issues There is a section at the end of the preceding chapter on blow jobs that is similar to this, only it is addressed to men. You might look over the parts titled "Attitude Issues." If the shoe fits...

Humor Next to bathing, humor is the most important sex aid there is. Try not to forget this.

Oral Sex during Menstruation

Some couples are fine with oral sex while the woman is menstruating; others wait a few days until the menstrual flow has stopped. Here are four possibilities if you want the action but not the mess:

Instead or The Keeper These are tampon-alternatives that fit over your cervix in the same way as a diaphragm. They work well for oral sex and intercourse during your period. Pop one in before oral sex and it will catch most if not all of the bloody flow. These are not for birth control.

Tampons A woman who is menstruating can douche and insert a couple of tampons before a man goes down on her. The tampons will usually catch most of the flow, assuming that you don't attempt to tickle the woman's cervix with the tip of your tongue. If you douche, which might do more harm than good, consider using a gentle solution with a lower pH.

Diaphragm Some women get a diaphragm for the sole purpose of having sex during their periods. The diaphragm becomes a barrier that traps the menstrual flow. Some couples use the diaphragm for oral sex but not for intercourse, since menstrual secretions can help make intercourse feel extra nice.

Plastic Wrap A simple way of dodging menstrual flow is by putting plastic wrap over the woman's vulva before going down on her.

NOTE: Little if anything is known about the risks of AIDS transmission when doing oral sex on a woman who is menstruating. A conservative approach is in order if the woman has any sexually transmitted infections. You should never do unprotected oral sex on a partner if you have a chancre sore or active oral herpes in your mouth, or if your partner has a herpes outbreak on his or her genitals.

Sixty-Nine

69 is when a man does oral sex on a woman at the same time that she does oral sex on him.

There are plenty of couples who enjoy oral sex but don't necessarily like doing 69. That's because when a person is on the receiving end of oral sex, he or she might want to kick back and not have to worry about getting the other person off.

On the other hand, there might be times when 69 is great fun. Some couples enjoy it as their favorite way of having sex. They love the feeling of simultaneously sucking and being sucked. 69 might also be good for people who can't tolerate receiving pleasure without giving it at the same time, or vice versa.

69 should also be avoided if either partner involuntarily clenches his or her jaw when having an orgasm.

Readers' Comments

Advice on Giving Oral Sex

"Lick around the area of the clitoris, not directly on it, until I am more aroused and then only part of the time."
female age 35

"Get a good rhythm going, don't suck or lick too hard on the head of the clit. Also, either be smooth-shaved or have a beard, but no in-between. Beard burn really kills down there!"
female age 45

"Stubble on the face is not welcome in tender areas down below." *female age 48*

"Please quit when I say so; it gets really tender and ticklish after I come." *female age 43*

"Start out slowly, working around the outer area with your tongue. Don't just push in. Do a lot of gentle rubbing and caressing on the insides of the leg. Gradually probe the vulva with your tongue. Develop a rhythm and keep going until I come." *female age 32*

"If my partner's tongue gets tired, he uses his finger and sometimes it feels the same." *female age 25*

"I like a man to first shave me smooth, then gently kiss and finger me." *female age 34*

"It's great when he puts a finger into my rear while giving me oral sex. It makes for quite the explosion!" *female age 38*

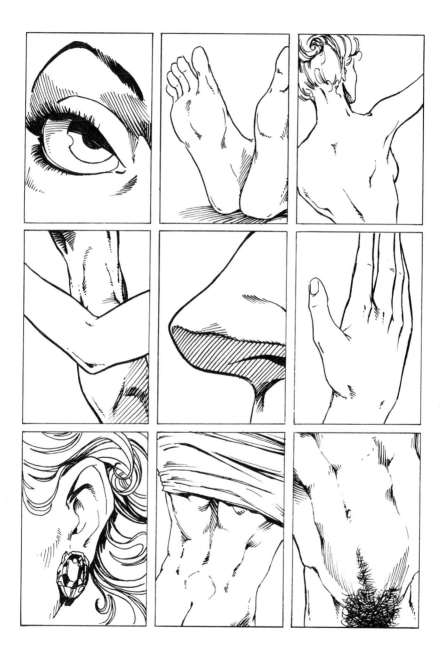

Massage, Back Rubs, Body Rubs
The Ultimate Tenderness
Chapter 24

In doing research for this book, almost every way that human adults get each other off was considered. Attempts were made to view sex through the eyes of mate-swappers, gays, lesbians, Tantric sex masters, conservative born-again Christians, bondage enthusiasts, and those whose sex lives are really boring. Having left no sexual stone unturned, one and only one universal truth about human sexuality emerged:

No matter what your sexual beliefs, fantasies, kink, or persuasion, nothing beats a good back rub.

Nobody, absolutely nobody, had a single bad thing to say about a good back rub. Ditto for foot massage.

Hard vs. Soft? Male vs. Female?

Just about every book ever written on sex loves to state that men touch women too hard, and that women touch men too soft. Baloney, says a straw poll taken by the Goofy Foot Press. There are two types of touch that both men and women like a great deal:

Feather-light to Light: This is where the fingertips lightly dance across the surface of the skin, resulting in a delightful tingling sensation that may or may not raise goosebumps. It can also be done with the flat of the hand doing light, long, gentle strokes. Optimal feather-light touch time: from five to fifty minutes. Some of you who were held down as kids and mercilessly tickled might not like this kind of touch.

Deep & Hard: This is when muscles are kneaded with a strength and authority that chases away stress and tension. The men commented that they often fear they are doing this too hard, but their female partners almost always say it's just right or to do it harder. Optimal deep-and-hard massage time: from half an hour to however long the giver wants to keep giving it.

Fortunately, numerous books on touch and massage have been published in the last twenty years. There are also several nicely done videos on the subject. An hour spent reading one of these books or watching a tape will probably do more for your relationship than a lifetime of looking at *Playboy* or *Penthouse.* Pay special attention to the chapters on foot rubs, hand rubs, and scalp and facial massages. These body parts are often ignored because they aren't considered blue-chip erogenous zones.

Spectators vs. Participants

Some people struggle to get fully into their bodies. Some are perpetually stuck in "prepare to defend" mode and have trouble relaxing enough to enjoy what is being shared with them sexually. They need to be hypervigilant about what is going on around them. The same thing happens when a person always needs to perform and has difficulty becoming passive enough to allow sexual things to happen to his or her body.

Learning to massage and be massaged is one way that might help you to relax your body's armor. This might be anxiety-producing at the start, so go slowly and try to enjoy the gains you are able to make.

Combining Sex & Massage

One reader comments: "My husband often massages my shoulders while I'm giving him head. It feels wonderful and serves to relax me so I can become more easily aroused." Another reader ties her naked partner's hands together above his head, lets him watch as she slowly removes her satin underwear and then caresses his entire body with it. A third reader drags her long hair across her lover's naked body and eventually wraps it around his genitals. One man reports that the best way to drive his partner into total ecstasy is for him to brush her hair or massage her scalp with his fingertips. Another couple takes long, candlelit showers together, shampooing each other's hair and soaping each other's body.

Perhaps you have your own favorite ways of combining massage with sex play. Whatever your inclination, if there is only one thing you take from this book, take the resolve to make massage an integral part of your sexual relationships. Touch and massage might be the most important aspects of human sexuality, outside of the occasional need to replenish the species.

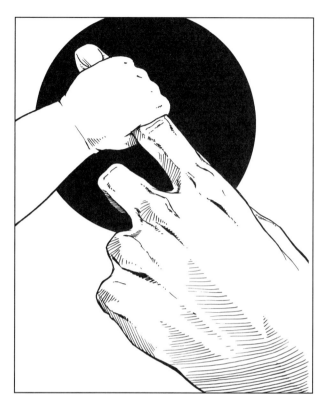

Intercourse Alert

There are a number of fun, exciting, and highly satisfying ways of sharing sexual pleasure besides vaginal intercourse. Many are listed in this book.

If you are not fully prepared to become pregnant, to support ($$$) and parent a child for the next eighteen years, to give your baby up for adoption, or to have an abortion, then you shouldn't be having vaginal intercourse. [1]

Even the best birth control methods fail. In our culture, we value the creation of human life too much to ignore the responsibility and consequences of what may follow.

Intercourse can also be an easy way of passing on STIs.

---

[1] Unless you are past menopause or have been properly snipped!

This illustration was inspired by photographer Trevor Watson. Books by artists like Mr. Watson are considered by many couples to be far more creative and sexy than the glossy fare of traditional porn mags. Known as "Erotic Photography" or "Erotic Fine Art Photography," you will find samples in the galleries at websites such as LibidoMag.com, Nerve.com and Salon.com.

Horizontal Jogging (Intercourse)
Chapter 25

closed caption

Intercourse can mean different things to different people. As presented in this chapter, it's an intensely private, delicious act. You can use it to honor and expand your relationship at the same time that you are doing really nice things with your body. It's also what couples do when they want to create new life. We don't take it lightly, and we try to present it with a level of feeling and intelligence not normally found in popular books on sex.

Dick, Laura & Craig

To learn more about the role of intercourse in sexuality, this book has invaded the privacy of three young adults, Dick, Craig, and Laura. Laura used to go out with Dick, and now she's involved with Craig. Here are their goofy stories:

DICK

Dick is a very nice-looking guy who won his fraternity's "Mr. All-America" title two years in a row. Dick has a nice job, a nice social manner, drives a nice sports car, wears nice clothes, has nice biceps, triceps, and pecs, and goes out with nice women. Since this is a book about sex, you might as well know that Dick has a tree trunk of a penis that stays rock hard from dusk to dawn. A former girlfriend referred to it as "the sentry."

CRAIG

Craig is the same age as Dick. Craig is a sportswriter. Craig is no longer eligible for the Mr. All-America contest. During a football game a few years ago, Craig went airborne to catch an overthrown pass. On the way down he got sandwiched between two spearing linebackers.

Craig's spinal cord snapped and he hasn't been able to walk or have an erection since.

LAURA

Laura is a fine young woman who just left a big corporation to form her own company that makes sporting gear. Laura's had sex with both Dick and Craig. Let's see what Laura has to say about these two different men.

> "Dick's the kind of guy that many American women have been raised to worship. Parading him around your friends or taking him home to your parents would win you the female equivalent of the Breeder's Cup. I've always really enjoyed sex, and until recently I could never understand why a woman would want to fake an orgasm. But it didn't take too many nights with Dick before I started faking orgasms. There was Dick, Mr. Right Stuff, making all that picture-perfect love. I didn't want him to think there was something wrong with me since I couldn't get into it like he was, so I started faking orgasms."

> "Craig is nowhere near as perfect as Dick, but he has a great sense of humor and he is genuine. Craig is able to laugh at himself, which Dick never could. Craig has taken the time to learn exactly how to kiss, touch, and caress me, and the sex I have with him is great. When I'm with Craig I don't need to fake a thing."

> "This may not seem relevant to your question about sex, but I work in a totally male-dominated business. I have to think like a guy from morning to night. Sometimes it leaves me feeling alien from my femininity. With Craig it's easy to find it back again. Craig never wakes me up at 3:00 a.m. with a hard-on poking in my back, but he feels just as masculine as Dick. With a lot of guys there's a huge difference between how they treat you in bed and how they treat you the rest of time; with Craig that's not the case. Maybe that's another reason why sex is so nice with him, even if it's not intercourse."

Okay, so here we have Dick, more functional than a Sidewinder missile. He fulfills everybody's definition of what a sexual athlete should be. Then we have Craig, who redefines the term "sexually dysfunctional." If Craig had the same erection failure but no spinal cord injury, psychologists and sex therapists would collect a small fortune trying to make him "normal." At the very least, they would have him munching down blue boner pills as if they were M&Ms. And probably Prozac, too.

And finally, there's Laura, a woman who enjoys sex a great deal. She's saying that the guy who can't get it up is a more satisfying lover than Mr. Erectus Perfectus.

In telling you about Laura, Dick and Craig, the intent was not to dump on intercourse. Intercourse, when it's good, can be one of the sweetest things there is. What this book is dumping on is the assumption that intercourse is good just because it's intercourse and that a man is a man because he can get hard and fuck, or that a woman is a woman because she can get wet and fuck him back.

When Ms. Dworkin Has Intercourse

These days, certain groups of women are referring to any and all kinds of intercourse as evil. They say that even if a woman wants intercourse badly, it's only because she has been brainwashed by men into thinking it is pleasurable. To explore this issue in greater depth, we asked our women readers the following question: "What does it feel like when you have intercourse?" Mind you, these women are describing intercourse with partners whom they care about.

What Does It Feel Like When You Have Intercourse?

"Oh God—It's like describing the universe. It feels like I might explode and can't wait to but at same time want it to last forever. Breathless, hot, turned on in the extreme. I want to engulf and squeeze his penis, get it in me as much as possible. I love the connection of it."   *female age 48*

"When his penis first enters me I want to feel every inch of it because it is exquisite. I feel like I need it inside me and I don't know if I can describe that. The actual sensations of his penis sliding in and out of me are sometimes over-powered by the pleasure I feel all over my body, so I don't necessarily concentrate on the intercourse."   *female age 23*

Intercourse in the old days.

"As he enters me I feel myself spreading open to accommodate him. Emotionally it feels right that he is inside of me. I have a feeling of fullness when he is inside me. I can feel the head of the penis as it slides in and out and can feel my vagina collapse or expand around him. If he plunges deep I can feel the head of the penis bump my cervix, a not altogether unpleasant feeling. From rear entry I can feel the penis more acutely rubbing the top of my vagina." *female age 37*

"It feels different every time. Sometimes it is very satisfying. Sometimes it hurts inside my vagina if I'm not lubricated enough. And sometimes when his penis hits my G-Spot it takes my breath away!" *female age 34*

"At first I feel the light pressure of my partner's penis against my unopened vagina. It is often deeply pleasurable to feel the head penetrate, and then a slow, smooth slide all the way in, and a jolt of excitement when my lover's penis is completely inside me. The most sensation is around the outer part of the vagina, but there is also a pleasurable feeling of fullness when he is fully inside me. My hips want to move and match his strokes, or create my own rhythm for him to match. Different types of strokes and rhythms create different sensations."
female age 47

"The first thrust is the most vivid for me. I like to slowly slide down his cock and feel it go up me. I love it when he is trying to hold back from coming; I can feel him get more swollen and hard and I get very excited when I feel that. It actually is the time when my vagina gets the most pleasure from intercourse."
female age 23

"It depends on how sexually excited I am and whether I'm in the mood or if I'm just doing it because he wants to. If I'm into it, it's like ecstasy!" *female age 43*

"I enjoy the pumping and grinding a great deal. I love it when we are rubbing our pelvic bones together and when the penis is in deep." *female age 21*

"My favorite part of intercourse is when he comes, his entire body stiffens."   *female age 55*

"I'm strictly a clit person. I love having sex with men, but I don't like intercourse."   *female age 36*

At the Start — New Relationship or New to Intercourse

For a lot of couples it takes time and familiarity for intercourse to get that kind of sloppy-intimate-erotic edge that makes it so much fun. This means that intercourse won't necessarily knock your socks off at the start. It may not even feel as good as masturbation.

Also, each partner brings his or her own hopes and expectations, as well as physical anatomy and body rhythms. Patience can be a virtue. For instance, some couples who are having dynamite intercourse during the fifth year of their relationship had lousy intercourse during the first year. And even if the sex is great at the start, chances are there will be periods in any relationship when sexual desire falls flat. Hopefully you continue to grow as a couple during those times.

Your First Intercourse

In a study on first intercourse that included 659 college students, researchers Schwartz, Sprecher, Barbee, and Orbuch found this:

While 79% of the men reported that they had an orgasm during their first intercourse, only 7% of the women reported having an orgasm.

Males had far more overall pleasure than females.

The mean age for first intercourse was sixteen and one-half years, although those who waited until they were seventeen or older reported having a better experience than those who were younger. Not that anything gets better with age automatically, but sometimes a year or two of added life experience can go a long way when you are only sixteen.

Both males and females reported more pleasure if they had intercourse for the first time in a more serious or long-term relationship than in a casual or brief one.

Individuals in long-term relationships reported having less guilt during their first intercourse than those in more casual relationships, although they experienced more anxiety, perhaps from having more at stake.

People who used alcohol during their first intercourse (about 30 percent of the total) reported significantly less pleasure and more guilt than those who did it sober.

Those who used contraception reported more pleasure than those who didn't.

On our own sex survey at goofyfootpress.com, we've asked hundreds of women to compare how their first intercourse felt with how it feels now. While most of these women say it feels great now, it's a very unusual woman who says she enjoyed her first intercourse, even if it was in a loving relationship.

Suggestions for a First Intercourse

If Robert Dickinson is even remotely correct in his classic book *Sex Anatomy*, there's a lot of rearranging that goes on in a woman's pelvis the first couple of times she has intercourse. If you combine that with not enough lubrication, extreme stress, fear that it's going to hurt, and a lot of young women who say "Ick" if you mention a birth control method where they have to stick their own finger inside their own vagina, then you truly have a recipe for inept intercourse. Add to that the fact that the young woman's partner is often just as much in the woods as she, and that it's unlikely she has ever talked to her mother about what it feels like to have intercourse—not good news.

One optimistic reader suggests that a young woman bring a vibrator to have an orgasm with before intercourse, pillows for under her butt to improve the angle of penetration, and gobs of lubrication. However, the day American mothers start making suggestions to their daughters about such matters will be the day there's a real man and woman walking on Mars instead of mechanical Mars Rovers.

If you haven't had intercourse yet, our readers offer plenty of suggestions at the end of this chapter. Also, keep in mind that you need birth control and that you can also become pregnant from having unprotected intercourse during your period.

The Approach

Sometimes you're both so horny that you hardly get your shoes and socks off before you are doing the wild thing. But a lot of the time, one of you is ready for intercourse before the other. If it's the man who isn't ready, it's a no-brainer where the attention needs to focus.

If he's the one who's ready first, it wouldn't hurt to tease and caress his partner until she genuinely wants to be entered. And if that doesn't work, then it's time to enjoy a little masturbation.

A man can always get extra mileage before taking the big plunge by letting the head of his penis caress the lips of her vulva. She'll know it's there, but she won't know when it's going to go in.

Also keep in mind that some women enjoy intercourse more if they have an orgasm before the penis goes in. This won't make sense to a lot of guys, because after orgasm a penis often wants to pack it up and go home.

One in the Hand. Who Sticks It In?

"I generally prefer to put it in; otherwise we seem to miss a lot."
female age 32

"I always want him to put it in." *female age 25*

"I like to put his penis in me because it seems no matter how many times we have had sex, he still misses a little bit when aiming. Also, I find it exciting to hold him while he thrusts into my vagina." *female age 23*

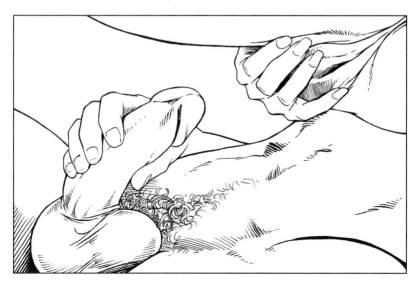

"It's really whoever grabs ahold first."   *female age 36*

"He prefers to put it in, because if I do, he thinks I think he doesn't know where in the heck that hole is."   *female age 38*

"She always does. No matter how many years we've been doing this, I still manage to miss!"   *male age 43*

This may seem like a dumb thing to talk about, but the issue of who sticks the penis into the vagina can sometimes be significant. A rule of thumb, so to speak, is that the woman should be the one who sticks it in—at least for the first few times until both partners have their signals in sync. That's because only a woman knows when she is ready to have a penis inside, and all those years of inserting tampons have taught her exactly where the head of little Tonto needs to go. Of course, some women might be shy about grabbing a guy's penis and guiding it in for a landing. This kind of reticence is silly, but understandable.

If it's the man's job to put the penis in, he should wait until getting a go-ahead signal. At the very least, he should check out the readiness of his partner's vagina with a finger. If it's not particularly wet but the woman still wants him inside, he should lube himself up with a water-based lubricant such as KY. Also, a wad of saliva slapped on the head of the penis is a time-honored antidote for a willing but arid vagina.

If you are using a water-based lube and it dries out half way, add a few drops of water or saliva rather than more lube. A drop or two of water will give it new life, while more lube will just gum things up. The women at Good Vibrations suggest keeping a water pistol handy for just this purpose, although women without humor will find this to be offensive, and wives of NRA members should be careful not to grab the Glock 36 by mistake.

The First Thrust

As we were reading the questionnaires of our women readers, an amazing pattern emerged. A large number of women said that the part of intercourse they liked best was the first stroke. For a lot women, it seems like the first stroke is a nearly religious happening, assuming they're primed and eager for the thrusting to begin.

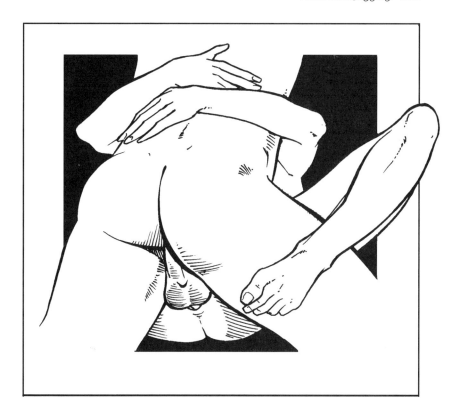

Do not hesitate to ask your sweetheart how she likes you to do your first stroke. Does she like you to start by teasing her with a series of short little thrusts, going in only an inch or two? Or does she like one big straightforward glide for the gold?

Legs Bent or Straight, Open or Closed

The biggest single variable in the physics of intercourse is often the position of the woman's legs—whether they are straight or bent, open or closed, over your shoulders or in your face. When the woman's legs are straight, penetration is not as deep, but the tip of the clitoris might receive more stimulation. When a woman bends her legs and brings her knees closer to her chest, the penetration is deeper. This can be nice if she likes more pressure in the back part of her vagina. It also changes the angle of the penis in the vagina, causing a different feel for both the man and the woman.

If the woman's legs are together, the penis is hugged more snugly. This might offer better clitoral stimulation, because the extra snugness may push the inner labia more tightly against the shaft of the penis as it goes in and out. If the woman's legs are open, there is greater skin-to-skin contact between her vulva and the man's genitals. This can also result in more bouncing-testicle action if the man is on top.

Some couples enjoy intercourse with one leg straight and the other flexed. And some women like to reach between their legs and push the clitoris against the penis with their fingers.

And if this isn't confusing enough, some women keep their legs straight and together while flexing their thighs to help push themselves over the top.

Legs Bent or Straight, Anatomical Consideration

A woman's decision to keep her legs straight or bent might also vary with the length and thickness of the man's penis. A woman whose partner has a really long penis may find that she gets poked in the cervix if she opens and bends her legs during intercourse, while a woman whose man has a short penis might prefer the feeling of deeper penetration that bent knees allow.

Porn star Nina Hartley has a shallow vagina and can't take guys who are really long. Mind you, "shallow" and "long" are defined differently in the world of pornography than in the average bedroom. Ms. Hartley suggests that women can add another inch or two of thrusting room by using positions that allow the penis to move into the space behind the cervix that is called the fornix. You will need to experiment on your own—Nina doesn't say what these space enhancing positions might be.

Apologies: Sex books these days don't use the term "short penis." Instead, they say a penis that isn't overly long. The latter phrasing is meant to protect the allegedly fragile male ego, yet this guide hates to think that today's male is so fragile that he can't say "I've got a short one" without experiencing a crisis of character. As for the sentiment expressed by the 20 Fingers song "(Don't Want No) Short Dick Man," making peace with body parts is discussed in a latter chapter entitled "Techno Breasts & Weenie Angst."

Thrusting—Shallow vs. Deep

The walls of a woman's vagina change shape with each thrust of intercourse. This means that with each stroke, thousands of nerve endings are being pulled and tugged, which, neurologically speaking, can feel quite nice. (This doesn't feel half bad for guys, either.) The most sensitive part of the vagina is usually at the opening, up to an inch or two deep. This also becomes the snuggest part of the vagina when it is aroused.

Shallow thrusting encourages the snuggest part of the vagina to wrap around the most sensitive part of his penis, just below the head. Shallow thrusting also allows the ridge around the head of the penis to stimulate this sensitive part of the vagina. An exception might be if the man's penis has a compact head and is thicker around the middle part of the shaft, in which case the woman may prefer the thicker part to be in the vaginal opening.

Deeper thrusting offers its own advantages: 1. Unless the man's penis is really long or the woman's vagina is shallow, deep thrusting can help to position his pubic bone in direct contact with more of her clitoral area. Rubbing against a man's pubic bone helps some women have orgasms during intercourse. 2. Deeper thrusting may allow the penis to pull on the labia minora (inner lips) for a longer period of time, providing more stimulation to the clitoral area. 3. The deeper part of the vagina is often sensitive to pressure. As some women approach orgasm, they find it pleasurable if there is a penis or penis-like object in the back part of the vagina that it can contract around.

The Zen Police Talk Thrust

Some Tantric and Oriental sex masters caution about deep thrusting during intercourse. They feel that the vagina does best with a ratio of five-to-one or nine-to-one shallow-to-deep thrusts. This is an interesting observation, given how they don't allow women to be monks or masters and they don't even allow them to enter business meetings unless it's to bring tea, but they have no shortage of suggestions for pleasing them sexually.

Anyway, the nine shallow for every one deep thrust is a pattern that pretty much wins you the Tantric intercourse exacta. Then, as your partner becomes more aroused, increase the ratio to two deep for every four shallow, or live dangerously and go for one shallow to one deep.

This is definitely something to experiment with, but if your partner starts threatening you with serious grief if you don't knock off the shallow stuff, you can safely assume she wasn't an Asian princess in a past life.

Battering Ram or Pleasure Wand? Mosh Pit or Symphony?

Some men use a penis as a kind of battering ram, believing that women enjoy being slammed during intercourse. Other men, perhaps a bit more sensitive or experienced, realize that there are different thrusting rhythms that can help make intercourse feel more symphonic than metallic. A lot of it also depends on what style or styles of thrusting the woman enjoys. Maybe she will like it slow at the start but strong at the end.

An excellent way to find out what works best during intercourse is when the woman is on top. That way the man can feel what she does with his penis, how she moves up and down on it and what parts of her vagina she focuses the head on. For instance, does she thrust rapidly with it, or does she keep the penis deep inside of her and rub her clitoris on the man's pubic bone? Does she like to massage her clitoris or breasts while a penis is inside of her, or would this be an unwelcome distraction? Where does she like to look, and what does she do with her mouth? There are certainly other ways that women use to help orchestrate the rhythm and speed. Sometimes a hand pushing on a man's hip or rear end can speak volumes.

Eager for Beaver — Intercourse as Two Separate Acts

If you are feeling terminally reflective and have nothing else to do, it might be helpful to think of intercourse as two separate acts—the thrusting or rocking part and the orgasm part. If the sole purpose of the former is to achieve the latter, then the intercourse might not have much emotional depth to it. That's because it is during the thrusting part of intercourse (before orgasm) when feelings of love, friendship, and gratitude are often shared.

Most couples have a variety of thrusting modes—hot and furious, fun and playful, giggly, tearful, passionate, powerful, passive, and maybe even angry at times. This becomes part of the private language that lovers share.

Studies show that guys who help out around the house get laid more often than guys who don't, causing speculation that Windex and 409 are better aphrodisiacs than oysters, expensive cars, and a medicine chest full of Viagra.

Missionary

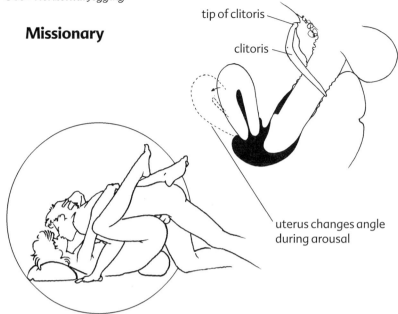

tip of clitoris

clitoris

uterus changes angle
during arousal

Using Your Head

The first inch or so of a woman's vagina is sensitive to touch. That's why a bit of gentle finger or penis-head action around the rim can be a nice way to begin. The art, of course, is in making those shallow little thrusts without pulling out too far and having your dick fall out. If it falls out enough times, she'll start thinking your middle name is "Goober," or maybe she does already and she loves you still.

Beyond the first inch or so, you need to start thinking pressure. That's because the back part of the vagina feels stretching and pressure more than it does light little touches. This is when it's wise to learn which parts of her vagina respond best to pressure when the head of your penis pushes against it. You'll find that you can combine certain positions with certain angles to put pressure on the different parts of her vagina if she likes.

A good way to learn about a woman's genitals is with your fingers as well as with your penis. This will give you a better understanding of what needs to be done with your penis. (As one female reader says, "It wouldn't hurt for women to know this about themselves.")

Popping Out

During some orgasms, the vagina contracts enough to expel a penis. When asked about this, most women advise, "Push It Back In!!!"

Rear Entry

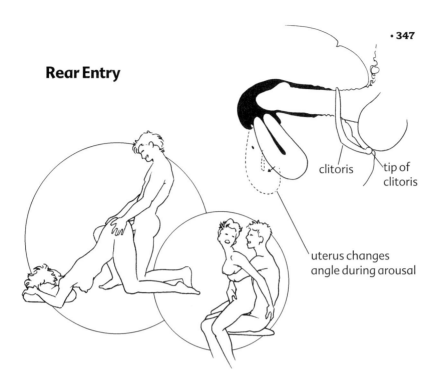

clitoris · tip of clitoris

uterus changes angle during arousal

With this kind of contraction, it feels good to have a penis deep inside a vagina, even if it takes quite a thrust to keep it in or get it back in.

Thrustless in Seattle

Some couples don't thrust at all during intercourse, but move their entire bodies in sync. Or the man might do a circular motion with his penis or pelvic bone grinding against the woman's vuvla. Some couples occasionally stay really still during intercourse and simply try to coordinate their breathing. For instance, one partner breathes in at the moment that the other breathes out.

You don't have to be a yogi master to achieve wonderful experiences with breathing instead of thrusting. You don't even need to meditate or stand on your head while chanting mysterious incantations. All you need to do is be in sync with each other.

Another way of enjoying intercourse without thrusting is to play "squeezing genitals." This is based upon the anatomical fact that when the male squeezes or contracts his erect penis it momentarily changes diameter, and when the woman squeezes her vagina it hugs the penis—sometimes rather snugly and with memorable results. To play "squeezing genitals," partners alternate squeezing their genitals. This can be extremely satisfying if your pelvic muscles are in really

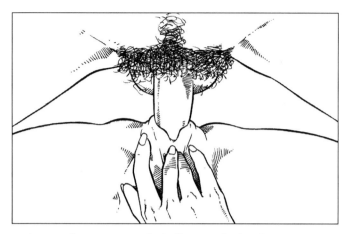

Plenty of women use their fingers during intercourse.

good shape, and it doesn't require a particularly high I.Q. or a daring sense of adventure.

Riding High—Tom Landry Remembered

Each year a new book comes out that promises to reinvent the wheel sexually. For instance, one entry talked about a radical "new" way of having intercourse. The couple starts by assuming the traditional missionary position with the man climbing on top. Right before the thrusting begins, the man makes a quick shift toward the head of the bed, like the Dallas Cowboys used to do at the line of scrimmage before the set call, back when they were America's team and Tom Landry was coach.

During this quick shift, the male pushes his entire body a couple of inches forward over the head of the woman. This puts him in the position of being able to say, "Honey, your roots are showing something awful, time for a new weave job." This new intercourse position is supposed to bring the man's penis in more direct contact with the woman's clitoris, assuming his poor weenie doesn't snap off between the down and set call.

There is no in-out thrusting in this new form of intercourse. The couple simply move their hips back and forth in synchronized form, like those women swimmers at the Summer Olympics. Fortunately, the founder of this new position says nothing about wearing ugly swim caps or Dallas Cowboy football helmets.

This intercourse position does attempt to maximize clitoral stimulation by making the man "ride high." Guys who are sensitive lovers figured this one out long ago, although an occasional man may have had the knowledge forced upon him by a rambunctious lover who rode so low that she made him wonder if his penis would survive the night. Her riding low is the equivalent of his riding high. Again, a good way for a man to learn what angles his partner prefers is to pay close attention when she's on top. Or ask.

Nasty Reflections

Watching your genitals at work or play during intercourse can be an amusing and fun way to pass time. "Sexy and hot," adds a woman reader. There are several positions which allow one or both partners to watch the vagina swallowing up the penis and then spitting it out again—oops, passionately enveloping it. A good-sized hand mirror can offer a nice view of genital play until one of you accidentally kicks it over. Also, try using the magnifying side of the mirror. It will make you look huge! A woman reader comments: "That's a frightening thought."

Some couples also like to pull out the Camcorder and tape themselves when having intercourse. Entire books have been written on this subject. Precautions for making home movies are mentioned in the fantasy chapter, such as putting a big X on the cassette and keeping it in a separate place from the movies that go back to Blockbuster. There are also special video locks that can be put on tapes of mom and dad having sex so the kids don't accidentally watch and suddenly have the ammo to blackmail you out of every last dollar in your retirement fund. And who knows these days with those secret hidden spycams...

Kissing When Thrusting—Size vs. Intent

Sometimes there's nothing nicer in the world than kissing passionately when your genitals are locked in a loving embrace, but this simply isn't possible for some couples. For instance, if a woman is 5'1" and her partner is 6'4", there is no way her tongue is going to play inside his mouth when they are having intercourse unless she has a really deep navel or a tongue from a sci-fi horror flick.

One reason why it's impossible to make recommendations regarding intercourse positions is because different couples come in different sizes. Some positions will feel better for couples who are relatively the same height and weight, while those positions might be a disaster for a union between Twiggy and the Jolly Green Giant. Likewise, certain positions will feel better or worse depending on the size and angle of your respective genitals. And some positions that feel best during the first part of a woman's menstrual cycle might give way to other positions during the later part of her cycle. And that's just physical differences. It really gets complicated when you factor in each partner's emotional desires and needs.

Signaling

Sex seldom works well when a partner is too passive or inhibited to let the other know what feels good and what doesn't. Fortunately, signaling during intercourse doesn't need to include words, because hands on a partner's hips or rear end can be great rudders—as long as the partner with the hips is hip to the hands.

To Come or Not to Come...

People have this silly notion that women are supposed to come during intercourse and by thrusting alone. The fact is, way fewer than 50 percent of women have orgasms during intercourse. As you will see from their comments, many women who do come during intercourse need a little help from either their own or their partner's fingers.

"I very rarely have orgasms with intercourse, unless I'm playing with myself at the time. The best way for me is oral sex or using a vibrator." *female age 36*

"I don't usually have orgasms during intercourse. In a very open relationship, I can have an orgasm after intercourse by manually stimulating my clitoris or by rubbing myself on his flaccid penis." *female age 26*

"I usually have them with intercourse if my husband is rubbing my clitoris or using a vibrator while he is thrusting. Sometimes when I am really excited, I can have one just with thrusting." *female age 35*

"I come faster sometimes when he's inside me, but I always have to rub my clit to climax." *female age 25*

A woman can love the feelings she gets from intercourse, both emotional and physical, but still not have orgasms from it.

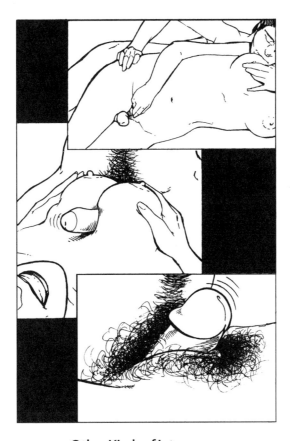

Other Kinds of Intercourse

*Intercourse between the thighs, intercourse between
the breasts, and femoral intercourse—where the penis
is slid up the vulva without going into the vagina.*

When Is Intercourse a Success?

Most books imply that intercourse is a success if you give each
other orgasms and a failure if you don't. Hardly. This guide takes the
position that intercourse needs to convey certain feelings between
partners that are too primal for words alone. These feelings rest on
the boundary between body and soul and are transmitted from one
person to another in many different ways. If orgasm is part of that
process, fine, but having an orgasm is no guarantee that anything
special has taken place. Yet it's possible to have intercourse with no
orgasm at all and experience it as being wonderful or enchanting.

When is intercourse a success? Intercourse seems successful when it leaves you feeling a little more solid, less grumpy, more able to face the day, and less afraid of the world when it's an overwhelming place. Intercourse is successful when it allows you to both give and get something from your partner that makes you feel more whole or wholesome and secure.

When is intercourse a failure? This book's criterion for failure is waking up at three or four in the morning, looking at the person who's sleeping next to you and thinking "I wish I were home in my own bed, ALONE." This can be a particularly nasty dilemma if you are married or living together. Also, intercourse that conveys less pleasure than when someone leaves you a free hour on a parking meter is not necessarily worth having.

Pillows on Parade

Don't underestimate the power of a pillow under the rear to enhance intercourse. Changing the angle of the hips can dramatically change a person's experience of intercourse, sometimes for the better. Experiment to find what placement might be good for you.

If you like intercourse from the rear, keep a lookout for the right big pillow that will provide support and raise the woman's rear end to an angle that is comfortable and inviting. The more humongous the pillow, the more fun. Experiment with bolsters and cushions.

Environment

If intercourse is seeming a bit stale, it might help to scout out some new locations. Of course, it never hurts if that new location happens to be a four-star hotel somewhere in Europe, but if you haven't saved up quite that many frequent flyer miles, here are a few other possibilities:

The Kitchen Always a fine place for intercourse until you have kids. But once the kids reach school age, the kitchen is usually free for an occasional nooner.

In Front of the Fireplace There's nothing quite like doing it in front of the fireplace, until the woodsman delivers wet pine instead of seasoned oak and a slew of hissing, burning embers shower your naked back and rear end.

The Yard It's a shame to spend all that time and money making the grass grow and never fuck on it.

In Water   Hot tubs, bathtubs, pools, and other large bodies of water can be great places for people to do all sorts of nasty things. But intercourse in water provides its own unique hazard because water washes away natural lubrication. The best solution is a silicone-based lubricant. In fact, why hot-tub manufacturers don't include samples of silicone-based lubes is beyond us. Another solution is to slip the penis inside the vagina while both sets of organs are outside the water. Then slither your way under the surface, penis-in-vagina. Aquatic intercourse will be possible if you limit yourselves to a muted kind of thrusting. Also, to help facilitate underwater hand play and other forms of sexual groping, coat your genitals with something oily while they are still dry-docked.

Sex at the Office   Sex at the office often has the right elements of risk and mischievous fun. One reader is a commercial real estate agent who has keys to some of the finest offices in all of Los Angeles. When he and his girlfriend want a dramatic change of scenery, they check out the upper floors.

Candlelight   An old standby for erotic ambiance is candlelight. Make sure that the candle wax doesn't drip on your carpet, because it will cost you a fortune to have it commercially removed. (A reader kindly comments: fold up a paper towel a few times and place it over the cooled wax on the carpet. Then put a hot iron on top of the towel. It will melt the wax into the towel and the carpet is wax-free! Another reader cautions that some types of candleholders get hot enough to scorch furniture.)

After Intercourse—The Drip Factor

Unless a guy is wearing a rubber or pulls out and squirts to the side, he usually leaves ejaculate inside a woman's vagina during intercourse. Okay, so where does the ejaculate go?

"Runs down your leg," says one female reader. "It usually drips out," replies another. "Like water in a cup that's turned upside down," says a third. This might not be a problem if you are going to sleep, except for the wet spot on the mattress, but what if you had intercourse in the morning or at lunchtime? "You can usually get it out in the shower" was one response, while another woman says, "Not true. It tends to drain out at its own pace, and all the showering in the world isn't going to hasten it along." Either way, what if you already took a shower or

don't want to take one just then? "Sometimes I'll wear a panty liner," said one woman, "but it's not worth a tampon." All of the women who were asked said they know of other women who douche right after intercourse even when they have it at bedtime. Most thought this was silly and unnecessary. As one woman said, "It's not dirty; I put the stuff in my mouth!" Another woman said, "I don't have sex with a man unless I really care about him. While this might sound a little weird, I find the occasional dripping to be a sweet and sometimes exciting reminder that he's been here."

As for why the ejaculate drips out rather than slowly oozes, you can find the answer in the chapter titled "The Glands Down Under."

Top Dog

It has been said that people who always need to be on top during intercourse are basically insecure, while people who have it more together are happy to switch off. If this is true, then intercourse is no different from life in general.

Also, feminists claim that intercourse usually follows a prostitute model of sex—once the male comes, the sex is over. It seems like a shame to end that way. It's also rude. Perhaps the two of you can talk about ways to help the woman get her share of pleasure if the man comes before she's ready to stop.

On Not Pulling Out

Staying inside your sweetheart after the thrusting is done can sometimes feel magical. Since most men lose their erections after coming, the two of you need to be somewhat clever, keeping the fading member in while getting comfortable enough to stay in each other's arms. Some couples like to fall asleep this way.

The desire to stay inside your sweetheart after ejaculation is one of the downsides of using a rubber. A man who is wearing a rubber needs to pull out soon after he's come. Otherwise he might leave the rubber inside his partner.

Missed the Train Again

Men who have trouble coming tend to pump faster during intercourse, hoping this will provide extra stimulation to help them ejaculate. This is a bad idea. The rapid thrusting desensitizes the penis, and it's possible the female partner won't be able to walk right for a few days afterward. Delayed ejaculation is discussed in the chapter "When Your System Crashes" which begins on page 689.

Passive Intercourse vs. Masturbation

This section was included with an awareness that only some couples might be interested. Other couples will find that it has no place in their relationship or that it might even seem perverse.

Let's say a woman wakes up at 5:00 A.M., horny as can be, and would like to have intercourse. Her partner, on the other hand, is not a morning person and is pretty much comatose until noon. Assuming he's just slow to rise and not an early-morning grouch, he might allow her to stimulate his penis to a point of erection, or maybe he's already got an early-morning (REM-state) hard-on. They then have intercourse in a position where he can be passive while she is active, or she massages her clitoris while his penis is inside of her. In a sense, she is using his penis as a dildo.

Or let's say it's nearly midnight and this woman's partner is feeling sexually amped, but she is pretty much dead to the world. She doesn't mind his using her vagina for intercourse, but doesn't want to have to be into it either. So she rolls on her side and allows him to have rear-entry intercourse.

Ah, you might say, why didn't the horny partner simply masturbate instead of bothering the one who is zoned out? Sometimes a partner honestly doesn't mind being "used" for sex as long as he or she isn't expected to get all turned on. He or she might even enjoy the other's pleasure. However, it is essential that the passive partner feels comfortable saying, "Naw, not now," if that is the case, and the horny partner should be willing to masturbate. And it requires a sex life that is fairly rich at other times, given how an entire diet of passive sex might leave the active partner feeling unvalued or the passive partner feeling used.

What's the Frequency, Dan?

When it comes to frequency of intercourse, people who ask "What's normal?" usually aren't asking the right question. If you are in a relationship, good questions to be asking are "Do we have intercourse as often as each of us likes?" "Do we have intercourse more often than one or both of us likes?" The reason these questions are far more important than "What's normal?" is because the only thing that matters about sex is what feels best for you—whether it's three times a day or three times a decade.

Betty On Intercourse

What better way to wind down a chapter on intercourse than with a few passages from Betty Dodson's book *Sex For One*? These quotes refer to things that transpired during Ms. Dodson's sex groups for women. Part 1 is a summary of women's experience with orgasm, part 2 describes a role-playing exercise where Betty Ann had the women take the man's role in intercourse, and part 3 includes general comments on intercourse.

1. On Orgasms

Some women had good orgasms with oral sex but not with intercourse. Others could come with intercourse but couldn't get off alone. Still others were having orgasms with themselves but not with a partner. All of the orgasmic women agreed on one thing: Their experiences of orgasm varied greatly from one orgasm to the next.

2. On Pretending You're a Guy during Intercourse

One amusing and informative exercise was called "Running a Sexual Encounter." It involved reversing sex roles with the women on top. We made believe that our clitorises were penetrating imaginary lovers, and we had to do all the thrusting. I would set the egg timer for three minutes, a little longer than the Kinsey national average. As the fucking began, I would participate and at the same time comment on everyone's technique. 'Keep your arms straight; don't crush your lover. You're too high up; your clitoris just fell out. Don't stop moving, you'll lose your erection. Don't move so fast; you'll come too soon. And don't forget to whisper sweet things in your lover's ear between all those passionate kisses.'

Watching the egg timer, I coordinated my theatrical orgasm with the ding of the bell, frantically thrusting for the last ten seconds. Then, falling flat on my imaginary lover, I muttered, 'Was it good for you?' and promptly began snoring loudly. It was always hysterically funny. Panting and exhausted, the women all exclaimed, 'How do men do it?' Complaints included tired arms, lower-back pain, and stiff hip joints. Most of the women had fallen out long before the bell went off. After that, there was always more empathy for men, and the women showed an increased interest in other positions for lovemaking.

3. Odds & Ends

Some of the women talked about experiencing pain with deep thrusting intercourse, while others claimed to want a hard fuck. In my youth, I'd confused hard pounding intercourse with passion, and experienced internal soreness afterward…. While I enjoyed a strong fuck when we were two equal energies in sync, I also loved the slow intense fuck.

Another problem the women complained of was lack of lubrication and the pain of dry intercourse. Some women felt inadequate if they weren't wet with passion. My experience varied; sometimes I lubricated when I wasn't even thinking about sex. Other times I could be dry even though I felt sexually aroused…. (from *Sex for One* by Betty Dodson, Harmony Books, New York, New York)

Readers' Comments

Some of your favorite intercourse positions?

"My favorite position is doggy style, with me on my hands and knees, and him behind me. I like this best for two reasons: my vagina is tighter this way, and I can easily rub my clitoris and have an orgasm. I also love to sit on a guy while he is sitting up. This just feels wonderful. Our bodies are so close."

female age 26

"Good old missionary, with me on the bottom and him on top!"

female age 32

"One of my favorite positions is sitting in his lap in a chair. He can kiss my neck or armpits, which drives me nuts, and I can move freely. If we are on the bed, I can also lie back and touch my clit if I want." *female age 38*

"My favorite position is sitting on top of him. That way I can stroke my clitoris or I can watch him do it." *female age 43*

"I enjoy having him on top but recently discovered that if we lie on our sides with me in front and I throw my upper leg over his, he can enter me from behind and it's very exciting." *female age 45*

"I like it best when we're doing it doggy style and I hold the vibrator and rub my clit with it. The sensation is wonderful!" *female age 25*

"I like to bend over a table and have my partner insert his penis from behind. We get great penetration this way, and he is also able to hit something in there that makes me feel really good!" *female age 34*

"I like to be on my back with my legs up while he is on his knees entering me and rubbing my clitoris. We started using this position when I was pregnant and I still like it best." *female age 35*

What do you like the most about intercourse and what do you like the least?

"Worst part—the big wet spot. Best part—making the big wet spot." *female age 27*

"It is wonderful when we first start having intercourse and I love the cuddling after. I don't like how, if you don't clean up afterward, the ejaculate runs out of you (sometimes cold) and drips down your butt onto the sheets." *female age 30*

"I like it when he first inserts his penis into my vagina the best. The thing I like least about sex is having to really work for a long time to get him to orgasm when he's had too much to drink." *female age 34*

"I like the beginning the most and orgasm, of course. If somebody takes too long, the middle gets dull." *female age 25*

"The first moments of penetration are the best. The wet spot on the bed, the worst." *female age 44*

"The part I like best is when my man spends a long time getting me hot until I want him so badly I can't wait and he finally sinks his penis into me. It's such a relief to finally be joined together. I like it least when he enters too soon and comes too fast and says, 'I'm sorry' when I had my hopes up for more." *female age 38*

"I love feeling him on top of me, kissing and caressing, and I love the feeling of his penis inside me. The part I don't like is the mess." *female age 35*

Women readers offer their suggestions about having intercourse for the first time

"Make him read the *Guide To Getting It On* first!" *female 30*

"I would have waited until I was in college, or maybe even after. I would have saved myself years of painful, uncomfortable, inexperienced, or hurried sex—often without pleasure for me. And while it just felt good to be close to the guy, I realize that I haven't thought of most of them in years. Girls, you ain't missing nothing!" *female age 32*

"Be choosy. Take your time. Touch and explore everything, maybe tie him up and you take total control; it's amazing the feeling you get by doing that." *female age 36*

"Make sure you really want it and it's not about being pressured. Masturbate together first. Be comfortable together. My first time was painful and humiliating; there's got to be a better way." *female age 38*

"It was very hard to do, but I waited until I was 18 to have intercourse. It was with a guy who I know cared deeply about me, which made my first experience very fun and comfortable." *female age 36*

"Relax and don't expect it to be like the romance novels." *female age 32*

"Make him go slowly and be sure that you are aroused sufficiently before you let him enter you because it will probably be a little uncomfortable the first time. If he rushes, it will hurt and you won't enjoy it at all." *female age 35*

Extra Odds'N'Ends

Some couples enjoy it greatly when the woman uses a vibrator during intercourse. The sensations can be very pleasing for both partners. This can work in any number of the usual positions, or you can get all artsy and try doing it like the couple in the illustration in the vibrator chapter.

A woman who is on top and facing her man's feet can watch his penis as it goes in and out of her vagina. She can also reach forward and play with his toes, or reach down and play with his testicles.

Rear-entry positions allow the head of the penis to focus on different parts of the vagina than missionary positions. Rear entry also provides extra padding, which can be very welcome if one or both of you is really bony.

Rather than thrusting, some couples find that rocking back and forth with a penis inside can feel quite pleasant.

Some couples enjoy taking an intercourse break in order to have oral sex; other couples like to have oral sex after intercourse.

In Veronica Monet's video of women masturbating, some of the women used dildos. However, it was not unusual for the woman to run the dildo between her labia rather than pushing it into her vagina. Some women enjoy a well-lubricated penis moving between their labia in this way, like a hot dog going back and forth through a hot dog bun. The ridge around the head of the penis can feel especially nice as it glides back and forth over the clitoris. The woman can increase the pressure by pulling the penis tighter against her vulva with her fingertips. This is also called femoral intercourse.

In the highly recommended book *Tricks — More Than 125 Ways to Make Good Sex Better*, author Jay Wiseman suggests having the man lie on his back and the woman place a pair of her panties over his penis. The penis sticks through a leg hole, with the panties draping down over his testicles and between his legs. The couple then has intercourse with the woman on top. If the panties are silky or rayon-like, the material might stimulate him with each stroke.

Some couples find a well-trimmed and freshly bathed big toe to be a fun penis substitute. (No, this was not a suggestion submitted by Dr. Scholl.) Also, a heel that's jiggled back and forth rapidly can be used to stimulate a woman's genitals.

There are couples who like to gently bite each other's shoulders or run their teeth along each other's skin while having intercourse. This works best when the skin is well-lubricated and the lovers let each other know when it starts to hurt.

Some men and women particularly enjoy the feeling of intercourse after a woman has had an orgasm rather than before.

If for some reason a vagina doesn't get as wet as a couple might want, keep some water-based lube handy, or pick up glycerin suppositories from the drugstore that can be put into the vagina ahead of time. If vaginal infections are a problem, you might experiment with water-based lubricants that have no glycerin. As the former baby boom generation hot flashes its way through the new century, a plethora of pricey new "personal moisturizers" will be flooding the market.

Women might not lubricate very well for the first couple of months following pregnancy. Extra lubrication can also help if the woman is taking drugs such as antihistamines, alcohol, or pot, and if the man is wearing a condom or the couple is playing with sex toys.

Why not try feeding each other while having intercourse? That's what nature created papaya for.

Some couples enjoy a finger, thumb, small vibrator, or butt plug on or in each other's anus during intercourse.

Most sex stores sell little plastic thingies that fit over a man's penis and provide extra stimulation to the woman's clitoris when she rubs up against his pubic bone. There is also a plastic vibrating cock ring that some couples enjoy, and a special vibrator in a harness can be strapped in place over the clitoris for use during intercourse.

Some vaginas make fartlike noises during intercourse. This is due to air that has been pushed into the back of the vagina. If you get embarrassed about these sounds, it might be helpful to remember that the noise was the result of the two of you doing wonderful things to each other.

 There is one position where the man sits on a chair and the woman sits in his lap, wrapping her legs around his waist. While this doesn't work for heavy-duty thrusting, the penetration can be really deep. Sitting up also allows more blood to pool in the pelvic region, which can help some men get better erections. You might try a similar position where the man sits in the chair and the woman sits on his lap but facing away from him (sitting spoons position?).

Warning: This can hurt you! Really.

Certain kinds of intercourse injuries can cause your penis to forever bend in a strange way. Most of the injuries occur when the woman is on top. Urologists strongly suggest that when using this position, the woman be well-lubricated and that she restrict her up-and-down motion. This helps decrease those instances where she sits down on your penis, but at a funny angle, or when it comes out on the upstroke and gets crunched on the downstroke instead of sliding in easily the way it's supposed to. A good way to compensate for the decreased thrusting is to put a pillow under the man's rear end. This can help make his pelvic bone more accessible, and his partner might delight more in pushing down against it (grinding) than in moving up and down. That way she's got the penis deep inside and gets her clitoral area worked too. She might also try squeezing, as if she's peeing and trying to stop the flow.

Up Your Bum — Anal Sex
Chapter 26

The following recollections are those of a seventy-one-year-old woman: "I grew up in the country.... We had neighbors, Amos Wheatley and his wife. One night while washing dishes, Mrs. Wheatley told my mother that she let Amos 'use the other hole.' Then they had a baby girl, and I heard my father comment that Amos must have got it right at least once. Sometime later, Amos, who was uneasy about the expense of having a new baby, told my father he'd rather have had a team of horses. My father said, 'Isn't that expecting rather a lot of Mrs. Wheatley?'"

As told to Julia Hutton in her wonderful book,
"Good Sex: Real Stories from Real People" Cleis Press, San Francisco

Anal Sex — Statistical Lowdown

Some couples would rather drink goat sweat than try anal sex; others enjoy an occasional rectal soiree. Most people say that the reason they like doing it has more to do with how it feels than just with the perverse thrill of it all. This is why some heterosexual women and men, as well as some gay guys, like having their rear ends plowed.

Anal sex—*Penis into Rectus*—is often associated with homosexuality. However, according to various statistics, thirty percent to forty percent of all heterosexual couples in this country have tried anal intercourse, with up to half of these continuing to do it on an occasional basis. While two to five million straight American couples are said to practice anal intercourse with regularity, only about fifty percent of gay males are into backdoor sex. Of course, straight or gay, these statistics refer only to anal intercourse. The following reader comments indicate there are other ways to tickle your hemorrhoids than with just a penis:

> "My boyfriend likes me to rub a finger on his anus while I give him oral sex. Gentle pressure and a rotating finger add a lot to his pleasure." *female age 23*

> "I hate admitting this, but I like it when Dave wets one of his fingers and slides it into my anus. It is a huge turn-on, and there are times when it makes me orgasm. The only problem

is pulling out. It always hurts coming out and usually throws off my bowel movements for the next few hours. It feels like I have to go...." *female age 26*

Whether you are straight, gay, or somewhere in between, the chances are good that at some point in your life you might try anal sex. That is why the topic is covered in this book, although it may catch severe grief from the self-righteous and anally oppressed. Please be aware that this guide couldn't care less whether you do or don't practice anal sex, but it does have a few suggestions in case curiosity nips you in the rear.

Why Do People Do It?

Why do people have anal sex? Some women offer anal sex as a way of keeping their virginity. Some men offer anal sex as a way of getting work in the entertainment industry. Some couples like anal sex because it's forbidden. But the most obvious reason why people do anal sex is because they enjoy the way it feels.

"Anal sex helps me feel a whole different part of my vagina and vulva. The fact that it is so tight and kind of nasty is a turn-on to me too." *female age 23*

"My wife asks for anal intercourse on occasion, usually late at night when she is very aroused and her inhibitions are down."
male age 41

"I can come from anal intercourse, but not from vaginal intercourse." *female age 32*

"When Hillary is all worked up, she sometimes really likes me to massage her anus. When I slip a lubricated finger inside her, it is often the thing that puts her over the edge. If I have a finger inside her vagina and one in her anus, she reacts very well to the sandwiching of the wall when I press the two together. Other times, she really hates it when I touch her there. I can never quite guess when it's going to be a green light." *male 25*

"Both of us like it. I will sometimes put a finger in her anus while we are having intercourse. It's very exciting for her, and I can feel my penis through the wall, which I find to be very erotic." *male age 39*

A lot of people have the notion that the only reason women do anal sex is to please a male partner. Not a single woman in our survey who does anal sex mentioned anything about pleasing a partner. Each one said she did it because she liked the way it feels. Aside from the obvious reason, which is that the anus is filled with lots of nerve receptors, it seems that the wall between the vagina and rectum may swell when the woman is sexually aroused. This wall might tug on the same nerve that transmits vaginal orgasms to the brain. As a result, some women experience extra-pleasant sensations on the wall between the rectum and vagina during anal intercourse that they don't get otherwise. Some women report getting an extra-intense orgasm when they stimulate their clitoris at the same time that they are having anal sex. This makes sense, since the extra anal stimulation might intensify the orgasm signal that is going to the brain, as well as providing extra stimulation to the pelvic nerve. It might result in what is known as a blended orgasm.

As for men's pleasure, some enjoy having their anus massaged or penetrated, and some report having memorable orgasms when their prostate gland is being pressed. Seldom do men have an orgasm from anal stimulation alone. Usually it includes penis stimulation as well. It is certainly possible that anal stimulation lights up extra nerve pathways that help amplify genital orgasms.

A final reason that some couples do anal sex is for birth control. It is possible that anal sex is practiced as birth control in countries that take seriously the Catholic Church's opposition to contraception. Perhaps this isn't what the Vatican had in mind. Or maybe anal sex would be a hot concept in these countries regardless of where they pray. Is anal sex an effective means of preventing pregnancy, or can ejaculate run out of the anus and into the vagina? Pregnancies from anal sex are common enough that the term "splash conception" is used to describe them. Perhaps this is how people with anal-retentive personalities are conceived.

Big Mama Nature & The Human Backside

When Big Mama Nature designed the female body she gave it a vagina that's rough, tough and durable. She made the walls of the vagina so they would stretch, swell, lubricate and straighten out at times of sexual excitement. This allows objects of desire to slide in and out with a fair amount of ease and enjoyment.

Mother Nature was working from a different set of blueprints when she built the human rectum. That's because the rectum's main purpose is for elimination rather than romance. As a result, the walls of the rectum don't stretch and lubricate like those of the vagina, although they comfortably fit objects that are even larger than a penis on a nearly daily basis. Think about it. Reports that anal sex will damage your rectum are not backed up by medical fact as long as you use lots of lubrication and leave your crowbar in the toolshed.

Another difference between the rectum and the vagina is that nature included a pair of pugnacious sphincter muscles to guard the gates of your anus. These muscular rings were designed to facilitate outgoing rather than incoming objects, although they can be taught to yield in either direction. The anal sphincters are two of the most important muscles in the human body as long as you plan on living and working in the vicinity of other human beings.

A Brief Historical Summary Of The Structure & Function of the Human Rectum from the Time of Cro-Magnon Man Until the Founding of Ancient Greece

If you consider the history of the human rectum, say from the time of Cro-Magnon man until the founding of Ancient Greece, its sole purpose was to hold things in. It wasn't until the Ancient Greeks invented sodomy that our bums became multipurpose. (In giving credit where credit is due, the Old Testament may have had an interest in the subject of anal sex that possibly predated the Ancient Greeks. At the very least, one of the early Biblical plagues visited upon the Egyptians apparently included hemorrhoids.)

Down & Dirty at the Acropolis

Thanks to the inventiveness of the Ancient Greeks, we now have things in our lives like politicians, lawyers, doctors and anal sex. The only one of these that should never cause you any pain is anal sex. If it does, you are doing it wrong, says psychologist Jack Morin, who has written the bible on the subject called "Anal Pleasure and Health" (Down There Press, San Francisco, 1998). It is doubtful that you will find this title at your local B. Dalton.

The key to pleasurable anal sex is training the anal sphincter muscles to open for incoming objects. One set of these muscles is under conscious control. It's what people use to maintain their dignity when waiting to use the bathroom. The second set of sphincter muscles is a total free agent that automatically closes whenever something pushes against it. In order to have comfortable anal sex, the second set of sphincters must be taught how to relax when you ask.

Rectal Aerobics —One and a Two and a...

"I like it when a guy stimulates my anus with his fingers or a dildo before entering it with his penis. It's much easier to take him that way. It's a very intense feeling, and can be very pleasurable, but it has to be slow and gentle; otherwise it's too painful." *female age 26*

This section has been written as if the male is doing the inserting and the female is receiving. Far be it from this guide to say how it is in your own relationship. Make sure that your fingernails are trimmed

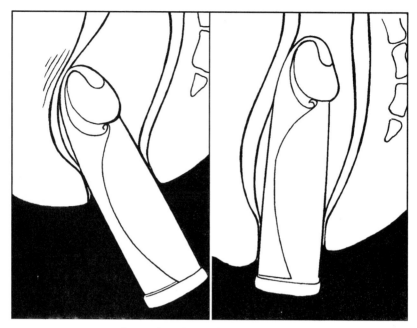

Location, Location, Location

and your hands are washed. Wearing a latex glove and/or condom is recommended. Also, some people prefer to give themselves a quick enema ("short shot") with a bulb syringe or a prepared store-bought solution before having anal sex. Others might equate this with removing the patina from the Statue of Liberty.

Psychologist Morin suggests the following technique for teaching your rectum to relax: Each night for a week or so the male partner lubes up a clean finger and gently inserts it in the female's rear, pushing very softly and slowly.

Rectal expert Erik Mainard—known as the Avatar of Ass—encourages a gentle massage of the anus and suggests angling the finger slightly upward toward the tailbone, since that's how the rectum curves. He says to push in quite slowly and only as the resistance eases. This kind of digital exploration should feel very good for the receiver; otherwise the person who is inserting the finger is either rushing it or being a brute.

One way to help relax the anal area is for the receiver to push down as though she were trying to move her bowels. In addition to relaxing the sphincters, this adds a bit of suspense to the exercise.

However, anal purists say that with the help of a patient, caring partner, one needn't trick the sphincters into relaxing.

The receiver should feel comfortable with finger penetration before attempting any further unnatural acts. It is also suggested that the receiver try inserting her own finger, for instance, when she is in the shower, so she can get a better sense of how her second sphincter works. This will help her to better bond with her rectum. It is not until the second sphincter learns to relax that anal sex will feel comfortable, and if it doesn't feel comfortable, you shouldn't be doing it. If there is any discomfort other than a feeling of fullness which shouldn't be painful, spend an extra week doing the finger exercises or give up the concept of anal intercourse entirely.

Butt...

> "I like to have my anus stimulated when I'm receiving oral sex. I like to have one finger inserted, but it doesn't have to be very far—just past the sphincter muscle will do. And rather than sliding all the way in and out, it is better if there is just a slight tugging movement. It adds one more sensation to the myriad of sensations involved in oral sex." *female age 37*

If you want anal stimulation, you need to ponder the profound question of exactly how you want it. Do you want it thin like a finger, or wider like a penis or dildo? Do you want it to move in and out, or do you want it to go inside and stay there? When it comes to purchasing sex toys, the former activity would call for a dildolike object; the latter would be best be served by a butt plug. When it comes to toys for anal sex, there are more choices than at a Marks & Spencer After-Christmas Sale. For more on sex toys, see the chapter "Oscillator, Generator, Vibrator, Dildo."

Rear-end connoisseur Erik Mainard claims that people tend to stick fingers or a penis into a partner's rectum ("rosebud") when they would be better off spending more time massaging and caressing the external butt and anal parts. Until watching Mr. Mainard's *Rosebud Massage* video, we'd always assumed that a man either left his sweetheart's rectum alone, which seemed like a fine idea, or tried to stick a finger or penis up it, assuming that's what she wanted. But

Mr. Mainard teaches several different ways of massaging a partner's anus which seem pretty interesting if the two of you are into backdoor stimulation. For information on Mr. Mainard's videotapes, contact www.eroticmassage.com.

Romancing the Rear

Any kind of anal play, be it using a butt plug or a real-life penis, goes best with relaxation. Make sure the receiver receives a long, lingering massage, a candlelight bath or whatever it is that you do to get really relaxed. That's because one of the places in our body where we tend to carry a lot of tension is between our butt cheeks. If you are going to do anal sex, you want that area to be as relaxed as possible before anything goes in. That could well be the difference between an experience that is pleasing and one that is painful.

The Partner Matters

"I truly hated anal sex the two times I had tried it before. But I agreed to do it with my new boyfriend and it feels incredible with him! Am I weird, or are there any other women who enjoy anal sex?" *female age 28*

You've gotta love our readers. We posted this reader's question on our sex survey at www.goofyfootpress.com and found a surprising number of women who said they'd had a similar experience. Many said the two key elements were being able to feel totally relaxed with the guy and feeling exceptionally horny. Here is one of the responses that not only met the previous question, but upped it by six inches:

"I have had anal sex intermittently. It's okay. I was double penetrated twice and THAT was the most incredible thing, but it was a dangerous science to get the positioning just right."

female age 28

Playin' the Back Nine? Bag It

Straight or gay, single or married, monogamous or slut, you are always wise to use a condom when having anal sex. There are good reasons for this that extend even beyond concern about AIDS.

Fluids deposited in the rectum are absorbed more easily into the body than fluids deposited in the vagina. In other words, deposit a wad of male ejaculate up a partner's rear, and chances are her hungry colon is going to slurp it up. Heaven only knows how her immune system is going to respond, and science won't be helping straight couples answer this question any time soon. If you bag the penis before it goes up her bum, you've eliminated a potential source of concern.

Also, males can get prostate infections from having anal sex without wearing a condom. Our prostate consultant, who is nobody's prude when it comes to matters of sex, nearly comes unglued at the thought of sticking an unbagged penis inside a rectum. That's because the same bacteria that are prevalent in the bum can also cause a difficult case of prostatitis. He feels that the reason more men don't get bladder infections from doing anal sex is because the infection settles in the prostate. Also, no matter how hard you wash your penis after a rectal rendezvous, little pieces of poop still remain inside the urinary opening if you haven't used a condom. This is not good for either of you, and at the very least can give her an infection if you follow with vaginal intercourse. If you are going from anal intercourse to vaginal intercourse, not only should you wash the penis, but be sure to take a hearty leak as well.

When it comes to condom use up your bum, consider these:

Avanti or *Trojan Supra:* These polyurethane condoms should be a butt pirate's dream; however, they have not been approved for anal-sex usage by the FDA. These are made thinner than traditional latex condoms and can be used with oil-based lubricants. Also, they may have a higher rate of breakage than the old latex war horses.

Latex condoms with water-based lube: Silicone lube is the water-based lube of choice for anal sex. It won't harm latex condoms and you get a lot more slide for your buck than with KY or other water-based lubes. It also won't dry out as fast as most water-based lubes.

Do not used ribbed or studded condoms for anal sex. It's always a good idea to put a new condom on any sex toys that go into the rectum and to wash the toy afterward. If you do like toys for anal play, dedicate some just for that purpose so they never see the inside of a vagina.

Beware the Buttman

If you like the thought of doing anal intercourse, the chances are good you like to watch anal-sex videos. In her book *The Ultimate Guide to Anal Sex for Women,* Tristan Taormino warns that anal intercourse

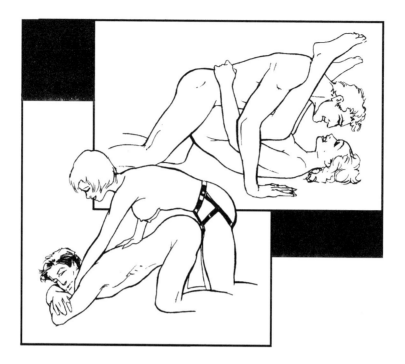

requires lots of patience and a slow, relaxed approach. This is the part that the anal-sex videos leave out. Even when making X-rated movies, they don't just go plowing some porn starlet's rear end without lots of preparation and anal foreplay—none of which the viewer actually sees in the video. So while it's fine to enjoy the hot action shown in *Anal Invaders Number Six Million and Thirty-Two,* don't for a moment try to replicate it in real life with a real partner, unless she's inflatable.

In Slow—Out Slow

No matter what you are putting inside a rectum, it needs to go in very slowly and come out very slowly.

Most people have no difficulty grasping the former, but they don't realize that anything being pulled out of a rectum, whether it's a finger, penis or butt plug, needs to be pulled out slowly. Otherwise, extreme discomfort and even physical damage might result.

Anal Intercourse Alternatives

One of the most sensitive parts of the human body is the skin that surrounds the outer rim of your anus. It's easy to stimulate this area with a thumb, finger, tongue or butt plug without sticking a penis all the way up it. For instance, some women who are receiving vaginal stimulation enjoy it when a partner puts pressure on their anus with a thumb or finger. Just be sure to avoid putting something that's been up an anus into a vagina.

All Things Considered: Zucchini Revenge

It's only fair that if a guy wants to stick his penis up a partner's rectum, she should be able to stick something of comparable size up his. If vegetables are used, don't forget to check with your grocer or family doctor as to which are safest and most suitable. You don't want a vegetable breaking off and taking up permanent residence inside your man's rectum. Couples who are less organically inclined might use a silicone penis substitute known as a dildo or butt plug.

Butt Plugs Galore

Butt plugs are dildolike objects made specifically for the rear end. They have flared bases to keep them from getting lost on the Hershey Highway. Butt plugs come in many different sizes, and some even vibrate. People use butt plugs to give their rear ends a feeling of fullness. They are much better suited for this purpose than a dildo, which is made for thrusting.

Dildo Deluxe

So you thought you finally had this sex-toy thing under control when suddenly your old man informs you that he wants you to do him up the rear. What's a girl to do? Pull out her real-life rubber version of porn star Jeff Stryker's monster dong? Or does she use her silicone Rocketeer, or what about her Billy the Kid with the vibrating head?

When it comes to violating a loved-one's rear end, wisdom has it that a dildo which curves upward is the way to go. That's because our rectums tend to curve. The nice thing about using a dildo instead of a real-life penis is that you can turn the dildo upward or downward to hit the right spot. Check out places like Good Vibrations or Blowfish to find which dildos are best for anal penetration. They'll also be able to tell you which dildo will fit into your new Malibu two-strap harness. (Your classic Jeff Stryker dildo won't—it's too big!)

If you plan to use a dildo for both vaginal and anal recreation, it is a very good idea to get a separate one for each port of entry. Having dedicated dildos helps decrease the chance that fecal matter will get into the vagina.

"Bend Over Boyfriend"

> "My boyfriend of five years actually made the suggestion that I penetrate him anally. I lubricated the finger with the shortest nail on it and slowly slid it into his anus. He enjoyed it so much that he asked for two fingers and then three. While doing this, I also alternated sucking and manually pumping his cock with my other hand. He had a mind-blowing orgasm. He tells me it's the kind you feel deep down to your toes…. I'm now looking for a strap-on that stimulates me as well as him!"
>
> *female age 40*

Some people feel that only gay guys like things up their rears. Yet straight men have rectums that are every bit as sensitive as those of gay men. While plenty of straight guys would just as soon be boiled in oil as have a dildo or butt plug put up their rear, other manly guys enjoy the feeling tremendously. In fact, there's a popular new series of straight adult videos titled *Bend Over Boyfriend.*

As for penetrating their men anally, some women hold a dildo with their fingers; others put it in a dildo harness and propel it with their hips. A dildo harness looks somewhat like a jock-strap and holds the dildo in the same position as a man's erect penis. This allows the woman to thrust in and out, more or less. Learning how to use a dildo in a harness is an acquired art that takes time and patience. Also, keep in mind that a man's anal sphincters need just as much rectal foreplay as a woman's.

Consider trying a harness that straps to your thigh. It might be easier to control than the model that goes over your crotch.

Toy Precautions

Rectums are hungry little orifices. Make sure that anything going up them is firmly anchored on the outside of the body so it can't get sucked up inside. Dildos or butt plugs with flared bases are best for anal play, as it is unlikely you will need the assistance of an emergency room crew to get them out.

🐑 Be sure that anything inserted into the rectum is smooth with no points or ridges.

🐑 Anal beads consist of five large beads on a string. They resemble worry beads, but each bead is held in place on the string so it doesn't slide. While anal beads can certainly be used to count your worries on, people usually stick them up their butt. They are slowly pulled out, often at the point of coming, which is said to make for a super-charged orgasm. Anal beads can be as small as mothballs or as big as tennis balls (okay, golf balls). If the beads are plastic and have sharp blow-mold edges, be sure to file them down first. Also, it is wise to encase them in a condom before inserting. That's because they are very difficult to fully clean.

Prostate Stimulation

A number of straight men experience pleasant sensations from rectal and prostate stimulation. Yet the only time most straight men get anal stimulation is during a physical exam. Then and at tax time.

Men who are curious about feeling their own prostate can do so by reaching between their legs and sticking a well-lubricated finger up their own wazoo. It can be both weird and neat to feel a part of your body that you've never touched before. Pressing on the prostate will probably cause a dull, subtle sensation in the penis. Some men find that the physical contortions necessary to reach their own prostate can result in unanticipated trips to the chiropractor. To avoid this, you can purchase specially curved sextoys that help a guy to stimulate his prostate, if that's what you want to do. This book has a separate chapter on the prostate. See "Glands Down Under" starting on page 245.

Rimming

Rimming is a slang word for kissing ass, literally. It means sticking your tongue up or around your partner's deep-space nine. Keep in mind that it's probably not a good idea to rim just anyone, unless he or she is your boss or the chair of your dissertation committee. One reason to avoid indiscriminate rimming is that it can be an effective way of getting hepatitis and various parasites. It's the sort of thing to save for long-term relationships if you are so inclined, or cut a condom lengthwise and lay it over the person's anus before licking. Good hygiene is also a plus.

One gastroenterologist has said that by the time a couple has been together for a couple of years, they pretty much share the same anal flora. This means you probably won't get anything more from licking your partner's asshole than you would from licking your own. On the other hand, if you are in anything that even resembles a casual relationship, use a barrier before licking ass.

For advice on rimming, see "Gnarly Sex Germs" page 593.

Anal Fisting

Yes, Martha, there is such a thing. It can be very dangerous if done by the inexperienced. If you absolutely must have someone else's fist up your ass, the best book on the subject is said to be Bert Herrman's *Trust: The Hand Book—A Guide to the Sensual and Spiritual Art of Handballing*, Alamo Square Press, San Francisco, 1991. Be sure to check with a physician first, perhaps one from your local gay and lesbian health center. Even if you're not gay they are more likely to know about the practice than a regular family practitioner. There are also organized groups of fisters in large cities who sometimes offer talks and demonstrations—in Powerpoint and then some.

Rules of the Rear—A Pocket Guide

Here's a list of precautions for anal sex:

🐑 Straight or gay, married or in transition—if you are doing anal intercourse, use a condom.

🐑 Make sure that anything about to go up your rectum is both clean and well-lubricated. Reapply the lube often. See page 180.

🐑 The human rectum curves in a funny way and your partner won't know which angle feels best unless you specify. This means that you'll need to discuss which positions and angles feel best. Positions are similar to those used with vaginal intercourse.

🐑 Remove anything you have placed in the rectum very slowly. This includes a penis.

🐑 Don't stick a finger, penis or other object directly into a vagina when it's just been up an anus. Wash it first with soap and water. Make sure that your nails are well-trimmed.

People who have anal intercourse should occasionally get a rectal swab done to check for VD, yet few individuals own up to doing anal sex, so they don't tell their doctors. It might be easier if doctors simply asked, "Have you ever tried anal sex?" but it seems unlikely that the answers given would become a barometer of truth.

Never, ever have anal sex unless your rectum is in 100% good health. Do not do anal sex if it is painful. Unless you are sure of what you are doing, check with a physician or qualified expert first.

The author of this book went to a university with a top reputation in the sciences. Many of his classmates became medical doctors. A number of these did not seem equipped to deal with questions about sex, anal or otherwise. If you have medical questions about any kind of sex, it is possible that you won't be comfortable asking your private physician. An alternative is to call your local free clinic or national sex hot line. And as mentioned on the prior page, while you may not be homosexual, a friendly place to call with questions about anal sex might be the nearest gay and lesbian health center.

Additional Anal Tips

Make sure the receiver is aroused in other parts of his or her body before knocking on the backdoor. One of the keys to enjoyable anal sex is having your entire body relaxed and receptive to sex. Do not hold your breath. Breathing deeply will help you to stay relaxed. Once your get your finger, penis, dildo or whatever inside your partner's rear end, don't start thrusting with it. Leave it in place and gently start making circular motions. If and when your partner wants you to start thrusting, pull out slowly and as far as possible, and add more lube. Then you can start thrusting slowly. A woman might like her clit massaged at the same time she is having anal sex, as it may extend the feeling throughout her pelvis. Using a latex glove helps fingers slide in more smoothly, using a condom helps a penis slide in more smoothly. You might try inserting an anatomically shaped butt plug and then applying a strong vibrator to the base of it. Don't have anal sex when you are drugged or drunk. Your rear end is more easily damaged by sloppy sex than other body parts. Anal sex requires that the driver as well as the passenger be alert and sober. Likewise, don't use a lube like *Anal Ease* that numbs your butt.

If you are into enemas as part of anal sex, use plain tap water and make sure it's not too cold, unless you enjoy giving yourself cramps. Some people suggest a bulb syringe with a pinch of non-iodized salt.

"Do I like anal? It truly depends on how relaxed you are with the person doing it. He must take his time and understand your sensations. You can't do it like a porn star. It just doesn't feel good that way. When it is done right, the orgasm makes me scream!" *female age 26 [Note: other readers who are less enthusiastic about anal sex says it makes them scream, too!]*

Resources: If you are into anal recreation, consider the following:

Jack Morin's *Anal Pleasure and Health* (San Francisco: Down There Press, 1999). Morin's book is not shy on the "love your anus" mantra, but anyone who is having anal problems of any kind will find it to be helpful. He really does get you thinking about your anus in a different way, and if you have any kind of stress-related anal problem (especially hemorrhoids), this book will be more than worthwhile. It's also a highly regarded book to read if you are thinking about trying anal sex. It may not help heal your inner asshole, but it does an excellent job with your outer one.

Tristan Taormino's *Ultimate Guide to Anal Sex For Women* (San Francisco: Cleis Press, 1998). In spite of its title, this book is just as informative for men as for women. Tristan Taormino's infectious zeal and zest for life and sex provide a welcome backdrop to all things anal. If you are looking to expand your sexual horizons beyond Uranus, she's done an excellent job with her *Down and Dirty Sex Secrets* from Reagan Books, 2003.

Been down on your butt? Try *Anal Massage for Relaxation and Pleasure* from www.eroticmassage.com. Expect to see couples of all ages and all orientations massaging each other's butt cheeks and anuses. Don't expect to be aroused. However, if your goal is to be a pro at all things you can do when you are naked together, you will definitely learn a thing or three from this quietly-paced DVD.

Chapter Notes: If anal sex puts people at higher risk for AIDS, why do a chapter on it? Driving a car puts most straight couples at far greater risk for death than having anal sex. This guide would be more reckless asking most of you to start your car than writing on anal sex. Thanks to the late Dr. Bruce Voeller, Mariposa Foundation, for help.

Playing With Yourself

Chapter 27

Before the 1960s, people who wrote books on sex stated with an almost religious fervor that playing with yourself (masturbation) was a very bad thing to do. Today, people who write books on sex speak with the same kind of religious fervor, only now they say that playing with yourself is a very good thing to do.

It doesn't seem as though anything has changed. That's because none of the experts are asking you what you want to do. When it comes to the question of whether you should or shouldn't be masturbating, this book doesn't have any answers. It's your hand and your pants; if you want to stick one into the other, that's totally up to you.

What we can tell you is that as teenagers we felt certain that masturbation was an adolescent thing, something people get over when they become adults. Silly us. You will find there are times when you will do it a lot, and times when you'll hardly do it at all; times when it feels great, and times when it's a letdown. But during those times when the world doesn't seem like such a nice place, masturbation can usually be counted on to help take off some of the edge. It's also a wonderful nighttime aid that helps ease the transition between wakefulness and sleep, and contrary to what you might think, it will sometimes play an important role in relationships even when the sex between you and your partner is totally satisfying.

Playing with yourself can be a way to explore and pamper your body, as well as to explore the sexual feelings that you might be having about someone else. And some people find that their bodies simply work better if they have an orgasm every day or two, with masturbation being a natural way to help this happen. (Do you ever get into a certain state of mind where you need to masturbate just to relax enough so you can get the rest of your work done?) Whatever the motivation, if you are going to get yourself off by hand, why not try to get the most out of the experience? That is the focus of this chapter.

Vital Statistics

The following was told to Harry Maurer by a young woman for his book *Sex: An Oral History*, Viking Press, New York, 1994:

> "My mother has a vibrator that my father gave her one year. When I used to come home from college, I knew where she kept the vibrator, and I knew they never used it, so I would put it into my room and use it for the vacation. One summer I came home and it wasn't there. I was going crazy, I'm really a vibrator addict. Finally I was just so horny I said, 'OK, Mom, sit down. Where's the vibrator?' She's like, 'What!' I said 'Look, here's the deal. I've been stealing your vibrator for three years, and I need it now.' She was blown away, but she goes into her room, comes back with the vibrator, and says, 'By the way, have you ever used the jet in the hot tub?'"

According to just about everyone who has ever researched the subject, somewhere between 80% and 95% of guys eventually masturbate. Depending on whose statistics you look at, between 50% and 85% of women do the same.

Contrary to what you might think, people don't masturbate any less as they get older. In fact, many people who are married or deeply involved in a sexual relationship still get themselves off by hand. Masturbation doesn't decrease a person's desire for shared sex. For some people, it increases it. And some people report that they masturbate more when they are in a relationship rather than less.

How often do we masturbate? It varies from a couple of times a day to sometimes never. As for the number of orgasms per effort, researcher Thore Langfeldt interviewed children in Norway from kindergarten through high school about sex. Langfeldt found that the younger boys and girls could give themselves multiple orgasms when they masturbated. But as they got older, the boys started reporting fewer orgasms per attempt, while the girls reported more. This is a trend that continued with increased age and experience.

What the Sandman Knows about Masturbation

> "In my younger years, it usually took an hour or so before I had an orgasm. Now, if I'm especially hot, five minutes with a vibrator can do it, or about fifteen to twenty minutes by hand.

Sometimes I like to keep things slow; I prolong it by starting and stopping. Other times, I just want to get off as fast as I can. Sometimes I masturbate, but not to orgasm. It feels good and relaxes me without wanting to come." *female age 47*

According to the Sandman, the most common time when people masturbate is at night before they go to sleep or before taking a nap. It makes his job much easier. People get themselves off at other times, too. For instance, it sometimes feels good to masturbate after a work-out, since workouts can be sexually arousing. Plenty of people masturbate as a study break or when they have to spend long hours doing a paper or a project. It helps them refocus and return to the work at hand. Some people masturbate before a date so they will be more intellectually present. Women sometimes masturbate during their periods to help relieve cramping, or before intercourse to help it feel better. Some people wake up feeling really horny. They sometimes masturbate early in the morning, when the cock crows, before having their Wheaties®.

Some Seriously Twisted Lunacy from Kellogg's of Battle Creek

The last line of the last section should have read "Corn Flakes" instead of Wheaties, since Kellogg's Corn Flakes were created to give children more stamina so they wouldn't want to do horrible things like masturbate. John Harvey Kellogg, M.D., founder of the flake, told anyone who would listen that masturbation was a worse sin and "more immoral" than adultery. He called it the "most heinous, revolting, and unnatural vice."

Kellogg proposed a six-point program for every American male that included taking cold enemas every day and wearing a wet girdle to bed every night to help prevent masturbation.

His advice for parents whose children were caught masturbating included bandaging the genitals and covering them with cages, tying the child's hands together, and circumcision without anesthesia. He felt that the pain would be a helpful punishment for the horrible act that had been committed. Whatever foreskin was left should be sewn shut over the glans of the penis to keep the young man from having erections.

Kellogg's cereal is still known as "Kellogg's of Battle Creek." Battle Creek was the name of Dr. Kellogg's mental asylum where he served his special cold cereals to help the inmates to keep from masturbating. Of course, the finest medical minds of the day couldn't quite agree on what kind of physical horror masturbation would cause. Some physicians claimed it caused a man to become feeble, lackluster, and feminized, with side effects including impotence and underdeveloped genitals. Other physicians claimed that masturbation had the opposite effect, turning the young man into what fanatics today call sexual addicts, with the man blowing the family fortune on prostitutes and other excesses caused by uncontrolled eruptions of lust. If you look over the Police Gazette ads from 1892 that are on page 88, you can see how they refer to "the excesses of youth" and "underdeveloped genitals." These are what physicians in the day of Dr. Kellogg believed would happen if you masturbated.

To keep Dr. Kellogg spinning in his grave, this book encourages its readers to occasionally masturbate while eating a bowl of Kellogg's Corn Flakes.

How Guys Learn

"When I was ten, an older friend showed me how to masturbate. He had a full ejaculation; nothing came out of my penis except for a few drops of clear fluid. This was back in the day when astronauts were first orbiting the earth. I believed that technology could fix anything. So I pulled out my erector set and decided to create a jack-off machine. Planning and building it kept me busy for days. Unfortunately, it didn't make anything more come out of my penis than my hand did. Time, rather than technology, was the answer to that problem." *male 45*

A lot of guys learn to masturbate from other guys, often a big brother or friends. One shows the other how he does it, or the experienced whacker might put his hand on the novice guy's penis and jerk it off for him. Guys who don't learn about jerking off from other guys eventually learn on their own. That's because a teenager has to be pretty numb to himself to miss the obvious connection between soaping the thing up in the shower and the nice feelings that result. Also, when lying face down on a mattress with a hard-on, most guys are eventually compelled to hump or rub. Males eventually learn to masturbate because the penis, of all human organs, pleads to be yanked, stroked, lubed, and squeezed. (Anyone who has ever raised a little girl in a non-repressive environment might disagree, saying that those little clitoral hoods get a pretty good working out.)

Of course, if they haven't been taught about ejaculation, some guys will experience anything from concern to terror the first time they ejaculate, e.g., "Oh no, I broke something," to "Please God, I'll never ever do it again! I promise, just make it okay." And then they do it again the next day.

The Group Thing

"I can understand all sorts of things about guys' sexuality, except why they jerk off together. It seems so gay. Why do they do it?" *female age 23*

Good question. First of all, the majority of men will tell you they never jerked off with another male. And for those who have, maybe it has to do with the maturation process. Most young guys need little encouragement to take their pants off and explore. Getting naked can be so exciting for some boys that they get hard-ons from that alone. It's also natural for boys to share experiences, whether it's checking out an abandoned house or cave or showing each other the things you do with your dick. After all, you'd want to show your best friend the model you just built or take turns doing the latest skateboard trick, so why wouldn't you want to jerk off together and see what happens when you get hard or come?

"When we became teens, some of us boys would get together for a masturbation meeting in the treehouse, but it was more the thrill of something exciting and forbidden than anything else." *male age 26*

Again, plenty of men will shake their heads and say, "No way. You'd never catch me jerking off with another guy when I was a kid." Others will say, "Sure, that's how we did it." And some might even say, "It was neat back then, simpler, and a lot of fun."

As for masturbatory etiquette, some males have guy-like tea parties called circle jerks where they stand around and masturbate. There might be games connected with this, like who shoots the farthest or who comes the fastest (it's interesting how priorities change as you get older!). It's even been said that some young men feel excluded until they have been allowed to beat off with members of the local gang. The urge to beat off together seems to peak before high school age and drops off significantly after that. However, there are some adult males who, while identifying as heterosexual, enjoy masturbating together. Perhaps this isn't as much of a contradiction in terms as it seems. Straight men sure enjoy watching other men ejaculate in porn movies. Perhaps it's acceptable to be curious about another guy's ejaculation if he's just had his penis in a woman's body, but not acceptable if it's just two guys together.

The following answers to a survey in the newsletter *Sex & Health* help to summarize some of what's involved:

> "While partying with fraternity brothers, someone suggested a contest to see who could ejaculate the farthest. Each of the five of us took our turn in a tiled shower room. Surprisingly, the least endowed among us won!"

> "Sometimes when I'm camping with a couple of my buddies and our girlfriends are otherwise occupied, we get to joking about sex. We soon get so aroused that when one of us whips it out to pee, we start joking and the others whip theirs out, too. Then we just start stroking ourselves and talking about our favorite techniques. We don't touch each other, but we do comment on each other's members and may cheer one another on to climax. We're all good friends and have become much closer sharing our sexuality this way."

Sex & Health had a large straight male readership. Ninety-five percent of the men characterized themselves as strictly heterosexual; most were married and many had children. Still, a number reported fantasizing about masturbating with other men, e.g., 'Although I'm happily married with two children, I do sometimes fantasize about masturbating with friends. I've thought about asking one friend in particular, but I haven't had the nerve.' "

How Girls Learn

> "When I was young, climbing a flagpole always brought on such intense tingling feelings that I was only able to hold on tight and my legs would clamp around the pole. When the feelings subsided enough, I would resume climbing." *female age 37*

> "It was my freshman year of high school. I was kissing this guy and was getting really turned on. He put his hand on my inner thigh and I was going crazy! This was my first heavy petting session. I didn't quite know what to make of it. When I got home, I went to the bathroom. My underwear was very wet. I went to touch myself and BAM!—instant orgasm! My very first. I've never had it that easy since." *female age 27*

> "When I had my first orgasm I kept saying, 'Oh my God!' over and over. I was really shocked because I didn't know I could do that to myself!" *female age 25*

When it comes to masturbation, girls don't do "show and tell" nearly as often as boys. They tend to learn about masturbation on their own or by reading about it or seeing a woman do it in porn. Some women learn how to masturbate from the sensation they experience while cleaning their genitals, from climbing trees, poles, or ropes, while on swings or when riding bicycles. Some learn by putting a pillow between their legs or by leaning up against something such as the washing machine when it's on the spin cycle. It might also happen when they have a sex dream and wake up before it's over—the sensation is still alive in their genitals and all they need to do is reach down and rub. One woman reported learning to masturbate by pushing a sanitary napkin against her vulva; another by stroking the shaft of her clitoris with a pencil. The possibilities for discovering how to masturbate are way too numerous to name here. Here are some of the ways they do it now:

> "I did it in front of a mirror with a condom-wrapped candlestick, and another time with the end of a comb." *female age 21*

> "Bathtub, vibrator, boyfriend's fingers (my own don't work). Electric toothbrush handle, my ex-husband's hammer (the handle), even celery once." *female age 26*

"I get the most intense orgasm by leaning on a hard surface like a counter and wiggling around till I come. I also use a dildo, and I use my fingers to massage my labia and clit, occasionally fingering my vagina." *female age 37*

"I use a finger, then fingers." *female age 49*

"Occasionally I use my hands, but usually I use a running faucet before I take my bath." *female age 19*

"I rub my clit in a circular motion with my fingers or use a trusty old Prelude 3 [vibrator]. I've tried putting things inside my vagina, but so far that's been a very neutral experience — I need my lover's hand or torso to be attached to what's going inside. Sometimes I gently rub my chest as I masturbate, or run a soft piece of cloth over my nipples." *female age 47*

"I do it while reading a book or having a fantasy. Usually I stimulate my clit directly with one or more fingers. Only rarely do I put anything inside my vagina, although I do like the feel of a tampon. I also like anal stimulation. That will make an orgasm more intense and more diffused." *female age 36*

It is virtually impossible to list all of the different ways that women masturbate. A lot of women use their fingers while lying on their backs or sitting in chairs. Some do it on their sides, or while lying face down so nobody can see what they're doing. Some women may even occasionally prefer to squat.

Men sometimes have the fantasy that a woman who is masturbating sticks her fingers inside her vagina. Some women do, but many don't. Instead, they might squeeze the lips of their vulva together or push against it in ways that create pressure rather than penetration.

Plenty of women use lubrication when they masturbate, either their own (vaginal or saliva) or store-bought. Lots like to use vibrators for masturbating, and some use dildos. Some like to masturbate by using the faucet in the bathtub. After you get the water temperature just right, lie down in the tub and push your bum against the wall of the tub where the faucet comes out. It might help if you have an inflatable pillow to put under your rear to get the angle just right. Some women say it works better if they spread their labia open with their fingers so the water cascades onto their awaiting clitoris. Water Safety: When masturbating with a water jet in a whirlpool or Jacuzzi, sit back at a distance and aim the jet toward your genitals. The current might be stronger than you think, so approach slowly. Some women like to pull their labia apart; others don't. Do not get extremely close to the jet and don't aim it up your vagina or rectum.

A woman who has responsive nipples may make nipple stimulation an enjoyable part of her masturbation.

Thigh High

The woman writer who contributes to the female part of Jackin-World.com suggests that some women can teach themselves to come by squeezing their thighs together. She suggests that you start by masturbating in the normal way, but press your thighs together when you start to have an orgasm. After a few weeks of doing this, masturbate yourself to the point where you almost have an orgasm, but pull your fingers (or whatever) away at the last minute and try to finesse yourself into orgasm by squeezing your thighs together. Once you are able to do this successfully, start with the thigh-squeezing action a little earlier each time. Some might prefer doing this with tight jeans on so they get an assist from the seam in the crotch.

Additional Ways

One of us knew a woman who could have an orgasm by doing thirty-seven stomach crunches (mini sit-ups). What an incentive for keeping your abs in shape!

Other women get off by humping pillows or water bottles, swinging on swings, tugging on underwear, rubbing up against things, using peeled cucumbers, and riding a bike down bumpy roads. Some like to stimulate their anus, either by putting pressure on it or by sticking a finger or butt plug inside it. Some like to look in mirrors, some get turned on by wearing their boyfriend's or girlfriend's shirt or underwear. Heck—fill in your own blanks.

Say It Ain't So!

Tennis elbow is a form of tendonitis. One reader, a female physician, suspects that some of her patients with tennis elbow actually

got their tendonitis from—gulp—the number one repetitive finger motion that many women do. So if you are having tendonitis or repetitive stress syndrome on the arm that you masturbate with, try using a vibrator for masturbating and see if the problem doesn't improve. Ditto for lovers who routinely masturbate their female partners. This physician adds that guys with unexplained tendonitis might try masturbating differently, too. If you do it dry, you might try using lube. The hand motion can be quite different.

Rubbing the Nub? Beating the Bush? Giving Girl-Masturbation a Name

There are numerous slang terms for male masturbation. This is not the case with female masturbation (Diddle? Jill off? These are not exactly universal terms). Since women don't usually masturbate together, they haven't needed to establish slang to convey what they are doing. In fact, it has only been during the last forty years that our society has even acknowledged the existence of women's masturbation. Maybe it's time that women adopted a universal slang term for masturbation. Perhaps one of the women's magazines could have a contest, or maybe the First Lady could announce what she calls it.

Women Rock'n'Rollers Touch Themselves—Even Britney!

While there are several rock'n'roll references to male masturbation, there were only a few until recently that mention women's masturbation (on a major record label, anyway). One was Cyndi Lauper's "She Bop" and another was a hit song by the Divinyls "I Touch Myself." While there's nothing hidden about the joys of female masturbation in "She Bop", "I Touch Myself" is another story. It's about a woman who touches herself when she thinks about her lover. According to the lyrics of this song, the woman is so into her man that she doesn't seem to have much of an identity without him. This amplifies an age-old double standard: guys can masturbate because it feels good, but women need to frame their sexuality with love for a man.

While Cyndi Lauper made no secrets about the subject of her song, Christina from the Divinyls said in a Rolling Stone interview that the song doesn't refer to masturbation. Perhaps she hadn't seen her own video. While it's perfectly normal and natural to masturbate over the love you feel for a partner, that used to be the only way women were allowed to have a dripping depth of sexuality—if it were all about her man and limited only to him.

Women, Masturbation & Intercourse

Some women give themselves orgasms during intercourse by pushing against a partner's pubic bone or by reaching down with their fingers and playing with themselves while the penis is inside of them. Is this masturbation, intercourse, or both? It doesn't matter, given how it happens so often and is totally normal.

Also, it's not unusual for a woman to masturbate before intercourse to help her genitals be more into it, or after intercourse because she wants more stimulation or simply enjoys the feeling. It is unfortunate that women often hide this and think that their partners might not want to know about it. It seems like a sign of a good relationship when a woman feels free to finish what we couldn't, or when we help her get started and she takes it from there.

It's also nice when a partner feels free to masturbate on his or her own. Far from being a sign of deficit, this might be an indication there is a great deal of love and understanding in the relationship.

Girls, Their Horses & the Fifty-Minute Hour

"My first orgasm? I was riding my horse and I felt a strange sort of pleasure between my legs. I felt like I wanted it to stop so I could concentrate on my riding, but it felt so good." *female 18*

"I was standing in the barn with my horse when I had a spontaneous orgasm. I gushed and everyone laughed at me for peeing in my pants. I was fourteen or so. I didn't discover masturbation until I was twenty, and then I thought orgasm was so incredible, I wanted one every day." *female age 37*

"My first orgasm ever was when I was riding a horse. I thought I was perverted and never told anyone. Then at a slumber party one of my close friends who also horseback rides admitted that she'd had a similar experience." *female age 18*

Having grown up in a farm town, your author knew from a young age that it was unwise for any man to come between a woman and her horse. But can you imagine his amazement years later when an occasional female patient would describe the euphoria she gleaned from the back of her favorite gelding? It's information that's usually relayed in hushed tones of revelry and delight—warm, pleasing, primal sensations with one of nature's most magnificent creatures between her legs. Women rarely speak about their husbands or boyfriends with the kind of knowing sensitivity that is reserved for their favorite horse.

From Trigger to Hitachi

After having an orgasm, women's genitals often stay primed. Some women experience waves of orgasm that can be finessed for the better part of an hour. Other women find a single orgasm to be very satisfying.

Because of the different possibilities, one woman might masturbate on and off for an entire evening, reaching between her legs every page or two while reading a book. Another woman might masturbate with the sole purpose of reaching a single, discrete orgasm, going from beginning to end without pause.

Of course, there are plenty of women who don't like to masturbate. Some never feel the urge. For others, touching themselves implies an uncomfortable investment in their own sexuality. Sex with a man makes it okay to be a sexual rocket ship, but masturbation might feel dirty. This might be true even if their body badly needs an orgasm to help it unwind. There are also women who like to masturbate but don't like to touch their genitals. They might use a vibrator or masturbate with their fingers on the outside of their underwear.

The Limitations of a One-Grip Rhythm (for Both Sexes)

If you always use the exact same touch and rhythm when you masturbate, you might be teaching your body to expect that and only that. Given how it's difficult for someone else to do you in precisely the same way that you do yourself, you might consider occasionally mixing it up. For instance, if you usually get yourself off dry, you might try it with lotion. If you use your right hand, experiment with your left or try it with a vibrator one time and another time in the bathtub, but not with a vibrator in the bathtub unless your vibrator is waterproof.

On Sucking Air (for Both Sexes)

Learning to breathe right is an essential part of being an athlete, unless maybe your sport is billiards. It's no different with sex.

When you are in the process of having sex, be it solo or with a partner, you might occasionally pay attention to your breathing. The Tantric types encourage taking long, slow, deep breaths where you imagine pulling the air all the way into your groin. This helps some people to have a more intense experience. From this book's more geriatric perspective, the extra O_2 helps keep us from having a coronary.

Guy Tricks—"First, Nuke a Jar of Miracle Whip, Then..."

"I made a false pussy out of bicycle tire inner tubes, and it worked quite well. I have also used banana peels, watermelons, and a hole in a piece of wood." *male age 42*

A lot of guys use their hands to jerk off with. Some do it dry and some add lubrication which includes saliva, soap, hair conditioner, *Vaseline,* vegetable oil, coconut oil, baby oil, and anything else under the sun that can make their pecker slick. Guys do better using an oil-based lubricant, and some even use a special type of facial cleanser called *Albolene* which is greatly admired for its jerk-off properties. The trouble with standard moisturizers is that they dry up quickly, as do water-based lubes when exposed to air. If you use a water-based lube, try adding a few drops of water or saliva as it dries instead of adding more lube. Otherwise, you might end up with two sticky messes instead of one.

A lot of guys masturbate in the shower using soap as a lubricant, but that's kind of iffy because the soap can get up your peehole and irritate the living daylights out of you. A fine substitute is hair conditioner, or you might start each stroke by grabbing your penis around the base and pulling outward only. As soon as one hand reaches the head, grab the bottom of your penis with the other to keep an uninterrupted rhythm going. The hand motion is the opposite of what you would be doing if you were pulling in a rope. (Female shower mates, take note!)

Another way that guys sometimes masturbate is by lubricating the inside of a condom with a water-based lube like KY. They slide the condom on an erect penis, wrap their fingers around it and pump away. A variation of this is to lube up the inside of a Baggie or plastic bag and put it between your pillows or mattress and box springs. You then get on your knees and hump the bag, being careful not to get your mattress pregnant.

If you make an artificial vagina and heat it in a microwave, be cautious. It could feel nice and warm around the outside, but could sizzle your little pecker when you stick it in the center.

Rushin' Roulette (for Men)

Guys tend to rush themselves when they are masturbating. There are a couple of reasons for this. First, a man who is jerking off often wants to get to the heavy duty pleasure part as soon as possible. Second is the matter of privacy, or lack of it, when you are growing up. The last thing most guys want is for someone to walk in on them when they are stroking themselves, so they teach themselves to come quickly and quietly. Also, if they are doing it in the shower, the extra speed helps them finish before the hot water runs out.

In employing the basic theorem of jack-off relativity, $M = Q^2$ (masturbation = quick x quiet—Betty Dodson), the body becomes numb to anything but the rush of coming. This might desensitize a man to some of the more subtle sensations that can feel so wonderful when he is sharing sex with a partner.

This young buck is taking his time.

Learning to Live in the Zone of Subtle Sensation

Taking extra time when masturbating might help a man learn about subtle sensations that he won't notice if he's red-lining it. For instance, if he slows down as ejaculation approaches, he might discover a rush of feelings in his stomach, bladder, or rectum. Instead of going for the big squirt, he might try to back off a bit, teaching himself how to live in the zone of subtle sensation. If allowed to emerge slowly, pre-squirt feelings can be quite intense and last for long periods of time without becoming an actual ejaculation. Learning to stay with these feelings might help a man experience deeper levels of intimacy when he is with a partner.

Also, instead of reaching for his crotch each time he masturbates, a man might start by touching or massaging other parts of his body: scalp, face, neck, shoulders, chest, hands, feet, etc. This can be a way of reminding himself that sex is a full-body activity rather than something that just happens between his legs. (One female reader says that this section should have been written for women as well as men.) For new ways of stroking yourself that you might not have thought about before, check out the "Extreme Hand Job" part of the chapter "Different Strokes for Different Blokes" on page 220.

Intercourse Spoilers

Grip of Death Guys tend to grip themselves tightly when masturbating. Yet few vaginas can come close to generating that kind of squeezing action. This might be one reason why some men have more intense orgasms when they masturbate than during intercourse. You might try masturbating with a lighter grip, at least occasionally.

Face Down The last thing we want to do is amplify internet rumors, but our urology consultant said he's dealt with this as well. It seems possible that some men who always masturbate face down have erection problems when trying to have sex with a woman. So, if you are having erection problems and masturbate face down, try to limit your jerking off to sunnyside up. And if you masturbate face down and have erections of steel each and every time, have a good laugh over this paragraph of caution.

Socks or Tissue?

In case you were wondering, *Sex & Health* reports that younger men tend to use socks to jerk off into, while older men prefer tissue. Now that guys are wearing darker underwear that doesn't show cum stains, it is likely that more socks are being spared during bedtime masturbation by guys who sleep in the buff and use their shorts for cleanup.

Warnings

URETHRA SAFETY Some people, both men and women, are tempted to stick things up their urethra (pee hole) when they play with themselves. This can be a dangerous thing to do. It may end up requiring an embarrassing visit to a hospital emergency room and maybe even surgery if the object gets lost in your bladder. If you absolutely must do this, find a physician or nurse who can show you how to correctly use a catheter and get sterile ones from a medical supply house or one of the mail-order houses that include fetish and kink. Even then, you might end up getting infections.

BUTTHOLE SAFETY Some men and women enjoy sticking things up their butt holes when they play with themselves. Be sure it is well-washed and has no sharp edges. The advantage of using a finger is that it's not likely to get lost up there. Always wash your hands ahead of time and make sure that your fingernails don't look like Elvira's. A good alternative is to use a butt plug.

REALLY TWISTED STUFF Over the years, people have tried some seriously dangerous and life-threatening ways of getting themselves off. If you are into that sort of thing, there are two ways to go. If you need to act out scenes or levels of kink that are risky, search out a community of caring, thoughtful people who are into similar things and can help you to do it as safely as possible. The other way is to get yourself some therapy from a sex-positive psychotherapist or sex therapist.

Chapter Notes: Dr. Tom Szasz made a presentation which was similar in content to this chapter's introduction. This similarity was discovered after this book was already written and is a pleasant coincidence.

Readers' Comments

Guess which answers are men's and which are women's.

Have you ever needed to masturbate while away from home?

a. "I have done so occasionally in the car, while driving. Tricky, but doable." *age 37*

b. "I would pretty much masturbate anywhere if I could. I know it sounds silly, but when I am on the beach or catching a killer wave I get kind of horny." *age 23*

c. "Yes. Although never at my current job, I have masturbated at work." *age 26*

d. "Yes. I've masturbated driving in my car; the urge was just too great and I had to deal with it right then." *age 36*

e. "It has happened. I feel pressure like I'll go nuts if I don't get relief, and I'll sneak off." *age 38*

f. "Except for when I was on a long vacation, I've always been able to wait until I got home." *age 26*

g. "One time I was driving and I had a terrible urge, so I brought myself to orgasm. I've also done it at work once." *age 43*

h. "I was once on a long-distance bus trip and a teenage boy was next to me. I don't remember why, but I got very aroused, so I put my coat over me and masturbated while he slept." *age 45*

i. "While my partner lived in a different city, I used to all the time. I would lock myself in the bathroom and put my feet on the wall while sitting on the toilet, with my legs bent and above my head. It was most satisfying this way." *age 37*

j. "I was using the computer at my brother's house when no one was home. While on the net, I was talking to someone who was so hot that I had to masturbate to release enough tension so I could keep talking online." *age 27*

a. female b. female c. female d. female e. female f. male g. female h. female i. female j. female Darned stereotypes....

Oscillator, Generator, Vibrator, Dildo

Chapter 28

In the introduction of yet another new book on sex toys, we are told how sex toys changed the author's life. Interestingly, they did. She's sold them for years and now has a book about them. Sex toys are changing other women's lives. But the changes aren't so much from what's happening for them sexually, rather it's in an economic way. Selling sex toys has become a new way for women to make money while working out of their homes.

As for sex toys having a major impact on your sex life, this *Guide* has always been wary. The most obvious use for a "sex toy" is as a vibrator. Vibrators were one of the first electric machines created back in the 1800s, and there was no question about their intended use. The same can be said for dildos, as long as you realize that the number of people who enjoy using a dildo is a small fraction of those who enjoy vibrators.

When it comes to other sex toys besides vibrators and dildos, all bets are off. For instance, sex toy sellers can't sing highly enough the praises of two new toys for men. One is an alleged prostate massager. Our experience with it was "why in the heck would someone want to pay $40 for a $1 piece of plastic that hurts you when you stick it up your butt?" We'd rename it the Prostate Annoyer. And then there's the darling of sex toy enthusiasts, a thick sleeve-like device that you stick your penis into that feels like the vagina of a woman who's been dead for two weeks. Over the years we've tried a $1200 sex toy device that had nothing on a $20 vibrator. We also tried a $600 male masturbating device that made you appreciate just how good your own hand feels.

To offer guidance in dealing with the new cottage sex-toy industry, we've included a Naked Truth column on this subject at the front of this chapter. The rest of the chapter is a helpful look at vibrators and dildos for people who would like to explore their use.

Dear Paul,

Our holiday edition is coming up. Please write an article for us on buying your partner a sex toy.

Pam, editor of the Daily

Dear Pam,

If you are trying to get a sex toy for a partner, the first thing to do is to think about the kinds of things that turn him or her on. If your gift doesn't resonate with some inner fantasy, it will end up being just another buzzing piece of plastic or strange suggestive object without any sexual oomph.

Another thing to do is to ask yourself, "Would my partner prefer flowers and the latest book by her favorite author?" "Would he like it better if I got him a new computer gizmo or brake cable for his mountain bike?" If the answer to either of these questions is yes, consider dumping the sex-toy idea. You will end up having better sex if your partner knows that you went out of your way to get something that he or she really wanted.

As for sex-toy specifics, let's say you are a woman who is trying to rev up her partner's interest. You could be uncreative and buy one of those sleeve things that he sticks himself into, but even the best of these feel cold and strange. Instead, what about giving him a gift that helps create a shared adventure?

There are plenty of great sex toys that hardly cost anything. For instance, you can make a series of coupons that you give your partner. Each lists a special thing you are willing to do, from giving her a special bath and full-body massage to things we can't even print in the *Daily*. She gives you the coupon when she wants you to do what it describes.

Another idea is for each of you to describe a sexual scene that is a personal turn-on. Then go shopping for props to make the scene happen. For instance, if one of you has the fantasy of being stopped and frisked by an officer in uniform, you can go to a used-clothing store and buy the perfect uniform for acting out the scene, perhaps including handcuffs. If the fantasy concerns a visit to the doctor, do your shopping at a medical supply house.

If you don't like that idea, try surprising your partner with a sex toy that's found at your local pet store. When your lover comes home, you can be standing there in your underwear with your new dog collar around your neck; hand her the leash and say, "I'm yours for the night!" But don't forget to attach a bow to the collar, as they do at the fancy pet groomers, and pray that she isn't bringing her parents home for a surprise visit.

There's a new world of erotic books and literature that you and your partner can read together or to each other. Collections of short stories by competent writers abound. The quality is leagues above the typical letter to *Penthouse;* think *Vanity Fair* or the *New Yorker* instead. Some will get you going, others will fall short, but it's nowhere near as bleak as it used to be. A collection of erotic short stories might be the best sex toy you ever gave or got!

If your partner feels his penis is adequate, consider getting a kit from your local art supply store that allows you to make a mold of his little soldier. Best to tell the clerk that you want to make a mold of your son's foot or hand. It's the same kit and won't cause you unnecessary embarrassment. You and your lover will be laughing yourselves silly as you make the mold and the whole thing becomes an adventure. He might even be paralyzed with excitement when you use the finished product on yourself or place it proudly on your bookshelf.

You can find a kit that's specially designed to mold your man's penis on the web at www.artmolds.com. Put the words "intimate" or "penis" into their search engine once you reach their site.

If you are still sold on getting traditional sex toys, make a deal with your partner: she selects a toy for you to use on her, and you select a toy for her to use on you. Then go shopping together.

The neat thing about using toys in this way is they help you reveal new things about yourself to your partner, and vice versa. Sex can get boring when you think you know all there is to know about the person you are sleeping with.

Oscillators, Generators Vibrators and Dildos

Some people claim that the light bulb is the most important electrical invention of the last 150 years; others say it's the vibrator. The rest of this chapter is about vibrators and dildos. Its emphasis is on the use of these devices by couples as opposed to individuals, although many people use them for solo sex. Please keep in mind that there are lots of people who don't like to use sex toys. They should be spared the sometimes evangelical prodding of sex-toy enthusiasts.

Confusing Vibrators with Dildos

People often confuse the vibrator with the dildo, which is like confusing a rhino with a giraffe. Both are native to the bush, but that's where the similarities end.

Vibrators are valued for their buzzing properties and are usually rested on the outside of the genitals rather than placed inside them. Dildos are penis-shaped and are used as such. Most don't vibrate like a vibrator, but are made to be kept inside the vagina to give a feeling of fullness or to be thrust in and out. They can also slide up and down between the lips of the vulva.

The common battery-operated plastic vibrator is sometimes thought of as a dildo. While some women use them as such, the vibrating part of these little devices is usually located on the tip, which means a woman can't insert it deeply inside her vagina and expect it to keep her clitoris happy. These are also made of hard plastic, and some of them don't pack much of a wallop compared to the more adequately appointed AC models. Most of these novelty devices aren't in the same league as a well-made dildo or vibrator, although some highly devoted users would clearly disagree. One of these is illustrated on the prior page. It is to the right of the dildo.

Vibrators, Dildos & Couples

Most guys have no problem with a partner who uses sex toys; many find the situation a total turn-on. However, some males worry that their sweetheart will start preferring the vibrator or dildo to them. Some believe that a sex toy means they aren't hung well enough or can't deliver the goods.

On the surface, these are not irrational fears. First of all, the vibrator keeps running long after most men have delivered the mail, and nobody's ever heard of a dildo that couldn't get it up. Also, women can put the vibrator or dildo anywhere they want and totally control the proceedings. But strangely enough, if you are a considerate, caring, real flesh-and-blood guy, most women will still want you regardless of how often they fire up the old magic wand. In fact, it's hard to have a meaningful conversation with a vibrator, and no dildo has ever played catch with the kids or gotten up in the middle of the night to feed the baby. Also, sex toys aren't the sort of thing that you can cuddle up next to and feel safe with—not that you can with all men, either.

In purchasing a new vibrator or dildo, a woman who is in a relationship should consider making her partner a part of the selection process. This way, her partner won't feel left in the dust, resentful or inadequate. On the other hand, good luck getting a guy to attend an all-woman's sex toy party.

Perhaps it might not hurt to show your partner this chapter, which encourages men to take pride in a woman's sex toys. It might also help to let him know that women who buy vibrators and dildos are often extremely happy with their male sex partners.

Making Friends with Your Lover's Toys

Rather than feeling at odds with your lover's vibrator or dildo, ask her to show you how she uses it. Hold her tight while she's getting herself off with it. If she has a vibrator, why not let her use it on you? And for heaven's sake, be sure to have her use it during intercourse. Some couples find the sensations to be sensational. It's even possible to combine vibrator play with oral sex. The man pushes a small battery-operated vibrator against the bottom of his tongue while the tip of his tongue is touching his partner's clitoris. Or you can gently push a dildo in and out of her vagina while planting wet kisses on her clit.

Vibrator Bits & Pieces

Here are a few vibrating facts that might be helpful if you have never used a vibrator. (People with medical conditions such as phlebitis should check with a physician before using a vibrator.)

Coil vs. Wand When it comes to vibrators that plug into the wall, there are two different types of vibrator design: wandlike vibrators with longer bodies and large heads, and coil vibrators with compact heads. Each type delivers a unique sensation. For instance, coil vibrators are smaller and nearly silent. The sensations they produce tend to be more localized. The more popular wand vibrators are bigger and make a distinct humming noise. Newer models are rechargeable and will hum for up to an hour per charge. Some come with two heads which can be used for a variety of purposes, including on your genitals and bum at the same time, as well as for up and down your spinal column. The Windmere coil vibrator was specifically designed for sex play and its vibrations are a bit more gentle than the Wahl or Sunbeam.

Be a Brand-Name Snob While some people swear by the little battery-operated vibrators, plenty of other people swear at them. The beefier AC-powered vibrators, such as those crafted by Hitachi, Oster, Wahl, Panasonic and Windmere, deliver more bang for the buck and won't let you down at critical moments. They are also well made and have warranties.

First-Time Users If you are new to a vibrator, be sure to use it on the lowest possible speed at first while you learn to navigate the head around your pubic bone. Some new users have actually bruised their pubic bones by plopping the head of a vibrator on a bony pelvis.

Geography Some women move a vibrator around the entire vulva rather than parking it in one particular place; others find a favorite spot and leave it there as though it were welded.

Muffled Sensations Some users like the sensations full blast; others like to muffle the vibrator with a towel or even a pillow, and some hold the vibrator in a way that allows their fingers to transfer the vibrations. Some vibrators have variable speed controls.

Hands Some vibrators strap on the back of your hand. Your fingers deliver the vibrations. These can be great fun to use, but they do tend to numb out the fingers temporarily.

Fingers The Fukuoko vibrators fit on your finger. They are incredibly small and almost unnoticeable.

No Hands Some women rest a vibrator between their legs so they can use their hands for other things such as holding a book, playing with their nipples, touching a partner's body or channel surfing. There are special harnesses which hold the head of a vibrator snugly between your legs. There is even a small vibrator with built-in straps that is sometimes called Joni's Butterfly. It can be worn during intercourse, in public, at work, on a date or wherever a woman might want to get a private buzz in a public place. However, this type of vibrator can sometimes be heard in super-quiet places like elevators or libraries, so plan accordingly. (One woman says that when she gets really bored she tucks a vibrating phone in her underwear and calls herself.)

Positions Unlike most men, vibrators are meant to be abused. Be sure to try different positions with it on top of you, with you on top of it, with it between your legs and as you lie on your side.

Vibrator Vacations People sometimes worry that a woman will become used to the vibrator and want only that. This seldom happens, but if you are concerned, consider taking vibrator vacations for one week every month.

Attachments There are a number of vibrator attachments for both coil and wand vibrators. These have names such as the G-Spotter, Clitickler, Twig and Wonder Wand Plus. They can deliver a finger of vibration to any specific location a man or woman wants.

Vibrators and Boys Women aren't the only ones who appreciate an occasional mechanical assist. Some boys learn to wrap a towel around their dad's hand-held vibrating sander and hold it against their genitals for a quick and easy orgasm. Just about anything around the house that vibrates will eventually find a young man leaning against it to see how it feels. Likewise, some girls first learn about good vibrations by leaning against the washing machine when it's on the spin cycle. Leaning against the handles of some vacuum cleaners can also be enlightening.

Vibrators and Men Given how many times the average male masturbates during his lifetime, it makes a certain amount of sense to try out a couple of gadgets that are made for that purpose. Some are interesting, most are disappointing, and many are nowhere near as convenient as using your own hand. For instance, there is a special attachment for certain types of vibrators called a come cup which fits over the head of the penis. (Be sure to lube up the cup first.) To make a come cup of your own, push the head of a vibrator against your hand as it is holding your penis. Some men wrap a vibrator with a towel and lean into it. The towel helps to muffle the sensation, since some vibrations can be too much and you're left with a numb dick and no orgasm. There are even vibrating sleeves that a penis can fit into. Beware of sleeves that vibrate or suck, though. Of those we've tested, none came close to using your hand and five cents-worth of lotion. We also tried a vagina substitute that's shaped like a big flashlight. Sticking your penis into cold mud would have been more fun.

Battery-Operated Personal Massagers There are many different vibrators crafted in every possible shape known to woman, from interesting contours and cute little lady bugs to vibrating silver bullets and even vinyl hummingbirds. Some of these hold up well and are made by reputable companies.

Flying High When viewed through X-ray, vibrators can resemble detonating devices on bombs. Airport security will make you open up purses, briefcases and suitcases that have vibrators in them. Resist informing them about what your vibrator does and doesn't detonate.

Dildo Logic

Vibrators have become so socially acceptable that most department and drug stores display them. Few manufacturers mention why people buy vibrators, although most of the boxes show scantily clad women using them on their calves. With dildos, there are fewer options for subterfuge and denial. Big stores would be hard-pressed to advertise that dildos help relax tense muscles, although they clearly do. And if people hear a woman say the word "dildo" in a public place, they are more likely to think that she is referring to a man she used to date than to something that gives her pleasure.

The next couple of pages offer enough information about dildos so you won't be in the dark even if you use them in the dark.

Dildo vs. Penis

It is a biological fact that the human penis when fully anchored to the human crotch imposes certain limitations upon a woman's sexual pleasure that the silicone dildo does not. A real penis can't be radically flipped upside down without necessitating a trip to the hospital for the man whose body it is or was attached to. There is also the matter of hardness: the male penis isn't always hard when a woman wants it hard, nor for as long as she might desire. And finally, a penis is not like a car that you can trade in every couple of years. Even if her spouse's penis might not be the best size and shape to fit her psyche or anatomy, a married woman is pretty well glued to it till death or divorce does them apart. Fortunately a woman needn't ditch the man she loves just because she prefers a Chevy-type penis when nature gave him a Ford or, gulp, a Yugo. She can purchase a dildo instead.

In Search of the Perfect Dildo

Dildos are made from a large variety of materials, including jade, acrylic, alabaster, latex, leather, glass, brass and wood. However, the most highly regarded dildo material is usually silicone. Silicone has a soft but firm texture with a smooth surface that is durable and easy to clean, although it doesn't stand up to cuts too well. The silicone material also warms up rather nicely, which is an added plus unless you like cold things in your vagina.

Since there is a fair amount of craftsmanship involved in producing a high-quality dildo, be sure to purchase dildos from places that carry only proven products and take pride in pleasing their customers. Check how long they've been in business and how well they support their products. As for dildo particulars, here are a few to consider:

Price Expect to pay from $45 to $90 for a good-quality silicone dildo. Vinyl or rubber dildos are cheaper, but each has its own set of drawbacks. For instance, rubber dildos have little divots in the surface which make them next to impossible to keep clean. You should always use a condom over rubber dildos.

Size The most important consideration in sizing a dildo is width. One strategy for determining which width is best for you is suggested by the women at Good Vibrations. They say to buy different-sized zucchinis, carrots or cucumbers that have an inviting width. Steam or nuke them for just a few seconds so they won't be cold, wash them, and put condoms over them. Add lubricant and try them in your vagina. Don't hesitate to use a vegetable peeler to fine tune the width. When you find one that feels just right, cut it in two and measure the diameter, which will most likely be somewhere between one and two inches. If you are the one who will be inserting the dildo, order one that's sized just right. However, if a friend will be doing the inserting, consider getting a dildo with a slightly smaller diameter. As for length, a four- to five-inch-long dildo should be just right if you plan to keep it stationary inside your vagina, while a six- to eight-inch length might be easier to handle if you like thrusting.

Shape When it comes to dildos, there are plenty of variations within a basic theme. Some dildos are made to look like penises, complete with veins and testicles, some look like dolphins or bears, and some have ridges. Dildos also have different-sized heads. With a small amount of effort, you are likely to find the dildo of your dreams.

Lubrication No matter how wet you might be, it's best to lubricate the dildo and yourself before inserting, but don't lose track of where you put the tube of lube. You may need to add more as you go.

What to Do With It Women don't necessarily use dildos for thrusting in and out. A woman might like a dildo to be stationary inside her vagina while she uses her fingers or a vibrator, or while a partner provides her with oral or anal attention. Or she might enjoy running the dildo up and down between her labia.

Numbers Some women have one favorite dildo; others have dildos of different shapes and sizes for every day of the week.

Clean Dildos should be washed and dried after each use or used with a condom over them. If not properly cleaned, the porous surface of some dildos will grow microorganisms that are best not introduced or reintroduced into you body. If you are sharing sex toys, sterilize your dildo with hydrogen peroxide, rubbing alcohol or a light bleach solution (nine parts water to one part bleach).

Anal Play If you use the dildo in your arse, be sure to wash it with soap and water before putting it into a vagina. Better yet, slap a condom on it before it goes up anyone's rear. Also, it is wise to limit your anal play to dildos with a flanged end or use a butt plug which won't get lost up your rear end (bum bummer). People who enjoy both anal and vaginal penetration are wise to have dedicated dildos for each orifice.

Dildo Harnesses Dildos with a flared base can be worn in harnesses which make them appear like erect penises. With a moderate amount of skill and effort, the person wearing the harness can use the dildo to penetrate a partner. This can be disappointing, though, because the dildo isn't connected to the wearer's nervous system like a real flesh-and-blood penis and she can't feel what the dildo is feeling. (Talk about an existential crisis!) Nonetheless, there are plenty of couples, both straight and lesbian, who enjoy using a dildo in a harness. The best harnesses are made of leather or nylon webbing. The actual geometry of harness construction and fastener application can be tricky; the catalog of Good Vibrations is full of advice about the do's and don'ts of dildo-harness buying and wearing. Also, there are other kinds of dildo harnesses such as those that fit on the thigh. Users of these marvel at the versatility of such an arrangement and claim that the human penis should have been attached to the thigh of the male rather than between his legs. There is even a dildo mounted on a beach ball that a person can bounce up and down on.

Dildo Harnesses for Inner Wear Let's say you're shopping at the supermarket or have a hot date and want to spice things up a bit. Now you can do it with your favorite dildo sticking inside of your vagina and no one will ever know. That's because they now make dildo harnesses that hold the dildo inside a vagina so it won't pop out when you are at WalMart or when making a special presentation to that hugely important client who just flew in from Algiers.

Doubles? A double dildo is worn in a harness, with one end going up the wearer's vagina and the other end sticking out in front like a penis. There are a couple of highly-rated double-dildos on the market.

Techno Dildo Some dildos are motorized and move in circles. Some have vibrating appendages that can be parked over the clitoris.

Beware Of Gumby-Like Dildos Some dildos are embedded with wire rods to help keep whatever shape the person bends them into.

Be aware that if the wire separates from the dildo material, it will become embedded in the wall of your vagina or rectum.

Menopause Masturbating with a dildo fully inserted might help some menopausal women without partners to keep their vaginas in good shape.

Full-Court Press Some women like to be penetrated in both the front and the rear at the same time. In lieu of doing a threesome, the dildo can penetrate one gate while her partner fills the other.

Suction Cups There are even dildos with suction cups on the bottom so the woman can stick them on a wall or the floor while she moves her entire body up and down or forward and back while the dildo remains stationary. These can also be planted on the wall as decorations for your home or office.

Sex-Toy Layering—Dildos & Vibrators

Some women who have never enjoyed masturbating with their fingers or a vibrator go to town once they get the right dildo. The dildo provides an internal fullness that makes it much more satisfying when they stimulate the vulva with their fingers or a vibrator. Some like to rest the head of the vibrator on the end of the dildo. Other women consider this to be sex-toy overkill, and do just fine with their fingers or vibrator acappella.

Backdoor Men & Women

Good Vibrations reports that about half of the dildo harnesses they sell are to heterosexual couples in which the woman wears the dildo to do her man in the rear.

Chapter Notes: Was David Bowie's *TVC-15* about a vibrator that was made in the UK? Special thanks to the Good Vibrations catalog for technical help, to the *Good Vibrations Guide To Sex* by Cathy Winks and Anne Semans (San Francisco: Cleis Press), and to those movers and shakers who shared their personal tips.

How we deal with the bad in life is often what defines us.
The following letter is a reminder.

Dear Paul,

I was diagnosed with breast cancer at the age of 31. My boyfriend asked me to marry him ten days after that. Knowing that he still loved me and wanted to marry me after hearing such devastating news was so incredible to me.

I elected to have a double mastectomy which was a scary thing to do because the thing that defines you the most about being a woman is your breasts. It was strange thinking that the thing that I had criticized the most about my body was now feeling like the most precious part of it. I immediately had reconstructive surgery after my double mastectomy so I never experienced life without breasts, but the ones I woke up with were made of silicone and had no nipples. My skin was ultra sensitive, and at first I didn't want to wear a shirt let alone be touched. After a few days I had no sensation in my breast area at all.

Before my surgery I had LOVED having my nipples played with and I used nipple clamps frequently. It was so devastating to lose such an important part of my sexuality to cancer. It was hard to imagine enjoying sex as much without my nipples and the sensations they had produced in my whole body — a tingle that goes from your head all the way to your toes. I felt so ugly and disfigured. I really couldn't fathom that my fiancé would even want to have sex with me. Proving to me yet again what a wonderful man he is, we ended up having sex just a few days after I was discharged from the hospital. It was one of the most therapeutic parts of my sexual healing. Just seeing the devilish sparkle in his eyes as he looked at me with so much love and longing warmed me from the inside out!

It's been almost 1½ years since my surgery and I feel sexy despite my cancer and reconstructed breasts. My husband has continued to be turned on by me and we've found other areas of my body that are as sensitive (if not more sensitive) than my nipples used to be. It really goes to show that being sexy is more a mental attitude than a physical trait and that facing your fears about sex after such trauma can be a very positive experience.

A Changed Woman

Basic Brain Weirdness & the Mind-Body Interface

Chapter 29

This chapter is about mental events that can get in the way of having a good sex life, or just having a good life. Some people would call these mental glitches; others might say they are a normal part of the human condition.

Shyness

Shyness is a funny thing. Sometimes it sits like a shroud over everything you do. Other times it is highly selective, making only certain parts of your life sheer hell. Shyness can take many different forms and can be a great deal more mysterious than people give it credit for. For instance, shyness can make you babble like a fool and say really stupid things or it can make you seem cold and aloof when you're really not.

To illustrate what happens when shyness gets the better of you, consider the following true story of Andrew. Andrew is now pretty old, but he used to be really young.

It was a beautiful spring day about a month or two before the beginning of a somewhat magical time that later became known as the Summer of Love. This was the same year when nearly half a million young people gathered at a now-famous farm in upstate New York for three days of rock'n'roll that became known as Woodstock. It was a time when other people gathered on other farms throughout the country to do more mundane things like milk cows and tend crops. Andrew was more than three thousand miles away from that very special farm in New York. As for the Summer of Love, he had never even put his hand up a woman's shirt.

None of this stopped him from having an overpowering crush on a very popular young woman who was older than he. (Back then, younger guys rarely dated older women.) This female heartthrob just happened to be the local homecoming queen, or Future Farmers' Princess, or whatever it was that a young woman became in a small town when everybody claimed to like her. She was so special that he was too embarrassed to tell even his best friend about his lick-the-mud-off-her-shoes-if-that's-what-she-wants crush. Instead, he focused his energies on trying to act cool whenever she passed by.

To make matters worse, the young goddess was constantly surrounded by senior guys who had their own cars, lettered in football and baseball, and got drunk and never even threw up. He, on the other hand, saw himself as just another underclassman who had less than a snowball's chance in hell of attracting this woman's interest.

One day about an hour after school, some strange and peculiar force caused this special woman to toss her books and pompoms into the back of her car and aim it for the very address where this young man lived. When the doorbell rang he figured it was probably the paper boy or a Jehovah's Witness selling "The Watchtower." When he walked outside and saw who it was, his lower jaw dropped so radically that a big wad of drool nearly fell out of his mouth. All things considered, he did well to maintain bladder control.

He stood staring at this babe like a deer in front of headlights. He felt so paralyzed that he couldn't even mobilize the words to invite her inside. When he did start talking, it was in an almost glib way that didn't allow the slightest bit of closeness. He was clearly blowing it. After about ten awkward minutes of trying to deal with the situation, the young goddess blew the baffled boy a puzzled kiss and drove away never to return.

Many years have passed since this fellow botched the Summer of Love. He still feels just as clumsy and awkward when he meets a woman whom he is really attracted to. He doesn't expect it will get any better in a few more years when he's trying to talk to the nurses in the old folk's home.

One-Night Stands & Back-Seat Bangers

You will simply have to find out about things like one-night stands on your own, and even then you may disagree with this book's stand. But working up a good fantasy and getting yourself off by hand tends to be less of a headache and is often just as satisfying as most one-night stands. The fantasy of a one-night stand is usually better than the reality of it.

Counterpoint: One reader from London clearly disagrees: "A one-night stand can be an immensely exciting and rewarding experience which you may remember your whole life." Hopefully in a good way.

On Being a Sex Object

People usually associate "being a sex object" with being a woman. However, this is about a guy named Steve whom women treated as a sex object. Steve was tall, blond, blue-eyed and had a perfect body. In addition to being a fine surfer, he was a male model who was actually straight.

Everyone was thrown into total shock one night at Steve's tearful lament that he wished women would stop wanting him just for sex. It's a problem none of us could relate to. Steve was in a total funk because women were constantly diving for his crotch.

It's difficult to imagine that physical attractiveness can get in the way of leading a happy life, but people who are physical 10s are sometimes rather lonely. Friends of the same sex are often envious and sometimes feel threatened by the attention that the 10 seems to get. Members of the other sex tend to stare or else act bizarrely. People who are extremely attractive sometimes marry simply for protection.

What's Wrong with This Picture?

The opposite problem of being a 10 is when you are less than beautiful and having someone who is drop-dead gorgeous show a romantic interest in you. Instead of responding romantically, you might be saying to yourself, "Naw, can't be true. Big mistake here." While the physical 10 may be begging for romance, the less-than-10 is turning a great opportunity into a self-fulfilling prophecy of doom.

People Who Claim "The Opposite Sex Is Worthless"

Some people choose sexual partners who can't supply any of their emotional needs. It's as if they would be horribly overwhelmed to find someone who could be both a friend and a lover, and therefore not quite so "opposite." Perpetual victims such as these claim that they are more mature and able to love more than their moron partners.

The fact is, people who have a healthy self-regard do not suffer the presence of fools and jerks, let alone sleep with them. The perpetual victim is just as immature and has as many problems with intimacy as does the jerk whom he or she dates or marries. Neither has much to brag about.

Giving Friendship a Chance

The male-female relationships that we usually teach our children to value are those with romantic potential. As a result, men and women tend to approach each other as potential sex partners rather than as potential friends.

Platonic male-female friendships are a wonderful thing, but they sometimes become endangered if one person starts to feel sexual and the other doesn't. A lot of male-female friendships never happen because people are unable to work it out when one of them wants sex or romance and the other just wants friendship. Knowing that a friend wants romance when you don't can be uncomfortable. However, if he or she were given the time and understanding to cool his or her jets, the nonsexual friendship might be able to flourish for years to come. As for the person who feels smitten and then bitten, keep in mind that a platonic friendship often lasts for years, while that is not always the case with romantic affairs. You might be losing out on something special if you aren't able to accept the person as a friend instead of as a lover. (Another factor that often destroys male-female friendships is their jealous spouses or partners.)

Counterpoint: One reader comments, "This is a cursory and shallow discussion of this issue." We apparently struck a nerve. She's right; the matter is often far more complex than what's presented here. Sometimes it is filled with all kinds of hopeful expectations and excruciatingly painful disappointments, when one person feels romantic love and the other feels "only" friendship.

Initiating Sex When Holding Is What You Need

Some people find it hard to acknowledge that they simply need to be held, since asking to be held might make them feel weak, wimpy, vulnerable or frightened. Instead, they sometimes initiate sex when what they really may have wanted was physical tenderness and comfort. Fortunately, the desires for sex and tenderness often overlap, which allows them to receive both at the same time. But sometimes they need more of one than the other. Hopefully you can evolve a set of clear signals that will help your partner know what it is that you need, assuming you know yourself.

Fuck Buddies or BuddySex

Everybody seems to know somebody who is having BuddySex—which is when two people decide to sleep with each other for the sex only. That's certainly been the response when we've asked the question on our sex survey at goofyfootpress.com. However, a couple of very interesting trends have emerged.

While everybody knows somebody, or while they've done it themselves in the past, very few people said they were currently doing it. If BuddySex were really the rage that the media wants us to think, you'd think that everybody would be doing it themselves, or everybody who did it in the past would still be doing it. Perhaps it's one of those things that works a little better on paper than in real life. Or maybe it's something people resort to when they'd prefer romance in their lives but the romance isn't working out.

The second trend we noticed was how many people said they had done BuddySex, but weren't doing it anymore because the two of them fell in love and ended up getting married.

The biggest "hazard" for BuddySex is when one person starts having feelings for the other person who they are having sex with. Imagine that. So if you are thinking about having BuddySex, be sure that you talk about this possibility ahead of time. There were certainly people who said they'd had an excellent experience with a BuddySex partner, and that they were still friends. But few said they were still buddies in a sexual way.

In Love but Out of Sync

It's the saddest thing in the world when people have powerful feelings for each other but can't make their relationship work. For instance, one of you might become more settled and grounded earlier in life than the other. You may feel like putting down roots or becoming established while the other is still an emotional tumbleweed who needs to experience the outside world and soak in whatever it has to teach. The lack of synchrony forces a breakup, or maybe there's a level of sensitivity or maturity that one partner won't have for several more years. While you may not have any desire to get back together, there might always remain a place in your heart for the other person.

Breaking Up

Breaking up is the sort of thing that you write a whole book about. Otherwise, you risk being trite about a phenomenon that can leave even the strongest of hearts and minds crippled.

The one thing we will mention is that breaking up doesn't always happen with a big fight or a hell storm of hostility. In fact, sometimes you spend your last hours together holding each other tight, with tears flowing and a kind of desperate, profound sadness in your hearts. And even if you are the one who is doing the leaving, the final steps toward the door can sometimes feel horrible. Right, but horrible.

Forgiving Yourself

Every once in a while we say or do something so stupid that even friends talk about having us committed. This can be particularly devastating when it results in the loss of friendship or love.

The best thing you can do in these situations is to figure out how and why you messed up. Then do what you can to mourn the loss and get on with your life. While there is much to be gained from introspection, there is little to be gained from beating yourself up. On the other hand, if you suffer from a perpetual case of foot-in-mouth, it is possible that there is a chronic confusion or anger in the depths of your soul that prevent you from using good sense. In that case, the input of a respected friend, teacher, colleague, relative or therapist might be an important thing to seek.

Stupid Mistakes — Young vs. Old

If anyone ever tells you that making stupid mistakes is a part of being young and will pass as you get older, don't make the really stupid mistake of believing them.

True, you usually don't make as many mistakes as you get older, but that's only because your brain doesn't work nearly as fast. As your brain slows down, you simply don't have the opportunity to make mistakes with the same lightning speed that you once did.

The Fantasy of Love & Commitment

When you feel particularly empty inside, it's easy to have the illusion that things will be better if you can just find someone to love.

Love is a special way of sharing friendship that can bring tremendous joy. It allows you to think and worry about someone other than yourself, which can be a much-needed relief. It also lets you know that there is someone who believes in you when you don't particularly believe in yourself. But in spite of all its pluses, it's unlikely that love will take away your fears and insecurities, organize your chaos, cure your bad habits, help you lose weight, stop smoking, get in shape, or turn you into a better human being—not in the long run anyway. These are personal demons that we need to conquer on our own.

The Dark Side — Nights of Quiet Despair

Sometimes you get hit by a certain mood, one that's a quiet mix of frustration, hopelessness and despair. It's when something deep inside you isn't working right, something incredibly human, but you can't put a finger on it. Being in a relationship does not always help the bad feelings to go away.

Sometimes it becomes a contest between you, the despair and the beer, pills, sleep, food, sex or whatever it is that helps make you feel better. Presidents' wives tell you to just say no, the disc jockey on the all-night radio station never plays the song you need, and a river of pain cuts your heart in two.

Nights of quiet despair sometimes go away by morning.

Readers' Comments

One-Night Stands vs. Long-Term Relationships

"Not to sound like a dick, but a one-night stand is all about me. I am there to get and to be fucked. Sex in a relationship is about both of us. Adding in love and respect makes sex in a long-term relationship better." *male age 25*

"In one-night stands, the expectations far exceed the experience. I'm not in tune to what turns my partner on sexually as I would be in a long-term relationship." *male age 39*

"In a one-night stand, sex can be exciting because you just don't know what you're gonna get." *female age 25*

"Sex in a one-night stand has its own excitements. But most of those are related to the 'naughtiness' of the situation and having to live with the thoughts and fears of possible exposure to STIs, as well as guilt concerning 'what type of person do I want to be.' " *female age 37*

"I am a very horny person and I was surprised that I could not get wet when I was with a one-night stand. It was almost like a business deal. I felt no release and passion that I do in my relationship with Chris." *female age 23*

"My one-night stands have varied; some guys pass out drunk, or they plain just can't get it up no matter what you do. I really haven't had much luck with one-night stands." *female age 36*

How Does Sex Impact Your Long-Term Relationship?

"I find that if we go without sex for a few days it throws my boyfriend and I off and we lose our common wavelength. After sex we are right back in tune with each other, and there's nothing like that." *female age 23*

"Sex enhances just about everything in my life. It relieves my stress and anger, and it increases our love and romance. It leaves me happy and with a certain glow. It's as though I can conquer anything!" *female age 36*

Dear Paul,

Ever since I graduated from college my sex life has taken a big nose dive. I have had sexual intercourse ONCE between then and today! I had a healthy sex life in high school complete with true love and several short-term physical relationships. That was when I wasn't even legally an adult. Now I am almost 30 and for most of my twenties my sex life has been NO life at all. I am not at all physically unattractive, although I am somewhat shy and keep very

For instance, if you had volunteered in a program where you helped people learn to read, you might get comfort from remembering some of their smiling faces when they read their first sentence. If you coached a baseball team and helped keep kids out of trouble, or helped build a park, or did something that makes your community a better place, those are the things that might give you solace. If you created something that is helpful to others, that's what might be important in your waning moments. It's what you have done to make yourself a better person that counts the most in life. So instead of wasting your time trying to find a bed partner, why not do things that will make you a better person? Please, don't think I am suggesting that you do altruistic-appearing events as a thinly disguised sham for meeting women. There is nothing more obnoxious than people who volunteer for things with the ulterior motive of trying to find love or sex.

Improve yourself, and maybe love will come. Maybe it won't. But it seems that people who are vitally involved in life tend to have an energy that attracts others. This is not as true for people who spend their evenings in front of a TV set or who think mostly of themselves from morning to night.

Not to overdo the death thing, but the best advice I ever received after the age of thirty had nothing to do with sex. It was just three words, "Grow or die." It's something I remind myself of often, especially when the couch potato in me threatens to take over. Since there is nothing about cruising for women that is particularly growth-promoting, my advice is to go for the bigger picture. Do what it takes to improve yourself as a person. Hopefully, the other things in life, like finding relationships, will fall into place.

Counterpoint: Several months after publishing this column, I received an email from someone who said he was dying and begged to differ. He said that the thing he was enjoying most was memories of sex. A week later, when I tried to reply, there was no answer.

Better Mating Through Internet Dating

Chapter 30

There must be some person somewhere who can make small talk with a total stranger and walk away with a phone number. He or she shouldn't waste a dime on Internet dating. For the rest of us, finding a date through the Internet can make good sense. It gives you access to a huge segment of the singles in your area without requiring you to ever attend a singles' dance or social. And you can stop pretending you are some sort of cool fool in bars where the customers are the main course.

In fact, Internet dating should go down with the discoveries of penicillin and chocolate if it's able to put an end to social events that have the words "for singles" in the title. Not only can Internet dating make this painful form of public humiliation more private, but it also helps to make the process of meeting someone more dignified and less random. It doesn't mean you have to stop splashing on the Drakar or Armani and never go cruising again; it just gives you an added venue in case you want one.

NOTE: There's usually a big difference between using the Internet to find a real-life date and wanking to porn in cyberspace. Please see Chapter 31: *Sex In Cyberspace* for more on the latter.

Virtual Logistics

You might be a wonderful person who anyone would be lucky to date, but it doesn't mean you are going to be a natural at Internet dating. So before you join any Internet dating services, take a hint from your old friends at Goofy Foot Press—read at least two very helpful books on the subject. As of press time, these are the two titles that got the Goofy nod:

I Can't Believe I'm Buying This Book—A Commonsense Guide To Successful Internet Dating by Evan Marc Katz, Ten Speed Press, Berkeley, California, 2003.

Virtual Foreplay—Making Your Online Relationship a Real-Life Success by Eve Hogan, Hunter House, Alameda, California, 2001.

The Katz book is a very funny, well-written guide that will tell you exactly what you need to know, from how to choose Internet dating services to ways of writing your personal profile that will make it more effective. No, you don't need to do a single thing the book says, but before blazing your own creative trail it's a good idea to have a sense of what works and what doesn't. Katz does a great job of laying this out for you, much better than any other book on the subject.

Virtual Foreplay takes a more psychological look at the emotions involved in Internet dating. Eve Hogan is a therapist who has made Internet dating her area of expertise, and she's done a good job with it. She speaks often about the need to have compassion and respect, and many of the tips she offers are excellent. However, people around here nearly gagged at statements such as, "The attention is placed on aligning your virtual presence with your real essence and using the experience as a process for growth." Does anybody have any idea what that means? And if anyone at Goofy Foot Press ever uses the word "soulmate" in a serious way, just nuke us. In fact, be safe and nuke the entire state. Even with its occasional touchy-feely, new-age blather, *Virtual Foreplay* still gets a serious thumbs-up.

The Katz and Hogan books each have a different emphasis and compliment each other nicely. Reading both won't take you long and it will give you a keyboard up before you've made your first post.

What You Want and Where You Want It

You will be amazed at how many different types of Internet dating services there are. You will probably want to join a couple. But before you decide which ones to join, you'll need to decide what it is you are looking for. Are you looking for a buddy to have fun with on the occasional weekend date, or are you looking for someone to settle down with and eventually collect social security with? Are you in a "screw the ring, I want sex" mode? There are Internet dating services for people who are looking for other people to have sex with. There are also services that match people based on the kind of kink they are in to. Maybe you have no kink but lots of religion, or maybe you have both and would like to join a dating service for Presbyterians who enjoy having hot wax dripped on their genitals.

After you decide what type of relationship you want, it wouldn't hurt to check out a number of Internet dating services that fit the bill. With each service, see if there are plenty of members in your age group and in your geographic area. Just because a service says it has more members than the population of China doesn't mean there are any this side of Peking. Also keep in mind that some services might specialize in singles who are twenty-eight to thirty-five with college degrees, while others may have a stable full of silver-haired sexpots.

You will also want to compare and contrast the features that the different services offer. For instance, it's not uncommon for some-one who successfully hitches up to forget to remove his or her profile from the service. So a feature you might want is one that lists the last time the person visited the site. That way you won't waste your time responding to a cutie who has moved across the country or a death row inmate whose final appeal was denied a year ago.

Your Profile

Most Internet dating services will ask you to fill out a profile that shoppers—ah, members—get to read. It's how you present who you are. A lot of people don't take profile writing seriously enough. This is where Evan Katz's *Internet Dating* book truly excels, in helping you decide what's important to put in your profile and how to go about it. (If the males who have taken our survey at goofyfootpress.com are typical of how the average straight guy writes—in monosyllabic grunts—then some of you straight-boys-in-waiting might consider having a female or gay friend help you write your profile.)

For How Long and How Much?

Many of the better services charge around $20 to $30 a month, but they also offer discounted three-month and six-month plans. Strongly consider going for one of these longer plans. Give yourself time for the process to work, and if for some reason you find the part-ner of your dreams in the first week, consider the extra money as a tip for a service that was well provided. Beware: some services say they are for free. You usually get what you pay for.

Time For a Reality Check

Internet dating isn't going to be any easier than trying to find a date without the Internet, and it isn't going to make the competition disappear. Internet dating isn't going to keep you from feeling bad when someone says no. It's not going to make you seem any more appealing if you are short on social graces or high on the kind of behaviors that result in a psychiatric diagnosis.

What will be different is that the process is going to be more private and it may help you to have a more focused approach. It also gives you more choices. If you don't do well with romantic cold calling, being able to email back and forth and then talk on the phone might be a great help. But just because you find someone whose profile looks good doesn't mean they will answer you back, and it doesn't mean you would want to go out with them if they did.

Whatever your situation, assume that you will need several months of solid effort to make the process work for you. Things might start clicking right away, but it would probably make you the exception rather than the rule.

From Email to Phone Calls to Pressing Flesh

So let's say you find someone with an interesting profile and he or she finds yours to be interesting as well. Where to go from there? Nobody seems to offer any hard'n'fast advice. While it might be more desirable to email each other several times and then spend a few weeks trying each other out on the phone, someone might come along who is more aggressive and next thing you know, the person you've been having the conversations with is already hitched. When it comes to timing, making the move from online to in-person is a totally subjective call.

Eve Hogan's book lists several precautions that are a good idea to consider throughout the Internet dating process.

The Possibility Of Being Overwhelmed

It doesn't matter if you are twenty or fifty, occasionally someone will write a great profile and he or she is overwhelmed with responses.

Keep in mind that this is a good thing, and don't feel like you've got to respond in detail to everyone. As you start to see the type of people who are responding to you, you might want to establish a set of criteria that helps you in making a quick first cut. This way you can form a short of list who you'll want to spend more time responding to. Even then, you might not have the time to do so as well as you would like. Don't be afraid to tell people when you've been overwhelmed. Say that you won't be getting back to them for awhile.

Don't Be the Litter on The Side of The Information Superhighway

It's only the Internet. What's so wrong with stretching the truth a little, like when you say you've got a D-cup or 9 inches when you don't? Or how about saying you are well-read and sensitive when the only thing you've read in the past year was the mandatory handout at your anger-management class?

You need to set your own standards in life. If there's not much substance inside of you, then there's no point in setting your standards very high. But if you are a decent person, why should honesty be any less important in cyberspace than face to face? Why be an online off-beat? Think seriously about telling the truth, even if it's the Internet.

Next to telling lies about yourself, another form of dishonesty in Internet dating is to say you'll do this but then you do that. If you aren't interested in going any further with someone, have the decency to say so. Don't just disappear, and don't keep something going because you feel too guilty to say "no more." Have the courtesy to say "so long" or "it's been swell," and then disappear.

And Then What?

Whether we want to admit it or not, dating is a significant part of a single person's life. When a date truly clicks it can make you feel on top of the world, and when a date misfires it can make you feel down and deflated. Even if you swear off dating totally, it remains a significant part of your life because you have to work so hard to ignore the importance that our culture puts on it.

Internet dating is a little like arranging your own blind date. It is an attempt to meld high technology with Cupid's bow. It changes the process, but it doesn't change the feelings that people need to sort through once they actually meet.

Dear Paul,

I was originally writing you to say you forgot to cover threesomes in the last edition, and to ask for advice. But my husband and I have recently met up with a third person for sex, and the experience was great!

Bonnie from Bonneville

Dear Bonnie,

If you are wondering what a letter on threesomes is doing between *Internet Dating* and *Sex In Cyberspace,* it's because I forgot it and we'd already typeset the chapters where it might be more appropriate—not that the Internet is any stranger to threesomes.

Way back when I was doing research for the first edition of *the Guide,* I remember being surprised by a conversation I had with a young woman who was living with two men and having sex with both of them. One was her husband and the other was their roommate. This had been going on for a couple of years and they were one big happy family. The psychoanalyst in me kept thinking "How can this be?"

I've forgotten everything about our conversation except for two things: how totally normal she sounded and how happy she seemed. I've since learned that "threesome" might mean something entirely different to you than to your boss or tennis partner. Your threesome could be a once-in-a-lifetime event when your husband's old college roommate visited for the weekend. Or it might be something you do a couple of times a year, a couple of times a month, or?

The type of combination can also vary. Is it MMF or FFM? Do the MMs or FFs have sex with each other as well as with the partner of the other sex? Do you meet socially or just for sex? Is it an exclusive threesome? Are two of you coupled? And as one reader reminded me, why not include MMMs and FFFs? How thoughtless of me!

I've been surprised on our sex survey how many people say they have had at least one threesome, and that it was a good experience. Others were not so positive, and many threesomes seem to be done in an alcohol haze. So please be careful and do your homework first.

For advice on how to find a third, how to advertise and approach people, how to set up safeguards for dealing with jealousy, and much more, I highly recommend *The Ultimate Guide To Sexual Fantasy—How To Turn Your Fantasies into Reality* by Violet Blue, Cleis Press, 2004.

Sex in Cyberspace
From Sputnik to EatMyPussy.com

Chapter 31

The world wide web is part of a vast digital expanse known as the Internet. In January of 1994, there were less than one-thousand websites on the world wide web; in January of 2004, there were more than forty-six million. It's not unreasonable to assume that the world wide web has seen a bit of growth.

Technology and Sex

There's nothing new about using technology to get sex.

When the author of this book was a young boy, the best porn magazine collection in town was in the lobby of the two-story hotel that was named after the town's founder. There was one problem. The old man who ran the hotel sat behind a large desk that was next to the wooden racks that held the glossy goods. The old man took seriously his job of protecting the breasts and thighs from the pleading glare of the town's young. If you were under the age of twenty-one—or worse yet, under the age of twelve—the town's only porn stash might as well have been on the moon.

Fortunately, right across from the old man's desk sat the only elevator in town. It was an amazing, ornate contraption that was as old as the man himself. Using this piece of ancient technology required the old codger to leave his wooden perch, enter the ancient time machine, pull the shiny brass gates shut, and perform a ritual of knob-turning and lever-pulling that would nudge the geriatric lift from its slumber.

Whenever the boys in town needed reassurance about the true nature of the intimate parts of a woman's body, they would head over to the hotel and hide behind the oversized Morris chairs that populated the west end of the lobby. They would wait patiently until the old man had his back turned. Then one of the boys would do a crawl-sprint up the stairs to the second floor and ring the call button for the elevator. By the time the old man shuffled into the elevator and made its big piston rise, the boys would have two-and-a-half minutes to look through the glossy magazines. That's how long it took for the old man to return with his empty cargo.

Nowadays, if the author of this book wants to see porn, he slaps his keyboard with a stroke or two and there it is—an outrageous supply of naked this or that. Whether it's the Internet today or the clunky old elevator from years ago, sex and technology have never been strangers.

As for the old hotel with the antique elevator, there were other things of a sexual nature that went on upstairs that were beyond what the mind of a young boy could comprehend. They were curious things that helped some of the town's people keep their sanity, and others nearly lose theirs.

 ### Flower of the Military-Industrial Complex

If things have parents, then the sperm for the Internet was donated by the Cold War. If they have godfathers, the Internet's might as well have been Sputnik, a transmitter in a tin can that the Soviet Union snuck into space in 1957.

The launch of Sputnik put the fear of God into the U.S. government and it triggered a massive race in technology. The foundations of the Internet arose from this national fury which was the technological equivalent of going to the gym, getting buff, and winning the babe back.

The Internet was based on a new idea called "packet switching," which was the communications version of coming in spurts. It's how we upload and download everything from PTA schedules to X-rated streaming videos.

One of the false myths about the Internet is that it was designed as a communications cobweb that would keep working after places like Omaha, Washington, New York, and Chicago were buried by nuclear bombs with hammers and sickles on their sides. While no one at the Department of Defense would have minded such a stout creation, the Internet seems to have evolved as a way for computer programmers from the major universities and defense labs to share information. This was the womb that would eventually give birth to the world wide web.

Even if it wasn't created to be nuke-proof, thank goodness they designed the Internet to withstand a great deal of abuse. That's because during any given week, millions of people in this country will be masturbating while they are logged on to it.

Sex on the Internet: Two Different Forks

What's interesting about the flow of sex online is that it takes two very different forks. One fork provides a faster way of doing what books, magazines, Super-8 movies, and all kinds of catalogues used to do. The other fork is sometimes called cybersex. It taps into the new technology of the Internet to redefine how some of us get off.

The First Fork, Sex That's Not Interactive

There are several ways that people use the Internet for sexual purposes. Here are some of the ways that Heather does it. It involves using the Internet as a giant sex library or a huge mall or bazaar that's full of porn, sex toys, and Lord only knows what else.

Heather uses the web for sex information and misinformation. Let's say Heather's new boyfriend ejaculates too soon or she catches him wearing her bra and panties. Instead of picking up the *Guide To Getting It On!* for information, she goes on Google and puts in "premature ejaculation" or "transvestite." Hundreds of resources pop up. Or maybe she wants to know what other women think about swallowing. So she finds a couple of online forums that look legitimate and she posts the question. Or maybe she wants to learn more about different methods of birth control, or whether women should use pills to stop their periods, or how ecstasy effects people's sexual experience. These are some of the ways that many of us use the web as a source of information about sex.

Heather uses the web for reading arousing stories. She often goes to the Erotic Writers and Readers Association website. There she gets to read story after story about steamy sexual encounters from people who can actually write. She also gets to read people's personal posts about everything from orgasms to what kind of threesomes they prefer. Heather then visits one of the new sex blogs, but finds it kind of self-involved. She flogs the blog and checks out ScarletLetters.com.

Heather uses the Internet to visit fascinating websites that combine news, top-rate writing, erotic photography, and cool stories about sex. Not being a freeloader, she's purchased annual subscriptions to some of these sites including Salon.com, Nerve.com, CleanSheets.com, and Libido.com. Heather realizes that we aren't going to have sites like these for long unless she buys the annual subscriptions, so she allows

$200 a year out of her entertainment budget to support the creative websites that she likes to visit.

Like a growing number of women these days, Heather gets off on good porn, whether it's visual or text based. Sometimes she goes to groups on Yahoo! and MSN that cover everything from people who enjoy BDSM to those who like fisting, wearing diapers, or just about any topic under the sun that has to do with sex. Or maybe she likes to peek in on live webcams where people have sex in front of cameras and the images are refreshed every now and then. Heather also knows that Jane's Net Place (janesplace.com) is a great website to find out about all kinds of porn sites. Maybe she'll want to visit some seriously raunchy porn sites, or maybe she'll want to visit some really cool erotic art websites. The Internet is a great conduit to porn that's done by some of the world's top photographers.

Heather uses the web for buying sex toys. The people who sell sex toys consider Heather to be enlightened and evolved. Her friends think she's got a problem. Heather uses the Internet to buy the Hitachi Magic Wand vibrator, three silicone dildos, and a couple of different butt plugs. She also has a pair of vibrating nipple clips and a strap-on harness with a double-headed dildo. For her boyfriend, she's bought a vibrating cock ring and a Fleshlight masturbating device that feels like the vagina of a corpse, even though the websites that sell it say it's the best thing that's happened to men since the testicle. Luckily, she visits TinyNibbles.com for fun, info and advice.

It's easy and interesting to enjoy Heather's kind of sex on the Internet. Now let's look at cybersex.

The Second Fork of Sex on the Internet — Cybersex

Here are the accounts of cybersex by three readers who tell about two very different kinds of experiences:

> "We're in a long distance relationship, so masturbation in conjunction with cybersex is a great thing. Basically what we do is a 'This is what I'd do to you if I were there and horny.' There's an ongoing joke between us about 'Today was good, but it'd have been better if you were here naked,' and then the other person would ask 'What would you have done differently?'

Most of the time it's describing the various sex acts either one of us would like to perform on the other one, and the 'receiver' making the appropriate typed noises of pleasure. We both use AIM, but through a multi-IM protocol called Trillian. There have been swaps of risque digital pictures too, but that doesn't always coincide with cybersex." *female age 18*

"In answer to your question, I've tried many sex chatrooms, but they've been disappointing: lots of males chasing a very few females - or, just as likely, chasing males who are pretending to be female. A bit pathetic, really. Chat rooms with a webcam facility are as bad: a lot of males getting very excited over a very little exposed female flesh. Yahoo! has a webcam facility, but I've not yet found an intelligent user in any of the sex chat rooms, despite spending what must be many hours looking through user profiles. I'm sorry if that sounds harsh, but it's my experience. The rooms are also infested with advertising bots. Apart from chat rooms, I've found that newsgroups are better for porn than websites." *male age 51*

"From what I've seen in the IRC world, the male-to-female ratio tends to be about 20:1. And I have experimented entering a chat room as a woman just to see what would happen, and yes, you get pounced on." *male age 22*

When people are having cybersex, they are using the Internet to get each other off in real time. The way they do this ranges from typing text on the keyboard to masturbating in front of video cams.

When you compare cybersex to real life sex, one of the most striking features is how much is left out. In preparing for cybersex, you don't need to comb your hair or brush your teeth. You don't need to shave or shower. You don't need to figure out how you're going to get across town (or across the world) to his place or hers, and unless the person on the other end claims to be the Archangel Gabriel, you don't need condoms or birth control.

If you've never met your online partner in real life, you don't need to worry if he or she snores, has gas, or is seriously out of shape. You don't need to worry if your partner is single or married, rich or poor, male or female, or recently payrolled. Everything is just too perfect for words, as long as you are able to trick yourself into thinking that the hand in your pants is really your cybersex lover's and not your own.

In cybersex, people exist as words, sentences, and lines of text, unless you park a video cam between your legs and let the interface fly. And if you find yourself in a fantasy situation that starts to feel uncomfortable, relief is just a delete button away.

No Scratch'N'Sniff in Cyberspace

In real life, you are able to smell the person you are having sex with. Given how there is no scratch'n'sniff in cybersex, your sexual partner's smell is whatever you want it to be.

In real life, you touch your partner and your partner touches you back. In cybersex, it's you who is touching your body in the exact way you want to be touched. The touch you are giving yourself is fueled by an incredible level of fantasy that is untouched by the problems of everyday life or of living together.

Imagine a woman who somehow manages to find an eloquent guy online and they go into a private chatroom. She is highly aroused by the cybersex fantasy that they are weaving together and she is masturbating. Do you think there's a guy or girl on earth who could touch her genitals in the exact same way that she knows to touch her own at that moment? It makes sense when some people say they have more intense orgasms in cybersex than with real-life partners.

Liberation from the Real Body? Not Really

Some people say that the Internet is a medium where gender and looks are no longer factors. You can be whatever gender you want to be and nobody has to worry about being short, fat, young, old, bald or too hairy. That's because the only thing that supposedly counts is the persona you present in text.

This would be well and fine if it were anywhere near the truth. To paraphrase sociologist Dennis Waskul, when you look at the cybersex profiles that people create for themselves, you start to wonder if the only people who know how to use computers are women with large breasts and guys with 9" dicks. Good luck going through a cybersex chat room and finding someone who is 5' 2" and 250 lbs. Good luck finding the phrase, "Oh baby, let me suck your pathetically small dick!"

Not only does the body count a great deal in cybersex, we're talking a whole new religion devoted to the perfect person and the perfect lover. In cybersex, nobody comes too soon, can't get it up, or doesn't get wet. In cybersex, everybody gets an extreme makeover.

Cybersex proves that if given the opportunity, people will recreate themselves in the image that society says is the perfect 10. In cybersex, everybody looks as good as—gulp—the characters in the illustrations of the *Guide To Getting It On!*

A Sense of Community and Role Playing

There are countless numbers of forums and chat areas on the Internet where people form a very real sense of community. For example, there's a group of woodworkers who have a power tool forum where they give each other advice on the different kinds of equipment they use, from drills and planers to table saws and dust collectors. There are members whose names you learn to recognize and whose opinions you trust. In each new thread there is plenty of kidding and criticism, but always a sense of cohesion. When one member is struggling with a difficult project, other members offer an impressive stream of support and encouragement.

This same kind of community can be found in cyber groups that researcher Lori Kendall refers to as "Virtual Pubs." These are Internet portals where members interact in ways similar to a neighborhood bar. They rely on each other being there month in and month out and they offer the same kinds of intimate support and candor that would happen at any neighborhood bar.

An interesting thing about these non-sexual forums and chat rooms is that members tend to be honest about who they are. The expectation is that you are who you say you are, and your reputation online is often based on your honesty and integrity. It's not much different from life offline. Of course, this isn't to say that Builder Robert and Nail-Driver Ted don't meet in a private chat room where they drop their tool belts and stroke each other's powertools, but if that happens it's not part of the general forum and would surely create a big problem. However, when the focus moves to sex, that's when the fiction starts to fly.

Gender in Cyberspace

A woman's husband went into a chatroom one night while using her computer. He was logged on with her username. A political discussion occurred, and he presented his views on a subject rather strongly. This was no different than what he often did on his own computer using his male persona. But this night he was surprised to discover a strong negative reaction among the other members of the group. They assumed he was a woman because he was using his wife's username, and they didn't like that a woman would have such strong and forceful opinions.

There seems to be very little gender switching in non-sexual forums, although if a woman wanted to be taken seriously in the woodworker's power tool forum, she might consider saying she was a guy. On the other hand, when you are dealing with sex on the Internet, all bets are off. While there might be a hope that the woman on the other end really is twenty-five-years-old and wants nothing more than to have oral sex with you, it's just as likely that she's a sixty-year-old man with a wife and ten grandkids, or a fifteen-year-old high school student who's doing this instead of physics homework. And you don't want to assume that people who have usernames like "8inchElmer" or "StopStaringAtMyCock" are necessarily men.

Virtual Deception or a Real Reflection?

It's easy to be critical about the deception in cybersex, but it's not like there aren't precedents in real life.

For instance, in real life, Amy is an engineer who works for an aerospace firm. Amy used to have a bra-cup size that was an A. After $11,000 of cosmetic surgery, Amy's breasts are size D and the bump and bulge in her nose is history. She is wearing make-up, her hair has been bleached and permed, and she's got on $200 of underwear from Victoria's Secret. What's so real about any of that?

Or what about Fred. He works out at the gym three hours a day, leases a $90,000 car, and spends $3,500 at the Laser Hair Removal center each year to keep the hair on his chest and back at bay. He's in debt up to his plucked eyebrows and he drinks more than he should.

Fred and Amy have never tried chatrooms or cybersex, but are they totally real or do they have virtual parts themselves?

Beyond Text: Cybersex with a Videocam

If there are two things that will get the hackles up on a card-carrying feminist, one is when a person is reduced to a sexual object and the other is when that "gaze" thing goes in high gear—when a guy looks at a woman's boobs instead of straight into her eyes. Yet it's these very things that are the hallmark of televideo cybersex. In cybersex with a videocam, people are reduced to close-ups of their bodies, often just their breasts or genitals.

In cybersex, you've got people crossing a forbidden threshold which can be exciting. The risk isn't anywhere near what a flasher in a park has to face, unless a jealous former lover downloads pictures of you playing with yourself on the web and gives it to your fellow teachers or passes it out at your interfaith church group.

In fact, it's not all that often that you see a cybersex participant's face. The camera is focused on body parts being grabbed and rubbed. So you've got the thrill of watching and of being watched, of stripping and of being stripped for, and of being daring while feeling safe.

These and many other fascinating issues about sex in cyberspace have been raised by sociologist Dennis Waskul. For instance, in cybersex, you often see the genitals of the other person first and their face last, assuming you ever get to see their face. Yet in real life romance, you see the other person's face first and their genitals last, or at least that's the way we do it around here.

A notable exception that Waskul doesn't mention are some of the more high-traffic areas of gay sex. If you consider what goes on in some of the gay bath houses, on park trails, and in glory holes, the genitals tend to be what it's all about. Perhaps videocam cybersex is the heterosexual version of gay cruising. In fact, if you consider the paltry few females and the large number of males, a lot of videocam cybersex is actually a cyber-circle jerk.

Media Reports about Sex in Cyberspace

One of the truly fascinating things about sex and cyberspace are the statistics that people invent about it. For instance, a 2004 article in a college newspaper from Idaho made the following statement:

"While an estimated two-million Americans engage in cybersex, 200,000 of those people are addicted, which means it disrupts their professional or personal lives. The key to avoiding this pitfall is moderation, and a realistic perspective."

Really? Consider this:

1. There is no way of accurately knowing how many Americans engage in cybersex, so any figures you read are pure fiction.

2. How do you define "cybersex addiction?" Such a definition would need to have a consensus among Internet-savy sociologists and psychologists rather than the usual prattle of the addiction fanatics.

3. There have been no valid studies that have determined the number of "cybersex addicts," partly because none have ever been done and partly because there is no agreement on what "cybersex addiction" might even be. So any figures, be they two or 200,000, are a ridiculous fiction.

Of course, none of this stops the media from pretending that they are actual facts.

"Addiction" Is Relative–The Two Forks Meet

Let's say you spend five hours each night in Yahoo! or MSN sex-groups, or in sexually-oriented chat rooms, or checking out sexcams, or downloading porn, or reading steamy sex stories, or maybe having a cybersex jerkoff session with someone in Arkansas who claims he knew Monica Lewinski. There would be no end of alarmists with self-help books in hand who would say you are addicted.

Yet if you spent the same amount of time each night sitting in front of the TV, they wouldn't say a word. That's because you'd fit the national average for TV watchers. And no one would raise an eyebrow if you spent your evenings reading romance novels or books that Oprah recommends.

Mind you, there would be no protest from here if you started doing something better with your time than jerking off in cyberspace with a bunch of other guys who are hoping a woman will actually show up and flash a breast, but we'd say the same thing to the vast majority of the American public who sit like rotting potatoes in front of the television each night watching one dumb show after the next.

Privacy in Cyberspace?

> "You already have zero privacy. Get over it."
>
> —Scott McNeally, CEO, Sun Microsystems

If you honestly believe there is a single private thing about anything you put on the Internet, you are one big silly goose! It doesn't matter if you are in the most private of private rooms or a MOO on Mars. It doesn't matter if it's a blog in Bangkok or an MUDD in Madagascar, you need to be aware that if it's on the Internet, it's as public as if you wrote it in spraypaint on the side of the freeway. The same is true if you and your cybersex partner are masturbating for each other via a videocam, so play close attention to the accepted cybersex convention of showing no face when you're spanking your monkey.

Watch Your Financial Flanks

Before you hand out your credit card number to anyone on the Internet for anything to do with sex, visit janesguide.com and look at her "consumer tips." Jane, Jim, Peter, and Vamp know more about sex on the Internet than most people alive, and you would be well-served to spend a few minutes reading their warnings. Be especially aware when buying a "trial" subscription or a month on a website. It might take a year to stop the recurring charges, and do you really want to be calling the state's attorney general for help when you bought a month on ChicksWithDicks4U.com or CumOnACheerleadersFace.com?

RECOMMENDED: As of press time, the most insightful work on cybersex that crossed these desks was Dennis Waskul's *Self-Games and Body-Play—Personhood in Online Chat and Cybersex,* Peter Lang, New York, 2003. The only problem with the book is that the author speaks in two languages. In the main text, he uses a disembodied academic speak which makes the reader have to work too hard to understand anything he is saying. Yet in the footnotes he speaks in perfectly good English.

Dear Paul,

I have an online lover and the feelings I am having about him are the most powerful that I've ever had about anyone. I've never met him in person and the only sex we have is online. My husband doesn't know and I don't have any plans to leave him. But the feelings I have for my online lover are so strong and the sex is so incredible. Is this the same as adultery?

Laura in Washington, DC

Dear Laura,

While you were at it, you might as well have asked me the meaning of life, or the meaning of married life, anyway.

For some people, it's easier to have great sex and multiple orgasms with someone who you don't have to raise kids with and who you don't have to pay the rent with. This is one of the allures of cybersex. It's a pretty cool illusion, and the best sex we can have is usually grounded in fantasy and illusion. It comes from the erotic tension that we are able to create with each other. Marriage or long-term relationships can throw a lot of cold water on that. Hopefully there's a level of respect and love for each other that increases over time. This helps make up for the routine of married sex.

In some ways, I think your marriage would be on more solid ground if you and your husband were going to swinger's parties every weekend and having sex with couples who exchange partners. You would actually be having sex with other people instead of just fantasizing about it, which I think is less of a threat to a marriage that an imagined lover in cybersex might be. Plus, you'd both be in on it and it wouldn't be dishonest.

I'd be singing a much different tune if you and your husband had discussed your cybering ahead of the fact and had both agreed that it was okay. By discussing cybersex, I'm talking about something more honest than telling him it's like having a pen pal on the computer.

I've also heard people in your kind of situation say this never would have happened to them if it hadn't been for the Internet. But adultery is nothing new and if you are looking for a technology to blame it on, I'd be just as suspicious of the telephone and the automobile. After all, how much adultery happens without a phone or a car being involved?

I've also dealt with a situation where an angry, blaming husband says how cybersex stole his wife and made her a vacant mother to their three-year-old child, completely ignoring the point that she was an equally vacant mom before discovering cybersex. It's simply amazing that before her Internet indiscretions, he didn't regard her as a vacant mom when she sat on the couch all day watching TV.

You might want to tell me that what you do with your Internet lover is no different than someone who masturbates with a fantasy lover in mind, or that it's no different from when a wife fantasizes about the butcher when she's making love to her husband, the banker. Funny, though, how you and most of the other women on the planet who have been having these fantasies for years have never needed to ask me about them.

As for whether this is or isn't adultery, I don't think that's the point. Some people would say it is, others might counter that what you are doing is keeping you from really having adultery. Either way, it probably requires more effort to keep the sex in a marriage exciting than it does to find a cybersex lover.

It could be that if you told your husband about your cybersex experiences, it might be the kind of welcome shock that brings the two of you closer. Then again, maybe not. But you're not asking me for that kind of advice, and I honestly wouldn't know what to say.

Hopefully, readers who are venturing into cybersex behind their partner's back will take heed of your situation. Don't do it until you've discussed it with each other, including the possible ramifications and outcomes.

End of Chapter Note: The Russians are coming! For those of you who grew up under the shadow of the CD symbol on page 430 (CD = Civil Defense with CONELRAD radio broadcasts), it's a little amazing to think that the second largest publisher in the former Soviet Union is selling a Russian translation of the totally American *Guide To Getting It On!* WOWSKI!

busy. I think my problem is not meeting women. I dislike bars…. I do not feel my sex life is representative of a mature, healthy adult male, and the lack of physical intimacy bothers me considerably. Both of my house mates have the same problem and I know many other guys do. Paul, what is up with this problem, and besides offering your own valuable suggestions, can you direct me to some resources that might help me locate and meet available women?

Blue in Boulder

Dear Blue,

Regarding your question about helping you to locate and meet available women, I've added an entire chapter on internet dating. It follows this one. As for the other matters you listed, here's my personal take.

High school and college may not fill our lives with happiness and bliss, but they do provide an important social safety net. I can remember my own horror at finally having to leave college. I hadn't gotten into medical school, I didn't feel like doing grad work, and my girlfriend had just given me the boot. I didn't know it was possible to feel so awful. I got a job waiting tables—which is the equivalent of leaving school but not really. I wrote and floundered for a couple of years until I finally went back to graduate school when I was about your age. I don't remember getting laid much during that time. I also made the huge mistake of doing what you are doing—trying to find ways of meeting women. There is no shortage of books or manuals on that subject. But I'm not so sure they will help, and I don't know if they are what you need. In fact, I strongly encourage you to do something else with your time than focusing on how to meet women.

Please take a moment to imagine that you only have a couple of hours to live. I am willing to bet that even if you had been a stud lover and had created wet spots on mattresses all over Boulder, memories of your love life wouldn't bring you tremendous amounts of solace in the face of death. It's not how often you've had sex or who you had sex with that would make you feel like your life had been worthwhile. What's more important are the contributions that you've hopefully made in life.

Men's & Women's Experience of Sex

Chapter 32

Men's and women's genitals are generally found in the same location: behind the buttons of a person's blue jeans. But what about the way we experience sex? Do men and women experience sex differently? That's what this chapter is about. But first...

Forget Everything Else!

Forget penises, vulvas and chromosomes. The biggest difference between male and female sexuality throughout the ages has been the fact that men don't get pregnant and women do. Forget the "behavioral influences" of estrogen and testosterone — instead, consider how differently we might approach sex if men were the ones who got knocked up and had to carry a baby inside themselves for nearly ten months, and if men were expected to be the child's primary caregiver for the next eighteen years.

Of course, there are other factors that influence men's and women's experience of sex. While most of these have to do with cultural roles and expectations, some reflect differences in biology. For instance, there are subtle differences in brain anatomy which may influence behavior. Consider how the female brain responds to the smell and taste of chocolate. Think of how different life would be if the female brain responded to the penis with half as much craving as it often does for chocolate.

There are also claims about differences in the behaviors of male and female newborns. The author of this guide spent a number of years in graduate school holding and studying babies, from two-pound preemies to drug-addicted newborns of crack-smoking moms. He can assure you that the only difference between boy babies and girl babies that means a single thing is how the babies pee. Boy babies have the capacity to wipe out your favorite shirt, tie, glasses and note pad, while girl babies are more forgiving pee-ers. Working with boy babies requires a quickness of hand. Some women report this kind of skill is just as necessary when working with the babies' adult fathers.

Perhaps a more relevant finding of infant research is that girl babies are every bit as strong and healthy as boys at birth, if not more so. Yet we often treat girl babies as though they were more fragile. For instance, researchers have dressed the same baby as a boy and then as a girl. When caregivers thought that the baby was a girl, they said things like "Aren't you pretty and dainty." When they thought it was a boy, they said, "Aren't you a big one; look at how strong you are." Furthermore, if you want to know the sex of a baby from ten yards away, just observe how its daddy plays with it; girl babies get an abundance of hugs and kisses while boy babies get the rough 'n' tumble. With such profound differences in the way we raise our children, it's hard to imagine how subtle variations in neurology or genetics even matter.

Note: We use the term "opposite sex" when comparing men and women, yet there is not a single psychological test battery that can distinguish male from female test takers.

Typical Male Porn vs. The Newer Female Porn

What happens to these babies twenty years later when they are having sex? Do the women's experiences fall into the "pretty and dainty" category? Are the men's "big and strong"? Perhaps not, but our culture does have specific insults that it hurls at women whose sexuality appears to be "big and strong" and at men whose sexuality is "pretty and dainty."

To help illustrate possible differences in men's and women's experience of sex, we have included a few samples of pornographic writing. The following is a typical letter to a male magazine that is commonly used for masturbation. It had a monthly audience of around five million people before the Internet took the staples out of its sides.

> It wasn't long before a wet area began to appear in the front part of DeAnne's bikini panties. I slowly started to pull them down, at first revealing a neatly trimmed patch of silken blonde down, then the glistening tip of DeAnne's swollen clit, and finally the rest of her hidden steamy treasure. The mere sight made me so hot I nearly exploded.
>
> DeAnne must have sensed my excitement. Without saying a word, she ripped open my bulging blue jeans and started

ravaging my nine-inch cock with her pleading lips. Within seconds I was filling her hungry mouth with load after load of white hot cum. DeAnne kept sucking and slurping on my throbbing cock until she milked my big balls dry.

Okay, so getting your rocks off is the name of the game in traditional male porn, with the focus being on the particular body parts that get you there the fastest. There's also the premise that within every woman sits a raging nymphomaniac begging to wrap her lips and legs around the teeming bulge of the nearest available guy.

The next two passages are from *Erotic Interludes,* a collection of women's pornography—ah, erotica—edited by Lonnie Barbach (Harper & Row, New York, 1986):

J.B. tenderly caressed my breasts until I could feel the space between my legs grow warm and wet. His kisses were different than ever before, long and slow at first, then his tongue licked mine like fire dancing in the dark. His long, slender legs gradually, rhythmically inched mine apart. The tip of his cock played on my belly, and I couldn't resist rising up to meet him, opening my legs as far as the backseat would allow. A soft flash of red filled my vision when he entered me, his kisses wild on my face. I remember only the sense of infinite motion that followed. (Written by Sharon S. Mayes)

Amy groaned with pleasure as his large hand cupped her gently and his third finger came to rest on the one sweet spot he knew so well. As he touched it she felt an electric current flow from his hand into her. His energy swirled inside her till the whole universe seemed to start spinning around…. The spinning sensation rose up and flooded her whole body, pushing at the boundaries of who she thought she was…. Finally, unable to hold the energy back any longer, she let it explode through every cell in her body, cleansing her with light and pulsating out into the room. (By Udana Power)

Blinding light? Infinite motion? This has a different edge than "Within seconds I was filling her hungry mouth with load after load of white hot cum."

One female reader says that the samples of women's porn "left me bored," while she found the male passage to be "erotic for me until he wastes his cock in her mouth." Several female readers have echoed this same sentiment, but with phrasing that is somewhat more delicate. At the same time, a male reader says that he finds the women's passages to be more erotic. Perhaps it's not so easy to generalize about the preferences of men and women, although the samples could easily be tagged as typical male or typical female.

Is It Really Different?

Are men's and women's experiences really different, or do they just use different words to describe them?

Researchers asked men and women to write a paragraph describing their experience of orgasm. A panel of judges could not tell the women's descriptions of orgasm from the men's. So much for those charts on orgasm that make men and women look like they come from different planets. Nonetheless, studies have shown that there are some sex-related differences in the attitudes of men and women, but mostly when they are with members of the same sex. These differences decrease greatly when men and women are in mixed company.

But this isn't what Madison Avenue wants us to think. Advertisers work hard to make us believe that men and women are very, very different. That's because manufacturers can often charge more for products that are targeted to a specific sex, such as cigarettes, deodorants, and even hemorrhoid ointments which are for one sex only. It's a little surprising that we haven't seen toilet paper that's made just for a man's or woman's "special needs"—although one manufacturer, Kleenex, did try to sell man-sized facial tissues, which really were better for jerking off into than normal-sized tissue.

How Men and Women Experience Visual Pornography

It is often said that women aren't as turned on as men by X-rated movies, but this notions seems to be less pronounced in today's young adults. Research shows that rather than being turned off by visual pornography, women are turned off by the premise of most male pornography, which portrays females as submissive bimbos. When shown X-rated movies which are smart, fun and where the sexuality conveys affection, both male and female viewers prove to be highly aroused.

In research on pornography, college students were hooked up to devices that measure blood flow in the genitals. They were then shown X-rated movies. Although these devices indicated that the groins of the female students were as sexually aroused as the males, several of the women were not consciously aware of their arousal. This may have been due to an experimental glitch; on the other hand, it might reflect how women are often raised to ignore their body's sexual cues. Also, it is possible that males wouldn't be nearly as conscious of their own sexual arousal if they didn't have a penis that's difficult to ignore when it gets hard. Whatever the case, women used to rent about 40 percent of adult videos, and the absolute number of X-rated rentals were staggering. Perhaps they did this just to please their male partners, but from the responses we've seen on our sex surveys, this is unlikely. Nowadays, with the number of cable, satellite and Internet downloads, it's difficult to tell the sex of who's watching what.

Role Reversal—Fingers up Men's Rear Ends

Getting a finger up the rear during a routine physical exam makes many guys feel like they've been violated, yet they don't think twice about sticking their own fingers up a woman's vagina. It's possible that a woman's experience of sex might feel more private than a man's since her body is the one that is usually being penetrated. One woman reader comments:

> "Even if he's wearing a condom, it still feels like a man leaves something inside of me during intercourse. He's got to have something I really want inside of me, or I won't do it."

One of the few times when a woman gets to stick something of hers inside a man is during French kissing. Some men love the feeling of a woman's tongue inside their mouths, while other men are only comfortable with French kissing if it imitates intercourse, with the male's tongue doing the thrusting. Also, there is some body-cavity equality in those couples who are into certain kinds of anal sex where the woman penetrates the man's rear with her fingers or various kinds of sex toys.

Intimacy in Men vs. Women

In our society, we often assume that women are better at intimacy than men. Is this true?

The answer depends upon how you define intimacy. According to psychologist David Schnarch, women are often better at some levels of intimacy (sharing feelings, talking about how the day went, etc.), but when you get past the small talk, neither women nor men do particularly well with intimacy. When your definition of intimacy excludes feelings of dependency, a lot of women run from it as fast as men.

A Final Perspective

Some evolution experts believe that nature has programmed men to ejaculate into each and every available vagina, while women are programmed to couple with males who will offer the best chance to successfully raise a family (relationship material). The people who take these theories most seriously are the evolutionists themselves. They have a wild propensity to twist facts to fit their theories, and people who question the process are dismissed as fundamentalist quacks. It's interesting how with changes in economics and politics, more women are looking to catch more ejaculations from more men than they did fifty years ago.

In spite of what the evolutionist would want us to expect, a man who is straight and masculine-appearing might experience sex in a way that we would typically expect of a woman—sensitive, monogamous and intimacy seeking, while a very feminine-appearing straight woman might enjoy sex with numerous men, value it for the rush of sensation that it offers, and avoid long-term relationships. It's also possible that what we want at one point in our lives may be totally different from what we want at another. Perhaps it's dangerous to generalize about how any of us, male or female, experience sex.

The most important thing to be aware of about sexual differences is that your partner might experience sex differently than you do. Instead of pretending to know what that might be or making silly assumptions based upon even sillier generalizations, why not ask, explore, and find out for yourselves?

Also, as we get older, life keeps presenting us with opportunities for growth and change. Hopefully, you will be able to use these opportunities to increase the intimacy and satisfaction in your relationships, even if it means being more "male" or "female" in bed than your gender's stereotype currently allows.

What's Feminine, Masculine & Erotic
Chapter 33

To use the terms *masculine* and *feminine* as if they actually exist as real things is a bit out of fashion today. The thinking in many academic circles is that masculinity and femininity are constructed by society in the same way that a beer commercial or Victoria's Secret lingerie commercial might be. Likewise, once you start chipping away at traditional definitions of what's masculine and what's feminine, your assumptions about what's erotic for one sex or the other start to look a little silly. This chapter takes a brief look at matters that tend to be incredibly complex.

Linebacker-Dad Likes What?

In defining what's masculine and what isn't, let's consider Dave, the prototypical manly guy. Dave plays football, hunts, is a great dad and beloved husband. And there's one other thing. Every month or two, Dave gets together with an old guy friend who gives it to him up the rear. You know, anal sex. So what happens now to his rating on your scale of what's masculine? Does it drop some? A lot? Just a tiny bit? None?

Even if you said, "Just a tiny bit," please be aware that your definition of masculinity includes "what goes in and out of a guy's butt": 100% feces = 100% real man. Less than that, and he's not a real man. That's how many of us define it.

Masculinity, Then and Now

A little more than a hundred years ago, men who didn't have much money tended to work in jobs that required a good deal of physical labor. As a result, you could often assume that a man in 1900 who looked like he spent several hours each day in the gym didn't really. Those well-defined, masculine muscles were usually the result of a low-paying job. In fact, a well-dressed man with a pot belly was a pretty good catch for an attractive young woman. A big belly and nice clothes appeared quite masculine at the turn of the century.

Do you think things have changed just a bit? Nowadays, we assume that most men with buff muscles have enough leisure time to spend hours at the gym. It's unlikely that someone who is working two jobs as a janitor will be able to work out as well, and a guy who has a job as computer programmer may work out at the gym in an attempt to hide the fact that his biggest physical challenge at work is opening up his laptop. And the young woman of olde who may have viewed Mr. Portly as a good catch might very well be working out at the gym today with Mr. Buff and making as much money as he is. This would have confused people a great deal a hundred years ago.

What Different Societies Have to Say

Each culture has its own definition of what's masculine, feminine and erotic. Here are some examples of how these definitions differ from culture to culture year to year:

Women in Muslim cultures cover themselves from head to toe when appearing in public. Women in Hollywood appear in public wearing a few molecules of black spandex, designed more to tease than to cover. The women in Hollywood claim that their Muslim counterparts are sexual prisoners. The Muslim women feel that the real prisoners are the females in Hollywood. A neutral observer might call it a toss up. One female reader says that neither women are sexual prisoners, since they both use sex to control the people around them!

In Japan, it's a common practice for people to strip naked and bathe together. Nobody finds this kind of public nudity to be erotic or shameful, but Lord help two Japanese who kiss in public, at least until recently. In our society, it's nearly the opposite, with kissing being fine but public nudity being a legal offense.

Kim Edwards is a woman who taught English in a rigid Islamic country for two years and then moved to Japan. In the Islamic country, an exposed female body is considered to be the tool of the devil, and women cover it from head to toe to save the souls of men. After a few years in a rigid Islamic country, Ms. Edwards literally started hating her own body. When she finally moved to Japan, she was shocked to find herself treated as a normal person no matter what she wore. She could even bathe naked in public bathhouses, while she could

Who is the "Sexual Prisoner"?

a. The Muslim Woman
b. The Western Woman
c. Neither
d. Both

have been stoned to death for doing this in an Islamic country. (Kim Edwards's story is told in her work "In Rooms of Women," published in Laurence Goldstein's "The Female Body: Figures, Styles, Speculations" [University of Michigan Press, Ann Arbor].)

During the Summer Olympics, male gymnasts from the Russian team often celebrated good performances by kissing other male team members on the lips. Our U.S. male gymnasts wouldn't be caught dead doing that, not in public anyway.

In America, many straight women now wear their hair short, and straight men wear their hair long. Fifty years ago this meant that you were homosexual. And think of the public outcry if a 1950s professional baseball player appeared in billboard ads wearing a pair of red bikini briefs; or if his 1950s beehive-coiffed girlfriend went to the grocery store wearing Doc Martins and a pair of male boxers. Or what if a straight American male tried wearing a pierced earring before the 1980s, or routinely trimmed or shaved his pubic hair?

In America, there is nothing unusual about an unmarried eighteen-year-old woman having sex; but among more traditional Arab-Muslims, Christians, Druze, and Israelis in places like the Gaza Strip and the West Bank, such a woman risks being murdered for harming the honor of her family. This type of "honor killing," is supported by the girl's family as well as the rest of the village. Even the girl's mother and sisters support it because it protects the family name.

In Africa, millions of women have their clitorises and inner labia crudely cut out of their bodies as children. This type of "surgery" has been considered an important passage to womanhood which many African mothers have done to their young daughters. In the Western world, a mother who did such a thing to her daughters would be put in prison. Of course, African women might claim that the clitoridectomy is just as cosmetic and feminine as our Western penchant for mutilating female bodies with breast implants. Who knows what an African woman might say about liposuction.

In the Hispanic culture of East Los Angeles some males don't feel masculine until they have gotten a woman pregnant ("given her a child"). Likewise, some Hispanic females don't feel good about themselves until they have borne children. Twenty miles to the west, in Pacific Palisades and Malibu, the last thing a teenage couple wants to do is get pregnant. They often seek an abortion if it happens. Also, a Malibu woman who is pregnant often worries about losing her hard-earned, occasionally anorexic shape, while the pregnant Hispanic woman might relish the feeling of fullness that pregnancy offers.

Until the last couple of decades it was considered unfeminine for women in our society to enjoy sex as much as men. Valuing sex was a masculine trait, and some women even believed that it was unladylike to have orgasms. Yet there are plenty of other cultures which take it for granted that the sex drives of men and women are equally intense. In some cultures, parents even teach their children about enhancing sexual pleasure.

Masculinity & Femininity

For many of us, masculinity and femininity are concepts that make all the sense in the world as long as you don't try to define them.

For example, people in this country think of masculine as being rough-and-tumble and feminine as being dainty and nurturing. Yet this isn't nearly as true in preschools that require little girls to wear the same kind of clothes as little boys. Once freed from wearing dainty outfits, a lot of little girls get rough-and-tumble too. Likewise, if little boys had to wear outfits that needed to be kept clean, they would probably act more daintily.

Equally puzzling are all the rough-and-tumble men who become extremely nurturing and maternal when it's time to feed the baby. Do their aggressive male hormones suddenly dry up at dinner time? Do their brains change shape? And if you assume that women are less aggressive or the more nurturing sex, try talking to a random group of female lawyers, advertising execs or women in entertainment.

While hormones may have some impact in determining male and female behaviors, what we learn from culture about our respective sex roles is clearly the larger force in shaping the way we behave. That's why it is hard to talk about the definitions of masculine and feminine unless we also know the particular country, culture and year.

France Weighs In

From this guide's perspective, any culture's definition of masculine, feminine and erotic is arbitrary, transient and often artificial. Nonetheless, people take these definitions seriously and get really bent out of shape if you ignore their local customs. In some of the chapters that follow, we consider society's sacred-cow rules and traditions, as well as the perspective of people who don't abide by them.

Counterpoint: One reader from France writes, "You have done a great job in this chapter explaining cultural differences, yet you blow it with the first sentence of your final paragraph. In my mind, it's a culture's rules and definitions that make it unique. It would be a very boring planet if we were all the same, and especially if we were all like Americans."

Some days you're the mouse, some days you're the elephant.

Gay & Bi
Chapter 34

Let's face it, ours is a culture based on the great heterosexual dream—marriage, kids, own your own home and a rock-solid pension plan with no dot.com or Enron stock. Straight or gay, people who don't fully subscribe to the great heterosexual dream tend to feel left out. This is particularly true for teenagers who are gay, many of whom are desperately trying to fit in and behave like future breeders.

This chapter begins by looking at how we decide who is straight and who is not. But first, the following is from a very funny book *Who Cares If It's a Choice? Snappy Answers to 101 Nosy, Intrusive and Highly Personal Questions about Lesbians and Gay Men,* by Ellen Orleans, (Laugh Lines Press, 1994):

> **At What Age Do You Know You're Homosexual?** As you might imagine, this varies greatly. Guys seem to be aware of their sexuality early on. A single erection while watching Batman free Robin from the clutches of the Riddler provided many young men with their first clue. One gay friend told me that his childhood role models were Bert and Ernie. For others, it was Skipper and Gilligan.
>
> Women seem to discover their sexual orientation more from personal experiences. Although I didn't realize it at the time, my first clue was when I zipped up Bobby Wolinsky's fly for him in the second grade. My teacher said this was not proper—that that was a boy's private area. At the time, I didn't see what the big deal was. Guess I still don't.

One man in *Frontiers Magazine* said he knew he was gay when it became clear that he preferred masturbating to the men's underwear part of the Sears catalog instead of *Playboy.*

Gay, Straight or in Between?

We've received more than 3000 surveys at goofyfootpress.com, and approximately 80% of the women described themselves as "mostly straight," while about 80% of the men described themselves as "totally straight." A lot of the women said they'd had fantasies or were curious about what it would be like to have sex with another woman, while even the mildest hint of such a possibility resulted in angry flaming responses from many of the males, e.g. "NO FUCKIN WAY!" or "THAT'S SICK!"

So do we define "straight" differently for women than for men? In our society, we consider a woman straight until she conks us over the head with evidence to the contrary. But what if a guy slips up once or twice by showing behavior that isn't straight from a beer commercial? He gets hammered with taunts of "gay" and "faggot." It seems that we define "straight" differently for men than for women because for a guy to be straight, he's got to constantly prove that he's straight, or at least put up a good show. A woman can say she has fantasies about having oral sex with another women, and we still think of her as straight as long as she's got a boyfriend. But if a guy says he's got fantasies of giving another guy a blow job, we're not so sure anymore even if he's married and has six kids. And that's just for people who say or think they are straight.

What if the chairperson of the Lesbian Women's Caucus gets turned on while staring at the butt of the cute guy at the hardware store? Does that make her less of a lez or a damaged dyke? Or what if the gay homecoming king looks up a cheerleader's skirt with something other in mind than whether she waxed her bikini line correctly?

Where does the line between thought and action play into all of this? What if the chairperson of the Lesbian Women's Caucus is tongue-deep between the thighs of last year's Miss Akron when she's suddenly nailed by the fantasy of the hardware boy easing her down on a pile of new lawnchair cushions and giving her the nicest politically incorrect six inches a woman could ever want? This woman is a 100% card-carrying dyke, but she occasionally suffers from the fantasy equivalent of break-through bleeding. Do we need to account for this in how we label her? Does she need to account for this in how she labels herself? And what in heaven's name do we do if the gay homecoming king borrows a pair of the head cheerleader's panties from her workout bag and goes home one night and jerks off into them?

Confirmed gay and lesbian readers are probably throwing up by this point and thinking "Not on your life." And we can assure you that not one of those "I'm-totally-straight-but-I-protest-too-much" males has ever had a single moment in his life when he felt a sex vibe for another guy.

But what if Mr. Totally Straight gets tossed in the slammer for twenty years? What if he ends up having a non-exploitive and perhaps even tender sexual relationship with his cellmate, Little Bubba? Does this mean he was really bisexual the whole time, or was it a situational glitch and Little Bubba will be history once the parole board tells Mr. Straight to skedaddle?

Wet Panties Have Their Advantages

Here's just one of a hundred different possibilities to consider when deciding what's gay and what's straight:

If a woman becomes aroused at the sight, smell, or touch of another woman, she doesn't have to worry about being found out. If she's undressing with another woman and finds the situation arousing, she can smile inwardly and enjoy her feelings and not have to worry that something sticking up between her legs is going to give her away. But if a guy gets an erection in the locker room, there's going to be hell to pay. If he even gets caught looking in the wrong direction, there might be hell to pay. As a result, it's possible that straight guys learn to suppress any inkling of same-sex arousal early on. They don't even let themselves become aware of the possibility, and if it starts to bubble into consciousness, they quickly push it out. This is a standard that women don't have to abide by. Only men have to be men.

With this in mind, think about the many men who label themselves as totally straight, but who get angry at even the thought of sexual tenderness between two men. Is there a connection? Remember, society cuts guys no slack while women are free to roam. On the other hand, it could be that their angry response has nothing to do with repression or protesting too much.

Interesting: For a very plausible account of how this kind of repression happens on the basketball court, see Michael Messner's "Becoming 100% Straight" in the book *Inside Sports* edited by J. Coakley and P. Donnelly, Routledge, London, 1999.

Gay Bashers & Reaction Formation

The University of Georgia is one of the finer institutions of higher learning, and not simply because they have used the *Guide to Getting It On!* as required reading in their sex education classes, although it does speak well of them. The University of Georgia did a fascinating study on homophobia.

Psychologists gave a questionnaire about homosexuality to a group of sixty-four men. Based upon their responses, the men were divided into two subgroups: those who were homophobic and those who were not. The testers then showed the subjects hardcore X-rated videos of men having sex with women, and men having sex with men. They did this after placing sensors on the guys' penises to see if they were having erections while watching the different videos.

When watching the tapes of gay guys, 80% of the homophobic men had penile arousal, while only 34% percent of the nonhomophobic men did. This means that 80% of the men who strongly disliked gays may have become sexually aroused while watching men having sex with men. Naturally, almost all of the homophobic men denied feeling aroused while watching gay guys having sex.

Unfortunately, the penis does not always tell the truth, and studies using genital sensors tend to raise as many questions as they answer. For instance, we might wonder if the increase in the penis size of the homophobic men could have been from fear or rage rather than arousal, or perhaps it was from a combination of all three.

Statistics

It is estimated that at least 60% of the population is straight, that 1% to 40% or more might be bisexual and that 2% to 7% percent of the population is gay. You will find that the numbers derived from different surveys vary hugely, depending upon how the questions are worded and how each category is defined. For instance, how do you categorize someone who occasionally fantasizes about having sex with a member of the same gender but would never actually do it?

Of the various sexual orientations, which is best? We have no clue. There are times when life and relationships totally blow no matter what your sexual orientation; being straight is no guarantee of happiness, nor is being gay. Nonetheless, straight is what most people think they are, and it is usually easier to be part of the majority no matter what the subject. Easier, but not necessarily more satisfying.

Most studies measuring the satisfaction of straight, gay male and lesbian couples find few differences, although the data often suggest that lesbian couples are likely to be more satisfied than their heterosexual or gay male counterparts.

Straight Mouth, Gay Mouth?

While it's one thing to feel uncomfortable about another person's sexual orientation, it's quite another to make fun of them, occasionally beat them up and pass laws that discriminate against them. Yet that's what a number of straight people do to gays.

Consider the following: Straight or gay, most men enjoy having their penises sucked. Straights prefer that a woman does the sucking. But did a prophet come down from the mount and announce that a woman's mouth is better suited to suck a penis than a man's? Are her molars more penis-friendly than a man's? While it's important to a straight man that a woman suck his penis, and it's important to a gay man that a guy suck his, the distinction is strictly mental.

Statistically speaking, just as many heterosexual couples in this country enjoyed anal sex last night as did gay couples. Maybe even your minister and his wife enjoy anal sex, not to mention some of our country's ultraconservative senators and congressmen. Are they bad people because they enjoy an occasional butt fuck?

A mouth's a mouth and a butt's a butt—gender is of little consequence, unless it's got a penis in it.

Heather & Cher's Place

While this guide doesn't care what your sexual orientation is, it does care that you respect your sexuality. This puts it at odds with what has been happening in some of the more visible parts of the gay male community.

For instance, some years ago the author of this book moved to Los Angeles for graduate school. That's when he joined one of the glitzy health spa chains whose spokespersons were celebrities like Cher and Heather someone. We're talking years ago, before either of those bodies had seen a single surgeon's knife. Being a person who loved taking a steam bath after a workout, it's also when your author discovered that the steam room at Heather and Cher's place was where some of the local actor-wannabe types congregated to jack off.

Call it provincial, call it petty, but there's something really annoying about taking a steam bath and having to worry about sitting in a puddle of actor-wannabe cum. This was before people knew much about AIDS, so the complaint was strictly aesthetic.

Livestock sexuality can be a lonely thing. This is just as true for straight people as for gays cruising locker rooms with pumped-up dicks hoping to attract the hand or mouth of a nameless, faceless stranger. On the other hand, if you consider the history of homosexuality in America, being able to troll inside of Heather and Cher's locker room is quite an achievement. That's because before the 1960s, being a homosexual in America was a greater crime than being a robber or a rapist. Having gay sex in the privacy of your own home could land you in jail and leave you branded as a sex offender for life. Until 2003, it was still illegal to perform a homosexual act in more than twenty states, in spite of the fact that almost one out of four or five Americans will take part in a homosexual act at some point in their lives.

Given this rather frightening history of oppression, it's easy to see why gays may have viewed the freedom to jerk off in Heather and Cher's locker room as a tremendous victory. But there comes a time to stop measuring the present strictly against the past. Instead of encouraging its members to respect their sexuality, the gay community in the '70s and '80s went out of its way to sanction the practice of livestock sex. The implied message became "Love me because I'm gay," which is about as dumb as saying "Love me because I'm straight."

Of course, one doesn't criticize this sort of activity without being called homophobic or anti-gay. But maybe it's possible that this section was included out of love and an awareness that whether you are gay or straight, life is even more difficult without a sense of dignity and self-respect.

Counterpoint: A gay male supporter of this guide says that we are trying to apply a straight model onto a gay population, and that this isn't fair. He says that while plenty of gay men are monogamous, there are others who find it incredibly rewarding and fulfilling to cruise and

have multiple partners. Far from taking from their self respect, it adds to it. He suggests that the only reason why more straight men don't do this is because it's not as available to them as it is to gays. From his personal experience, he questions whether a one-night-stand can't have as much intimacy and closeness for some gay men as sex in a monogamous relationship does for some straights. He also questions that with a divorce rate of 50%, and with a large percentage of other married couples staying together just for the kids, whether the ideal straight model of monogamy is all it's cracked up to be.

Postscript—That's Entertainment

On a beautiful California day, your author walked past a group of young women who were swooning in front of the poster of a good-looking actor who had made it big. This actor has had quite an impact on the American public—women want to sleep with him; their boy-friends wish they could be him.

Your author couldn't help but chuckle because he rarely forgets a face, even if it was through the fog in the steam room of Heather and Cher's gym several years ago.

Straight Male Friends Can Be Important

Contrary to what some heterosexuals fear, the last thing most gay men want is to have sex with a straight guy. While there are exceptions, most gay men would be bored by the concept. And if you are a straight guy who gets hit up for gay sex, it's quite easy to say, "Sorry, but I'm one of those boring breeder types." If the person is really thick and persists, you might say, "Again, no thanks, but let me describe for you how much I love licking a woman's pussy, and what it looks and feels like." If that doesn't gag the guy on the spot, be careful. He's probably an undercover cop.

Straight men should also be aware that within the gay community, conversations sometimes boil down to one of three topics: sex, AIDS or gay politics. This is one reason why some gay men value their friendships with straight men. With straight men they are only friends and not potential sex partners, and they can have conversations about things like baseball scores and new car tires without the added postscript of who just died. Furthermore, their straight male friends aren't invested in the sometimes vicious politics of the local gay scene. Likewise, there are plenty of straight men who can use help with fashion, design or advice about women from their gay male friends. There's even been a TV show on this very subject.

Straight or gay, most men prefer to be known for what they are rather than whom they fuck. Yet there are large portions of both the gay and the straight communities where this is not possible.

Cruising on the Internet

It used to be if a gay guy was cruising to find sex for the night, he'd automatically try the bars, baths, clubs or trails. A good deal of that has changed in the past couple of years. Enter the Internet. We're talking log onto one of the Internet groups in your area, select, chat, agree, log off, drive to where you're going, and presto!

Condoms Fit in Fun Places!

In some ways, this leads to more intimacy, since it requires more interaction than just a nod and dropping trow. However, it takes anonymous sex outside of the watchful eye of the larger community, where there might at least be some rules and customs. It seems to have led to an increase in barebacking, which is a gay slang term for having anal intercourse without a condom. This is like telling yourself that it's more exciting to walk through the mine field than around it. It's almost as if the reality is so difficult to deal with that even the small but profound step of using a condom feels like a violation of your right to party and bond. Caring becomes confused with prohibition.

A Sad Note about Teenage Runaways and Suicides

Statistics show that up to 50% of runaway teenagers living on the streets of New York City are gay or bisexual. A disproportionate number of teenagers who commit suicide are also gay, and that's only counting the ones who came out before they killed themselves. Is there something about being gay that predisposes kids to be depressed or unhappy in their own homes? Does it make them unlovable or antisocial? Or is this an indicator that being gay is so alienating in our society that it disrupts even the bond between parent and child?

Whatever the case, teenagers can most certainly benefit from contact with healthy role models, both gay and straight. Unfortunately, we don't like the idea of our children having contact with gay men and women, especially gay Boy Scout leaders.

For more on coming out issues, see the columns at the end of this chapter, as well as our special reading lists.

Going Both Ways—Bisexual Considerations

If you are looking for information about bisexuality, there is only one thing that can be said with absolute certainty—the number of credible studies on bisexuality can fit between your thumb and forefinger with no stretching. There is virtually no science on the subject whatsoever. We don't know if the number of bisexuals in the population is 1% or 50%. We don't even agree on how to define bisexuality.

In theorizing about what bisexuality might be, you would do well to toss out the old notion of a single scale with homosexual on one end and heterosexual on the other. According to that way of thinking, one has gay feelings at the expense of straight feelings, and visa versa.

A better description would be two scales, one gauging homosexual attraction, and a separate scale that gauges heterosexual attraction. According to this view, someone who has no attraction to the same sex but a high attraction toward the other sex would be a ten on the straight scale and a one on the gay scale.

But what if a person has a ten on the straight scale and a ten on the gay scale? It doesn't mean he has a stronger sexual drive, or that his attraction to the other sex is any less than someone who is totally straight. It simply means that he or she has the capacity for intense gay and straight feelings.

The following words of a bisexual woman might be helpful in explaining how some bi people experience their sexual feelings:

"It's funny to talk about the difference between male and female partners, because we did a lot of the same things. If I've got the emotional, intellectual connections, then the physical stuff can be about the same.... There's a chemistry that happens, and I don't know if it's going to be with a man or a woman." From Julia Hutton's *Good Sex* (San Francisco: Cleis Press, 1992).

If you want to forget the scales and look at it practically, at one time or another many people have a homosexual feeling or ten. It's no big deal unless you are also homophobic, in which case your mind has to perform all sorts of mental gymnastics so you can live with yourself. Likewise, there are plenty of homosexuals who have heterosexual feelings. And there are people who have their primary relationships with members of one sex, but also have pronounced desires to get it on with members of the other sex.

For some, the extent of their bisexuality is simply to enjoy bisexual fantasies, while others want and need real sexual contact with both male and female partners.

People who give full rein to both hetero and homo desires are called switch-hitters and are said to go both ways. While the ability to switch-hit might win a baseball player an added bonus, this is not the case when it comes to human sexuality. Both the gay and straight communities regard switch-hitters with suspicion, and the switch-hitter often feels alien with both straights and gays. This is especially true in parts of the lesbian community, where a good lesbian isn't supposed to even think about having sex with a man. It's also true on college campuses, where students apparently regard bisexual males more negatively than they do homosexual males.

While bisexual women might by shunned by ardent lesbians, they fare better overall than do bisexual men. For instance, a former hit song by female singer Jill Sobule is all about how she kissed a girl. Do you think that a song like this would have ever been cut, let alone become popular, if it had been performed by a male singer and were titled "I Kissed a Guy"?

Interestingly, on our sex survey, we've been asking women what they would think if they found out their boyfriend had always had bisexual fantasies. Surprisingly, a number have said it would be no different than if he had fantasies about other women, and it was okay as long as he wasn't acting-out on them. Some of the women aged eighteen to thirty have even said they would find it arousing if their boyfriend got it on with another guy as long as they got to watch. While our survey isn't even close to being real science, it could be an indicator that some things are starting to change.

Life As a Lesbian, As If We Had a Clue...

People often think of gay men and women as being similar just because they are both homosexual. Silly them. To give you an idea of how dissimilar gay men and women can be, consider these statistics: while the majority of gay males in this country will have sex with at least a hundred different partners in a lifetime, the average gay woman has sex with a lifetime total of two to five partners. And while less than 20% of gay males have had sex with a woman, more than 80% of gay women have slept with a man.

Setting a stereotype for gay women is not possible, says sex researcher Ira Reiss. While common personality traits and pathways to homosexuality have been found among some groups of gay males, Reiss has found few among gay women.

Lipstick Lesbians

People sometimes think that all lesbians are bull dykes or motorcycle mamas. This guide is willing to bet its left foot that there were as many lesbians entered in last year's Miss America Pageant as were on the women's professional golf tour. Lesbians are just as feminine (or unfeminine) as straight women. A number of very hot-looking actresses and models are lesbians.

Equally off base is the notion that gay women make love in a delicate or particularly poetic way. Gay women get it on with as much passion (or lack of it) as straight women.

Beyond Brown & Yale

In the past, women who preferred women still dated and married men. And women who had lousy experiences with their fathers often replaced them with equally difficult boyfriends or husbands. It was usually expected that women remain in heterosexual relationships

even if they preferred being with women. There are at least five reasons why this is not necessarily the case anymore:

1. Mothers used to teach their daughters that it was hugely important to marry a man and have his children. This is not as true as it used to be. 2. Appealing lesbian role models used to be few and far between. There now exists a group of very appealing, successful, high-profile lesbian role models in sports, business, rock 'n' roll, and entertainment. 3. It is now acceptable for lesbian couples to have

children by artificial insemination, spawning a whole new market for turkey basters and adoption in most states. 4. It is now the height of academic chic for angst-filled coeds to have lesbian affairs at schools other than just Brown and Yale. 5. Straight women get no respect at the WPGA golf tournaments.

Mistaken Identity?

Women in our society can hug, hold hands or dance together and it is not considered a sign of homosexuality. As a result, they can have homosexual feelings without acknowledging them as that. The following statements by two lesbians help describe how this lack of labeling can impact female homosexual thought, from *Women's Sexual Development,* edited by Martha Kirkpatrick, (New York: International Universities Press):

> "I never thought of homosexual as relating to women, only to men...." and "Our sexual relationship we kept to ourselves, and I was more excited about it than anything else. I thought it was just a delicious secret. And at the same time I had a mad crush on a guy."

Avoiding a label of straight or gay seems like a refreshing idea in this current age when one's sexuality is considered part of the community agenda. On the other hand, there are times when it is important for people who are gay to band together en masse, especially when their civil rights are endangered.

Highly Recommended: If you can't have fun with the *On Our Backs Guide to Lesbian Sex* edited by Diana Cage, Alyson Press, Los Angeles, 2004, then you might be beyond help. Here are a few chapters: "Flirting Tips for Fat Chicks," "Pack Like You Mean It," "Rim Like A Gay Boy," "Beyond the Cucumber, Fun With Food," "How To Suck Dyke Cock," "Fag Sex That Will Make Your Dyke Dick Hard," and "No Ass, No Tail: Uniform Fetish Aside, Real Military Dykes Aren't Getting Laid."

Homosexual Lambs & the Biology of Sexual Orientation

Much has been written about how sexual orientation might result from biological factors. For instance, researchers have injected sheep with hormones that cause male-type behaviors. The female offspring of these sheep turned out to be stud-muffin lambs who displayed stereotypical male behaviors. Other researchers have claimed that

there are differences in certain structures of human brains which they believe cause homosexuality. And you can always count on twin studies to shake things up.

Stories like these tend to make headlines, except for the details about their research design and their inability to be reproduced in other labs. Scientists are still scratching their heads about the study that proclaimed gay men's brains are different, but the researcher managed to get a book deal out it. And if you look at the design of the twin studies and consider the parts that the press doesn't report, the results actually support the idea that homosexuality is the result of environment and not genetics. As of press time, there are interesting studies out of the University of Oregon about homosexual sheep and possible differences in their brains, but until you find gay men who are bleating and baaing, it's difficult to know what to make of this. At the very least, the origins of gender in humans is complex and has many different elements. We aren't even close to knowing what these all might be and how they fit together.

The sad thing about these studies is the way some people use them as an excuse for being gay, e.g., "My son had no choice about being gay." Does one need an excuse for his or her sexual orientation? Whose business is it anyway, and why the need to apologize?

When it comes to needing excuses, the vast majority of serious crimes in this country—from violent attacks and child molestation to bank fraud and illegal drug importation—are committed by heterosexual males. If anyone needs excuses, it's the straight males who commit these crimes and the parents who raised them.

Highly Recommended: For a well-researched and eloquent rebuttal to those who want us to think that homosexuality in humans is simply the child of a queer gene, pick up *The Trouble With Nature— Sex In Science and Popular Culture* by Roger N. Lancaster, University of California Press, Berkeley, 2003.

Thinking-About-It Reading List

Let's say you are a young adult and you would like to explore more about gay or bisexual feelings. If you check with your local Gay & Lesbian organizations, they will probably recommend one of the usual coming out books with pictures on the cover of a white kid, a black kid, a Hispanic kid, and an Asian kid, all smiling and happy. Sorry, but it didn't make the list.

We have devised the following reading list to help you have a fun time exploring gay feelings, while forestalling any lemming-like march into gayness or straightness. In constructing this list, one of the goals was to have books that would cause a stirring in your crotch or longing in your loins—titles with a decent hard-on or wet factor. Many do, but a few don't. Another important factor was that the books be well-written or intelligent and fun to read.

Of course, there will be problems. For instance, what if you have homophobic friends and parents and would like to read some of these books? You'll need to be clever and sneaky—unfortunately, having to keep hidden an important part of yourself. If you drive, maybe you can take a day trip to a library in another city and instead of having to check the book out, you can spend the day reading it there. Or maybe you have an aunt or uncle you can trust, or there's a priest or teacher who will keep your secret. Perhaps they can get the book for you and you can read it at their place. Just be sure it's not someone who is going to insist that you "come out" or that you "get help," unless you really do need to speak with a therapist.

Another problem is that there are probably a dozen other books that deserve to be on this list, but aren't. No one would be surprised if we missed a couple of exceptional titles. Also, some of the books will be out of print. You'll need to find them.

Finally, the body of lesbian literature for young adults seems a bit thin if you include the criteria of "fun" and "sexy." Tragic and angst-filled, no problem; boring and academic—we could fill a library. Fortunately, there's plenty of really excellent panty-drenching lesbian erotica, but that might be a little intense for someone who is just starting to explore. So here's the list. Please have fun with it.

Young & Wet

Annie on My Mind — Nancy Garden
Ruby Fruit Jungle — Rita Mae Brown
Fried Green Tomatoes — Fannie Flagg
Valencia—Michelle Tea
The Passion — Jeanette Winterson
Tipping The Velvet — Sarah Waters
Dive — Stacey Donovan
Strangers in Paradise — Terry Moore
Flaming Iguanas — Erika Lopez
The Wrestling Party — Bett Williams
Girl Walking Backward — Bett Williams
Dare, Truth or Promise — Paul Boock
Deliver Us from Evie — M.E. Kerr
Crush — Jane Futcher
Memory Mambo — Achy Obejas

Young & Hard

The Blue Lawn — William Taylor
Jerome — Wiliam Taylor
Geography Club — Brent Hartinger
Farm Boys — Will Fellows
Blind Items — Matthew Rettenmund
Boy Culture — Matthew Rettenmund
Telling Tales Out of School — Kevin Jennings
Jocks — Dan Woog
PINS — Jim Provenzano
Lawnboy — Paul Lisicky
The Arena of Masculinity — Brian Pronger
My Worst Date — David Leddick
The Front Runner — Patricia Nell Warren
Harlan's Race — Patricia Nell Warren
Changing Pitches — Steve Kluger
Execution Texas: 1987 — D. Travers Scott
Easy Money — Bob Condron
Smooth and Sassy — John Patrick
Gay Olympian — Tom Waddell and Dick Schaap
World of Normal Boys — K.M. Soehnlein
The Coming Storm — Paul Russell
Boys of Life — Paul Russell
Out on Fraternity Row — Windmeyer & Freeman
Enchanted Boy — Richie McMullen
Enchanted Youth — Richie McMullen
The Boys on the Rock — John Fox
The Persian Boy — Mary Renault
Angel, The Complete Quintet — John Patrick
Rainbow Boys — Alex Sanchez
Foolish Fire — Guy Willard
Now and Then — William Corlett
Dream Boy — Jim Grimsley
Sex Toy of the Gods — Christian McLaughlin
For a Lost Soldier — Rudi van Dantzig
Diary of a Hustler — Joey
The Milkman's on His Way — David Rees
My First Time — Jack Hart
Lawnboy — Paul Lisicky
Glove Puppet — Neal Drinnan
Boys Like Us — Patrick Merla

A Better Place — Mark A. Roeder
XY Survival Guide
Cody — Keith Hale
War Boys — Kief Hillsberry
Entries From a Hot Pink Notebook — Todd Brown

A SPECIAL THANKS to Matthew Torrey, who consults on gay literature for public libraries, Kayla Strassford, book buyer for Good Vibrations, and Dan Culliane from Alyson Press. If the list has half the heart, intelligence and humor as these three, it will serve you well!

Dear Paul,

I am seventeen and am on my high school football team. I'm also gay. Nobody knows about it except for me and my boyfriend who is also closeted. It feels like I'm living a lie, but I also know that my dad would explode if I came out, and when someone isn't giving 100% on the football field, coach calls him a fag. What do I do?

Mark in Athens

Dear Mark,

When I was putting together the Guide's list of cool books for gay guys to read, I received the help of a man who consults for public libraries on this subject. When we discussed a book by Dan Woog called *Jocks,* he said it's the one book in the library that gets stolen more than any other. *Jocks,* is real stories from young male athletes who struggled with exactly the same questions you are. It seems that plenty of guys your age want to read it, but are afraid of being found out if they check it out. So it's understandable that they steal it.

Let's break your question down into two parts—the dad part, and the coach part. A lot of the street kids who I used to see in Los Angeles were there because they'd been kicked out of their homes because they were gay. They filtered in from different parts of the country and ended up living on the streets, a lot of them selling sex to buy food and drugs. So the first thing I want you to do is to throw out any considerations about "living a lie." Consider where you would live if your dad kicks you out. If you aren't completely comfortable with that option, then consider chilling on any coming out announcements until you are ready and able to support yourself and to live on your own.

On the other hand, by not telling your dad right now, you might be cheating him of the opportunity to show his love and care for you no matter what your sexual choices in life might be. I can't tell you how he will react, but under no circumstances should you risk having to live on the streets. I can't emphasize this enough. If you plan on going to college, you also might consider waiting until you get there and are settled and financially independent.

Then there's your coach and teammates. You will find stories of high school athletes coming out and being supported by their team. But here's my guess—they are few and far between, and they aren't in football unless the player who comes out is the all-league quarterback and the team's only chance of making it to the finals. When it comes to that sort of thing, you'd be surprised how many coaches and teammates can convince themselves that heterosexual athlete rapists are decent guys and simply misunderstood, or that gay athletes are just confused and will probably get over it.

Again, if you don't come out, you will be cheating your coaches and fellow players from the chance of rising above it all and becoming princes among a gay man. You'll also be cheating them of the opportunity to defend you as opposing players try to "spear the queer."

I hope that this is all changing and that I'm being way too alarmist, but I'm also aware that in ours and in many other cultures, the way we convince ourselves that we are straight males is by hating anything that might be effeminate or gay around us. The fact that you're not willing to play that game can be pretty scary for guys who need to continually prove themselves.

Your chances of being accepted by your teammates would be better if you were in track or gymnastics than football or basketball, but that's just theory. Your chances of being accepted are better if you are white than black or Hispanic, and you'd probably get less flack if you were a female athlete who is a lesbian, since we expect that.

If you do come out you will need to deal with your teammate's concerns about what will happen in the showers and locker room. You can laugh and ask them what happened before you told them you were gay? You might also try kidding them by saying that gay guys don't have the low standards that straight women do, and that it would take quite some stud to get you to look twice in the showers.

In addition to Dan Woog's *Jocks,* please go online and visit www.coachgumby.com. This is an important website for gay athletes. You will find much of what you are looking for there.

Talking To Your Partner About Sex

Chapter 35

While most of us will see angels before we'll see our teenage years again, it never hurts to look at the truly unfortunate advice that *Teen Magazine* offers its 4.4 million American girl readers about sexual matters:

> When you're French kissing, it helps to let the guy take the lead. Part your lips gently, and let him explore your mouth with his tongue.
>
> *Teen Magazine,* "Kissing Anxiety? Lip-to-Lip Lowdown"

Teen's smooch advice gives the impression that we guys come out of the womb knowing how to French kiss. Don't the editors of *Teen* realize that the average American male's preparation for sex is jerking off to the centerfold of whatever dirty magazine he can successfully hide from his mother's grasp? This is supposed to teach us how to French kiss, or anything else for that matter?

And why are guys always supposed to know what to do? Why aren't men and women encouraged to explore sex together, teaching each other what feels good along the way? And why are magazines like *Teen* still trying to push the tired old notion that sex is something a man does to a woman—unless she needs something from him or wants a big favor? One way to avoid being a *Teen* type of lover is by learning to talk to your partner about sex, about what feels good and what doesn't, and by exploring beyond what's familiar. Unfortunately, that's not always easy to do. That's why we've included this chapter. It starts by exploring different parts of the problem and finishes with a concrete plan of action.

Naked & Tongue-Tied

Consider the following conversation between two people who are about to have intercourse for the first time:

"Uh, should I...?"

"I guess."

"Okay."

That's it. The intercourse begins. Less than ten words, most single syllables. Grunting cavemen were probably more expressive. And then there's the prolific verbal exchange at the end of the event:

"That was really good."

"Me too."

While most of us aren't too ashamed to have sex, plenty of us approach critical mass when it comes to talking about it. One problem has to do with the lack of a comfortable, shared vocabulary about sex. Many of us feel stuck using either stiff Latin terminology or sexual slang that is intended for swearing., e.g. "When I was giving you cunnilingus..." or "When I was sucking your cock..." No confusing these for Kodak Moments.

When talking to your partner about sex, it may help if you have a comfortable name or term for your genitals. For instance, a husband and wife were in sex therapy and the woman was asked to give her vagina a special name. She called it "Jewel Box." How sweet. Considering the state of their relationship, she should have named it "Jaws." But don't mind us. Whatever you want to name yours is fine, as long as your partner is comfortable calling it that too.

After Marriage — Grow or It May Die

Plenty of couples talk even less about sex after they've been married for a couple of years. Things like the interest rate on your credit cards or replacing the kitchen cabinets garner more excitement than finding new things that turn each of you on. Sexual desires start becoming hidden, and we sometimes feel embarrassed or shy about mentioning things that we would have stayed up all night trying a few years earlier.

After a while, sex has no room to grow. "I don't want him to know THAT about me" becomes more powerful than "It might be exciting if he knew that about me!" Perhaps we have too much to lose if a partner disapproves, or maybe we start giving our partners the kind of power that our parents once had to make us feel shame or humiliation.

Knowing vs. Asking

Imagine going to a restaurant where the chef served you what-ever he or she felt like fixing instead of giving you a choice. Imagine a gardener who never asked, "How do you like your bushes trimmed?" Imagine a laundry that didn't inquire, "Light starch, heavy starch, no starch, hangers or folded?" Yet when it comes to sex, many of us assume that we know what our partner wants, or we clam up instead of giving feedback.

After So Many Years...

Let's say after ten years of being sexually mute, you suddenly decide to raise the issue. Perhaps your partner will be happy that you finally spoke your mind. Or maybe he or she will be annoyed. "You mean it's been bothering you for ten years and you never said a word?" Or you might receive a suspicious reply, "How did you learn all of that new stuff all of a sudden?"

This kind of defensiveness wouldn't happen if you began talking about sex from the very start of your relationship. Unfortunately, a lot of couples are so satisfied by the newness of their sexual relation-ship that they don't see the value in learning how to talk to each other about it.

Learning to Speak

By discussing sex on a regular basis, if only every month or two, your partner will feel much less criticized when you suggest that he or she try something new. Fortunately, there are certain props that can make this kind of routine exchange easy and fun.

For instance, you might say to your partner, "Let's get a new book or magazine on sex every month." We're not suggesting glossy jerk-off tomes with the human crotch splayed wide, unless you're both into that sort of thing. Instead, you might try something that's classy and a bit upper end. What about those books with explicit black-and-white photos and stories that plenty of couples will find erotic? Laura Corn's *101 Nights Of Great Sex* (Park Avenue Press) has stood the test of time. It is action-oriented and good at giving permission if that is what you

need. You might pick up a couple of anthologies of erotic literature, there are some excellent ones out there. Why not browse through the erotica section of your local book store? Or go on an internet bookstore and pump in author names like "Alison Tyler" or "Carol Queen."

You can always highlight parts of this book that you find meaningful and would like your partner to know about. Or you can read parts of it to your partner, as some couples seem to do. It's amazing how a bit of humor helps any discussion that might otherwise be filled with anxiety.

Besides books and magazines, there are some really good sex videos and DVDs that are both informative and erotic. When searching for erotic videos, you'll find some winners and plenty of yawners. To help with the process, Violet Blue has written a book for couples, *The Ultimate Guide To Adult Videos,* Cleis Press, 2003. This book explains how to find movies that will make your titties tingle. She explains the different porn-film categories and she reviews hundreds of blue movies.

And why not get yourself on the mailing list of the big sex-related stores such as Good Vibrations, Blowfish, JT's Stockroom and Toys in

Babeland? We at the Goofy Foot Press have fun receiving what they have to send. Perhaps you will too.

Some couples find it fun to play board games that promote discussion about sex or physical exploration. The nice thing about these games is that none of the players are losers, not like with Monopoly, anyway. One game to consider is "Enchanted Evening". (We list other cool boardgames and ideas for couples at www.BoinkCentral.com under "Dates").

There are also internet magazines that publish interesting articles on sex. These can be great discussion starters. A great site that's been around for year now is www.cleansheets.com. After all, how can you pass up downloading an article that has text like the following:

> "Why is it that some men just can't deal with the idea that a smart, together, professional woman like me can actually deserve their respect and still want to be thrown down on the couch and pounded like a cheap steak now and then?
>
> By Hanne Blank in *Clean Sheets Erotica Magazine,* www.cleansheets.com.

Prevention

You'd think your sex life would be just as important as gardening, sports, business, travel and entertainment. Couples don't hesitate to get books and magazines on those subjects. They often value, appreciate, and discuss them with their partners. Not so with sex.

Of course, you might say, "Our sex life is fine right now. We don't need anything like that." Hopefully, your luck will hold, but therapists often see couples who had great sex lives two to ten years earlier. Things break down when we take them for granted, and the process of getting them right is not always pretty or fun.

A Few of Many Possible Resources

Good Vibrations www.goodvibes.com
Toys In Babeland www.babeland.com
Blowfish www.blowfish.com
JT's Stockroom www.stockroom.com

Be sure to visit our website at
www.BoinkCentral.com
This couple did!

I Knew the Bride
Long-Term Relationships
Chapter 36

This chapter is about marriage and long-term relationships. It doesn't pretend to be comprehensive, but it does speak about weddings, tradition, sex in marriage, fights, kids and divorce.

I Knew the Bride

One of the fun things about weddings is watching the white-laced bride taking her vows of marital bliss and wondering if she has ever handcuffed the groom and done some of the outrageously nasty things to him that she once did to you. The memory puts a smile on your face and maybe even makes you blush. But it's not the kind of question you ask as you are working your way through the reception line—not with everyone's parents standing there with an array of cold, clammy hands hanging out of pastel gowns and rented tuxedos.

Weddings—What's Love Got to Do with Them?

You don't have to go much farther than the average magazine rack to realize that weddings are big business. Plump, glossy zines with names like *Modern Bride* nearly bite your arm off as you walk by. The ads in these magazines reflect the many segments of our society that thrive on marriage-related businesses — bridal-wear shops, tuxedo rental centers, wedding gift registries, boutiques, kitchen appliance stores, caterers, florists, bakers, wedding coordinators, ministers, priests, rabbis, justices of the peace, churches, synagogues, reception halls, hotels, resorts, diet plans, etc.

In our society, traditions like marriage (and Christmas) have become an economic spectacle rather than a symbol of love and commitment. Today's marriages are so choreographed that you seldom get a feeling that two people are making a promise to be there for each other no matter what, to be inseparable partners on the great climb through life. Instead, what you often get is the familiar bride-to-be psychosis, where the future bride and her mother become so savagely obsessed about things like table centerpieces and bridal gowns that any sense of love and devotion is pretty much out the window.

482 • I Knew the Bride—Long-Term Relationships

What if couples put as much effort into improving the level of intimacy and fun in their relationship as they do selecting wedding invitations? And what about those bizarre, adolescent feeding frenzies known as bachelor parties? If guys need to see high-priced women getting naked or want to lick whipping cream off silicone-filled breasts, why not just do it? Why use weddings as the excuse?

Marriage is a big step, an important step. Hopefully you won't get caught up in our culture's expectation of marriage as a generator of crippling debt, and will instead work to make your union a safe haven in a world that is sometimes anything but.

And what if couples took the money they spent on weddings and set it aside for one long weekend each and every month, just to be with each other and have fun? No cell phones, no pager, no work, just an extended three-day weekend each and every month.

Sex after Marriage

Studies show that within a year of saying "I do," most couples start saying "I don't want to."

A recent study by Call, Sprecher and Schwartz investigated factors that influence how much sex we have in marriage. This well-designed study found that one reason why sex declines within a year after the wedding is because marriage makes sex legitimate. This might cause it to lose some of its erotic edge. It also seems that once the wedding ring is welded to the finger, people are less inclined to use sex to help make things better. Contrary to what they expected to find, the authors state:

> Couples who want to make time for sex do, even with the obstacles of schedules, fatigue and work-related emotional complications. The DINS dilemma (double income, no sex) may be a myth.

Styles of Problem Solving

Besides feeling love and friendship for each other, an important ingredient in keeping a relationship happy is a couple's ability to solve conflicts. Couples with a knack for problem solving tend to have happier marriages. (Duh!)

Such couples approach conflicts with a willingness to talk things over and work them out, and we are sure that such couples exist

somewhere. The rest of us occasionally resort to sarcasm, name-calling, stubbornness, making threats, automatically giving in, taking blame needlessly, becoming silent or pretending that there is no conflict when all hell is about to break loose.

Contrary to what you may have heard about the value of releasing anger, trying to resolve a conflict when you are still fuming at each other is not always productive. Sometimes it is best to wait until cooler heads prevail. Of course, some people will use this as an excuse to avoid confronting a partner altogether. Then nothing ever gets worked out.

The Good, Bad & Ugly

When you enter into a marriage or long-term relationship, the chances are good that you will discover hidden but wonderful aspects of your partner's character. Cherish, respect and admire these. To deal with the less fortunate parts of your sweetheart's character, consider the following:

1. Learn how to fight constructively. This means that no matter how nasty or unpleasant your fights might be, try to keep them issue-oriented so you can work your way toward a solution or compromise. This is quite different from fights that revert to name-calling or rehashing past hurts. These accomplish little, except to degrade whatever dignity you once may have had.

2. Fighting is preferable to indifference, unless you are getting violent.

3. Every once in a while, when you feel like wringing your partner's neck, do something really nice for him or her. This could end up being far more satisfying than fighting, and it might even get you laid.

4. Instead of blaming your partner for things that are going wrong or wishing that he or she would somehow change, try to eliminate ways that you might be setting your partner up to be the bad guy. Also try to make changes that will help you to be a better or more effective person. This doesn't mean that you should stay in a relationship that's no longer working, it just means that the things you control most in a relationship are those that you put into it. If your efforts to change yourself don't inspire changes in your partner, then there's not much more you can do.

Birds of a Feather Get Bored with Each Other

Long-term relationships can sometimes be a challenge to keep fresh and vital unless both partners make a constant effort to enjoy each other.

For instance, think about all the extra things you did to impress each other when you first met; you probably even cut your toenails or trimmed your bikini line. Why would there be any less need for

We sometimes forget about the potential of sex to create new life, sustain love, and offer hope.

The illustration above was in the first edition of this book. But some people got all worked up over the notion that the couple might be doing the nasty while holding junior, so we now include this revision as well.

romance and wooing after you've known each other for what seems like forever? If anything, mature relationships require more rather than less effort at romance and improvement—from cards, flowers and special dates to extra attempts at tenderness.

Single vs. Hitched

Being single makes it easier to maintain the illusion that you are a perfect human being. Long-term relationships force you to confront parts of yourself that many of us would rather not. For instance, in a long-term relationship, your husband or wife will probably get fed up with your worst faults and remind you of them at least six times a day. If you are the rigid type who is incapable of change and compromise, then you might not be well-suited for marriage. On the other hand, a reader from San Francisco comments, "It could be just what you need."

Sex after a Fight

Fights leave most couples worn out or sad. However, some couples enjoy sex after a good fight, given how their neurotransmitters are already fired up and ready for action. On a biological level, the body might confuse a fight with sexual excitement, thus eliminating the need for tender preliminaries. Hopefully, the reasons for the fight have been resolved and the sex isn't simply being used as a cover-up.

Your Partner's Bad Moods

Like colds and flu, occasional bad moods are part of the human condition. In better-functioning relationships, the partner who is in the good mood is sometimes able to maintain a healthy perspective when confronted with a partner's bad mood. He or she might even take steps that will help the other's bad mood to go away. But in difficult relationships, all bets are off.

In a difficult relationship, the partner who is in a good mood experiences the other's bad mood as a personal attack, even if it has nothing to do with him or her. Attempts to help are often filled with so much anxiety that they only make matters worse, and the partner in the bad mood might lash out at the other just for the heck of it. (Why not be nasty to the person who loves you? After all, no one else would put up with you.)

Such couples usually do better if one spouse has a job that keeps him or her on the road for long periods of time.

Sex after the Baby Arrives

Our society doesn't provide many role models for caring parents who are also sexual beings. We sometimes separate the two roles entirely, as though being a good mom or dad precludes your giving great head or loving the feel of your partner's naked body next to your own. Just identifying as a parent may make you feel less sexual than you really are. Hopefully you will take the time to talk this over with your partner before having children, as well as after. There is no reason why you can't be great parents and have great sex—although the latter might not be as spontaneous as it was before the children arrived. A married reader comments: "We had lots of sex during nap time and *Sesame Street*."

Also, never discount the extent to which exhaustion might erode the desire to have sex, and don't expect to have sex if you aren't doing your fair share of the child care and housework. While you've probably never considered vacuuming and taking the garbage out to be romantic acts, good luck getting laid without doing these sorts of things once the new baby arrives. One reader who is a prostitute adds, "And for heaven's sake, hire someone to help with the cleaning or wash before you spend the money on a prostitute."

Divorce & Your Children

Don't assume that kids automatically do better if their parents stay together. While some children feel a terrible sadness when their parents get divorced, others feel relief. It usually depends on how bad the marriage was, how bad the divorce is and whether the kid gets to live with his or her favorite parent, if there is one. The absolute worst arrangement for some children is spending half of a week or a month at one parent's house, and half at the other. This can be the psychological equivalent of cutting the baby in two.

What often destroys kids more than the actual divorce is the parental lunacy for years before and years after. In an emotional sense, children of divorce often end up having no parents at all because their parents are sad, joyless, hateful or frightening to be with. If you are getting a divorce, do what you can to reach through your own pain, remembering that children need to see at least some form of hope reflected in their parents' eyes. And remember that your child's psychological health will in large part be determined by how amicably you and your former spouse are able to co-parent when divorced. It is not possible to emphasize this point too much.

Dear Paul,

Friends set me up with a wonderful woman and we've hit it off really well. We have had sex four times and are building a caring relationship. Unfortunately, I went to her place for the first time last night. (Before that, we'd always gone to mine.) Her bathroom looked like it hadn't been cleaned for a year, and some kind of alien life form was growing from the tile in her shower. She appears clean and neat, but this is another side of her that's scary. Just so you'll know, I've never been a neat freak, and don't even buy antibacterial soap. What do I do?

Tyrone in Jackson Hole

Dear Tyrone,

Your letter would have gone straight into the wastebasket if you hadn't mentioned the slimy ooze growing from the grout in your girlfriend's shower.

Let me tell you a story about Bill and Nancy, a couple whom I feel proud and honored to have known for more than fifteen years. Their house has always been immaculate—I'm talking serious sparkle. Even the litter box smells clean. One night a few years ago, we'd been having too much wine and I mentioned how impressed I was with Nancy's ability to keep such a clean house. At that point, Bill started hyperventilating and nearly bled from the ears. He told me about the first time he went into Nancy's bathroom when they were grad students at the University of Chicago. It took him five hours of scrubbing and several gallons of bleach before he could reach terra firma on her shower floor.

My point, Tyrone, is the way your lover keeps her bathroom doesn't need to be a deal breaker. What's more important is the way you and she handle the situation. For instance, if you say nothing and continue to ignore her wanton disregard for Lysol and Ajax, then I'd say your relationship is in trouble. Likewise, if she is unable to handle your spending half of next Sunday scrubbing her bathroom, your relationship is also in trouble. But if you clean her bathroom and don't make her feel bad about it, and she returns the favor with the finest blow job you've ever received in your entire life, then I think you're onto something good.

Chapter Notes: Special thanks to the Rosewoman, Daphne Kingma, for thoughts on divorce. Ms. Kingma has written many books on all aspects of relationships, from the rise to the fall. And thanks to researchers Michael Metz, et al. for specifics on conflict resolution, and to Call, Sprecher and Schwartz for keeping the bar high and bringing a helpful dose of sanity where ever their researching eyes turn.

Sex & Sects

Chapter 37

Religion can be a way of making sense out of a world that sometimes seems overwhelming. It can give focus, meaning and hope to a life that might otherwise have none. It can encourage belief in something other than yourself.

Religion can also be used as a force of oppression. Perhaps that's why so many people refer to their personal beliefs as spiritual rather than religious. This allows them to believe in something greater than themselves without endorsing the kind of narrow thinking that has characterized so many organized religions throughout history.

Sex

It's interesting how some religious leaders obsess more about sex than even people who run adult bookstores.

It is sometimes helpful to remember that what religious leaders call "the word of God" is actually what is left over after the scriptures have been interpreted by men. For instance, the Koran states that women need to dress modestly in public. But it is a human religious leader who decided "modestly" means covered from head to toe.

As it turns out, interpreting religious scripture is a lot like interpreting the Constitution of the United States. It is generally done by a small group of males who have won positions of power and title. They often claim God is speaking through them.

Guns, Dollars & Faith

It doesn't matter if you are a Christian, atheist, Muslim or Jew, we live in a country that was founded with a Bible in one hand and a firearm in the other. As a result, many of our society's values are rooted in a rather strange combination of gunpowder and holy scripture. Faith is important, but it never hurts to have a Smith & Wesson handy.

If you believe that religion has no influence over your daily life, grab your purse or wallet or conk your piggy bank over the head. Pull out any form of U.S. currency, from a penny to a hundred dollar bill. Each piece of money bears two four-word phrases. One is "United States of America." Check out the other.

The Bible

There is no question that the Bible has much wisdom to offer. Take, for instance, the passage from Luke that reminds us how easy it is to love those who love us, but how important to love those who don't. And what about the story of the poor fellow who is mugged and left for dead? A priest passes by and does not help, nor does a man from a blue-blood religious family. (They are probably on their way to church.) Finally, a traveler from a much-maligned country stops to offer aid. And that's how we got the story of the Good Samaritan. The Bible abounds with many thought-provoking passages, including Matthew 18:23-35, which presents much wisdom about fairness and debt.

In addition to the many good things that it offers, the Bible is often blatantly unfair to women. Why does the Bible have such awful things to say about women and sex?

Virgins & Prostitutes

In the reference classic called Butler's Lives of the Saints, the name of each saint is written in bold black ink. Next to the names of the women saints is the additional inscription "virgin" or "widow." The sexual status of the male saints is not listed. It is fortunate for men like St. Paul and St. Augustine that women saints were the only ones who had to account for their personal sexual histories.

It is also interesting that the majority of women mentioned in the New Testament are either virgins or prostitutes. There was little room for virtuous women who enjoyed sex, nor was there any room for women to become priests, preachers or popes.

It seems that the Bible as we know it had many different sources. Some had more to do with war, politics and real estate than religious salvation. For instance, the Bible's account of the Creation goes out of its way to portray Eve as a total bimbo who cavorts with the snake and leads Adam into sin via the fruit-tree fiasco, thereby blowing the gig in the garden. This is the kind of story you might create if you were trying to discredit outlying tribes who believe in female gods.

Sex & The New Testament

The New Testament shows Jesus of Nazareth accepting women and speaking to them in a way that shocked some of his contemporaries. Yet if Jesus did show a loving acceptance toward women, some

Mayhem in the Garden. The beginning of the end.

of his followers failed to notice. Even Mary, mother of Jesus, wasn't considered a major player in church dogma until the 11th to 14th centuries, when a romantic wave of sentimentality toward women forced the church fathers to significantly upgrade her role. And during the early years of Christianity, the church forbade husbands and wives from enjoying sexual pleasure. For instance, St. Augustine proclaimed that husbands and wives were no different from pigs and geese unless they abstained from sex. Also, the church administered more punishment for oral sex than for premeditated murder, and a virgin daughter was accorded a higher place in heaven than her mother because the mother had to have intercourse for conception to take place. Rape was better than masturbation, because at least with rape there was a chance that the man's seed could create new life.

Fortunately, some modern religions, both Christian and Jewish, are moving away from their early anti-woman and anti-sex biases. However...

Women Are Subservient to Men, & Masturbation Is Really, Really Bad

You think certain thresholds have been crossed and then the Southern Baptists let us know that this modernization thing is out of hand. They've announced that men are the head of the household, and that is that. Now word has it that they are taking their message into Utah, trying to convert Mormons, who are having their own little fuss over the polygamy thing.

But that's nothing compared to a recent Catholic catechism for junior high students. It states in no uncertain terms that masturbation is bad. Really, really bad. Statute-wise, the Catholics have placed jerking off somewhere between shooting heroin and grand theft.

Bad Acts & Queer Angels

Religious leaders have often ranted and railed against certain sexual practices, from masturbation and oral sex to homosexuality, as though these acts were the handiwork of the devil. But what if God feels more honored when a person joyfully masturbates than when he or she says a speedy rosary or spends an obligatory hour in church? After all, God created orgasm, while prayers and churches are the creations of men. What if God receives more joy when an unmarried couple lovingly shares oral sex than when a church-going husband and

The Christian's Dilemma

wife have passionless, missionary-position intercourse? And who is to say that God hasn't created a group of homosexual angels to guard the gates of heaven? Maybe God has a sense of humor and brings out the queer angels whenever a redneck preacher or one of his intolerant parishioners has just died and is awaiting judgment.

Kindness & Warmth

The most important thing that this guide has to say about religion is something remembered from childhood:

There is sometimes a priest, minister or rabbi whom the children feel safe with and to whom they will tell the truth. To the other clerics they withhold or lie. Perhaps children are aware of something that we adults forget—that what's needed from spiritual leaders is warmth, kindness and understanding rather than the propensity to judge, preach and chastise.

As adults, we often forget how contagious kindness and warmth can be. In so doing, we forget the essence of God.

Chapter Notes: There are interesting similarities between the Bible's Eve and Greek mythology's Pandora. ⚸ The Mormons have a different take on the apple-biting incident in The Garden. They believe that Eve did us all a big favor by pursuing knowledge. Of course, this is not to imply that the Mormon church is the Rome of feminist thinking. ⚸ Carl Jung's *Answer to Job* provides a captivating exploration of monotheism of old. ⚸ The so-called pagans who worshiped a male and female god also practiced human sacrifice. While not such an inviting practice from a public relations point of view, it is hard to believe that the number of human lives lost in this way was even a fraction of those lost in the religious wars that have dominated the globe since the monotheists seized power. ⚸ There may have been a translation error involving the early Greek, Latin and Aramaic languages; the expression for "young woman" may have been confused with the term "virgin," perhaps explaining some of the Bible's jones for virgins. Also, the notion of the Assumption didn't exist until a church council in the mid-1800s decided to invent it. ⚸ Thanks to Elizabeth Berlese for spurring memories about warmth and kindness, to Presbytera Donna Pappas for mentioning how people often refer to themselves as spiritual rather than religious, to Carol Tavris for the Muslim "head to toe" example, to Robert VanSweden on the Mormons and Eve, and to the writings of David Schnarch and Paul Evdokimov. Evdokimov's writings were suggested by Father Andrew Barakos. Because these people are being thanked does not mean that they necessarily agree with the perspective of this chapter.

Culture & Kink

Chapter 38

On the surface, it seems that men in our society are more into kink than women. But maybe that's because we define kink differently for men than for women. For instance, a woman who wears her boyfriend's boxers or briefs is at the height of fashion, but if he wears her underwear we consider him to be weird. Our society relishes her kink, but gets very uncomfortable with his.

In our society women touch each other at will. However, if men were to touch each other with half the frequency that women do, they would be called queer. Once again, our culture labels men as being strange for something that women do all the time. In our society, most male-to-male touching is limited to handshakes and contact sports—which may be a reason why men feel such an affinity for football. For a guy to experience much physical contact with another guy, he needs to be a jock, a homosexual or both.

There are plenty of other things that are considered kinky when only men do them. For instance, a woman who routinely undresses in front of an open window is thought to be a neighborhood resource. Double that for a woman who plays with herself with the window shades up. But a man who does these things is considered to be a pervert and may even be locked up. There is also the biological fact that some women can masturbate without being noticed. Guys can't masturbate with that kind of subtlety. The occasional male who gets himself off in a public place is at much greater risk of being caught and labeled a pervert than the occasional female who does the same thing. One reader comments, "Not only is he labeled a pervert, but if convicted he would be forced to register as a sex offender."

Bondage Lite

The United States was originally settled by a group of religious outcasts, malcontents, criminals and slaves—the fact that we're not all into some form of bondage is a little amazing.

Bondage is the application of restraint, pain or humiliation in a way that some people find erotic or satisfying. One form of bondage includes having your arms or feet tied while being kissed, tickled,

caressed or otherwise made love to. In parts of Los Angeles, New York and Chicago this type of activity isn't considered bondage, but merely good bedroom technique.

Those who are into light bondage often enjoy it because they are rendered passive and have no choice but to totally enjoy what a partner is doing to them. They don't have to worry about being a "good" sex partner who provides pleasure in return. Performance anxiety is virtually eliminated.

If you are into light bondage, be aware that scarves and ties form tight knots that are hard to undo; wrists and ankles can be permanently damaged. Bondage enthusiast William Henkin says that professionally made cuffs may seem expensive to couples who simply like to tickle and spank, but they are much safer than the restraints that people improvise at home. In the event that professionally made cuffs aren't available on your TV's Home Shopping Network, check with places like Good Vibrations, Blowfish or The Pleasure Chest.

Painful Contradictions

You don't have to be into BDSM to appreciate the following social ridiculousness: here in America parents can spank a child and it is not called bondage or sadism. Yet fully consenting adults who spank each other are ostracized and even considered morally corrupt.

Spanking is a form of sexual kink that can be considered either light or heavy bondage, depending upon how it's done. For instance, some participants like their spanking hard and with a hostile edge, while others enjoy a little spank here and there when highly aroused.

Why do some adults enjoy spanking or being spanked? One theory states that people sometimes sexualize their childhood shame or humiliation. Turning shame or humiliation into erotic sensation helps it to become more bearable and even fun. What's particularly important is that they are now able to control the sexual scene, while as children they were helpless.

Another reason why some people enjoy an occasional swat on the rear is because they find that it feels good, as long as they are sexually aroused and it is their own personal choice to be in the situation. Who can argue with that?

Bondage by Choice—A Feminist Contradiction?

People who are feminists or socially progressive (whatever that means) sometimes feel that they are deserting their own cause if they enjoy being submissive or have masochistic fantasies. For instance, consider a feminist lawyer whose favorite fantasy is being tied up and sexually violated. She occasionally acts out this fantasy with her male lover. Does this contradict her political beliefs? No, since the relevant issue is the freedom to choose rather than what's being chosen.

The lady lawyer believes that each person should be able to choose what to do with his or her own sexuality. In acting out her bondage fantasy with her lover, this woman chooses to give up her position of equality, and she chooses the man whom she wants to give it up to. In the criminal rape cases that she handles in court, the rape victim had no choice. The act was forced upon her, rather than being part of a shared fantasy between two consenting adults.

Note: The term "feminist" no longer has the meaning that it once did and is rife with contradiction. For instance, some feminists are opposed to pornography and feel it demeans women, while other feminists believe that women should be proud of their bodies and free to display them sexually if that's what they want to do. Some feminists

hate men, others don't; some embrace lesbianism, others are alien-
ated by feminist groups who are more concerned with lesbian issues
than with those of straight working moms. Some feminists think that
intercourse is a form of oppression that women have been brainwashed into having by the patriarchy (straight white guys). Other
feminists view intercourse as a satisfying activity where a vagina is as
active and powerful as a penis. Some feminists consider motherhood
to be a form of slavery for women, while others welcome motherhood.
In fact, most women in this day and age describe themselves as being
feminists, regardless of their political, social or religious views.

Heavy Bondage — A Little Like Life?

Heavy bondage can get fairly brutal. It can be a world of whips
and chains and devices that might even put a chill up the spine of the
average high school PE teacher. When it comes to heavy bondage, the
only comment this guide knows that even comes close is "Toto, I have
a feeling we're not in Kansas anymore." (Acronyms: B&D = bondage
and discipline; S&M = sado masochism; D&S = dominance and submission; BDSM is a blanket term for all of it.)

In heavy bondage, having an orgasm isn't nearly as important
as the bondage scene itself, with its undercurrent of domination,
submission and sometimes humiliation. People into heavy bondage
process pain differently than people who aren't. Bondage lovers find
serious doses of sexual pain to be invigorating and intimate. They
speak about sexual pain with the same kind of clarity and relish as religious pilgrims who are describing a visit to a shrine or the Dalai Lama.

People into heavy bondage tend to be very serious about their
kink. In fact, there are even well-established bondage clubs like the
Chicago Spanking Society, the Boston Dungeon Society, the Society
of Janus in San Francisco, Houston People Exchanging Power, and Arizona Power Exchange.

There are mainstream bondage publications like *Domination-
Submission, Dungeon Master* (which probably takes the prize for being
the *Boy's Life* of kink), and *Prometheus: the Quarterly of the Eulenspie-
gel Society.* There are numerous magazines on latex fashion. There
are also bondage reference guides like *The Leatherman's Handbook*
and *The Lesbian S/M Safety Manual*—cross their hearts and hope to

Apologies for this, the second tie-up illustration in a row. But female readers wanted to know why the guy in the first illustration has been allowed to hog all of the tie-up fun. Also, look at how her wrists are bound. This can cause wrist damage and is NOT the way you want to do it. Splurge and get some fake sheepskin cuffs.

be humiliated. Several bondage references are included in the Kinky Corner of our website, www.BoinkCentral.com—from beginner books to videotapes on corsetry.

If you have an irrepressible need to get into heavy bondage, please consider the following advice: don't pick up a stranger who enjoys beating the crap out of people and confuse that with bondage, even if you are a woman who loves too much. In heavy bondage there are established rules and etiquette that keep the participants from getting seriously hurt. Mind you, the definition of seriously hurt is a personal matter. If heavy bondage is what turns you on, learn the rules and make sure that your partner knows and respects them.

In almost every large city in the United States you will be able to find an established bondage club. These clubs often have extensive calendars of events, including talks, demonstrations and social gatherings. Generally speaking, you will be far safer in joining one of these established clubs than by experimenting on your own. You might also be amazed at how many educated, kind and helpful people you will meet at the established clubs.

Even if you aren't into bondage, don't get roped into thinking that mild-mannered people prefer being bottoms (slave role) and that aggressive types prefer being tops (master/dominator/dominatrix). There are plenty of business executives, lawyers, doctors, politicians, policemen and even East Coast publishing types who prefer being on the bottom when it comes to sexual kink. In fact, it's a problem in the bondage community that a good top is hard to find. It's also true that a number of people into BDSM enjoy alternating roles between top and bottom. They are called "switches."

Lite or Heavy Bondage—Safety Considerations

No matter if you only use bondage once a year or are a full-fledged bondage brute, the S&M book by author Jay Wiseman titled *SM-101* (San Francisco: Greenery Press) makes the following suggestions:

🐑 Anytime a body part that is tied up feels numb or goes to sleep, untie it immediately. And never tie anything around a partner's neck.

🐑 In anticipation of catastrophes like fires, earthquakes or an unexpected visit from your mom and dad, be sure that you have a flashlight and a pair of heavy scissors handy. *SM-101* recommends paramedic scissors, which can be found at medical supply stores. They cut through almost anything except handcuffs. Keep the scissors and flashlights in a place that you can readily find in the dark. Ditto for the handcuff key if that's what you are using. Better yet, tie the key to the handcuffs with a string.

🐑 Never leave the person for long, and check them often. If any injuries were to occur, you would be legally and morally responsible.

🐑 Always establish a safe word or gesture which means to stop. Some people use "red" for stop and "yellow" for easing up a little. No one who is seriously into dominance and submission uses "stop," "don't," or "no more" for safe words, since any good bottom says them often but doesn't mean them one little bit.

Fetishes: An Overview

Several years ago, a singer named Randy Newman wrote a song whose lyrics entreat his lover to take off all her clothes, except her hat. If Mr. Newman couldn't enjoy sex unless the woman had a hat on, then we might say he had a hat fetish. The Glossary at the end of this book offers the following definition of fetish:

> FETISH—1. Reliance on a prop, body part, scene or scenario in order to get off sexually. 2. The prop can either be fantasized or exist in actuality. 3. One philosopher has described "fetish" as being similar to when a hungry person sits down at a dinner table and feels full from fondling the napkin.

If both people in a relationship enjoy a particular fetish, then acting out the fetish will be a welcome event. But if only one partner is into the fetish, the other person might feel that she or he is not nearly as important as the fetish itself. For instance, if the woman in the above-mentioned song loves wearing her hat while otherwise naked, then she has found the perfect man. Otherwise, she may start to feel like a human hatrack.

Fetish Specifics

Fetishes come in many different forms; some include objects, others include actions that need to be repeated over and over. What follows are examples where a woman's dirty words and a man's cross-dressing might be considered fetishes:

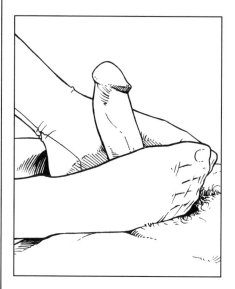

Is this activity:

a. fun
b. a fetish
c. both
d. who cares?

This wouldn't be considered a fetish if it's something you enjoy doing but can also do without. Psychologists would call it a fetish if the man couldn't become aroused without seeing or touching the woman's feet, or if her pantyhose were so important to him that he needed them rather than her to become sexually excited. How do psychologists know? Because they're as strange as everyone else.

Talk Dirty to Me Some couples enjoy saying dirty things while having sex. But what if one partner can't perform sexually without hearing the dirty words? This takes it beyond simple sex play and hints of a fetish, especially if the other partner feels stupid screeching things like, "Fuck me harder, fuck me harder, you big stud, Mama wants it all," or degrading things like, "You miserable, worthless little turd." Particularly troublesome are situations where the partner with the fetish needs to say degrading things to you, unless of course, you find something endearing about being called a smelly old cow, fat whore, or pencil-dicked imbecile.

What a Drag Some women occasionally dress up like men, to the point of wearing a fake penis. This is a form of accessorizing known as "packing." One woman reports that if she's been packing for an extended amount of time she even stops having her period—without taking a single male hormone. Once she is through packing and the fingernail polish goes back on, her periods become regular again. Some men feel a powerful need to dress like women, aka "transvestism" or "crossdressing." This might be fine with the guy's wife or girlfriend. However, problems could arise if he keeps stealing her favorite bra and panties to wear under his suit whenever his law firm assigns him to handle a high-profile case. (Crossdressing and other fetishes are discussed more fully at the end of this chapter.)

It is interesting how, in our culture, men with certain conflicts might deal with them one way while women sometimes give them a different spin. For instance, more men probably have foot fetishes than women, yet women seem to obsess about shoes more often and spend more money on them than men usually do. An obvious, time-honored solution is for men with foot fetishes to work in women's shoe stores.

People with fetishes usually love them immensely and resist giving them up. Therapy is seldom effective in loosening the love for a fetish. As long as the partner is fine with the fetish and it causes no harm to others, there seems to be little reason for abandoning it. On the other hand, if it violates criminal statutes and the wishes of others (e.g., flashing or being a Peeping Tom), or it introduces a level of weirdness that a partner won't tolerate, then the person with the fetish will face sad and serious consequences.

When 911 Isn't Enough to Put Out Your Fire

Ever wonder what goes on in phone sex, when a man pays several dollars a minute to get a good talking to? A young woman who worked as a phone-sex operator after graduating from an expensive private college was kind enough to offer the following description:

> "The fantasies ranged from men who wanted me to physically beat myself on the phone with a hairbrush, to those who wanted me to force them to have oral sex with other men and those who just wanted to hear me have an orgasm. What struck me is that men have more gay fantasies than I would have expected. There seems to be a correlation between men who have powerful jobs and their sexual fantasies—one client, who I later found out was a senior partner in a financial

firm always wanted me to 'force' him to do things—mostly to other men and sometimes to me. Others wanted to escape from their life, shed their responsibility and their maleness— they explored their imagination with me and pretended I was their dominatrix, their she-male, their whore. I gave them permission and encouraged them to be who they wanted to be and that's what they needed."

"I always wondered about clients. I was madly, madly curious. I wanted to know who they were, how much money they made, if they were married, if they were straight and if they were the kinds of guys I knew. And often, I'd 'interview' them and I'll admit that I looked up what I could find on Google—I couldn't help myself. I wanted to know why they were calling me, how it played into their real sex life and what I was to them. In some instances, I was the woman on the phone who was their mistress, but in the most controlled way and they would call on a regular basis. Some got attached to me and I was fired and then rehired and in my absence, I was missed (as I learned later)."

Piercing & Tattoos Pt. 1—On Pins & Needles

Is getting tattooed a sexual thing? Who knows. It sure is popular these days, especially among women who are sporting little butterflies, flowers and the like in highly private places.

If you are thinking about getting a tattoo, don't be impatient or impulsive. It's not like your skin is a canvas that you can throw away if you don't like what's on it or if you get tired of it. Keep in mind the following:

🐑 A tattoo is pretty much forever.

🐑 If you've thought about it for a long time and truly believe a tattoo is the right thing for you, save up your money and find the best tattoo artist you can possibly afford. Do lots of research.

🐑 Never, ever have the name of a partner or lover tattooed on your body. Why? See the next part about tattoo removal.

🐑 If you get a tattoo with the idea that you can always have it removed later, please think again. The removal will cost you far more money than the original tattoo and it is unlikely to be totally successful. The pain will be much greater than that of the original tattoo, and you may need to opt for cover-up instead of removal. Do lots of research and ask several tattoo experts their opinion before deciding on a specific removal process. A botched removal can leave an unsightly scar. If you go for a cover-up instead of removal, find a cover-up specialist who comes highly recommended. There are some cover-up specialists who do it often and do it well. There are others who will only make the tattoo look worse.

There is one internet resource that anyone who is considering getting a tattoo should read. It is up-to-date and is run by an incredibly conscientious man. It is the bodyart/tattoo-faq newsgroup and it just has text. It is not very pretty to look at, but has excellent information. The address is pretty hideous:

http://www.cs.uu.nl/wais/html/na-dir/bodyart/tattoo-faq/.html

Piercing & Tattoos Pt. 2—Body Modification

Piercing, like tattooing, has been around for a long, long time. Women have traditionally had their ears pierced, as have various pirates and sailors who have sailed the seven seas.

In a highly sexualized version of piercing, body parts like noses, navels, nipples and genitals are potential sites. People who are seriously into piercing will stick rings or posts through just about anything. Some do it for sport; others experience it as a personal high.

If you are into this kind of thing, please do lots and lots of research, and make sure the person who is doing the piercing has a great deal of experience. (The bmezine.com website is the Rome of all who are pierced.) If you must get pierced, be sure to have it done at a well-known establishment with a solid reputation. Not enough can be said for sterile technique and skill on the part of the piercer, as infections and botched insertions are common. There is also a fair amount of wisdom involved in selecting the proper ring or post for specific body parts, given how those that are too thin eventually pull out.

Please keep in mind that going through airport security with body piercings can light up all sorts devices that are best unlit. Also, if you have any piercings and are about to get any kind of medical procedure that involves an MRI or X-ray, you must remove the piercing jewelry.

This means all piercings, including naval, tongue, penis, clit, and labia. Otherwise, the X-ray can make the jewelry get hot and start to sizzle the skin around it.

Hopefully you will be very wary about piercings through the clitoris and penis. Most clitoral piercings don't really go through the clitoris, but through the clitoral hood. Getting a piercing through the actual clitoris can result in numbing and nerve damage, so hopefully you will do a great deal of homework and evaluation before considering it. As for male genitals, the head of the penis can be skewered in several different ways, and rings can be placed anywhere from the bottom of the testicles to the tip of the foreskin. Pain in the piercing site can last for months, and any piercings that go through the urethra may result in your having to pee while sitting down for the rest of your life.

This isn't to say that people don't like their genital piercings. Some people, who felt their genitals were ugly, begin to take pride in them once they have jewelry on them.

Women who are planning to have their nipples pierced should inquire about the kind of fabrics they will be able to wear. For instance, how will your nipple rings look under a conservative business suit? Lacy bras will probably be out, since the ring will constantly catch in the lacy material. Ditto for what kinds of shirts you will be able to wear to work. Concerns about underwear fabric also apply to labia and clitoral piercing.

Vaginal Fisting (Handballing)

Vaginal fisting is finger fucking times five, and then some. This guide first became aware of the concept when reviewing lesbian tapes produced by and for women. It seems that some women enjoy having a partner's fist inside their vagina.

The trouble is, that kind of fisting is usually being done by women for women. This is an important distinction, since most women have significantly smaller fists than men. A fist the size of a man's could take a potentially pleasurable experience and turn it into something akin to childbirth. On the other hand, a leading sex therapist has informed us that a number of straight couples are getting a fist up.

If vaginal fisting is something you want to try, please plan far enough ahead to read a book or two that covers the subject. Greenery Press publishes *A Hand in the Bush: The Fine Art of Vaginal Fisting* by Deborah Addington, (Greenery Press, San Francisco, 1998). This subject is also discussed in the *Good Vibrations Guide to Sex* by Anne Semans and Cathy Winks (Cleis Press, San Francisco, 2002) and in the *On Our Backs Guide To Lesbian Sex,* edited by Diana Cage, (Alyson Press, Los Angeles, 2004).

Please check with a health care professional before attempting any kind of fisting, and in no instance should you proceed if you experience anything but the slightest amount of pain. Perhaps you can find the name of a physician or nurse practitioner who is familiar with fisting through a gay and lesbian health center, since your local HMO might not be particularly well versed in the practice. You should never attempt fisting if either of you has been drinking or doing drugs, and you certainly shouldn't try it before reading the advice of women who do it.

Anal Fisting

Some couples, straight as well as gay, are into anal fisting. You shouldn't even think about trying this unless you really, really, really know what you are doing. Technically, this act is possible without causing physical damage, since surgeons occasionally stick an entire hand up a person's rectum. On the other hand, receiving an entire fist up the bum requires the kind of relaxation that is beyond the capacity of the average asshole.

Couples into anal fisting often recommend a book on the subject by Bert Herrman, *Trust—The Hand Book* (San Francisco: Alamo Square Press, 1991). There might also be organized groups of fisters in the nearest large city who give talks and demonstrations. Please check with a health care professional before attempting any kind of fisting, and in no instance should you proceed if you are not completely sober and experience anything but the slightest amount of pain.

Healthcare for Those into Kink

Finding a kink-friendly physician can be an incredible challenge, especially if you have to work within an HMO. A book that offers helpful suggestions is *Health Care Without Shame—A Handbook for the Sexually Diverse and Their Caregivers* by Charles Moser, Ph.D., M.D., Greenery Press, 1999.

Dear Paul,

Do you have any advice about going to a dominatrix?

Policeman by Day
Schoolboy by Night

Dear Officer,

When you visit a dominatrix you are engaging someone who will help you act out certain sexual fantasies. The fantasies often have to do with power. For instance, you enjoy being a policeman and having power when you are on the job, but you also enjoy becoming a schoolboy and giving a dominatrix power over you. Each has its own time and place in your life.

To help answer your question, I called my friend Lorrett, who runs a house devoted to S&M and fantasy play. She offers the following advice:

1. B&D or S&M is about creating a fantasy scene, and then acting it out. In creating the scene, you need to talk to the person you are hiring about things like boundaries, safe words, and how you want the scene to play out. You should feel comfortable with the person, and feel that they are comfortable with you in negotiating the scene. If they come off as being abrupt or domineering when setting up the scene, then what follows isn't going to be play. Instead, you are going to be acting out their agenda, and what follows will be anything but consensual.

2. Trust your instincts. It's fine to be nervous or anxious, but if you feel frightened or uncomfortable, go elsewhere.

In domination and fantasy games, the dominatrix doesn't actually get you off. You are free to get yourself off in her presence, but she won't actually give you an orgasm the way a prostitute will. That's why it's not illegal for you to hire a dominatrix.

For reading materials, try the catalogs from Greenery Press, QSM, Daedalus Press, Alamo Square Press, and the other resources listed at the end of this chapter.

Dear Paul,

I recently had my tongue pierced. I've got a barbell type of post, with a small steel ball on each side. Do you have any suggestions on how to best use it to please a woman sexually?

Beaufort from Biloxi

Dear Beaufort,

Sexually speaking, the best place for a piercing on your tongue is near the tip. The problem is, this tends to cause speech impediments such as lisping. You also run the danger of your tongue splitting in two which would result in a lifetime of surgical attempts at repair. And then there's the little problem of chipped teeth. So experienced piercers wisely place the piercing farther back on the tongue where it is safer for you but not as effective sexually, not that any human tongue has ever needed an accessory in order to be effective sexually.

Here's advice on the matter from women who have slept with guys who have steel balls:

Kissing (mouth to mouth): Unless you are careful, you can bang and perhaps chip your partner's teeth. So go easy and be aware that your new tongue needs more tooth clearance than one that is less accessorized. Also, women don't seem to enjoy being kissed by guys who slobber. Having a post through your tongue may keep you from sucking the saliva from it as well as you did pre-op. And some women aren't crazy about having foreign objects in the back of their throat. So when you French kiss, don't stick your tongue in very far, and remember to swallow.

Nipple Play: One woman says that dragging a steel ball across her nipples can be "a bit gnarly." Assuming your partner likes to have her nipples licked or sucked, make sure that you've coated her nipples with a heavy layer of loogie. Extra saliva on her nipples may help your ball glide rather than drag. Use the tip of your tongue when playing with her breasts and nipples. This will help keep the steel ball at bay. The best solution is to talk to your lover about this, with her giving you plenty of feedback.

Oral Sex: Here's where the real skill comes in, ball or no ball. It's possible to give wonderful oral sex, but only as long as you know where your ball is and what it's up to. Try flicking your tongue across the palm or back of your hand. This will help you learn to steer your ball better. The last thing you want to do is bang a steel object against a woman's tender nerve endings. You will need to flick your tongue more delicately than a guy who doesn't have a steel ball attached to the end of his. To paraphrase a woman who has dated a couple of different guys with pierced tongues, flicking a pierced tongue across a woman's vulva can feel really cool, but only if the man is extremely gentle and acutely aware of the impact that a pierced tongue has. She also cautions against probing inside a woman's vagina with a tongue that's pierced.

As for the piercing procedure, be aware that a newly pierced tongue can swell a great deal, as well as become infected. Piercing is a surgical procedure which requires the same sterile surgical technique that is used in hospitals. It's best if done by an experienced hand with good references. Learn about the physical risks and care requirements before having any body part pierced, think about it for a couple of weeks first and plan accordingly. It's not the sort of thing to do on the spur of the moment.

Dear Paul,

My boyfriend loves to feel my legs when I have pantyhose on. He's a really sweet guy and I enjoy the extra attention, but my friend says it's a "fetish." What do you think?

Penny from Paducah

Dear Penny,

From the sounds of it, I'm not hearing fetish, or at least it's not screaming at me. But what is a fetish? Let's say your boyfriend can't become aroused unless you are wearing pantyhose or maybe he gets off more and more by your pantyhose and you feel like a mannequin. Rather than being an erotic accessory that helps to spice things up, the pantyhose become way too important. That's when you're talking a fetish.

Some people have fetishes for certain objects or materials like leather, rubber, latex, underwear, shoes, socks, boots, smelly feet, hair, breasts and even diapers. Honest, there are websites with adults wearing diapers, and not because they need to.

Other people with fetishes have certain scenarios or fantasies that get them off, e.g., the guy who likes his partner to pee or shit on him (aka golden showers and scat or brown showers). Or the fetish might be as hidden and subtle as the kind of haircut his partner has. He suddenly goes bonkers if she changes it. (Ever notice how some guys only date or marry women who are the spitting image of each other? Is it the woman he loves, or a certain look that she has?)

People with fetishes get comfort from the fetish that they can't get from human beings. The fetish becomes the missing piece that completes their sexual circuit.

How can a pair of pantyhose, an enema or an extreme sex scene have the kind of allure that we normally find in a human partner? Maybe the object a man chooses for his fetish is connected to a situation that was once overwhelming, like where a young boy was raised by four sisters and an aunt. He chooses an arousing element that was part of the original situation, but unlike his childhood experience, it's something he can control.

He turns the fetish into a kind of sexual partner, one that could never be as demanding or humiliating as a real live human—a wish that most of us can relate to at one time or another. (It's far easier to control a pair of pantyhose than to control the woman who is wearing them!) The fetish provides temporary and exciting relief for the early psychological drama.

One problem with having a serious fetish is the loneliness that can sometimes be a part of it. No matter how many times you fondle them, a pair of rubber panties or woman's feet can only go so far in providing the closeness or friendship that many of us value in a sexual partner. In fact, some people refer to the fetish as a compromise between the fear of human closeness and the need for it.

Please be aware that I am a psychoanalyst and always will be. I work with people when the bottom has fallen out. I tend to see loneliness and isolation where those with fetishes see bliss and excitement. I suspect the truth lies somewhere in between.

For an academic but very interesting resource, check out *Fetish— Fashion, Sex & Power* by Valerie Steele, Oxford University Press, New York & Oxford, 1996.

Dear Paul,

Help! I think my husband is a crossdresser. How can this be? Please tell me what you know about this.

Virginia from Lawrence

Dear Virginia,

There are thousands and thousands of transvestites or male crossdressers in the United States, although they prefer to be described in the millions. Many are straight and appear quite masculine when they aren't wearing a bra and panties.

Contrary to what you might imagine, male crossdressers aren't drawn to professions that welcome a guy's feminine side. Instead, the average crossdresser is more likely to be a baseball player, fireman, policeman, auto mechanic or business executive than a hairdresser or florist. Research shows that a good many transvestites remember being dressed up as women or girls when they were growing up. This was done to them by other family members either as entertainment or as a form of punishment.

Most crossdressers value their macho side as much as their feminine side, but have never found a way to enjoy both at the same time. As young boys, they usually showed traditional male behaviors. As men, they are often heterosexual, married and the last guy you'd imagine would dress up like a girl.

A crossdresser gets sexual excitement by identifying with a woman, but he's still got the straight guy consciousness going on, so he puts on the women's clothes and underwear as a compromise. Psychologists might suggest that the bra symbolizes the actual breasts, and the panties symbolize her genitals. So there he stands, in front of the mirror, admiring his symbolic breasts and vulva, while sporting a fully masculine erection. Sexually, he's got his bases covered.

It is unlikely that therapy will change a crossdresser's need to crossdress. However, if the guy is compulsive about crossdressing, therapy can help him control that aspect of it. Many crossdressers hope that marriage will cure them of their desire to dress like a woman. But the envy and allure of their wife's underwear drawer will soon rear its satin head, and so much for good intentions.

Men who are reading this book while wearing their favorite DKNY dress might be concerned about being found out. This is a fear shared by many crossdressers who are not out of the closet. For more info, check out some of the following internet sites:

www.tri-ess.org www.tgfmall.com
www.pmpub.com www.brendat.com

As a wife or girlfriend who suddenly discovers that her man has a secret cache of frilly garb, try to give yourself a three-month chilling-off period before doing anything drastic. He must love you a great deal if he's worked so hard to hide something that he fears will disappoint you. If you can, check out the site of the Society for the Second Self or Tri-Ess at www.tri-ess.org. This national organization is for cross dressers, their wives and their families. Search out anything written by Francis Fairfax, particularly the Wives' Bill of Rights.

Given how this is not the sort of thing you can call your mom or sister about, see if there is a support group in your area for wives of crossdressers. The folks at Tri-Ess can help you find them. Talk to these wives about what they will and won't put up with. For instance, there are plenty of things you don't need to agree to, like meeting your man for lunch when he's dressed like Britney Spears. And if for some reason he thinks he can dress up in front of the kids or gets so deep into the crossdressing scene that he stops being a good husband or dad, crossdressers' wives will offer all the support you need to confront him. In other words, you don't have to condone what he's doing, but you don't need to divorce him either.

For a lot of women, it would be easier to accept their husband if he said he were gay. But to see him dressed up like Little Bo Peep and hear him say he's totally straight....

Part of your fear might be about losing the manly part of your crossdressing man. This usually won't happen. He'll be the same man he was in bed before you knew about the heels and A-line dress. Part of your fear may have to do with humiliation that someone else will find out.

One reason why I suggest that you wait a few months before taking any action is that once the shock wears off, you might be able to see that there are far worse things a man could do than wear women's clothes, fashion crime that it might be. You might also realize that he has the same good characteristics that he had before you found out about his hidden side.

Fortunately, there is no shortage of publications on crossdressing. Some people value the books by Peggy Rudd, a therapist and the wife of a crossdresser. Others aren't so comfortable with her crossdresser-as-visionary point of view. Two of the titles written by Dr. Rudd are *My Husband Wears My Clothes: Crossdressing from the Perspective of a Wife* (PM Press, 2nd edition, 1999) and *My Husband Wears My Clothes: Crossdressing with Dignity.* Talk about a quaint title for a series of books. Your public library may have them, but perhaps you'll want to try Amazon. Another book on crossdressing and drag that's received interesting press is *Girlfriend: Men, Women and Drag* by Holly Brubech and Michael Jones O'Brian (Random House, New York, 1999). Also see the references on the next page.

Knowledge may not make it hurt any less, but it does give you more options than simply saying goodbye.

If you need a gift for a man who enjoys wearing women's clothes, don't forget the book known as "The Tranny Bible." Find the latest edition of *The Tranny Guide* at www.wayout-publishing.com.

Resources

The *Guide* is not encouraging you to try alternative forms of sexuality. We have trouble enough dealing with old-fashioned vanilla sex and are not pointing anyone toward kink. If kink is what you want to explore, it might be better for you to explore these resources, some of which we know, than to list no resources and have you randomly search the internet. It is always risky including websites in a book, considering how half of them will be history before the ink even dries. Also, a site that is great today can become a spam hole tomorrow, so we offer no promises about the integrity of the sites that are listed.

Kink can be fun and kink can be dangerous. The wisdom and safety of what you do and how you do it are totally in your hands. If you are unable to distinguish what's safe from what's dangerous, then you have no business exploring alternative forms of sexuality.

www.altsex.org/ Helpful information about alternative sexuality, from BDSM and polyamory to transgender issues, homosexuality and safer sex.

www.sexuality.org Web home of the Society for Human Sexuality.

www.bannon.com/kap/   Check out Kink Awareness Professionals for healthcare related issues.

www.whatsyours.com Kink for the United Kingdom. A full-featured, link-loaded site that's hard to beat.

soc.sexuality.general Can handle a wide range of questions about most forms of alternative sexuality, assuming you can find it.

Publishers with catalogs to request.

Circlet Press Erotic sci-fi and different kinds of books on alternative sexuality. www.circlet.com

Daedalus Press Specializes in books on S&M and alternative sexuality. Prints *Consensual Sadomasochism* by therapists William Henkin and Sybil Holiday. www.bannon.com

Greenery Press Publishes a full array of books on S&M and alternative sexuality, from *Miss Abernathy's Concise Slave Training Manual* to *SM-101*. www.greenerypress.com

Mystic Rose Publishers prints *Screw the Roses, Send Me the Thorns* as well as S&M fiction and erotica. www.mysticrose.com

QSM Hundreds of books on S&M. www.qualitysm.com

Other resources to consider on alternative sexuality

The Black Book, An encyclopedia of kink-related resources, but not as thick. They also publish erotic anthologies and the humorous bi-queer sex zine *Black Sheets.* www.blackbooks.com

On Our Backs A fine mating of Lesbi-Kink. www.onourbacksmag.com

Sandmutopian Guardian www.aswgt.com

Chapter Notes: Thanks to the writings of Chris Gosselin and Glenn Wilson for some of the ideas used in the introduction to this chapter, and to the works of Carol Queen, Cathy Winks, Anne Seamans, Bert Herrman Jay Wiseman and William Henkin. Also, to Lorrett at Fantasy Makers in Berkeley and Janet at Greenery Press—two of the nicest, most wonderful people alive.

"She-Males," like the lady above, are different from other transsexuals. They try to look very feminine, will get breast transplants, take estrogen, and endure whopping amounts of electrolysis. But they love their male genitals and don't want to part with them. This is very different from other transsexuals who can't wait to have their pesky penises and testicles pried away.

She-Male prostitutes say they do a booming business in straight males who would never want to have sex with a gay guy. The straight male customers find something reassuring and exciting about sex with a "woman" who also has male genitals. Perhaps it is tied into a childhood concern that women may have been castrated, and this becomes reassurance that it just wasn't so.

Very Highly Recommended

Normal—Transsexual CEOs, Crossdressing Cops and Hermaphrodites with Attitude, by Amy Bloom, Vintage Books, New York, 2002.

The Man Who Would Be Queen—The Science of Gender-Bending and Transsexualism, by Joseph Henry Press, National Academies Press, 2003

Almost anything from the impressive Intersex Society of North America at www.isna.org/

Sex Fantasies
Chapter 39

Given how sex fantasies are nearly universal, it's a little surprising that we tend to be embarrassed about them. On the other hand, why bother fantasizing about something that everyone else approves of?

Some people know they're horny because of the sexual fantasies they've been having. For others, horniness is something they feel in their bodies, with very little mental imagery.

Some people have a single reliable sex fantasy that they go back to time and again. Others have a virtual toolbox of scenes and images that help get them off. The vast majority of people have fantasies during intercourse, and a lot people find it difficult to masturbate to orgasm without an arousing sexual fantasy.

The content of sex fantasies varies; some are sweet, kind and silly; others are weird, kinky and bizarre. Some are action-packed and exciting; others are really boring. Some sex fantasies are populated with past lovers, rock 'n' roll singers, people in uniforms, movie stars, teachers, priests, family members, total strangers and even furry friends from another species.

Believe it or not, one of the most popular sex fantasies involves doing stuff with your current partner! As for scenarios that people fantasize about, here's a partial list:

Being held or cuddled; doing all kinds of sex acts; having sex with more than one partner; having anonymous sex with a highly attractive partner or partners; being forced to have sex; watching a partner have sex with someone else; having gay sex when you otherwise feel straight; having sex with a male/female couple; role reversal where a guy fantasizes he's a woman having sex with other guys, or a woman fantasizes she's a man having sex with other women; watching or being watched having sex; being the one who dominates; being adored, desired, spanked, tortured, shamed or humiliated.

Fantasies of Rape

It is not unusual for people to have fantasies in which sex is forced, nor is it unusual to fantasize about sex with policemen, priests or others in uniform. Consider the following passage from Betty Dodson's fine book, *Sex for One* (New York: Harmony Books):

> A friend who considered herself a radical feminist got concerned that her sexual imagery wasn't politically correct because it wasn't "feminist oriented." I assured her that all fantasies were okay. Lots of people imagine scenes they never want to experience. I also pointed out that we can become addicted to a fantasy like anything else, and suggested she experiment with new ones. One of her new assertive fantasies is about moving her clitoris in and out of her lover's soft wet mouth while he's tied down. Whenever she gets stuck or is in a hurry, she brings out her old fantasy of being raped by five Irish cops and always reaches orgasm quickly.

Just because someone has a fantasy of being raped doesn't mean that he or she wants it to happen in reality. Sometimes being raped in fantasy is a way for the person to enjoy pleasure that would otherwise cause guilt. Sex that is out of your control keeps you from having to feel responsible for wanting it, and in a typical rape fantasy the rapist is usually someone whom the victim finds appealing and would like to have sex with anyway. It is also a way to feel sexually desired and valued, since the perpetrator would do anything to have you.

Men's vs. Women's Sex Fantasies

Young girls in our society are raised on fashion magazines that highlight gorgeous female models—gorgeous if you don't take into account how many meals these women barf up to stay slim and how much silicone they have surgically packed into their chests. As they look through these magazines, American girls often grow up thinking about other women's bodies, particularly the ideal woman whom they hope to someday become. Boys, on the other hand, often grow up fantasizing about doing things; for instance, being firemen, sports heroes, musicians, stuntmen and eventually stud lovers. It seems our society wants its girls to be admired for how they look, and its boys for how they perform.

Lucky's Home!

Psychologist Karen Shanor believes that when women see an erect penis in their fantasies, they often relish it as a sign that the man finds them irresistible, and not as an object of worship. In fact, Shanor speculates that many young women learn to include men in their fantasies as an afterthought, with the fantasized male being little more than a woman retrofitted with a penis. (Perhaps this is one reason why teenage girls so often fawn over totally androgynous male rock 'n' roll singers.)

When a woman walks into a formal affair like a dance or prom, the first thing she often notices is how the other women look and how she feels in comparison. The first thing a man notices is often the same thing: how the other women look. Men usually aren't concerned with how the other men look, unless they are actors or gay.

As focused as women sometimes are on other women, this theory does have its limitations. For instance, it doesn't explain why some women clearly prefer the sexual touch and feel of a man's body.

Comment: A reader writes that teenage boys before puberty tend to look androgynous, so maybe the girls' fantasies are right where they need to be in an age-appropriate sense.

Your Lover's Sex Fantasies

Every once in a while, one partner will tell the other about his or her private sex fantasy. Stranger things have happened. But don't expect to see the fantasy plastered on a billboard surrounded by neon lights. Most of us are a little embarrassed by our sexual fantasies, sometimes with good reason. As a result, we tend not to reveal our fantasies in a way that's particularly direct.

You Only Get One Chance

Let's say you are a guy and your sweetheart casually or jokingly makes an off-the-cuff statement that she likes seeing guys in jock straps. Boom, ball's in your court.

Now, if you have half a brain, and not many of us do, you won't laugh and tell her how much better you feel in boxers than wearing some old athletic supporter. Instead, you will consider buying about a dozen or so new jocks, maybe in colors, maybe one with a cup, what the heck. So there you are later that night, your sweetheart's warm familiar fingers are slowly popping the buttons on your blue jeans and bingo—she discovers that you are wearing a jock underneath! Before you know it, she's in sexual orbit and you are the happiest jock on your block! On the other hand, she might discover that her fantasy was best when it was only imagined and that it feels silly or loses its erotic edge when acted out in reality.

Beat the Rut

Sex can be really boring if you never vary the routine. Mind you, this hasn't stopped many couples from doing the exact same thing in bed week after week, month after month, year after year.

Adding variety to a boring sex life is a favorite topic of the magazines that people read in check-out lines at the grocery store, especially when the person in front of you pulls out an entire shoe box full of coupons and you suddenly find yourself with an extra half-hour on your hands.

Odds & Ends: Compromises, Big Xs & The Truth

While it's great that you and your partner might be open to hearing each other's fantasies, this doesn't mean that you need to act them out. When one partner has a jones to do something that the other finds loathful, you might try working out a compromise. For instance, it's likely that there are plenty of videos depicting whichever fantasies are currently oozing from the darkest recesses of your sexual mind. Why not rent one and use it as a masturbation aid? At other times acting out your sex fantasies can be great fun.

People occasionally have sexual fantasies about someone other than their partner. Sometimes it's prudent not to share these fantasies (e.g., "The reason I got so hot is because I pretended you were Mike"). Other times your partner might find these fantasies very arousing.

If you are going to make your own adult videos at home, keep in mind the fate of the poor sheriff from the Midwest who accidentally returned a custom-made X-rated video of him and his wife to the local video store.

There are special locks available that fit into the sprocket hole of videocassettes. By using these, you are safe even if your six-year-old accidentally grabs your homemade orgasmo-tape instead of *Toy Story* or *Shrek.* "Mommy, Mommy, you'll never guess what we saw Amber's mom and dad doing on videotape!"

Responsibility

Knowledge of your partner's fantasies is a trust that remains with you for life. This trust holds true even if you break up and otherwise find yourselves hating each other. No one forced you to be in a relationship with the person, so don't go blabbing personal stuff just to be hurtful. In the long run, it reflects badly upon you.

To put it another way, people who gossip about a current or former partner's sexuality are both shallow and deceitful. The laws of karma will someday haunt them, assuming there are laws of karma.

Readers' Comments

"At work I daydream a lot about sex and what it would be like with certain people that I am especially attracted to. Since I am about to get married, I sometimes feel bad thinking of others, but as long as you don't act on it, you're pretty much okay."   *female age 30*

"My sexual fantasies always involve my current real life lover. We're making romantic love somewhere that is new to us, a beach, forest, remote island, in front of a fire in a cabin."

female age 34

"I probably have similar fantasies to anyone who watches the Sci Fi channel too much."   *male age 30*

"My fantasies don't play a huge part in my life, except that I get confused why I have fantasies about other girls when I love penises and my boyfriend very much." *female age 23*

"I had always fantasized about my girlfriend being totally naked with her legs spread apart when I came into the room. One day she actually did this! It was awesome!" *male age 21*

"I don't have any clearly defined fantasy. They are more fleeting feelings and don't affect my life much." *female 38*

"As a working mother, I get sex and orgasms, but I rarely get romance, so that is what I fantasize about." *female 36*

"My husband and I have been married for ten years and still love to act out our sexual fantasies. Last month he was a customs agent and I was trying to sneak something across the border. After he completely searched me, I had to bribe him with sexual favors until he let me go. Later, I was a physician and he the reluctant patient. Acting out your fantasies can be great fun, and it keeps your sex life young!" *female age 33*

"I'd love to see my girlfriend get it on with another woman and I know it would be a turn-on to see her get it on with another guy, but I don't know if I could keep from getting jealous."
male age 39

Have you ever had homosexual fantasies?

"I used to fantasize about women all of the time. Finally, I decided to give it a try and had sex with one of my best female friends, who is mostly heterosexual. It was fun and every now and then we play with one another. I have never developed an emotional attachment to her or any other woman, and I no longer fantasize about women."   *female age 26*

"I fantasize about being with another woman often, but I also fantasize about my boyfriend and Brad Pitt!"   *female age 25*

"I am aroused by images of women with women; also by stories of multiple partners. On occasion, I use these fantasies to help me reach orgasm."   *female age 32*

"I've had no fantasies or gay experiences, although I wonder sometimes if I could get turned on by another guy."

male age 30

"Gay fantasies? I've never even considered being gay. I'm not gay. I swear it."   *male age 22*

Want help in making your sex fantasies become real? Try *The Ultimate Guide To Sexual Fantasy—How To Turn Your Fantasies into Reality*" by Violet Blue, Cleis Press, 2004. This book covers everything from role-playing without feeling silly to having sex in public and making your own private porn flicks.

Love Dreams, Sex Dreams & Sweet Dreams

Chapter 40

Some people have dreams of misty-eyed romance, the kind of dreams that leave you floating in the clouds until noon the next day. Some people have dreams that include sex. These are the dreams that this chapter is about. And some people have dreams that combine sex and romance. These are the dreams that we dream about dreaming — the rocket-fuel variety of dream that fills the soul and tugs at the edges of who we are.

Sex-Dream Statistics

Less than 10% of American parents inform their children about sex dreams, yet the majority of young adults at one time or another have them. More than 50% of women have sex dreams, yet many women don't start having them until they are in their twenties. With the male of the species it is different. Males often experience sex dreams as teenagers, with the frequency tending to decrease as they get older.

Sex-Dream History

In the mid-1800s, it was assumed that sex dreams were caused by immoral thoughts. Bizarre operations were proposed for the penises of men who had wet dreams, and all sorts of devices were patented for a man to wear on his penis at night to prevent him from having erections and the dreaded sex dreams that were thought to follow. One device was designed to wake him up by pulling on his pubic hair when he got an erection. Another machine poured cold water on him whenever he became erect during his sleep.

Dreamtime Sex Cinema—Pass the Kleenex, or Not?

During an average night of sleep, human genitals get hard or wet several times. This usually happens whenever you are dreaming, regardless of the dream's content, even if the dream is about your grandmother or someplace you once visited. A "wet dream" happens when you are actually dreaming about sex and have an orgasm.

Almost half of all "wet dream" orgasms are actually dry and don't include ejaculation, which makes the term *wet dream* a bit of a misnomer when it is used to describe men's sex dreams. However, it is an accurate description of what happens during women's sex dreams.

While having an orgasm in your sleep isn't much of a problem for a woman, it sometimes leaves a guy with a sticky mess. In a more understanding world, a male wouldn't have to feel embarrassed about wet-dream stains. But wet dreams often leave a splotch on the sheets or in your underwear, and what's a boy to say? Since there is no way of predicting when you will have a sex dream, packing your shorts with Kleenex at bedtime isn't going to help.

Sex Dreams vs. Masturbation

Talk about difficult bedtime decisions. When the author of this book was a teenager, he assumed that he would be more likely to have a wet dream if he didn't masturbate. He would hold out, trying not to masturbate for as many days as possible, in hopes of hastening a wet dream. Not so. Sometimes a person can have a wet dream the same night that he or she masturbates or has sex, but not masturbating won't increase your chances by one little drip.

There is simply no way to will yourself a wet dream, unless you are good at lucid-dream enhancement, or whatever the people at Stanford are calling it these days. A seminal book on the subject of lucid dreaming is *Lucid Dreaming* by Stephen LeBerge, Ballantine. Another helpful book (except for its dumb title) is *Lucid Dreams in 30 Days* by Keith Harary and Pamela Weintraub, St. Martin's Press.

Sex-Dream Complications

Not only are sex dreams a sign that you are growing up, but they are a great way of having sex when it is not readily available. Some people even have their first orgasms while asleep and dreaming. Still, some people feel upset by their sex dreams. For instance, you might have a sex dream that includes someone you know, maybe a friend, boss or teacher. This might make you feel a bit sheepish when you see that person in real life. Not to worry, you have done nothing wrong. This book's suggestion is to scope out the person from head to toe. Check everything from subtle mannerisms to what kind of clothes he or she is wearing. Then ask yourself: "Is he or she as good (or bad) in real life as he or she was in my dream?"

There can also be wet-dream downers. For instance, wet dreams can leave you feeling frustrated when the love of your dreams doesn't want anything to do with you in waking life. This can be particularly bittersweet when the person is a former lover and is now with someone else or is no longer living. Also, it is not unusual for heterosexuals to dream about having sex with members of the same sex. There are many ways of interpreting this sort of thing, e.g., the sex in these dreams might represent accepting part of yourself that the other person represents, with the actual sex being a metaphor for "taking in." But of course!

Whatever the content, it would be nice if your sex dreams could be a safe and welcome place to explore a full array of sexual activity that you wouldn't ordinarily do when awake.

The Family That Dreams Together...

People sometimes have sex dreams that include members of the family. This doesn't necessarily indicate a problem. Again, actions that transpire in dreams are often symbols for something very different than what meets the eye, so you can't assume that the sexual partners or the sexual activity in a dream truly reflects the deeper meaning of the dream. If, however, this happens on a regular basis and you are disturbed by it, consider seeking the help of a trained mental health professional.

Another reason to get outside help is if you usually end up frustrated, hurt, frightened or angry in your dreams. You don't have to be Sigmund Freud to realize that repeated dreams of a disturbing nature reflect an inner struggle of major proportion. The exception is with children, since bad dreams are quite common during the younger years. It is not unusual for children who are happy and whose emotional development is normal to have bad dreams two to four times a week. If, on the other hand, the child is also struggling during the waking hours, it might be prudent to seek a professional assist.

Techno Breasts & Weenie Angst

Chapter 41

People who feel sexually inadequate sometimes focus their angst on body parts. For women, the focus is often on breast size or body shape; for men it is on the penis and sometimes height. Of course, it is silly to obsess about something that you had no say in getting, yet that's what many of us do.

When generating a physical balance sheet, it might be helpful to remember that even Man-O-War had his weaknesses. It might also help to remind yourself that sexual attractiveness is not like a steel chain, where one weak link makes the whole thing useless. All of us have weak links sexually, as part of our bodies and minds.

Of course, this offers little solace to people who are convinced that their essential body parts are deficient. They will keep telling themselves, "Everything would be better if I just had a bigger this or a smaller that...." To address such fears, this chapter offers a lengthy discourse on men's genitals, then ruminates on breast implants and ends with a few suggestions about alternative strategies.

Body Concerns: Guys & How They're Hung

While most books on sex say that penis size doesn't matter, there are two groups of people to whom it does matter. One group includes almost every male alive. The second group includes every woman who derives sexual pleasure from intercourse.

In years past, women weren't supposed to care about the size and shape of a man's penis. That is because they weren't supposed to be interested in sex. But wouldn't you notice the size and shape of something that was about to get stuck into your body? As for how women respond to the actual dimensions of the thing, it clearly varies.

For instance, some women regard the penis as a trophy—the bigger the better; others couldn't care less. Some women prefer the feeling of fullness that a beefier penis has to offer; others prefer giving blow jobs to a partner who isn't particularly well hung, and some even prefer a smaller penis for intercourse. Plenty of women get the bulk of their pleasure from what a man is able to do with his hands, heart, tongue and intellect. They view the penis as just another body part.

For some women, a lover's penis becomes her penis or a part of her body when it's inside of her. Does this mean that she necessarily wants the biggest one in town? Not usually. After all, when women buy dildos, they tend to select medium- to smaller-sized units. (Sorry, but they sometimes upsize later.)

Of course, this isn't to say that women don't have their favorites. Ask a woman to tell you which lover's penis was her favorite, and she will probably be able to give a direct and clear-cut answer such as, "It was Alex's" or "There are two or three that stand out, but I'd have to say Todd's takes the prize." However, if you ask about the men behind the penises and which ones she loved the most, Alex or Todd might not be at the top of the list. Maybe the guy she was happiest with didn't have a memorable penis, but was able to put it together in other ways.

So while women might prefer one penis over the other, penis size usually isn't a deal-breaker when it comes to choosing a man. It is sometimes disappointing, but usually not the deciding factor.

Irony: While some guys grow up worrying if they are hung well enough, women sometimes grow up worrying that guys will be hung too well and might cause them pain or injury. Maybe we humans were simply programmed to worry.

Weenie-Enhancement Techniques

Surgery That Makes Your Penis Fat

There is a surgical technique for penis plumping in which fat cells are harvested from the lower stomach region and injected into the penis. The author of this book called three offices that advertise this procedure and was hit by a wave of sales pitches that he hadn't encountered since joining a health club.

The heavy sales pitch, which tried to capitalize on every sexual doubt known to man, made sense when you consider that these clinics charge $3,000 to $5,000 for a simple outpatient procedure that takes half an hour.

One clinic in Beverly Hills refused to even mail out information about the procedure. They claimed that a brochure had fallen into the hands of a child, resulting in great embarrassment. To prevent such a hideous event from ever occurring again, each caller had to make an office appointment where he could read the brochure and talk to a specialist. "Why an appointment?" "Because we process over forty men a day." As it turned out, the dreaded brochure contained no pictures or drawings and was embarrassing only in how it insulted the consumer's intelligence.

This fancy medical clinic insisted that it needed a social security number and health insurance information before discussing the procedure. Each visitor was also required to fill out a separate page about his penis. The wording was designed to make a man feel sexually insecure and blame it all on the size of his weenie.

The Beverly Hills clinic then treated your author to an interview with a clean-cut salesman masquerading in a physician's coat, perhaps so people wouldn't confuse him with the salesmen who populate used car lots.

None of the three offices offered any studies on the long-term safety of the procedure, they didn't agree on where the fat actually went, and none was willing to say exactly how a penis feels that is encased in a layer of fat.

It seems that if Mother Nature wanted an extra layer of fat on the penis, she would have put it there herself. Heaven knows, she put it everywhere else. Not even the hot dogs at Dodger stadium have as much fat as a penis that's been cosmetically plumped, and they cost significantly less than $4000—okay, they cost somewhat less than $4000.

The best we could conclude about this procedure is that a man pays $4,000 to give his penis cellulite. Also, some lawyers are specializing in lawsuits from men who were less than satisfied with the results of their surgically enhanced penises. And recently, the penis-enlargement ads in the sports section of the *Los Angeles Times* have been stating that there is a "new procedure" which is vastly improved over the one used in the past. Perhaps they have forgotten that only a year ago their ads for the "old" procedure used to boast about how safe and successful it was.

Would you trust your penis to these people?

The Vacuum Pump

There is an X-rated video called *How to Enlarge Your Penis* in which porn star Scott Taylor pumps himself up with a vacuum device that is supposed to make a guy bigger. Taylor uses the pump to plump his penis up fatter than a grain silo, which he then maneuvers into the apparently spacious vagina of porn starlet Erica Boyer. At no point does Scott's big salami actually get hard; he has to hold his fingers around the base to keep the pressure in. In spite of this "self-help" video, the vacuum pump is one of the options that urologists offer male patients who are having trouble getting hard. Also, inside-industry sources have informed Goofy Foot Press that the *How to Enlarge* infomercial took several hours to shoot, and even Scott Taylor couldn't stay hard for that long.

The penis pump was first patented in 1917. About sixty years later it became popular in the gay community, both for sex play and for organ enhancement. Some pumpers even started clubs, along the lines of Kiwanis or Rotary, where guys get together to pump. Straight men started using the pump in the mid to late 1980s. Pumping provides a sensation that some men find enjoyable. It also causes the penis to plump up bigger than usual. Most urologists think that there is no way a guy can make himself permanently bigger with a vacuum pump and that short-term gains occur because the penis is swollen. However, the people who manufacture the pumps claim that long-term gains are possible. They say that the vacuum pump expands the width of the penis by stretching the walls of the chambers that fill with blood during normal erection. The increase in penis length apparently comes from stretching the ligament that holds a third of the penis inside the body.

To achieve a "permanent" increase in size, pumpers say that a man has to pump at least a half-hour a day for almost a year. As for the safety of the vacuum pump, it has been approved by the FDA for use with erection problems, but not for use as a weenie-enhancement device, not that anyone has applied. Can you imagine the lab studies that the FDA might require, with hundreds of white rats having their penises pumped for hours on end to see if they got bigger?

For safety's sake, check with a physician before pumping for long periods of time. That's because there might be a difference between pumping for a few minutes to get hard and pumping for an hour to get bigger. Also ask yourself why you might be focusing so much insecurity on your penis. No matter what its size, your penis is still a marvelous gift from nature which provides tremendous feelings of pleasure.

You would think that the majority of men who pump for size would be those with smaller penises. Not so. A lot of pumpers are well endowed to begin with. Go figure.

The Bottom Line...

"I once had a lover with an enormous penis. It was a turn-on to look at it, and an ego trip that a man that huge was my partner. But the actual feeling of it inside me didn't give me one one-hundredth of the pleasure that my more modestly-sized present partner's does. While the size of a man's penis does create different sensations, it is the relationship I have with the man who is attached to the penis that determines what those sensations mean to me." *female age 47*

Before rushing out to get either a pump or surgery, consider the following: If your penis is average-sized or more, why do you need to be bigger? What's your problem anyway? And if your penis is closer to a finger than a phone pole, learn to give great back and foot rubs and become sublime at the art of loving a woman with your lips and tongue. Do this and it is likely that you will be admired by many women, assuming you are a decent human being to begin with. Also try using intercourse positions that might focus more stimulation on the parts of your lover's vagina that give her the most pleasure. The most sensitive areas of a vagina are often located in the first inch or two beyond the vaginal opening. And finally, try to avoid women who are confirmed size-queens. No sense in humiliating yourself needlessly.

A bantam-weight penis might feel longer if the female bends her knees during intercourse. This results in deeper penetration if that is what she wants. Keeping her legs together will help it feel more snug. A couple of positions that accommodate this are rear-entry intercourse with both of you on your sides (aka spoons) and where the woman is on her back and her ankles are resting on the man's shoulders instead of around his waist.

As for being embarrassed in front of your locker-room buds, sex experts say that it's not fair to compare nonerect penises, because penises that are smaller when they are soft tend to grow more when they are getting hard. In other words, it isn't a fair comparison unless all of you have hard-ons, and what kind of gym would that be? But reality checks are of little solace to a guy who's feeling insecure in the showers after football practice. Hopefully he will learn that there are other ways of earning respect besides having a big penis, assuming that big penises earn respect rather than envy.

Perhaps it might be good to remember that many things in life have a purpose. In case you are here on earth to learn something, your less-than-memorable member might be one of the keys that helps you find it, especially if it's a bit of humility.

A Note for the Extra-Well-Endowed

A small number of men feel angst because they were especially blessed behind the buttons of their blue jeans. Others just smile.

For those guys whose girlfriends scream in horror the first time they see the penis erect, relax. Talk about it before you get undressed or hand her a copy of the *Guide* and point to this chapter. Flatly rule out the possibility of intercourse for the first couple of times. This will allow time for your lover to become comfortable touching and playing with your trunk—uh—penis. Ray Stubbs's *Erotic Interludes Part 2* is a tastefully done videotape which shows a woman massaging the penis of a man who doesn't give much ground to the average race horse. And no matter what its diameter might be, a partner can get you off quite nicely with the oral sex technique which doesn't require her to take your whole penis into her mouth. It is shown in Chapter 22: "Oral Sex: Popsicles & Penises" on page 288.

There's an entire Naked Truth column at the end of this chapter that is crammed full of information on the ways of the big weenie.

Now, for ways that women mangle their bodies.

The Sound of Leaking Breasts

"I tried out for the cheerleading squad when I was a sophomore in high school. 'This isn't a beauty contest,' the advisor had told us, but we all knew better than that.... But you weren't beautiful, Julie Brown, and you knew it. Face facts. You even made a list one time, outlining your numerous faults: breasts too small, buttocks too big, teeth crooked, hair too thin, arms and legs too skinny, feet too long, four inches too tall, nose too bumpy. If you were wealthy, you could make the necessary corrections. If you had enough money, you could have the breast implants you needed, the braces, the nose job, the hairweaving, and with enough money the right cosmetics could be purchased, the ones you saw in the magazines, the ones that would render you flawless..." (Julie Brown, "Beauty" pp. 68—70, *Michigan Quarterly Review,* edited by Laurence Goldstein, Vol. XXX, No. 1, Winter 1991.)

Men aren't the only ones who worry that body parts are too small. Women often believe that the world would be a nicer and kinder place if only they had bigger breasts. Some women with petite breasts even feel they would get a better job or promotion if their A cups swelled into majestic Es. Hopes like these have inspired thousands of American women to have their chests packed with funky substances.

Aside from the sheer ridiculousness of getting breast implants, many questions have been raised about the safety of them. Silicone molecules seem to leach through the plastic implant pouches. However, it is possible that this isn't any more dangerous to your health than, say, living in Detroit or Los Angeles. Saline implants appear to be safer than the silicone, but far less so than the original equipment that Mother Nature saw fit to provide.

Note: Many women who have implants need additional surgery a few years down the line, and even the saltwater boobs make it difficult to screen for cancer. Of course, implants are truly a godsend if you've had cancer and are getting them following a mastectomy.

Silicone Sisters[1] and the Men Who Love Them

Here in America men with plastic brains are attracted to women with plastic chests. What a perfect combination. What a sad perception of womanhood.

Young women in America are raised on fashion magazines that highlight gorgeous female models, whatever gorgeous might mean.

---

[1]With apologies to Bruce Springsteen.

Having grown up under the shadow of surgically-enhanced breasts, American girls often confuse a combination of anorexia and a fake profile with what femininity is all about. As a result, breast implants and bizarre diets have become a way of achieving the fantasy of perfect womanhood.

Perfect womanhood is a costly and precarious myth to pursue. Even if you are able to achieve the right look, it tends to be short-lived and often comes crashing down by the time you reach age thirty-five and can no longer suppress that which in other cultures is considered to be a sign of wisdom. It's too bad America's teenage girls don't get to spend time with America's supermodels. They might get over the supermodel fantasy rather quickly.

The Placebo Effect of Store-Bought Boobs

Until recently, some of the biggest proponents of breast implants were the women who got them. Then they had to start spending all that time and energy convincing themselves that the darned things weren't killing them.

One reason women with plastic chests were so excited about their implants was because life really did get better for many of them. But the real reason life improved was the women's attitudes got better. It's how they saw themselves that made the difference, not whether their breasts were As or double Ds. Otherwise, women with naturally large boobs would seldom feel depressed or have a rotten day, and women with As would all be suicidal.

Feeling more attractive is what made these women be more attractive. Granted, there are plenty of men who like the way that big boobs look, but an increase in confidence without the implants would have brought similar results.

Microchip Melons—A New Generation of Breast Implant?

Unless there is a major shift in the consciousness of American men and women, it is likely that the medical world will find new ways to surgically mangle women's bodies. As long as that is the case, this guide suggests that the next generation of breast implants contain slots for video games and a couple of firewire ports. This will help turn the female chest into a full-fledged entertainment center, which is what some men and women expect it to be.

Exercise Video Alert—Truth in Advertising

Exercise videos have been very popular for the past decades. It only seems fair that any actress/model/whatever who does an exercise video ought to list how many cosmetic surgeries she's had to look the way she does. (Breast implants? Ribs removed? Liposuction? Face lifts? Tummy tucks? Breast lifts? Supplemental hormones?) The videos might then post a warning label such as the following:

> WARNING: With $22,000 worth of plastic surgery, a lucky role of the genetic dice, an eating disorder, and the exercises on this tape, you too can look more like your video host.

Alternatives for Both Men & Women

American advertisers spend millions of dollars to make us think, "If only I had this or that, I'd be sexier and happier." It is easy to see why many of us fall for these devious traps. The thought of instantly having bigger, smaller, hairier or balder body parts can be terribly seductive.

If cosmetic surgery is what you need, please choose carefully. Do be aware that if you haven't worked through feelings of inferiority, realigning body parts may not make you feel any better in the long run. You'll simply find new things to feel insecure about.

For alternatives, think about getting your body in good physical shape or dressing better. Breasts that sit on well-developed chest muscles sometimes look bigger, if that is what you are trying to achieve. At the very least, being in good shape makes most people feel and look sexier. A smaller penis will often look bigger if it isn't being dwarfed by a pot belly, or if the eyes are drawn to nicely developed shoulders and pecs. Also, why not find ways to expand your mind's creativity and intelligence? These are the kinds of measures that will make you a better and sexier person.

As for sexual performance, some of the best and most eager lovers are those without ideal dimensions. Since they have less natural endowment to fall back on, they sometimes learn to be extremely attentive and skilled in bed.

Considering any kind of cosmetic surgery? Please read Virginia Blum's book on the subject. This book will let you see a side of cosmetic surgery that is well-hidden from the viewers of the "Extreme Make-over" TV shows. It is by a woman who has had plastic surgery and has interviewed surgeons and patients. What would it hurt to read some of the information that you won't find in the glossy brochures at your plastic surgeon's office before making such a big decision? *Flesh Wounds, The Culture of Cosmetic Surgery* by Virginia L. Blum, University of California at Berkeley Press, Berkeley, California, 2003.

Chapter Notes: Some women have breast-reduction surgery because it can be severely uncomfortable to lug huge breasts around all the time. If this is what you are considering, be sure to consult at least two surgeons who specialize in breast reduction surgery. This is not a simple operation and can leave permanent scaring or disfigurement.

Dear Paul,
My boyfriend and I are both virgins and have been attempting to have intercourse, but we are having a few difficulties. First of all, I have no problem getting wet, but when it comes to penetration I am completely dry. This makes it very painful, as it aches and burns. I am also quite petite, and he, on the other hand, is quite tall and "fully equipped" (8 inches, and rather large in circumference). It seems that penetration is practically impossible as I am rather tight and do not enjoy being fingered. I was just wondering if you have any suggestions as we are getting a little antsy.

Athena from Olympus

Dear Athena,

None of the women I've slept with have had to come up with strategies for inserting an extra-large penis—not when they were with me, anyway. Nonetheless, I'll do what I can.

To put this size-issue in its truest, ugliest light, if the Penis Fairy arrived one night and offered to give all men an extra inch or an extra 10 I.Q. points, a lot of us would go for the below-the-belt enhancement without giving it much thought. In fact, until I'd written a book about sex, I never realized that toting around a huge penis can be a liability. We're talking about guys who need to wear specially made underwear, who are forever getting stares in the locker room and at the doctor's office, and for whom hopping into bed with a woman can be a trauma.

On the other hand, I have interviewed a woman who is as petite as can be. Her husband's penis was in the 98th percentile for size, and she never had any problem with intercourse. So you can't predict.

Size aside, medical factors can make intercourse uncomfortable. So I am assuming you have had a recent gynecological exam and have discussed this very matter. As long as you are okay physically, I would suggest that the two of you call it quits on any intercourse attempts for the next month or two. Fortunately, there are lots of ways you can please each other sexually besides intercourse. At the same time, you can be working on some or all of the following:

#1. It sounds as though each time you've tried to have intercourse there's been a fair amount of pain. I suspect that the muscles around the mouth of your vagina are now automatically tightening up whenever Mr. Jumbo tries to land. This would be your body's way of protecting you from more pain. Unfortunately, it's backfiring.

One thing to try is called "femoral intercourse," but it isn't intercourse at all. It is where your partner lies on his back and you lube up his penis. You then straddle him and ride back and forth along the length of his well-lubed penis as it is lying against his belly. (Your vulva is like a hotdog bun, and his penis is like a Ballpark Frank. You slide the bun up and down the length of the dog, enjoying the sensations without him trying to steal home. Be sure to use birth control even if he holds the Mayo. His penis is not going into your vagina, but your genitals will be rubbing together and that's reason enough to call out the contraceptives.)

It might help if you could learn to give yourself some orgasms this way or at least enjoy the sensations. It offers lots of nice stimulation to your clitoris. You are in complete control and there's no need to worry about intercourse. These pleasant experiences with his penis will help the muscles around your vagina learn to stop clenching in anticipation of pain. This also helps massage the tissues around your vulva, which leads to the next step.

#2. Have your partner squirt lube on his fingertips. He can then gently clasp the outer lips of your vulva between his thumb and forefinger and do a small circular massage on one area at a time. Tell him exactly what feels good and what doesn't. He should massage as deeply as feels comfortable to you, then move to an adjoining spot.

When the Tide Turns Red

Chapter 42

Once you get into a long-term relationship, menstruation is something that happens to both of you. That's why you'll do better in life if you try to understand more about it. The best way for a guy to find out about menstruation is to ask his partner. For instance, does she sail through her periods without much distress, or does she get all swelled up and bloated? Are there certain things she likes or dislikes when she's having her period? How long does her period usually last? For most women, it's from three to seven days. Does she bleed heavily or light? The total amount averages from two to four ounces. (The ancient Greeks thought it was several pounds!)

You might eventually ask her to tell you about the first time she menstruated. Almost all women remember their first period quite vividly. You might ask what she thinks about the controversial new trend of using birth control pills to eliminate three out of every four periods. Learn all she can teach you. The two of you might feel more connected as a result. Why not give her the laugh of a lifetime by trying to insert a tampon for her?

A Brief Historical Note

When people talk about the scientific discoveries that have given women more freedom and equality, the birth control pill is often the first thing mentioned. They forget that a couple of generations ago women had to use rags to collect menstrual blood, hence the term "on the rag." After the vulcanization of rubber in the 1800s, women could strap little rubber canoes between their legs to catch the dripping. Then came the sanitary napkin and decades later the tampon, which has had more of a positive impact on many women's lives than the birth control pill. While the sanitary napkin has pretty well held its same shape for the past century, modifications have left it more manageable to use as well as giving birth to the term "panty liner." (Many female readers say it still feels like wearing a mattress between their legs!)

> ## Let's be frank, everybody's knickers get a bit damp by the end of the day. It's just the way we're made.

From a 1994 Carefree Panty Liner ad.

Intercourse during Periods

Some couples fear intercourse during a woman's menstrual cycle. But menstruation causes no harm to either partner. In fact, the contractions of orgasm push accumulated fluids out of the uterus which helps decrease menstrual cramping. Still, can you imagine an American mother telling her fourteen-year-old daughter, "Honey, if you're having cramps, why not masturbate?" Instead, they buy Midol.

Intercourse with a menstruating woman sometimes feels extra-nice. Some of the reasons are: 1. Menstrual secretions can make the vagina feel super-lubricated. 2. Menstrual swelling can help a woman have a really nice orgasm. 3. Some women get extra-horny during their periods. This might have to do with a change in hormones, or perhaps they feel more relaxed since it's harder to get pregnant, although pregnancy is still a risk. (Women who don't enjoy having sex with their partner might look forward to their periods as a respite from sex!)

As for the aesthetics of midperiod intercourse, sheets with menstrual lovemaking on them usually wash clean, but so what if they don't? Guys shed blood during a hard-fought game of football and consider it a sign of courage.

If you are having intercourse during a period, consider some of the following:

 Put a towel down to catch the flow!

 Have sex in the shower.

He can use a male condom or she can use the female condom.

Wear a diaphragm. This stops most of the flow for the guy who doesn't like to see blood on his penis.

Use *Instead.* This is an over-the-counter alternative to tampons that fits over your cervix in the same way as a diaphragm. The people who make it say it's great for intercourse during your period. NOTE: Another produced called the *Diva Cup* is similar to *Instead* and it works well for oral sex. But it is not recommend for intercourse because it is bell-shaped and is worn low near the vaginal opening. Neither the *Diva Cup* nor *Instead* provide any protection from pregnancy or STIs.

If intercourse or oral sex during a woman's period isn't for you, you can always get each other off by hand, by using a vibrator or dildo, or you can enjoy watching each other masturbate.

Anal sex can be an option if both of you enjoy it, but it's hard to think that a woman who enjoys anal sex would have a problem with vaginal sex while she's on her period.

Important Health Notes: Do not wear a tampon while having intercourse! Chances are good you'll end up in an emergency room trying to get it fished out. And yes, you can get pregnant from intercourse while menstruating, so be sure to use birth control.

Oral Sex during Your Period

Some couples have no problem with oral sex during a menstrual cycle; others are a bit stand-off-ish. Last year someone complained that Goofy Foot Press is menstru-phobic because it does not actively encourage readers to give women oral sex while they are menstruating. Even if you are not from Transylvania, please accept our apologies. Here are ways that some couples enjoy oral sex while a woman's mensis is flowing:

Use tampons. Splash some water into your vagina while in the shower, then insert a couple of tampons before a man goes down on you. The tampons will catch most of the flow, assuming he doesn't attempt to tickle her cervix with the tip of his tongue. **NOTE:** if oral sex evolves into intercourse, be sure to take the tampons out first.

Wear a diaphragm. Some women get a diaphragm for the sole purpose of having sex mid-flow. The diaphragm becomes a barrier that traps the menstrual flow. Some couples start with it in for oral sex, but take it out for intercourse if they like the feeling of the menstrual flow.

Use *Instead* or the *Diva Cup*. These fit over your cervix like a diaphragm. Pop one in before oral sex and it will catch most if not all of the bloody flow.

Throwing plastic wrap over it. A simple way of dodging menstrual flow is by putting plastic wrap over the woman's vulva before going down on her. You'll need to experiment with ways of making this feel right. A little lube between the vulva and plastic wrap might help.

Feeling Unlovable

Some women have grown up in households that weren't particularly supportive of their biological processes. As a result, they may feel unlovable or unattractive when Aunt Flo visits. If this is true for your partner, find a time when she isn't feeling quite so unlovable and discuss it. It's one thing to feel bad when you have done something dumb, but there is nothing dumb about having a menstrual cycle. Besides, if you have ever had to wait out a menstrual period that is seriously late, you will learn to regard the monthly flow as a lover's best friend.

Stamp Out the Menstrual Cycle?

UC Berkeley scientist Margie Profet believes that menstruation evolved as a way of protecting the female's uterus from harmful bacteria and viruses that might be delivered by male ejaculate. Far from being a waste, she sees menstrual bleeding as the body's way of systematically preventing infection.

Others don't agree, and now there is a major move afoot to eliminate eight out of twelve menstrual periods a year. Mind you, the researcher who is heading this march is the same man who invented the DepoProvera shot that makes it possible. One would hope there would be a number of long-term studies on the subject done by labs that have no investment either way before this becomes the norm.

Also, some feminists will argue that this is one more attempt by modern science to subvert the natural processes of a woman's body, in an effort to make it more like a man's. Other women say they would be delighted to eliminate as many periods as possible.

Other Facts on the Period

It is said that in some primitive societies, the native women didn't start suffering from menstrual pain and cramping until they had been "saved" by Western missionaries and their American wives.

In the 1976 Olympics, an American swimmer won gold medals and broke a world record while on her period. Too bad she didn't get big bucks for endorsing her brand of tampons!

There is no evidence that a woman's intellectual or job performance is affected by her menstrual cycle. It may not feel great, but it doesn't compromise her ability to think or perform.

The Legacy of Bleeding

Children are taught from an early age that bleeding is what happens when you have a cut. Can you imagine the impact of menstrual bleeding on a young girl who isn't well-prepared? She would assume that there is something terribly wrong with her body. "Well-prepared" needs to include more than just the biological facts. It should also incorporate a sense of pride about the body and an awareness that menstrual bleeding is a sign of maturity and health. On the other hand, it is possible for parents to go a bit too far. One reader still cringes when she recalls the "Menstruation Party" that her mother proudly threw for her after her first period.

Where Do You Put It?

Another problem with menstruation is what to do with the blood. Few guys ever have to worry about bleeding through their shorts, but their girlfriends do. One very astute woman reader who is in her nineties still has dreams that she is menstruating and can't find a sanitary napkin. The feelings of panic remain fresh in her unconscious, although she last menstruated when Harry Truman was president, or was it Dwight Eisenhower? Another reader who had mercilessly heavy periods says she suspects the reason why some high school girls wear long shirts untucked is as a hedge against the embarrassment of bleeding through.

Feminist writer Gloria Steinem said that if men were the ones who menstruated, they would brag about how many ounces they bled each month and for how long. At least this would indicate pride!

Twinkies & the Onset of Menstruation

In the Western world, the onset of menstruation has been steadily occurring at a younger age. While this has generally been attributed to better nutrition, it may actually be due to poorer nutrition. Researcher Rose E. Frisch thinks that there is a relationship between the onset of menstruation and stores of body fat. Fat is one of the places in the body where estrogen is synthesized. As a young woman approaches puberty, her proportion of body fat increases. In order to start having menstrual cycles she seems to need around seventeen percent body fat, and to ovulate the figure increases to approximately 26%.

It could be our penchant for junk food and the sedentary life rather than healthy nutrition that is lowering the age of first menstruation. At the other extreme, women who are old enough to menstruate but are seriously overweight tend not to menstruate regularly.

It is also possible that all of the artificial hormones we ingest when eating meat is contributing to a younger onset of menstruation.

Women Athletes

It is not uncommon for women athletes to stop menstruating or have irregular periods. One reason is that their body fat is often lower than 17%. If a female athlete wants to get pregnant but is having difficulty, adding a few pounds might help.

Women athletes might also find that the start of menstruation is delayed due to metabolic reasons. Female athletes and dancers who began their training before the ages of nine or ten often start menstruating a few years later than their nonathletic peers.

It is with restraint that your author tells about the time during his freshman year of college when he lifted weights with the women members of the Soviet National Shot Put Team. He never thought to ask Olga, Svetlana and Georgia if they menstruated regularly.

Tampons, Sponges & Toxic-Shock Syndrome

Toxic-Shock Syndrome (TSS) is a rare but sometimes fatal disease caused by the toxins of bacteria that grow in the bodies of both men and women. TSS is now mainly associated with surgery and severe burn cases, but during the early 1980s some women died from TSS following the introduction of a new superabsorbent tampon called Rely.

Contrary to what scientists first believed, the killer tampons did not act as a breeding site for the TSS bacteria. Rely contained two synthetic fibers (carboxymethyl cellulose and polyester foam) that are thought to have irritated the vaginal lining in ways that triggered the TSS bacteria to produce a dangerous toxin. Tampons are now made from only cotton and rayon. As a result, the occurrence of TSS among tampon users is rare. Your chances of getting killed in a car wreck are 500 to 1000 times greater than the risk of death by tampon.

It was originally thought that wearing the same tampon for several hours increased your chances of getting TSS. Not so. But the risk does go up when you use nothing but tampons throughout your entire period, even if you change them every three hours. If you are a tampon user who wants to greatly reduce her chances of getting TSS, don't wear tampons throughout your entire period. For instance, alternate using tampons and napkins. Also, some people are naturally more susceptible to TSS. If you have ever had TSS or appear susceptible to it, you are better off not using tampons.

There is a slight increase in TSS among women who use barrier contraceptives, i.e., a diaphragm, cervical cap or contraceptive sponge. This risk is very, very, very slight.

One reader comments, "I was put on sea sponges back in the 1980s during the TSS scare. I had used Rely tampons and developed cell abnormalities. After ditching all tampons and inserting a clean sea sponge during my period, the abnormal cells disappeared."

There are Internet rumors that tampons contain dioxins which cause TSS. That might be possible if anyone could actually find dioxins in tampons, but the amount of dioxins in tampons is virtually nil. We are exposed to much higher levels of dioxins in the environment than from anything that comes in a box.

For First-Time Tampon Users

A number of our female readers have reported strange or painful experiences when they first tried using a tampon, including trying to pull out the tampon while it was still dry. This probably resulted from wearing a higher absorbency tampon that was needed. Tampons come in a couple of absorbencies. It's best not to use one that is more absorbent than you need.

Reader Comments on Tampons and Pads:

"I didn't realize the cardboard was supposed to come out (while the cotton wad stays in). It was a rather uncomfortable first hour, till I finally asked a girlfriend, 'What the hell?'" *f. age 28*

"I mostly use pads, but they used to get stuck in my pubic hair OUCH! Tampons are only useful for pools and hot tubs, otherwise it feels really weird walking around feeling like you have a soft dick stuck in you all day." *female age 21*

"Pads were so horrid, even though I used them for many years. they were just so gross, it felt like wearing a diaper, but I could never get the hang of applicator tampons, so I just used pads. When I got to college we got a free trial pack of OB applicatorless tampons and I fell in love instantly and have never looked back!" *female age 20*

"I hated pads because I felt gooey and gross when I wore them. The blood never absorbs like the commercials say it does. I hurt the first couple of times I put a tampon in, and had to force it, but eventually that stopped and I didn't have a problem anymore." *female age 21*

"I never had a problem using tampons, and I hate it when my pubic hair gets stuck to the bloody pad. YUCK. So I'm a tampon girl—though I have to use the slim kind, as the larger ones hurt." *female age 20*

Putting tampons where they need to go requires three steps—pushing in the applicator, pushing in the plunger, and pulling out the applicator, unless you're using OBs.

Tips on tampon insertion from our female readers:

Be sure to follow the instructions from the manufacturer. Check the instructions to see how often you should change tampons. Try not to leave it in longer than the manufacturer says.

Most tampons come with their own applicators or plungers. Some tampons, like OBs, use the inserting device that Mother Nature provided: your finger.

Buy or borrow the skinniest tampon you can find. You might try Tampax Lites or Playtex SlimFit regulars for your first time.

Some women put tampons in while standing with a little squat action or with one leg higher and out to the side. Other women put them in while sitting on the toilet.

It might help to coat the end of the tampon with a lubricant like KY Jelly. If you can't score the jelly, try dabbing a little saliva on it.

Find your vaginal opening. It's down there somewhere, honest. It's at the bottom part of your vulva. Spread the lips of your vulva and put your finger in a little way. This is where the tampon will go.

Spread your lips with the fingers of one hand, and insert the applicator into your vagina with the other. Aim it toward your tailbone and not up toward your stomach.

Insert the applicator so that the wider part of the barrel is almost all of the way in—with just enough sticking out to hold on to. If you don't insert the tampon far enough inside, the ring of muscles in the first part of your vagina can clamp it, making it feel uncomfortable.

Once you've got the applicator in, hold the barrel firmly with your fingers. Push the plunger in. Bingo!

As you pull out the applicator, try not to pull on the string or you'll pull the tampon out and you're back to square one. If this happens, push the tampon back in with your finger.

Make sure the string is hanging out of your vagina. If it isn't, don't worry. Squat and push down as if you are trying to take the mother of all dumps. Reach a finger inside your vagina to see if you can feel the critter. You can always use your thumb and finger to pull the string out. If you have no luck, ask your mom, aunt, grandmother or older sister for help, or call your healthcare provider and speak with a nurse. Again, it's not like the end of the world, but you will need to get the thing out in the next couple of hours.

Your vagina might be dry on the last day or two of your period. Don't hesitate to dab some lube on the tampon before putting it in.

Sorry to be repetitive, but do not have intercourse with a tampon inside. Lord only knows where in your vagina it will end up.

Dear Paul,

When did they invent tampons? What about sanitary napkins?

Fluffy in Florida

Dear Fluff,

Kotex, the first widely marketed sanitary napkin, was invented shortly after World War I. Before that, women used rags which they wadded up and pinned to the inside of their underwear.

According to the Museum of Menstruation, the modern tampon was born in the late 1920s or early 1930s. The first one was probably named Fax, and it was called an "internal sanitary napkin" because nobody knew what a tampon was. It did not have an applicator or a string. It was wrapped in gauze, which a woman pulled on to get it out.

Another early tampon was called Paz. In 1936, the Tambrands company bought the Paz company and started selling Tampax, which was the first tampon with an applicator. But for the genius of 1930s marketing, it might have been called Tampaz instead of Tampax.

One early problem was that using tampons required women to touch their genitals. There were fears in many circles that this would lead to wanton immorality. There were also fears that tampons would devirginize teenage girls. As late as the early 1990s, Tampax still ran ads to help dispel this fear. After Madonna and Britney Spears, even the people at Tampax gave up the virginity ghost.

So much for the past. If you are adventurous, there are a couple of newer menstrual products on the market. But first, a warning. New is not always better. For instance, a few years ago we heard about a new menstrual product called the "inSync Miniform." It was about the size of a tampon but fit between your labia. It was supposed to be used on light days, but who reads the instructions? Our research assistant volunteered to try it out. This nearly resulted in a worker's compensation claim against Goofy Foot Press.

With that said, one menstrual product website that seems to be pretty conscientious is www.lunapads.com. They distribute all sorts of reusable products that you stick on or up your crotch, including Luna Pads and Natural Sea Sponge Tampons. Their motto used to be "Go With The Flow," but then they got all fancy and lost their sense of humor. Another product that's seen several incarnations since the 1930s is the menstrual cup. I think of it as a cross between a diaphragm, toilet plunger and a shot glass. Two very similar menstrual cups are The Diva Cup (made of silicone) and The Keeper (made of gum rubber). Links to both can be found at www.keeper.com. There is another product called Instead that's more like a diaphragm. Find it at www.softcup.com. None of these products work as birth control.

Be sure to check out the amazing Museum of Menstruation website: www.mum.org. It includes anything you would ever want or need to know about menstruation. And if you are doing research on menstrual products patented in the United States from 1854–1921, get a copy of a paper of the same name by Laura K. Kidd and Jane Farrel-Beck, published in Dress, 1997 Vol. 24 pp. 27-41.

Chapter Notes: Special thanks to Dr. Anne Schuchat from the Center for Disease Control in Atlanta and Nina Bender at Whitehall Laboratories for their help on TSS. Also, thanks to Harry Finley at the Museum of Menstruation for consultation on the history of sanitary napkins and tampons, and to Jane Farrel-Beck for being so generous with photocopies of her articles!

Clean Jeans, Tight Jeans, Briefs & Boxers

Chapter 43

Some guys never recover from the defeat of being toilet trained and get their revenge by avoiding soap and water. It's so easy for a man (and woman) to be clean and smell nice. All it takes is a five-minute shower, deodorant and a toothbrush. If you have a foreskin, pull the thing back and wash around it.

If you are young or don't have much of a beard, keep your stubble shaved and no one will know the difference. The daily shaving ritual gets old really fast, so count your lucky stars if your beard is wimpy or late in arriving.

Clean & Girls

Regarding sexual hygiene for women, this book defers to Betty Dodson's *Sex For One* (Harmony Books) where Ms. Dodson refers to events that occurred in her women's groups:

> During "Show and Tell" we reviewed our concerns about episiotomy scars from childbirth, inner lips that didn't match, little bumps or moles that looked strange, clitorises that were thought to be too small, and the dreaded vaginal discharge. We talked about genital hygiene and how douching could be available but not as a compulsive routine.

> Since most women have some clear or white secretion, I always considered that normal. I never used harsh commercial douching preparations.... Usually washing the exterior genitalia and reaching just inside the vaginal opening was sufficient cleansing. Before making love, I inserted a finger inside my vagina to smell and taste myself, which made me feel secure.

Regarding Ms. Dodson's reference to tasting herself, it might seem a little strange to some women, but we guys taste you all the time. It's okay, honest. Some of the feminists might say, "If we're supposed to taste ourselves, why don't you guys taste yourselves?" Plenty of us have. Besides, what flavor do you think we get when we kiss you after receiving a blow job?

It's also helpful for women to remember that the hood of the clitoris collects the same kind of cheesy stuff as the foreskin of the penis. A Q-Tip dipped in mineral oil will help remove any of the deposits that might be stuck under the hood. Also try to use a low-pH soap on your genitals. More about this in "Oral Sex—Vulvas and Honeypots."

Bidet in a Can?

While we Americans don't allow anything as functional as bidets in our bathrooms, we have invented a totally useless substitute that not only causes irritation but harms the environment as well. It's called feminine hygiene spray.

Feminine deodorants, sprays, powders and commercial douche products with names like Cherry Orchard Breeze and Morning Dew are key players in Madison Avenue's relentless campaign to create and cash in on every conceivable form of human doubt and fear. The vagina is self-cleaning. Sprays and douches can actually cause odor by disturbing the natural flora and fauna of the vagina.

Women who douche more than three times a month are said to have a three times greater chance of getting pelvic inflammatory disease than women who don't.

Trimming the Triangle

"I wax and swear by it. Have it done professionally. It's worth the money and then you can start doing it yourself. I use hot wax, not with the strips. Ingrown hairs are sometimes a problem, but it beats having an entire snatch of stubble."
female age 25

"Shaving is painful and I look about 12 years old, it grosses me out. Trimming works! Borrow a beard trimmer and go for it! One crew cut coming up!" *female age 29*

"I shave and just deal with the irritation." *female age 26*

"I shave in the summer so that when I wear my bathing suit it doesn't show. Waxing or tweezing is less irritating. When you shave, it itches terribly when it starts to grow back."
female age 49

"My husband really likes to trim my pubic area for me. He gets turned on by this. I think it's highly arousing, too." *female 45*

"I'm more aware of myself and my sexuality when I'm shaved. It feels sensual, like the first time you wear silk underwear. It's too much trouble to keep up, though. If there was an easy way, I think I'd do it more often." *female age 36*

"I used to have this lovely, neat, wonderfully behaved triangle of pubic hair. And then I turned 30 and the thing started to spread..." *female age 32*

What's amazing about the comments above is that when the first editions of this Guide went to press, they made all of the sense in the world. But based on what's been going on lately, it seems that a lot of guys are now shaving or trimming their pubic hair. In fact, we thought it was pushing the edge a decade ago to say, "A prostitute who previewed this book reports that men trim and shave too. 'I see lots of this in my line of work. Yes, big-time execs, too.'"

A lot of women say it's easier to give a blow job when a man has trimmed a bit down below, which is something that men have often said about going down on a woman. So the line between "male—big and hairy" and "female—silky and smooth" is starting to blur. As for shaving rather than trimming, guys face the same problems with itching and stubble that women always have.

Either way, all you have to do is walk into your local drugstore and see products like "Bikini Bare" and special bikini shavers to realize that a number of people trim their pubic hair. Many American women trim their pubic hair and some shave it off during the summer when they are trying to wear bikinis without looking like they just stepped off a boat from the Ukraine.

Some sexual partners get really turned on by a slick vulva. Others view this as an attempt to deface the female body. They find a furry bush to be quite sexy and equate trimming the triangle with burning down the rain forest.

Five O'Clock Shadow Where the Sun Don't Shine

If you like a close-cropped look but don't want the itching or ingrown hairs from shaving, try a men's beard trimmer. If you do shave, experiment with different types of razors. Some people say to shave only once in each direction, first with the grain of the hair, then against it. Wait a day if it needs more; otherwise rawness will result.

Problems with bumps and tenderness often result from sporadic shaving and will decrease greatly if you shave frequently. Experiment and find what's best for you.

The pubic area seems to be more tender when you are menstruating, so wait until later for plucking, waxing or shaving. If you wax, put ice on it afterward. A lot of people don't like depilatory creams, even if these products claim to be for bikini lines. Some like waxing; others say waxing and electric depilatories are fine on legs, but can be problematic between them. Some even swear that the only way to do a pubic area right is to pluck it, hair by hair. Ouch!

The Lowdown on Electrolysis & Laser Hair Removal

For any questions about hair removal of any kind, we strongly encourage you to visit www.hairtell.com. This is an exceptional website with forums that are very helpful. For the Genital Hair Removal forum, go to the "mature" area and apply for permission. Once it arrives, you'll be amazed at the number of comments. As of press time, there seemed to be a general consensus that one should be wary about the claims surrounding laser hair removal. For most people, there is nothing permanent about laser hair removal, and in the long run it can end up being more expensive to maintain than electrolysis. But who knows what advances will occur in the years to come.

A very helpful and knowledgeable electrolysis expert found through the Genital Hair Removal forum at www.hairtell.com offers the following perspective:

> "In the pubic area, there are well over 20,000 hairs packed into that small area, so one would need to remove at least 2,000 hairs just to effect a 10% removal. Proper treatment requires longer and more frequent appointments in the beginning, and tapers off to minutes every 3 to 6 months at the end. If the aggressive schedule is not followed, one could go once a month for an hour for the rest of one's life and only get to a noticeable reduction."

Part of the problem is that at any one time, huge numbers of hair follicles are dormant. So you can zap an entire area clean, but six months later find that it's almost as hairy as before. So this expert is saying that you and an experienced electrolysist need to make a treatment plan and follow it. Don't just go in for an hour or two and think it's going to work. Also keep in mind that removing only 2,000 hairs will take hours of electrolysis.

The average electrolysist works on female upper lips and chins. They are not used to firing their machine up with somebody's dick, labia or scrotum in their hand. One way of finding a trained professional in your area who does pubic deforestation is by doing an internet search on the male-to-female (MTF) transsexual chats and forums. Any guy who's getting his crotch surgically reassigned needs to first have serious electrolysis done in his pubic area. Otherwise, he'll end up having pubes growing out of his new vagina. That's because surgeons do a tuck-and-roll between the legs to refashion a vulva and vagina from a penis and scrotum. The transsexuals will usually be very helpful in sharing information about which electrolysis people in your area do a good job on pubic hair. Also see what you can find on the Genital Hair Removal forum at hairtell.com.

Hair Removal and Pain

No one in their right mind would say that electrolysis in your pubic area is going to feel as bad as, say, being in an electric chair nicknamed Old Smokey. But getting hair zapped in the nether regions can certainly put you in touch with parts of your nervous system that you never knew existed. It seems that all of the nerves that make things feel so good down there can also make it feel pretty bad when someone is sticking an electrified needle next to them. One of the big problems is that topical pain killers that work great in your mouth don't absorb through the skin in the pubic area. So be sure to talk to your electrolysist ahead of time about pain management strategies, and don't go through the ceiling if they say a little tube of numbing potion costs $50. In a perfect world, you would visit your dentist on the way to the electrolysist and get a shot of novacaine in your pubic area, giving new meaning to the term "numb nuts" if you are a guy.

Rainbow Girl Muffs

Some highly adventurous women dye their pubic hair amazing colors such as bright blue, pink, purple or green. Can you imagine? This guide endorses the concept and would love to hear a woman announce the change by blurting out, "Hon, I was abducted by aliens today!"

Hopefully, adventurous ladies like these will go out of their way to use only approved nontoxic hair dyes that won't irritate their tender tissues or stain their boyfriends' teeth.

Tight Jeans & Infections

Of the things in life that are most irritating, bladder infections rate right up there with presidential campaign speeches, unemployment and earthquake aftershocks. They are not pleasant events. Guys usually don't understand them because they seldom get this type of infection, unless it's in the form of prostatitis.

Other common female infections involve an overpopulation of yeast cells in the vagina. This can happen when the vaginal environment becomes irritated or gets out of balance, as sometimes occurs when taking antibiotics. In fact, the vaginal environment tends to be out of balance when its pH goes above 5.5. This means that a healthy vagina is a bit acidic.

Yeast infections can cause a whitish discharge that may be clumpy. There can be a strong odor and possible itching. The first time you get a yeast infection you should definitely see a gynecologist to make sure it is correctly diagnosed and properly treated. Discuss with your gynecologist how to prevent yeast infections, how to diagnose them and what medications to use in the future.

There are some events that might increase the occurrence of both bladder and/or vaginal infections. One is having intercourse when the vagina isn't well-lubricated. Vaginal irritation can also result from using rubbers that aren't adequately lubricated. Putting a water-based lubricant on the outside of a rubber can help. Both partners usually enjoy the extra slip 'n' slide feeling.

There may also be a connection between yeast infections and wearing tight jeans, pantyhose, spandex leotards and even panties. These cause a woman to sweat between her legs. This allows bacteria from the rectum to hydroplane into the vulva. One solution is to trash your tight jeans or spandex crotch-huggers. But if you are a total slave to fashion, be sure to wear cotton underpants and try cleaning your bum with a moist towelette each time you defecate. This may help cut down on the bacterial version of moonwalking. Also make sure you wipe from the front to the back. Some women say that decreasing the amount of sugar or artificial sweeteners in their diet helps to decrease the number of infections. Lubricants that contain glycerine should also be avoided if you get frequent infections.

Male partners can sometimes carry the infection without having any symptoms themselves. If that's the case, they will need to take the same medication as the woman. Otherwise, the infection will simply ping-pong back and forth between partners.

If you get bladder infections often, you might try peeing right after intercourse. It could help flush out whatever little micro-mites are waiting to make your life miserable. Also, some women find that drinking cranberry juice that's fairly concentrated helps prevent urinary tract infections, while drinking lots of carbonated drinks helps to cause them. (Cranberry doesn't kill the infection, but it does seem to make it more difficult for the germs to drill into the bladder walls.)

And finally, it might be helpful if both men and women accept the fact that bladder and vaginal infections fall into the category of shared problems rather than just her problem. Guys who enjoy doing oral sex almost always know a woman's baseline state and can often detect changes before she might be aware of them. It might be nice if the woman felt comfortable enough to tell her lover, "I hope that you won't hesitate to let me know if the environment down there gets a little, uh, tropical." Of course, partners should know that the environment of the vagina changes with the status of a woman's menstrual cycle. For instance, the acidity of the vagina changes when she is ready to conceive and the discharge becomes more thin and clear.

Is Smoking Sexy?

There are plenty of people who make a phenomenal effort to keep themselves neat, clean and attractive but still fill their lungs with cigarette smoke. Living with a contradiction like this is testimony to how difficult it can be to break the nicotine habit, especially when some of the huge tobacco companies have apparently tried to increase the addictive properties of cigarettes.

While there has been a substantial decline in tar sucking among most of us, young women remain the one group who are still puffing away as much as ever. This fact hasn't escaped the attention of ciga-rette makers, who work hard to attract the interest of young women.

Studies show that people who don't begin smoking before the age of twenty-one aren't likely to ever start. As a result, more and more of the tobacco industry's advertising emphasis will be on getting teenag-ers to smoke. **UPDATE:** Smoking is up among all teens, male and female. Way to go, Joe Camel!

Cigarette ads are populated with shots of sexy women who seem happy, confident and in control, but you almost never see the ciga-rettes hanging out of their mouths, nor do you see them contorting their lips so they can try to blow the smoke out the side. These ads never have scratch and sniff patches to let you know what your breath will smell like once you begin smoking, nor do they offer free coupons to the cleaners, whom you will be visiting way more often if you smoke. Young women are also impacted by the fact that most women's maga-zines make huge revenues from cigarette ads. As a result, women's magazines are hesitant to boycott cigarette ads or run articles about the health hazards of smoking. They'll harp on every tragic disease in the world except cigarette-related heart attacks and cancers.

Cigarette smoke and birth control pills that contain anything more than progesterone combine to create a major health risk in women above the age of thirty-three. And women who take birth con-trol pills and smoke have a greater incidence of bruising. (What about nonsmoking pill takers who are exposed to ambient cigarette smoke? Does the ambient smoke put them at extra risk? One should assume the answer is yes until credible research is done that proves the oppo-site.) Even dogs who live in homes with cigarette smokers die signifi-cantly sooner than those with nonsmoking masters.

You won't believe how bad her breath smells after just one cigarette.

Chapter Notes: Thanks to Kate at www.cleansheets.com for some of the depilatory tips used in this chapter.

Dear Paul,

My boyfriend says that his finger starts to sting when he's had it in my vagina. It hasn't stopped him from wanting to have sex, but I'm worried that I have an infection or that my vagina is too acidy inside. I had an exam at the doctor's, and she says everything is okay. But I still think something is wrong. There are things I can buy at the drugstore for vaginal infections. Do you have any advice?

Amber in Auburn

Dear Readers,

I can't give Amber medical advice. However, I can suggest that we all shrink until we are very, very small, so we can take a trip up Amber's vagina. Given how a healthy vagina is fairly acidic, some of you might think of this as an acid trip. (If Amber's boyfriend gets his prayers for sex answered before we're done, it will probably feel like an acid trip.)

One reason for this venture into Amber's vagina is to show why her boyfriend's fingers sting when exploring inside her maidenly folds. Another reason is to show how unwise it can be to assume that over-the-counter drugs will automatically make a vaginal infection go away, even if Amber really had one. Vaginal infections are not all the same. The way to cure a bacterial infection can be nearly the opposite from how to treat a yeast infection.

So let's look at what makes Amber's vagina hum, besides flowers and kisses from her boyfriend.

While we could think of Amber's vagina as a warm, wet, heavenly place that a lot guys and some of the girls she knows would like to visit, it's also instructive to think of it as an underground jungle or a massively complex rainforest, an incredible ecosystem with bacterial flora and fauna that keep the whole thing in balance.

One of the most important residents of Amber's vagina is a bacteria called Lactobacilli. Actually, there are several different types of Lactobacilli, and too much of it can cause as much discomfort as too little. When things are in balance, friendly families of Lactobacilli produce hydrogen peroxide and lactic acid in amounts that are helpful.

The hydrogen peroxide helps kill undesirable bacteria when they try to intrude. The lactic acid helps to maintain the acidic environment that's so essential for healthy functioning. It also makes the fingers of Amber's boyfriend sting when they have been basting inside of her vagina. This is a property of all healthy vaginas. Their acidic nature will make most people's fingers sting if they stay in there long enough.

Another positive effect of the Lactobacilli is that they have tiny projections that stick out from their cell bodies. These projections clasp onto the cell walls of the vagina. This prevents other bacteria and germs from attaching at these points. You might think of it as aluminum siding for the inside of Amber's vagina.

If anything happens that causes the Lactobacilli to stop reproducing, the stage is set for infections and uncomfortable conditions. For instance, let's say Amber starts taking antibiotics for a lung infection. This kills off the wicked bacteria in her chest, but it also starts to kill off the friendly bacteria in her vagina. As a result, the lactic acid that's produced by the good bacteria will decrease and the alkalinity in Amber's vagina will increase. The increased alkalinity or rise in pH will cause fewer Lactobacilli to reproduce. A nasty spiral is created where the population of the good bacteria stars falling faster than a dropped ball.

As the population of the good Lactobacilli begins to crash, another of its important by-products (hydrogen peroxide) will suddenly be in short supply. Unfriendly bacteria will have an easier time taking up squatter's rights in Amber's vagina. Also, the Lactobacilli shield that was protecting the walls of Amber's vagina will weaken. Unfriendly anaerobic bacteria with names like Gardnerella and Coccoid will be able to invade the cell walls in Amber's vagina. When this happens, the woman gets what is called bacterial vaginosis or BV. One of the most common symptoms of BV is a discharge with a fishy odor. This can worsen during menstruation and with the friction of intercourse.

Another kind of vaginal catastrophe can occur from virtually the opposite situation, when the population of Lactobacilli suddenly rises and too much lactic acid and hydrogen peroxide are produced. Natural sugars start being fermented into carbon dioxide, alcohol, formic acid and acetic acid. This causes itching and irritation. The official term is

564 • Clean Jeans, Tight Jeans, Briefs & Boxers

cytolytic vaginosis or CV. When this occurs inside of Amber's vagina, her boyfriend will need more than prayers and flowers to get between her legs.

CV shares the same symptoms as a yeast infection: itching, burning, painful intercourse and a slight discharge. As a result, it is often misdiagnosed as a yeast infection. This is one of the reasons why a woman who is having problems with recurring vaginitis needs both a sharp gynecologist and a good knowledge of how her vagina works. Over-the-counter drugs for yeast infections won't touch CV.

A third problem that can occur in Amber's vagina is when she really does get a yeast infection, commonly referred to as Candida. A fourth type of infection is caused by a protozoa known as Trich or Trichomonas Vaginalis. Yet another kind of vaginitis is known as Noninfectious Vaginitis. Instead of being caused by funky organisms, the source of irritation for Noninfectious Vaginitis can be anything from feminine hygiene spray and regular body soap to perfumed toilet paper, laundry detergent, exercise bikes and tampons.

We've had a more intimate look inside of Amber's vagina than most, and some readers will wonder why we didn't stop and play with her G-Spot. But it never hurts to reach a little farther and learn a little more.

Abortion? Adoption?
Chapter 44

A large percentage of women who get abortions were using contraceptives at the time of intercourse. That's because even the best contraceptives occasionally fail, or sometimes a rubber breaks, or sometimes we forget to take a pill.

If you are pregnant, there are a number of different things you can do. This chapter talks about a couple of them.

What If You Just Found Out You Are Pregnant and Didn't Want to Be?

There are plenty of people who will offer advice. Some of it will be helpful. One of your challenges will be in finding someone who will listen and help you think things out instead of feeling the need to tell you what to do. In addition to talking to your partner, you might try to find a level-headed friend, family member, doctor, nurse or teacher who you trust. You can also call your local family planning center. They deal with this all of the time and tend to be helpful.

The one thing you want to avoid are "crisis pregnancy centers." These are often run by anti-abortion groups and they have a very specific agenda.

There are many people who have opted for abortion and many who have had unplanned children. Most will tell you that they did the right thing. Whichever way you decide, keep in mind that millions of people have had to face the exact same thing that you are— even though you may feel like the loneliest person on the face of the earth.

In case you are wondering about the emotional aspects of having an abortion, studies show that most women who have abortions don't report an increase in depression (as a group) for any more than a week or two after the abortion, if that. One of these studies was funded by a very biased agency that was hoping to find the opposite result. On the other hand, your own personal beliefs might not allow for abortion, in which case your options will be whether to raise the baby yourself or give it up for adoption. There are plenty of agencies that will help with the latter, but not many that will help the parent of an unplanned child who is trying to raise it on her own.

Please be aware that some of the strongest anti-abortion proponents are highly supportive while you are still pregnant, but are quite stingy and punitive when it comes to helping the unmarried mom of a toddler or older child. To many of these groups, you are only of value as the physical vessel that is incubating the unborn child. Once the baby is born, they won't want to have anything to do with you.

Whether you choose to have an abortion or to have the baby, it's important that you make your mind up as soon as possible. Many people who are faced with unwanted pregnancies tend to be indecisive and don't act as soon as they might. If they opt for an abortion, it is sometimes later in the pregnancy when the procedure might be more complicated. And if they decide to have the baby, they sometimes don't go for prenatal care until later in the pregnancy. This is especially true for teenagers, and it places them at high risk. Delaying prenatal care will endanger both yourself and your baby.

If you decide to keep the baby, make sure you have a support system in place to help after the baby is born.

A Special Note on Giving Your Baby Up for Adoption

There are thousands of loving couples who can't have a baby of their own and desperately want to adopt one. These couples tend to have been married for quite a while. Most have stable homes, good relationships and solid incomes. They will give your child a lifetime of love and care. Unfortunately, many of these couples must wait as long as seven years before they can adopt a baby, since not many single parents are giving their babies up for adoption these days. Part of the problem is that younger moms are often encouraged by their nonpregnant peers to keep the baby (easy for them to say!). Unwed moms often have the unrealistic fantasy that keeping the baby will make their lives better, or that the baby's father will want to marry them. This seldom happens.

One of the really nice things about adoption in this day and age is that the pregnant mom gets to interview the couples who want to adopt her baby. She gets to decide which couple she wants to raise the baby. That way she will know her baby is being raised and loved by people she likes.

If you have medical questions or want to schedule an appointment with the nearest Planned Parenthood, call toll-free 1-800-230-PLAN.

The Birth Control Case–Sperm V. Egg
Chapter 45

Why is it that some men will care for a car or favorite baseball glove with meticulous detail, but forget about birth control when they are having intercourse? Why do so many of America's women go nearly insane over one little zit or take hours getting dressed for a party, but throw all caution to the wind about getting herpes or HPV? And why is our nation's rather feeble program to educate its young about sexually transmitted infections little more than a thinly veiled attempt to discourage them from having sex? It is a program that talks about disease, but rarely mentions pleasure. Does it need to be this way?

To Use or Not to Use

Researcher Meg Gerrard spoke to college students about sex and birth control. Later, she gave a series of follow-up tests about what she had presented. She found that students who felt less comfortable about their own sexuality remembered significantly less about birth control, even if they were *A* students in other subjects. On the other hand, students who scored highest on measures of sexual self-esteem were able to remember the most about birth control.

These findings were just as true for men as for women. Gerrard found that while being uncomfortable about sex is not enough to keep a person from having sex, it is enough to keep him or her from using birth control.

One way that people who are ambivalent about sex get around this conflict is by having sex that isn't planned or discussed ahead of time. That way, they can plead temporary insanity if they have to deal with a harsh conscience, or a real-life mom and dad if they are still living at home.

This Book's Approach to Birth Control

Most books on sex have birth control chapters that read like a Chilton manual. Not this one. *War and Peace* maybe, but not a Chilton manual.

Sharing the responsibility for birth control often increases the sexual trust and enjoyment in a relationship. It's the sort of thing that people do when they care about each other, rather than just making it the responsibility of the woman or ignoring the need altogether. Making birth control a mutual project could be the ante for having better sex.

This chapter looks at several ways of keeping a guy's wad from sliming a girl's egg. Keep in mind that one of the factors in choosing a birth control method is whether or not you are at risk for getting a sexually transmitted infection. Sexually transmitted infections are discussed in the chapter that follows.

Also, please contact your healthcare provider or local Planned Parenthood office for complete information about birth control. Your best bet is to speak with someone who works with birth control day in and day out, and who can use his or her practical wisdom to help you select a long-term option that will work best for you.

Finally! The New Birth Control Halo for Your Cervix

The chances are good that many of the women who are now taking the pill will eventually be switching to the NuvaRing. The NuvaRing has lots in support of it:

> You put it in your vagina on day one and take it out on day twenty-one. That's all she wrote. No pills to take, no patches to put on and pull off, no mess, no hassle.

> The amount of hormones in the NuvaRing are much lower than what you get from most pills or the patch. Because the hormones absorb directly into the blood stream, the dosage in the ring is even lower than most birth control pills.

> It doesn't cause some women to gain weight like the pill or patch. That's because the dose is so low.

> You'll be hard-pressed to find a method of birth control that's more effective, more reliable, and more user-friendly.

What are the downsides? You've gotta touch yourself, just like if you were popping in an OB Tampon. It's truly amazing how many women will let some guy with a fast line stick his penis inside of them, but go "ICK!" when it comes to putting their own finger inside their own vagina. Go figure. If guys had vaginas, we wouldn't be able to keep our fingers out of them.

The NuvaRing sits in the same place as a diaphragm, only you don't have to worry if it's exactly in place because it wasn't designed to be a barrier. If it moves around, fine. Also, one size fits all.

If for some reason you are still having your period at the end of day 28 when you need to pop in the new NuvaRing, it's no problem. You can wear a tampon at the same time that you are wearing the NuvaRing; it won't impact the absorption. Maybe the NuvaRing and tampon can enjoy a conversation or do some intravaginal bonding.

As for aesthetics, think of the NuvaRing as a cross between a cockring and a smaller version of an angel's halo, not that anyone is going to think that the pope canonized your cervix.

At this point you might be wondering how the NuvaRing stays put in the back of your vagina. Is it an anti-gravitation device? Maybe. But the muscles in your vagina will hold it in place, and most women can't feel it. In fact, one nurse practitioner tries it out on some women's vaginas when she's giving them exams. Most can't even feel it. And due to some strange law of intercourse physics, few guys can feel it either. But if for some reason your partner can, you can easily take it out for up to three hours at a time. If he can't finish doing his business in three hours, send him to the bathroom with a jar of hand cream and a dirty magazine, and pop your NuvaRing back where it belongs.

Hormonal Birth Control Patch, a.k.a. OrthoEvra

Remember seeing pictures of pirates who wore a patch over one eye? Now you can wear your own patch and be just as bad. Approved in late 2001, this is another hormonally-based contraceptive that eliminates having to take birth control pills.

The new patch, sold under the brand name OrthoEvra, is a small 2-inch square that is applied to the skin. It can be placed on the hips, butt, abdomen, upper arm, or shoulder blade, but not on the breasts or extremities. The patch contains a dose of hormones similar to birth control pills. However, instead of having to swallow them in pill form, the hormones are absorbed through your skin and you only have to deal with it once a week. Once the patch is on, you leave it on and forget about it for seven days. When the week is up, you take it off, put a new one on and you're good to go. After three consecutive weeks with a new patch, you go patch-free for a week to have a period. (Yippee!) Then you start over again, so it's a 28-day cycle overall.

When used correctly, the new patch is up to 99% effective in preventing pregnancy. While it is a great new method for some women, it has similar concerns, good and bad, that regular birth control pills do. Therefore, it's not for everyone. But it's still a good alternative that many women are trying.

While the patch can cause skin irritation, its biggest problem is that it currently comes in only one color: Fake Caucasian. Hopefully the people at Ortho will come to their fashion senses and start producing the patch in all kinds of neat shapes and colors. How about a pretty rose, a pair of bright red smooching lips, or a patch in the shape of a lightening bolt? Or maybe even a big sperm with a gun to its head…

NOTE: As of press time, they still didn't make a "patch grande" with enough hormones for the larger loving lady. So if you weigh in at over 198 pounds, the patch is not yet for you. The reason why it won't work on bigger babes is because the hormone has to make its way through the skin and through the fat layers before it is effective.

The Pill

There are more than fifty different kinds of birth control pills. Most are a combination of estrogen and progesterone, although the original birth control pill was made of progesterone only. Progesterone-only pills are called POPs or mini-pills.

Women over thirty-five who smoke or who have certain health risks should not take birth control pills that contain estrogen. However, they might do just fine with pills that have progesterone only, or the DepoProvera shot.

DepoProvera—Three Months at a Shot

DepoProvera is a progesterone-only pill-in-a-shot that lasts for twelve weeks. Women seem to either love it or hate it. But if you end up hating it, you are stuck with it for an entire three months, since there's no way of getting it out of your body once it's inside. A smart way to approach taking Depo is to first take a progesterone-only pill for two or three cycles. If that works well, then try the shot.

One of main side effects of Depo is irregular bleeding. Some women bleed a lot, some don't bleed at all. If you do have irregular bleeding on Depo, it usually stops after the first three to six months. One of the benefits for some women is that Depo stops their periods altogether for three months. Also, it has an extremely low rate of failure as long as you remember to take the shot every three months.

Because Depo only releases progesterone, it can be safe for women who smoke or who are in high risk groups.

There's Nothing New about Seasonale

The idea of stopping menstrual periods for three months at a time is nothing new. Women have been doing it for years by taking certain monophasic birth control pills for eighty-four straight days. This is often prescribed for women who have serious difficulties with their periods. Now, all women are being given the option of eliminating two-out-of-three periods, although there is a lot of debate about his.

With Seasonale, you get eighty-four monophasic birth control pills. You take one each day. Then you take seven placebo pills at the end so you can have a period. This makes it a ninety-one day cycle. The trouble is, Seasonale is currently so expensive that few people are using it. If you want to eliminate your periods but don't want to pay dearly for the privilege, talk to your healthcare professional about what kind of regular birth control pills you should take and how to go about it. These will end up being the same kind of pills that are in Seasonale, but without the added cost. They will be normal, monophasic estrogen/progestrone pills that you take for eighty-four straight days. Nothing fancy there. ("Monophasic" means the dose in each pill is the same.)

If you have trouble remembering to take pills, do not try to eliminate your periods in this way. If you've forgotten to take a couple of pills early on, you might have to wait nearly three months to find out if you are pregnant.

What About the Tampon and Pad Manufacturers?

You do the math—if women have only four menstrual periods a year instead of twelve, that's several zillion fewer tampons and pads each year. While it is wise to have a rigorous debate about eliminating menstrual periods, it will be interesting to see if the tampon and pad manufacturers play a role in making sure that the "period-once-a-month" argument is well-heard and well-funded.

Forget to Take a Pill?

If you forget to take your birth control pill, check with your physician's office right away. They will tell you if you should double up the next day. If it's been less than twelve hours since you were supposed to take it, some physicians will recommend taking one when you remember and one a few hours later.

Depending on the timing and the circumstances, it is possible that some form of emergency contraception might be helpful. Emergency contraception is discussed at the end of this chapter.

Why Some Birth Control Pills Can Zap Your Zits and Your Sex Drive

You will be hard-pressed to find a woman whose sex drive goes up after she begins to take birth control pills. That's because the pill reduces free testosterone in the body. It's the reduction in free testosterone that helps clear up the skin in about 50% of the women who take certain types of birth control pills. But as your zits dry up, so might your sex drive. Fortunately, this is not the case for all or even a majority of women.

Research on pill usage and libido (sexual desire) is strange and contradictory. The impact of the pill on a woman's sex drive can range from nothing at all to being so severe that she can no longer stand to be touched by her partner. In one study, women who took triphasic birth control pills actually reported higher libido and sexual pleasure than other pill takers, but this study has not been replicated.

An excellent choice might be the NuvaRing, which delivers a much lower dose of hormones into your body than most birth control pills. Another good choice for women who have already had a baby might be the Mirena IUD.

If you have less desire after taking the pill, tell your healthcare provider and at the very least try a different type of pill. It is unlikely that the problem is in your head, unless you discovered that the bum was two-timing you at the same time you started taking the pill.

Breast Feeding & Birth Control

Millions of women who breast feed their infants also enjoy having sex. While breast-feeding appears to provide natural birth control, there can be significant exceptions, especially if the infant is older than six months, is sleeping through the night, or is taking solid foods. If you do take birth control pills while nursing, you might want to avoid pills that contain estrogen, since estrogen can suppress milk production. Some people also fear that it might find its way into the milk supply. Birth control pills that contain only progesterone usually do not decrease the milk supply. In fact, your body uses its own natural progesterone to help keep you from getting pregnant while you nurse.

If you don't want to get pregnant, be sure to discuss the matter of nursing and birth control with your healthcare provider.

IUDs—The Most Reliable & Cost-Effective Birth Control

There's a new kind of IUD called the Mirena. It delivers a very low dose of progesterone and is highly effective. It is placed in the uterus and can be left there for five straight years, or you can have it removed earlier. IUDs can be an excellent birth control choice for women who have had at least one child. They are extremely safe and there is virtually no user failure, although there can be a lot of cramping the first few days after installation.

The only part of an IUD that can be felt is two little nylon strings that hang down from it. The strings are there so a woman can reach up and feel them after each period to make sure the IUD didn't slip out. If a man is able to feel the little strings during intercourse, ask your health care provider to snip them shorter.

IUDs are recommended for women in long-term, monogamous relationships because the strings can make it easier for sexually transmitted infections to get into the uterus. However, it's fine to have casual sex partners while wearing the IUD as long as condoms are worn. The strings do not bother the condom.

In a recent study of different types of birth control, the IUD was considered to be the most cost effective and reliable method over a five-year period. However, the initial cost is higher than with other methods such as birth control pills. Unfortunately, while many insurance companies will cover the cost of sterilization, they won't cover the cost of IUDs. Perhaps this is why IUDs are much more popular in Europe than in the United States.

Diaphragm This

Diaphragms used to be as common as sex itself, but now not many women use them. They are not as reliable as some methods and they require the old goop-and-insert routine each and every time. However, when hormonal methods don't work or you have a medical condition that makes hormonal methods unsafe, don't discount the diaphragm. It has no hormonal side effects. And think of the fine-motor skills you'll learn in getting the thing in and out. The diaphragm might also be good for a woman who doesn't need to use it often, for example, someone who has a long-distance partner where most of the sex is on the phone anyway. For those of you with latex allergies, they are finally making nonlatex diaphragms out of silicone, which is the same material that finer dildos are made from.

Some women find it frustrating to get the diaphragm into place and you shouldn't use it if you have a reaction to spermicide. It also has to be fitted and it can cause a feeling of pressure on the bladder. You have to leave it in for eight hours after your last intercourse. If your man is the kind who does a rapid reload and fire, you'll need to squirt in extra spermicide. For some strange reason, the failure rate of the diaphragm is much higher if you have already had a baby.

Cervical Cap

The cervical cap is a like a rubber thimble that forms a suction on your cervix. For some women it feels better than the diaphragm and it doesn't put pressure on the bladder. Other women don't like the feeling of suction on the cervix. After intercourse, you'll need to leave it in place for eight hours. As with the diaphragm, the failure rate is much higher if you've already had a baby. You aren't going to find many healthcare professionals who know how to fit a cervical cap, and the rate of effectiveness isn't going to overwhelm too many people.

Rubbers & Rubber Wisdom

After much painstaking research, we have come to the conclusion that what you slop on the outside of a condom is almost as important as what you stuff into it. In the sections that follow, we'll tell you more about that as well as describing different cuts of condom and what to do when your rubber is a lemon.

Nowadays, rubbers or condoms can be purchased nearly every-where except for maybe your local post office or Christian Science Reading Room. But you still need to hand them to a cashier before they are yours to wear, unless you get them from a vending machine or buy them by mail.

For some people, the ability to purchase a rubber depends upon who's working the cash register. This is especially true in small towns where there is no such thing as retail anonymity. In some small towns, a person would attract less attention knocking off the local bank than buying a pack of rubbers.

Getting rubbers by mail order helps alleviate this problem, but in some households plain unmarked envelopes garner as much attention as a singing telegram.

Rubber Scoop

Back in his academic days, the author of this book was particularly fascinated with the study of slow viruses. As a result, he figured something serious was brewing when reports of a lethal new sex germ started trickling out of San Francisco. Knowing what happened each night in the bars and baths up there, he assumed it would be an epidemiological nightmare for both gays and straights. Fearing the worst, he began using rubbers before it was fashionable.

When he first started bagging himself, his girlfriend scoffed, hissed, puffed, and all but threw him out of bed and into the nearby LaBrea Tar Pits. "Those damn things give me bladder infections," she snarled. Sure enough, she got a bladder infection. And that's when he learned that the word 'pre-lubricated' on the outside of the package is someone's idea of a joke. No matter how wet she might be, it's best to add lubrication when using a condom. Otherwise, the added friction can cause a woman to have bladder or vaginal infections.

To help put the slip back in your slide, slop some water-based lubricant on the outside of your rubber before you have intercourse. This will help compensate for a number of rubber ills, and it will help intercourse with a bagged penis feel much, much sweeter.

The extra lubrication also helps to make up for the loss of precum or natural lubrication that normally drips out of the penis. The condom catches the precum, like everything else.

And as long as you've got the lube handy, it never hurts to put a dab on the head of your penis before throwing the condom over it. Along with your precum, this will help the head of your penis get an extra ride with each stroke, as it slides against the condom material.

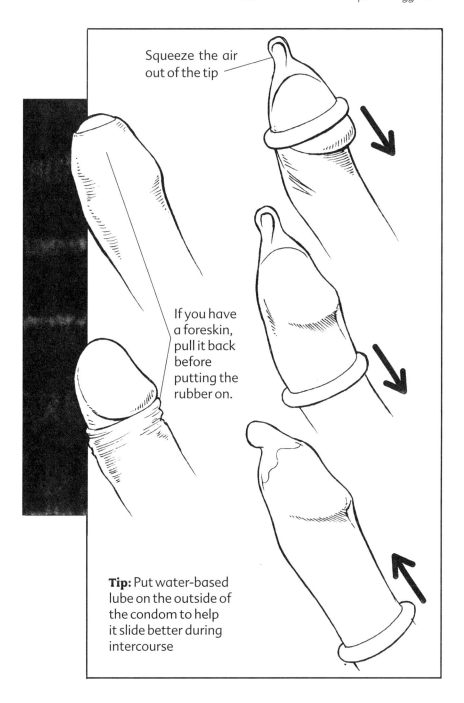

Squeeze the air out of the tip

If you have a foreskin, pull it back before putting the rubber on.

Tip: Put water-based lube on the outside of the condom to help it slide better during intercourse

For the Ride of Your Life!

Chronic Rubber Busters

Researcher Bruce Voeller and associates studied a group of young men who were chronic rubber busters. Contrary to what you might think, these chronic rubber busters weren't hung any bigger than the average guy and they hadn't used Vaseline as a lubricant. Petroleum jelly, i.e. Vaseline, is an oil-based lubricant that does to latex rubbers what AIDS does to the body.

Voeller and associates found that almost all of the chronic rubber busters were using ordinary hand creams like Nivea, Johnson's Baby Oil, Vaseline Intensive Care, Corn Huskers, or Jergens to lubricate the outside of their rubbers. These guys assumed that since the hand creams washed off easily they weren't oil-based. WRONG. Almost any type of hand cream will weaken a latex rubber by ninety percent in less than sixty seconds, especially those that contain mineral oil. The same can be true for body powders. The safest lubricants are contraceptive jellies or water-based products like KY Jelly sold at supermarkets or drugstores. For more on lubes, see the chapter "Sex Fluids."

Another thing that can help make a rubber break is if you don't squeeze all of the air out of the tip before rolling it down your penis.

If a Condom Breaks or Doesn't Come Out When You Do

Nasty, nasty, nasty. If you were using a condom for birth control and discover that it broke while in service, consider taking Plan B (see "emergency contraception" on page 585). Plan B is a morning-after pill that is reasonably effective in preventing pregnancy.

In the meantime, do not inject birth control foam or jelly into the vagina. The pressure might push the ejaculate up into the cervix. The same is true for douching. Instead, try inserting a contraceptive suppository if you've got one. Wash your external genitals and pee. And for heaven sakes, if you honestly think that douching with Pepsi or Coke is going to do anything but prove that you're the world's biggest fool, nothing this book has to say is going to count for much.

Fear of Condoms

If you have deep feelings for your partner and fear that using a condom will ruin your spontaneity or somehow dampen the moment, please read the following to him or her:

"I love you way too much to risk putting our relationship through the strain of having to deal with an unwanted pregnancy. I also love you way too much to risk giving you something that I may have gotten from a toilet seat somewhere. (Leave out who you were on the toilet seat with.) So if we are both serious about being together, let's work on a timetable for ditching the condoms. To do this, we need to get tested for sexually transmitted infections, and we have to start using an effective method of birth control. Then we can work on dumping the condoms."

Condoms That Cum in Fifty-five Different Sizes

Condoms that come in fifty-five different sizes—really? Why not get latex gloves that come in fifty-five sizes as well?

Ah, the wonders of the internet. As of press time, one of the rages on the internet was being able to buy condoms that come in fifty-five sizes. You download a sizing kit, measure away, and place your order. Interestingly, the main proponent of the fifty-five sizes is a man by the name of Adam Glickman. Mr. Glickman has written a number of fear-mongering articles about why men supposedly need fifty-five sizes. Often absent is mention that Mr. Glickman is president of the company that makes the fifty-five condoms.

Also, in order to get the sizing kit, you need to supply your email address. Then, if you order the condoms, Mr. Glickman's company also has your mailing address. As for why men might need so many sizes, nobody has a clue except for Mr. Glickman.

Extra Large Condoms

If you are really lucky and need a bigger size condom than the rest of us, there are several choices on the market. But keep in mind that normal rubbers can inflate to the size of a watermelon.

Also, if the reasons you are buying the bigger rubbers is to impress your friends or a partner, the truth is going to come out once your pants are down. So why create an added expectation that you might not be able to fill? Plus, if you get the extra large size and don't need them, they are more likely to slip off during intercourse.

Baggy Rubbers?

Some condom companies are now manufacturing rubbers that are extra-baggy around the head. They fit snugly around the base of your penis, but the top inch or two bags out like the Tommy Hilfiger pants that the gangbanger wannabes wear. This lets the head of your penis slosh around inside the rubber, which, believe it or not, can feel really nice. (Baggy-headed rubbers are different from those with reservoir tips, which have a little finger-like tip at the end of the rubber that supposedly collects cum.)

Baggy-headed brands include the Pleasure Plus, the Trojan Ultra Pleasure, Lifestyle's Xtra Pleasure and the Inspiral. Each has its own sensation and it is fun to experiment. Who knows, you might just find that good-old-fashioned rubbers with none of the fancy features suit you just fine.

The one place where rubbers need to fit snugly is around the base of the penis. Otherwise, they might slip off. The penis usually starts shrinking right after ejaculation, so a guy shouldn't keep thrusting after he comes. He also needs to hold on to the edge of the rubber with his fingers when he's pulling out.

So what about all those situations when a man comes before his sweetheart? What about her sexual pleasure if he's supposed to pull out? Help her come before intercourse. That's why Father Nature invented vibrators and oral sex. Or once you begin having intercourse, one of you can reach down with your fingers or a vibrator to help her get more stimulation. Another way to increase the stimulation is for the woman to be in a position where she can push her clitoris against her partner's pubic bone. Also consider oral sex after intercourse.

Reservoir Tips?

Some rubber brands make a big deal about having reservoir tips to hold a guy's ejaculate. There are a couple of problems with this concept. The first is that most reservoir tips hold about 2.9 ml. of ejaculate. While half of all guys produce 2.9 ml. or less, there's still another fifty percent of guys who produce more than 2.9 ml., which means their tips runneth over.

The other problem with reservoir tips is the assumption that they really do hold the fluid. Reservoir tip or not, it's a good idea to leave a half-inch or so of space at the end of the rubber. Just be sure to squish the air out of it before rolling it down the shaft of your penis.

Rock'n'roll question: Did the geezer-rock band *10c.c.* take their name from what they assumed was the volume of the average male ejaculation? If so, they guessed way too high.

Throat Hygiene

With the apparent increase in oral sex, healthcare professionals are seeing more sexually transmitted infections in the back of people's throats. To avoid something disgusting like a gonorrhea infection where your tonsils ought to be, consider bagging a penis before sucking on it. The only trouble is, condoms aren't known for their appetizing flavors. Worse yet, a lot of the condoms that call themselves *flavored* taste truly disgusting.

The flavoring on condoms isn't embedded into the latex, so it comes off as quick as some guys. And most condoms are pre-lubed, which means you get to enjoy the bitter taste of the pre-lube.

As of press time, one brand of flavored condoms that seemed to taste okay were those made by Trustex. If you can, find nonlubricated rubbers for blow jobs. If the initial taste of latex bothers you, rinse your mouth out with something like mouthwash, cognac, or toothpaste first, but make sure it's not something that reacts with the latex.

Other Rubber Tips & Trivia

A guy who doesn't feel comfortable using rubbers during intercourse might try wearing them while jerking off. This could help him get used to the feel.

One book on sex cautions against using colored rubbers, since some of the dyes may not be safe or colorfast. They might turn a penis or vagina red, green, blue, yellow, magenta, or maybe even hot pink. If you are buying colored condoms, just make sure they come from a name-brand manufacturer.

Some guys tie off the end of a spent rubber before throwing it in the trash. This is similar to tying the end of a balloon, but for slightly different purposes.

Don't recycle your rubbers. Use a new one each time you have intercourse whether you come or not. Don't carry them around in a wallet. Don't put them in the glove compartment of a car. They don't like that kind of heat.

His goal is not to stretch the skin, but to get the blood circulating deep inside of the folds. He should do your entire vulva, including the outer lips, inner lips and the clitoral hood. Then, if it's comfortable, he can gently insert a well-lubricated thumb into the opening of your vagina and rest it there. His forefinger should be on the outside, resting on the skin that's between your vulva and anus. He then clasps the tissue that's between his thumb and forefinger and massages. This stimulates the part of your genitals that stretch wider when you have intercourse. (The ceiling of a vagina doesn't stretch as much as the floor part because the pubic bone is right above it.)

#3. Consider purchasing two or three penis-shaped objects or dildos that range in size from small to large. Start by lubing up your vagina in addition to the smallest dildo. Once you become comfortable inserting that and moving it around inside your vagina, move up to the next size. This process should be done over several weeks and not all in one night. The women who run www.touchofawoman.com can be very helpful with this process and they have products especially designed for this.

#4. Once you are comfortable with these steps, have your partner rest the head of his well-lubed penis at the opening of your vagina, but no farther. A day or two later, have him move in about a quarter-of-an-inch if it is comfortable for you. Try just a little extra each time you are together, as long you feel comfortable with it. As for intercourse positions, you'll want to be really conservative. Stay with the classic missionary position where you are on your back and your legs are slightly spread. Avoid rear-entry positions and stay away from anything where your legs are flexed. Any flexing of the knees tends to compress or shorten the available thrusting space in the vagina. Also, you might find that having an orgasm before intercourse helps a great deal.

#5. Using store-bought lubrication is an absolute must. It can be fun to experiment with different types of lube. Some offer more sensation, some more cushioning. Rub them between your fingers to see how they impact your ability to feel the ridges. I would also caution you against using any lubes that have glycerin in them. While this is not a problem for many women, it does create the potential for vaginal infections. Why tempt the Fates with another negative association to sex?

Do experiment with different brands until you find one that you like best; however, don't use the ones with ribs or nubs if you are having anal sex. The next time you want to have extra fun with your friends, sacrifice a couple of latex rubbers by blowing them up really big. If you have helium, you can fly them to the moon.

Reality Hits the Skids

There is a female version of a rubber that's inserted into the vagina rather than rolled over a penis. It's called Reality in the US or Femidon in the UK. (Femidon—what a hideous name for something they want you to stick into your most private space, not that Reality makes you wet with anticipation.) In spite of early hopes, Reality hasn't made much of a splash.

Reality is made from polyurethane instead of latex. Because it sits in the vagina, the man doesn't have to pull out as soon as he comes. It helps women to feel that they have more control in protecting themselves, and some women report that the ring around the outside of the condom stimulates the clitoris during intercourse.

Unfortunately, Reality's birth control properties might be less than optimal and it isn't cheap. It is kind of big and strange, but if you're the type who's already been abducted by aliens and had your genitals probed with interplanetary sex tools, this should be no big deal.

The woman's condom is also being used by some straight and gay couples for anal intercourse, although it's doubtful that the instructions include this small detail.

Polyurethane Rubbers

A few years ago there was a lot of hype about the new polyurethane rubbers with names like the Durex Avanti and Trojan Supra. The idea was that a condom that crinkles like a plastic grocery bag might work better than one that blows up like a circus balloon. In the ensuing years, plenty of guys have put their groceries in the Avanti and Supra, and the results haven't been earth-shaking. Early studies showed that these condoms break more often than latex rubbers. Given that they don't grip the penis as well, they are more likely to slip off. Also, because they are made of polyurethane, it was assumed that they would do a better job of transferring the warmth of the vagina onto the penis.

This has not proven to be the case for most couples. However, they are a fine alternative if you are allergic to latex, and somewhere between 2% and 10% of people really are allergic to latex.

Spermicides —Films, Foams, Suppositories & Jellies

Spermicides are chemicals that are used to kill sperm and hopefully reduce the risk of pregnancy. They come in various forms to be placed inside the vagina before intercourse, including films, foams, suppositories, and jellies. Most are made with the chemical nonoxynol-9 (N-9). When used by themselves, spermicides are much less effective than other birth control methods, including condoms. If you are using spermicides for protection against pregnancy, it is best to use them along with condoms.

Spermicides can be bought over-the-counter, and they might be a good alternative for women who can't use hormonal methods. However, they can be messy and they taste really nasty. They can also cause irritation in either partner. This means that spermicides should only be used by monogamous couples where there is no chance of exchanging sexually transmitted infections. Spermicidally-lubricated condoms can cause the same kind of irritation and should only be used by true-blue couples for the sole purpose of preventing pregnancy.

Tubal Ligation for Women, Vasectomy for Men

Tubal ligation and vasectomy are permanent forms of birth control. They have a failure rate of 1% or less and both are done on an out-patient basis. Neither procedure will cause the slightest change in your level of horniness, and many people report they enjoy sex more once they don't have to worry about pregnancy.

In tubal ligation, a thin tube-like instrument is passed through a small incision that is slightly below your belly button. The surgeon seals your fallopian tubes with clips, rings, or electrical coagulation. In order to see your fallopian tubes, a harmless gas is put into your abdomen. The gas is let out once the tubes have been sealed and the eggs from your ovaries can no longer reach your womb. The total procedure takes about fifteen to twenty minutes. Unfortunately, tubal ligation does not stop a woman's periods. It only stops her fears about becoming pregnant again.

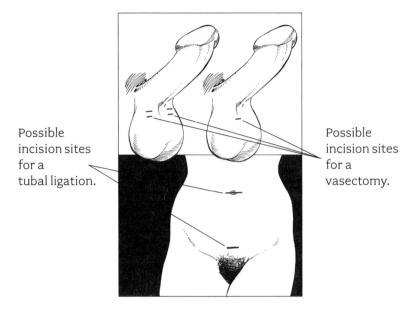

Possible incision sites for a tubal ligation.

Possible incision sites for a vasectomy.

With a vasectomy, a small incision is made in the scrotum. The physician reaches the vas deferens or sperm-carrying tubes through the incision with a thin instrument. The tubes are then sealed, so that sperm does not mix with your ejaculate. The procedure should take less than twenty minutes. Since sperm makes up less than 1% of each wad, your ejaculations will have the same volume as before. Neither you nor your partner will notice anything is missing, except for the contraceptives.

How Many Pregnancies Are Unplanned?

In the United States, fifty percent of pregnancies in women under the age of thirty-four are neither planned nor intended. The number rises to seventy-five percent for women over forty. More than eighty percent of pregnant teens had no desire to be that way. Also, twenty-six percent of people who use abstinence as their method of birth control become pregnant each year.

Sexually active people often fall into one of two extremes: those who have intercourse often and those who don't. Believe it or not, the once-in-a-blue-moon group has the lion's share of unwanted pregnancies. There are several reasons for this which could fill an entire book. Please take it on faith that if you have intercourse sporadically rather than regularly, you are in a high-risk group for getting pregnant.

When it comes to choosing a birth control method, please check with your physician or family planning center. This book's information may be out of date by the time you read it.

Emergency Contraception and Morning After Pills

Let's say the condom broke, or you were raped or pressured into having intercourse, or your level of passion suddenly overwhelmed your level of sanity and the condom never went on or the diaphragm never went in. Believe it or not, there is a simple, relatively safe way of decreasing your chance of becoming pregnant by 75%. It's been known about for thirty years, but until recently was referred to as *The Nation's Best-Kept Secret.*

In the early 1970s, a Canadian gynecologist by the name of Albert Yupze discovered that taking two birth control pills within 72 hours after unprotected intercourse, and then two more birth control pills twelve hours later, greatly reduced the chance of getting pregnant from unprotected intercourse. The type of birth control pills he pre-scribed were not an esoteric blend that needed to be snuck across the border in someone's shoe or briefcase. They were a common brand of birth control pill that was being prescribed for women all over the world during the 1970s.

However, the strength of birth control pills that were given then was much higher than those given now, and who knows what brand you'd need to take to get the right combination. So there is now a specific pill called Plan B or "the morning after pill" which is the right strength for emergency contraception.

Don't let the term *morning-after pill* fool you. It works just fine if you take it up to five days after having unprotected intercourse. You will need to take one pill within 120 hours after the sperm train has left the station, and a second pill twelve hours after that. The side effects are minimal and the hassle is almost nonexistent compared to getting an abortion.

Another option for emergency contraception is a device called the copper-T intrauterine device (IUD) aka Paragard. It can be inserted up to five days after unprotected intercourse and can reduce the risk of pregnancy following unprotected intercourse by ninety-nine percent. It can also be left in place to provide effective contraception for years.

Except for the Copper-T IUD, emergency contraception should not be used as a routine method of birth control. However, they are readily available and safe to take.

How to Get Emergency Contraception

A concern about emergency contraception is that people would rely on it rather than using regular birth control. Yet in Britain, where Plan B has been available for years over-the-counter and in schools, studies have shown that it is being used only as intended—for an emergency back-up.

Plan B emergency contraception is so safe that an FDA advisory panel unanimously voted to allow it to be sold over-the-counter in the United States. However, the "advisory" panel was just that: advisors and not politicians. As of press time in 2004, the current US President and his conservative cabinet apparently vetoed the recommendation of the FDA advisory panel. As a result, women still need to have a prescription to get Plan B.

If Plan B is not available over-the-counter when you read this and you need emergency contraception, call toll free (888)668-2528 or go to http://not-2-late.com.

Gyno Visits—Use a Condom the Night Before

Most women would be happy if they never had to spread their legs in a physician's office again. However, if you do have an appointment for a pelvic exam, your partner should wear a condom the night before. Male ejaculate can mess with pap smear results, and it won't help the doctor make an accurate diagnosis of possible infections.

Wanting to Be Pregnant for All the Wrong Reasons

No matter how much we know about birth control, some of us have unconscious fantasies about getting pregnant and having a baby. Some of these fantasies might keep a woman from using birth control. Here are some possibilities: getting pregnant will make her feel "grown up," the baby will love her unconditionally, it's one thing she can do "right," it will help her be respected, it will free her from her parents, the baby's father will want to marry and care for her, or she'll be able to care for the child in a way that she wasn't. Unfortunately, most of these fantasies come crashing down once the girl has the baby in her arms and reality rears its uncaring head.

Dear Paul,

They've had birth control pills for women for years. Why haven't they invented a birth control pill for guys?

Georgia in Georgia

Dear Georgia,

At the end of last year, major news outlets including the BBC and CNN reported that a new male birth control pill was about to be released. Feeling particularly suspicious, I contacted the chief researcher at one of the two medical centers in this country where trials on male birth control are being run. Here is her response:

"The most likely hormonally-based male contraception preparation that will be available will be injections once every two months, we hope. This may be available in 5 to 7 years (2009 to 2011). I think the next available preparation may be an implant. The testosterone patch will not be used as a male contraceptive method."

As for your question about why it's taken so long, one reason why there's a pill for women but none for men has to do with biology. Stopping an egg versus a wad of sperm is like stopping the Hindenburg as opposed to the Viet Cong. Eggs are the easier target.

In an average month, a woman produces a single egg. In an average day, her boyfriend produces 10 million sperm. Worse yet, once a sperm is created, it is warehoused down in Scrotumland for more than two-and-a-half months. This means that if you gave your man a pill that would magically stop him from producing any new sperm, he would still be fertile for another seventy-five days. (When the vet castrates one of our llamas, we still need to keep him from the lady llamas for several weeks. Even without his testicles, he is still fertile.)

Another problem for researchers is whether to stop sperm production altogether or to find a substance that allows sperm to be produced, but interferes with their ability to mature.

Pills for guys may also have unwanted side effects. They might make us even more moody than we already are. So scientists are trying to develop synthetic hormones that will decrease sperm production without these troubling side effects.

Researchers are also trying to create reversible vasectomy procedures. These include inserting mini-plugs or micro-valves inside a guy's scrotum. The valves might be regulated with a magnetic or electrical impulse. This could be problematic if the valves got turned on each time we went through a metal detector or rested a laptop computer you-know-where.

A social issue in the use of male birth control has to do with trust. It would require females to trust men in the way we have to trust you when you say, "Don't worry, I'm on the pill." You have more to lose by virtue of who is left carrying the placenta. On the other hand, if I were designing the media campaign for a male birth control method, I would show attorneys who handle paternity cases. I'd have them explain just how much it's going to cost a guy for the next eighteen years if he doesn't put a cork in the sperm fountain. And then I'd end it with a slogan such as "Love your lady, trust yourself."

End Of Chapter Note: Technically speaking, the term "progesterone" only refers to the naturally occurring hormone. Since hormones in contraceptives are synthetically made, they are actually called "progestins" For the sake of simplicity, the term "progesterone" is used throughout this chapter, albeit incorrectly.

Special Thanks: A very special thanks to Angela Hoffman, birth control and sex education expert, for help above and beyond the call of duty with this chapter.

Gnarly Sex Germs

Chapter 46

Some people believe that AIDS is the most deadly sex disease that ever was. Sadly enough, the prize goes to syphilis. Even a couple of popes died from syphilis. That's why this chapter begins with a discussion of syphilis and then works its way to other diseases that are associated with sexual contact.

Syphilis—The Great Pox

Before 1492, when Columbus came to America, there had been no recorded cases of syphilis in Europe. But syphilis did exist in the part of the New World where Columbus and his crew landed. Shortly after Columbus's return, a vicious strain of syphilis began to spread throughout Europe, quickly killing a sizable portion of the population. During its first fifty years in Europe, from about 1493 until 1550, syphilis was a savage killer. Smallpox got its name because the lesions it caused were small compared to those of The Great Pox syphilis. It seems that the Spanish army sent syphilitic prostitutes to infect the Italian army, which is one of the first recorded instances of biological warfare.

After 1550, syphilis went from being a quick killer to a slow killer, more like the syphilis we know today. Instead of finishing off its victims in short order, syphilis began to linger in the body for years after the initial infection, eventually targeting organs like the heart or brain. Syphilis remained a potent killer for four hundred more years (from 1550 to 1940), with almost half of all hospital beds worldwide filled with its victims. Syphilis is less of a problem today because it can now be treated in its early phases by antibiotics, which weren't discovered until the 1940s.

Nobel Note: In the 1920s, a medical doctor received the Nobel Prize for infecting syphilis patients with malaria. The high fever caused by the malaria helped burn out the stubborn syphilis infection. Unfortunately, there was no cure for the new cure. Some scientists speculate that more people died from the attempts to cure syphilis than from syphilis itself. Until the discovery of antibiotics, popular syphilis therapies included treatment with arsenic and mercury.

Lonely Shepherds, Scared Sheep—Sounds Like AIDS?

Folklore has it that syphilis was originally caused by lonely shepherds who prodded their sheep with something more personal than carved wooden staffs. The reason for the sheep/shepherd rumor is a matter of simple poetry. In 1530, a great physician, poet, and scholar named Fracastor wrote a poem about the disease of syphilis which hadn't been named syphilis yet. In the poem, a sixteen-year-old shepherd boy named Syphilis made the horrible mistake of building an altar on the wrong plot of land and praying to the wrong gods. This was the 1530s equivalent of wearing the wrong colors in a gang-controlled neighborhood. It angered the god Apollo, who struck the youth's genitals with a chancre-laden thunderbolt. Fracastor's poem tells about the rapid spread of the "new" disease:

> "I sing of that terrible disease, unknown to past centuries, which attacked all Europe in one day and spread itself over part of Africa and Asia..."

Sounds a little like the spread of AIDS. But syphilis behaved and still behaves very much like a sexually transmitted disease. That is not the case with AIDS.

AIDS

AIDS is a disease or cluster of diseases that involves a shutdown of the immune system. Several factors may be involved in its spread. AIDS is both horrible and fascinating. Hopefully, you will stay aware of it and try to learn more about it.

AIDS has yet to follow any predictions that are based upon our knowledge of sexually transmitted infections. For instance, it has never made the highly anticipated crossover into heterosexual populations in North America. Sexually transmitted infections have been soaring in straight populations, so why not AIDS? If AIDS behaved like any virus the world has ever known, straight college students in North America would be dying from it left and right.

We have also been warned about AIDS running rampant in Africa. Yet severe malnutrition can result in AIDS symptoms. Some people have suggested that we would save more lives in Africa by helping to stop malnutrition and by installing water purification systems than by exporting billions of dollars of toxic drugs.

What is disconcerting about our handling of AIDS is how little dissension has been tolerated in the scientific community regarding the current medical models. Can any of the current models explain why so few straight people in this country have AIDS while gay men are unfortunately at such high risk? Can any of the models explain why so few female prostitutes get AIDS as long as they are not abusing drugs? And how is it that straight people in Africa are showing AIDS-like symptoms but not straight people in the United States?

You would think that researchers would question a model with holes like these. Yet this kind of attitude is not unusual. Until 2003, anyone who questioned the safety of giving women hormone replacement drugs was scoffed at by physicians. Then, after decades of making women feel like wrinkled prunes if they didn't take hormone replacement therapy, scientists suddenly said "Oops!"

Unfortunately, some straight people will think this means they don't need to take an informed stance against the spread of AIDS. This is a gamble none of us, straight or gay, should be willing to take.

Why Should Straight People Continue to Be Cautious?

Many people have become wise to the fact that hardly any of their heterosexual peers are coming down with diseases like AIDS. More of their straight peers are dying from drugs and alcohol.

One of the reasons for being cautious about sexually transmitted infections is called HPV. HPV is a virus that can cause cancer of the cervix and it has now been implicated in cancer of the penis. Unlike AIDS, HPV behaves like a real virus. If you have more than a couple of lovers, you are probably going to get it. And when it comes to herpes, it's pretty easy for a penis or vulva to get a lifelong case of herpes when a partner with a loving tongue and lips has a simple cold sore.

Defining an Acceptable Level of Risk

Each year more than 40,000 Americans die in car accidents. Thousands more are seriously injured. Yet most of us consider driving to be an acceptable risk. On the other hand, if people were told about a new sexually transmitted disease that took 40,000 American lives each year, there would be a great outcry against sex.

Perhaps we believe there is something inherently good about driving and something inherently bad about sex. Or maybe we get more satisfaction from driving. Whatever the case, you can greatly decrease your chances of being killed in a car accident by not drinking or doing drugs when you drive, by wearing a seat belt, and by driving sensibly. The same is true for having sex, except for the seat belt.

Other Diseases of Mass Destruction

You honestly don't know what's out there. So rather than focusing on one type of disease, why not try to keep your entire body healthy?

First and foremost, this means never, ever do recreational drugs such as poppers (nitrile inhalants) or shoot anything into your veins. Poppers and crystal meth remain extremely popular in the fast lane of the gay sex scene. In fact, crystal meth is so popular that even young guys are taking Viagra to help reverse the effects of "crystal dick", which is meth-related impotence. The reason for avoiding recreational drugs is there is a strong association between using recreational drugs and getting AIDS.

Keeping your entire body healthy means staying fit, eating well and avoiding all nonessential drugs. It also means using rubbers if you are having anal sex, whether you are heterosexual or homosexual. And if you aren't true blue and monogamous, it means using rubbers during oral and vaginal intercourse as well. This will help decrease the spread of chlamydia, syphilis, and perhaps HPV and herpes. It will also help decrease your chances of getting any new diseases.

The Importance of Sex

For many of us, an important part of staying healthy is having sex. On the other hand, there would be a significant drop in the number of sexually transmitted infections if people dated for a few weeks or months before getting naked together. By then, you would know more about a potential partner than simply how they fill out their blue jeans. Perhaps the sex would be better, too.

QUESTION: Would you be safer from getting a sexually transmitted infection by going to a party with no condoms but remaining sober, or by having a pack of condoms but also drinking or doing drugs?

As for staying well when your pants are off, consider this:

Oral Sex (mouth-to-crotch) You would think that if AIDS were easily transmitted by oral sex, women who blow men for a living would be getting it in droves, but prostitutes aren't unless they also shoot up drugs. While your chances of getting AIDS from oral sex are quite low, you can get and give plenty of other sexually transmitted infections while doing oral sex. Using a condom while blowing a guy makes a lot of sense if you are not in a long-term relationship. (See the condom section for which condoms don't taste as bad.) Using a dental dam or plastic wrap over a woman's vulva when giving her oral sex also makes sense, but nobody is going to do it. Just be aware that if there is a cold sore in your mouth, you stand a good chance of giving herpes to the person you are having oral sex with.

Oral Sex (French kissing) Besides being a delightful thing to do, French kissing is a way of contracting anything you might get when someone with a cold or flu sneezes in your face.

Oral Sex (rimming or booty lickin') Rimming is when you use your tongue on your partner's anus. If you are in a long-term monogamous relationship, you share many of the same intestinal flora, fauna, and bugs, so there's probably not a big risk associated with rimming. But in more casual relationships, you should be concerned about getting things like hepatitis, E-coli, salmonella, shigella, amoeba, giardia, and cryptosporidiosis. So, if you enjoy rimming but aren't in a long-term or true blue relationship, get yourself a hepatitis vaccination. It does not matter if you are straight or gay; if you enjoy rimming with casual partners, you are being really dumb not to get vaccinated for hepatitis. As for other bugs and germs, a dental dam would make sense, but tongues that like to rim really like to rim. So a good strategy is to hop in the shower together before the games begin. (A post-doc fellow at UCLA did a study on germs and hand-washing. She discovered that if you soap-up a second time after the first rinse there will be a huge decrease in the amount of germs. We assume the same is true with your anus, but this was in the pediatrics department and it is unlikely that rimming was part of the protocol.)

Hand Jobs Researcher Bruce Voeller says the chances of catching a sexually transmitted infection from doing your partner by hand are about the same as breaking your neck from falling out of bed, unless you get the fluid into an open cut. Voeller comments: "A good way to know if you have an infectable cut is to rub a piece of lemon or lime over your skin. If a place burns, then you've got a cut that might conceivably get infected." An efficient way to dispose of the lime is into a glass of tequila that has been rimmed with salt. What you don't want to do is take a hand with a partner's sex fluids on it and then rub it on your genitals, unless neither of you has an STI.

Intercourse (vaginal) Do you really believe that the cute fraternity guy you are about to go to bed with is going to say, "Oh, by the way, I'm totally low-risk except for that little butt-fucking incident last month with the captain of the wrestling team"? Or what about that sweet-looking former high school cheerleader? Do you honestly believe she will cop to having spiked heroin while going through her rebellious phase last summer? Keep in mind that other people might not be as responsible about what goes on with their bodies as you might be with yours.

Be especially sure to use condoms when sleeping with partners who drink or do drugs, even if it's just brewskis or pot. That's because these substances numb the part of the mind which we count on to keep us out of trouble. It's the sober part that says, "I'm not even sure if I like this guy, but he's got one hand under my shirt and the other down my pants; what's wrong with this picture?" It's the polluted part that says "Condom schmondom, ain't nothin' bad gonna happen."

NOTE: Pulling out and squirting off to the side may win you the *Birth Control From The Middle Ages Award,* but it won't keep you from getting a disease. Also, try to put a rubber on as soon as you get wood. A hard penis usually starts dripping before it gets to where it's going.

Intercourse (anal) Let's say you are in a long-term, true-blue relationship and you have no concerns about sexually transmitted infections. In that case, barebacking (anal sex without a condom) is probably okay except for three possible concerns. The first is that there might be immune-suppressing factors in male ejaculate that help it in its quest to fertilize an egg. What happens when this sits in the rectum, where it's absorbed into the blood stream? Will it eventually start to impact the receiver's immune system? On the other hand, people have been butt-fucking since the beginning of time. The second concern is that males might be getting urinary tract or prostate infections when fecal matter gets into the urethra. The third concern is that even if you wash the penis, fecal matter still might stay in the peehole and end up shooting into the vagina if you don't pee before having regular intercourse. Of course, there isn't a single study we know of that examines these concerns, but you still might be ahead of the game if you bag it before plowing your partner's back forty. Also, you can't use enough lube to help reduce possible tissue trauma.

Urine Play If you are into water sports and not in a monogamous relationship, don't shoot urine into any body cavities. Using a partner as a urinal is something that needs to wait for marriage or a long-term relationship.

Drugs It is a sound idea to eliminate all non-essential drugs from your body, whether prescribed or recreational. This includes anything from meth and cocaine to antibiotics and antifungals. Since some members of the gay community were a wee bit promiscuous during the past, sex diseases and parasites were passed around like bongs at a Grateful Dead concert. As a result, antibiotics and antifungals were prescribed in huge amounts, often as a preventive before a guy spent a weekend at the baths or cruising the trails. No one knows what long-term effects this might have had on the immune system; at the very least it helped create increasingly drug-resistant organisms. Whether you are gay or straight, avoid taking any drugs that are not essential, whether they are legally prescribed or not. Also take precautions so you don't have to be prescribed all sorts of nasty drugs.

Diet There is no way the immune system is going to work well if you are malnourished. Many intravenous drug users are malnourished, and people who are severely malnourished can start showing symptoms of AIDS.

Exercise Exercise is more important than we like to think. Studies have shown that most people who exercise rigorously often have a delayed onset of serious AIDS symptoms. Also, several of the patients waiting for heart transplants at a major medical center were recently put on a program of exercise; fifty percent of them no longer needed the transplant by the time it became available. In most studies on aging, men and women who exercise regularly show a significant decrease in the number of problems typically associated with getting old. They also have sex more often.

AIDS & God

Some people claim that AIDS is a message from God about sexual "immorality." If this is true, then why does God allow millions of church-going, heterosexual Americans to die each year from cancer and heart attacks—diseases that take far more lives than AIDS? What's the hidden moral message there?

And what about young children who are dying from cancer and various immunological diseases? Is God punishing these two- to ten-year-olds for being immoral? How can people say that one disease is caused by the wrath of God while others aren't? Perhaps the real disease is in the minds of those who are willing to cast the first stone.

Monogamy Only Works for Some People

Monogamy would be fine if people would actually stay monogamous. But for some men and women who have had lots of sexual partners, the chance of remaining monogamous is low.

Don't try to fit yourself into a monogamous space if you belong in a round hole. Whether you are straight or gay, don't stop using condoms in a relationship if there is even the slightest chance that you or your partner might have sex outside of the relationship. And if your partner wants the two of you to keep using condoms, do yourself a huge favor and don't resist. "Monogamous" only works for some.

Know yourself, enjoy yourself, and protect yourself.

Not So Deadly Sex Germs & Scruffy Sex Critters

There are several germs and sex critters that owe their very lives to people who indiscriminately make love. A highly annoying but non-fatal sex critter is crab lice.

The author of this book first learned about crab lice years ago while listening to a radical student leader at UC Berkeley. The radical leader was speaking to a group of not-so-radical students at a pizza place on the southside of campus. Throughout the entire speech, the radical leader kept scratching his pubic area with the ferociousness of a junk-yard dog. He could barely keep his hands out of his pants long enough to light a Gitanes. Gitanes are French cigarettes that smell really unpleasant. People with bad teeth, radical politics, and itchy balls seem to enjoy them.

At the end of the speech, your author asked a friend if he had noticed something a little, uh, unusual about the radical's social manner. The friend's more experienced face scrunched and spit out two ugly words: *crab lice.* Crab lice are infectious little mites that live in body hair. They can cause serious pubic, as well as public, itching.

There are other sexually transmitted infections besides crab lice that can be either very mild or very annoying. Some have names that can hardly be pronounced, and more than just radical student leaders get them. Even lawyers and sorority girls get herpes, venereal warts, thrush, candida, and chlamydia.

If you are sexually active, please keep this in mind: whenever your genitals, anus, or mouth sprout warts or grow tiny cauliflowers, lesions, or strange-looking pimples, when there's discomfort as you pee, when your urine is constantly cloudy or has blood in it, when there's a weird discharge, or when things don't feel quite right, get yourself to a doctor or a clinic. Most of these problems can be treated without much pain or hassle. But without treatment you could become sterile from an otherwise treatable problem. You can also pass on sexual infections to your partner without experiencing any symptoms yourself. This is not cool.

Anyone who has been in more than one sexual relationship during the past year should take his or her genitals to a clinic or a private practitioner for a checkup. Be sure to include a throat culture if you have been doing oral sex and a rectal culture if you've been taking it up the rear. It's a good idea to get routine checkups even if you use rubbers and don't have symptoms. Sorry to say, but plenty of people who were using condoms have walked away with a case of herpes or HPV.

If symptoms of an STI suddenly go away, do not for a moment assume that the disease has gone away! Keep in mind that the most common symptom of a sexually transmitted infection is no symptom at all. It is very common to have an STI and not be aware of it.

Herpes, Etc.

The reason this book doesn't include more about sexually transmitted infections is it would take many pages to do a decent job. As for herpes, more than 20 million people have it and there are entire organizations that do nothing but supply help and information on the subject. Just because millions of people have herpes is no reason to be laissez faire about it. Avoid it by using condoms and sleeping with fewer, rather than more, partners.

Herpes is a buff DNA virus that causes eruptions of small painful blisters on the skin and mucous membranes, usually around the mouth and genitals. Some people also experience flu-like symptoms. Herpes likes to take long siestas, sometimes for years at a time. Then it emerges like a creature from the underworld. Stress can trigger outbreaks, and it helps to have a sense of humor about it. If you've got it, you've got it. Getting all freaked out about herpes isn't going to help matters one bit. Be wise and stay informed. Let yourself become the master of it rather than the other way around. Or, as the Zen folk might say, you and the herpes are sharing the same body, so learn to get along.

If you are having your first outbreak of herpes, get to a doctor right away. Proper treatment of the initial herpes outbreak can significantly reduce the severity of future outbreaks. For more information about herpes, phone the National Herpes Hotline at (919)361-8488 or the National STD Hotline at (800)227-8922.

If you have herpes or any other potentially contagious disease, never, ever have sex without telling the other person first. If the shoe were on the other foot or, more appropriately, if the germs were in the other mouth or crotch, you would want them to inform you.

Highly Recommended *The Updated Herpes Handbook* by Terri and Ricks Warren, The Portland Press, Portland, OR, 2003. This little book is less than forty pages long and costs only $3.00 plus postage. It will tell you everything you need to know about herpes, and the authors are good about keeping it updated. To get it, call (503)226-6678.

Sexually Transmitted Infection Recap

In the United States, STIs used to be called Sexually Transmitted Diseases or STDs, while in Australia they were called STIs or Sexually Transmitted Infections (same germs, different accent.) Now we all call them STIs! No matter what part of the world you are in, failure to get treatment for most STIs can lead to complications beyond your wildest imagination. Here are a few STIs and some of their symptoms:

AIDS The symptoms can range from unexplained weight loss and extreme tiredness to night sweats, fever, chronic diarrhea, dry cough, pneumonia, seizures, skin blotches, and swollen glands.

Chlamydia With over 4 million new cases each year, this is one of the most common STIs today. Four out of five women don't know they have it until they get serious complications such as Pelvic Inflammatory Disease. With males, it's a similar picture, except for the PID. This is why all sexually active people should be tested for chlamydia at least once a year. MEN: Few symptoms or liquid discharge and painful peeing. It can cause Nongonococcal Urethritis or NGU. WOMEN: Usually no symptoms, but there can be burning or itching in your vagina with or without a discharge.

Genital Herpes Transmission: contact with an infected area during oral, anal, or vaginal sex. MEN: Painful blisters on the penis, scrotum, and sometimes anywhere from your navel to your knees. WOMEN: Red bumps in and around the folds or lips of your vulva that turn into painful blisters. Can also appear on the cervix, thighs, navel, or anus. MEN AND WOMEN: Sometimes flu-like symptoms. Can also cause painful peeing. Other times, there might be no symptoms, and symptoms often come and go.

Genital Warts See Human Papilloma Virus (HPV).

Gonorrhea Often no symptoms at the start, but complications will cause pain in the groin or stomach and you can end up with anything from swollen testicles or Pelvic Inflammatory Disease to brain infections. Cases of gonorrhea in the throat are also being found. MEN: There might be a burning discharge from the penis. WOMEN: Possible green or yellow discharge from the vagina, abnormal vaginal bleeding, or pelvic pain. Pelvic Inflammatory Disease, tubal pregnancy, and sterility are real possibilities if not treated.

Hepatitis A, B, or C Often there are no symptoms, or there can be yellowing of the skin and the whites of your eyes, nausea, fever and soreness of your liver, and/or your urine can get dark and your feces can turn lighter or grayish. You can be totally incapacitated for several months and even die. Liver damage is a common complication. Different types are spread in different ways, from simply kissing on the lips to butt-fucking and nearly every kind of sexual act in between.

If your sexual boundaries are a bit porous or you enjoy barebacking and rimming with all kinds of partners, please talk to your physician about getting a hepatitis vaccination.

Human Papilloma Virus (HPV) Including Genital Warts There are more than seventy different strains of HPV that can attack anywhere from your larynx and lungs to your cervix and anus. One of the strains of HPV that can impact your sexuality is genital warts. These are like little cauliflowers that grow where the sun don't shine. They are often spread sexually. It is nearly impossible to tell when or whom you got them from. They cause small, hard, wrinkled bumps that are sometimes big enough to be seen with the naked eye. MEN: Warts from HPV can spring up on the head or shaft of your penis, on your scrotum, or in your anus. Genital warts are sometimes confused with pearly penile papules, which is not an STI. (Can you say "pearly penile papules" three times in a row out loud?) HPV has also been implicated in cancer of the penis and throat cancer. WOMEN: Warts can be in the vagina, on the vulva, or in or on your anus. HPV can also cause cervical lesions, which can lead to cancer of the cervix if not treated. These lesions are usually discovered when a pap smear comes back with abnormal or precancerous cells, which is another reason why a woman who is sexually active should get gynecological exams often.

Nongonococcal Urethritis (NGU) This is an infection in the urethra that can be caused by different germs including chlamydia. MALES: Discharge from your penis can be milky, thin, clear, or watery. BOTH SEXES: You might feel a burning sensation when peeing.

Scabies and Crab Lice—Pthirus Pubis or Crab Louse (Ever hear the insult, "You louse" or "He's a louse"?) Crab lice are mites that are highly contagious. They can cause itching beyond belief. Crab lice can be found anywhere on the body that has hair; scabies burrow under your skin and can cause itchy sores that look like poison ivy. Talk to your pharmacist or healthcare provider about scabies or louse-killing potions. Grab everything that isn't nailed down and dry clean or wash and dry it at the highest heat possible. If you can't wash it, store it in a tightly closed plastic bag for two weeks.

Syphilis You can get syphilis in your throat, anus, or genitals. About a third of untreated sufferers eventually get tertiary syphilis and die from brain, heart, or nerve damage. There are often no symptoms, which is why sexually active people should be tested every year.

Vaginal Infections (Trichomoniasis, Bacterial Vaginosis, or Yeast Infections/Candida Albicans): Symptoms: foul-smelling discharge, painful peeing, or no symptoms at all. You can get it from sexual activity or in other ways, like sharing an infected person's towel or bathing suit. Bacterial Vaginosis (BV): symptoms can include a creamy discharge and fishy smell after intercourse, sometimes itching and painful peeing. Yeast Infections or Candida Albicans: symptoms can include itchy genitals and a heavy, whitish, clumpy discharge that can smell like yeast. Yeast infections can happen on their own, when the woman is taking antibiotics, when she's been wearing tight pants, panty hose, leotards, or anything that doesn't allow her crotch to breathe. With some vaginal infections, it is important that the male is treated also. Guys can get vaginal infections in the penis, even if it is a serious contradiction in terms.

Dear Paul,

I'm a pretty responsible and selective guy. I get tested for AIDS every year and make sure that my partners have been tested too. Is there any need for me to use condoms?

Clean in Colorado Springs

Dear Clean,

I just returned from a speaking engagement at Portland State University, where campus health workers estimate that fifty percent of the student population has a sexually transmitted infection known as papilloma or HPV. One of the problems with papilloma, besides the fact that there are more than seventy known strains of it, is that it causes up to 95% of the cases of cancer of the cervix and it has been linked with cancer of the penis and cancer of the head and throat.

Another study in Baltimore found that 40% of inner-city teens have chlamydia, which is also a sexually transmitted infection. So, if you are traveling to Portland or Baltimore, you'll probably want to put a condom on in the morning, right after you put on your socks.

As for your own state of Colorado, I was recently there and didn't notice anybody who looked like they had a sexually transmitted infection. They weren't frothing at the mouth or sporting big skin lesions. However, STIs like papilloma, chlamydia and herpes don't usually announce themselves to friends and potential lovers. It's possible to have a serious STI and not even know it. Symptoms can take months to develop, if they ever do. This means that Amber, who sprouted genital warts after sleeping with Dave, might have actually gotten the virus from her former squeeze Mike.

What I'm saying, Clean, is just because you look clean or feel clean doesn't mean you are.

Also, did I mention your anus? Condom or no, vaginal fluids that slosh around during intercourse can carry STIs to a guy or girl's rear end. So if you end up with anal discomfort or warts in your anus, take your entire pelvis to a clinic and have its various entries and exits probed, poked, and cultured. Some men feel uneasy about having anal warts checked out, fearing that the physician will suspect they've been receiving anal sex. Not to worry. The medical profession knows that straight guys get anal warts. Honest.

NUMBERS:

For your nearest Planned Parenthood center: (800)230-PLAN
National Herpes Hotline: (919)361-8488
National STD Hotline: (800)227-8922
National AIDS Line: (800)342-AIDS
For AFTER intercourse/emergency contraception: (888)668-2528

For STIs, Birth Control, Adoption and Abortion, please check out the resources part of our website at www.goofyfootpress.com.

Special Thanks: A special thanks to Angela Hoffman, birth control and sex education expert, for help above and beyond the call of duty with this chapter.

Trying to Get Pregnant

Chapter 47

Dear Paul,

> *My wife and I have been trying to get pregnant, with no luck. The doctor wants me to get a sperm count. Do you know anything about this?*
>
> *Hank from Thunder Bay*

Dear Hank,

If personal experience is of any use, here's the skinny on getting a sperm count.

First, a sperm sample needs to be less than an hour old in order for an accurate test to be done. In fact, the fresher, the better. That's why they may want you to produce the sample on location—at the same lab where you go for routine blood tests.

Unfortunately, your little sperms don't suddenly appear for roll call and that's that. There's a whole procedure that needs to be followed. Like handing the proper authorization form to a total stranger in a white coat who will automatically yell in a loud voice, "Whadda ya here for?"

That's when you will become acutely aware of just how many people are sitting in the crowded waiting room less than five feet behind you. There will be a mom with a couple of kids, two teenagers, an older gentleman, and maybe even a nun—all waiting to hear your answer just like the people before them waited to hear theirs. You will clear your throat and say as quietly as possible, "I'm here for a sperm count," after which the person in the white coat will immediately say in the loudest voice possible, "SPERM COUNT?" as if for some reason you were really there for a barium enema, but said sperm count just for the heck of it.

The person in the white coat will then yell to another person at the other end of the lab, "Louise, where are the specimen cups for doing a sperm count?" at which point Louise will yell back "WHAT?" to which the person in the white coat will respond even louder, "I NEED A SPECIMEN CUP FOR THIS GUY TO GIVE A SPERM SAMPLE."

Now maybe Louise will yell back, "Top shelf in the cupboard on the right." Or maybe she'll yell "WHAT?" once again, and then the person in the white coat will look up at you shaking his or her head, expecting you to offer a sympathetic nod.

Eventually, they will find the correct cups and hand you one. If you are lucky, they will open the door and direct you to a bathroom down the hall. Otherwise, they will tell you to have a seat in the waiting room, where twelve sets of eyes will be staring at your face and then at the plastic cup that's in your sweating hand. And then the little five-year-old, who is sitting with his mother, will ask, "Mommy, what's a spurn count?" and the woman will glare at the child with her most intense "Don't-ask-me-that-now—OR EVER!" stare, and the little boy will protest, "But that man has to have a spurn count. Is something wrong with him?"

I am still not sure what the correct response should be when the person in the white coat finally summons you to the bathroom down the hall. Do you smile, make eye contact and say, "Thank God!"? I marvel at the man with gumption enough to look at the specimen cup and ask, "What do I do with this?" or better yet, "It won't be big enough."

Of course, if you are anywhere near to being a normal guy, harvesting your own sperm in a locked bathroom is nothing you need instructions about. On the other hand, when you are producing sperm for an official sample, thoughts may enter your mind that never have before. For instance, "How long should I take?" You don't want to return in two minutes, deed done. On the other hand, you don't want to take half an hour, because you know that Louise and the person in the white coat will be giving knowing glances to each other, as if they aren't already.

To top that, no one has ever given you a grade on what actually came out. This time, not only are they scoring you on the number of sperm you're about to produce, but your wad will be graded on how well your sperm swim and on how full you fill the cup. So suddenly you'll be asking yourself, "Is there some way I should be doing this for optimal results? Should I be squeezing my testicles at the moment of truth? How do I get the most out?" I don't know what to suggest, except if you want to save yourself the embarrassment of scoring in the lower percentile of men who have ejaculated in plastic specimen cups, save up for a couple of days. You'll never believe how large a specimen cup looks when you are trying to fill it with sperm.

Finally, when you are done, you might smile inwardly and walk down the hallway looking for the person in the white coat. That's when you discover she is drawing blood and you'll need to hand the cup to Louise. Oh God. During your entire lifetime there may have been dozens of different ways that you've delivered sperm to a woman, but never in a plastic cup and never has she held it up to the light and swirled it to inspect its contents, and never has she stared so blankly and never have you felt quite so strange.

Anyway, Hank, that's what I know about sperm counts. Good luck to you and your wife.

P.S. If a couple is trying to get pregnant, it takes an average of eight months before hitting conceptual gold. If a couple is NOT trying to get pregnant, it only takes one night.

Dear Paul,

I've heard that couples who are trying to get pregnant are not supposed to use any sort of synthetic lubricant, and I've even heard that saliva can kill those little guys who are trying to get the job done. However, I am not one of those women who lubricates very much naturally, and we use K-Y on a regular basis. Are there any options that you know of besides using egg whites (eewww) as a lubricant—which I've been told might help?

I am asking because, well, getting pregnant has not been as easy as I thought it would be. Funny how many years you can spend trying to avoid it, then how many months you can spend taking your temperature, watching your body, taking folic acid, etc., with no results! After a while, sex actually got to be a drag. I really don't want to add "dry" sex on top of that. So I guess another question is, do you have any tips to keep sex fun, even after months of carefully monitored (schedule-body-clock wise) frolicking?

Mary in Virginia

Dear Mary,

It's amazing how sex can become such an unpleasant chore when you and your partner start having a menage'a'trois with a basal thermometer. My wife and I went there for a couple of months and decided to give it up. We became foster parents and eventually adopted.

In researching your question, I am once again reminded of how often the "science" of fertility can also be the voodoo of fertility. For instance, there are all kinds of self-described fertility specialists pontificating about the very question you are asking. Some say you can use lube, but most say absolutely not. One specialist who has written four books on fertility avoids the question altogether by blaming the lubrication problem on the male, saying that any woman can lubricate perfectly well if she has a partner who gives her enough foreplay. I don't think so. I'm also a bit flabbergasted how Dr. Sensitive managed to forget that when a man and woman are concerned about fertility, sex can feel a wee bit pressured and stressful.

So rather than asking medicine men, I went to the horse's mouth—the people who make K-Y. This happens to be a small pharmaceutical concern by the name of Johnson & Johnson. J&J says, "We are instructed to tell all people who call about this to consult with their medical doctor" to which I said, "But you make the darned product!" to which they replied, "Yes, and we've never done any studies on KY and couples who are trying to get pregnant, so we can't answer your question."

And that's my point, no studies have been done, but that doesn't stop medical doctors from pretending there have been. At least Johnson & Johnson has the integrity to say, "We don't know." And that's what I find missing in so much of the medicine of fertility—integrity. How can we trust these people on advice with major issues when they are clearly faking it on the simple ones?

So regarding your question about using lubricant when trying to conceive, no one knows. As for idle speculation, the vagina tends to be acidic. This is not good for sperm, although given the world's population, it's apparently not all that bad for sperm, either.

Around the time of ovulation, the uterus creates an alkaline mucous that flows into the acidic vagina. This is nature's way of rolling out the welcome rug for sperm. Artificial lubricant is made to be acidic, to match the acidic nature of the vagina. Some people think that store-bought lubes slow down the sperm and cause them to cook in the vagina's acid rather than allowing them to hop on the alkaline welcome rug. One lube advertises that it doesn't slow sperm down, but this lube is just as acidic as the others. Could it conceivably make a difference? Perhaps. But it would be nice to have some science here so we aren't just guessing.

A lot of couples use saliva for added lube, but that, too, is kind of acidic and might not be enough to make the intercourse feel good. As for using egg whites, I'm worried that your child might come out of the womb clucking instead of crying.

You also ask how to make conception-driven sex more fun. I'm sorry but I don't have an answer. I never could figure out one for myself. My best suggestion is to leave Mr. Basal in the medicine cabinet and enjoy intercourse for the sake of intercourse and not as some sort of Moonie-like march of sperm toward Fallopia. Your love for each other needs to be respected and enjoyed as much as the love you might have for any child that you may or may not be creating. Couples who are desperate to get pregnant sometimes forget the importance of this.

Mind you, others might have very different feelings about the fertility business. If you are doing reading or research, keep an eye out for anything with the name "Sandra Leiblum" attached. I'd trust almost anything she puts her name to, and looking up resources she has written or edited might be an excellent place to start.

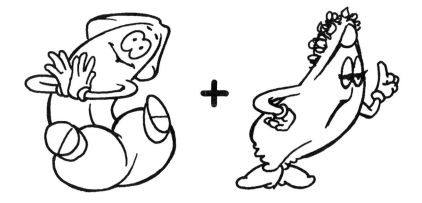

Twist and Shout!

Sex During Pregnancy

Chapter 48

If you hadn't noticed by now, each woman has her own unique way of looking at the world and you can't really predict how she will react to the man who knocked her up. Some pregnant women will want more intimacy than ever before, while others will want space—sometimes huge amounts of space. This can be confusing for a dad-to-be, as he is never quite sure if the love of his life wants to snuggle or pluck his eyes out. Also, don't think that the dad-to-be isn't experiencing his own set of pregnancy-related emotions. These may cause him to hesitate sexually while his child-to-be is turning somersaults half a penis-length away. The mom-to-be might be wanting to rip his clothes off, and he's suddenly all prim and proper.

The chapter that follows is about sex during pregnancy. It covers all of these issues and more, from orgasm-related uterine contractions and swelling vulvas to fetal brain development and having sex after your baby is born.

Please! No matter what you read in this chapter or anywhere else, you absolutely must discuss the matter of having sex while pregnant with a healthcare provider who is familiar with you and your pregnancy. That's because in some cases it might be prudent to alter some of the more outrageous ways that you and your partner enjoy sex. But for most couples, anything that felt good before conception is perfectly okay after, including anal sex, bondage, vibrator play and even good old fashioned vanilla lovemaking.

Talking to Your Healthcare Professional about Sex

Think about this for a moment: you go to a physician, get totally naked, spread your legs wide apart and let your doctor put her fingers in places where even the IRS doesn't. Yet many of us are nearly paralyzed by asking the simple question "Is it OK for me to have sex while I'm pregnant?"

Plenty of physicians encourage couples to have sex during pregnancy. And obstetricians like the one you are probably seeing rely on people having healthy sex lives in order to keep from going broke. So do pediatricians, gynecologists, Lamaze instructors and everyone else in the healthcare industry. There is no way your physician wants you getting out of practice with intercourse as long as the possibility exists that you might have more kids further down the line. So don't be afraid to ask.

If your health-care provider says it's okay to have sex, go to it. If the answer is "No, it's not okay to be having sex," then it is important to ask more questions. The first is "Pork hay?" which is Spanish for "Why not?"

If your healthcare provider is one of the few remaining dinosaurs who doesn't believe that pregnant women should be having sex, get yourself a second opinion. Most physicians feel that having sex during pregnancy is a completely normal thing to do, unless there are specific reasons not to such as having a prior history of miscarriages or premature labors, the placenta is attached near the cervix (placenta previa), your water has broken or there is bleeding of unknown origin.

If the physician gives a specific reason for why you shouldn't have sex, ask two more questions:

1. "How long should we not have sex—for the next few weeks, months, or for the entire pregnancy?" All too often, when a physician says, "No sex," the couple assumes this means for the entire pregnancy, when the intent was "No sex for the next couple of weeks." If you were to ask the same question in a month, the physician might say, "It was just a precaution. Based on how well you are doing now, I see no reason why you shouldn't have sex."

2. "Does 'no sex' just mean intercourse, or does it include all sexual contact?" For instance, intercourse might pose a concern, but it's fine to have orgasms orally or by masturbating. If all orgasms are a potential problem, ask if you can still have intercourse as long as you don't have an orgasm. For some women, this would be a cruel and unusual compromise, while others might welcome the extra intimacy that intercourse allows, orgasm or not.

Urge Surge—The Mood Swing

Moodwise, some women stay pretty even throughout their pregnancies, while others push the mental envelope. An interesting feature of pregnancy-related moodiness can be the intensity of the mood and the amplitude of its swing. For instance, some pregnant women

who are horny feel so intensely horny that they find it hard to think about much but sex and literally attack the dad-to-be the second he walks through the door. The intensity can be so great that some men feel a little used, while others seize the moment. Other pregnant women don't feel like having sex at all, and some might feel horny one moment and weepy the next. Keep in mind that a pregnant woman has the potential to feel hurt by comments that few women in their nonpregnant right minds would find offensive.

For the woman whose moods fluctuate, there might be moments when she blames her man for her condition and other times when she feels elated about being pregnant and is quite happy to know and love the guy who got her that way. Also, it is normal for a pregnant woman to feel moments of depression alternating with feelings of elation, and to have dreams of her child being a perfect baby as well as fears of it being handicapped.

Much has been said about the disruptive effects of hormonal changes on a pregnant woman's mood, and this might be quite true. On the other hand, oxytocin levels rise throughout pregnancy, and oxytocin is said to make for better moods. It also causes contractions of the uterus which may help to prepare the woman's body for labor, and it is thought to be involved in a woman's orgasms whether she is pregnant or not.

Beautiful or Gross?

How you feel about yourself can be an important factor in determining whether you want to have sex. Some pregnant women look in the mirror and feel fat and gross. Others feel they have never been more beautiful. Most women who are pregnant fall somewhere in the middle of these two extremes.

No matter how a woman feels about her pregnant self, it never hurts for her to receive loving reassurance from her partner. While a hard penis and a willing heart might be physical evidence that a man finds the mother of his child to be desirable, loving words and other romantic gestures speak to a different part of her soul. Do your best to always be available if not always near.

No Fear

One of the nice things about being pregnant is not having to worry about getting pregnant. You can put the diaphragm in the deep freeze, keep the condoms in the bottom drawer or forget about taking pills each morning. This can make sex during pregnancy particularly relaxed and easy to enjoy. If pregnancy is what you wanted, there's no more "We have to do it now because my most fertile three-and-a-half minutes during the entire next quarter of a century is about to pass." Even if you didn't plan on getting pregnant, the fact that you can't get pregnant again for nine more months allows some couples to relax and enjoy sex in ways that they might not when consequences are a concern.

Genital Swelling—Slip & Slide

Around the fourth month of pregnancy, most women's genitals begin to swell. And swell. And swell. This swelling can lead to full-time lubrication and can make some pregnant women feel very horny. The increased swelling is due to the growing vascular capacity in the pregnant woman's pelvis. As a result, her vulva often becomes a deeper color and her labia thicken.

Couples find that the added swelling may lead to a delightfully snug feeling during intercourse. Genital swelling during pregnancy can also up the intensity of the woman's orgasm. More on this in the pages that follow.

Orgasms during Pregnancy

Plenty of women have no interest in sex or orgasms when they are pregnant. Others not only want orgasms, but report coming in awe-inspiring bursts that are more intense than their most memorable pre-pregnant efforts. For some women, sex during pregnancy presents a slight contradiction: even if she is more easily aroused and her orgasms are more intense, she might take longer to reach orgasm. For some couples, the payoff is worth the extra effort.

One reason for whopper orgasms during pregnancy might be the increased level of engorgement in the abdomen. With all the extra blood in there, her uterus stays hard for a few minutes after orgasm. As a result, a woman who had single orgasms before pregnancy may experience two or more at a time while pregnant. But by the end of the pregnancy, some women find that the swelling in their genitals causes a congested feeling that makes coming feel more frustrating than relieving. Other women continue to have awesome orgasms throughout their entire pregnancies.

Also, it is normal for a pregnant woman to have cramps or Braxton-Hicks contractions either before or after orgasm. These cramps can last for a half-hour or more. The cramping might be due to the extra blood flow in the genitals, it might result from prostaglandins in the man's ejaculate, or it may stem from emotional concerns. Some healthcare professionals believe that these cramps help improve the muscle tone in a pregnant woman's uterus. If the cramping becomes too uncomfortable, you can eliminate one possible cause by using a condom during intercourse or by having the man pull out before he is about to come. See if this makes any difference over a couple of weeks. Another approach that may help relieve cramping is for the woman's partner to give her a loving foot massage or back rub.

Another unexpected source of orgasms during pregnancy may be the prolific array of sex dreams that some women report having. "Never had one before, never had one after, but had a large number of sexual dreams during."

Prostaglandin Note: Prostaglandins are what physicians give to help induce labor (e.g., pitocin). Nature has included very low doses of prostaglandins in male ejaculate. However, if these prostaglandins influence labor, it wouldn't be until the cervix is ripe and ready for labor. This is why some women who are near their due date intentionally have lots of intercourse believing that the prostaglandins work in synergy with a ripe cervix to provide a more gentle labor. A recent study has shown that intercourse during pregnancy does not contribute to premature birth; if anything, the opposite might be true. Still, if you are concerned about this or any kind of contractions during pregnancy, be sure to consult your healthcare provider.

Breasts: Tenderness, Expansion & Leakage

Breast tenderness can happen in any phase of the pregnancy, especially during the first trimester. This means that breasts which used to cherish firm handling might suddenly prefer a light kiss, caress, or no direct stimulation at all. Fortunately, some breasts that are painfully tender during the first trimester morph into major arousal zones during the second trimester. These kinds of changes make it important for pregnant couples to have frequent discussions about "what feels good this week..."

It is normal for the breasts of a nonpregnant woman to swell when she is sexually aroused. However, when a woman becomes pregnant, her breasts may remain swollen all the time. As a result, she may get swelling on top of swelling when she is sexually excited. This might feel painful, or it may feel wonderfully pleasant, depending on the woman and the stage of her pregnancy. Also, dietary salt might contribute to the swelling.

For some couples, breast tenderness will make the missionary position a thing of the past long before expansion of the abdomen does. Another potential problem or potential delight, depending on your point of view, might occur if the woman's breasts start to leak during the latter part of pregnancy. This is an ever-so-natural event and is simply a preview of what's to come.

Intercourse Concerns Part 1—Fetal Concussions

It is not uncommon for couples to worry that the head of daddy's thrusting penis is going to bop junior on the fetal brain and somehow knock him senseless. While it might be nice for dad to think his penis is that powerful, the fetus sits in a sac filled with a fluid that absorbs shocks and provides superb protection. To make it even that far, dad's penis would have to get through mom's cervix and uterine walls.

The most important consideration during intercourse is to find positions and thrusting styles that feel good for mom and her swollen reproductive organs. If it feels good for mom, chances are that the baby will do just fine.

As for questions about squirting junior in the eye with dad's ejaculate, the uterus is sealed off by a mucus plug that is a bit like the cork in a bottle of wine. The amniotic sac provides a secondary barrier that helps keep the ejaculate at bay.

Intercourse Concerns Part 2—"The Baby Will See Us"

Believe it or not, the human fetus is not taking notes on your every action and won't be emotionally scarred by the things you feel or do during pregnancy, even if you listen to—gulp—rock'n'roll instead of classical music. Exceptions, of course, are excessive drinking, smoking, or doing certain drugs that may compromise the infant's developing brain.

The fetal brain is not like a miniature of the adult brain. Its memory units (neurons) are hardly functional at birth. There is simply not enough developed brain structure for the fetus to say, "Oh my gosh, Mom and Dad are having sex and isn't that disgusting" or on a more positive note, "Mom and Dad are having sex, isn't that wonderful!"

Why Don't They Make Sexy Lingerie for Pregnant Moms?

Sex doesn't stop being an expression of love and intimacy just because a baby is on the way. Yet you get the feeling that pregnant moms are supposed to be more interested in changing tables and what color to paint the baby's room than in being lit up sexually or wondering what the new guy at the office looks like naked. You have to search far and wide to get the message that pregnant moms can feel sexy and that some moms and dads find pregnancy to be sexually exciting.

For a lot of pregnant women, nature turned up the horny knob instead of turning it down. Granted, not all women feel like having sex while pregnant, but enough do that it's difficult to believe that nature would have allowed this urge to go unchecked if it weren't for the benefit of the pregnancy or the species in general.

Intercourse

Some pregnant women cherish the feeling of having both the baby and the baby's father inside of them at the same time. Other women feel like three's a crowd. Dads, too, have their own issues about sex during pregnancy, some of which are discussed later in this chapter. As long as you feel like having intercourse while pregnant, the most important elements are a shared sense of humor and a willingness to explore. Here are some particulars to consider:

Clothes On Some couples who are trying new positions do so first with their clothes on. This helps them focus their collective energies on the engineering feat at hand, and it allows them to appreciate the humor of the situation without having to worry about feelings of urgency or declining erections. There's always time to get naked and actually go for it once the target positions have been mapped out and a strategy is planned.

Penetration Some women who are pregnant have a desire for penetration that's deep and assertive, while others prefer a more gentle approach than usual. Whatever the case, different phases of pregnancy may require different styles of penetration while the proverbial bun is in the oven. Also keep in mind that the swelling of the cervix and uterus can make certain kinds of intercourse feel uncomfortable, at least the kind where she rides you like a wild bull or clasps her ankles around your neck and shouts, "Harder, you big stud." Let

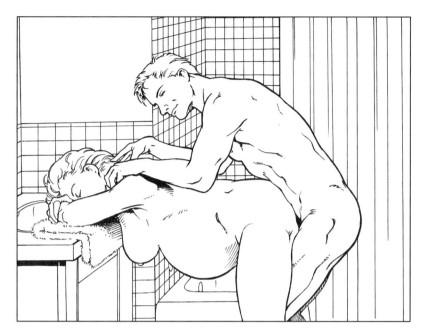

the woman control the thrusting depth, and if you feel that this some-how cramps your style, be mindful that there are plenty of dads-to-be who aren't getting any at all.

Lubrication Some women seem to lubricate all the time when they are pregnant. However, there are plenty of exceptions. If that's the case for you, try adding KY Jelly. Be sure your lubricant contains no contraceptive goop, as that might cause vaginal stinging.

Dizziness Some pregnant women experience dizziness or indigestion in certain positions or during certain phases of the pregnancy. This can be particularly true when a woman is on her back. Doing it on her side, on all fours, or while on top might suit her better.

Romancing the Cervix The cervix of a pregnant woman often swells due to the extra blood flow into the uterus. It becomes soft, and can sometimes bleed with deep penetration. Try shallower thrusting or use positions where the head of the penis romances the cervix more gently. This may be especially wise during the later months of pregnancy when the cervix starts to ripen. If you have questions or if there is any bleeding, be sure to consult with your healthcare professional.

Third-Trimester Stretch By the third trimester, the cartilage in the pelvic region has had months of pregnancy-related hormones thrown at it. It becomes softer as a result, as part of nature's conspiracy—ah, plan—to ready the pelvic floor for the joys of childbirth. As a result, a woman may find that pressure on her pubic bone feels a little weird. This is another reason why couples need to be creative in their search for comfortable intercourse positions.

Bag It or Let It Fly? Some physicians believe that a man should wear a condom during the last month or so of the pregnancy, but others think this is silly. Some experts believe that male ejaculate helps a ripening cervix prepare for an easier labor. Be sure to check with your own healthcare provider for advice.

Too Much Swelling For some women, genital swelling may eventually increase to a point where intercourse feels uncomfortable, while for others the desire to have intercourse never wanes. Experimenting with positions where the woman has her legs apart might help.

Backaches & All Fours With the muscles between her ribs being slowly pried apart and her pelvic floor feeling trampled on, the pregnant female has been known to suffer an occasional backache. Some women find that the rocking motion of intercourse while on all fours can help soothe pregnancy-related backaches. It can also soothe the throbbing between her partner's legs, resulting in a win-win situation for both parties.

The Penile Vice (Okay—Vise) Grip

Some healthcare professionals think it's good for a pregnant woman to tone and exercise the muscles in her pelvic floor by doing Kegel exercises. What better way to accomplish this than by having a man insert his penis into your vagina, keeping it stationary while you squeeze it with your pelvic muscles? Most guys would be more than happy to lend a helping penis. This is an exercise that you might keep doing after the baby is born. (It has been said that some of the finer prostitutes in Asia are able to "massage" a man's penis to ejaculation by squeezing it in this way. Of course, it's easier to pretend this really happens by placing the prostitute in some foreign land. If it is possible, achieving this kind of proficiency might take months of practice, but would add a new dimension to any woman's bedroom technique.)

When to Stop

Most physicians in this day and age say it's okay to keep having intercourse until your water breaks. Some couples have intercourse until labor itself begins.

There are at least four factors which should influence you on when to stop having intercourse: 1. It doesn't feel good any longer. 2. Either partner has a genital infection. 3. The woman experiences bleeding or new discharge. 4. Your healthcare provider says to stop.

Oral Sex

The extra lubrication caused by pregnancy can give the vaginal area a stronger taste or smell, which some men notice when giving their pregnant wives oral sex. However, there are no medical reasons to stop giving or receiving oral sex during pregnancy unless the pregnancy is at risk for other reasons.

Recently, one European medical journal reported that women who went down on their partners before becoming pregnant had a significantly lower incidence of pre-eclampsia during pregnancy. Pre-eclampsia is a condition in which the pregnant woman's blood pressure can rise to potentially dangerous levels. The origin of pre-eclampsia is not known. One medical journal several years ago found that pre-eclamptic conditions decreased significantly in women whose obstetricians were able to make a solid emotional connection with them, thus pointing to possible psychological factors in pre-eclampsia. Concerning the more recent study, one would want to know if the decrease in pre-eclampsia was limited to women who swallowed their husband's ejaculate, or if it included those who ducked and let it fly across the sheets. The latter might suggest that the preventive factor is a stronger emotional bond with the husband rather than the ejaculate itself.

Nipple & Perineal Massage

One of the nice things about being pregnant is that when the dad-to-be is complaining about all the things he usually complains about, you have the perfect excuse to say, "Shut up and rub my nipples!" That's because as the final months of pregnancy approach, it might be helpful for a woman to have two areas on her body massaged—well, three areas if you count each nipple as having its own private domain. Put a little lotion on each nipple and massage and knead it, assuming it isn't too painful. This will help condition the nipples for nursing, and it may also help release extra oxytocin into the system, which seems to be a good thing as the due date approaches. The other area that massage might help is the perineum, which is the small piece of real estate between a woman's vagina and her rectum. Some pregnancy aficionados believe that massaging this area may help to make it more pliable and reduce the need for an episiotomy.

Bleeding

During the first couple of months of pregnancy, bleeding may occur during the time when you would normally have your period. This is usually less reason for concern than bleeding that is random. Be sure to check with your physician when there is any bleeding, just to be on the safe side.

Touch vs. Sex

Some women may experience a decreased desire for sex during pregnancy, but an increased need for touch and cuddling. This can be difficult for the dad-to-be, because all of the cuddling and touching might make him feel extremely horny. To help him make it through these lean times sexually, his pregnant partner can cuddle beside him and caress his thighs, chest or testicles while he does himself by hand. Or he can do what a lot of other guys do—jerk off in the shower.

Besides being an important time for holding and touching, pregnancy is a fine time for partners to reassure one another about their feelings of love and attraction, hopefully for each other.

Fears That Bubble Up from
The Deep Dark Recesses of the Human Psyche

Contrary to how you think you should be feeling, it is not uncommon for perfectly good parents-to-be to have mixed feelings about the baby-to-be. For instance, you may have planned for years to have this baby and wanted it with the deepest of convictions, but then suddenly start feeling, "Oh my God, what have we done?" Feelings like these can be fleeting or last for weeks. One reader says that both he and his wife were shocked to discover such feelings, given that their pregnancy was better planned than the average moon walk. Fortunately, they did not experience their bummer moods at the same time. As a result, the one who was feeling good about the pregnancy was able to comfort the one who was feeling tragic.

It is perfectly normal for us humans to be overwhelmed by inner conflicts. These can be especially intense during pregnancy, when so many new demands are about to be placed on you. These are not the sorts of feelings that make us want to have sex. It can be very helpful to talk over these conflicts with a friend, partner or even a counselor if you are feeling particularly jammed by them. One reader adds: "Worries about child care, job security, and having to go back to work after only six weeks can be overwhelming."

Recognizing Dad's Role

During pregnancy, all attention usually focuses on the mom-to-be, which is as it should be. But this is also an important time for the pregnant woman to acknowledge the dad-to-be's role. Potential problems can occur when the woman feels that the baby is her creation alone. This can lead to problems in the relationship between father and child as well as between mother and father. It is likely that the child will be made to feel guilty when he or she finally attempts to separate from mom.

Dad's Emotional & Sexual Issues during Pregnancy

There are plenty of books devoted to the various feelings that pregnant moms experience. Yet dads-to-be experience their own set of pregnancy-related emotions. According to researcher James Herzog, dads-to-be tend to fall into two groups: more attuned and less attuned. The pregnancy spurs the first group of dads onto a path of personal growth, while the latter group feels threatened by the pregnancy and is not particularly fortified by it.

One factor that impacts how a man responds to his wife's pregnancy is the influence of his own father or father substitutes. Herzog noticed that during the second and third trimesters of pregnancy, a number of pregnant dads turned toward their own fathers in an attempt to reconnect with them. They felt that reconnecting with the "good dad" from their early childhood would help them be better dads to their own children. Men in the less-attuned group tended to experience a high degree of "father hunger"—growing up without an involved and caring father figure. These men tended to act in unsupportive ways, such as becoming competitive with their wives or being sexually promiscuous; some had sexual relations with other men. If you find yourself feeling unsupportive or disconnected from your pregnant wife, it might be a great idea to spend extra time with a friend or acquaintance whose fathering skills you admire. Tell him you are feeling on shaky ground; ask him how he manages as a dad when he's feeling uncertain or overwhelmed.

Other things that Herzog found about pregnant dads included the following:

The Right Stuff Upon learning of the pregnancy, a number of dads-to-be feel quite good about themselves in a masculine and sexual way. The fact of the pregnancy may help allay fears that they didn't have the right stuff to make a pregnancy happen. With the excitement of being pregnant, a number of couples enjoy sex that is quite intense and intimate, as though sex itself now has a different meaning.

Nourishment As the pregnancy progresses, some men feel as if they are nourishing or symbolically feeding their wives during intercourse, especially when they come inside of them. On some level, the dad-to-be might view his semen as a kind of milk that will help nurture both mother and infant.

Coming Harder Some men report feeling more depth to their orgasms when their partners are pregnant, with more physical and emotional awareness both before and after ejaculation. At the same time, the dad-to-be might be rethinking who he is; he's a man whose personal identity is expanding. At times this can be exhilarating, at other times a frightening burden.

Dreams Etc. There are plenty of ways that dads unconsciously identify with a pregnant spouse or wonder about what's going on inside of her. For instance, by mid-pregnancy, some fathers experience dreams or fantasies about being penetrated as well as being the one who penetrates. Some dream or start to wonder about their own inner body parts. Some put on extra weight or feel a kind of gastric fullness or upset. Some men have toothaches during this time that land them in the dentist's office. When a man has a toothache of an undetermined origin, some dentists know to inquire if the man's wife is pregnant.

Character Evolution   Being a dad-to-be can help a man shed unwanted or outdated parts of his character. The pregnancy becomes an excuse and a stimulus to mature and become more responsible. Of course, not all men use pregnancy in such a constructive way, nor do all women.

Sex after Giving Birth

Some parents experience the first three to six months after the child's birth as being the most demanding and difficult time of their lives. They might not feel like having sex, or if they do, they might be too exhausted to actually do it. Other couples enjoy sneaking in quickies while the baby sleeps.

There are hugely important considerations that affect the frequency of sex among new parents, like whether dad does his fair share of the work around the house and with the baby, and whether mom welcomes his help or is nervous and critical whenever he gets near the baby. If one parent is an obvious klutz with the baby, there are plenty of ways that he or she can be helpful other than with actual hands-on baby care. In a few months, the baby may have grown enough that you feel more comfortable handling it.

Even with the best intention and desire, there will be plenty of times when new moms and dads are way too exhausted for sex, especially if there are other children in the family besides the baby. Keep in mind that plenty of couples struggle when it comes to adapting to their new roles as parents and sexual partners.

Hormones & Libido

Some women don't feel like having sex after pregnancy due to anti-horny hormones that might be surging through their veins. Women who are nursing are said to produce more anti-horny hormones than women who are bottle feeding, yet statistics show that nursing mothers want sex more often than those who don't nurse. Go figure.

Talking about Sex Before the Baby Is Born

Some of the best advice this book has to offer is that you talk about sex before the baby is actually born. For instance, "I've heard some new parents don't feel like having sex for a few months after giving birth—what are some of the ways we might handle that if it happens to one or both of us?" Or "What do we do if you've got a raging hard-on and I want to be held and cuddled but don't want to have intercourse?" Or "What if I want sex but you start seeing me as a mother type and don't find me exciting?"

One of the worst things you can do about sex after pregnancy is to pretend it is not a problem if it actually is. Nothing is to be gained by rolling over and pretending you are asleep to avoid having sex, by getting defensive or by feeling attacked. As with other aspects of your relationship, this is a time to redefine and put things in a new perspective. Where sex was once taken for granted, it may now need to be planned or scheduled. There will be plenty of times when sexual desire is a casualty to exhaustion. For a while, you might end up masturbating more often.

When Can We Start Having Intercourse?

After the placenta comes out of the womb, it takes time for the place where it was attached to heal. The woman is going to be vulnerable to infections. This is why it might not be such a good idea for things like male ejaculate and store-bought lube to be working their way up there. Also, it might take a couple of weeks for the vagina to heal after it's been stretched from here to China. Some physicians worry that intercourse before the vagina is healed can cause scar tissue to build. This is why most physicians feel it is wise to wait at least a few weeks after birth before you start doing the nasty. Check with your healthcare provider for specifics. This is particularly true if the woman had an episiotomy, with stitches that need to heal, and don't even think about having intercourse after a C-section until the doctor waves the checkered flag, or should that be green flag?

Birth Control

Be sure to stock up on birth control products before the baby is born. Do not leave this important detail for after the birth, as you will have your hands full dealing with other things and are likely to let it slip. It is not fair to you or the new baby to have a repeat pregnancy sooner than you want. Also, don't for a moment believe that moms who are nursing are unable to get pregnant. Nursing moms get pregnant all the time. Ditto for couples who have unprotected sex during mom's period.

Lubricated condoms and condoms with contraceptive chemicals can irritate tender vaginal tissues. If dryness is an issue for you and you are concerned about irritation, check with your obstetrician's office for advice.

Designated Night Out

Once the baby is three months old, you might be wise to plan at least one evening a week where you and your spouse go out together, without junior in tow, for at least a couple of hours. There are a couple of ways to engineer this, with willing grandparents being top on the list. Every Wednesday night they get the baby and you get each other. If grandparents aren't an option and a baby sitter is either too hard to find or too expensive, call couples from your Lamaze class or find other parents with young babies and arrange to co-op the baby sitting. For instance, they take yours every Tuesday, and you take theirs every Thursday.

Children know when something important is missing in their parents' relationship. If there is a lack of intimacy or unity among their parents, they can suffer almost as much as the parents. Do not make the mistake of focusing all your energy on being parents and no energy on being lovers. By the time you notice that something is wrong with your relationship, it may be difficult to repair.

Painful Intercourse?

You may need to work your way up to intercourse. If time permits, you might try taking showers or baths together and sharing a beer or bottle of wine beforehand. Also, it never hurts to have a giant-sized tube of lube on the night stand. Some women who have never had a problem getting wet find they need an assist after giving birth. For other women, it can be just the opposite.

Beware the "Husband's Stitch"

Physicians sometimes do a "husband's stitch" when sewing a woman up after delivery if she had tearing or an episiotomy. This is essentially a little tuck that's done at the opening of the vagina. The physician assumes it will make intercourse feel better for the husband. While the sentiment is nice, the "husband's stitch" is better used in upholstery shops than on women's genitals. Tightening the entrance to the vagina just makes the opening smaller and is liable to make intercourse feel painful for the woman. If a woman is concerned about vaginal tone following pregnancy, she would do much better to practice Kegel exercises, which help to tighten the entire vagina rather than making the opening more difficult to get into. It never hurts to discuss this with your healthcare provider.

Readers' Comments

"When I was pregnant, I wanted sex more, and felt more free."
female age 44

"I was extremely horny during my pregnancy and I felt very sexy until the last month or two." *female age 26*

"I had no sexual desire at all." *female age 36*

"I was constantly horny when I wasn't nauseous."
female age 35

"I viewed her expanding body as just more to love, hold and caress." *male age 41*

"Intercourse can hurt toward 39-40 weeks when the baby's head is lower. Sometimes foreplay was just as satisfying."
female age 25

"I was more horny than anything. Because of the pregnancy, we needed to start using new positions. Some worked so well that we are still using them today." *female age 25*

"We didn't do anything different during pregnancy, except we didn't have to use rubbers. Yea!" *female age 38*

"For intercourse while pregnant, I was pretty much always on top." *female age 45*

"Don't worry about the baby. If it is firmly implanted, no orgasm will dislodge it." *female age 35*

"If anything, I admired her more for being able to 'do' a pregnancy. It's a real turn-on to feel an essential part of one."

male age 43

"When I was pregnant, sex felt extremely good and multiple orgasms happened all the time. They would sneak up on me. Things would be feeling good and if I concentrated hard I could have another and another." *female age 26*

"My wife seemed to be more lubricated, which was great. She seemed more relaxed also." *male age 38*

"Be gentle, be considerate, encourage her to lead. As for sex after the baby's born, that depends on whether she's in a private room or not." *male age 40*

Sex after the kids are born?

"Sex after the kids are born? Babysitters, movies for kids, grandmother's house and motel rooms...." *male age 44*

"Lock the door, turn the music up, and put *The Lion King* on the VCR." *male age 39*

"When you've got kids, bedtime is the most convenient time for sex, but it's not always the most exciting time for me. If I wake up early and am horny, I wake my husband up, which is something he loves, to have sex when he's just waking up."

female age 45

"You have to make it clear they can't interrupt. Sometimes I'm just very upfront with what we are doing and she knows not to come in." *female age 25*

"Cut to the chase: I am an RN and have seen hundreds of uncircumcised males. No turn on. But when my most recent lover happened to be such it was so totally unexpected that my sexual arousal rate went up 200%. I am very turned on by stroking him to expose the head, kissing and licking it and then covering it again by pulling the foreskin back up. Sucking ever so gently with the skin covering the head gives him pleasure, but pulling it down near the base of his penis completely exposes him and his reaction is amazing. All it takes is tender gentle swirls to drive him crazy…. The wanton horny bitch that resides within myself has now been released and owes you all at the Goofy Foot Press gratitude and the author the best blow job ever!" *female age 27*

The author responds:

"Drive south on I-5 until you reach the Corvallis exit, go west…"

Fun With Your Foreskin

Chapter 49

Medically speaking, routine circumcision makes about as much sense as removing a kid's eyelids or cutting out the labia of a baby girl. So why are so many American boys routinely circumcised?

During the 1880s, a few influential men like John Harvey Kellogg, physician and founder of a famous American cereal company, started preaching that boys masturbate because the foreskin rubs on the head of the penis. Until that time, most American men were not circumcised. As a leading anti-masturbation fanatic, Dr. Kellogg believed that boys who were circumcised at birth would be less likely to play with themselves. His influence helped circumcision to become a routine operation in America. Swell guy that he was, Dr. Kellogg also recommended that girls who masturbate have their clitorises burned out with acid.

Is There a Medical Need for Circumcision?

America's medical establishment has tried to justify its hand in circumcision by saying that it prevents cancer of the penis, cancer of the cervix and numerous other medical calamities. If this were true, why would physicians in England decide that the operation is not such a good idea? Less than 10% of the newborn blokes in the UK have their dicks docked. As for cancer of the penis and cervix, it now seems that a strain of the HPV virus is the culprit. Either way, there is no evidence that circumcision prevents cancer of the penis. In fact, in circumcised men who do get cancer of the penis, the cancer tends to break out on the circumcision scar.

Women who live in countries where men aren't circumcised have no higher rate of cervical cancer than women in America. The only penis-related item that increases a woman's chance of getting cancer of the cervix is having numerous male sex partners, circumcised or not. Condom use might help decrease this risk, but circumcision has no impact.

Cancer of the penis is extremely rare. More men get breast cancer. In evaluating cancer risks, it is twice as dangerous for a woman to have intact labia than for a man to have an intact foreskin.

In Sweden, where few men are circumcised, cancer of the penis is just as rare as in the circumcision-happy United States. It would be interesting to compare the number of penises lost to cancer with the number of penises mutilated through botched circumcisions.

As for other claims, one study years ago did show that circumcised males were less likely to get urinary tract infections during the first year of life. However, in that study the parents of the uncircumcised babies were instructed to pull back their foreskins and wash under them. Yet parents should do just the opposite, because nature did not intend the foreskin to retract before one year of age. It is quite likely that the instructions given to the parents were what caused the higher rate of infections among the uncircumcised boys. But even if those figures are correct, the number of urinary tract infections is still much greater in female babies, and no one is recommending preventive surgery for them.

There have also been claims that uncircumcised men are more apt to catch sexually transmitted diseases, including AIDS. However, European men don't show any greater incidence of these diseases than American men, and European men are mostly uncircumcised. Until recently, American men who were uncircumcised tended to be from poor families. Whether circumcised or not, poor people often get diseases at a higher rate than those who are rich.

Finally, there exists a myth that large percentages of uncircumcised babies will have foreskins that don't retract (phimosis), and that these males will need surgery when they grow older to correct this condition. In reality, fewer than 1 out of every 100 uncircumcised men have this condition, and a foreskin-friendly urologist can almost always help to resolve the problem without having to cut the kid.

So Why Do They Keep Doing It?

A physician in the US makes between $150 and $300 per circumcision. Doing one circumcision per day, five days per week, at a fee of $150 each minus time out for a six week vacation nets a physician an extra $34,500 per year for a procedure that takes less than ten minutes. And that's only one a day at the lower rate. No wonder why pediatricians and obstetricians used to fight over who got to do the circumcision!

Another reason for doing circumcisions is medical bias. Until recently, physicians in this country have had a long-standing bias that hysterectomies are good for women and circumcisions are good for men. Before managed health care, they also had a bias for C-sections over natural births, given that C-sections were much more profitable and easier to schedule.

In short, there appears to be no medical reason besides possible income enhancement for doing routine circumcision. There does, however, appear to be a very good reason why nature equipped the penis with a foreskin. Not only is the foreskin rich in pleasure-producing nerve endings, but it also keeps the head of the penis moist, and the extra skin provides added sliding pleasure during intercourse and masturbation. The foreskin is extremely elastic and is said to be as sensitive to touch as the human lips. Far from being unnecessary, a foreskin is usually a nice thing to have.

How They Do It

During male circumcision, they stick a prodding instrument into the foreskin to tear it away from the head of the penis. One-third to one-half of the skin on the penis is then cut off. Traditionally, male circumcisions have not been done with anesthesia, but even when anesthesia is used, there is still pain from the raw scar on the penis.

Religious Considerations

Some people will say, "But circumcision is done for important religious and cultural reasons." The same is true for female circumcision, which we refer to as genital mutilation.

Some people say this is being disrespectful of an important ritual in the Jewish faith. This is true. We are also disrespectful of the Catholic Church's ban on birth control and masturbation. If Jewish men want to be circumcised as an expression of their faith, why not let them wait until they are eighteen years old and able to call the Mohel themselves? That would be a far greater expression of faith than having the end of your penis chopped off when you're only a few days old and can't tell the Torah from a phone book.

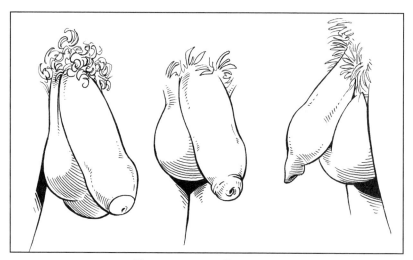

Different Guys, Different Foreskins

According to psychologist Ronald Goldman, not all Jewish men are circumcised. Theodore Herzl, the founder of modern Zionism, did not allow his own son to be circumcised. Even Moses did not circumcise his son, and circumcision was not done during the forty-year period in the wilderness. It is quite possible that this custom arose out of the Egyptian practice to circumcise their Jewish slaves. Over time, this became a ritual or custom, and eventually became associated with the Covenant.

The ultimate goal of circumcision, according to ancient rabbis and Jewish religious scholars from Philo to Maimonides, was to decrease sexual pleasure for both men and women. This would give men more time to study the Torah, and result in women receiving less sexual pleasure from a man who was circumcised.

In 1843, Reform Movement leaders in Frankfort, Germany started a mini-house revolt against circumcision. This group of intellectuals and professionals argued that 1) Circumcision had not always been practiced among Jews; 2) It was not commanded to Moses; 3) It's not unique among Jews, given how Muslims do it as well; 4) It is only discussed once in the Mosaic law and not repeated in Deuteronomy; 5) There was no comparable practice for females.

Perhaps one of the most interesting elements of circumcision in the Jewish religion is that for the first 2000 years of the practice, only the tip of the foreskin was cut. This was called Milah. It was only after the first 2000 years of Milah that they started whacking off the entire foreskin.

Resource: A very helpful book on this subject is *Questioning Circumcision—A Jewish Perspective* by Ronald Goldman, Ph.D., Vanguard, Boston, 1998.

For Parents—Foreskin Care

Do not try to retract the foreskin of a young boy unless there is a specific medical reason. During infancy and childhood, the inner surface of the foreskin is physically attached to the skin on the head of the penis. This protects the opening of the penis from irritation, infection and ulceration. Over time, the cells that attach these two surfaces together will start to dissolve on their own. By trying to retract the foreskin prematurely, you are ripping apart these delicate tissues that nature has "glued" together.

A young boy will often push his foreskin away from his body. As he gets older, he will begin to pull it toward his body. A number of males don't fully retract their foreskins until they into their teenage years. This is normal and will usually happen without any coaxing or encouragement from mom and dad.

Parents do need to tell their teenage sons about cleanliness. They should explain that once a boy is able to retract his foreskin he should clean it every day in the shower. Enlightened parents might also explain that boys who don't keep their genitals clean don't get nearly as much oral sex as boys who do!

Resources:

Circumcision Information And Resource Pages
www.cirp.org

National Organization of Circumcision Information Resource Centers (Includes a list of foreskin-friendly physicians)
www.nocirc.org/

No Harm
www.noharmm.org

Circumcision Resource Center
www.circumcision.org

Doctors Opposing Circumcision (D.O.C.)
2442 NW Market Street, Suite 42
Seattle, Washington 98107
http://faculty.washington.edu/gcd/DOC/

Pictures of intact foreskins
www.foreskin.org

Reader Comments

"I'd never even seen an uncircumcised penis until my current lover, but I've decided now that it's the best thing since sliced bread. The foreskin makes hand jobs 100 times better and easier because it slides over the penis so you don't need lube. I was kind of nervous about it at first but then I realized how stretchy the foreskin is even though it looks kinda fragile. For blow jobs, I pull the foreskin down to the base and massage it there and go to town." *female age 18*

"The only Jewish guy I ever slept with was also the only uncircumcised guy I ever slept with. He seemed to have more stamina than any of the others, but that might just be a coincidence." *female age 21*

"For a blow job, pull the foreskin up over the head and stick your tongue down inside of the opening and swirl it around." *female age 38*

"Just ask the guy how he likes it. Some guys like you to pull the foreskin tight, others say this hurts." *female age 20*

"I use my foreskin to massage her clitoris. This might only be possible with a partner who has a larger than normal clitoris. You need to be able to get hold of it." *male age 65*

"Once my wife and I are ready for penetration, I roll my foreskin all the way shut. I press it gently against her labia while spreading them slightly, and push the glans in just a little. Then, I withdraw the glans back inside the foreskin, never exposing it to open air. What this does is spread her lubricant all over the first half of my penis. After several strokes like this, I am able to slip inside easily. Sometimes we find this so pleasurable that we continue a good long while before penetrating farther." *male age 38*

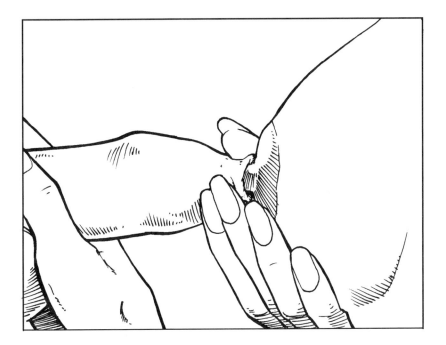

"A partner should know that the inside of a foreskin is where there is the most feeling, so gentle movement of it over a cock-head and down the shaft feels great. The best part of getting a blow job is what a tongue and mouth can do with that inside lining of a foreskin." *male age 59*

"One thing I find particularly stimulating is to lubricate a finger or thumb, slip it between the foreskin and the head, and massage the glans. It feels really, really great." *male age 19*

"When did I first retract it? I was around ten. I would slowly pull it back every day in the shower. After about two weeks I was able to pull it all the way down." *male age 22*

"Letting the foreskin balloon is quite nice both when peeing and when enjoying the pool jets." *male age 37*

"I like to do the trick of clamping the end shut while peeing and making it swell up. Also, a similar and a more satisfying experience is to leave just a bit of the end open and put it under a strong flow of water so that the water flows in but has a place to get out." *male age 20*

"My fiancee does all the foreskin movement for me, its such a turn-on when she pulls it back and then returns it to normal. She does this with her mouth constantly while she gives me a blow job." *male age 19*

"There is nothing worse than cracking an erection in your pants and not being able to make it go away because your foreskin is retracted and the head of your cock keeps on rubbing on your pants." *male age 18*

Somebody took my hat!

The First Time—Not What You'd Think

Chapter 50

Why would a parent want to read about teenagers and their attitudes on sex? Trust the *Guide.* There's more to this than meets the eye.

Researchers Newlyn Moore and J. Kenneth Davidson recently questioned hundreds of young women about their sexual experiences and corresponding feelings of guilt.

You would think that young women who felt the most guilt and shame about their sexuality would be motivated to sleep with fewer guys. You would think they would be losing their virginity at an older age than girls who feel better about sex.

Shock of all shocks, the opposite is true. Girls with the most negative attitudes about their sexuality are doing it younger, with more partners and in less committed relationships than girls who feel the most positive about their bodies and their sexuality.

Also, the guilt girls are the most likely to have their first intercourse with an "occasional dating partner" or with a "person just met," a pattern they continue to repeat as they get older. And they tend to have their first intercourse when drinking or stoned.

As you might expect, the girls who feel the best about their bodies tend to masturbate more. But you'd think these feel-good masturbators would be more promiscuous. Not so. The girls who masturbate the most and feel the best about sex actually wait the longest before having their first intercourse and they have it with more committed partners. Most importantly, when they do have sex, it's part of a conscious decision. Not so with the girls who feel bad about sex and their bodies. More often than not, they just let sex happen to them, without thinking it through first.

So who are these high-guilt, more-promiscuous girls? High-guilt girls tend to grow up in families where the mother and father are less affectionate toward each other. They tend to regard their dads as being overly strict and they are from homes that are more religious, rather than less religious, than girls who don't sleep around as much.

Perhaps the girls who have the least sexual acceptance at home go searching for it elsewhere. The trouble is, they go about it in such a destructive way that they end up reinforcing the bad feelings about themselves that they grew up with, and they end up with partners who are just as constricted as their dads.

Who knew that the daughters of the self-righteous would be more likely to sleep around and do it drunk than daughters of parents who have a more open, honest approach to sex and sexual feelings? It's certainly not what the self-described moral majority would have us believe. Perhaps there's more to waiting longer than the just-say-no abstinence-only proponents want us to think.

Girls vs. Boys — Feelings about Sex

For a boy, puberty usually brings freedom. It also leaves a young man feeling more positive about his body, more independent and more masculine. Not so for girls. Menstruation itself often leaves a girl with a feeling that her body is out of control.

According to Dr. Martin: "The girls whom I interviewed gave only negative descriptions of their menstruating bodies. Their bodies made them feel 'yuck' or 'sick,' or as if they had 'shit their pants'.... While plenty of girls look forward to having their first period, a lot become ambivalent after the first couple of periods have come and gone."

Teenage boys may struggle with wet dreams and unwanted erections, but not many would equate these with shitting in their pants. On the contrary, a boy's growing body often makes him feel more grown up and effective in the world, while a girl's growing body brings parental warnings about the evil intentions of men and physical restrictions on everything from climbing trees to learning to sit like a lady. These warnings can make the world seem scary.

For a girl, her growing body represents loss as much as it represents gain. For instance, the mere fact that she suddenly has breasts causes changes in her relationship with her dad and every other man she meets. No longer will her dad be as physically affectionate, and no longer will she be as unconscious about her body. Ever hear that upbeat song from the early 1960s, "Sweet Sixteen"? It talks about a girl who was just a normal kid next door until suddenly she grows boobs and hips, and her former big-brother figure up the street has a hard-on and a hit song. Maybe the girl was happier before puberty when the universe didn't revolve around what her body looked like.

Dr. Martin tells about asking teenage girls to describe themselves:

> When I asked girls, especially working-class girls, to describe themselves or asked, "Tell me about yourself," they described their bodies and had a difficult time describing any other aspects of who they were. "Can you describe an important goal you achieved?" "I love my hair. My hair's my accomplishment..." "What kind of things make you feel good about yourself?" "When someone like pays me a compliment on something, you know. Like says that I look nice or have on nice clothes or something."

It was totally different for most of the boys. The boys felt good about themselves because of things they had done or things they felt they could do in the world. Of course, if most of these boys were more in touch with the reality of their "effectiveness" rather than their fantasies of it, they might not feel so confident. But still, when boys want to have sex, it is often with confidence and good feelings about their bodies, while girls often feel the opposite. In terms of sexual economics, we're talking the U.S. versus Peru.

So how does this reflect itself in the feelings that boys and girls have about sex?

"Boys thought sex would be pleasurable, and many said they looked forward to it or were curious about it.... No girl said that she looked forward to sex or that she expected it to be pleasurable. It is a rare teenage girl who has sex because she wants to."

The majority of teenage girls whom Dr. Martin interviewed expected sex to hurt or to be painful or scary. If this is true, why did the girls have sex?

"No matter how you look at a girl's reasons for having sex, the vast majority break down to the same simple reason: they are afraid the boy will leave, they are afraid they will lose him, or afraid he won't like them anymore."

More than half of the working-class girls and a quarter of the middle-class girls in Dr. Martin's study seemed to have an ideal or exaggerated love for the boys they were dating or wanted to date. Feelings like these will make a girl do anything to keep her man in tow. The boys, on the other hand, did not report looking for romance or ideal love. They seemed to want a combination of friendship and sex in their relationships, although it is possible that the boys kept their romantic feelings to themselves. (For a teenage boy to tell an interviewer about feelings of romantic love might be admitting to less than manly aspirations. Or as the boys at Dartmouth might say, "Whadda you, a faggot or something?")

When it comes to teenagers and sex, boys and girls often have different wants and expectations. Far more boys think that the sex will feel good, while far more girls believe it will hurt. Far more girls idealize their boyfriends and feel they can't live without them, or they need the boyfriend as an affirmation that they are attractive and worthwhile. For this, they are willing to have sex, which they expect to be painful. Due to the inexperience of the parties involved, it often is.

As for masturbation, many teenage girls feel it is something that boys do, and do not associate it with femininity. Nor do they seem very interested in exploring their own bodies. As Dr. Martin comments, "Their boyfriends were allowed more access to their bodies than they allowed themselves." And this study was done in the 1990s, not the 1950s.

Perhaps one of the most frightening findings of Dr. Martin's research is that almost all of the teenage girls felt better about shaving their legs than they did about the sex they were having with their boyfriends. It seems that being able to shave their legs provided a happy identification with their mothers or older sisters. It made the girls feel grown up in a good way.

Few and far between are the teenage girls who feel in control of their bodies and who have sex because they expect it to feel good. But those girls who did tended to have good relationships with their mothers which included lots of conversations about sex. They had good relationships with their dads and they were also more involved in extracurricular activities like sports or 4-H. They seemed to place more value on the size of their IQs than on the size of their waists. They knew their own bodies better and felt more in control of their sexuality.

If as many teenagers did as badly with computers as they do with sex, the President and Congress would be in arms. The last thing they would be telling teens is "Just Say No To Your Computer!" Will one less teenage girl have sex because of so-called sex education programs that preach abstinence? Not if the reason she has sex is to keep her boyfriend. On the other hand, if she feels she has a good mind and she understands how wonderful sex can be, maybe she'll make better decisions when it comes to sharing sex with others.

While we can't help you with the countless hours and effort that it takes to raise a child with a good mind, this guide can help with suggestions for raising children who feel that sex is healthy and valuable. That's what the next chapter is all about.

Counterpoint: A reader writes: "Sex for me was definitely not because I was afraid of losing the guy. I don't even know if it was really about my feelings for the guy. Mostly it was my curiosity about how sex felt. Few of my friends were dating and none were having sex so it wasn't about fitting in."

If readers would like to send in their thoughts about this, we will add them with each new printing as space permits, as well as post them on our website.

Chapter Notes: Moore and Davidson's thoughtful and thought provoking paper, *Guilt About First Intercourse: An Antecedent of Sexual Dissatisfaction Among College Women* was published in the Journal of Sex and Marital Therapy, Vol. 23, No. 1, Spring 1997, pp. 29-46.

Karin Martin's study is titled *Puberty, Sexuality and the Self* (New York: Routledge, 1996). ISBN: 0-415-91425-6. While this 118-page book is addressed to academic types, the actual quotes and observations make it an essential read for anyone studying teenage sexuality.

Explaining Sex To Kids

Chapter 51

Let's say that little Billy has gone shopping with his dad for the afternoon and you steal half an hour to lie on your bed with stereo headphones bolted to your ears, eyes closed and fingers massaging a very important place between your legs. You are all alone and the sensations begin to feel wonderful. Next thing you know, the headphones are being yanked off your head by little Billy, who is asking, "Mommy, what color napkins were we supposed to get for the birthday party?"

Or perhaps you assume that little Amber is fast asleep and you begin enjoying an all-too-rare moment of sex when a little hand suddenly taps you on the shoulder and you hear the words "Daddy, how come Mommy's sucking on your penis?"

The pages that follow don't pretend to have all the answers about children and sex; they are simply a way of getting you to think about the subject long before most parents do, which is sometimes too late for an effective response. Topics range from talking about genitals and masturbation to menstruation, sex play and even sex on the internet.

Children's Sexual Development

People often think of sex as something that happens once we become teenagers. Not true. Most of us started having sexual feelings when we were little babies. Each time someone changed our diapers and powdered our private parts we had sexual feelings in the most basic sense—nice physical sensations down where the Pampers go.

As children get a few years older, they often enjoy playing sex games with friends and relatives, same sex or otherwise. Sometimes they just compare and contrast; other times they enjoy doing things that big people do, like sucking on each other's genitals or sticking fingers, penises and heaven knows what else up each other's front and rear ends. Eventually you might encounter a third-grade child who's sitting there with both hands in his or her pants, happily rubbing away, while claiming how yuckie it would be to ever kiss on the lips.

As children's minds grow and become more complex, so does their ability to have sexual fantasies that include others. With time, the thought of making love doesn't seem so "yuckie" anymore. Eventually, they might even want to read books like the *Guide to Getting It On!* In the meantime, one parent might wonder if it is normal for her four-year-old boy to be playing with his penis, while another might say, "Thank heavens he's got his penis to play with. It's a never-ending source of pleasure for him!"

Telling Children about Sexual Enjoyment

Parents usually tell their children all there is to know about things like blowing noses and wiping rear ends, but rarely do they mention that genitals can be the source of good feelings. As a result, children learn that it's okay to seek their parents' wisdom on just about everything but sexual feelings. This is most unfortunate, because kids need their parents' guidance on sexual feelings as much as they do on wiping their rear ends or learning to drive a car.

Some parents assume that a three-year-old who is rubbing her genitals has the same intent and fantasies as a twenty-three-year-old. They either try to stop her or simply pretend that nothing is happening. Perhaps it would be helpful for parents to understand that their masturbating three-year-old isn't thinking about how good Johnnie, her day-care buddy, might be in bed! The child is simply touching her genitals because it feels good. It is perfectly normal for little hands to reach between little legs when a child is happy or excited, at naptime or even when you are reading Dr. Seuss to her. All a parent needs to do is say an occasional "It feels good to touch yourself there." This gives mom and dad credibility about such matters and lets the child know it will be safe to talk to the parents about things of a sexual nature.

Also, little boys have erections from a very early age, yet parents seldom explain to them that males get erections when they are having fun with their penis, as well as at other times like when waking up in the morning. Parents tell boys that they have nice eyes, ears or even feet, but they avoid telling a boy about his penis or saying anything nice about it. Nor do they tell a girl positive things about her genitals or let an older girl her know that her vagina will sometimes get wet. Yet girls get wet as often as boys get erections. (Parents who explain such matters to their children may need to distinguish between the sexual kind of wet and the peeing-in-your-pants kind of wet.)

Nanny Interruptus

Everyone these days is worried about nannies shaking their baby to death or kidnapping it or being lazy when no one else is around. Few people think to ask the nanny how she responds if she encounters junior playing with his or her genitals.

What if you are trying to encourage a healthy attitude about sex, but during the nine hours a day when you are away, Consuela is slapping the kid's hand and warning of a thousand curses that will happen if your child ever touches him or herself again?

Ask about this when you are interviewing for a nanny. Otherwise, much of your hard work may be for naught.

Opportunity Knocks, and Knocks, and Knocks

four-year-old girl: Daddy, how come boy's have penises?

dad: I don't know. But I do know that boys and girls are both really lucky to have something between their legs that feels so good when they play with it!

The wonderful thing about explaining sex to kids is that you usually don't have to bring up the subject. It comes up on its own. Whether it's dogs mating in the backyard or your kid rubbing her genitals while you read her a good night story, opportunities abound to make talking about sex a normal and natural part of growing up.

Unfortunately, parents who explain sex in an open and honest way should be prepared for nasty glares from other adults, because their children won't know it is bad to talk about sex; e.g., "Mr. Johnson, my daddy gets erections. Do you?" or "Sister Mary Elizabeth, does your vulva tingle when you feel excited?"

Ultimately, this kind of embarrassment is nothing compared to what you will feel if the first time you talk about sex is when your fifteen-year-old daughter informs you she is pregnant. (In Sweden, where children have better access to sexual information and birth control, the rate of teenage pregnancy is one-sixth of what it is in the United States. Also, the kids there don't start having sex any earlier than they do here.)

Playing with Themselves

Since many parents don't talk about masturbation, their children may regard it as a dirty secret.

You can explain masturbation to a younger child by saying, "Masturbation is when you touch yourself between your legs in a way that feels good." If your child asks for details and you feel comfortable about it, you can make a pretend penis with a finger while saying, "This is how boys do it" or point two fingers downward and rub the knuckle part to explain how girls do it. Or you can say "It's what you've done since you were really little when you put your hand between your legs and pull and rub, I'd say about nine-hundred times each day." Also, it might be reassuring for an older boy to hear his father say, "I started masturbating when I was your age" or for a girl to hear her mother say, "I masturbate, too."

Keep in mind that masturbation is very common for kids between the ages of 2 and 11, and it's not unusual for a child to occasionally hump or rub their genitals up against just about anything that suits their fancy.

Public vs. Private

In doing research for this book, the author met with a class of high school students to talk about sex. Before he had even introduced himself, one of the boys yelled, "Do you masturbate?" It's not the sort of question he is used to being asked, let alone by a young punk with baggy pants and a strange haircut. Embarrassing? You bet, yet to have said anything but "Sure" would have created a serious credibility gap, and it would have been dishonest. Beyond that, it would have been inappropriate for him to have discussed details about his private sex life with the young and restless. Hopefully, parents will keep in mind that it is neither necessary nor advisable to discuss the details of their private sex lives with their children. On the other hand, it is fine for parents to let their children know that sex is a fun and important part of their lives.

Younger children may need constant help in learning the difference between public and private. You may need to remind your three- or four-year-old numerous times that they aren't to play with their vulva or penis in the yard. Hopefully, you will never hear them reply, "But you and daddy do!"

Liberal Parent Alert For super permissive parents who feel that putting limits on children destroys their little spirits, keep in mind that children won't feel safe with their sexuality if it is allowed to explode all over the place. If a child won't stop masturbating or exposing himself or herself in a public place, there is no harm in saying, "I know that feels really good, but the place to do it is in the privacy of your own room and you should consider stopping it right now if you ever want to eat ice cream again as long as you live." Also, older children who constantly rub their genitals might be dealing with emotional anxieties that have little to do with sex. Before getting too concerned, you need to consider how the kid is doing with the rest of his or her life. Is this one of many things that isn't going right, or is it simply an isolated problem that needs loving but firm guidance?

Naming Private Parts

Modern parents usually have no problem telling little boys that they've got a penis and testicles between their legs, although little boys rarely refer to these items by their proper names. For that matter, neither do big boys.

Female sexual anatomy is mislabeled from practically day one. First of all, what you see from the outside is not a vagina, but that has become the generic term for what is nestled between a woman's legs. What you see from the outside is a vulva, which means lips. The vagina doesn't appear until after the vulva is spread open, and even then you only see the outer rim of it. It is also helpful for parents to identify the clitoris.

Parents might do well to inform boys about girls' genitals and vice versa. This way, girls' genitals won't seem like such a mystery. Also, it is through such talks that parents can teach boys to respect and care about girls' genitals. Otherwise, how are boys expected to learn such things? In a locker room?

The Difference between Cum and Pee

When you are ready to explain the concept of ejaculation to an older child, he or she might assume you are talking about pee. After all, that's what comes out of a penis, right? Kids will likely surmise from early talks about the birds and bees that the man pees into the woman to make her pregnant. One way of avoiding this confusion is to explain that there is a big difference between pee and ejaculate. Pee is thin and mostly clear like water and there is a lot of it, while ejaculate is white and thick, and there is only a teaspoon or two of it at a time. It won't hurt to explain that nature was very smart about all of this and made it so that a man can pee when his penis is soft and have an ejaculation when his penis is hard. You can say that when a man has intercourse and his penis is hard, there comes a certain point where his penis feels really good and warm and the ejaculate starts to squirt out. That's the stuff that can get a woman pregnant. Let them know that boys don't start making this fluid until they go through puberty, which happens sometime between the ages of eleven and sixteen. Also explain that a man can't get a woman pregnant by simply hugging her or kissing her.

Child-Abuse Warnings

Now that our society is so revved up about child abuse, we've got parents and teachers telling young children, "Don't let anyone ever touch you down there!" Think about this.

In this day and age, the first time parents mention sex to children is often through warnings about sexual abuse—complete with those deep, measured parental tones that barely hide mom and dad's fear and concern. Consider how dumb it would be if the first thing parents told kids about bike riding is how many scraped knees, broken bones and fractured skulls they are likely to get. At best, the child would learn to hide his excitement and questions from mom and dad. And if the kid did have a bad encounter on the bike, it is only natural that he or she would try to hide that, too, and perhaps feel horribly guilty.

Why not establish a good rapport about sex with your child from early on? Then your child can take in your eventual warnings about child abuse with intelligence rather than guilt or trepidation.

As for an actual strategy, try giving young children a sense that their bodies belong to them and no one else. Tell them they don't need to give hugs or kisses if they don't want to. If parents respect this in their interactions with the child, then the child will learn from an early age that it's okay to say NO to unwanted physical touching. This is a far better approach to preventing child abuse than the stern fear-based warnings that some parents give.

When your child is older and able to speak with you about sexual matters, you can say, "No one should touch you in a sexual way unless it's what you want." Let your child know that no adults should ever touch their genitals and bottoms or ask to see them undressed unless it's at a doctor's office when mom and dad are present, or it is with a helping teacher whom mom and dad say is okay. If anyone ever touches them anywhere on the body or takes pictures of them and says to keep it a secret, they should tell you anyway. Also encourage them to tell you about any kind of touching that makes them feel strange or uncomfortable. And tell them if a stranger ever asks for their help in finding a lost pet, to come straight home and get you.

Some parents tell their children that there are "good kinds of touch" and "bad kinds of touch." This is too abstract and is seldom helpful, as children often confuse "good touch" and "bad touch." Any child abuser worth his or her salt will be able to turn this around to his or her advantage.

One of the greatest tools you have in combating child abuse is to spend lots of time with your child, being a real and vital part of his or her youth. Children who only get limited amounts of time from their parents (aka "quality time") are far more likely to be interested in the attention that child abusers have to offer. Child abusers are very savvy in their ability to select children who aren't getting enough attention at home or who have lots of unanswered questions about sex. They then become the involved, exciting and understanding adult figure that the child longs for. Unfortunately, they end up doing your job for you, and more.

Children's Questions about Sex

Some parents have the fantasy that children will ask about sex as the need arises. But when parents volunteer information about all things under the sun except sexual feelings, children grow up sensing that questions about sex are off-limits.

What children need to know are the proper names of the things that they can see or touch, and an acknowledgment that touching or rubbing their genitals can feel quite nice. The latter isn't anything that kids don't know, but it gives them a message that it's OK to talk to mom and dad about things that are sexual.

Also, some parents overwhelm young children with biological facts about sex. Folks, a five-year-old can't understand the concept of fallopian tubes!

If a child under the age of five asks, "Where do babies come from?" it's fine to say that the baby grows in mommy's uterus and point to your abdomen. And then they might want to know how the baby gets out. You can explain that there's a another hole between their poop hole and pee hole where the baby comes out. Honestly, if you ever think there's a time when they won't make your jaw drop with questions like these, think again.

Between the ages of five and eight, children will probably want to know how the sperm gets to the egg, and we're not talking via the stork. They'll want specifics on how it got from daddy's body into mommy's body. (For the sake of political correctness, remember to say, "Mommy and Daddy place Daddy's penis inside of Mommy's vagina," and not "Daddy places his penis inside of Mommy's vagina." When you explain sex, try to make it a "we" thing when possible.)

For birds and bees stuff, find a book with fun illustrations that you enjoy and then read it together with your child.

Once a child asks a question about sex, he has often created a scenario or answer to the question in his own mind. As a result, you may want to pause and ask Junior to tell you what he or she thinks the answer might be. That way, you may get more clues about what the child needs. If there is no evidence that he or she is courting a hidden hypothesis, proceed to answer the question the best you can.

When it comes to questions about sex, or anything else for that matter, don't be afraid to tell a child that you don't know the answer. Acknowledge that it's a really good question, and tell Junior that you will do your best to find the answer. Then ask a friend, find a book or call one of the national sex lines. This way your child will feel that you take his or her questions seriously and will feel free to ask for your opinion in the future.

Keep in mind that you may be asked the same question about sex ten or twenty times. It could be that young children have a profound need for repetition, or maybe they get a secret sense of joy from seeing mom and dad break down in tears after they've been asked the same question a billion times. Also be aware that you will be giving a very different answer to a five-year-old's question about intercourse than you will to the same child when he or she is ten or fifteen. Just because you answered a question when your child was five doesn't mean you won't be answering the same question every couple of years, but each time in a slightly different way.

A wonderful and hopefully helpful book on sex for children age ten and up is *It's Perfectly Normal* (Cambridge, Mass: Candlewick Press, 1996) ISBN: 1-56402-159-9.

A Normal Five-Year-Old's Feelings about Sex

"In second grade, a little boy kept squeezing my vulva and it felt so good and tingly and warm and throbbing that I waited quite a while until I told my teacher!" *female age 23*

As part of his training, the author of this guide followed the growth of several normal children from birth on, discussing child development quandaries with their parents as they arose.

One of those children was a five-year-old girl whose lifelong best friend had been a boy of her own age. The girl's mother was shocked one day to find both kids buck naked with the little boy's fingers on her daughter's vulva. The mom's first thought was to break every bone in the little boy's hand, but her daughter was just as happily involved as he. So she went into the kitchen and forced herself to count to twenty. She then decided that the last thing she wanted to do was respond as her own mother would have. Needless to say, your author got a phone call asking for help.

The mom and he discussed how blanket prohibitions about sex often teach children to hide their sexuality from their parents. The child then loses the advantage of having a parent's wise counsel about sex. So rather than being guided by her initial response to protect her daughter, the mother asked the little girl how she felt about the way her friend had been touching her. Realizing that it was safe to answer truthfully, her daughter replied that it felt so wonderful she simply couldn't find a way to say no!

Since then, this little girl has asked her mother questions about who can touch her genitals and how to say no if she doesn't want them to. She asked these questions on her own initiative without being prompted by her parents. Few moms and dads have "perfect" answers for such questions, but just letting your child know that these are good questions and making an effort to discuss them can be amazingly helpful. This kind of discussion helps the child learn how to use reason when dealing with sex.

It is likely that when this little girl becomes a young woman she will have more respect for her own sexuality than the vast majority of her peers. Her sexual decisions may even be the result of good judgment, instead of the all-too-common adolescent rush to just do it because the opportunity presented itself. Also, it seems that she values herself and won't be agreeing to sleep with a boy out of fear that he will go away if she says no.

Please, don't for a moment think that this guide is saying to avoid setting limits on your children's sexual behavior. Parents who set no limits on their children's behavior tend to raise obnoxious brats. Instead, why not think about strategies that might be more effective than simply yelling NO!—although there are times when a contemptuous glare or a straightforward no are fine parental responses. Hopefully, you will encourage your children to think about their sexuality in ways that are constructive, rather than raising kids who are mindless about sex or have as their criteria "What can I get away with?" or "If I don't have sex with him, he'll start going out with someone else."

When Children See (or Hear) You Having Sex

If a young child walks in when you are having sex, cover up slowly and try not to look like you were doing something bad, because you weren't. One of you should take the child back to his or her own bed and tuck the kid in. It's a good idea to ask the child in a fun voice, "What did you think Mommy and Daddy were doing?" This will help you to know what they saw and how they interpreted it; e.g., "Daddy was hurting you!" Please resist saying, "I'd be a very happy person if daddy hurt me like that more often."

If the child has a negative read on what he or she saw, be sure to disagree with his or her interpretation and give it a positive spin. And no matter what the child answers, you might also say in a reassuring voice that you and daddy were having sex which was a lot of fun and you will be happy to talk about it in the morning. Even if the child doesn't ask, make sure that you raise the issue the next day.

Also, parents who make a fair amount of noise when they are making love should consider telling their young children about it, saying that mom and dad sometimes make noises at night when they are sharing sexual feelings. Explain that these are happy noises which are very different from the noises that mom and dad make when they are fighting. This is an important distinction to make.

The good thing to know about being seen by your kids is that Dr. Paul Abramson and colleagues at UCLA just completed an eighteen-year longitudinal study of "Early Exposure to Parental Nudity and Scenes of Parental Sexuality." Eighteen-year-olds who, as kids, had walked in on mom and dad when they were having sex showed no differences from other eighteen-year-olds on measures of self-acceptance, relations with peers and parents or other adults, antisocial and criminal behavior, substance use, suicidal ideation, quality of sexual relationships and problems associated with sexual relations. In fact, young boys who walked in on mom and dad actually seemed to demonstrate a better long-term outcome than those who didn't. Hmmm.

"Why Can't I Watch You and Mommy Have Sex?"

You've worked hard to be an open, honest parent about sex and your child suddenly rewards you with the statement, "I want to watch you and Mommy have sex!" Instead of convulsing with panic, regard this as yet another opportunity to talk about privacy and sex; for instance: "One of the things that makes sex so special for Mommy and Daddy is that it's private, just between the two of us. Since sex between us is private and personal, I wouldn't feel comfortable having anyone else watching." "Well, what about that time I saw you kissing Mommy's vulva. Will you kiss mine?" "Your vulva is very sweet and nice. But I wouldn't feel comfortable kissing your vulva like I kiss Mommy's because it's a private sexual thing that I only do with her."

Nudity at Home

"Nudity was a normal part of bathing, dressing, getting up in the morning or going to bed at night. I think this is ideal. Kids get a lot of reassurance and education from the occasional observation of natural (not contrived) nudity." *female age 35*

"My daughter always felt comfortable walking around the house naked, but my teenage son is so modest that nobody can remember seeing him naked since he was five years old!"
male age 65

Is nudity around the house good or bad? A retrospective study of college students compared how much nudity they reported when growing up with their current levels of sexual activity. There was no correlation between high levels of nudity at home and sexual promiscuity at college age. Interestingly, kids who reported higher levels of nudity at home seemed to report more feelings of warmth or security when away at college. Perhaps one reason for this is because it's easier for them to adjust to communal bathroom and shower situations that are so common in college life. It's also possible that they feel better about their bodies, which can help a person feel more self-confident in social situations.

Parents' Sexual Feelings about Their Children

Our society gives parents little guidance about sexual feelings toward their children, except blanket condemnation. Hopefully, you will find this to be a helpful discussion of the matter.

Children of all ages are able to evoke sexual feelings in parents, from a nursing experience that leaves a baby's mother with pleasant genital sensations, to an older teenage son whose developing body gives mom an occasional sexual stirring—perhaps reminding her of the excitement she used to feel when seeing the boy's father when he was the same age. The problem isn't in having occasional sexual feelings about your children, which plenty of parents feel at times; it's in what to do with the feelings.

For instance, let's say that a dad is playfully wrestling with his young daughter and finds that he is getting an erection. A healthy dad might think to himself "Oops!," beg out of the roughhousing, and say to his daughter something like "Why don't you grab the mitts so we can work on your pitching?" or "How about a game of Scrabble?" A less healthy dad might keep doing the same activity over and over without adjusting to the reality of the situation.

Unfortunately, upon discovering the start of an erection, some very good dads withdraw from physical and sometimes even emotional contact with a child. In these cases, dad's own harsh superego can ruin a very important parent-child relationship. This can be quite sad for both parent and child. On the other hand, there are some parents who could use a more highly developed superego—or at least develop enough boundaries to recognize that children are not meant to be sexual partners.

As for mother-son feelings, let's say that mom enjoys rubbing her teenage son's back, but finds that she is starting to have a sexual response. Maybe it's time to give Junior a quick hug instead and realize that it is more appropriate for him to have his back rubbed by girls his own age. Or maybe mom enjoys the way her son's teenage body looks. This is fine, but it starts to cross the line if she ends up in his bedroom whenever he is getting undressed. Particularly troublesome are lonely moms who encourage their sons to share the bed with them, unless such conditions are dictated by abject poverty. The same is true for lonely dads.

Problems sometimes abound in families where the parents' sexual relationship is not a particularly good one. One of the children might decide that it's up to him or her to be a replacement spouse. What's amazing about this kind of mutual seduction is if a therapist suggests that something might be askew, both parent and child may glare at the therapist as though he or she were some sort of twisted pervert. Especially destructive are those situations where the parent alternates between being seductive and puritanical.

All things considered, it's not possible to set specific rules and standards for all households. For instance, nudity in one family might be perfectly healthy, while nudity in another family might be part of a syrupy, seductive mess. And while it might be best for parents to put boundaries on one child's sexual expression, another child might do well with the opposite kind of response. For instance, a teenager who is an exhibitionist with his or her naked body can clearly use some limit setting, while a highly inhibited child who is embarrassed about his or her body might find it helpful to hear that it's okay to be naked. Another example involves a young child who enjoys masturbating before naps or when tucked into bed as mom or dad are reading a favorite story. This is perfectly normal. However, another child who rocks and masturbates anxiously throughout the day needs help.

It would be nice to say that common sense should prevail, but when it comes to sexual development within the family, there doesn't seem to be an abundance of collective common sense in our culture.

Explaining Puberty

"When I got my first period I was excited, but then my mother wouldn't let me climb trees or play with the guys anymore."

female age 55

"My mom had always been really open with me, so I was prepared when my body started changing. I was even glad to get
my period." *female age 19*

"I started growing awfully fast and none of my clothes fit anymore. I'd consume everything in the refrigerator and would
still feel hungry. My armpits had never perspired or smelled.
Suddenly, it was like someone had turned on a faucet under
each one. I dreaded being called on in morning classes, because
I'd often have a raging hard-on. My beard was really strange,
mostly boyhood fuzz with man hairs growing through it. So
I appropriated one of my dad's razors and started shaving.
I didn't know why I was suddenly having wet dreams, and I
used to hide my underwear and wash them myself so my mom
wouldn't see the stains. I was sure I was damaging myself by
masturbating once a day, but couldn't stop to save my life.
Hair started growing from my neck down. And suddenly there
were zits. That's what I remember of puberty. It would have
been nice if a parent or some adult had taken a moment to
explain some of these things to me."

male age 44

It never hurts to let your children know that their bodies will
change as they get older. Of course, you will need to address the issue
in different ways depending on the child's age. For instance, you can
tell your seven-year-old that puberty is what happens when you stop
looking like a kid and start looking like an adult—that boys get taller,
their voices deepen, they start getting hair under their armpits and
around their genitals. You can also say that girls' hips start to get
wider, they grow breasts, and their armpits and genitals get hair too.
For more about teenage boys and their unwanted erections, see the
chapter "On The Penis."

When your child is a few years older, you can explain that puberty
is a process that takes a couple of years to complete and that it usually starts to happen for girls when they turn ten or eleven and for
boys when they turn twelve or thirteen. Of course, let them know
that puberty is a little like the repair people from the phone company:

sometimes they arrive when they're supposed to, sometimes they are awfully late, and occasionally they get there before you expected. You can mention that puberty is the time when girls start to menstruate and boys start to ejaculate when they have orgasms, and that everyone's genitals start to look more adult like (bigger and hairier).

Keep in mind that kids can be awfully cruel toward other kids who are in the throes of puberty. Let your child know that you'll ring his or her neck if they ever make fun of another kid whose body starts to change sooner than theirs, or if they taunt a kid who is really late.

Menstrual Bleeding

"Puberty was not a really big deal for me. I read *Are You There God, It's Me Margaret,* so I knew what my period was when I got it, although my Mom never bothered to tell me."

female age 25

"I was afraid that I would just start bleeding sometime and that it might go through my clothes and I would be embarrassed."

female age 49

"My first period was a celebration. I was at my friend's house and I noticed bleeding between my legs. I rushed home to tell my mother, fully aware I was having my period. She was thrilled, and we went out to dinner to celebrate."

female age 18

The only time when many parents mention sex to their daughters is while explaining menstruation. What an unfortunate association, bleeding and sex. Now it's even worse, as the first thing young girls often hear about sex from their parents is a warning of sexual abuse.

As children, we learn that blood is a sign of bodily injury. We are never told that some bleeding is good for us. So when girls start menstruating, the blood that drips from their vulvas is often equated by the unconscious mind with injury or internal damage. When explaining menstruation, girls should be informed that the bleeding which comes during their menstrual periods is a good thing, and that menstruation is the body's way of keeping the walls of their reproductive organs clean and fresh.

Keep in mind that girls are now menstruating at ages twelve or thirteen; their grandmothers started menstruating when they were three to four years older. The bodies of these young girls are more developed than their grandmothers' were at the same ages, but their emotional development is about the same. This means they will need plenty of encouragement and support from their parents in negotiating the puberty process, especially if they begin menstruating earlier or later than most of their friends.

Growing Girls

Young girls tend to be very self-conscious about physical changes, especially around fathers and brothers, so don't be talking about tampons and training bras when the guys are around. If they mature earlier than their friends, you'll need to be aware that other girls might shun them and boys might tease them. Keep reminding them that things will be fine in a couple of years when everybody else has started to mature. Make sure they are involved in activities like sports, science, 4-H—anything where value is placed on their achievements and abilities.

If your child is comparing herself in negative ways to actresses on TV, let her know that many of the allegedly "perfect" girls on TV are, for the most part, self-absorbed lunatics who think nothing of barfing up a perfectly good meal so they won't get "fat." These are people who have more surgery than a BMW in a Tijuana chop shop, and in spite of the stories that their publicists send to *People Magazine,* few have off-screen lives that are particularly happy. Double ditto for models who are in magazines like *Seventeen.*

Teenagers & Sex

"I used to pretend my friend Heather was another boy that I liked in school in fifth grade and we would touch each other's vulvas and breasts and have a lot of fun until my Mom found out and sent me to a psychiatrist for being a lesbian!"

female age 24

If you ask a group of sixteen-year-olds if they are emotionally ready to have sex, most will say yes. If you ask their parents whether their sixteen-year-olds are emotionally ready to have sex, most will say no. Chances are your teenagers do not view sex the way you wish they would.

As a parent, you can't expect a teenager to be verbal about sex just because you have suddenly decided to offer wise counsel. Having an open dialogue about sex is an option that some parents lost when the child was three to five years old. If mom and dad ignored the existence of sexual feelings back then, it might be very uncomfortable for the child who is now a teenager to suddenly start talking about sex. If there is tension between you and your teen, or if the kid is engaged in reckless acting-out behavior, you might do better to solicit the help of a favorite aunt, uncle, teacher or therapist to whom the teen is more apt to open up to. And if there are problems, you'll need to become more involved in their lives than you might currently be.

When Teenagers Ask on Their Own

Let's say your teenager asks you a question about sex: "How do you know if you're gay?" or "What if you get so nervous before having sex that you feel like throwing up?" or "Would I have to leave home if I got pregnant?" Don't assume that she or he is thinking about being gay, is about to have sex or is pregnant. Maybe your kid heard something on the TV or radio and is putting him or herself in the other person's place.

Try to respond by saying things that will help expand the question into a discussion, such as "What are your thoughts about that?" or "I'll be able to give you a better answer if you could tell me more about your question." This buys you precious time, which parents can never have enough of when being asked questions about sex, and it helps you squelch any potential screams that are about to explode from the depths of your parental being.

You might take solace from the following words by one of the top sex educators in the country, Debra Haffner: "Like most parents, I have found myself at a loss for words when a question I never expected popped up. Indeed, there have been times when I have responded in ways that I later regretted. For instance, I struggled with how to respond to my daughter when she asked questions about the Bobbit case, and then about Michael Jackson, and Monica Lewinsky."

Don't think that you need to come up with perfect answers. The most important thing is to provide an atmosphere where the child can ask questions and know that it's okay to think out loud about sex.

Wouldn't It Be Nice If...

Here are the kinds of questions that you probably never asked yourself before having sex, but hope that your teenager will ask him- or herself. Perhaps these questions can act as guides when you are helping your child think about what they might want from sex.

Why does this person want to have sex with me? Is it experimentation, fun, romance, a personal quest?

Does having sex mean something different to him or her than it does to me?

What would we do if we had intercourse and became pregnant? To whom would we turn ? How would we tell our parents? Would we face it together? Am I ready to be a parent? No kid should begin dating without seriously discussing these questions with his or her parents.

Do I know what it feels like in my body to be sexually excited? Have I fantasized about being naked with this person? Do I want to have sex because I am physically excited about it, or is it just to please a partner or to keep him or her interested in me?

What kind of stimulation does a woman need before intercourse so it feels good instead of bad?

Are there ways we could please each other sexually without having intercourse?

How do I say no to someone who is pestering me for a date, or no to sex without feeling like a coward or geek?

If we do have sex, how do I get genuine feedback from my partner about what felt good and what didn't? How do I tell him or her what feels good and what doesn't for me?

Will I feel good about myself the next day?

Who sticks what into where when we have intercourse, and how can we do it in ways that will make it feel better?

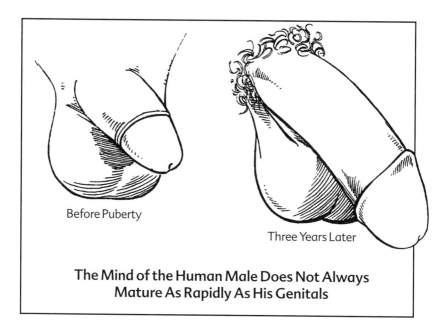

Before Puberty

Three Years Later

The Mind of the Human Male Does Not Always Mature As Rapidly As His Genitals

Toward Higher Expectations

The mere thought of asking an eleven-year-old what qualities she would want in a sexual partner would send most American parents racing to the bathroom for a hit of Tagamet or Imodium. But let's think about it. If you as a parent don't introduce the notions of chivalry and respect in sex, where else are your children going to learn them? From MTV?

There is nothing wrong with talking to your child about the difference between a partner who's just trying to get laid and one who is going to be a caring and loving sexual companion. For instance, does a partner who is going to be a respectful lover say, "I won't go out with you anymore if we can't have intercourse"? Is he or she responsible and caring toward family and friends? Are his or her friends good people? Do they drink or get loaded a lot? And what about introducing the expectation that a truly desirable partner is one who is trustworthy and dependable and says things such as, "I'd really like to please you. What can I do?"

Of course, none of this is going to stop your kid from shacking up with one of the local Hell's Angels, but it does kick into motion the idea that an important part of self-respect means choosing your sexual partners carefully. With enough intelligent concern and involvement on your part, your kid may even search out a sexual partner who has some of the characteristics and values that you do. Hopefully that's a good thing.

Condom Advice — For Teenage Boys

Give your teenage boy a couple of condoms and a tube of lube, saying that these are for him to put on when he's alone to see what it feels like. If you have a straightforward relationship with him, you might suggest that he try masturbating with a condom on, which is the condom equivalent of taking a test drive. Tell him to pay attention to how long it takes after he ejaculates before his penis starts to shrink and the condom gets baggy. That's how much time he has to pull out; otherwise the condom might stay in his partner's vagina. Tell him that the shrinking penis factor is why he needs to clasp the condom around the base of his penis as he is pulling out. Maybe you could try reading the instructions together. Let him know that the lube is to put on the outside of the condom to help it slip and slide better when he is having intercourse.

Condom Advice — For Teenage Girls

Give your daughter a couple of condoms, a tube of lube and a penis-sized banana. Tell her that one of the condoms is for her to practice putting on the banana; the others are for whatever she wants to do with them. If you have an open relationship with her, try putting the condom on the banana together. This should result in a number of giggles and laughs. If it doesn't, you're being way too serious. Explain that she needs to leave a an extra half inch at the tip of the penis so it can fill with ejaculate when the guy comes. Also explain that as soon as a guy ejaculates, his penis starts to shrink. This means that she should clasp the condom with her fingers and push it against the base of his penis as he withdraws so he won't leave it inside her. Let her know that it never hurts to put a little lube on the outside of the condom before having intercourse. This will help it slip and slide better. Maybe you can try reading the condom instructions together.

By the way, teenage girls who know what kind of birth control their mother uses are more likely to use birth control themselves.

Odds'N'Ends

If you have a son, make sure he's got a big box of Kleenex next to his bed, and when it's all used up in three days don't make smart remarks like "I didn't know you had such a bad cold." Better you have to stock up on Kleenex than he is out knocking up some young thing!

If your child begins to wash his or her own underwear or pajamas, be sure they have proper information about menstruation, masturbation and wet dreams. While most of us know what happens when boys ejaculate, we forget that some teenage girls get major wet spots in their underwear when they become sexually excited.

Abstinence-only programs do not significantly delay the onset of intercourse. Unfortunately, the entire "just say no" approach had no significant impact on drug use, either. The "just say no" approach works about as well on teenagers as it does on adults! If you don't want them to be doing this or that, you need to get them involved in activities that will fill their time.

Let your kids know that it's fine to wait until they are older before having sex with a partner and that masturbation is what you do in the meantime, which is why the Good Lord gave us humans two more fingers than ET.

Inform them that what they see on TV about sex is usually pretty twisted, exaggerated and outright incorrect, unless they're watching reruns of *Married With Children*.

Final Word about Boundaries

If you think your younger teenagers would do better to wait a couple of years before sharing sex with partners, then you might do something other than tempt the fates.

One thing is to talk to your kids about sex and encourage them to talk to you. That way, if they're going to become sexually active, it won't be just to get one up on a mom or dad whose head was stuck in another century. Another thing that helps delay sexual activity is getting teenagers involved in activities that challenge their minds and bodies—we're talking about things like science fairs and playing soccer or building things. You're thinking, "Isn't that about the tenth time they said that?" You betcha!

Understand that good kids do not always make good decisions. If you give them enough rope to hang themselves, most will. On the other hand, no kid ever lost a friend because their parents insisted on knowing where they were and with whom. No teenager ever died because his or her parents set a curfew on weekends. No kid ever shriveled up and blew away because one parent called another parent to make sure that an adult would be home when their kid was sleeping over.

Your kids will have plenty of time to do whatever they want once they are legal adults. Until then, it is your job as parents to get them there safe and sound.

Dear Paul,
Last night I discovered that my 11-year-old had bookmarked a number of porn sites on his web browser. I checked out these sites and was shocked at what I saw. I am not a prude, but I am concerned at the negative messages that my son might be getting in the name of sexual excitement. I don't know how to handle this.

Lucy in Allentown

Dear Lucy,

The first time I used a web browser I put the word "erotic" in the search engine. About a zillion sites popped up, so I selected the first site on the list. Moments later, a close-up photo of a smiling, attractive woman with her mouth wide open started to fill my screen. A stream of liquid was flowing into her mouth, and then a penis appeared. What I ended up with was a close-up of some guy peeing into the mouth of a young woman who could have been the girl next door. The second site on the list showed a close-up of a woman's pelvis with one penis sticking up her rear and another in her vagina. As an experiment, I entered "Beanie Babies" in the search engines. I got a number of sex sites from that.

This is different from what we saw as kids. We'd masturbate for months over a tattered page from *Playboy*, and while *Playboy* may not show the most accurate representation of what nature put on the average woman's chest, it's at least an approximation of what you'll get if you're going to have sex. I had no idea that someone would ever want to pee into another person's mouth until I moved to Los Angeles and started meeting people in the entertainment industry.

So what concerns me, Lucy, isn't that your son is seeing pornography, but that the pornography he is seeing is so darned twisted.

I wouldn't want anybody's son or daughter to see some of the porn that's out there today. But I don't believe there is an effective way of keeping kids from seeing this type of stuff. Even if you have the most effective screening program in the world, your kid's friend down the street will have found a way to circumvent it, or they will get on his parents' computer when his mom and dad are at work (from 7:00 a.m. to 8:00 p.m.). If they can't access this stuff on the internet, there are plenty of videos floating around that show some of the same things.

And that's where you need to enter the picture. As a parent, you are not going to keep your kid from seeing some of today's seriously demented porn. So instead of just ignoring it, consider this an opportunity to be the emotional anchor your son needs to develop a healthy and caring sexual self.

One strategy is to let your kids know that it's perfectly normal to be curious about sex, and despite your best efforts, they might see things on the internet that are seriously weird and way out of the range of normal. If your kids know that you won't suddenly transform into a total lunatic when the subject comes up, you might ask them about some of the weirdest things they've seen on the net. If they have seen sexual sites and are able to tell you about them, your response might vary from "That sounds really strange; you're not describing any sex acts I'd ever want to do" to "I know it seems weird now, but maybe it's something you'll like to do when you get older," depending, of course, on what they describe.

Assuming they don't fess up about what they've been seeing, you can always tell your kids that there's sometimes a big difference between looking at pictures of people having sex and what happens when two people actually have a good sexual relationship. Sex with a real-life partner is full of tender and caring moments. You rarely see any of this if you are watching sex on the internet or in a video.

Also, keep in mind that even regular intercourse or oral sex can be scary or disturbing for teenagers. They'll try to dismiss it by saying, "Oh mom, I know all about that," but they can still be very anxious about it.

Your job, Lucy, is to help your son digest some of what he will be seeing in the next couple of years—from twisted porn to bizarre and disturbing video collections of people killing themselves or getting wasted in accidents. (You wouldn't believe what my teenage patients tell me they see.) Through your attitude and willingness to be involved, you can help your son sort through the bizarre and twisted images that he will most likely be seeing. Otherwise, the disturbing images may stay trapped within his consciousness and interfere with healthier ways of relating. And years later, he'll end up spending thousands of dollars on shrink-types like me to help sort the mental wheat from the chafe.

If your children are spending countless hours on the web, it might be due to loneliness and isolation in addition to normal curiosity. On the other hand, there are whole communities of people on the internet who can be better friends and a better influence than some of the kids he's probably meeting in school. If it seems like your son is spending hours on sex sites, you won't get it to stop by taking a "just say no" approach. Try to get him involved in extracurricular activities where his time is structured and he's doing things that make him feel good about himself. If he's really isolated and the computer is an emotional lifeline, you might try to get him involved in a computer class. Use it as a bridge.

Dear Paul,

I am 14 and my mom, who is totally cool, just got me birth control pills. My boyfriend and I are totally committed to each other. Do we still need to use a condom?

Heather from Humbold

Dear Heather,

I am not fourteen, but I am a fairly liberal guy and have produced one of the more liberal books on sex ever written. I want to disagree with your first statement. I don't think your mom is totally cool because she got her fourteen-year-old daughter birth control pills. I think she's misguided.

You're not going to like this, but I don't think fourteen-year-olds should be having intercourse and I don't think their parents should be condoning it.

Of course, you might feel I am being hypocritical, given how I encourage parents to speak with their children about everything from masturbation and orgasms to ways of telling a partner what you like in bed. But this assumes that talking about sex encourages kids to do it sooner. I don't think so.

One reason why I feel you should wait is because our minds handle abstract concepts a lot better at age seventeen or eighteen than at fourteen. And believe it or not, there's a lot of abstract stuff to cope with when you are in a relationship and having sex. You might be the most mature and responsible person in your entire class, and I think it's great that you are thinking about birth control and condoms, but I also think you'll appreciate sex a lot more when your mental equipment catches up with your physical equipment, which doesn't happen for a few more years yet.

In the meantime, your mom could help you get involved in community activities, like volunteering at an old folks home or an animal shelter. She should help you get something under your belt other than your boyfriend's penis. This is just one man's opinion, but I feel it's really important for someone your age to channel your sexual energy into expanding your mind and creativity. Then, after you graduate from high school, the sex you have will complement who you are as a person rather than define it, as is often the case when fourteen-year-olds are having intercourse. I am concerned that it's just too big, too soon right now.

And yes, Heather, if you do have intercourse, it's a good idea to use a condom in addition to taking the pill. Once you are in a time-tested, true-blue relationship, you can ditch the rubber.

Chapter Notes: Thanks to *Not with My Child* (Carson City, Nevada: United Youth Security, 1999) for insight into how child abusers think. And to Debra Hafner's *From Diapers to Dating: A Parent's Guide To Raising Sexually Healthy Children,* (New York: Newmarket Press, 1999) for a reminder about nannies and other things mentioned in this chapter.

Sex When You Are Horny & Disabled

Chapter 52

Astory recently appeared on the internet about a twenty-two-year-old man with cerebral palsy who has virtually no control over his body's movements. The guy started using his wheelchair antisocially, as a ramming device. He was running over anything he could. Eventually, this young man wrote on his word-board that he was so horny he couldn't stand it anymore.

Although his body has the same sexual urges and desires as a fully able twenty-two-year-old, he has no ability to walk, talk or masturbate like the average twenty-two-year-old. He can't even turn the pages of *Playboy* or stick an X-rated movie into the DVD.

As quickly as they began, this young man's wheelchair tantrums stopped. The reason? A nurse's aide mercifully began giving him hand jobs. But then she was caught and fired instantly. The board-and-care home threatened to file a complaint against her for sexual abuse.

Sexy & Disabled?

If you think you have a good attitude about sex, consider a quadriplegic who wheels by in an electric wheelchair. The person drools a little and steers the chair with a joy stick that's strapped to his forehead. Do you think of this person as being sexual? Do you think he has the same sexual needs and desires as you? Chances are you'd wonder how good his jump shot is before you'd think of him as having the same sexual needs and desires as you.

Many people not only disapprove of sex for the severely disabled, but might find the concept offensive. They might even feel that we need to protect people who are disabled from sex.

Dear Paul,

I'm a paraplegic from Ohio. From where I sit, I have women's rears and crotches in my face nearly all day long. You have no idea how much restraint it takes to keep my hands to myself. Last week I copped a feel but quickly apologized and blamed it on my "bad driving" and "spastic hand."   Dude from Dubuque

Dude,

Just to let you know, there's not an able-bodied guy on the planet who could come face-to-tail with as much anatomy as you do and not want to reach out and touch some. P.S. You must consider a crowded elevator to be a gift from God.

Counterpoint: I recently received a letter regarding my response to Dude because I didn't chastise him for his inappropriate actions. "I am really disappointed that you suggest in your response that a man couldn't be expected to withhold his sexual desire and that it's fine to occasionally use a woman's body for your own purpose." Hmmmm.

One reason why so many of us blanch at the idea of a disabled person having sex is because the advertising industry spends billions of dollars each year trying to narrow our concept of what sexual attractiveness is. Never do advertisers tell us that sexual appeal might have something to do with integrity and character, given how those can't be paid for with a credit card. Forget even existing sexually if you are missing a few fingers or an entire leg, slur your words when you talk or are paralyzed from the chest down.

A huge hurdle for many disabled people is being able to accept themselves as being sexual. If you don't accept yourself as being sexual, it is unlikely that others will.

Roll Models

"Prior to my becoming blind, the only person who was blind that I had seen was a beggar. I was horrified to think that this was the only option available to me as a person who was blind." From an article on women who are blind by Ellen Rubin in *Sexuality and Disability,* 15(1), 1997.

One of the more discouraging aspects of having a disability is that positive role models are few and far between. For instance, if you ask people to name a famous disabled person, just as many will say the Hunchback of Notre Dame as Franklin Delano Roosevelt. Of the two, FDR was a real-life American president who provided people with a real sense of sanctuary, although he was unable to walk unaided. There were reasons why FDR tried to hide his disability. When he was a young man, disabled people were considered a success if they could get a job in the circus.

Different Ways That Disabilities Happen

When people are disabled from crashes and accidents, it is often because the spinal cord was damaged. About 85% of spinal-cord injuries happen to men, many in their teens and twenties. That's because men have a penchant for doing things that involve speed or collisions. For instance, if a boy says he needs "pads," you might assume he's talking about something to put under his football jersey. If a girl says she needs "pads," it's likely that she's referring to sanitary napkins or something to stuff into her bra. In addition to sports and car crashes, disabilities might come from gun wounds, stabbings, fistfights or a serious bonk on the head.

Diseases that cause disabilities include arthritis, which can make intercourse painful or cripple your fingers so much that you can't masturbate. Polio can make it nearly impossible to walk or breathe and it can result in all kinds of problems later in life (post-polio syndrome). Diabetes can keep a guy from having an erection but it usually doesn't keep him from having an orgasm. Multiple sclerosis can be mild and manageable or severe and debilitating. Cancer and the various treatments for it can impact a person's ability and desire to have sex.

There are many genetic or congenital disorders that can cause disabilities. Certain chromosome disorders can damage a person's physical growth and/or mental development. Congenital disorders might result in being a midget (top-shelf challenged). Medications taken during pregnancy can result in the birth of infants with severe disabilities. Parental exposure to pollutants and chemicals can cause birth defects. Disabilities can also result from things like strokes and heart attacks or cerebral palsy and muscular dystrophy.

Spinal-Cord Injury (SCI) Shorthand: When people with spinal-cord injuries are talking to other people with spinal-cord injuries, they sometimes use a shorthand such as "I'm a C-4 quad" or "I'm a T-3." This

code refers to the location on the spine where the injury occurred. For instance, a C-4 injury occurs higher up on the spinal cord (in the neck) than a T-3, so it is likely that a person with a C-4 is paralyzed from the shoulders down (quadriplegic), whereas a T-3 has the use of his or her arms (paraplegic), and an L-4 most likely has more use than a C-4 or T-3 because the injury happened at a point on the spinal cord between the ribs and pelvis. Another factor is whether the injury was complete or incomplete, with the latter supposedly being less severe.

Quad Note: Thanks to Tom Street for this info. Tom is a C-4 quad from an auto accident in 1988. Tom manufactures a computer mouse for quadriplegics called the QuadJoy. This special mouse, combined with extra software that Tom has written, allows the user to run the entire computer including keyboard by mouth. The full range of clicking and dragging happens by virtue of puffing and sucking on the end of the joystick. This can be particularly helpful for a quad who would like to interact with others in chat rooms or who would like to see internet porn in PRIVATE and without the help of an attendant. Tom can be reached on the internet at www.quadjoy.com.

Chronic vs. Acute

There are certain disabilities that happen all at once. They don't keep getting worse. This is true of most spinal-cord injuries. There are other disabilities, usually caused by diseases, which have symptoms that get worse over time.

For some people, it is easier to have a disability that stays the same. For instance, once a person with a spinal-cord injury is able to learn how to deal with his disability, he can be pretty sure that his condition won't worsen and he won't have to learn a whole new set of skills just to keep even. However, people with chronic illnesses have a more uncertain future and may have to constantly readapt as the illness progresses. The uncertainty of a chronic illness makes it more difficult to get on with your life, as you never know when your disease is going to pull the rug out from under you. Of course, you can say that none of us has any guarantees for the future, but the uncertainty of everyday life is much easier to cope with than the uncertainty of a disease that may be getting worse.

674 • Sex When You Are Horny & Disabled

Even the recovery process is different for someone with an acute injury as opposed to a chronic illness. For instance, consider a person who had his leg amputated after being run over in the parking lot at the 7-Eleven as opposed to having a leg amputated due to complications from diabetes. Outside of not getting to finish his Slurpee, the person who lost his leg at the 7-Eleven had no pre-existing condition and must only face the problems associated with the amputation itself. The person with progressive diabetes has to cope with numerous problems caused by the diabetes in addition to those that are specific to the amputation. Mind you, neither situation is enviable.

Also, the treatments for certain disabilities or illnesses can cause sexual problems. For instance, tricyclic antidepressants are often prescribed to help with the neurogenic pain that can occur after spinal cord injury. These drugs can decrease the desire to have sex as well as the ability to have an erection and to ejaculate. The same is true for certain cancer treatments that adversely affect the sexuality of both men and women.

Double Your Trouble

As if it weren't bad enough to have your spinal cord injured, accidents that cause the damage are often severe enough to also cause traumatic head injury. Not only does the person have to cope with possible paralysis from the spinal injury, but he may also experience low sexual drive, poor impulse control or unpredictable behavior from the brain injury.

Can Guys in Wheelchairs Get Hard-Ons?

It's interesting how people wonder if guys in wheelchairs can get hard-ons, but they don't wonder if women in wheelchairs can get wet! Why's that? Contrary to what you might think, a lot of guys who are in wheelchairs are able to get erections. The stimulation for the erection will often need to come from direct physical contact with the genitals rather than from feeling horny, as the link between the horny center in the brain and the genitals is often damaged. Guys with disabilities can often get good erections with the help of vacuum pumps or injections. Men with higher-level spinal-cord injuries (usually quads, not paraplegics) tend to get reflex erections. These happen when the penis is being touched and have little connection to feeling horny. They usually go down as soon as the touching stops, but some couples learn how to keep the stimulation going so they can have intercourse.

Able-bodied men often become aware of their own sexual arousal by feeling their penis grow. Men who are paralyzed have to rely on other signals to know when they are aroused, e.g. nipples getting hard, goosebumps, heavier breathing and a heart that beats faster. These aren't any different from what able-bodied men experience, but how many guys notice subtle physical clues when their dicks are screaming, "Touch Me! Touch Me!"

Women with spinal-cord injuries may find that the sexual wetness in their vagina is decreased or absent. Using a lubricant during intercourse can be very helpful. Many women with spinal cord injuries are able to have orgasms. Bregman and Hadley (1976) interviewed a number of women with spinal-cord injuries and found that their descriptions of orgasm were similar to those of women with no spinal-cord injury. This suggests that orgasms can be generated by nerves in the body that do not run up the spinal cord. Also, some people with spinal-cord injury have orgasms that are referred to as "para-orgasms," which are different from genital orgasms but are quite compelling. Para-orgasms can be so strong that women who are injured above the T-6 level need to be aware of rapid changes in their blood pressure.

Both women and men who no longer have traditional orgasms can learn to experience a type of orgasm that is called an emotional orgasm. This kind of orgasm results in a rush of relaxation and calm in the rest of the body that's like the afterglow of a good hard come.

Whether a person can or can't have an orgasm, the good feelings that most able-bodied people get from being touched and loved are still massively satisfying for someone who is disabled. One person with a spinal-cord injury reported in a video that "before my accident I couldn't get enough stimulation from the waist down; now I can't get enough from the waist up!" When a person is paralyzed in other parts of the body, areas such as the back of the neck and arms can become extremely sensitive in a sexual way. Also, plenty of disabled people report that watching a partner doing something sexual to them can be

676 • *Sex When You Are Horny & Disabled*

very satisfying even if they can't feel the actual sensations. The brain is able to fill in the missing pieces.

Vibrator Note: Vibrators can be a very helpful sexual aid for men and women with disabilities. They can supply the necessary stimulation when a hand is unable. If you tend to be incontinent, consider getting a vibrator that's rechargeable or has batteries. Urine is a far better conductor of electricity than water, making plug-in models a wee bit risky. If your hands are too crippled to use a regular vibrator, it's possible to embed one in a nerf ball.

"Will I Be Able to Have Children"

This seems like a simple, straightforward question. But it is often an indirect way of asking, "Will I be able to have sex?" "Will anyone want to have sex with me?" "How in the blazes do I have sex now that I'm like this?" The answer to all of these questions is usually yes, unless the person stays in a full-time funk and never transitions out of asking "Why me?" Try as they might, nobody but God or nature has an answer to the "Why me?" question, assuming there is an answer at all.

Most women with disabilities are able to become pregnant. This is why most disabled women need to use birth control, even if they are paralyzed from the shoulders down. Many men who are paralyzed have problems ejaculating. Physicians are having some success helping these men to ejaculate by sticking electrodes up their rears and shocking the bejesus out of nerves in the prostate region. Some guys with spinal-cord injuries above T-12 are able to ejaculate with the help of a vibrator on the penis.

Born with It vs. Got It Along the Way

Unless they are in a rock'n'roll band, most people who make it to adulthood have probably achieved certain developmental milestones, aka "maturity." But if a person was disabled at an early age, it is possible that this has gotten in the way of achieving the level of maturity that he or she needs in order to behave as a responsible and caring adult. For instance, how does a kid who is disabled at age sixteen progress through the usual steps toward independence if he or she needs a parent to get them out of bed and dressed each morning? If he or she is in a rehab center, how do they get the privacy to explore sexually as other kids do? If their hands are crippled, how do they masturbate?

Consider the following questions posed by a therapist who works with the disabled: "How does a young girl in a wheelchair learn how adults are sexual if her parents are afraid to be that way in front of her? How does she explore her parents' drawers when they are out and find books, movies, condoms, sponges, lingerie and so forth—as many youths do—if she cannot get into their bedroom? How can she find her brother's copies of sexually explicit publications if she cannot get under his bed where they are stashed?" (From "Performing a Sexual Evaluation on the Person With Disability or Illness" by Kenneth A. Lefebre in *Sexual Function in People with Disability and Chronic Illness*, Marca Sipski and Craig Alexander, Aspen Publishers, 1997.)

People who are disabled at a young age will become adults with the same sexual drives and desires as anyone who is not disabled. However, they may be missing a sense of sexual orientation or knowledge of responsible and appropriate ways to satisfy their sexual urges. To help fill in the missing pieces, parents and educators of disabled kids need to be more open about sexual issues rather than less.

Sex & People Who Are Developmentally Disabled

It is not likely that people who are developmentally disabled will be reading this book, although we know of one such woman by the name of Linda who loves looking at the pictures! People with developmental disabilities have the same sexual urges and desires as people without disabilities. They simply go through the stages of sexual development at a slower pace.

The developmentally disabled pose special problems when it comes to sexual training, because they may need a good deal of repetitive explanation about things that many adults feel uncomfortable saying just once. Also, in their drive toward sexual pleasure, developmentally disabled kids may be even less apt to use birth control than their nondisabled partners in crime.

If you are the parent of a disabled child, or you work with people who are disabled, you might be at a loss for finding good references to help you in dealing with your child's sexual growth. One book that might be helpful is *Doubly Silenced: Sexuality, Sexual Abuse and People with Developmental Disabilities* by Patricia Patterson. Also, *Sexuality: Your Sons and Daughters With Intellectual Disabilities* by Schwier,

Melberg and Hingsburger, Paul H. Brookes Publishing Company, Baltimore, 2000. The Paul H. Brookes catalogue has a number of excellent books on disability.

Body Image

If a person has been disabled for a long time, particularly from a young age, his body image might also include a wheelchair or braces, scars from various surgeries, hands that are twisted and not particularly dexterous, a voice that slurs words, a head that doesn't sit straight on its shoulders or other features that aren't always like those of models in *Vogue* or *GQ*. It may be very difficult for a person who is disabled to feel attractive and effective if they can't see themselves as separate from the devices that help them to survive. As a result, they might need plenty of feedback that you value them as a person in the same way that you do someone who doesn't have a wheelchair, braces or disfigurements.

Dear Paul,

We both have spinal-cord injuries and are disabled. Yet we like watching porn that shows able-bodied people having sex. Is this weird?

Rhonda from Rolling Hills

Dear Rhonda,

None of us have eight-inch penises, last forty-five minutes, come in buckets or have partners who like taking it ten different ways, but we like watching pornography, too. If most of it weren't so darned boring, we'd watch it more often! Keep in mind that pornography is a fantasy. It helps us go places in our minds where many of us wouldn't go in reality even if we could. Now here's a question for you: I'll bet you aren't worried about watching able-bodied actors in TV or movies, so why when it comes to porn do you suddenly worry about being crippledly correct?

Explaining Yourself & Educating Others

"People do have all these kinds of curiosity, and you have to find ways of making them feel more comfortable around you at first."

Steve, on the videotape *Sexuality Reborn*

Just like people who are able-bodied, people who are disabled need to learn their own sexual strengths and weaknesses and then teach a partner what they need. They also need to receive plenty of feedback. For instance, for someone who has had a stroke, it might be important to lie on their affected side so they can use their active arm for caressing a partner. Likewise it is important for their able-bodied partner to give them feedback, as someone with a stroke might have a "visual field cut" which causes them to ignore one side of their partner's body. (This example by way of social worker Sharon Bacharach.)

When it comes to enjoying sex, different disabilities pose different challenges. For instance, if you can't use your hands in a way that allows you to masturbate, then figuring out how to do that will be one of your first challenges. If you need help breathing but want to give a partner oral sex, you might need to alternate sucking on your partner's genitals with sucking breaths of air from your respirator hose. If you can't have intercourse, then you'll need to work out ways of pleasing both yourself and your partner without it. (This book has plenty of chapters that describe ways of doing that.) Perhaps your disability has left you with little nerve sensation in your genitals, but the opening of your anus is still sensitive, and stimulating it might bring you to orgasm. Perhaps your neck, lips, cheeks or nipples are highly sensitized to touch. Maybe it helps if you take a warm bath or shower or have a beer or glass of wine before having sex. This is just as true for able-bodied people.

Goodbye to Spontaneity

Some able-bodied couples don't like to use a condom because the thirty seconds it takes to put it on somehow destroys the mood for them. Think of how resilient "the mood" has to be when it takes all sorts of preparations and maneuvers to be ready to have sex! Think of how resilient the mood has to be if one partner cries out in pain and adjustments need to be made in order to continue.

One of the things that people who are disabled lose is the kind of sexual spontaneity that some able-bodied couples take for granted unless they are parents with kids who are still at home. Consider the following advice that was recently posted on the internet:

"Patience is truly a virtue in disability-related sex. Disability often destroys something in sex, spontaneity for one thing. Drugs, fatigue, depression, neurological impairment can also be a destructive force. Utilizing the turn-on can sometimes partially make up for what has been taken away. Sometimes erotic books, photos or videos can enhance the performance. The type and degree of disability often demands traveling that extra mile or two. "

PeterLove@primenet.com

Getting into Relationships

"Why would any man want this body?" "No woman's going to want this!" Some people who have disabilities feel that nobody will find them sexually attractive. As a result, they might push away people who do or, at the other end of the spectrum, offer themselves to the first person who shows interest, even if it is not someone they particularly like or trust. A disabled person without a solid sense of self might be starved for affection or desperately need to prove that he or she is desirable. Of course, one doesn't need to be disabled to have these sorts of hang-ups, but it can be extra-difficult when your physical ducks aren't in the same row as everyone else's.

Regarding the subject of dating and people with disabilities, a woman with cerebral palsy recently commented, "I think women are more accepting of differences than men. I see a lot more dis-abled men married or in serious relationships. I see a lot more disabled women just giving up." There are plenty of disabled men who say it's equally tough for them. Another disabled woman says one of the reasons she fell in love with her husband "was the idea that here was a person who looked and acted okay, wanting to have a relationship with me." (Both quotes are from "Dating Issues for Women with Physical Disabilities," *Sexuality and Disability,* 15, no. 4 [1997]) by Rintals, Howland, Nosek et al. Original source: T. Due, *Houston Chronicle,* May 24, 1995.)

People with disabilities sometimes shy away from dating other people who are disabled. When you are disabled yourself, there can be a kind of hatred of other people who are disabled—an inner need to say, "I'm not like them." There can also be the added problem of social

acceptance. Two people in wheelchairs humming down the sidewalk garner far more stares from able-bodied pedestrians than does one.

The Disabled Couple

Perhaps the most difficult aspect of being in a relationship where one or both members is disabled is that ultimately the couple has to face the same kinds of fights, squabbles, disagreements and difficulties as couples who have no physical disability! As for how disability affects a couple, keep in mind that some able-bodied couples stay in love with each other only as long as each partner is able to mirror the other's sexual attractiveness. If one member starts to look older than the other, slows down a bit or becomes disabled, the relationship may quickly dissolve. With other couples, there is a deep love and friendship that transcends physical change.

When there is a new disability, it is not uncommon for both partners to experience frustration, anger, fear, disappointment, and helplessness. Roles within the relationship may undergo serious changes. Neither the able-bodied member nor the one who is disabled should be afraid to seek help and advice from social workers and rehab staff.

When it comes to experiencing sexual intimacy, a couple with a new disability may need to learn anew. This might actually be a relief to your partner if you weren't as good in bed as you thought you were! The good news is that couples who had a rewarding sex life before the disability usually find a way to have a good sex life after.

If you are a couple whose primary expression of sexuality was through intercourse, you may have a good deal of adjusting ahead. It will be easier if you are a couple whose sexuality included a full range of sensory experiences, like enjoying the beauty of a sunset, holding hands and caressing each other.

Also, if you can afford it, it would be wise to hire an attendant to perform caretaking functions. Otherwise, a parent/child dynamic can evolve between you and your partner which can intrude on feelings of sexual passion.

With a Deaf Ear & Twinkle in His Eye

A woman who is a friend of the Goofy Foot Press works with deaf people and has also had sex with one or two deaf men. She said that she never realized how much she relies on verbal cues from a partner until she was romanced by a deaf man. For instance, when you are with a deaf person, there is no hearing without seeing. Whether it's being in another room or looking down when you are having a bowl of soup, the necessary conditions for connection are suddenly missing. She said that the lack of verbal give-and-take is particularly noticeable during sex, whether it's oral sex or intercourse.

People who are deaf are obviously more comfortable with verbal silence during romance and lovemaking than are people who can hear.

If our friend is sleeping with a man who is deaf, she lets him know that she needs more input than he might be used to giving a partner who is also deaf. She also says that it is important to have some of the lights on when you are making love to a deaf person, so they can either see you sign or read your lips. On the other hand, deaf people sometimes sign on each other's skin, or if they are in a spoons position, the person in the back can reach around his partner's body and sign in front of her where she can see it.

Attacking Their Own

It's interesting how people sometimes attack their own. For instance, while many people who are disabled would welcome an increased awareness that they are just as sexual as anyone else, some clearly don't. A year ago, when a mainstream glossy magazine for disabled people ran a story on sex and the disabled, some disabled readers were so upset that they canceled their subscriptions. When hearing about this, you might think that the story was *Hustler*-like and included photos of the naked disabled doing things that would have pleased Caligula. In reality, the article was so tame that it could have been published in *Parade* magazine or even *House & Garden*.

Perhaps the subject of sex brings up huge amounts of frustration and sadness for some disabled people, to the point where they simply get angry at sex itself.

So You Won't Have to Read The "Sex during Pregnancy" Chapter of This Book Unless You Want To

Women can get pregnant in a wheelchair just as easily as they can get pregnant in any other chair. Don't think for a moment that just because you are disabled or paralyzed from the shoulders or waist down you somehow can't get pregnant. Be sure that you speak to each other and to your physician about birth control. Note: Until recently, it was believed that birth control pills, shots and implants might be unsafe for some women who are in wheelchairs. It's not the wheelchair that's the problem, but proneness to circulatory problems and blood clots that can be increased by the birth control pill. However, the newer low-dose pills and shots are thought to be quite safe. If your gynecologist isn't used to working with women who have disabilities, check with the National Spinal Cord Foundation for a referral.

Attendants and Caregivers —The Good and Bad of It

Powerful feelings can develop between people who are patients and those who are hired to care for them—both loving and hateful. It is beyond the scope of this book to explore the various possibilities, except to say that it does little good to turn a blind eye to the dynamics that can arise between caretaker and caregiver.

If you are able-bodied, consider for a moment the issue of privacy. The kind of privacy that able-bodied people take for granted might not exist for someone who is disabled. This can range from bathing and completing bowel movements to preparing for masturbation and sex. It may be necessary for a disabled person to share private aspects of themselves with an attendant that some able-bodied people don't feel comfortable sharing even with a partner of many years.

Considering the level of dependency that some disabled people have, opportunities for abuse by attendants are rife. This is a huge issue, and abuse is unfortunately quite common. It is important that disabled people speak up against assistants who are abusive. If this is a concern for you, please contact your local center for independent living.

Helping The Helpers

In order to have fulfilling sex lives, people with disabilities often need the help of several different medical subspecialities. These might include neurology, psychology, urology, oncology, endocrinology, physical and rehabilitative medicine and sex therapy. Unfortunately, getting medical specialists to work together in a collaborative effort requires that professional egos be set aside. This can be as difficult as getting Catholics, Mormons, Jews and Southern Baptists to join forces. The problem multiplies when the issue is sex, since many of the professionals who need to work together might be ever so uncomfortable with the subject at hand.

If you are a disabled person who is struggling to get assistance with your sexual needs, maybe it will help if you give your healthcare provider a copy of this book opened to this chapter. Perhaps it will help them feel more at ease in aiding you with sexual matters. After all, it's quite likely that they, too, enjoy sex and would be more than happy to help you if they were just able to feel more comfortable.

Rehab Note: When rehab therapists get around to mentioning sex, it is usually in combination with discussions about bowel and bladder functioning. This is quite unfortunate. People who are newly disabled need access to positive information about sexuality early in their rehabilitation. Even if they reject the information, it is something positive that will remain in their consciousness, to be accessed at another time.

Stroke Studies — Interesting for a Number of Reasons

Stroke survivors, as a group, experience a decrease in sexual activity. Until recently, this was thought to have physical, rather than emotional, causes. However, a study of stroke survivors by Buzzellie, di Francesco, Giaquinto and Nolte concluded that "psychological issues, rather than medical ones, account for disruption of sexual functioning in stroke survivors" ("Sexuality Following Stroke," *Sexuality and Disability,* 15, no. 4, [1997]).

It is especially significant that the researchers found no differences in the sexual functioning of people with right-brained lesions as opposed to left-brain lesions or contralateral lesions. This contradicts our modern tendency to view behaviors as coming from one side of the brain or the other. This study indicates that sexuality is neither "right-brained" nor "left-brained."

Resources on Sex for People Who Are Disabled

Please check out the Resources section at goofyfootpress.com, for a listing of resources for people who are disabled. If you don't have internet access, you can call us at (541) 563-7550 and we will try to find the resources you need. There are some pretty clever solutions out there. For instance, if your fingers are too crippled to hold a vibrator, you might be able to negotiate one that is embedded in a Nerf ball.

Recommended Videotapes

Sexuality Reborn is an excellent video in which four likeable and articulate couples tell about their personal experience with sex and disability. At least one person in each couple is wheelchair-assisted. Very helpful for both disabled and able-bodied viewers. College instructors who use the *Guide to Getting It On!* in their classes are highly encouraged to show this tape to their students. A great deal of humanness is conveyed without a moment of pity or self-absorption. There is something about the honesty and genuineness of the couples who speak in this video that gives able-bodied people a more realistic and grounded perception of people who are disabled. There are parts of the tape where the couples are naked and having sex, but it isn't in a pornographic way that's going to ruffle the feathers of your dean or regents. The only criticism that reviewers had was that the occasional comments by the talking-head medical specialists seemed unnecessary and perhaps detracted from rather than added to the tape's effectiveness. To order, call (800) 435-8866.

Untold Desires shows interviews about sex with people who have all kinds of disabilities. This award-winning documentary contains no nudity and makes an excellent companion tape for *Sexually Reborn*. We seriously hope that anyone going through a rehab program would get to see both tapes. Included is a wonderful interview with a woman who has severe cerebral palsy. She is astute, funny, and energetic. The tape provides subtitles when she speaks because her speech is so CP-involved. The interviews with other disabled people are equally valuable. As an additional bonus, there is spectacular footage of one chair-assisted guy skiing down a steep mountain and a disabled dude racing down stairs and streets. Redefines the term "No Fear." Highly recommended for people with disabilities as well as those without.

Beware the Magic Bullet!

Chapter 53

Before long, modern medicine will be selling a pill that can increase the blood flow into even your great grandmother's genitals. Women will be plunking down $10 for something the size of an aspirin that promises a chemical solution to whatever ails you sexually. But what about the silliness and fun that some of us look for in sex? What about the tenderness? Does that automatically happen because you paid your pharmacist $10 to get your genitals all puffed up?

Maybe not. A research group from Italy found that while men who took Viagra reported increased sexual satisfaction, their female partners didn't necessarily. It seems the wives and girlfriends of these men discovered that there is more to being sexually satisfied than having a partner with a hard salami.

A social scientist recently studied surveys of older people and found that the critical factor in maintaining a woman's sexual desire is the attraction and lust that her partner feels for her. You can pickle a man's penis in Viagra, but if he doesn't make his partner feel good about herself, she won't have much desire for sex.

Still, many people are looking for an easy cure—a pill or cream or whatever. It doesn't matter if you've been angry at your partner for the past twenty-five hours or twenty-five years, or if he or she falls asleep watching television every night at nine or hasn't tried a new thing in bed since Jimmy Carter was president. With pills that can increase the blood flow to our private parts, all resentments will suddenly disappear! Or so they say.

Research papers are already being released with claims such as "sixty-five percent IMPROVEMENT FOR WOMEN ON VIAGRA!" What they mean by "improvement" is an increase in blood flow into a woman's crotch. What they don't tell you is that most women can achieve this by sitting on a washing machine when it's on the spin cycle.

In spite of what some of us may be wishing for, sexual satisfaction in long-term relationships is usually more involved than having an erection or a swollen vagina or popping a pricey pill.

If you want to keep your sexlife silly and satisfying, you might take a closer look at how you spend your time together when you aren't having sex. Does sitting together in front of the TV for hours each night make you feel more excited about your partner? Maybe if she gives you a hand job during reruns of *Law & Order*, but don't expect that to keep happening for long. Sitting in front of a television is no more helpful to your relationship than having a heroin addiction.

Just because the sex was hot during the first year doesn't mean it will be hot during the tenth. If you want to keep your intimacy alive, you need to talk, share things and do things together that you enjoy. If you want your sex life to stay healthy, do things that make you like and admire each other when you have your clothes on. And don't expect a pill to make up for what you haven't been doing.

Take note from early on what's exciting about your relationship. Then you scream like the blazes if you see it starting to fade away.

Chapter Notes: Special thanks to Sandra Leiblum, Marian Dunn and Leonore Tiefer for their help and input.

When Your System Crashes

Chapter 54

While this is a chapter on sexual problems, please keep in mind that it's only a brief overview. Hopefully you will find it to be an intelligent overview. You are encouraged to read articles and books on sex that offer a more traditional perspective, and check with a sex therapist or physician as indicated.

This chapter starts with male trouble & ends with female trouble.

Mr. Softy—The Bummer in Your Pants

It is amusing to look at the impotence ads in the sports section of major newspapers. They are usually located next to the ads for hair removal and hair restoration, above the ads for nude female mud wrestling and sometimes on the same page as the penis-enlargement ads. Most of the men in the impotence ads are older. Does this mean that erection problems are a part of old age, or are these men simply bored with the type of sex they've been having for much of their lives?

Contrary to what the erection ads show, hard-on problems (hard-offs?) happen to men of all ages, from teenagers on up. For instance, it's not unusual for erection problems to occur at the start of a sexual relationship. Call it performance anxiety, call it fear—it's not unusual for a guy to need a couple of weeks or months to find a comfortable groove. Giving him any less time to get it up is silly and shortsighted, as long as your relationship is solid and there is a strong sense of mutual attraction. The real danger is not with the lack of erection, but with what each of you makes of it. Short-term problems can become long term-problems if the man sees himself as a failure or the woman needs his erection to validate that she's desirable.

Several kinds of erection failure are discussed in the pages that follow—from those caused by physical impairment to penile paralysis that is fueled by soft thoughts and limp emotions. Whatever the cause, hopefully a man will be able to utilize these moments of hydraulic failure as an excuse to explore and please his partner with his hands and mouth, and as a time for her to be intimate with him in other ways than by having him stick his penis inside of her. Lips and fingers can feel just as good on a penis that's soft as on one that's hard, and there are plenty of sexual fantasies the two of you can act out that don't require a penis at all.

Some people feel that it's best to focus attention on other body parts when a penis stalls out. But if you decide to keep stimulating a pokey pecker, make sure your only intent is to give it pleasure rather than trying to squeeze an erection out of it. Otherwise, the guy will feel like a total dud and will probably have performance anxiety next time around.

It can really help if the woman seeks his assistance in other ways. This might include necking for a long time, finger fucking, oral sex, using a vibrator or dildo, tying each other up, or maybe she can try masturbating while he watches or holds her. That way, a potential downer might evolve into something sweet and hot.

Often, the biggest problem with impotence isn't the lack of erection. Rather, it's a lack of playfulness and resourcefulness on the part of the man and woman when they are confronted with a hard-on that's a no-show.

Trouble in Deadwood—When Your Posse Won't Ride

Books on sex often use terms such as "self-hatred," "self-loathing" and "devastating" to describe how a man feels when he is—gulp—impotent. You know, the horror when he can't get it up.

Perhaps this guide is way out of step or maybe it's just insensitive, but devastating is what happens when your wife or child dies or when you've just been told that you only have six months to live. Self-hatred is what you feel if your business flops or if you've just blown your life's savings. Self-loathing is what you experience when you've had a major stroke or accident and can't feed or bathe yourself anymore.

Call us callous, call us rude, but we can think of about a thousand things worse than if a man's hard-on takes a hiatus, even if it's forever. Sure, it's frustrating and even humiliating at times, but so are a lot of other things in life. The fact is, you still have your fingers and mouth for giving pleasure, and you still have what's in your heart to love your partner with. And if you can't count at least five things in your life to be thankful for, even if your dick never gets hard again, then your priorities are in seriously bad shape.

Contrary to what you'll read elsewhere, this guide believes that erection problems, regardless of the cause, are an opportunity to have better sex rather than worse. Fortunately, there are plenty of ways that modern medicine can help a recalcitrant penis to get hard, but it seems a shame to employ a quick cure without allowing yourself and your relationship to grow in the process. You won't believe how many times Viagra-like pills will result in better erections but not in better sex for either partner.

A woman who is overcoming orgasm problems has to welcome a new way of embracing her body and her sexuality. It's a journey, a process. People who survive heart attacks and cancer learn to approach life differently as a result of the disease. Impotent men, on the other hand, just want their dicks to get hard—no learning, no journey.

The Sufis have a saying that you have to let yourself die before you are truly born. Sometimes a guy has to give up his penis as a symbol of masculinity before he can get on with his life. Sometimes he has to realize that there's more to being a man than getting a hard-on, and there's more to sex than just intercourse. Then he sometimes has to convince his wife.

This is not to say that a man shouldn't inquire about the various remedies that modern medicine has for erection problems. He should also have a full physical to make sure that the erection problem is not a symptom of something else. If there are medical problems, they need to be treated. At the same time, it's worth noting that some medical problems are the body's way of making a statement. Perhaps the man has important lessons to learn about himself and the world around him. If he and his partner are able to accomplish the kind of changes and growth that are necessary, then maybe he'll start getting hard again. But by then it won't matter as much, because he and his partner will have discovered new ways to give each other sexual pleasure and emotional support.

Note: No kidding about getting a physical exam. Men who begin to experience a gradual increase in impotency might be seeing the first signs of an impending stroke or heart attack. Impotence may be

a greater predictor of stroke or heart attack than the highly-regarded stress test. It seems that the arteries in the penis start to gum up before those in the rest of the body. A physical exam may allow physicians to help a man before something really bad happens to his most important organs—the heart and brain. ALSO: Researchers are now finding a high correlation between obesity and impotence.

A Modern Medical Approach To The Great Groin Grinch

If your penis is impotent, it is likely that you are muttering under your breath that we can take our Sufi logic and stuff it where the sun don't shine. You want a traditional Western approach. You want a magic bullet that does not require introspection or lifestyle changes. Good enough. The advice that follows is a spoof on a modern medical approach to fixing erection problems. While it conveys some wisdom, it still focuses on fixing the penis instead of helping the man behind it and the woman in front of it. It is an approach that attempts to turn the clock back to a time when the penis worked just fine. It's a regressive fix rather than a step forward, one that is oblivious to lessons that might be learned or frontiers of trust that are waiting to be crossed.

Dear Dr. Goofy,

My bowling partner recently started having erection problems and is too embarrassed to seek help. Can you offer advice?

Bob from Boston

Dear Bob,

If your bowling partner has stopped throwing strikes for more than a couple of weeks, it's a good idea for him to take his pokey pecker to a physician for a checkup. It's smart to rule out underlying medical conditions.

Modern medicine has decided that more than 99.999% of erection problems are strictly due to physical causes, from diabetes to who-knows-what. We can fix almost anything, unless your friend is a cigarette smoker. If that's the case, he might as well call a mortuary and have himself interred. Cigarette smoking is as bad for your penis as it is for your lungs.

Is your friend able to get erections at all, like in the morning upon waking, or when he jerks off? To explore this further, we might send him home with a device he attaches to his penis when he sleeps. The device won't help to get him off, but it does tell if he has erections in his sleep and for how long. If a man can get a sustained erection in his sleep or while masturbating, the problem may reside in his psyche, although certain types of depression can keep a man from getting an erection even in his sleep. Yikes. Did I say "psyche?" With the help of our friends in the pharmaceutical industry, we have declared that the psyche no longer exists. There are, however, neurotransmitter issues that we can throw pills at.

Speaking of pills, some physicians will send your friend home with samples of Viagra—or Levitra or Cialis if they have stock in Glaxo or Lilly. If the pills don't work, then they'll do a work-up. Or they might give your friend's penis an injection that's a pecker-picker-upper. Don't worry, no one's going to pull out a syringe with a hollow nail for a needle and say, "Drop your drawers." It's an itty-bitty wisp of a shot that hurts less than getting a pubic hair stuck in your zipper. If the penis gets hard and is able to stay hard, then the plumbing is intact and the problem can probably be fixed with a prescription.

If the shot does not make the penis hard, or it gets hard but doesn't stay hard, then it's likely there is a circulation problem. This can range from hardening of the arteries (strange term for when it happens in the penis!) to leaky valves. More tests would need to be done to peg the exact cause, but don't worry, we know a fine surgeon.

It is also possible that there is a neurological problem which is disabling the body's ability to begin the hard-on process. This is similar to when you turn the ignition key on your car and nothing happens.

Another thing we sometimes remember to check is if your friend is taking medications that might be cold-cocking his rooster. Suspicious meds can range from alcohol and heroin to prescriptions and over-the-counter drugs. Some even say that Tagamet can do a dick in.

Finally, if you insist, we will consider the highly unlikely possibility that your friend's erection problem stems from emotional causes or a combination of something emotional and physical.

To check that mental thing, your friend needs to do some private detective work, or detective work on his privates. For instance, what was going on in his life around the time when his soldier stopped marching? Did his ability to get an erection decline gradually, like the fall of Rome, or did it shut down all at once, like the Bank of Boston? Was there a change in his job status? Did his insurance company cancel him without cause? Did his team not go to the Superbowl because of a lousy call in the closing seconds of the final playoff game? Was there a change in his relationship with his partner? Did his wife leave him for another man? Did she leave him for another woman? Was he pulled from an important project, or did he lose a promotion he had his heart set on? Did he receive an unkind inquiry from the IRS?

Also, it is helpful to inquire about his relationship with his spouse. If he instantly says, "Naw, it's fine," ask him to describe some of the things that are fine about it. See if he conveys a sense of love and fondness, or if he sounds like he's reading the instructions on a bottle of Kaopectate. If the relationship has fallen on—dare we say—hard times, then he and his wife need to focus on fixing that rather than on fixing his penis, which is merely the messenger.

Don't worry, we're working on Husband-Wife Combo pills and patches for whatever ails them. In the meantime, in order to treat erection problems that are caused by relationship problems, your friend and his partner might try to forget all they know about each other and start over again as if they'd just met. This can be difficult, especially if they have had some really lousy times together. They might try taking a month or two doing things like hugging, touching and talking, with no attempt at intercourse. They also might try sharing romantic dinners, movies and the types of things they enjoyed doing when they first met. How about racking their bowling balls and taking a trip around the country in the Winnebago? They might discover that there really is life after bowling. On the other hand, some couples do better when they spend less time with each other. This can be especially true when they are newly retired and suddenly find themselves in each other's face for 24 hours a day. Other couples do well with the extra time together.

There is also the possibility that your friend had erection problems before he and his wife met. Then he might find it helpful to get some psychological help on his own.

And if none of that seems to help, there's this Sufi saying ....

Viagra & Friends

You've heard of Niagra® right? It's a spray that starches your shirts when you iron them. They've managed to put something very similar into a pill, and they called it Viagra. Instead of starching your shirts, it starches your schlong. And there's more. Remember how Barbie had friends like Skipper and Midge? Viagra now has little pill friends too, with names like Levitra and Cialis.

One of the finest quotes about Viagra is from *Boston Globe* columnist Ellen Goodman:

> "I can't help wondering why we got a pill to help men with performance instead of communication. Moreover, how is it possible that we came up with a male impotence pill before we got a male birth control pill? The Vatican, you will note, has approved Viagra while still condemning condoms."

A urologist in Colorado wonders why they don't combine Viagra with Prozac to make a pill that cures everything. And even some women are taking Viagra, perhaps to help with their erections too.

If you and your partner have been low on sexual intimacy for a few years and suddenly discover that pills or injections can help with his hard-on, please schedule a couple of sessions with a sex therapist first. All sorts of issues need to be dealt with before you slide a rusty penis inside a vagina. Questions about intimacy, romance, attraction, and excitement may have been buried under layers of anger and frustration. They will need to be addressed first. On the other hand, if you and your partner have been enjoying orgasms and physical intimacy, but just no intercourse, go for it and see what happens.

Viagra in the Cockpit

Pilots are not allowed to take Viagra less than twelve hours before a flight. The FAA does not want the co-pilot to accidently grab the pilot's erection instead of the landing-gear controls. Viagra also inhibits an enzyme in the penis which helps the blood vessels dilate. A similar enzyme works in our eyes and is impacted by Viagra. This is why taking Viagra can result in altered color perception. Pilots who are taking Viagra have apparently seen vaginas in the cockpit.

Levitra as a Thrill Pill?

At least the Viagra people have had the decency to market their drug toward older guys who might actually need it. No such claim can be made by the makers of the more recently-released Levitra, which is clearly going for the younger guy who gets it up just fine. In one of their ads, they show a young guy trying to throw a football through a tire. It bounces off to the side. Then, after Levitra is mentioned, the guy gets the ball through the tire several times, and is finally joined by his smiling wife or girlfriend.

First of all, if you equate sex with a woman with throwing a football through a tire, you don't have a clue about sexual intimacy or have been watching way too much sports on TV. And if you honestly think that taking a hard-on pill when you are young is going to make you a better lover, then you are wasting your time reading this book.

Other Chemicals That Make You Hard

There are come compounds which cause a diehard erection when injected into the penis, assuming the penile plumbing can maintain an erection once the penis gets hard. A compound called Papervine was formerly used for this purpose, but now there are different combinations of ingredients used in the injections. For example, one popular combination includes papervine, phentolamine, and prostaglandin E1.

Also, there is a kind of prostaglandin which a man shoots into his urethra (peehole) before he needs an erection, like one of those fertilizer sticks that you shove in the soil next to your droopy houseplants. It has not turned out to be as popular as was hoped.

There are other orally-prescribed drugs that can help some men to get hard. One drug that is sometimes prescribed is called yohimbine. Yohimbine is native to Africa. It can often be found in health food stores. Since the cost of yohimbine isn't much more in prescription form, why not get it from a urologist? That way you will be monitored for side effects and you will be sure that you are getting the yohimbine in consistent doses, which is not true for the yohimbine in health food stores. The urologist can also rule out other possible causes of the erection problem. Other drugs for impotence are currently being tested, including some that are administered in cream form. The problem is getting the cream to penetrate through the part of the penis that surrounds the vascular tissue. Another problem seems to concern stiffness in the fingers after applying the cream.

Mechanical Devices for Getting Hard

Some men find that the vacuum pump is a useful erection aid. It is a little bulky and cumbersome, but worth a try if you are in search of a lost erection. It might also be wise to try the vacuum pump first before subjecting your genitals to various types of surgery, including implants. What do you have to lose? Some surgeons are happy to tell you about their surgical successes, but don't expect them to show you pictures of their failures. There are different suppliers for vacuum pumps. Be sure they include special gaskets which keep your scrotum from getting sucked up into the tube.

Surgical Implants

There are different surgical implants, from semi-rigid shanks to implants with little pumps that give you an erection. Please research this subject carefully before making an incision—ah, decision.

Lousy Hang Time—Premature Ejaculation

The term "premature ejaculation" didn't exist in our society before the 1960s. That's when sex researchers realized that a woman might want more than a couple of thrusts during intercourse.

The next chapter of this book is titled "Dyslexia of the Penis—Improving Your Sexual Hang Time." You'll never guess what it's about.

Pharmaceutical Sex Assassins

You wouldn't believe how many over-the-counter or prescription medications can mess with everything from your ability to get wet to your feelings of desire. For instance, just taking a common antihistamine can keep a woman from lubricating. Extending this into a worst-case scenario, the woman starts having painful intercourse because she isn't lubricating due to the antihistamine. Because of the pain, the muscles in her vagina tense up whenever her husband's penis gets hard. The automatic muscle contraction continues to make intercourse painful long after she's stopped taking the allergy medicine. Because of the constant pain, she experiences a decrease in desire, which causes her insecure husband to have an affair. She finds about it and files for divorce. All because she took a couple of Sudafed! Or maybe she's taking an antidepressant which decreases sexual desire, and who wants a divorce because of Prozac?

At the top of the list of sexual suspects should be any medication that says, "May cause drowsiness. Do not drive or operate heavy equipment." *Heavy Equipment* is a subliminal reference to the penis (in the copywriter's dreams!) Your heavy equipment might not work so well when taking this medication. Ditto for having your sex drive bulldozed, whether you are a male or female.

Whatever your sexual problems or concerns, the absolute first thing to do is to make a list of all the medications you are taking—from simple over-the-counter drugs to prescription medications to herbal teas and vitamin concoctions to heroin, cocaine, pot, poppers, ecstasy, meth, or alcohol. Then check these over with a pharmacist.

Medications may not be the cause of the sexual problem, but they're the first and most obvious thing to rule out.

The Tour de France in Your Pants

In the past few years, physicians have found a relationship between extensive bike riding and malfunction or numbness of the nuts and penis. Dr. Robert Kessler, a urologist from Stanford, provided the following update: "Both our studies and other studies show that cycling greater than six hours per week is not only associated with Erectile Dysfunction (ED) but also perineal pain and voiding systems. When you compare similar groups of men who are engaging in aerobic exercise (cyclists with runners, for example), there is an increased incidence of ED in the cyclists." Other researchers found that conventional biking produced a dramatic, though temporary, drop in the oxygen supply to the penis, from 60 to 18 mm Hg. Recumbent biking produced no change at all. While most bicycle-related numbness appears to be temporary, a special surgery has been devised to help those men whose penises have suffered permanent injury. There are now special seats that help absorb road shock. These or recumbent bikes are a wise choice for the serious rider of either sex.

Also unkind to the sexual safety of male bike riders are incidents where the crotch goes crunch on the bicycle frame, handlebar stem, or seat. The *Dictionary of Mountain Bike Slang* refers to this kind of catastrophe as "CROTCH-TESTING—the sudden impact between a male rider's private parts and something very hard and pointy."

'Gasm Spasm

One of the nice things about being naked together and having sex is getting to experience an occasional orgasm or two. Of course, most couples realize that there are times when either orgasms don't happen or you need to supply your own afterward. This is so normal that it would be silly to call it a sex problem. On the other hand, there are some men and women who don't orgasm at all, or it only happens when they are alone and not in the presence of a lover. That's what the next couple of sections are about.

Not Being Able to Come with a Partner

Some guys, called retarded ejaculators (honest), are able to get hard and have intercourse for hours, but can't reach orgasm during intercourse to save their lives. These men can usually come while masturbating, but not while having intercourse. Men with this sort of problem often try to thrust faster and harder, thinking this will help. This is one of the worst things to do, because after you've been thrusting for a while, going harder and faster tends to desensitize the penis.

Men who are taking drugs that are commonly used for urinary problems and high blood pressure, including alpha blockers, minipress, hytrin, cardura, and flomax who started having delayed ejaculation after taking these drugs should let their doctors know what's happening, or what's not happening. However, the causes for delayed ejaculation are seldom medical.

Very rough estimates of the problem have somewhere between 6% to 8% of men experiencing this problem at one time or another. Men with delayed ejaculation fall into two groups, those who have had it all their lives, and those who have it situationally. The lion's share of men with the problem fall into the second group.

Usually it's some sort of emotional trauma, especially of a relationship nature, that will cause the problem to rear its ugly head. Let's say a guy tends to be a bit obsessive to begin with, and then finds out that his wife has been sleeping with the gardener. And with his lawyer. And with her gynecologist. Get the picture? Would anyone be surprised if he had sexual problems in his next relationship? There can be plenty of other reasons for delayed detonation, including concerns about losing control or becoming too vulnerable, or even an unconscious fear of getting a partner pregnant or causing her damage.

One of the cures for retarded ejaculation is to start having sex in unusual places, like the back seat of your car or any place else that is a bit strange, unfamiliar, and possibly exciting. The goal is to try to draw the guy out of his comfortable environment where he's become a master at blocking sensation. Making him a bit nervous seems to allow more excitement and sensation to break through.

Strange as it may seem, the chances are good he can masturbate just fine, even if he couldn't launch a load during intercourse to save his life. So the two of you might work on masturbating together, with the woman eventually doing some of the stroking. He might also start to masturbate with a different grip and a lighter touch. Just before he's about to ejaculate, he should get into a position that he usually doesn't come in and finish himself off that way. Also, he might try alternating between intercourse and masturbation, e.g., thrust a little, jerk a little, thrust a little, jerk a little. Or when he's just about ready to come from masturbating, pop his slow stick into his partner's vagina and start thrusting away.

Another way to help is to focus on other parts of his body rather than on his penis. He's clearly king at keeping his Johnson under control, so maybe you can work on raising his excitement level in other ways. For instance, you might spend some time tickling his inner thighs and groin with a feather, silky fabric, fingers, or lips. Or if you are into kink, slip on a dildo and do him up the rear, or turn into Doreen, Dominatrix from the Dungeon of Hell, and make him beg for sexual favors. Anything to throw him off balance, sexually speaking.

While you are at it, try consulting a few books whose focus is on treating sexual problems. Some couples have found Barbara Keesling's *Sexual Pleasure* from Hunter House to be helpful. And don't hesitate to visit a sex therapist.

While the man is the one with the delayed ejaculation, it's the woman in his life who can get a bit nutzoid about it. She might assume it's perfectly normal when a woman doesn't have an orgasm, but can get seriously bent out of shape if she can't make him waste his wad. This is something you should definitely talk about. If he finds his partner to be a sexual turn-on, he needs to verbalize it often. That's because his body is giving signals to the contrary.

When A Woman Can Come on Her Own But Not with a Partner

Sometimes a woman is able to give herself orgasms when she is alone, but can't generate one in the presence of a man even if he stimulates her to near perfection. The reasons for this might be similar to those mentioned in the preceding section about men with delayed ejaculation. Also, some women are so frightened by men or angry at them that they would sooner give birth to triplets than have an orgasm in a guy's presence. The vulnerability is just too much. Other women aren't hostile but feel there is something about their sexuality that needs to be hidden, or they might feel frustrated or absent in the presence of a man. Therapy can often be helpful if that's what you want to do.

As for coming during intercourse, plenty of women need more stimulation than thrusting alone. But with the right kind of fingerplay, oral sex, or a vibrator, they are often able to have an orgasm in their man's presence.

A Question of Desire

Some people think that "low desire" is a sickness like the flu that a woman needs to get over. They assume that she's cured of her low desire if she can happily hop on her partner's erect penis. But low desire can mean different things, some of which require a reworking of the relationship outside of the bedroom before there will be any changes between the sheets. The mind-set of trying to turn the clock back is not a productive one when dealing problems of desire. Of course, this won't stop us from giving a woman Viagra or gluing a testosterone patch on her hip—to hell with years of pent-up anger and frustration, often on the part of both partners.

Highly Recommended for Everyone, Not Just Women with Low Desire: Remember the finger that you used to masturbate with? Why not put it to use by turning the pages of Kathryn Hall's truly helpful book *Reclaiming Your Sexual Self: How You Can Bring Desire Back Into Your Life,* John Wiley & Sons, New York, 2004. Kathryn Hall is an excellent sex therapist and she treats low desire as a messenger rather than as a disease. Men and women both will be able to find approaches in her book that can help them better understand and give meaning to lost desire. She presents a number of ways of approaching desire. Fortunately, she is not beholden to the drug companies and she realizes the short-sightedness of automatically throwing pills or patches at whatever ails you.

When Excitement Is Too Much

Some of us can't tolerate much excitement. Somewhere along the line we got the feeling that sexual excitement is dangerous or disorganizing. As a result, we experience conflicts when becoming sexually excited. People with this problem sometimes numb themselves between the navel and the knees. That way they don't have to face the anticipated dread that sexual excitement holds in their imagination.

People who want to work through excitement problems need to experience pleasurable feelings slowly and without goals such as having an orgasm. Pressure to feel sexual takes them out of the moment and makes them feel numb. With time and effort, sexual excitement can be tolerated in the here and now, assuming that's what you want.

Some people have trouble managing sexual excitement when they are alone. They can't masturbate or even feel sexual on their own, but do just fine when they are with a partner. Perhaps they need to experience a partner's excitement about them before they can feel their own excitement.

Orgasm Fears & Tears

Although orgasms are usually welcome events, this is not always the case. For instance, young girls or boys who are having their first adult-like orgasms might feel that they have done something wrong or broken something inside.

Adults can have mixed feelings about their own orgasms, especially when sadness, loneliness or guilt are triggered by the orgasm. The sadness can sometimes be about a former real-life partner, or maybe the orgasm taps into a deep emotional pain that suddenly gets released. Some people cry after a good come because it touches a sadness that's deep inside.

There are also people who treat their own orgasms with cold detachment, especially when they feel a need to masturbate. Perhaps the need for sexual relief brings up feelings of weakness or self-loathing. Whatever the case, they are not particularly gentle or tender when handling their own genitals. There are also people who dislike orgasms because they experience them as a form of losing control.

It's a fine testament to the power of orgasm that more people in our society don't have problems with them, given how we tend to be a bit sexually repressed.

Painful Intercourse

Pain during intercourse can happen to both men and women, but is more often experienced by women. The causes can be physical

704 · *When Your System Crashes*

or emotional, or the problem may originally have been physical, but has evolved into an emotional struggle.

If you are having pain during intercourse, be sure to check with a physician or perhaps a couple of physicians. If you are a woman, try to determine whether the pain is at the opening of the vagina or is caused by deep thrusting. Deep-thrusting pain is sometimes caused by constipation or pelvic inflammatory disease. Shallow thrusting pain has a larger range of possible causes, from adhesions under the clitoral hood or episiotomy scars to yeast infections, herpes sores, or vaginal changes associated with menopause.

Painful intercourse might also occur when there is a poor match in sexual anatomy between male and female (see pages 540-542 on dealing with a jumbo penis). It is also possible that the couple is a bit clumsy. Of course, most sex books assume it's the man who is clumsy, but a passive female who accepts a male's clumsiness is just as sexually challenged as he. Maybe both partners are trying the best they can, but need a little extra help. Whatever the case, it is the couple, rather just one of them, who needs the assist.

Other questions to explore about painful intercourse include whether it happens all the time, how long it has been happening, if it happens with all partners or just one, and if added lubrication helps. It might be wise to consult with someone whose expertise is human sexuality. At the very least, read up on the subject in a couple of books on sex problems and see what they have to say. Common terms for this are vulvodynia or vaginal pain disorder.

This kind of pain is very real and it can have horrible effects on a relationship. The woman (and couple) who is experiencing it needs the same kind of support as anyone who is experiencing a chronic pain disorder.

In the meantime, the couple needs to get past their frustration and try to enjoy their sexuality in other ways besides just intercourse. There are many wonderful ways to please each other besides sticking a penis inside a vagina.

Ladies: Beware of What You Hear about Female Sexual Dysfunction

If you were preparing to sell a drug into a new segment of the population, you'd want to have statistics that demonstrated an overwhelming need for the drug such as "43% of American women complain of sexual dysfunction." Perhaps it's pure coincidence, but at a conference on female sexual dysfunction which was partially funded by the company that makes Viagra, a number of the presenters who were studying the effects of Viagra on women began their presentation with this exact statistic.

Of course, there's just one problem. Where do statistics like these come from? For instance, if we at Goofy Foot Press wanted to come up with statistics that said, "95% of the American public needs to read the *Guide to Getting It On!*" it would be easy to do as long as we structured the questions cleverly enough. We could also pay a research team to re-interpret findings of other studies to give them the spin we want.

So when you hear that 43% of American women complain of sexual dysfunction, be a heads-up consumer and start asking, "What do they mean by sexual dysfunction?" "Are they trying to sell me something that I don't need?" "If I do have 'sexual dysfunction,' could it have more to do with the shortcomings of my relationship than a shortage of blood flow into my crotch?"

Women's Orgasm Problems

Plenty of women don't have orgasms with thrusting during intercourse. This doesn't mean that they have sexual problems. All it means is that both partners need to explore what gets the woman off and include it as part of their lovemaking, unless it happens to be the man's best friend, and some couples might enjoy that, too.

Also, there is no question that a history of sexual abuse can cause significant sexual problems. However, some therapists automatically assume this was the case when any woman presents with a significant sexual problem. Yet plenty of men and women who never had a shred of sexual abuse still have sexual problems. For instance, being raised in some religious households can cause sexual problems that appear very similar to those of sexual abuse, including the person's feeling vacant, depersonalized, or numb when having sex. Such a person might find it extremely difficult to have an orgasm.

For women who haven't had an orgasm yet, the classic reference book remains *For Yourself: The Fulfillment of Female Sexuality* by Lonnie Barbach.

Vaginismus—Gridlock in Your Groin

Vaginismus is when the muscles surrounding the vagina close so tightly that they won't allow anything to go inside. The reaction can be so severe that a woman can't even insert a tampon.

Vaginismus might result from something as simple as a lousy experience at the gynecologist's office, to the body holding onto scary memories from something that was too overwhelming to be processed by the mind.

If you have this kind of problem, try reading up on the subject. There are simple behavioral techniques that can be used to help the vagina eventually relax. Depending on your sexual history, you might also do well to seek out a psychotherapy consultation. If you had a traumatic past, vaginismus might be a powerful statement that your body is holding onto something that needs to be worked through. Or it might just have been a reaction to one isolated experience that had little to do with sex or sexual repression.

Not a Sexual Problem Per Se, But Still...

When people are diagnosed with certain terrible diseases, or tragic things suddenly happen, they sometimes try to blame it on things they have done.

For instance, they might interpret their cancer as punishment for past sexual enjoyment, or for masturbation, incest, abortion or anything we might have felt guilty about. In some ways, it is easier for us to believe that there was a cause of the cancer such as masturbation than to realize that bad things can happen in a totally random way.

It often makes us feel too helpless to admit that there was nothing we did to cause the cancer or the tragedy. That would mean the world is totally random with no regard for human effort or struggle. So we create a personal myth that allows us to place the blame on past forms of sexual enjoyment.

In our culture, sexual pleasure is still a dangerous commodity with dangerous overtones. It's the first thing we toss overboard during life's various storms. We forget that it's as much a part of us as the need to eat and breathe.

Chapter Notes: Special thanks to sex therapist Joe Marzucco, Ph.D in Portland and to Julian Slowinski, Linda Banner and Barbara Keesling.

Dyslexia of the Penis
Learning to Improve Your Sexual Hang Time

Chapter 55

Slow down, Pud!!!

Would if I could, Labby!

Welcome to the *Goofy Foot Academy of Premature Ejaculation. Early admissions are warmly accepted!* Coming too soon is an unkind joke that a man's body plays on itself. His penis suddenly feels like it has had twenty minutes' worth of intercourse before his partner barely has her panties off. He loses out on lots of fun and intimacy.

Equally frustrating is the numbing effect that premature ejaculation can have on a woman's level of excitement. That's because she often holds back in an attempt to help the man last longer. In cases where she wants to wrap her ankles around her lover's neck and have him thrust away at a hefty clip, she learns to lie still; and if she wants long, deep strokes, she learns not to ask.

A lot of women feel that rapid ejaculation is "his problem," so he's the one who needs to fix it. However, coming too soon affects both partners, and this chapter takes a partners' approach to solving it. For instance, it talks about the need for a couple to increase rather than decrease the level of sexual excitement in their relationship.

It offers exercises that can help some men learn to tolerate a depth of sexual feeling that they probably don't know exists. It also suggests that a couple's entire relationship can be strengthened when the woman helps the man to improve upon a problem he has been helpless to fix on his own.

This chapter uses the terms *coming too soon, premature ejaculation, PE,* and *rapid ejaculation* interchangeably, like balls in a juggler's bag. They all mean the same thing.

Why Does It Happen?

There have been many different theories about why men come too soon. One theory blames the masturbation habits of teenage boys, saying that they teach themselves to come quickly by jerking off as fast as they sometimes drive. But plenty of guys who jerk off lickety split can last as long as they like during intercourse. Another theory says that our bodies confuse anxiety and sexual excitement. So the Peter-meter on a guy who is anxious tells him it's time to come when he's only had a couple of thrusts. But no research has ever shown that guys who come fast are any more or less anxious than anyone else. A third theory says that a man with PE holds tension in his pelvis. This results in constant muscle contraction that makes for a quick come. A fourth theory says that some men's penises are more sensitive than others, making it impossible for them to get past the early innings. A fifth theory says that the part of the brain where orgasm is triggered gets hyper in guys who come too soon. And finally, there is a zoological perspective, which says that plenty of male animals ejaculate after only a few thrusts. This helps them to live longer, since a steamy two-hour lovemaking session in a jacaranda tree greatly increases the chances that a pair of mating primates will fall off a limb or be eaten by predators, and we're not talking oral sex here.

Some women have the theory that guys can last longer if only they tried harder. But a man with rapid ejaculation can no more will his wad to wait than he can will good weather or world peace.

Whatever your theory, P.E. is a problem that keeps men from being able to enjoy the sensations in their own bodies. That is what the rest of this chapter addresses.

Different Types of Premature Ejaculation

Premature ejaculation has different causes in different groups of men. For instance, males who are beginning to have intercourse for the first time tend to come too soon. But after time and experience, they get a handle on it. Men with rapid ejaculation never get a handle on it, or sometimes they are inconsistent about when they squirt, feeling more like clowns with a firehose than lovers with a reliable penis. Here are some possible subgroups of men with rapid ejaculation:

Pronto Penis Subgroup #1. Typical of this group is the guy who has never been able to last for more than a minute or two, unless he goes frightfully slow and manages to squeeze out a few more minutes before his sausage starts to spasm.

It is possible this man's penis is more physically sensitive than most. If so, he might talk to a physician about trying 25 mg or 50 mg of Clomipramine (Anafranil) four to six hours before intercourse. Since many of us have no clue if we'll be getting laid six hours from now, some men simply take the drug every day.

As of press time, few doctors and healthcare practitioners are familiar with the medical treatment of rapid ejaculation. Don't be surprised if they are uncomfortable prescribing this medication. This is an "off label" indication for this drug, which means the FDA has not reviewed it for PE. While prescribing "off label" is often done in medicine today, this doesn't mean your healthcare professional will know about it when it comes to premature ejaculation.

One drug that is currently in clinical trial for premature ejaculation is called Dapoxetine. It is a selective serotonin reuptake inhibitor (SSRI) that acts quickly in delaying the ability to orgasm. The owner of the patent hopes to have it on the market by 2006.

Currently-prescribed SSRIs such as Prozac, Paxil and Zoloft are prescribed like M&Ms for people who feel depressed. While there are questions about how well these drugs work for depression, users have found that a frequent side effect is delayed orgasm. It seems they interfere with the neurotransmitters in the brain that result in orgasm (a.k.a. the "Oh-God" neurotransmitters.) Other side effects of these medications can include sleepiness, dry mouth, decreased libido, and problems with erection or wetness.

There are also over the counter creams for desensitization. They aren't particularly helpful, although some prescription creams for oral pain are said to help delay ejaculation. You rub them on your penis before dipping it into its favorite cavity. However, you will be at cross-purposes if the numbing potion gets on your partner's clitoris.

There are even condoms to help with rapid ejaculation. People at condom factories squirt special numbing stuff inside the condom. Some brands are Trojan Extended Pleasure and Durex Performax.

Pronto Penis Subgroup #2. Typical of this group is Mr. Inconsistent. His penis is the proverbial loose cannon. Sometimes he lasts as long as he and his partner might want, other times he's quicker than Trigger. He might benefit greatly from the exercises listed in this chapter. While drugs may help him become more consistent, they will mask the larger problems he has with not being aware of his body's sensations. He might also be having anxieties about sex, or perhaps he has issues about his partner or long-term commitment.

Pronto Penis Subgroup #3. In this group is the man who is struggling with newly acquired premature ejaculation. He is usually older. But a closer look at his sexual history raises suspicions that he might also be having erection problems. Rather than trying to treat the premature ejaculation, it would be wise to first treat the erection problem and see if the premature ejaculation doesn't go away on its own once his boner gets buff.

Danger! Danger!

Using these kinds of examples in this way gets into a dicey area where we are treating the penis without looking at the entire relationship. It could be that the man's partner has a different take on the situation. Perhaps from her perspective, there are important relationship issues that impact her far more than whether he ejaculates in two minutes or in twenty. Wouldn't that be something?

When looking at any kind of sex problem, you will often discover that a different story emerges when you include the perspective of both partners rather than just one. But that's not how modern medicine usually does it, especially when the physician is allotted fifteen minutes to see you. If a pill can't fix the problem, good luck. Also, sex therapist Joe Marzucco says, "The man with PE is frequently too shy to be seen with his partner present, or she says it's his problem to fix."

What Is It, Anyway?

Different people define premature ejaculation in different ways. Some say if you are fine if you can last for five to ten minutes of intercourse, thrusting at a rate your partner finds satisfying. Or if you shift gears after five minutes, offer other kinds of stimulation, and then thrust for another five minutes, you are fine. Others say that minutes are irrelevant, and that your mutual pleasure is the defining line.

All of this assumes that you are not silly enough to think that all women can come from intercourse alone. Plenty do, but plenty don't, and it doesn't matter how long you last.

There are other ways of defining rapid ejaculation. If you have to think about baseball while barely moving your hips, then you probably come too soon. Or maybe you do things that make your lover incredibly satisfied before intercourse ever begins. Perhaps both of you are perfectly happy and neither cares how long you last for intercourse.

Since few researchers seem to agree on exactly what premature ejaculation is, it's hard to say how many men are rapid ejaculators. Estimates range from 30% to 40%, but a big factor in deciding whether you come too soon is how you and your partner feel about it.

Increasing Madame's Sexual Excitement & Enjoyment While Sir Speedy Is Learning New Skills

One of the keys in helping a guy who pops prematurely is for him to become more aware of what is going on inside of his body. This requires retraining.

Retraining the man behind a dyslexic penis can take months, so it's a fine idea to consider his partner's pleasure during the process. The couple should explore ways that Mrs. Pronto can experience high levels of sexual satisfaction outside of intercourse. That way she won't feel resentful, he won't feel guilty, and both partners will get to experience what it is like when she can open up sexually, no longer needing to mute her excitement to help him last longer.

Plenty of men learn to compensate for PE by becoming really good at pleasing a woman with oral sex and different kinds of massage. It also might help if the woman will masturbate while he holds her. This allows Sir Speedy to feel her body in his arms as she experiences intense levels of sexual pleasure.

What Not To Do

Whatever the cause(s) for coming like greased lightning, men with PE often go from erection to ejaculation without very much awareness of the steps in between. They try to prevent ejaculation by thinking about something unsexy, which is about as productive as a race-car driver thinking about golf to help lower his anxiety as he's entering a high-speed turn. All of us are occasionally distracted when having sex, but this is not a good way to last longer.

The Other 97% of Your Body

It can be very helpful for a man with a dyslexic penis to become more aware of the sensations in his body—and not just the part that he pulls out when he pees. Not enough can be said about allowing a partner to touch you from head to toe while you let your body relax.

It also helps to learn the difference between inside and outside. For instance, put your hand on your penis and start playing with it. After a few minutes, describe how your penis feels. If you use words like "hard" or "big," go directly to jail, do not pass go, do not collect $200. The reason you got dinged is because you were describing what your hand was feeling rather than what your penis was feeling. If you came up with words like "tingly," "ticklish" or "throbbing," then you described what was going on inside your body, and this is good.

Learn how it feels in the head of your penis, on the right side of the shaft, on the left side, in the front or back of it, in your balls, in your butt, in your shoulders, thighs, face, etc. Rather than trying to numb or ignore what's going on inside you, you want to know and experience it as you never have before.

Calibrating The Penis — Teaching an Old Dog New Tricks

Men who come too soon often believe that they feel too much rather than too little, when the opposite is often true. If a man can learn to tolerate a fuller range of sexual feeling, then greater amounts of pleasure are less likely to make him splooge.

The mechanics of calibrating the penis are fairly simple. A guy can try it on his own, or he can have a partner help.

This begins with the woman caressing his penis in any way that she and he enjoy. It can be done with the penis dry or lubed, with oral sex, or even with a vagina, although the latter is usually not recommended until the man has mastered the basic maneuvers. How you stimulate the penis will also depend on how quickly he comes. Some guys who come quickly with intercourse can last forever when being given a hand job. The woman's arm could fall off before her partner comes. She might find it more fun to calibrate her partner's penis orally or by lubricating it and massaging it.

The scale of calibration is from 0 to 10, with 0 representing no arousal whatsoever, e.g., "Your grandmother just slipped you the tongue." 10 represents orgasm and ejaculation.

As the woman stimulates her man's penis, he tells her where he senses himself to be: "1," "3," "5," "6, "8." At first he will just be guessing, but after a while he'll have a good sense of where he is on his own personal scale. Guys who come too soon often go from 3 to 9 in one fell swoop, while pro ejaculators can stay at 6 or 7 for several minutes.

As the man lands on a specific number, his partner should try to keep him there for a few minutes, and then back off before going higher. She shouldn't hesitate to call it a day and let him ejaculate after fifteen to thirty minutes of this torture. With time, he will be able to tolerate hovering at a constant 6, 7, or 8 for prolonged periods, but don't expect him to achieve this rapidly. That's because his body might resist staying at a 7 or 8, since these levels are currently experienced as mere bleeps on the way to a fast cum.

In addition to spitting out numbers, he should tell her at various points how the different parts of his penis feel, including the head, front and sides, and he shouldn't forget his testicles, stomach, rear end, and shoulders. This may seem extreme, but there's no other way for him to learn how his body feels.

The Point of No Return

To successfully calibrate the penis, it is helpful to recognize when the man is approaching the *Point of No Return.* This is when nothing short of stepping on a land mine will keep him from ejaculating. The point of no return is usually an 8.5 or 9 on the scale of 10. Signs that the big squirt is eminent include: the veins in his penis start to bulge, or his love log might give a sudden throb, the color of the head may darken, his testicles might suck up into his groin, his muscles will tighten, his hips may thrust, and he might start to groan like a dying bull or invoke the name of God or Allah. Appreciate how well you are doing when you can keep him close to the point of no return for several minutes without letting him go over the edge.

When first calibrating a penis, a woman should probably stop all stroking as a man approaches the point of no return. She waits about ten seconds before starting again. A goal to shoot for is when she can switch stroking techniques rather than stopping the stimulation. For instance, if she is rubbing the shaft and finds that the thing is about to blow, she might switch and begin to rub only the head. The change in focus becomes a cue that helps him power through the urge to come. But don't try this until you have spent a couple of months and feel really comfortable with the prior routine. Rushing through the process contradicts everything you are trying to achieve.

As for erections, don't worry about them. What you are interested in is trying to tolerate more sensation. Some men will start to get hard at only a 3 on the sensation scale, while others won't stiffen until a 7 or higher. So don't be confused by the presence or absence of hardness. It is possible to come without an erection at all.

What's Your Sign?

As you become more aware of yourself, you may discover new signs when an orgasm is on its way. These might be felt in other parts of the body rather than in your penis. For instance, you might feel a tingling or tightening in your stomach, thighs, feet, rear end, or someplace else as the point of no return approaches. This information helps you know when to change your pace.

Deep Breathing and Relaxation

When it comes to rapid ejaculation, shallow breathing is the tool of the devil. As you are learning to tolerate higher levels of sensation, you want to teach your body to relax and to breathe deep.

Penis Pull-Ups

There is much hype about genital squeezing exercises called Kegels. Unfortunately, some people in the sex business claim that doing Kegel exercises will make the dead walk and the blind see. No research has ever shown that Kegel exercises can cure premature ejaculation or impotence, nor will they allow a man to dial a phone or lead an orchestra with his penis. However, Kegel exercises can help a man become more aware of the feelings in his penis and pelvis.

Kegel exercises are simple and straightforward. They involve squeezing the muscles that stop the flow of urine—the ones you squeeze when the phone begins ringing after you started taking a leak and you think it might be a really important call. Here are four ways to help build up these muscles:

Squeeze as you would when you are peeing and want to cut off the flow of urine. Do this nine or ten times in succession. For the first couple of weeks hold the squeeze for only a few seconds. After a month or two, try holding the squeeze for up to ten seconds. (The peeing reference is so you will understand which muscles to squeeze; it's best not to do these exercises when actually taking a leak, lest your urinary tract begins to revolt.)

Try the above exercises without pause, squeezing and relaxing the muscles in rapid sequence, like when shooting at ducks in an arcade game.

Change the tempo. Squeeze for a couple of seconds and then push all the way out as if you were trying to have a bowel movement. Try this a couple of times. **Note:** The first two exercises can be done just about anywhere: at work, at school, at church, inside a crowded elevator, or when commuting. However, do this third exercise in privacy, as the push-out part might cause you to loudly pass gas.

Optional exercise for guys who have way too much time on their hands: When your penis is erect, sit or stand with your legs apart and try wagging the thing up and down or sideways by squeezing the muscles in your groin. Some wives and girlfriends find this amusing to watch. Eventually toss a washcloth or small towel over the penis to add resistance, but be careful that you don't strain. Before upping the weight, check with your physician or personal trainer first, and never attempt anything that causes pain or strain.

Possible Benefits of Doing Penis Pull-ups

At first, most men won't be able to isolate the different muscles in their pelvis. They end up tensing the whole thing, including the rectum.

With time, they can learn to isolate the different muscle groups, distinguishing the ones that stop the flow of urine from the ones that wag the end of the penis. This can help a man become aware of when he might be tensing these muscles unintentionally. Some people believe that tension in the anal sphincters contributes not only to premature ejaculation, but to hemorrhoid formation—two conditions that are greeted with similar amounts of glee. Some sex therapists say that one of the keys to lasting longer is being able to relax the muscles in the pelvic floor.

Including Intercourse

It can take a month or two to fully calibrate the dyslexic penis. By then it's time to start having intercourse, after you can keep the penis between 6 and 7 for at least ten minutes.

Having intercourse can be tricky. Mrs. Pronto might be tempted to fall into old habits of muting her sexual excitement to help Mr. Pronto last longer. And he can't be expected to make his new skills work without easing into it. Keeping this in mind, it might not be a bad idea for the couple to help her have orgasms before or after intercourse.

Penis Tip #1 He should avoid using the muscles in his rear end for thrusting. Perhaps the reason why some men last longer when the woman is on top is because they don't have to thrust as much and it allows them to relax their pelvic muscles. The same has been said for when a guy is standing. If it feels okay, you might try using more of your back instead of your butt to propel your thrusting.

Penis Tip #2 Consider starting with femoral intercourse for a few weeks before doing full penetration. This is where the shaft of the penis glides through the lips of the vulva, like a hot dog in a bun. The penis doesn't go into the vagina but does need to be lubricated. Femoral intercourse can also be done with the woman on top.

Penis Tip #3 The start of intercourse may cause a backslide and return to old habits. As you feel her lush, warm, wet vagina starting to suck every drop of ejaculate from your helpless loins, do not run from the sensation. Stay with the feelings in all parts of your penis and body. Ignoring the feeling never helped before, and it won't help now.

The Realm of Sensation

A lot of people teach their bodies to ignore subtle sensations. A man might have learned to block out his body's more subtle sensations when he was a boy. Perhaps this happened the first time he had to throw himself in the path of a charging linebacker.

To help rebuild this capacity, some couples enjoy using a variety of materials and fabrics to massage the body from head to toe. Good results can be had with a feather or furry mitt, as well as a silk scarf or piece of rayon. Some couples might be into leather, latex or rubber. Others find the feel of a partner's fingertips to be exquisite. As this happens, try to be aware of the sensations in your body.

The Squeeze Technique — No Squeezin' Way!

Sex therapists since the time of the Ming dynasty have recommended doing one form or another of the squeeze technique to help relieve premature ejaculation. To do the squeeze technique, the woman brings the man close to the point of no return and then squeezes his penis to stop the impending orgasm.

While sex therapists used to claim a 95% cure rate with the squeeze technique, this was only in the short term. The problem returns in almost all men who have used the squeeze technique. There is simply no way to squeeze a man's Johnson into submission.

The Most Important Ingredients

In helping a man to last longer, patience, love and a tolerance for frustration are essential for a woman to have. That's because her man is probably fighting a private battle with his own penis that doesn't include much kindness. And for heaven's sake, don't forget to have a sense of humor. Humor is the sexual lubricant for the soul.

Visualization Exercises

Visualization is not a traditional exercise for premature ejaculation, unless the man is trying to visualize something that's totally nonsexual in an attempt to last longer. Here are a few visualization exercises designed to help a man stay in the saddle by becoming more, rather than less, aware of his body's processes. If they make sense to you, give them a try.

Close your eyes and feel yourself having intercourse. After you are able to feel yourself thrusting in and out, concentrate on relaxing the muscles in your butt cheeks, anus and genitals. Each time you feel these muscles tense up, concentrate on relaxing them.

Repeat the prior exercise, only this time concentrate on your breathing. Try to relax by taking slow, deep breaths. Breathe by expanding and contracting your abdomen instead of your chest.

Close your eyes and feel yourself having intercourse. Keep thrusting until your mind starts to wander or you visualize yourself ejaculating. At this point, start to visualize something pleasant and nondemanding, such as lying in the warm sun on a private beach. Relax in this way for a few minutes and then let your senses have another go at intercourse. Keep returning to the pleasant, nondemanding place whenever you feel conflicts arising from intercourse. The point of this visualization is not to decrease sexual sensation, but to help reduce anxiety that might be causing you to tense up.

Extending Your Awareness

With all of this focus on the man's body, you might be wondering about his awareness of his partner's body. An ideal balance is for him to alternate focusing on his and then on his partner's body. This way, he never loses contact with one or the other for long.

Relationship Fears & Resistances

It is reasonable to expect that a man might be shy about seeking his partner's help with his premature ejaculation. It is also possible that his partner may have resistances or fears about what might happen if her man is able to last longer.

In her book on premature ejaculation, sex therapist Helen Singer Kaplan says that most of the men who were unable to successfully complete her program for rapid ejaculators had wives or girlfriends who did not necessarily want them to last longer.

The three gentlemen mentioned below were rapid ejaculators as well as readers of earlier editions of the *Guide.* They were kind enough to share their personal stories.

Zeus suspected that his wife didn't want him to improve his sexual function and that she would resist helping him do something about it. As it turned out, he was right. His wife didn't enjoy sex, and the faster he came, the better. In addition, she didn't want him having sex with anyone else. She assumed that he would be less likely to have extramarital affairs if his problems remained intact.

Lancelot was afraid that his girlfriend wouldn't want to invest the time and effort in helping him to last longer. He was mortified to even ask. As it turned out, he was wrong as could be. She was happy (and relieved) that he wanted her help in solving the problem. They took on the problem together, with historic results.

Heathcliff had a secret and didn't know if Catherine would want to help. While caring greatly for each other, their sex life had never been a central part of their relationship. After several years, he finally asked for her help with his premature ejaculation. He received an unexpected reply. She told him that she often masturbated after he went to sleep, keeping her sexual needs to herself because she didn't think he was interested. They began masturbating together and started feeling sexually intimate for the first time in their lives. Eventually they worked to solve his problems with premature ejaculation. By this time, Heathcliff had become such a changed man that not even his neighbors could recognize him.

Rather than bulldozing ahead with the exercises that are mentioned in this chapter, why not start by having a couple of long talks about it first? The two of you might do well to talk about your entire sexual relationship and any fears or concerns that you are having.

Get a Grip—Stop Apologizing

Some of the most annoying aspects of premature ejaculation that women report are the constant apologies and self-criticism that men express after coming too soon. They say that this whining and bellyaching puts them off. If you decide to work on these exercises together, the man needs to promise that he will no longer apologize or berate himself for coming too soon!

Health Note: If you went for years without coming too soon, have had no change in relationship or other major life changes, and have suddenly become a two-minute man, please get a physical exam before trying to treat the premature ejaculation. As for purported associations between premature ejaculation and prostatitis, we don't buy it. Others do.

Resources: Helen Singer Kaplan's short little book titled *PE: How to Overcome Premature Ejaculation* (New York: Brunner/Mazel, 1989) is a good resource. Unfortunately, Dr. Kaplan suffered from a premature departure and is no longer with us. Another very helpful book is Barbara Keesling's *Sexual Pleasure: Reaching New Heights of Sexual Arousal and Intimacy.* (Alameda, Calif.: Hunter House, 1993).

Special Thanks: Joseph Marzucco, Ph.D., who has many years in urology under his belt, has been very helpful with this chapter. Thanks also to Dr. Michael Metz. Dr. Metz is one of the country's finest sex therapists and most thoughtful experts on rapid ejaculation. He recently co-authored a book on the subject. It is a very thorough and complex presentation; *Coping With Premature Ejaculation* by Metz & McCarthy, New Harbinger Press, 2004.

Pud & Labby say,
Don't forget to visit our free and
mostly wonderful website
for updates & advice."
www.BoinkCentral.com

Kink in the Animal Kingdom?

Chapter 56

Are humans the only animals who have sex just for pleasure? Do the others only have sex for reproduction and dominance? Is there no kink in the rest of the animal kingdom? Until recently, that's what the biologists had told us.

Fortunately, some biologists have been reconsidering the party line that humans are the only animals who have sex just for the heck of it. So for the rest of this brief chapter, let's pretend you are a biology professor who wants to study sex in the jungle.

Sex in the Jungle (No, Not Manhattan)

After spending years of applying for grants, you have finally gotten your project funded. Your plane is about to set down in a third world country where you hope to observe bonobos in the wild.

Discovered in 1929, the bonobo is one of the Great Apes. In terms of genetics and evolution, the bonobo is closer to the human than most other living creatures; closer than even the savanna baboons and chimpanzees. It's not that bonobos are identical to humans, but they are found swinging on 98% of the same limbs of the evolutionary tree. Girl bonobos don't give birth until they are thirteen or fourteen years of age, reaching full maturity by age fifteen. When they do have babies, bonobos nurse and carry them around for up to five years.

So while they don't ride around on skateboards or listen to rock'n'roll, it can safely be said that bonobos are more like humans than, say, white mice or pigs.

Your Lab in the Bush

You are finally able to set up camp in an area where you can watch bonobos do what bonobos do. You write in your notebook that you have successfully paid off the local officials and insurgent rebels haven't captured, killed, or raped you. (You think we're kidding?)

And then it happens—your first sighting. Not only do you see bonobos having heterosexual sex, but you notice one big male has his hand on the erect penis of another male and he's giving his bonobo buddy a hand job. Eventually you see two bonobo women rubbing their genitals together, like in lesbian porno flicks. You also observe two males rubbing their penises together in a pleasurable way, and you then you see a male and female having face-to-face intercourse.

After your first year of observing bonobos, you decide that they're certainly not sex maniacs, but that sex appears to be an essential part of their social interactions.

After spending two years in the jungle watching bonobos, you find yourself desperate for a little sea air, so you apply for another grant that will allow you to watch dolphins and whales have sex.

After two more years at sea, you long to go back to the jungle, only this time you apply for funding to watch giraffes have sex. By now, people at the various foundations are saying "We'll be darned if we're going to give any more money for that pervert professor to watch another species have sex." So instead of funding your project, they spend millions of dollars trying to teach sexual abstinence to students in inner city high schools. Fortunately, your Great Aunt Clarice recently died and left you enough money to return to the jungle to watch giraffes have sex.

After a few more years, you sit down and try to make sense of all your findings. There's simply no way around it—your years of research tell you that the homosexual encounters you have described were not limited to acts of aggression and dominance. The same animals who one day were having a homosexual tryst might be enjoying hetero-sexual loving the next. And in spite of years of being told this can't possibly be, you get the sense that these animals were having sex for the mere pleasure of it. Good God, you say to yourself, I'll never get tenure now. So in order to make your findings more palatable to your colleagues, you report that animals have sex in order to resolve con-flict, for tension regulation, and as appeasement behavior. There, you didn't use the words "fun" or "pleasure," even if that's exactly what you've been watching for the past six years.

Your findings show that not only does a full range of pleasure happen, but animals don't spend a lot of time having an identity melt-down because they were displaying their finest mating behavior for a member of the same sex. Nor did you notice any animals with white collars and bibles who were telling their fellow animals that they would burn in hell for their ungodly sins. That kind of behavior is only found at the "top" of the evolutionary tree.

Recommended: For more on bonobos, see the wonderful writing of Frans B. M. de Waal. For more on sexual behavior in other species, an incredible resource is *Biological Exuberance* by Bruce Bagemihl, St. Martin's Press, New York, NY 1999.

Tyrannies Having Sex

This is an artist's conception of how the tyrannosaurus had sex. While tyrannies were clearly meat eaters, it is difficult to imagine them giving or receiving oral sex. In the Mesozoic Era, the term "I got some tail last night" was more descriptive than misogynist. (Special thanks to brilliant dinosaur artist Luis Rey for inspiration.)

Sex on the Interstate & in the Woods

Chapter 57

For some people, there's nothing like cruising down a deserted highway with one hand on the wheel and the other on their lover's sweet spot. It doesn't matter if you are rich or poor, mongrel or blueblood, this is one time when our motor-driven culture nips you in the rear and makes you feel good all over.

The Rolling Monotone of a Nebraska Back Road

It might be particularly nice when your brain's in a narcoleptic funk and your sweetheart slyly grabs your free hand and slips it into the warm, wet space between her legs. Or maybe you're taking that long drive from Texas to Washington D.C. and the wind's not the only thing that's doing the blowing.

About ten years after the fact, one of you will occasionally say, "Honey, remember that time going 'cross Kansas..." and you'll both stop whatever you are doing, smile, and shut out the rest of the world for a precious moment or two.

The best way to use a car for sex, besides for driving to your sweetheart's house to get some, is when parking at a romantic spot and seeing how quickly you can steam the windows up. People who live in the inner city often don't have cars, so they sometimes find a favorite rooftop or "tar beach" with a romantic view where they can make love. Just be sure it's not a spot where junkies like to shoot up; you don't want to roll over on someone's stuff.

Winnebegos on the Continental Divide

While it's important to do things that inspire fond memories, it's also nice to stay alive so you can enjoy them. Keeping your bearings on the road while sharing certain types of physical pleasure is a talent that few people should ever attempt. Don't even think about it if you aren't an excellent driver to begin with, or if your eyes clamp shut and your body twitches and spasms when you come. No matter how much driving experience you have, it's really stupid to be messing around when road conditions require your extra attention, like on a busy freeway or when you're taking a Winnebego over the Continental Divide. Also, your state might have laws about sex behind the wheel. Why not call and ask?

On the other hand, just about anything that wakes you up when you're on a rural road might be safer than trying to drive when you feel sleepy, and driving with your head up the tailpipe has to be safer than trying to drive while dialing a cellular phone. **Note:** Thousands of people die each year from falling asleep at the wheel. We'd love to keep you as readers of future editions, so please, if you find yourself feeling sleepy, get some coffee or pull far off the road and take a nap.

Sex on the Rail of the Hoover Dam

Some people like to have sex in public places where other people will see. While this might be a fine form of release for all parties involved, it is not what this section is about. What's being described here is that rare moment in life when you and your partner get to make love in a natural setting which is so magnificent that nature's sweet vibration nearly explodes inside of you. What transpires can be so expansive that it's difficult to think of it as just sex, or maybe it's what sex was meant to be before we started living in high rises and condominiums.

Sex in the Outdoors

There are plenty of natural settings where you don't have to be too cautious about getting it on, like in a meadow filled with wildflowers, on a deserted beach, or under a god-sized rainbow in the Montana Big Sky. But there are other equally compelling locations, like dams, bridges, trains, planes, and various national monuments, where a well-honed sense of cunning and mischief is absolutely essential. The following are but a few suggestions that you might find helpful:

Bug repellent. Don't forget the bug repellent if you are baring your all next to some humid bog or anyplace where the average mosquito would take one look at your naked butt cheeks and think it had died and gone to heaven.

For sex in public places, it can be more than helpful if the woman wears one of those full 1950s-type dresses or sundresses. It's the equivalent of wearing her own private dressing room. She won't need to take a single thing off except for her underwear, unless she's not wearing any.

If you are doing it at the beach or on a sandy river bed, be sure to take two large blankets. There's something about being on top of two blankets instead of one that helps keep sand from getting inside your crotch. Also, extra lube might help take the abrasive edge off any sand that makes its way inside.

Sex in water provides its own set of challenges, given how water washes away natural lubrication. Try coating your genitals with a silicone-based lube ahead of time. Also, according to *How To Have Sex In The Woods* author Luann Colombo, intercourse in the water tends to pump the vagina full of water, so women will save themselves embarrassment if they will squat to let their crotches drain as they are emerging from the deep.

Ms. Colombo recommends carrying your condoms in a thermal cooler bag to keep them from freezing or frying. Even if you don't ordinarily use condoms, using them in the outdoors will help decrease the drip factor and will help keep your sleeping bag dryer. Consider packing a disposable blue hospital pad for when you are doing the nasty in a sleeping bag. It's absorbent on one side, but waterproof on the other. Ms. Colombo says that for sex in a sleeping bag, more "in" and grinding results in a smaller wet spot than lots of in-out.

Very Highly Recommended: *How To Have Sex In The Woods,* by Luann Colombo, Three Rivers Press, New York, 1999. In addition to being extremely wise, practical and lots of fun, this book makes a great gift for friends who like to hike and pack. Some of Ms. Colombo's other books include "Dead Guys and Gals of Science," "Make Your Own Superballs," "Sleepover Madness," and "Gross But True Germs."

Caution

One reader comments, "A close friend of mine went to jail for having sex in public; it was her first arrest and very traumatic." So please be aware that while it's perfectly legal for a couple to have a really loud and nasty fight in public, having sex in public (or maybe even in your backyard) is likely to break local, state and federal statutes and might get you arrested. Of course, some people say that the risk is half the fun.

A Goofy Goodbye
Chapter 58

This is the final chapter of the *Guide to Getting It On!* It talks about things like hippies, cash flow, meaning and integrity, and then it says goodbye.

What Puff the Magic Dragon's Tears Were Really All About

Back in the 1960s, a small group of hippies suddenly appeared in this country. These hippies didn't think like the rest of us and probably arrived from another planet. The nation became infatuated with them.

After the arrival of the real hippies, there suddenly appeared millions of hippie wannabes. These were often college students who didn't have to work because they were getting money from home. They spoke a great deal about love and peace, but you had the feeling they didn't know much about either. They were going to save the world from anything that was even remotely like their moms and dads.

By the time the 1980s rolled around, the hippie wannabes started getting degrees in fields like law, business and medicine. Guys started cutting their hair and women stuffed their breasts back into bras, all in preparation for an important American ritual called "the job interview." Words like "marketing" and "standing to sue" took the place of "bitchin'" and "groovy." Designer labels became more important than flowers and beads.

Few people had time anymore to hold hands, take walks or talk about a problem before it became a major crisis. Instead, there was the constant specter of work, often sixty hours a week, with a person's whole life mapped out according to which rung of the corporate ladder he or she planned to hang from.

It may seem strange that a book on sex would mention things like jobs and money, but in the course of our lifetimes most of us will fret more over money than love. The people at MasterCard will probably know more about us than our sex partners do. Yet no matter how much money or social status you acquire, you can never leave who you are or what you've become on the floor at the edge of the bed. Sex may be a wonderful thing, but it can't make up for an existence that has little integrity, value or meaning.

A Better Place

There are still a few of us from way back when who didn't abandon our hopes and dreams for a better society. We weren't radical or reactionary, we simply hoped to leave the world a better place than we found it. This book is an attempt in that direction.

This guide may not have the head rush of good drugs, and it doesn't pretend to have many answers. But it is a more advanced view of sex than most of us had when we first started getting it on. Thank you for being patient with its efforts to be more than just another how-to manual on sex.

This book has 782 pages, and it still can't define sex. Hopefully you will be able to define it on your own, or at least have a beautiful time trying.

Vaya Con Dios!

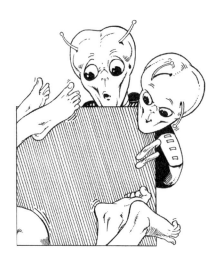

Thanks! Thanks! Thanks!

Laura Corn, Joe Mazucco, Bob Francoeur, Sue Palmer at the Eugene Register Guard, Sarah Rosenberg, Tracy Fortini, Lance Tilford, Kim Wylie, Kevin Votel, Elise Cannon, Judi Baker, Jill Kamada, Chris Schrader, Sabrina Young, Heather Cameron, Charlie Winton, Paul Rooney Jerry Delaria, Becky Kaapuni, Cyndy Perlich, Meagan, & all at PGW (past and present) who do such a great job of distributing the Guide to bookstores in a region known as North America, Dave Hite, Dave Fleming, Jeff Ochs, Renee Lane, Jill Esch, Carleen Rogers, Vickie Jedele, Kerwin Leader, and all the fine people at McNaughton & Gunn in Saline, Michigan who print this book, Theresa "T" McCracken, Scott McCann, Bev Cutler, Cyrus Farivar, Kayla Strassberg from Good Vibes, Adrienne Benedicks, Inger Klekacz, Rich Siegel and the Bare Bones, Ryan Hanson, Todd Hawley, Dan Cullinane, Trena Jayne, Leslie Rossman, Michael Meller, Franka Schmidt, Ralph Bolton, Dmitri Siegel, Denise Westmoreland, Rose Reed, Harry Gilmartin & Karen Kummerfeldt at Entrenue, Janet Hardy, Jay Wiseman, The Fine people at the Boulder Book Store, Powells, Waterstones and Virgin, Matt Torrey, Dan Culliane, Kirk Groeneveld, Mr. Verne Graham

A very special thanks to Drs. William Erwin & Donald Marcus and *to my wife, Toni, who endures patiently and offers wise guidance, she makes sure that every attempt is better than what came before and she helps me to be a better person.*

More thanks... To Gary Todoroff, who made national distribution a reality, Janice Hamilton who got the whole academic ball rolling, Dr. Larry Hedges, Barbara Keesling, Debra Hanson, Steven Wales, Dr. Avedis Panajian, Dr. Bill Young, Rob Hill, Nevada's own John & Miss Kelly, Shane, Nancy "Professor B" Carmel Eyes, the wonderful copy editor Carol Bee, to Ron, Steve, Linda & Jeanette at Old Town Printers,

Jon Westover, Morgan & Burce Yarrosh, Suzanne LaPlacette, Mike Fischler, Wanda Moore, Veronica Monet, Monte Farrin, Rebecca Wood, Catherine, Peter & Claire Gilson, Dixie Marquis, Mike Conway, Karen Saliba, Carol Tavris, Michael Kogutek, Katherine Almy, Richard Curtis, BJ Robbins, Ken Sherman, Bob & Kim Otto, Linda Szymialis, Kristi Walsh, Duncan & Lilly Rouleau, Tom Reynolds, Bill Applebaum, Nancy Reaven, Bruce Voeller, Andre Deuschanes, Meridith Tanzer, Roan Singh Sidhu, Evan Rapostathis, Kenny Wagner, Ross Rubin, Barry Richmond, Carolyn Andre, Paula Samuels, Daphnicious Delicious Rosewoman-Kingma, Cathryn Michon, Diane Driscoll, Billy Rumpanos, Ben Fiorino, Ray Calabrese, Paula & David Wayne, John Van Dixhorn & Members of the Newport Psychoanalytic Institute, Janet Snow, Don DeFrancisco, Diana Heiselu, Judy Seifer, Randi Lockwood, Michael Meller, Anke Vogel, Franka Schmidt, Brent Ryder, Breta Hedges, Emily LeBeff, Ken Stubbs, Loren & Steve Kapelo, Laurel Shaffer, Brent Myers, Ron Goosen, Pat Lincoln, Alison Rosenzweig, Marty Gilliland, Val Littou, Krista Foley, Lee Horn, Mat Honig, Mike Mansel & Eric Ruiter at Argo, Sheryl Palese, Chip Rowe, Rodney Fingelson & Steve Frankiel, Kathy Herdman, Jack McHugh, Todd Seigel & Jessica, Alex Foti, Adam Moore, Pat Patterson, Dana Smart, Laura Corn, Elizabeth Olsen, K.C. Rourke, Pam Winter, Bill Brent, Dan Poynter, Judy Linnan, Theresa Benedick, Brandon Klock, Joe Sparling, Carol Queen, Lily, Bill & Louie at Sir Speedy, Monte at Input/Output, the staff at Book Soup, How at Kinko's Westwood, Nathan & Bob at Kinko's Ventura, the librarians at UCLA (Biomed, URL & the former Ed/Psych) & LA County Library, staff at A Different Light bookstore (West Hollywood), Brentano's (Century City & Beverly Hills), & Borders (particularly Fawn in Honolulu), Joe Marsh at the Earthling (R.IP), the managers and staff at the wonderful Waterstone's Book Store chain including Matt Comito, Christine, Maura, Jill, Sandy, Dave, Peter, Jay, Doug, Terry, Travis, Ann, Betty, Jane, & Eric Horndog Deville (a sad & tragically premature R.I.P.), Mike Moskowitz, Juliann Popp & Jason Aronson, Bill & Beryl Johnson, Karen Seemueller, Lew & the staff at Font Shop in San Francisco, Christianna Billman and Lisa Blai .

Jan Nathan at PMA, Peter Handel, Carol Fass & Eda Kalkay, Leslie Rossman, Patricia Holt, Kim from LA, Doug Abrams, Susan Naythons, Renee Sedliar, Mr. Peter Stoller, Steve DuPont, the staff and owners of Montgomery Management, super romantic Adrienne Benedicks, Victoria Snider, Edie Moore at the Society for Adolescent Medicine, Michael Rakusin, Dale and Ewa from Tower Books Down Under, Jarred Gunn at Tower Books up here, Carol Floyd, Ms. Heidi Cotler, Chris & Dennis at Portland's Printer Place, Marcia papier mache Binnendyk, Babs Adamsky and Kevin Samsel at Powell Books, Pam White & Mark Collins, Ben & Joe & Grace at C&L Graphics, Shannon & Gaylen at Lightbourne, Kris Lorret Rourke, Dodie Ownes, Ben Saltzberg, Whitney Thomas from Barnes & Noble, Stacie Herndon, Phil Bruno, Rob Fogel, Marge Clifton from Cal Western Freight, Genanne Simply Wonderful Walsh, Rachael Cart, Joanie Blank & Constance Claire at Good Vibrations, Dr. Andrea Best—best emails since the wall came down, Gretta and Heather from Blowfish, Bettina Nibbe, Zev Lewis, Mr. John Davis from Koen Book, Leonore Tiefer, Marian Dunn, Michael Metz, Julian Slowinski, Udi Tagari.

Without their efforts, you'd probably be having to read this book on one of those useless little e-book devices and we all know what happens when a big wad of whatever hits their little motherboards, to Dave Fleming, Mike Viso, Jay, Jill, Carlene and all of the McNaughton folks who do such a great job of putting the words on the paper and gluing up the sides, Dana & Linda at Loves, Mardi Link at Foreword, John McHugh, Stan Mitchell & Lynn, Dr. Adam Moore, Dr. John Money, Dr. Rob Hardy, Dr. Beverly Whipple, Kristen Kemp, Carol Briezke, Esther Crain, Julia Gaynor, Carol Edington, a very helpful Paul Harrington.

The Goofy Glossary

Animal Husbandry

AARDVARKING—term for sexual intercourse coined by B-movie-reviewer extraordinaire Joe Bob Briggs, e.g. "Absolutely no plot to get in the way of the story. Thirty-four breasts. Multiple aardvarking. Gratuitous hot-tubbing. Man in a cheesy lizard suit. Sorority hosedown. Gratuitous topless dancing at a radio station. Slapstick Fu. My kinda movie. Two stars."

AC/DC—1. someone who is bisexual; enjoys bedding members of either sex; aka "switch-hitter," "ambisexterous" or "versatile." 2. former metal rock'n'roll band whose members are now really old; aka "geezer rock."

ACORN—the glans or head of the penis.

AFRODESIAC—sexy-looking black man.

AFTER MARKET—a biological female who's had her genitals surgically changed to look like those of a male, as opposed to being "factory-equipped" or having "original equipment;" aka: "F2M transsexual," "frankendick," or "SRS."

AFTERNOON DELIGHT—sex in the afternoon; aka "a nooner."

AGE PLAY—sexual role-playing where one partner pretends to be older and in control while the other pretends to be much younger.

AIRHEAD—1. perfect date for a guy who is easily overwhelmed by intelligent women. 2. in a discussion on the effects of global warming, an airhead would want to know how it would affect her tan lines; aka "bimbo" or "fern" (having the intelligence of one).

AMERICAN BOYZ—"an organization which aims to support people who were labeled female at birth but who feel that is not an accurate or complete description of who they are and their significant others, friends and families."

ANIME—animated art or cartoons from Japan with a distinctly Japanese style and aimed at a more mature audience than american cartoons; characters have large eyes, wonderfully wild facial expressions, women have multi-colored hair and breasts that are so big they look like they are going to pop. often has nudity and violence, but stops short of being considered porn in japan; aka "Japanimation." Amine that crosses the line into porn is "hentai."

ANABEL CHONG—former convent-school student turned porn starlet, whose claim to fame is having intercourse with eighty different men on the same day; heaven help the poor guy who had to clean up the movie set afterward!

ANAL—1. referring to the anus, as in anal sex, anal play, rimming; aka "brown eye." 2. describes a person who is anal retentive or of constipated psyche.

ANAL BEADS—worry beads for the rectum, to be pulled out as orgasm is starting; for some people it's like pulling the pin on a orgasmo grenade, for others, it's just another pain in the rear; aka "pearl string."

ANALINGUS—"kissing ass" minus the metaphorical intent; aka rimming.

ANDRO DYKE—a lesbian who is neither butch nor fem, aka "butch lite."

ANDROGYNOUS—1. not clearly masculine or feminine. 2. can you name three androgynous rock'n'roll musicians?

ANGEL FOOD—a gay pilot.

APHRODISIAC—1. substance that is given (or taken) to increase sexual desire. 2. be wary of anything that is called an aphrodisiac because it is usually people and not chemical concoctions that turn other people on.

ARSE—British for ass, e.g. "piece of arse," "up your arse," "arse wipe," "Tom's an arse," "arsing about," "arse-over-tit" (a bad fall), or "tight as a duck's arse."

ASS BLOW—"rimming" or sticking your tongue into the chamber of horrors.

ASHRAM—1. mansion where a guru lives. 2. important to know in case your sweetheart forsakes volleyball and string bikinis for incense and meditation.

ATROPHY—1. scientific term for "use it or lose it." 2. fear that many guys have concerning their penis, especially when they haven't had sex for an epoch or two. Atrophy happens to muscles; the penis, for better or for worse, does not seem to be one. The penis often gets a better workout from jerking off than from intercourse, so if you are worried about atrophy...

AUTOFELLATIO—1. to suck one's own penis. 2. makes dating an option rather than a necessity. 3. requires an extremely long schlong or incredibly nimble spinal column or both.

AUTOPEDERASTY—1. when a guy can stick his own partially-erect penis into his own anus, requiring a long penis, a long anus or both. 2. "pederasty" is when an old guy has sex with a young guy, so why this is called "autopederasty" makes no sense at all.

AYUGA—1. warning sound that a submarine makes when it's about to dive. 2. make this sound and give a wink when you are about to go down on a guy.

A2M—1. means "ass-to-mouth" or rimming. 2. sucking on a penis after it's been up your butt or someone else's.

BABE RATIO—ratio of people who you find sexually attractive to the total number of people in the room; e.g. if you are nineteen and visiting a meeting of the AARP (American Association of Retired Persons), your babe ratio will hopefully be zero; if you are seventy-five and visiting the same meeting, your babe ratio might be 25% or higher.

BAD LESBIAN—1. among politically stiff lesbians, a bad lesbian is a gay woman who has sex with a man or fantasizes about it (heaven forbid). 2. writer Carol Queen attributes this kind of rigid thinking to "the lezzie thought police."

BALL—to have intercourse with; past tense is "balled."

BALLS TO THE WALL—a state of mind where one powers through a situation with tenacity and guts; origin: the air force.

BANGER—British for sausage or penis, with a "banger hanger" being a vagina.

BAREBACKING—1. anal intercourse without a condom. 2. describes a gay male whose ability to connect cause with effect has been seriously compromised.

BARDEX NOZZLE—the John Deere of enema tubes.

BARTHOLINS GLANDS—two small glands at the bottom part of the vaginal opening which help secrete lubrication; explains why you should reach to the bottom of the vaginal opening to bring lubrication up to coat the clitoris.

BDSM—1. umbrella term for people who are into power play, bondage, discipline, spanking, certain types of fetish play, whatever. 2. now encompasses the older acronyms of B&D (bondage and discipline) and S&M (sadism and masochism), plus a little D&S (dominance and submission) for good measure. 3. while BDSM is sexual, genital orgasm and stimulation is not its focus.

BEAR—1. large, mature male with lots of body hair and a fondness for other males. 2. term used in gay male porn and dating to describe big hairy guys.

BEARD—date or marriage arranged for a homosexual to make them appear straight; important for when mom and dad are in town.

BEARD BURN—1. inner-thigh hazard that women face who receive oral sex from men with five o'clock shadow. 2. can be prevented by draping thighs with towels or plastic wrap, or by a quick shave on Thor's part.

BEAT OFF or BEAT YOUR MEAT— (male) to masturbate or tickle your pickle.

BEAUTY PAGEANT—event where beautiful women get to meet other beautiful women.

BEAVER—1. someone who attends Oregon State University 2. refers to the female sex Oregons. 3. "split beaver" is porn-speak for when a woman spreads her labia wide open. 4. great bumper sticker: "Eat a Beaver, Save a Tree."

BEEFCAKE—nude males in photos.

BEN WA BALLS—1. a pair of metallic balls that are inserted into the vagina for sexual pleasure while rocking back and forth or squeezing the thighs together; more hype than reality since they don't work for most people. 2. the ultimate ben wa story comes from Good Vibrations in San Francisco: a woman who had inserted a pair of ben wa balls just before a flight was apprehended by airport security personnel as she tried to pass through the metal detector.

BESTIALITY—when your sexual partner has four legs and a tail; aka "farm sex," "K-9" and "animal training." The Spanish called it "the Italian vice."

BICURIOUS—someone who is interested in exploring sex with a member of their own sex, but hasn't gotten around to it yet or it isn't a raging priority.

BIDET—1. oval-shaped porcelain bowl that is plumbed with a fountain of water over which a woman squats to clean and sometimes stimulate her genitals; found in traditional European bathrooms, but in few American bathrooms. 2. for the insistent reader from Key West, YES, bidets are also used for anal hygiene and pleasure.

BIKINI LINE—how girls in modern America refer to their vulvas, defining them on the basis of what needs to be plucked in order to look good on the beach.

BIOLOGICAL CLOCK—procreational urge that overwhelms some people between the ages of 34 and 44.

BISEXUAL—1. person who is able to feel sexual arousal for both sexes. 2. the bisexual breaks the rule that you have to desire either a man or a woman, and often pays a social price for blurring the sexual boundaries that a lot of people need in order to feel safe with their own identity and sexuality.

BLADDER INFECTION—1. when totally obnoxious bacteria with a painful kick establish residency in the human bladder; aka "cystitis." 2. a person so affected would be willing to pawn her great grandmother's wedding ring for a hit of antibiotics. 3. is more common in women because the passageway from the bladder to the outside of the body is much shorter, allowing bacteria easier access. 4. things that might help prevent vaginal and bladder infections include avoiding soaps with fragrances and high alkalinity, wearing underpants with cotton crotches, wiping from front to back, peeing after sex, and washing your hands before playing with your genitals.

BLENDED ORGASM—1. orgasm from stimulation with a blender, supposedly enjoyed by Betty Crocker 2. term for an orgasm that's both clitoral and g-spot; 3. an extra-intense orgasm that is triggered by stimulation of two different areas at the same time, such as nipples and clitoris, or clitoris and g-spot area. 4. when a woman wins the daily double between her legs.

BLIND DATE—aptly named social event; see "Loch Ness monster."

BLOOD SPORTS—1. rugby. 2. extreme BDSM play where blood is drawn.

BLOW—cocaine

BLOW JOB—oral sex that's done on a guy; aka "hummer;" see "ayuga."

BLUE BALLS—1. refers to a condition where a male has been sexually stimulated but not to orgasm. 2. sometimes actually hurts and is rumored to cause a blue tint to the scrotum. 3. can easily be cured by jerking off. 4. at one time was thought to cause physical damage, but recent evidence does not support this fear. 5. get used to it, dude.

BMS—acronym for "baby-making sex" or rolling the genetic dice.

BODY SHOTS—when doing tequila shooters, you suck the salt from whatever part of your lover's body he or she puts it on, and then suck the lime from his or her mouth. Somewhere in between, you gulp down the tequila.

BODY MODIFICATION—1. things people do to change their bodies in primitive ways, including piercing, tattooing, branding, binding, cutting, castrating, nullification, or even corset training. 2. does getting a boob job count?

BOFF or BOINK—1. to have intercourse. 2. to visit our totally free and mostly wonderful website at www.BoinkCentral.com, aka "cyber-boinking."

BONDAGE—when someone gets a sexual high from that which the rest of us try to avoid.

BONE—1. term used by less than gentle men in referring to intercourse; e.g., "to bone a babe." 2. the dominant partner in a prison relationship. 3. penis.

BONEYARD—area in prisons where conjugal (sex) visits occur with spouses.

BOOSTER SHOT—a one-night stand.

BOOTH TROLL—guy who cruises other guys in the video booths at the cheesier adult sex stores. This is where they have anonymous sex with each other, often viewing straight porn flicks to give the appearance of being straight, with the added risk and excitement of being busted by the vice squad.

BOOTY—1. means "rear end," "bum" or "caboose." 2. can refer to having sex, but not anal sex; go figure.

BOOTY CALL—desperate, late-night phone call or email pleading for sex.

BOOTY CHECK—prison slang for "rectal cavity search;" aka "finger wave."

BOTTOM—1. means "sexually submissive," a BDSM term; see "top and bottom." 2. the receiver of the penis during anal intercourse, aka "catcher."

BOXERS OR BRIEFS?— a question every guy ponders at one time or another, but often ends up wearing what his mother originally dressed him in.

BRA HOOK—1. no single device known to humankind has caused more guys (and some women) more angst than the hook of the bra 2. legend has it that Obewan Kinobe originally taught Luke Skywalker about "the force" in order to help him unhook Princess Leia's bra. Given that they eventually turned out to be brother and sister, it's fortunate that Leia's bra hook proved even tougher than the force.

BRAZILIAN—1. waxing to accommodate wearing a thong; differs from a usual bikini waxing because it goes all the way back to the butt, including deforestation of the asshole. 2. people mistakenly think that a brazilian has to do with how the vulva is done, butt the key element in a brazilian waxing is that the perineum and butt are plucked bare, as well as the sides of the labia; the mons pubis can be left with a landing strip, waxed bald, or whatever, as long as your kitty's whiskers aren't hanging out the sides or top of your thong.

BREEDER—a gay term for a straight person.

BROWN SESSION—where defecation becomes sexualized; "scat," "coprophilia."

BROWN SUGAR—refers to a sexy black woman or to having sex with her.

BUCK WILD—rap term, to have wild sex or to act crazy; aka "buckwildin."

BUDDY BOOTH—booth in an adult sex venue where there's a window to the next booth. There are sometimes curtains in the windows and buttons that raise them. This lets you watch the person in the next booth stripping or doing whatever, as long as you both raise each other's curtains, so to speak.

BUDDY SEX—see "fuck buddy."

BUFF—1. having well-developed muscles. 2. having a chest and arms (guns) that are pumped up but still cut. 3. the result of spending an ungodly number of hours at the gym.

BUGGERY—1. an academic tradition. 2. anal sex that's done to boys and young men in boarding schools as well as other places where men are warehoused.

BUKKAKE—a japanese term that refers to showering the face of the receiver with the ejaculate of many men. Legend has it that in ancient Japan, a woman who was unfaithful was tied up in the town center where the male citizenry ejaculated on her face to show their distaste. Perhaps they were angry because the adultery happened with some other Samurai and not them. Has since become a fetish with some japanese porn depicting the act; aka "facial."

BUM— British term for rear end.

BURNING BUSH—1. female genitals that are sexually aroused and full of heated passion. 2. God was so pleased with His creation of the burning bush that He hid inside of one when speaking to Moses (Exodus 3:1-6). He figured if this didn't grab Moses' attention, nothing would.

BUSH—1. female pubic hair or genitals. 2. former U.S. presidents.

BUTCH—1. a lesbian who has adopted the male role and run with it. 2. an exaggerated form of manliness, a few notches beyond macho.

BUTCH-FEMME—1. an alluring woman who combines the no-nonsense strength of a stone butch with the steamy "make your crotch drip and throb" attraction of a femme fatale. This is a woman who can ride in on a hog wearing tattoos and leather, and ride out with men and women tripping over themselves to get her in bed. She blurs sex boundaries and gender boundaries, yet you would never use the word "androgynous" to describe her. The butch-femme is played well in some movies by actress Angelina Jolie. 2. term that refers to the community of women who would describe themselves as being butches, femmes, stone butches, stone femmes, TGbutches, transmen, and FtMs.

BUTT PLUG—1. a diamond-shaped object that goes in the rear end to give a feeling of fullness. 2. usually made of plastic or silicone with a special flanged end so it won't get lost where the sun don't shine. 3. plugs come in different sizes and shapes, some even vibrate.

C2C—take your pick: gay term meaning "cock-to-cock;" computer term meaning consumer-to-consumer commerce on sites like eBay; computer hardware term referring to a type of compiler; famous bicycle route that goes across Northern England from the Irish Sea Coast to the North Sea Coast ("sea-to-sea" or "coast-to-coast"); or a train company in London.

CABOOSE—last guy when a woman is pulling a train; see "gang bang."

CAMEL TOES—crotch cleavage: when a woman's clothes (pants, shorts, bikini bottom, etc.) dig into her crotch and you can see her labia bulging along the sides of the crease. can also apply to a male's genitals as well.

CAM WHORE—person who spends way too much time in front of his or her webcam, sometime with clothes on, sometimes with clothes off.

CARGINITY—what you lose when you have sex in a car for the first time.

CASTING COUCH—entertainment industry term referring to a process where certain directors and producers receive sexual favors in exchange for casting an actor/actress in a movie or TV show.

CELLULAR PHONE—male equivalent of breast implants, important to use in public wherever you go.

CERVICAL CAP—1. birth control device or little rubber beanie that sits on top of the cervix to discourage male ejaculate from entering. 2. differs from a diaphragm in several ways: it's smaller, stays in longer, is usually not filled with birth control jelly, and is not as effective for most people.

CERVIX—1. hat rack for a diaphragm. 2. the cervix is the bottom part of the uterus found in the back of the vagina. It can be as small as a cherry in a woman who has not delivered a baby through her vagina, or it can be much bigger. 3. the cervix usually feels softer when the woman is ovulating. During that time, mucus passes through the cervical opening and bathes the vagina. 4. male ejaculate passes through a small passageway in the center of the cervix on its way to do the conception dance.

CHAKRAS—an eastern concept (India, not New Jersey)—fuse box of the body, seven points said to regulate energy.

CHERRY—1. virginal or like new. 2. hymen. 3. maidenhead (in case you read Shakespeare).

CHEW TOY—someone you are having sex with, usually quietly or on the side.

CHICKEN & CHICKEN FOX—chicken refers to a boyish looking young man who wants to be picked up and cared for (or purchased) by an older man who is known as a chicken fox.

CHICKEN OF THE SEA—a young gay sailor.

CHICKS WITH DICKS—1. persons who appear to be women in many ways except for the genital region. Can be transvestites, partially fixed transsexuals or hermaphrodites (possessing both a penis and a vagina). In the latter case, the clitoris may have been enlarged prenatally due to a late dose of male-type hormones bathing a female fetus. 2. there can be many reasons why a gender bending boy would still have a penis: perhaps he/she is an MTF who can't afford the surgery, or he/she could be a guy who loves his dick and loves having the rest of himself looking like a girl; aka "she-he," "shemale" or "he-she;" see "transgender."

CHIGGER—blood-sucking little mite.

CHLAMYDIA—1. called "the silent sexually transmitted infection" because women often don't know they have it, although men usually have symptoms. 2. there are about three to five million cases each year. 3. although often without symptoms, chlamydia can cause sterility and also increases the chances of having an ectopic pregnancy. Sexually active people, especially adolescents, should get a test for it every year. 4. sexually active women can easily have the test done during pelvic exams. The test is inexpensive and doesn't hurt a bit. 5. treatment involves giving antibiotics to both sexual

Hmmm. Would this be a CIRCLE JERK or a CALVIN KLEIN underwear ad?

partners, not just the one with symptoms; otherwise, it won't work. 6. you can carry chlamydia for years before displaying symptoms of the infection.

CHOCOLATE—1. one of the few adequate substitutes for really good sex; traditionally used in the wooing process 2. may impact the female body on a physiological level as an anti-depressant, honest-to-goodness.

CIRCLE JERK—guys masturbating together.

CIRCLE JERKS—semi-notorious punk band of the 1980s.

CIRCUMCISION (GOYIM)—1. an often unnecessary medical procedure where the foreskin of the penis is sliced or chopped off; the foreskin comprises up to a third of the skin on the entire penis. 2. originally done in this country to prevent masturbation; more recently done to enhance the profits of the physicians who do it. 3. there is no scientifically valid reason that justifies routinely circumcising young males.

CIRCUMCISION (JEWS)—1. "the way a Jewish mother lets her son know who's in charge"—jmw. 2. you decide: a profound statement of faith or when a father won't stand up to his own father to protect his son. 3. what's the harm in allowing Jewish boys to wait until they turn eighteen and are able to phone the mohel themselves? Why not let them decide if being circumcised is a way they want to express their faith?

CLAMPS—see "nipple clips."

CLAP—1. gonorrhea, one of the old timers in the field of sexually transmitted infections. 2. can cause burning sensation when peeing as well as an unusual discharge. It is easily treated, but can do severe damage if not attended to.

CLINTON'S LEGACY—when someone who's had oral sex doesn't think they've had sex at all.

CLITORIS—1. Latin for "darned thing was here just a second ago." 2. the only organ in either the male or the female body whose sole purpose is pleasure— which from a biological perspective might indicate that the female genitals are more highly evolved than the male's. 3. sometimes regarded as the Emerald City of women's orgasmic response. 4. not to be approached in haste. 5. sometimes wants to be caressed with vigor, other times can hardly tolerate being breathed upon. 6. while the clitoris is a fine organ to lavish huge amounts of attention upon, qualities such as tenderness, playfulness and respect also contribute largely to orgasmic response. 7. in Ebonics, it is called a "click;" UK slang for an aroused clitoris includes the term "budgie's tongue."

CLUBBING—a term that is sometimes used in porn movie making. When the person who is receiving a blow job uses his penis to whack the side of the face of the person who is giving the blow job. For most couples, this would not be a big deal, but with the size of the average porn star's penis, extreme facial trauma can occur and the possessor of the penis could risk being charged with a "brandishing" offense; aka "a danza."

CLUSTER FUCK—1. army term for being in a bad situation. 2. three-way sex.

COCK AND BALL TOYS— 1. little harness-like assemblies that snap around the base of the male genitals to pull the testicles up and apart. 2. some men hang weights on these things to stretch or pull down the scrotum.

COCK AND BALL TORTURE— 1. some men just can't get enough abuse from life in general; they need to find a guy or girl who will hit or slap them in the testicles, or who will zap their testicles with electric devices or crunch them in big vices, or will tie them up until they swell and look like they are going to pop, or... aka "CBT." 2. add an extra "T" (CBTT) and you get "Cock and Ball and Tit Torture."

COCK RING—1. a ring made of rubber, steel or leather that fits tightly over the base of a hard penis or over the penis and testicles like a halter. 2. the purpose is to help maintain an erection when the mind and body are otherwise unwilling, or to make the male genitals appear larger. 3. supposedly holds shut the veins near the surface so none of the penile blood pressure can escape. 4. of dubious value. 5. don't wear one for more than 20 or 30 minutes without taking it off for a few minutes. Otherwise you may risk permanent damage; as for using rings made of steel, think about it—if it gets stuck on your swollen penis, you will have to go to a hospital to have it removed before it causes damage to your penis and testicles. What if they have to call in a locksmith or welder? This is why it's best if the ring is made of rubber or leather.

COCK SOCK—1. vanilla: slang for a condom. 2. gender bending: if your girlfriend decides to go out dressed as a guy, or has FTM fever and wants to become a guy, she'll probably wear a cock sock or jock-like harness which is designed to hold a soft pack (penis and balls) between her legs; see "packing."

CODE MONKEY—a software programmer.

COITUS—scientific term for sexual intercourse, taken from the root word "coit," which is a carpet and drapery cleaning business in Northern California.

COJONES—Spanish for "testicles" (it's not "cajones" which means "big boxes").

COKE WHORE—person who is so strongly addicted to cocaine that he or she will do anything (or anyone) to feed the habit; also "meth whore."

COLORED CONDOMS—1. just so you'll know, some of the color pigments used in colored condoms might be carcinogenic, and others may leave permanent stains on your skin. 2. if you want to change the color of your schlong, why not take it to Earl Scheib and have them sand, paint, bake, and buff it?

COME—to have an orgasm.

COME CUP—1. device that attaches to the head of a vibrator and fits over the glans of the penis. 2. use lots of lube.

COMING TOO SOON—when a male sexual partner has lousy hang time; aka "premature ejaculation," "PE" or "rapid ejaculation."

COMPUTER BULLETIN BOARDS (BBS)—a place in cyberspace for all kinds of interchanges via computer modem. There are specific computer bulletin boards to download porn, have conferences, get dates, etc.

CONDOM—1. fancy name for a rubber. 2. a rubber by any other name is still a rubber 3. only jerks brag about having to wear extra-large condoms.

CORNHOLE —1. term that means the anus or anal sex 2. probably originated from the use of dried corn cobs in the place of toilet paper. 3. not to be confused with the term "cornhusker" (can you name the cornhusker state?)

COTTONTAIL—term that nude sunbathers sometimes use for a person who wears a bathing suit; see "textile."

COWGIRL—1. intercourse position where the girl is on top facing the guy; see "reverse cowgirl."

COWPER'S GLANDS—tiny structures near the urethra inside the base of the penis which produce the clear, silky drops of fluid known as "precum."

CRABS—1. what people often see on Card 10 of the Rorschach (ink blot) test. 2. funky little creatures that hang out on body hair (pubic or otherwise); can sometimes make you itch to the point of near insanity. 3. reason for turning bright crimson when your pharmacist yells across the store "Harvey, can you show this young person where the shampoo for crab lice is located?"

4. washing your pubic hair and external genitals with alcohol (70 percent) will likely zap the crab lice, although it may sting somewhat; be sure to consult your healthcare provider first.

CRACK A FAT—Australian term for "have an erection."

CRAMPS—1. rock band whose cult hits include "What's Inside a Girl," "Bikini Girls with Machine Guns", "Can Your Pussy Do the Dog", and "Don't Eat Stuff Off the Sidewalk." 2. abdominal pains women sometimes get when menstruating, the intensity of which can sometimes be diminished by orgasms.

CRANK—1. speed (methamphetamine). 2. the nasal decongestant propylhexedrine, often used to get a quick rush.

CREAMPIE—1. a woman's vagina with male ejaculate dripping out of it; aka "a wet deck." 2. porn-speak for when a man comes inside a woman's vagina or rectum instead of doing the standard 'money shot' where he pulls out and shoots his load on her body—how unusual; however, you see it dripping out.

CROSSDRESSING—when a person of one sex makes a serious attempt to dress like a member of the other sex—and we're not talking about a woman simply wearing her boyfriend's shirt or boxer shorts, aka "transvestite."

CRUISING—1. primarily a gay term, when guys are on the prowl for a quick sexual encounter; aka "jonesing for bone." Cruising spots can include parks, parties, bars, baths, or where ever it's known that guys are looking for sex. 2. besides the thrill of it all, cruisers risk being robbed, beat up or busted by the vice squad. 3. in traditional cruising, there is no conversation or small talk; business is business. 4. In many ways, the cruising of the 70s, 80s and 90s is now being replaced by "meeting" first on local Internet chat rooms, and then meeting in person fifteen or twenty minutes later for whatever gets you off. Even more immediate is "toothing," where cruisers use Bluetooth-enabled cell phones and PDAs to hook up for an immediate and anonymous quickie.

CRUMPET—1. British term for sexual activity. 2. bakery product.

CRYSTAL DICK—impotence caused by taking crystal meth. A lot of gay men who use crystal as a party drug also take Viagra to counter crystal dick.

CUM (COME)—1. male ejaculate, white sticky stuff that usually squirts out of a penis during male orgasm, much of which is produced by the seminal vesicles and prostate gland. 2. most males average about a teaspoonful of cum per ejaculation. 3. varies in consistency and taste among different guys.

CUNNILINGUS—1. "cunnus" is Latin for vulva (the part of a woman's genitals that is on the outside) and "lingere" means to lick—put 'em together and see what you get. 2. has any living human being ever used the term "cunnilingus" outside an academic setting, except of course for telling the renowned "Connie Lingus" jokes?

CUNT—from the Latin "cunnus" (meaning vulva); traditionally a derogatory term for women's genitals, but currently being used by feminists as a term of positive self-reference or positive reference to the genitals.

CUP—1. plastic device that manly guys wear to protect their genitals from potential calamities like dick-high line drives, bad hops or catching for pitchers who throw screwballs and split-finger fastballs. 2. there are now two styles of hard cup, and a cup made of softer material for sports with less severe contact. The old style of hard cup is somewhat pear-shaped, while the new style is banana-shaped—reflecting changes in the shape of male genitals since the women's movement of the 1960s. Both types of hard cup are held in place by a special type of supporter 3. wearing a cup over shorts (briefs, boxers, etc.) may help it feel less strange; for instance, a friend of this guide who has been a baseball catcher for more than twenty-five years wears an old-style cup in a supporter over his briefs, and then puts on a pair of lycra sliding pants (a little like bicycle shorts) to hold it in place better.

CUPID'S HOTEL—a vagina.

CURVED DICK—1. a penis that curves as it gets hard, most likely due to a tight ligament. This is perfectly normal unless it causes physical pain, in which case it should be taken to a physician for consultation. 2. since some guys with curves feel self-conscious, consider the following pearl of information: one highly-experienced woman explained that the best sex she ever had was with an Italian guy who had a curved penis. 3. if you've got a curve, experiment with different intercourse positions that might provide an advantage over guys who don't have a curve. Especially effective might be a position that allows the head of your penis to massage the roof of the vagina.

CUT—1. referring to a guy who has been circumcised. 2. weightlifting term for muscles that have great definition.

CYBERSEX—when two or more computer users sexually excite each other with an exchange of words, images or both; aka "tinysex" or "cybering."

CYBERTRANNY—1. a guy who goes into chatrooms and pretends to be a woman, "I was having the hottest sex of my life for three months on the Internet with this hot babe from Harvard who turned out to be some fifty-year-old cybertranny with a beard." 2. Chicks-with-dicks online.

CYSTITIS—see "bladder infection."

DAIRY QUEEN—a gay guy who likes to suck on men's nipples.

DANCING WITH MYSELF—just about every male band in creation has done a song about masturbation or has lyrical references to it, and plenty of female bands have as well. Two of the songs in rock history that are in everyone's "Top Five Songs About Masturbation" list are Billy Idol's "Dancing With Myself" and the Divinyls "I Thouch Myself." Amazingly, the artists who wrote and performed these two songs say they weren't about masturbation!

DARKROOM—designated place in clubs, bars, baths, parties where gay men can enjoy orgy sex.

DAISY CHAIN—sex involving multiple participants where lots of crotches are being pleased in lots of different ways.

DATE—without this event, men might never cut their toenails.

DELIVERING THE WOOD—to have intercourse with. The term "wood" refers to—ah, what could it possibly be referring to?

DEPILATORY—cream for removing body hair.

DEPTH PLAY—1. refers to liking your dildos placed deep inside your favorite orifice. 2. this means you'll need an extra-long dildo, maybe even a foot or more and perhaps one with a special shape.

DIAMOND CUTTER—1. the mother of all erections, a ten on the 'Rector scale; it's so hard it feels like you could cut diamonds with it. 2. thank goodness only a small percentage of erections are diamond cutters, because the pressure inside your penis gets so intense it can actually hurt. 3. at the other end of the erection spectrum from a "half-master," "chubbie," "softie" or "floppy dog."

DIAL-A-PORN—1. phone sex at the rate of $2.00 or more a minute. 2. masturbation enhancement for those who like their stimulation over the phone; aka "dial-a-fuck." 3. the women who give phone sex usually work with the caller to create his favorite role-playing fantasy, often something he is too embarrassed to act out with a real-life partner.

DIAPHRAGM—1. cross between a condom and a frisbee, having the flexibility of the condom and the aerodynamics of the frisbee. 2. contraceptive barrier device that holds contraceptive jelly against the cervix.

DICK—1. male equivalent of the clitoris, urethra, vagina and inner labia. 2. a person who is being a jerk; aka "dickwad."

DICK-HEAVY COMPANIES—businesses where the bosses are men and the secretaries (oops! administrative assistants) are women.

DICKNOTIZED—when a girl has a serious crush on a guy, and her life becomes defined by wanting to hold him, touch him, talk to him and be with him.

DIEN BIEN PHU'D—("phu'd" sounds like food) 1. getting your butt kicked. 2. town in North Vietnam where the French were soundly defeated in 1954. The 72-day siege at Khe Sanh during 1968 nearly became America's Dien Bien Phu. 3. if we hadn't been so arrogant and ignorant, we might have looked at what happened to the French in Viet Nam and said, "No way are we getting involved in that mess!"

DIESEL DYKE—1. manly lesbian, aka "bull dyke," "butch." 2. opposing term is "lipstick lesbian" or "femme."

DILDO—person who is being a jerk or a moron.

DILDO HARNESS—1. jockstrap-like device that a dildo attaches to. 2. gives a dildo penis-like properties of suspension and thrustability, but with only a fraction of the maneuverability of the real thing.

DILDONICS—1. cross a dildo and a droid or robot and have it controlled by someone in cyberspace, and you might have a flavor of what dildonics could someday be. For now, dildonics is little more than a vibrator that someone at another computer controls remotely with a mouse (yawn!). 2. when people on a webcam can control each other's electronic sex toys.

DOCKING—1. when an uncircumcised male pulls his foreskin over the head of another man's penis 2. no reason why it can't be pulled over a woman's nipples, assuming she's into it. 3. cyberslang for "having sex," aka "to dock."

DOGGIE STYLE—1. intercourse from behind, not to be confused with intercourse in the behind 2. more popular than the missionary position in some parts of the world 3. often results in better stimulation of the vaginal roof, which some women prefer 4. can also refer to anal intercourse, but not usually.

DOGGING—where couples who like to be seen having sex log onto special dogging forums and announce that they'll be having sex in their car at a certain remote location at a certain time. People who show up get to sneak peeks of the couple who is having sex. Takes the risk and long hours of waiting, but apparently not all of the thrill, out of being a voyeur. Started in the UK.

DOG'S BOLLOCKS—an expression in the UK which means "The best!" such as "Marty's new car is the dog's bullocks!" aka "the mutt's nuts."

DOM—a dominatrix.

DO-ME QUEEN—1. in the world of BDSM, a bottom whose entire existence revolves around getting the attention of others, while giving nothing in return 2. in the entertainment industry, an actress or actor.

DOOBIE—a joint.

DORK—a whale's penis.

DO THE WILD THING—to make love.

DOUBLE ANAL—simultaneous penetration of the anus by two penises.

DOUBLE BAGGED—1. wearing two condoms at once. 2. not a good idea.

DOUBLE DILDO—dildo that seats two.

DOUBLE PENETRATION—1. penises in the vagina and rear end at the same time; aka "sandwich." 2. two penises in the same vagina at the same time.

DOUCHE BAG—1. gravity-driven device for feminine hygiene. 2. less than complimentary term for a woman or gay man. 3. women who douche three times a month are three times more likely to develop pelvic inflammatory disease than women who don't douche at all.

DOWNLOW—slang term in the black community for a gay or bisexual black man who is not out but who goes out. Often he can be married or have a girlfriend but the man-to-man sex is kept very quiet so he isn't kicked out of the black community.

DRAG—when a man wears women's clothing.

DRAG QUEEN—1. men who love to dress up and become a female character. 2. they are not transsexuals and would never say they felt like "women trapped in the bodies of men" and they don't have a core female identity. 3. they aren't transvestites, who are often straight men who like to wear women's clothes. 4. a drag queen often refers to her female character as if she were another person, "Cynthia had a bad day and is feeling like a total bitch" or "Crystal was dressed to the nines tonight!" 5. a drag queen loves her male genitals as much as her female character. 6. drag queens tend to be a bit more boisterous than either transsexuals or transvestites; when you are in a room with a drag queen you often know she's there because she so loves giving life to the female character she is playing. 7. sometimes known as a "she-male." 8. mind you, just when you think you've got these gender classifications such as "drag queen" sorted out, someone comes along and proves you to be totally wrong.

DRESSED TO THE RIGHT OR LEFT—1. guys who wear boxer shorts have to make a very basic decision in life: on which side of the fly to rest their genitals. This is no big deal (sorry) unless you get your Wrangler's tailor-made, in which case the tailor will inquire, "Sir, do you dress to the right or to the left?" He will then leave extra denim on whichever side you indicate. 2. deciding which side your package should rest on is usually a no-brainer for most guys, since it naturally feels better on one side or the other, unless you are amballdexterous.

DRY HUMP—1. traditional sport of young couples, especially at Italian wedding receptions, where pubic regions are feverishly rubbed together while both participants are fully clothed. 2. can result in severe chafing, irritation, orgasm or all three; aka "frottage."

DVDA—means "double vagina, double anus" and we're not talking one woman with two of each. This refers to the penises of four men simultaneously penetrating a woman's vagina and rectum. How can this be? It can't, but it was gloriously alluded to in the b-movie satire "Orgazmo." Hopefully, if anyone actually tries this, there will be a chiropractor in the house, if not a coroner.

DYKES ON BIKES—a type of all-girls motorcycle club.

EAT OUT—neat oral thing that a man or woman does to a woman; see "muff diver," "go down on" and "cunnilingus."

ECTOPIC PREGNANCY—1. pregnancy in which the embryo implants into the wall of the fallopian tube instead of the uterus. 2. a very dangerous condition which can result in maternal death.

EDGEPLAY—in the world of BDSM, there's your mainstream whip, chain and collar stuff, and then there's the edge, which refers to the edge of what is safe and what isn't. People into edgeplay are willing to take the extra risk of permanent harm or death for the extra thrill they receive. Most people who enjoy BDSM are able to get their kicks without having to push the edge.

EIGHTY-SIX'D (86'd)—1. put out of commission. 2. left behind. 3. dropped. 4. term used in restaurants to signify that they are out of a particular menu item, or that the item has been pulled from the menu because it has caused at least three customers to throw up before reaching the parking lot. 5. can also refer to someone who is being thrown out of a bar or restaurant.

EJACULATION—1. the big squirt. 2. usually accompanies orgasm in the male and often precedes orgasm in the female.

ELBOW GREASE—brand of lubricant often used for masturbation or anal play, well known in the gay community.

ENGLISH CULTURE—to get off sexually from spanking or caning.

ENURESIS—1. peeing in your sleep. 2. happens to almost as many girls as guys and can last until adulthood. 3. a really lousy thing to have, sometimes very difficult to shake.

EPIDIDYMIS—1. tightly coiled tube that sits on the top and back of the testicles; acts as a storage space where the sperm can mature. 2. a finishing school for young sperm, or the scrotal version of oak barrels where wine or whiskey mellows and ages.

EPIDIDYMITIS—when your epididymis gets an infection.

EPISIOTOMY—1. an incision made in the bottom of a woman's vaginal opening to increase its size so she can deliver a baby without tearing herself. 2. the delivery room equivalent of "We've got to destroy this village in order to save it." 3. in America, up to 90% of first-time mothers are given episiotomies; in the Netherlands, only 20% to 30% of first-time mothers are given episiotomies. There is speculation that American doctors don't understand the second stage of labor and sometimes mismanage deliveries. On the other hand, if it's a nine-pound baby...

E-PLAY—using electricity in a mutually acceptable way that both parties find sexually exciting. Can be mild (e-stim or e-jo electrical jerk off), or painful for BDSM effects.

EROTICISM—state of tension fueled by sexual desire; can be temporarily resolved through sexual contact that quenches at least some of this desire.

ESCORT— fancy term for a prostitute, gay or straight; aka "massage."

EUNUCH—guy without balls, literally; sometimes without a penis as well.

FACE SITTING—when a woman straddles the face of the person who is giving her oral sex; see "queening."

FAG HAG—woman who hangs out with gay men, claims to be heterosexual, but seems to fear sexual intimacy with straight men; aka "fruit fly."

FARANG—Thai term for tourists who visit for the main purpose of having sex or shacking up with Tai locals. Not to be confused with what goes on in Cambodia, which is usually but not always much more pathetic.

FARMER TED—term for an undesirable male who is trying to make a move on you; from a character in the movie sixteen candles, "Oh crap, it's farmer ted."

FAYGELEH—Yiddish term for gay male.

FANNY—in Britain and Australia, the vulva or vagina; in America, the arse.

FANNY MAGNET—British for something that attracts swarms of women, "You should see his brother's car, a right fanny magnet!"

FAUXMOSEXUAL—man who appears gay by his mannerisms, but who sleeps with women; aka "metrosexual."

FEEL UP—to touch or stimulate a partner's genitals with your hand.

FELCHING—when a guy sucks or licks his own ejaculate out of whichever of his partner's orifices he shot it into; can be out of an anus with a straw.

FELLATIO—from the Latin "fellare" meaning "that which stops after marriage."

FEMDOM—1. term born from the fusion of "female" and "domination." 2. where a woman has more control or dominance in a relationship because both partners enjoy it and want it that way. 3. can be as extreme as full-time mistress & slave including serious cock'n'ball torture, or it might only include occasional role-playing and perhaps a bit of foot worship, bondage or queening. 4. the degree of domination depends on the desire of the players.

FEMALE EJACULATION—with extra stimulation in parts of the vagina, some women squirt extra fluid from the urethra as part of having an orgasm.

FEMORAL INTERCOURSE—when a lubricated penis slides back and forth between the labia like a hot dog sliding up and down the length of a hot dog bun.

FEMME—feminine-looking lesbian as opposed to butch; aka "lipstick lesbian."

FETISH—1. a particular prop (leather, rubber, underwear, shoes, etc.), body part (feet, hair, breasts, etc.), or a scenario that a person relies on to get off sexually. 2. the prop can be fantasized or exist in actuality. 3. one philosopher has described a "fetish" as when a hungry person sits down at a dinner table and feels full from simply fondling the napkin; don't you wish! 4. a lucky charm or object that is believed to have special or magical powers.

FIFTY-FOOTER—1. someone who looks hot from across the room, but starts looking less attractive with each approaching step.

FIGMO—military term meaning "fuck it, got my orders;" used when someone wants you to do something but you are already doing something else.

FIST FUCKING (FISTING OR HANDBALLING)—1. placing a fist into the rectum or vagina, hopefully with lots of lube. 2. can be a male fist or a female fist, but if you hold the average male hand against the average female hand, some people might prefer the woman's, while those with a skosh more room in their orifices might prefer the male hand. 3. the term is a misnomer, since the hand goes in with the fingers extended and fingertips bunched together rather than in a fist. However, once it's inside, all bets are off.

FIVE ACROSS THE FACE—to slap.

FLAGGING—at one time there was supposedly an elaborate set of codes in the gay and BDSM communities where potential partners wore flags or hankies in their pockets to denote their particular kink. For instance, a yellow hankie hanging out of the left pocket meant you liked to be on top for golden showers, while the same hankie hanging from the right pocket meant you liked to be peed on (you'll never guess what a brown hankie meant). Theoretically, you could have all sorts of hankies hanging from all sorts of pockets, since a lot of people enjoy a variety of kink, both doing and receiving.

FLAMING—1. descriptive term for a male with an extreme case of unmanly mannerisms and behaviors. 2. extreme and perhaps pointless argument in an internet chat room; aka "flaming out."

FLAPPER—term used to describe a sexually liberated woman during the 1920s who flaunted her unconventional approach to life.

FLOG THE LOG—to masturbate.

FLUFFER—1. person who keeps male porn stars erect when they are not on camera 2. not used very much any more, as today's male porn star either has trained wood (erects on cue) or is out of a job.

FORESKIN—1. male equivalent of the clitoral hood. 2. flap of skin that extends from the shaft of the penis over the glans to keep the latter moist and safe; aka "lace curtain." 3. part that gets chopped off during circumcision.

FORNICATION—intercourse between people who are not married.

FRAZIER—1. manliest lion to ever live in captivity; once had intercourse more than 160 times in less than three days. 2. died shortly thereafter.

FREEBALLING—when a guy isn't wearing any underwear.

FRENCH—term for oral-genital contact, not to be confused with "French kiss" (however, one often leads to the other).

FRENCH EMBASSY—place where there's lots of gay sex going on.

FRENCH KISSING—1. kissing with mouths open as opposed to closed 2. usually involves transfer of tongues (in the nonbiblical sense)

FRENCH TICKLER—any form of condom that has little bumps, projections or ridges, marketed to increase a woman's sexual pleasure. Perhaps it works for Frenchwomen, but not for anyone we know. Instead of buying French ticklers, spend the extra money on flowers and you'll both be happier.

FRENULUM—extra-sensitive part of the penis just below the head on the side of the shaft that faces away from the abdomen when the penis is erect.

FRIG—British for jerk off; aka "wank" or "five-against-one."

FROG KISSER—person who believes that she can turn a loser into a winner.

FROTTAGE—see "dry hump."

FUCK BUDDY—friend or acquaintance you occasionally (or often) have sex with; while the sex might be serious, the relationship isn't; aka "buddy sex."

GANG BANG—when a woman has intercourse with several men in rapid succession, at her invitation (as opposed to gang rape, which is sexual assault); aka "pulling a train." 2. it's interesting how a man who has sex with five women in the same room might be considered a stud, lucky, or at the worst wild and reckless, while a woman who has sex with five men in the same room is considered trash and risks being given a psychiatric diagnosis.

GANG BANGER—member of a street gang.

GANG OF FOUR—1. the name of a very solid post-punk rock'n'roll band. 2. Jiang Qing, Wang Hongwen, Yao Wenyuan, and Zhang Chunqiao; if you don't know who they are, Google "Gang of Four;" it won't do you any harm.

GANG RAPE—when several men rape a woman, demonstrating incredible cowardice and supporting the notion that we humans reside on a limb far from the top of the evolutionary tree.

GENDER-BENDER—person of one sex who is becoming the other sex, or who enjoys alternating or fence-sitting between the sexes; see "transgendered."

GENDER DYSPHORIA—when the genitals you have and the genitals you wish you had are not the same. 2. when a guy seriously wishes he were a girl and a girl seriously wishes she were a guy. may lead to taking hormones of the desired gender and sex reassignment surgery (SRS).

GENITALS—part of yourself that you play with under the blanket; in the UK, the term "bits" is often used, especially for female genitals.

GETTING OFF—coming or having an orgasm; aka "getting your rocks off."

GIVE HEAD—to perform oral sex; often synonymous with giving a blow job.

GLANS—head of the penis.

GLORY HOLE—1. a crotch-high hole in a partition between two enclosed areas that a penis can be stuck through. Located in places where gay guys cruise: the baths, video booths, tea rooms, etc. The penis can be sucked or played with by whoever is on the other side of the glory hole, or the other person can watch what you are doing. Can also be used for anal sex if the giver is long enough, and hopefully wearing a condom. 2. why not call city hall first to see if this is legal in your town? 3. it is apparently not wise to ask a guy on the other side of a glory hole to go outside and have sex in your car, as sex in cars that are parked anywhere but your garage is illegal in most municipalities and why would you want to invite someone you've never said two words to into your car? (Some people would ask why you would want to have sex with someone who you've never said two words to, but that's a different discussion for a different time.) See "cruising" and "glory hole protocol." 4. origin of the term might be from British ships, where a "glory hole" was a small storage space between decks where treasure or unwanted items were hidden or stored.

GLORY HOLE PROTOCOL—one shouldn't indiscriminately stick his penis through a glory hole and hope for the best. He might try looking through it first. If the guy on the other side is hard and stroking, he might then poke a finger through. If a finger from the other side returns the gesture, it's time to play ball. Or he might stroke his own penis as a sign of availability until a guy on the other side bites. All is nonverbal. There is no room for small talk in the world of cruising and glory holes, or any talk for that matter.

GO DOWN ON—to perform oral sex on.

GO-GO DANCER—ask your grandparents.

GOLDEN SHOWERS—1. peeing on or being peed on as a sexual turn-on; aka water sports. 2. a tree of the legume family, native to India, whose Latin name is cassia fistula. 3. the kinky cousin of golden showers is called "golden enemas" or "golden douches" where the peeing penis is the nozzle.

GONAD—sex gland, aka "nads," "wank tanks," "testicles " or "ovaries."

GONZO PORN—1. means "low budget and over the top;" is one step up from total amateur, but has none of the gloss and—Lord forgive us—production values of high-budget porn. Actors are brash, highly enthusiastic and definitely playing to the camera. More in-your-face and more immediate than scripted porn, and probably more fun. 2. in journalism, the term "gonzo" is associated with Hunter S. Thompson, who tended to blur the line between reality and hallucination. 3. the origin of the word gonzo can't be gorgonzola cheese (gor-gonzo-la)? 4. porn directed by Seymore Butts or John "Buttman" Stagliano.

GREEK—usually refers to anal intercourse.

GROMMET—1. a rookie surfer who often substitutes gumption for intelligence, and hyperactivity for poise; aka groin, surf rat, or weed 2. Surfing mag reports

History of the Cold War

that sex is a matter of great concern and mystery for the young groin: "What does one do?" "For how long?" "Is it all right if I don't get completely naked?"

GROUP SEX—see "swinging," "Roman culture" or anything with "poly" in front.

G-SPOT—1. place on the roof of the vagina named after the lucky man (Grafenberg) who claims to have discovered it. 2. area of potential sensation for some women. 3. more accurate if it had been called G-area than G-spot.

G-STRING—oh, about a quarter of a bikini bottom.

GUSHER—term for when a man has an orgasm at the same time that his prostate is being stimulated; some men say it feels spectacular.

GYNECOMASTIA—when boys appear to be developing small breasts; happens to about 20% of boys during puberty; usually goes away in two years.

HPV—human papilloma virus; has more than seventy different forms. hangs out in moist genital skin and can increase the risk of cervical cancer. also causes genital warts. condoms can help but won't stop the spread of HPV.

HANDBALLING—see "fist fucking."

HAND JOB—bringing either yourself or a partner to orgasm with your hand.

HAND WARMERS—Australian term for breasts, perhaps explaining something about the way Australian men regard Australian women.

HARDBODY—person who is in great physical shape.

HARD-ON—1. male erection; aka "wood." 2. for a rap variation, Dr. Dre might say, "Ya dick's on hard." 3. UK: "stiffy" or "pitch a tent;" Aussie: "crack a fat."

HAVING IT OFF—1. British slang for having sex, "My roommate and his girlfriend were having it off while they thought I was asleep;" aka, "Have a naughty."

HEART—1. that which contains all love, caring, passion, tenderness, happiness, courage, loyalty, gentleness, awe, hope, beauty, feeling, play, laughter, trust, charity and joy. 2. an important thing to have.

HENTAI—animated Japanese pornography, Japanese cartoon porn, or graphic novels in the anime, manga, or doujinshi forms. We're talking "amine" with all orifices occupied by large penises and young woman with huge breasts that are unaffected by the forces of gravity. In Japanese, hentai means "pervert" or "abnormal;" see "anime."

HERMAPHRODITE—1. person born with both male and female sex organs in varying degrees. 2. sometimes caused by too much androgen (male-type hormone) during pregnancy, and sometimes by an androgen insensitivity. 3. Some possibilities include genetic males with ambiguous or female-looking genitals, and genetic females with a clitoris that looks like a penis. 3. In modern times the parents often get to choose which sex to raise the child, leading to some really nasty confrontations when the kid grows up. 4. in spite of what your friends tell you, you're probably not a hermaphrodite.

HERPES—1. virus that affects the mouth and/or the genitals with a rash, lesions or chancre sores; also can cause flulike symptoms. Herpes is usually harmless when hibernating inside the body, which is most of the time, but occasionally surfaces with a vengeance. It hibernates deep in the nerves that surround the mouth and/or genitals. 2. avoid sex without a latex barrier when there are active herpes lesions, because that's when it is usually transferred back and forth from the mouth to the genitals, mouth to mouth, or genitals to genitals. However, it is possible to get herpes when there is no apparent lesion. 3. if you have herpes, spend time reading up on it and learn as much as you can; that way you become the master of it rather than it becoming the master of you.

HERSHEY HIGHWAY—refers to "anal sex" or the anus or rectum.

HICKEY—1. love bite resulting in a bruise. 2. for some, a cause of embarrassment and reason to wear a turtleneck no matter what the weather; for others, an advertisement of desirability; see info on page 71.

HIRSUTISM—male pattern hair growth in women.

HIT A HOME RUN—to have intercourse.

HOLMES—gang talk for "dude."

HO CAKE—rap term for "vagina."

HO STRO—rap term which means "whore stroll," which refers to a street or neighborhood where prostitutes work.

HOOCH—1. illegal liquor. 2. a hut or shack, often where a prostitute lives.

HOOKING UP—prison slang for when a jocker enters a relationship with a punk. The daddy (aka "jocker" or "pitcher") controls the relationship and provides protection for the submissive punk who provides anal and oral sex at the whim of the dominant daddy jocker. Even if the punk is 100% straight and masculine, the jocker may want him to act more feminine so he can deny that the punk is a male. The jocker sometimes shares the punk with others, or can keep him all to himself. Hooking up can sometimes evolve into a loving, protective and caring experience—given the bizarre and twisted world of prison culture, or it can be an extension of life in hell; see "punk."

HORNY—1. having the sexual urge. 2. refers to a situation where "she's got to have it" (hi TJ!) or he's got to have it. 2. the term in Australia is "randy."

HOT-PILLOW TRADE—1. slang used in the hotel business for people who rent rooms just for sex. 2. Hotels where the parking lot is not visible from the street do more hot-pillow trade than hotels where the locals can recognize your car from simply driving by.

HUMAN VITAE—the pope's master plan for man's semen. Says that every act of intercourse must be open to conception and that sexual behavior that has no hope of resulting in conception is held by the church to be wrong. The no-nos include gay sex, oral sex, intercourse with birth control, and masturbation.

HUMP—the way a poodle or dachshund often greets the arm or leg of an unsuspecting human; see "dry hump" and "frottage."

HUNG—refers to a male whose sex organs displace more space than most. correct use of this terms eliminates the need to complete the simile; you simply say "melvin is hung" instead of "melvin is hung like an elephant."

HUSTLER—male prostitute, usually gay; aka "rent boy," "joy boy" or "escort" with a client known as a "john."

IMPOTENCE—when a guy can't get it up on a regular basis.

INCEST—sex among immediate family members who are blood relatives.

INCOMPETENT CERVIX—1. a cervix that just can't get it right. 2. when a cervix is weakened and can't hold the fetus in the uterus to term.

IRIE—rasta or reggae term meaning cool, relaxing, calm, and collected; how you hopefully feel after making love.

JACKING OFF—stroking your genitals in ways that cause pleasant or wonderful sensations; aka "jerking off," "beating off," "wanking," "masturbating," "Code 20" (prison slang —from Texas Dept. of Corrections Offense Code).

JACK'N'JILL PARTIES—1. gatherings of sexually uninhibited men and women who attend in their underwear and masturbate in front of each other. 2. by-product of concern about AIDS.

JADE STALK—Chinese Taoist term for penis.

JANEY—lesbian slang for vagina.

JELLY ROLL—jazz term for female genitals.

JOANI'S BUTTERFLY—a small vibrator that can be strapped in place for use during intercourse or when out on the town.

JOCKSTRAP—jog bra with only one cup.

JOHN—someone who pays a prostitute for sex, aka "trick."

JOHNSON—old-fashioned term for penis.

JOHN THOMAS—British term for penis; aka "old fella."

JUNKIE—1. a heroin addict. 2. anyone who's infatuated with someone or something; not necessarily a negative term.

KEGEL EXERCISES—1. genital aerobics—when you squeeze or contract the muscles surrounding your genitals in a way that would stop the flow if you were taking a leak. 2. some people claim that these exercises will fix everything from a floppy penis to an uninspired vagina. Research results do not support these claims; however, the exercises can be useful in becoming more aware of genital sensations, and some people say they result in stronger orgasms.

KILLER PUSSY—1. rock'n'roll group who sang the cult classic hit "Teenage Enema Nurses in Bondage" as well as "Pepperoni Ice Cream," "Pocket Pool" and "Bikini Wax." 2. how guys occasionally refer to a vagina that feels extra wonderful. 3. how guys occasionally refer to steamy-looking women; always plural with this usage, e.g., "They've got some killer pussy over at the White House," in reference to a stable of interns and to how the women look in general, as opposed to "She's got a killer pussy," which refers to only one intern and mostly to the part between her legs—of which it is assumed the speaker has intimate knowledge.

KINDNESS—perhaps the greatest sex aid of all.

KINK—beyond vanilla.

KINSEY AVERAGE—1. oh, about two and a half minutes. 2. the amount of time sex researcher Alfred Kinsey estimated that it takes the average American male to come during intercourse; because of increased public awareness, the Kinsey average has probably increased in the last thirty years, perhaps even doubled.

KNICKERS—1. undergarments worn by your great-great-grandmother. 2. what your great great grandfather dreamed of getting into. 2. British for "panties."

KNOCKED UP—pregnant.

KNOCKING BOOTS—1. rap term for "having intercourse;" the "boots" part means "booty," and the "knocking" refers to the slapping sound that a man's hips make when hitting the woman's thighs while doing it doggie style. 2. can also mean "anal sex."

KOW TOW—to show submissiveness or groveling deference; some say it was an attempt to suck one's penis in front of the Chinese Emperor to show submissiveness. True or not, this makes a fine story.

KY JELLY—1. a brand name of a water-soluble lube that a lot of people use to help increase the all-important slip'n'slide coefficient during intercourse, especially when wearing a rubber. 2. use the new KY Personal lubes for sex as opposed to the old tube of lube that's still used for medical procedures. 3. if it starts to dry out during use, add a few drops of water, not more KY.

LABIA MINORA—the inner lips of the vulva, which also attach to the underside of the clitoris. Tugging gently on the inner lips of a sexual partner can be a fine way to stimulate the nerves of her clitoris without overwhelming them.

LANDING STRIP—medium-to-severe form of bikini waxing where the pubic hair is done in a small rectangle.

LAPAROSCOPY—visual examination of the ovaries, fallopian tubes and uterus with an instrument that's inserted just below the navel.

LAWRENCE V. TEXAS—2003 supreme court decision declaring it constitutional for one man to suck the cock of another man in Texas; ditto for anal penetration. If you have ever been anywhere in Texas outside of Austin, you will immediately appreciate the magnitude of this decision. Since the court's majority decision focused on the right of liberty rather than on the right of privacy, we must assume that the court was speaking directly to the liberties that Mr. Lawrence was taking with Mr. Garner's rear end. How this decision will be interpreted by lower courts in other decisions is yet to be known, but it appears that it is no longer a crime for a woman to use a vibrator in Alabama, although it may still be a crime to sell one.

LAY PIPE—rap term for having sex, "I lay pipe with all the lonely bitches while their husbanz hard at work."

LEFT HAND—what a right-handed person sometimes uses to masturbate with so it feels like someone else is doing it.

LEG SPREADER—1. a bar with ankle cuffs on each end that keeps a woman's legs spread open; aka "spreader bar." 2. drink where no two recipes are even remotely the same; often includes several of the following: Bacardi 151, Wild Turkey, Jack Daniels, Tequila, Vodka, sweet vermouth, and a cherry of course.

LESBIAN—woman who prefers sex with women.

LIBIDO—what Freud said is the fuel for our desire to make an emotional connection with others; he did not limit the term to erotic or horny feelings as is often done in the present day and age.

LIFESTYLES ORGANIZATION—1. large organization for couples who like to have sex with other couples (thousands of couples belong), based in Anaheim, California, pride of Orange County, home of God, Country and eating your apple pie between someone other than your wife's legs. 2. if you went to one of the weekly dinners or dances sponsored by this organization, you would think you were among a group of police or teachers. 3. interestingly, a large number of police and teachers really do belong.

LINGAM—Sanskrit term for penis.

LIPSTICK LESBIAN—what a cutie! "There she goes, Miss America...

LOCH NESS MONSTER—1. a rather frightening mythical creature of Scottish origin; aka: "Nessi" 2. sightings of the Loch Ness monster are sometimes reported by men and women who have just returned from a blind date.

LONG FLANNEL NIGHTGOWN—very effective birth-control device worn by American women.

LOPPY TUNA—surfer term for women's genitals, first coined between Redondo and Hermosa beaches.

LOVE—a special and precious way that we have of relating to one another.

LUCKY PIERRE—a gay or bisexual term, referring to three-way sex; lucky Pierre is the person in the middle.

MAGIC WAND—Hitachi's laptop for women; has two speeds, a big round head and vibrates like a Federation freighter at warp 9.

MAINTAIN—1. a level of behavior one attempts to achieve when dealing with parents, teachers and officers of the law. 2. product you slap on your dick to numb it out and supposedly help it last longer during intercourse.

MAN'S SHIRT—1. object of male clothing which girlfriends often lay claim to and love wearing, especially to bed. 2. the very feel and smell of it gives the lovelorn woman comfort. 3. any man who had a similar attachment to a piece of woman's clothing would be called weird or kinky.

MAP OF TASMANIA—slang term in Australia for "women's genitals" or "vulva."

MASOCHIST—1. a person who invites pain and passively controls others in the process; a bottom or submissive. 2. the term "masochism" was coined by Havelock Ellis and named after Leopold Von Sacher-Masoch, a 19th century author who begged his wives to whip and humiliate him. an ideal day for Leopold began with a good whipping; otherwise, he struggled to get into a productive groove.

MASTURBATION—a date with your own genitals.

MATANUSKA THUNDER FUCK—non-sexual term used in Alaska, Matanuska being a region in Alaska known for its herb production.

MEAN QUEEN—a drag queen who is into BDSM.

MENAGE A TROIS—(sounds like "may-naj-ah-twa") 1. when three French people are sharing sexual intimacy. 2. includes either two men and a lucky woman or two women and a lucky man; aka "threesome."

MERCY FUCK—intercourse done from a sense of duty or pity rather than burning desire.

MERKIN—wig for the pubic area; supposedly originated in past centuries to hide syphilis lesions. Was held in place by toupee glue or a small G-string.

MILE-HIGH CLUB—to have had sex in a plane.

MILF—1. acronym for a "Mother I'd Like to Fuck," which is when you have lust in your heart for a PTA mom, a soccer mom, or any mom; aka "yummy mummy." 2. used in "American Pie" where the term refers to having a hard-on for a friend's mom, but origin may have been the movie "Milk Money."

MISSIONARY POSITION—1. intercourse position where the man and woman are horizontal and face to face, usually with the man on top. 2. term possibly coined by savages who associated this position with conquering missionaries.

MISTRESS—used to be "the other woman," now is BDSM term for dominatrix.

MONEY SHOT—the heart of traditional porn movies, where the male unloads a big white wad somewhere on his partner's body; aka "cum shot."

MONILIA—type of vaginal yeast infection that can be very uncomfortable for the woman. can cause thicker discharge than is normal, extreme itching, and painful intercourse.

MONS PUBIS—fleshy mound at the top of the vulva from which pubic hair grows.

MONTGOMERY NODES—little bumps that often form on the nipples after puberty, especially prominent when you feel a chill or are sexually aroused.

MORNING-AFTER PILL—pill which can be taken up to 72 hours after unprotected intercourse which greatly reduces the chances of becoming pregnant. especially helpful if the rubber broke.

MOTHER FIST AND HER FIVE DAUGHTERS—British masturbation term; the equivalent American term is Rosie Palm and her five sisters, and the Australian term is Mrs. Palmer and her five daughters.

MOUSE POTATO—person whose whole social life occurs while he or she is online; aka "compusexual" or "A-O-Looser."

MUFF DIVING—1. lip service. 2. going down on a woman.

NAPPY DUGOUT—1. slang for "female genitals"—the "nappy" refers to the pubic hair, and the "dugout" is the recessed part of a baseball stadium where the players sit. 2. in rap it refers to what a woman will do sexually, e.g. "Those ho's give up the nappy dugout." Why a woman would want to have sex with a man who calls her a "ho" is beyond the cultural appreciation of this Guide.

NELLY—an effeminate male.

NIPPLE CLIPS—1. variation of a roach clip that is placed on each nipple as part of sex play aka "nipple clamps." 2. used by people who like to have their titties tweaked. 3. applies varying degrees of pressure, depending on the type of clip used. 4. there are many styles, including vibrating and electrified nipple clips. 5. some people like them on their labia or scrotum. 6. B. Cohen, formerly of the *LA Weekly,* claims to use them as sweater guards.

NOCTURNAL EMISSION—sexual dream of the male that includes ejaculation; aka "wet dream."

NONOXYNOL-9—1. active ingredient in most contraceptive foams and jellies that renders the male ejaculate infertile by changing its ph (acid-base balance). 2. should only be used by monogamous couples who are not worried about the spread of STIs, as it has been known to irritate tender tissues which makes them more vulnerable to STIs. 3. not recommended for teeth brushing, but if you happen to swallow some during oral sex you're not going to die.

NORDIC COMBINE—a member of the other sex who is fair-haired, blue-eyed, and physically gifted; term coined by author Dan Jenkins.

NPVA—acronym for "No Practical Vertical Application," which refers to a person who is good for sex but not much else.

NSU (NONSPECIFIC URETHRITIS)—common infection of the urinary tube.

ONANISM—means "masturbation," named after the Bible's Onan, who spilled his seed (pulled out and came on the side). Yet Onan was clearly doing coitus interruptus rather than jerking off. Maybe God was annoyed because Onan came before helping his wife have an orgasm.

ONE-EYED—slang terms for the penis in the UK and Australia often begin with "one-eyed," such as "one-eyed wonder worm," "one-eyed trouser snake," "one-eyed pant python," "one-eyed willie," etc.

ON THE RAG—means "to be menstruating." Before tampons and sanitary napkins were invented, rags were used to catch menstrual flow.

OUTING—a vicious process where gays publicly expose gays who aren't out of the closet, supposedly to show the straight world that some of its biggest heroes and stars are really gay.

PACKING—1. when a woman who is cross-dressing wears a penis-shaped object in her pants to make it look like she is well hung. 2. worn by some male rock'n'roll singers 3. more realistic when made of a soft material rather than silicone (a good packing device does not make a good dildo).

PANDERING—pimping.

PANTY LINER—extra-large tampon that's been flattened out like the insole of a shoe, has stickum instead of string, and is worn on the outside of the body rather than inside.

PAPERVINE— drug injected into the penis which causes it to get hard.

PARAPHILIAS—kinky stuff.

PEARL NECKLACE—coming on a woman's chest.

PECKER CHECKER—prison slang for a guy who looks at others guys' genitals in the shower, aka "shower shark" or "peter gazer."

PEDERAST—man who has sex with boys or young men; aka "chicken fox."

PEEING WITH A HARD-ON—1. a misery inflicted on the human male in the morning, though much worse when he's a teen. 2. a very difficult act to achieve, since the passageway to the bladder is closed off when a male gets an erection. Even if you can pee when it's hard, what do you do—stand back three feet and hope the arc ends in the toilet? 3. phenomenon that originally caused Hindus to invent meditation, with the earliest mantra being "Lord, let this hard-on subside before my bladder bursts."

PEGGING—when a girl does her guy in the rear with a dildo, see "strap-on."

PELVIC INFLAMMATORY DISEASE (PID)—inflammation of the female reproductive organs, often the fallopian tubes, usually caused by a bacterial infection.

PERINEUM—1. demilitarized zone of the human crotch. 2. the area between the bum and genitals in men and women. 3. Taoist types get all weak in the knees about the perineum, which they consider to be quite sensitive.

PHILISTINE— smug, jock-like jerk with a bad attitude.

PIERCING—placing jewelry, a safety pin or facsimile through a person's nose, lip, nipples, navel, genitals, or anywhere skin grows; a form of body mod.

PINK PEARL—pink, bullet-shaped vibrator; can be inserted into the vagina.

PILLOW BITER—when receiving anal sex is painful.

PISTON SHOT—in porn, when the camera is doing such an extreme close-up that you can see the woman's inner labia slide in and out with each stroke of the penis; related terms: "gyno shot" and "P&P (pimples & penetration)."

PITCHER—guy who's throwing his balls into the catcher's big brown mit.

PIT JOB—intercourse using the armpit as a vagina.

POCKET POOL—1. rubbing the testicles or penis when you have your hands in your pockets. 2. it often looks like a guy is doing this when he isn't.

POLYAMORY—1. in this form of lifestyle, people have sex in committed relationships with a set number of different partners. 2. different from swinging, where you have sex with anyone who is there and who wants to have sex with you. 3. can include everything from open marriage to polygamy.

POLYMORPHOUS PERVERSE—kinky

POONTANG—word of dubious origin that refers to a woman's genitals or what one received from them if he is a male.

PONY BOY—1. BDSM-speak for a man who pretends to be a horse while his master or mistress rides him, hopefully with crop in hand. There are specially made halter gags, pony tail butt plugs and leather pony feet trainers for Pony Boys and Pony Girls. 2. "pony training" is BDSM for teaching a submissive.

POOFTER—British term for a gay male; aka "anal amigo," "bum chum," "starfish trooper," "sausage jockey" or "on the other bus."

POP A COD—to seriously injure a testicle.

POPPERS—1. sold over the counter as a liquid air deodorizer, poppers were originally made of amyl nitrate (which is for heart patients). Then the formula was switched to butyl nitrate because the amyl formulation could no longer be legally sold over the counter. When butyl nitrate was outlawed, popper makers switched the formula to a type of isopropyl alcohol which is fairly dangerous, but legal nonetheless. 2. poppers are very popular in the gay community. 3. popper vapors are inhaled immediately before orgasm with the resulting sensation described by some as amazing and indescribable. 4. one problem with poppers is that the current formulation can kill you if you have hidden heart problems. It is especially dangerous to combine poppers and Viagra, as both lower blood pressure. Some people feel that popper usage might weaken the immune system, but there's no research on the matter.

PRECUM—slick, clear fluid that drips out of the penis when it is excited. Most people assume it is nature's own form of KY Jelly; however, precum helps to neutralize or deacidify the urethra. This makes it easier on the ejaculate. Precum also makes the walls of the urethra more slick so the wad has less resistance. In all, it helps to get your girlfriend pregnant. It also helps the foreskin slide more easily over the head of the penis; see "Cowper's glands."

PREPUCE—the foreskin.

PRIAPISM—1. a hard-on that won't quit. Not a good thing. Having an erection for more than four hours straight without its going down can result in permanent penile paralysis. While priapism is not a common occurrence, emergency room visits should be planned accordingly 2. named after Priapus, son of Aphrodite and Dionysus, god of male reproductive power. 3. can occur in boys between the ages of five and ten (causes include leukemia, sickle-cell disease, or physical injury), as well as in older males, where causes can range from the side-effects of drugs or black-widow spider bites to bicycle injuries, disease or a kick between the legs while martial-arts sparing. In many cases, the cause is not determined. 5. there are two types of priapism, low-flow and high-flow. It is very important for the physician to diagnose which type it is, as this can help determine proper treatment and follow-up. Low-flow is often more dangerous. 6. in some types of priapism, the glans or head of the penis is not erect, though the shaft is. 7. often has nothing to do with sexual arousal.

PRINCE ALBERT—male genital piercing where the ring goes in through the urethra and comes out on the underside of the penis (dare we say "ouch"?). Allegedly named after the husband of Queen Victoria, who had it done so he could strap his rather well-endowed penis to his leg to keep it from showing through the tight-fitting trousers that were in fashion. But this is probably more rumor than truth. Queen Victoria never mentioned it in state papers.

PROMISCUOUS—term for a person who is having more sex than you, often said with an attitude of moral superiority.

PROSTATE—1. walnut-shaped gland located on the floor of a man's rectum nearly a finger's length up his bum. 2. it generates about 30% of the fluid in each ejaculation. 3. contracts seconds before orgasm, resulting in an fine feeling. 4. enlarges with age. 5. sometimes becomes inflamed and can crimp make it difficult to pee. 6. some men (straight, gay—it doesn't matter) enjoy the feeling that results from having the prostate rubbed. others would sooner die; see chapter 19: "The Glands Down Under" which starts on page 245.

PSA—1. what Southwest Airlines used to be called. 2. abbreviation for "prostate specific antigen," which tends to be elevated in men who have prostate cancer. Can be checked via a routine blood test, but is never definitive by itself.

PUDENDA—anatomical term for women's external genitals (vulva); from the Latin word "pudere," which means "to be ashamed."

PULLING A TRAIN—see "gang bang."

PUNANNY—rasta or reggae term for sex; "I wan' punanny!"

PUNK—1. a prison term for a submissive and often younger guy who is on the receiving end of anal sex; aka "catcher." The punk is seldom in the relationship because he is gay or because it is his choice; see "hooking up." 2. The term punk was adopted in the late 1970s to describe a movement within rock'n'roll. Punk bands had a rougher, more direct and immediate edge.

PUSSY POSSE—the vice squad.

PUSSY WHIPPED (PW)—a mental illness whereby the male hovers, grovels and begs in excess of what is normally required to have sex.

PUSSY WHIPPER—a sexual partner who is very controlling and rarely satisfied. She often wishes aloud that her man would be more aggressive, yet would annihilate him the second he dared.

QUEEF—a vagina fart.

QUEENING—when a woman straddles a man and rubs or grinds her vulva into his face; aka "face sitting."

QUIM—British term for vulva or vagina.

RANDY—Australian term for horny.

RAPE—1. sexual bodily assault. 2. because the developmental arrest is so profound and the capacity for empathy is so diminished, rapists rarely seek psychotherapy or respond to it. 3. there are men who are capable of committing rape and an hour later going home to have what appears to be normal sex with their suburban wives. 4. most rapists don't view their acts as being criminal or brutal and are apt to justify themselves by saying that the woman wanted it, needed it or deserved it. 5. the only good news on this front is that juvenile sexual offenders can often be helped. This is one of many reasons why they should never be placed with hardened adult offenders.

RAPE FANTASIES—1. when a person is aroused by images of being raped, but would never want it to happen in real life. 2. the "rapist" in rape fantasies is often a person whom the "victim" would very much like to have sex with anyway.

RAW DOG IT—have intercourse without protection.

REAM JOB—licking the anus; aka "rimming" or "reaming" 2. what a conscientious plumber does to the inner lip of any pipe that he or she has just cut.

RED WINGS—1. Detroit's team in the National Hockey League. 2. what a man earns when he's performed oral sex on a woman who is menstruating.

RETARDED EJACULATION—when a guy's sexual hang time is so long that his partner has mentally filled out a year's worth of shopping lists before he ever comes; aka "delayed ejaculation."

RETROGRADE EMISSION—1. when an ejaculating penis backfires. Can be caused by prostate problems or because a man clamps the end of his penis shut when he's jerking off. 2. an important reason why socks, Kleenex and toilet paper were invented was so guys could have something to shoot their wad into when masturbating. Otherwise, some guys who don't have the luxury of leaving a wad will clamp the penis shut when they come so nothing shoots out. ouch. 3. can cause severe plumbing problems and should only be done in the most dire of circumstances, unless you want to end up at the doctor's office doubled over with pain having to answer some really embarrassing questions.

REVERSE COWGIRL—1. intercourse position where the female is on top, facing the man's feet. 2. since she is on top and facing south, this allows her to watch her partner's toes curl with delight each time she squeezes the muscles in her crotch; she might also get to see his testicles rise up and hug the shaft of his penis when he begins to ejaculate or she can reach down with her hand and feel them do this (in some guys this is more pronounced than in others).

RIMMING (RIM JOB)—kissing ass, literally, aka "ass-blowing," "tossing salad" or "E-coli pie"(a great term for oral-anal from supervert.com).

ROAD ERECTION—unwanted wood can happen any time to a guy who is sitting in a vehicle that vibrates (bus, car, tractor, etc.). It is caused by a combination of the vibration, which sends extra blood into the penis, and sitting, which tends to shut the veins that carry blood out of the penis.

ROMAN CULTURE—refers to swinging and group sex.

ROOFIES—refers to any number of drugs that are used in date rape, sometimes rohypnol, sometimes GBH, maybe even ketamine. Using drugs for date rape may be as much of a media creation as anything else, when you consider that the vast majority of women who experienced date rape had been drinking lots of alcohol. So if you want to significantly lower your chances of date rape, don't drink at parties or in places where bad things might happen.

ROID RAGE—unpleasant mood occurring in some people who take steroids.

RUBBERS—common name for condoms; origin: before the invention of latex, condoms in this country were made of vulcanized rubber.

SADOMASOCHISM—where people find it erotic when there's an imbalance in power in a relationship and one person submits while the other dominates.

SAFE—prison slang for "vagina" or place to hide drugs or contraband.

SANGER, MARGARET—(1883-1966) famous birth-control advocate at a time when dispensing information about birth control was illegal in America.

SAPPHO—poetess on the island of Lesbos noted for her use of nonphallic imagery.

SAFE WORD—in BDSM, a special prearranged word or gesture that the submissive bottom can say to the dominant top which means to stop.

SCAT—when brown is a turn-on and the phrase "Look at that sexy shit!" means just that; aka "coprophilia."

SCHLONG—Jewish term for penis.

SCUM BAG—1. condom. 2. term for someone you don't like.

SEA FOOD—a gay sailor.

SEVEN-OF-NINE—see her on reruns of Star Trek Voyager. Human thinking may be illogical and flawed, but human crotches collectively swell when this piece of Borg perfection becomes one with the screen. Assimilate, ejaculate—resistance is futile. So who's resisting?

SEX—stands for "sign extend," an assembly language mnemonic used in the incredible and venerable DEC pdp-11s.

SEX BEFORE THE GAME—1. refers to masturbating or having sex less than twenty- four hours before taking part in a major sporting event 2. Mirkin and

Hoffman in *The Sports Medicine Book* have looked into the topic and found there's no correlation between sex before the game and decreased athletic performance. They report that in a recent Olympics that an athlete had sex approximately one hour before the event and won a gold medal; another Olympian had sex right before his event and ran a sub four-minute mile. Mirkin and Hoffman quote Casey Stengel on the matter: "It isn't sex that wrecks these guys, it's staying up all night looking for it" 3. Ansell International, the official supplier of condoms for the 2000 Olympic games, originally stocked the village where the athletes lived with 50,000 condoms. Halfway through the Olympics, they discovered that there were only 20,000 condoms left and had to do an emergency restocking. Durex, official supplier of condoms for the 2004 Olympics in Athens stocked the village with 130,000 condoms and 30,000 tubes of lubricant.

SEX DREAMS—nature's way of making sleep more interesting.

SEX-ON-THE-BEACH SHOOTERS-—1. on the West Coast, a drink consisting of vodka, peach schnapps, OJ, and cranberry juice 2. on the East Coast, a drink consisting of melon liqueur, raspberry liqueur and pineapple juice.

SEXUALITY—an altered state of mind that's often quite enjoyable. Usually includes varying degrees of erotic or sensual feeling.

S.F. JACKS—1. notorious men's jerk-off club in San Francisco. 2. a by-product of extreme horniness, a desire to socialize, and concern about AIDS.

SHAKE 'N' BAKE—to make love; do the wild thing.

SHE-HE or HE-SHE—see "transgendered," "hermaphrodite, "and "transvestite."

SHORT-ARM INSPECTION—1. military term for examining an enlisted man's penis. 2. supposedly for the detection of VD.

SHORT HAIRS—pubic hair

SHOT MY WAD—ejaculated; aka "cum," "pop," "came," or "blow a load."

SHRED BETTY—a woman who excels at what she does, particularly in volleyball, surfing and frisbee tossing.

SIXTY-NINE (69)—1. when a man and woman perform oral sex on each other at the same time. 2. when French people do 69 they call it "soixante-neuf."

SIZE QUEEN—1. a woman who likes guys who are hung like elephants 2. a guy who likes guys who are hung like elephants.

SKANK—a person who is short on physical and social graces; hard or harsh.

SKIN FLICK—porn film

SLICK—1. refers to male or female genitals that have been shaven. 2. some people enjoy being slick as a sexual turn-on. 3. women who shave often do so to often to accommodate thongs and bikini bottoms.

SLOPPY SECONDS—intercourse when you are not first in line.

SLOW DANCING—1. event that sometimes causes guys to get erections, especially during the teenage years. 2. when girls congregate in the women's rest room during dances, do they tell each other things like "Billy got a raging boner while we were slow dancing" or do they limit themselves to mundane stuff like "This new bra is killing me"?

SEXTASY—refers to when people combine Ecstasy and Viagra; aka "trail mix." The Ecstasy is not good on wood, so Viagra is used to help. No one knows the long-term effects of this combination, nor what's really in the Ecstasy or Viagra that you get on the street.

SMEGMA—1. cheesy stuff that forms beneath the foreskin and under the hood of the clitoris; aka "knob cheese." 2. calling someone "smeg" is an insult.

SNAP-ON TOOL—1. brand name of shop tools. 2. slang term for a dildo that some women wear in a harness and use as if it were an erect penis.

SNOWBALLING—when a guy swallows his own ejaculate after it's been somewhere else; for instance, his partner gives him oral sex, he ejaculates in his partner's mouth, and then he kisses his partner and his partner transfers the ejaculate back into his mouth.

SODOMY—any kind of sex that is declared illegal by local statute. In some areas, it can be oral sex or regular intercourse, in others, it is specifically anal sex.

SOUTHERN COMFORT—sex with someone from the south.

SPANDEX—that which gives bikinis their zing.

SPANISH FLY—1. alleged aphrodisiac made from powdered blister beetles; causes severe irritation of the bladder and urethra (peehole) and can be very toxic. Women have died from it. the effect is not dissimilar to drinking Draino 2. giving her roses and a foot rub will get you much further and won't endanger anyone's health.

SPASM CHASM—vagina, aka "gristle gripper."

SPECTATORING—describes what happens when a person is worried or obsessing about his or her sexual performance instead of being able to enjoy it; can be experienced by women who can't reach orgasm or by guys who have trouble getting it up, or who come too soon or too late; aka "performance anxiety."

SPLASH CONCEPTION—getting pregnant from doing anal sex without a rubber, after the male ejaculate oozes out of the woman's rear end and drips into her vagina. Are people conceived in this way doomed to be anal retentive?

SPREADER BAR—see "leg spreader"

STRAP-ON—abbreviation for "strap-on dildo," usually worn and used by women on men (aka "bend over boyfriend" or "pegging") or on women, but can also be worn by men for double penetration or if their own penis can't get hard.

SURFING—to have sex with waves.

SWEET DEATH—literary term for intercourse.

SWINGER—partner swapping, enjoys having sex with lots of people.

SWING LOW—rap term for "oral sex."

SWINGERS—couples in committed relationships who enjoy having sex with a variety of sexual partners.

SWITCHES—people into BDSM who enjoy alternating between the top and the bottom roles.

TAR BEACH—rooftop of a tall building where people do things like sunbathe, grow plants, make out or shoot up drugs.

TEA-BAGGING—when a man lowers his testicles into a partner's mouth.

TEA ROOM—public rest room where gay men go to have sex; in Britain they are called "cottages," in Australia they are known as "beats."

TEDDY—women's lingerie that is a combination of tank-top and panties, sometimes snaps at the crotch, usually made of silk, lace, acetate, or leather.

TEXAS TWO-STRAP—highly regarded brand of dildo harness.

TEXTILE—term that nude sunbathers sometimes use for a person who wears a bathing suit; see "cottontail."

THIGHBROW—pubic hair that's sticking out from the sides of a bikini or thong.

THIRD DEGREE CLEAVAGE—1. refers to breasts that are quite large 2. some guys salivate over the third degree, some couldn't care less, and some are more aroused by women with petite breasts 3. a good personality and big heart are usually sexier than big boobs, unless you are trying to get a job mud wrestling. Unfortunately, a lot of flat-chested women don't understand this and develop complexes or get surgical implants

THREESOME—sex with two women and a man or two men and a woman. see "menage a trois" or as we misspelled it in earlier editions, "manage a trois." Is it possible that having a menage a trois is as complicated as spelling it?

THRUSH—vaginal infection caused by candida or monilia fungus. Men can also get it, but not in the vagina.

TINY.SEX—refers to various kinds of cybersex, but used to specifically refer to cybersex on a tinymud. Got that?

TIPPED UTERUS—1. a woman's uterus is usually parallel to her spine; a uterus that is tipped points somewhat toward the back 2. depending on the severity of the tipping, the ability to conceive or wear a diaphragm can be affected. 3. has little effect on sexual enjoyment; experiment with pillows under your butt.

TIT-FUCKING—when a well-lubricated penis is thrust back and forth between a woman's breasts; aka "Russian."

TOOTHING—Bluetooth-enabled cruising; a situation where someone can anonymously message anyone with a bluetooth-enabled cell phone or pda who is in the same room (bar, train car, bus or Starbucks) with an invitation to meet and have a quickie. The problem, or fascination, is that you can't be sure who in the room you are messaging or who is trying to contact you. That's where ingenuity or cunning comes in, unless the message says "I'm the guy with the blue LA Dodgers cap and green polo shirt." Since you don't know if the person on the other end is straight, gay, young, old, male or female, making eye contact is an important supplement to digital contact. Started in the UK, its highest use will probably be gay males who are cruising; aka "bluejacking."

TOP AND BOTTOM—1. a top is someone who prefers doing and a bottom is someone who prefers having it done to them. 2. in BDSM, the top is the master, mistress or dominator; the bottom is the servant, submissive or slave. 3. in anal sex, the bottom is the one who is catching or receiving (split end).

TOSS or TOSSING SALAD—1. licking a lover's anus, aka "rimming." 2. UK term for masturbating, "to toss off" or "toss oneself off."

TOXIC SHOCK SYNDROME—very rare and sometimes lethal infection sometimes associated with tampon use.

TRAINED WOOD—1. necessary requirement of a male porn star, meaning he can pretty much get an erection on cue. 2. failure to get it up on cue means you've got "untrained wood," which puts you and your big bulge in the same unemployment line as most of the legit actors in town.

TRAINING BRA—training wheels for the waking chest.

TRANNY—1. that which helps give your car its go; 2. a transsexual aka, "tranny boys," "drag kings" and "transmen;" see "transgendered."

TRANSGENDERED—1. when the sex you were born as is different from the sex you want to be; aka "TS" or "gender bender." 2. don't assume that gender identities are fixed and remain stable throughout life. Who is to say that a rigidly gay-phobic straight guy doesn't occasionally have fantasies of what it would be like to be a woman who is getting fucked? He would never consider this to be a gay fantasy, because it isn't two guys, but it does involve gender-bending gymnastics. Or what about a woman who wonders what it would be like to have a penis and to fuck a gay guy? Or what about a straight guy who dresses up as a woman but only likes sex with women? The possibilities are many and most people keep gender-bending fantasies to themselves. It is the few people who publicly bend the rules that we notice. 3. people who are transgendered challenge our notions of what it is to be male and female or masculine and feminine. They also make us feel uncomfortable, because few are able to convincingly make the switch. So what we often see isn't a "male" or "female," but someone who is truly their own man or woman or whatever.

TRANSSEXUAL—person who uses surgery, makeup, electrolysis, and hormones to correct mother nature's little mistake.

TRANSVESTITE—a crossdresser; when a man gets more joy from wearing a woman's clothes and make-up than she does, often a straight guy who is happy being straight, not to be confused with a transsexual.

TRAUMA QUEEN—person who is highly skilled at finding or creating chaotic scenes, then feeds on it and fans it, complaining the whole time, of course.

TRIBADISM—1. two women rubbing their vulvas together, resulting in sexual pleasure; aka "tribbing." 2. the way they 'shake hands' on the island of Lesbos.

TRICK—1. customer of a prostitute; aka "john" 2. sexual act as done by a prostitute; "turning a trick."

TRIPLE PENETRATION—porn-film term for where there's a wealth of penii and only one taker; aka "triple play."

TROLL—when a Phil Hendrie wannabe gets on the Internet and posts messages that are designed to piss people off. Examples of trollness listed on Wikipedia include posting cat-meat recipes on a pet-lover forum, posting "I think 2001: a Space Odyssey is Roman Polanski's best movie" on a movie-lover's forum, or posting messages about how all dragons are boring in the usenet group alt.fan. dragons. To those who respond, the reply will sometimes be YHBT.YHL.HAND which means *"you have been trolled, you have lost, have a nice day."*

TROPHY WIFE—physically stunning woman who appears to be the ultimate entertainment industry or corporate wife. The relationship between a trophy wife and her husband is sometimes described as consensual parasitism. Trophy wives are often involved in charities for dying children when they are not messing up their own. It would be a mistake to throw all trophy wives into a predictable group of status-and security-seeking barracuda. Some trophy wives are complex people, capable of far more than simply abusing maids, caterers, florists, and gardeners. Trophy wives can be downright hospitable, especially if you are able to help their husband's career. Sexually speaking, it's possible that some trophy wives do feel sensation between their legs, but this is frowned upon because allowing sexual feelings might result in making sloppy decisions when selecting a mate. Trophy wives view wealth, power and security as the ultimate orgasm, as do the men who bed and wed them.

TUBAL LIGATION—female sterilization where the fallopian tubes are sealed.

TWINK—a young and cute gay guy.

UM-FRIEND—according to the people at Boston Poly, this is a person no one else knows you are having sex with, "This is Dan, my—um—friend."

UNCUT—not circumcised.

UPSKIRT—porn shot up a supposedly unsuspecting woman's dress.

URETHRAL SPONGE—cushions and protects the urethra when a woman's vagina is being penetrated; is associated with G-spot stimulation.

UHSE, BEATE—giant German porn and erotica chain founded and run by Beate Rotermund, a formerly destitute woman who, with her young son, stole a plane and cleverly escaped the Russians as they were pulling into Germany at the end of World War II. She funded one of the finest museums of sexuality.

UNDERWEAR SWAPPING or TRADING—1. in Japan, there is such a large market in the sale of unlaundered teenage girls' underwear that the legislature recently outlawed the sale of used underwear by teenagers. Japanese teenage girls could go to small stores called "burusera" and sell their soiled knickers for $20, $30 or more per pair (the more fragrant or soiled, the higher the price). 2. Some gay and straight guys enjoy swapping underwear of the desired sex as a turn-on or fetish, and only clueless neat-freaks would launder them.

VAGINAL MOISTURIZER—as the former "love generation" hot flashes its way through the next decade, we will be seeing more and more special potions that get squirted into dry vaginas to help make them slippery.

VAGINA—according to Hunter Thompson and Andrew Dice Clay, it's the box a penis comes in, although most women would say it does just fine without the penis accessory; aka: "gristle gripper" or "spasm chasm;" see "vulva."

VAL—1. San Fernando Valley (Southern California) version of a bimbo or airhead, unique in that this particular species of bimbo has evolved its own tribal dialect, perhaps caused by the added weight of lip gloss and braces, or it is possible that tanning-booth rays adversely affect the speech center of the brain. 2. immortalized in song by Moon Unit Zappa and icon dad Frank.

VANILLA SEX—how some people describe sex that doesn't include kinky stuff.

VARICOCELE—collection of varicose veins in the scrotum where the blood flows the wrong way. This causes a swelling in the top and back of the testicle, and results a warmer scrotum which isn't good for sperm production. 85% of the time, it occurs in the left testicle and is the leading cause of infertility in men.

VASECTOMY—snip, snip

VASELINE— that which melts condoms 2. should not be used as a lube, as it seems to interfere with the vagina's ability to self-clean 3. the reason Vaseline melts latex rubbers is because both are made of petroleum by-products. The Vaseline acts as a solvent and dissolves the latex rubber.

VERTICAL REENTRY—1. difficult but important surfing trick which involves coming out of the wave and doing a skateboard-like maneuver to get back in. 2. a similar maneuver is used during intercourse when a guy pulls out too far.

VIBRATOR—electrical device which makes some women very, very happy.

VIBRATING SLEEVE—1. soft, tubelike device with a vibrator in the end which men stick a lubricated penis into. 2. masturbation device.

VOYEUR—person who enjoys watching other people undressing or having sex.

VULVA—1. the external female genitals. 2. people often say "vagina" when they are referring to the vulva. 3. what you're looking at when you cop a beaver shot; aka "beaver," "snatch," and in the UK "fanny."

WAD—male ejaculate; aka "splooge" "spunk," "jiz," "load," "cum" etc.

WAKING WITH A HARD-ON—here are possible reasons why guys often wake up with hard-ons: 1. during REM (dream) sleep, males usually get hard-ons and female genitals swell and lubricate; since we humans have a much greater proportion of dream sleep toward the morning, men frequently awaken in the morning with REM-related hard-ons. 2. when a male has an erection, the entrance to the bladder is clamped shut so his ejaculation can squirt out of his body instead of backfiring into his bladder. Erections may serve double-duty, keeping a sleeping man with a full bladder from peeing on himself; but then, why don't sleeping girls pee on themselves? 3. many males awaken with elevated levels of sex hormones in their blood; while this doesn't necessarily make them hornier, it's possible it may contribute to the morning erection; aka "morning glory;" see "peeing with a hard-on."

WANK—1. UK term for masturbation with many uses, such as "I'm desperate for a wank," "I don't give a wank!" or "He kept wanking on about Marxist theory until the whole class nodded off;" aka: "to toss off."

WANKER—name that the Queen of England calls Andy and Charlie when they are being lazy or bad, e.g. "Go suck on a pig's nose, you royal little wankers!"

WANK MAGS—UK term for porn; a hidden stash of porn mags is a "wank bank."

WATER SPORTS—when pausing to take a leak does not signify a break in the love-making action, but is part of the main course; see "golden showers."

WEBCAM—you would think, with all of the people on the Internet who are naked in front of their webcams and who are watching other naked people in front of their webcams, that the webcam would have been invented by voyeurs. Not so, according to Will Judy. The first webcam was built in 1993 by Cambridge University computer science students who didn't want to walk several flights of stairs to see if there was coffee in the building's only coffee maker. So they devised a cam that allowed them to spy on the coffee pot from any terminal in the building, proving that laziness is the mother of ingenuity!

WEST HOLLYWOOD—the darnedest place, where buff construction workers wear cock rings and hard hats and actually mean "cat" when they say "pussy."

WET DREAM—sex dream; isn't totally accurate because people often have orgasms in their sleep without ejaculating.

WET SPOT—1. caused by a mixture of male and female sexual fluids, resulting in a wet patch on the sheets or mattress. 2. couples sometimes go through very complex negotiations to determine who sleeps on the wet spot.

WHITE MAN'S DISEASE—when a person has absolutely no sense of rhythm.

WOOD—1. an erection   2. "How did Pinocchio find out he was made of wood? His hand caught fire," attributed to Hunter S. Thompson.

YEAST INFECTIONS—1. group of party-hearty fungi (yeasties) that live in warm, wet places like vaginas, between toes and sometimes in the folds of your skin if you are a serious buffet junkie. 2. when environmental conditions get out of balance, the yeasties go nuts, causing major discomfort.

YIFF—internet slang that refers to sex or something that is sexy, e.g. "Wanna yiff?" or "I'm feeling yiffy." Originally a gaming term that represented the sound of mating foxes, was created in the domain of the furry community.

YOHIMBINE—1. tropical plant from Africa thought to help men get erections. 2. not exactly the Viagra of the Bush, but helps some men rise to the occasion.

GLOSSARY RESOURCES

Here are just a few of many excellent slang resources:

The excellent and highly-recommended PseudoDictionary
www.pseudodictionary.com

Strafe's Guide to Streetspeak
www.strafe.com

Probert Encyclopaedia
www.probertencyclopaedia.com/
slang.htm

Matt & Andrej Koymasky's
Gay Slang Terms
http://andrejkoymasky.com/
lou/dic/a.html

Swingers Board Dictionary
www.swingersboard.com/
?swing=dictionary

Roedy Green's Gay & Black Glossary
http://mindprod.com/
ggloss/ggloss.html

Australian Slang
www.koalanet.com.au/
australian-slang.html

The Sex Dictionary
www.thesexdictionary.com

A Prisoner's Dictionary
http://dictionary.prisonwall.org/

Online Dictionary of
Playground Slang
www.odps.org

The Urban Dictionary
www.urbandictionary.com

A Glossary of the Low Life
www.notfrisco.com/
prisonhistory/glossary/

Boyz Behind Bars
www.boyzbehindbars.com/
connections/dictionary.html

Brainy Dictionary
www.brainydictionary.com

Roger's Profanisaurus
www.viz.co.uk/profanisaurus/
profanis.htm

Index

Also check the Glossary!